count, that the Buyer of my Almanack may confi-
der himfelf, not only as purchafing an ufeful Uten-
fil, but as performing an Act of Charity, to his
poor *Friend and Servant*   R SAUNDERS.

The Anatomy of Man's Body as govern'd by the Twelve Conftellations.

The Head and Face

Neck	♉		♊	Arms
Breaft	♋		♌	Heart
Bowels	♍		♎	Reins
Secrets	♏		♐	Thighs
Knees	♑		♒	Legs

♓ The Feet.

To know where the Sign is.
Firft find the Day of the Month, and againft the
Day you have the Sign or Place of the Moon in
the 5th Column. Then finding the Sign here, it
fhews the part of the Body it governs.

The Names and Characters of the Seven Planets.
♄ Saturn, ♃ Jupiter, ♂ Mars, ☉ Sol, ♀ Venus,
☿ Mercury, ☽ Luna, ☊ Dragons Head and ☋ Tail.

The Five Afpects.
☌ Conjunction, ✳ Sextile, ☍ Oppofition, △ Trine,
□ Quartile.

Common Notes for the Year 1739.

| Golden Number | 5 | Cycle of the Sun | 6 |
| Epact | 25 | Dominical Letter | G |

From
the Library
of

Gina Petermann Sidransky
bought July 4, 2003

Happy 227th Birthday U.S.A.

July 4th 2003

Happy Birthday

W. S. Y.

Kissinger: A Biography

The Wise Men: Six Friends and the World They Made
(with Evan Thomas)

Pro and Con

BENJAMIN FRANKLIN

AN AMERICAN LIFE

WALTER ISAACSON

SIMON & SCHUSTER

NEW YORK   LONDON   TORONTO   SYDNEY   SINGAPORE

SIMON & SCHUSTER
Rockefeller Center
1230 Avenue of the Americas
New York, NY 10020

For information regarding special discounts for bulk purchases,
please contact Simon & Schuster Special Sales at
1-800-456-6798 or business@simonandschuster.com

Designed by Jaime Putorti

Manufactured in the United States of America

10   9   8   7   6   5   4   3   2   1

Library of Congress Cataloging-in-Publication Data
Isaacson, Walter.
  Benjamin Franklin : an American life / Walter Isaacson.
    p. cm.
  Includes bibliographical references and index.
  1. Franklin, Benjamin, 1706–1790. 2. Statesmen—United States—Biography.
3. United States—Politics and government—1775–1783. 4. United States—
Politics and government—1783–1789. 5. Scientists—United States—Biography.
6. Inventors—United States—Biography. 7. Printers—United States—Biography.
I. Title.
E302.6F8I83   2003
973.3'092—dc21
[B]   2003050463

ISBN 0-684-80761-0

To Cathy and Betsy, as always . . .

CONTENTS

Benjamin Franklin

An American Life

CHAPTER ONE

BENJAMIN FRANKLIN AND THE INVENTION OF AMERICA

His arrival in Philadelphia is one of the most famous scenes in autobiographical literature: the bedraggled 17-year-old runaway, cheeky yet with a pretense of humility, straggling off the boat and buying three puffy rolls as he wanders up Market Street. But wait a minute. There's something more. Peel back a layer and we can see him as a 65-year-old wry observer, sitting in an English country house, writing this scene, pretending it's part of a letter to his son, an illegitimate son who has become a royal governor with aristocratic pretensions and needs to be reminded of his humble roots.

A careful look at the manuscript peels back yet another layer. Inserted into the sentence about his pilgrim's progress up Market Street is a phrase, written in the margin, in which he notes that he passed by the house of his future wife, Deborah Read, and that "she, standing at the door, saw me and thought I made, as I certainly did, a most awkward ridiculous appearance." So here we have, in a brief paragraph, the multilayered character known so fondly to his author as Benjamin Franklin: as a young man, then seen through the eyes of his older self, and then through the memories later recounted by his wife. It's all topped off with the old man's deft little affirmation—"as I certainly did"—in which his self-deprecation barely cloaks the pride he felt regarding his remarkable rise in the world.[1]

Benjamin Franklin is the founding father who winks at us. George Washington's colleagues found it hard to imagine touching the austere general on the shoulder, and we would find it even more so today. Jefferson and Adams are just as intimidating. But Ben Franklin, that ambitious urban entrepreneur, seems made of flesh rather than of marble, addressable by nickname, and he turns to us from history's stage with eyes that twinkle from behind those newfangled spectacles. He speaks to us, through his letters and hoaxes and autobiography, not with orotund rhetoric but with a chattiness and clever irony that is very contemporary, sometimes unnervingly so. We see his reflection in our own time.

He was, during his eighty-four-year-long life, America's best scientist, inventor, diplomat, writer, and business strategist, and he was also one of its most practical, though not most profound, political thinkers. He proved by flying a kite that lightning was electricity, and he invented a rod to tame it. He devised bifocal glasses and clean-burning stoves, charts of the Gulf Stream and theories about the contagious nature of the common cold. He launched various civic improvement schemes, such as a lending library, college, volunteer fire corps, insurance association, and matching grant fund-raiser. He helped invent America's unique style of homespun humor and philosophical pragmatism. In foreign policy, he created an approach that wove together idealism with balance-of-power realism. And in politics, he proposed seminal plans for uniting the colonies and creating a federal model for a national government.

But the most interesting thing that Franklin invented, and continually reinvented, was himself. America's first great publicist, he was, in his life and in his writings, consciously trying to create a new American archetype. In the process, he carefully crafted his own persona, portrayed it in public, and polished it for posterity.

Partly, it was a matter of image. As a young printer in Philadelphia, he carted rolls of paper through the streets to give the appearance of being industrious. As an old diplomat in France, he wore a fur cap to portray the role of backwoods sage. In between, he created an image for himself as a simple yet striving tradesman, assiduously honing the virtues—diligence, frugality, honesty—of a good shopkeeper and beneficent member of his community.

But the image he created was rooted in reality. Born and bred a member of the leather-aproned class, Franklin was, at least for most of his life, more comfortable with artisans and thinkers than with the established elite, and he was allergic to the pomp and perks of a hereditary aristocracy. Throughout his life he would refer to himself as "B. Franklin, printer."

From these attitudes sprang what may be Franklin's most important vision: an American national identity based on the virtues and values of its middle class. Instinctively more comfortable with democracy than were some of his fellow founders, and devoid of the snobbery that later critics would feel toward his own shopkeeping values, he had faith in the wisdom of the common man and felt that a new nation would draw its strength from what he called "the middling people." Through his self-improvement tips for cultivating personal virtues and his civic-improvement schemes for furthering the common good, he helped to create, and to celebrate, a new ruling class of ordinary citizens.

The complex interplay among various facets of Franklin's character—his ingenuity and unreflective wisdom, his Protestant ethic divorced from dogma, the principles he held firm and those he was willing to compromise—means that each new look at him reflects and refracts the nation's changing values. He has been vilified in romantic periods and lionized in entrepreneurial ones. Each era appraises him anew, and in doing so reveals some assessments of itself.

Franklin has a particular resonance in twenty-first-century America. A successful publisher and consummate networker with an inventive curiosity, he would have felt right at home in the information revolution, and his unabashed striving to be part of an upwardly mobile meritocracy made him, in social critic David Brooks's phrase, "our founding Yuppie." We can easily imagine having a beer with him after work, showing him how to use the latest digital device, sharing the business plan for a new venture, and discussing the most recent political scandals or policy ideas. He would laugh at the latest joke about a priest and a rabbi, or about a farmer's daughter. We would admire both his earnestness and his self-aware irony. And we would relate to the way he tried to balance, sometimes uneasily, the pursuit of reputation, wealth, earthly virtues, and spiritual values.[2]

Some who see the reflection of Franklin in the world today fret about a shallowness of soul and a spiritual complacency that seem to permeate a culture of materialism. They say that he teaches us how to live a practical and pecuniary life, but not an exalted existence. Others see the same reflection and admire the basic middle-class values and democratic sentiments that now seem under assault from elitists, radicals, reactionaries, and other bashers of the bourgeoisie. They regard Franklin as an exemplar of the personal character and civic virtue that are too often missing in modern America.

Much of the admiration is warranted, and so too are some of the qualms. But the lessons from Franklin's life are more complex than those usually drawn by either his fans or his foes. Both sides too often confuse him with the striving pilgrim he portrayed in his autobiography. They mistake his genial moral maxims for the fundamental faiths that motivated his actions.

His morality was built on a sincere belief in leading a virtuous life, serving the country he loved, and hoping to achieve salvation through good works. That led him to make the link between private virtue and civic virtue, and to suspect, based on the meager evidence he could muster about God's will, that these earthly virtues were linked to heavenly ones as well. As he put it in the motto for the library he founded, "To pour forth benefits for the common good is divine." In comparison to contemporaries such as Jonathan Edwards, who believed that men were sinners in the hands of an angry God and that salvation could come through grace alone, this outlook might seem somewhat complacent. In some ways it was, but it was also genuine.

Whatever view one takes, it is useful to engage anew with Franklin, for in doing so we are grappling with a fundamental issue: How does one live a life that is useful, virtuous, worthy, moral, and spiritually meaningful? For that matter, which of these attributes is most important? These are questions just as vital for a self-satisfied age as they were for a revolutionary one.

CHAPTER TWO

PILGRIM'S PROGRESS

Boston, 1706–1723

THE FRANKLINS OF ECTON

During the late Middle Ages, a new class emerged in the villages of rural England: men who possessed property and wealth but were not members of the titled aristocracy. Proud but without great pretension, assertive of their rights as members of an independent middle class, these freeholders came to be known as franklins, from the Middle English word "frankeleyn," meaning freeman.[1]

When surnames gained currency, families from the upper classes tended to take on the titles of their domains, such as Lancaster or Salisbury. Their tenants sometimes resorted to invocations of their own little turf, such as Hill or Meadows. Artisans tended to take their name from their labor, be it Smith or Taylor or Weaver. And for some families, the descriptor that seemed most appropriate was Franklin.

The earliest documented use of that name by one of Benjamin Franklin's ancestors, at least that can be found today, was by his great-great-grandfather Thomas Francklyne or Franklin, born around 1540 in the Northamptonshire village of Ecton. His independent spirit became part of the family lore. "This obscure family of ours was early in the Reformation," Franklin later wrote, and "were sometimes in danger of trouble on account of their zeal against popery." When Queen Mary I was engaged in her bloody crusade to reestablish the Roman Catholic Church, Thomas Franklin kept the banned English Bible tied to the underside of a stool. The stool could be turned over on a lap so the Bible could be read aloud, but then instantly hidden whenever the apparitor rode by.[2]

The strong yet pragmatic independence of Thomas Franklin, along with his clever ingenuity, seems to have been passed down through four generations. The family produced dissenters and non-conformists who were willing to defy authority, although not to the point of becoming zealots. They were clever craftsmen and inventive blacksmiths with a love of learning. Avid readers and writers, they had deep convictions—but knew how to wear them lightly. Sociable by nature, the Franklins tended to become trusted counselors to their neighbors, and they were proud to be part of the middling class of independent shopkeepers and tradesmen and freeholders.

It may be merely a biographer's conceit to think that a person's character can be illuminated by rummaging among his family roots and pointing out the recurring traits that culminate tidily in the personality at hand. Nevertheless, Franklin's family heritage seems a fruitful place to begin a study. For some people, the most important formative element is place. To appreciate Harry Truman, for example, you must understand the Missouri frontier of the nineteenth century; likewise, you must delve into the Hill Country of Texas to fathom Lyndon Johnson.[3] But Benjamin Franklin was not so rooted. His heritage was that of a people without place—the youngest sons of middle-class artisans—most of whom made their careers in towns different from those of their fathers. He is thus best understood as a product of lineage rather than of land.

Moreover, Franklin thought so as well. "I have ever had a pleasure in obtaining any little anecdotes of my ancestors," reads the opening sentence in his autobiography. It was a pleasure he would indulge when he journeyed to Ecton as a middle-aged man to interview distant relatives, research church records, and copy inscriptions from family tombstones.

The dissenting streak that ran in his family, he discovered, involved more than just matters of religion. Thomas Franklin's father had been active, according to lore, as a legal advocate on the side of the common man in the controversy over the practice known as enclosure, under which the landed aristocracy closed off their estates and prevented poorer farmers from grazing their herds there. And Thomas's son Henry spent a year in prison for writing some poetry that, as one descendant noted, "touched the character of some great man." The inclination to defy the elite, and to write mediocre poetry, was to last a few more generations.

Henry's son Thomas II also displayed traits that would later be evident in his famous grandson. He was a gregarious soul who loved reading, writing, and tinkering. As a young man, he built from scratch a clock that worked throughout his life. Like his father and grandfather, he became a blacksmith, but in small English villages the smith took on a variety of tasks. According to a nephew, he "also practiced for diversion the trade of a turner [turning wood with a lathe], a gunsmith, a surgeon, a scrivener, and wrote as pretty a hand as ever I saw. He was a historian and had some skill in astronomy and chemistry."[4]

His eldest son took over the blacksmith business and also prospered as a school owner and a solicitor. But this is a story about youngest sons: Benjamin Franklin was the youngest son of the youngest sons for five generations. Being the last of the litter often meant having to strike out on your own. For people like the Franklins, that generally meant leaving villages such as Ecton that were too tiny to support more than one or two practitioners of each trade and moving to a larger town where they could secure an apprenticeship.

It was not unusual—especially in the Franklin family—for younger brothers to be apprenticed to older ones. So it was that Thomas II's youngest son, Josiah Franklin,* left Ecton in the 1670s for the nearby Oxfordshire market town of Banbury and bound himself to a pleasant older brother named John, who had set up shop there as a silk and cloth dyer. After the dour days of Cromwell's protectorate, the restoration under King Charles II led to a brief flowering of the garment industry.

While in Banbury, Josiah was swept up in the second great religious convulsion to hit England. The first had been settled by Queen Elizabeth: the English church would be Protestant rather than

---

* See page 495 for thumbnail descriptions of the main characters in this book.

Roman Catholic. Yet she and her successors subsequently faced pressure from those who wanted to go even further and to "purify" the church of all Roman Catholic traces. The Puritans, as these Calvinist dissenters who advocated this purge of papist vestiges came to be known, were particularly vocal in Northamptonshire and Oxfordshire. They stressed congregational self-governance, emphasized the sermon and Bible study over the liturgy and ritual, and disdained much of the Anglican Church's adornments as lingering pollutants from the Church of Rome. Despite their puritanical views on personal morality, their sect appealed to some of the more intellectual members of the middle class because it emphasized the value of meetings, discussions, sermons, and a personal understanding of the Bible.

By the time Josiah arrived in Banbury, the town was torn by the struggle over Puritanism. (During one of the more physical battles, a mob of Puritans toppled Banbury's famous cross.) The Franklin family was divided as well, though less bitterly. John and Thomas III remained loyal to the Anglican Church; their younger brothers, Josiah and Benjamin (sometimes called Benjamin the Elder to distinguish him from his famous nephew), became dissenters. But Josiah was never fanatic in pursuing theological disputes. There is no record of any family feud over the issue.[5]

ERRAND INTO THE WILDERNESS

Franklin would later claim that it was a desire "to enjoy the exercise of their religion with freedom" that led his father, Josiah, to emigrate to America. To some extent, this was true. The end of Cromwell's Puritan rule and the restoration of the monarchy in 1660 had led to restrictions on the Puritan faithful, and dissenting ministers were forced from their pulpits.

But Josiah's brother, Benjamin the Elder, was probably right in attributing the move more to economic than religious factors. Josiah was not zealous about his faith. He was close to his father and older brother John, both of whom remained Anglican. "All evidence suggests that it was a spirit of independence, coupled with a kind of intellectual liveliness and earthy practicality, rather than controlling doctrinal persuasions, that led the only two Franklins, Benjamin the Elder and Josiah, who became Puritans, to follow that course," wrote Arthur Tourtellot, author of a comprehensive book about the first seventeen years of Franklin's life.[6]

Josiah's greater concern was supporting his family. At age 19, he married a friend from Ecton, Anne Child, and brought her to Banbury. In quick succession, they had three children. With his apprenticeship over, he worked on salary in his brother's shop. But there was not enough business to support both fast-growing Franklin families, and the law made it impossible for Josiah to go into a new trade without serving another apprenticeship. As Benjamin the Elder put it, "Things not succeeding there according to his mind, with the leave of his friends and father he went to New England in the year 1683."

The story of the Franklin family migration, like the story of Benjamin Franklin, gives a glimpse into the formation of the American character. Among the great romantic myths about America is that, as schoolbooks emphasize, the primary motive of its settlers was freedom, particularly religious freedom.

Like most romantic American myths, it contains a lot of truth. For many in the seventeenth-century wave of Puritan migration to Massachusetts, as in the subsequent migratory waves that made America, the journey was primarily a religious pilgrimage, one that involved fleeing persecution and pursuing freedom. And like most romantic American myths, it also glosses over some significant realities. For many other Puritan migrants, as for many in subsequent waves, the journey was primarily an economic quest.

But to set up such a sharp dichotomy is to misunderstand the Puritans—and America. For most Puritans, ranging from rich John Winthrop to poor Josiah Franklin, their errand into the wilderness was propelled by considerations of both faith and finance. The Massachusetts Bay Colony was, after all, established by investors such as Winthrop to be a chartered commercial enterprise as well as to create a heavenly "city upon a hill." These Puritans would not have made an either/or distinction between spiritual and secular motives. For among the useful notions that they bequeathed to America was a Protestant ethic that taught that religious freedom and economic freedom were linked, that enterprise was a virtue, and that financial success need not preclude spiritual salvation.[7]

Instead, the puritans were contemptuous of the old Roman Church's monastic belief that holiness required withdrawal from worldly economic concerns, and they preached that being industrious was a heavenly as well as earthly imperative. What the literary historian Perry Miller calls "the paradox of Puritan materialism and immateriality" was not paradoxical to the Puritans. Making money was a way to glorify God. As Cotton Mather put it in his famous sermon "A Christian at His Calling," delivered five years before Franklin was born, it was important to attend to "some settled business, wherein a Christian should spend most of his time so that he may glorify God by doing good for others, and getting of good for himself." The Lord, quite conveniently, smiled on those who were diligent in their earthly calling and, as Poor Richard's almanac would later note, "helped those who helped themselves."[8]

And thus the Puritan migration established the foundation for some characteristics of Benjamin Franklin, and of America itself: a belief that spiritual salvation and secular success need not be at odds, that industriousness is next to godliness, and that free thought and free enterprise are integrally related.

A MAN OF SOLID JUDGMENT

Josiah Franklin was 25 years old when, in August 1683, he set sail for America with his wife, two toddlers, and a baby girl only a few months old. The voyage, in a squat frigate crammed with a hundred passengers, took more than nine weeks, and it cost the family close to £15, which was about six months' earnings for a tradesman such as Josiah. It was, however, a sensible investment. Wages in the New World were two to three times higher, and the cost of living was lower.[9]

The demand for brightly dyed fabrics and silks was not great in a frontier town, especially a Puritan one such as Boston. Indeed, it was a legal offense to wear clothing that was considered too elaborate. But unlike in England, there was no law requiring a person to serve a long apprenticeship before going into a trade. So Josiah chose a new one that had far less glamour but far more utility: that of a tallow chandler, rendering animal fat into candles and soap.

It was a shrewd choice. Candles and soap were just evolving from luxuries into staples. The odiferous task of making lye from ashes and simmering it for hours with fat was one that even the heartiest of frontier housewives were willing to pay someone else to do. Cattle, once a rarity, were being slaughtered more often, making mass manufacture of tallow possible. Yet the trade was uncrowded. One register of professions in Boston just before Josiah arrived lists twelve cobblers, eleven tailors, three brewers, but only one tallow chandler.

He set up shop and residence in a rented two-and-a-half-story clapboard house, only thirty feet by twenty, on the corner of Milk Street and High Street (now Washington Street). The ground floor was only one room, with a kitchen in a separate tiny structure added in the back. Like other Boston houses, it had small windows so that it would be easier to keep warm, but it was brightly painted to make it seem more cheerful.[10]

Across the street was the South Church, newest and most liberal (relatively speaking) of Boston's three Puritan congregations. Josiah was admitted to membership, or permitted to "own the covenant," two years after his arrival.

Church membership was, for the Puritans at least, a social leveler. Although he was merely a struggling tradesman, Josiah was able, because of his membership in the South Church, to become friends with such colony luminaries as Simon Bradstreet, the onetime governor, and Judge Samuel Sewall, a Harvard fellow and diligent diarist.

A trusted and paternalistic figure, Josiah rose within Boston's Puritan/civic hierarchy. In 1697, he was tapped to become a tithingman, the name for the moral marshals whose job it was to enforce attendance and attention at Sunday services and to keep an eye out for "nightwalkers, tipplers, Sabbath breakers . . . or whatever else tending toward debauchery, irreligion, profaneness and atheism." Six years later, he was made a constable, one of eleven people who helped oversee the tithingmen. Although the posts were unpaid, Josiah practiced the art, which his son would perfect, of marrying public virtue with private profit: he made money by selling candles to the night watch-men he oversaw.[11]

In his autobiography, Benjamin Franklin gives a lapidary descrip-tion of his father:

> He had an excellent constitution of body, was of middle stature, but well set and very strong. He was ingenious, could draw prettily, was skilled a little in music and had a clear pleasing voice, so that when he played Psalm tunes on his violin and sung withal as he sometimes did in an evening after the business of the day was over, it was extremely agreeable to hear. He had a mechanical genius too, and on occasion was very handy in the use of other tradesmen's tools. But his great excel-lence lay in a sound understanding, and solid judgment in prudential matters, both in private and public affairs . . . I remember well his being frequently visited by leading people, who consulted him for his opinion in affairs of the town or of the church . . . He was also much consulted by private persons about their affairs when any difficulty oc-curred, and frequently chosen an arbitrator between contending par-ties.[12]

This description was perhaps overly generous. It is contained, after all, in an autobiography designed in part to instill filial respect in Ben-jamin's own son. As we shall see, Josiah, wise though he undoubtedly was, had limited horizons. He tended to dampen his son's educational, professional, and even poetic aspirations.

Josiah's most prominent trait was captured in a phrase, deeply Pu-ritan in its fealty to both industriousness and egalitarianism, that would be inscribed on his tombstone by his son: "Diligence in thy call-ing." It came from Josiah's favorite piece of Solomonic wisdom (Proverbs 22:29), a passage that he would quote often to his son: "Seest thou a man diligent in his calling, he shall stand before Kings." As Franklin would recall when he was 78, with the wry mixture of light vanity and amused self-awareness that pervades his autobiogra-phy, "I from thence considered industry as a means of obtaining wealth and distinction, which encouraged me, though I did not think that I should ever literally stand before kings, which, however, has since happened; for I have stood before five, and even had the honor of sitting down with one, the King of Denmark, to dinner."[13]

As Josiah prospered, his family grew; he would have seventeen children over a period of thirty-four years. Such fecundity was common among the robust and lusty Puritans: the Rev. Samuel Willard, pastor of the South Church, had twenty children; the famous theologian Cotton Mather had fifteen. Children tended to be a resource rather than a burden. They helped around the house and shop by handling most of the menial chores.[14]

To the three children who accompanied them from England, Josiah and Anne Franklin quickly added two more, both of whom lived to adulthood: Josiah Jr., born in 1685, and Anne Jr., born in 1687. Then, however, death struck brutally. Three times over the next eighteen months, Josiah made the procession across Milk Street to the South Church burial grounds: first in 1688 for a newborn son who died after five days; then in 1689 for his wife, Anne, who died a week after delivering another son; then for that son who died after another week. (One-quarter of all Boston newborns at the time died within a week.)

It was not unusual for men in colonial New England to outlive two or three wives. Of the first eighteen women who came to Massachusetts in 1628, for example, fourteen died within a year. Nor was it considered callous for a bereaved husband to remarry quickly. In fact, as in the case of Josiah, it was often considered an economic necessity. At the age of 31, he had five children to raise, a trade to tend, and a shop to keep. He needed a robust new wife, and he needed her quickly.

A VIRTUOUS WOMAN

Like the Franklins, the Folger (originally Foulgier) family was rebellious but also practical, and they shared the same mix of religious and economic restlessness. Descended from reformist Flemish Protestants who had fled to England in the sixteenth century, the Folgers were among the first wave of emigrants to depart for Massachusetts when Charles I and his Archbishop of Canterbury, William Laud, began cracking down on the Puritans. The family of John Folger, including his 18-year-old son Peter, sailed for Boston in 1635, when the town was a mere five years old.

On the voyage over, Peter met a young servant girl named Mary Morrill, who was indentured to one of the Puritan ministers aboard. After their arrival, Peter was able to buy her freedom for £20 and take her as his wife.

Having found religious and personal freedom, the Folgers were restless for economic opportunities. From Boston they moved to a new settlement up the river called Dedham, then to Watertown, and finally to Nantucket Island, where Peter became the schoolmaster. Most of the inhabitants were Indians, and he learned their language, taught them English, and attempted (with great success) to convert them to Christianity. Rebellious in nature, he underwent his own conversion and became a Baptist, which meant that the faithful Indians whom he had led to Christianity now had to follow him through a ritual that required total immersion.

Displaying the robust resistance to authority that ran in both the Folger and Franklin families, Peter was the sort of rebel destined to transform colonial America. As clerk of the court on Nantucket, he was at one point jailed for disobeying the local magistrate during a struggle between the island's wealthy shareholders and its growing middle class of shopkeepers and artisans.[15]

He also wrote a near-seditious pamphlet, in verse, sympathizing with the Indians during what became known as King Philip's War in 1676. The war, he declared, was the result of God's anger at the intolerance of the Puritan ministers in Boston. His passion overpowered his poetic talents: "Let Magistrates and Ministers / consider what they do; / Let them repeal those evil laws, / and break those bonds in two." Later, his grandson Benjamin Franklin would pronounce that the poem was "written with manly freedom and a pleasing simplicity."[16]

Peter and Mary Folger had ten children, the youngest of whom, Abiah, was born in 1667. When she was 21 and still unmarried, she moved to Boston to live with an older sister and her husband, who were members of the South Church. Although raised as a Baptist, Abiah joined the congregation shortly after her arrival. By July 1689, when the well-respected tallow chandler Josiah Franklin went there to bury his wife, Abiah was a faithful parishioner.[17]

Less than five months later, on November 25, 1689, they were married. Both were the youngest children in a large brood. Together they would live to unusually ripe ages—he to 87, she to 84. And their longevity was among the many traits they would bequeath to their famous youngest son, who himself would live to be 84. "He was a pious and prudent man, she a discreet and virtuous woman," Benjamin would later inscribe on their tombstone.

Over the next twelve years, Josiah and Abiah Franklin had six children: John (born 1690), Peter (1692), Mary (1694), James (1697), Sarah (1699), and Ebenezer (1701). Along with those from Josiah's first marriage, that made eleven children, all still unmarried, crammed into the tiny Milk Street house that also contained the tallow, soap, and candle equipment.

It might seem impossible to keep a watchful eye on so large a brood in such circumstances, and the Franklin tale provides tragic evidence that this was so. When he was a toddler of 16 months, Ebenezer drowned in a tub of his father's suds. Later that year, in 1703, the Franklins had another son, but he also died as a child.

So even though their next son, Benjamin, would spend his youth in a house with ten older siblings, the youngest of them would be seven years his senior. And he would have two younger sisters, Lydia (born 1708) and Jane (1712), looking up to him.

A SPUNKY LAD

Benjamin Franklin was born and baptized on the same day, a Sunday, January 17, 1706.* Boston was by then 76 years old, no longer a Puritan outpost but a thriving commercial center filled with preachers, merchants, seamen, and prostitutes. It had more than a thousand

---

* See page 503 for a concise chronology of events in this book. Franklin's birthdate of January 17, 1706, and all dates unless otherwise noted, are according to the Georgian calendar in use today. Until 1752, Britain and her colonies were still using the Julian calendar, which then differed by eleven days. In addition, they considered March 25, rather than January 1, to be the first day of a new year. Thus, under the Old Style calendar of the time, Franklin's birth was recorded as Sunday, January 6, 1705. Likewise, George Washington was born on February 11, 1731, on the Old Style calendar, but his birthday is now considered to be February 22, 1732.

homes, a thousand ships registered at its harbor, and seven thousand inhabitants, a figure that was doubling every twenty years.

As a kid growing up along the Charles River, Franklin was, he recalled, "generally the leader among the boys." One of their favorite gathering places was a salt marsh near the river's mouth, which had become a quagmire due to their constant trampling. Under Franklin's lead, the friends built themselves a wharf with stones intended for the construction of a house nearby. "In the evening when the workmen were gone home, I assembled a number of my playfellows, and we worked diligently like so many emmets, sometimes two or three to a stone, until we brought them all to make our little wharf." The next morning, he and the other culprits were caught and punished.

Franklin recounted the tale in his autobiography to illustrate, he said, his father's maxim "that nothing was useful which was not honest."[18] Yet, like many of Franklin's attempts at self-deprecation, the anecdote seems less designed to show how bad a boy he was than how good a leader he was. Throughout his life, he took palpable pride in his ability to organize cooperative endeavors and public-spirited projects.

Franklin's childhood days playing along the Charles River also instilled a lifelong love for swimming. Once he had learned and taught his playmates, he tinkered with ways to make himself go faster. The size of people's hands and feet, he realized, limited how much water they could push and thus their propelling power. So he made two oval palettes, with holes for his thumbs, and (as he explained in a letter to a friend) "I also fitted to the soles of my feet a kind of sandals." With these paddles and flippers, he could speed through the water.

Kites, as he would later famously show, could also be useful. Sending one aloft, he stripped, waded into a pond, floated on his back, and let it pull him. "Having then engaged another boy to carry my clothes round the pond," he recalled, "I began to cross the pond with my kite, which carried me quite over without the least fatigue and with the greatest pleasure imaginable."[19]

One childhood incident that he did not include in his autobiography, though he would recount it more than seventy years later for the amusement of his friends in Paris, occurred when he encountered a boy blowing a whistle. Enchanted by the device, he gave up all the coins in his pocket for it. His siblings proceeded to ridicule him, saying he had paid four times what it was worth. "I cried with vexation," Franklin recalled, "and the reflection gave me more chagrin than the whistle gave me pleasure." Frugality became for him not only a virtue but also a pleasure. "Industry and frugality," he wrote in describing the theme of Poor Richard's almanacs, are "the means of procuring wealth and thereby securing virtue."[20]

When Benjamin was 6, his family moved from the tiny two-room house on Milk Street, where fourteen children had been raised, to a larger home and shop in the heart of town, on Hanover and Union Streets. His mother was 45, and that year (1712) she gave birth to the last of her children, Jane, who was to become Benjamin's favorite sibling and lifelong correspondent.

Josiah Franklin's new house, coupled with the dwindling number of children still living with him, allowed him to entertain interesting guests for dinner. "At his table," Benjamin recalled, "he liked to have, as often as he could, some sensible friend or neighbor to converse with, and always took care to start some ingenious or useful topic for discourse which might tend to improve the minds of his children."

The conversations were so engrossing, Franklin claims in his autobiography, that he took "little or no notice" of what was served for dinner. This training instilled in him a "perfect inattention" to food for the rest of his life, a trait he deemed "a great convenience," albeit one that seems belied by the number of recipes of American and French culinary delights among his papers.[21]

The new home also allowed the Franklins to accommodate Josiah's brother Benjamin, who emigrated from England in 1715 when he was 65 and his namesake was 9. Like Josiah, the elder Benjamin found the New World inhospitable to his craft of silk dyeing, but unlike Josiah, he did not have the drive to learn a new trade. So he sat around the Franklin house writing bad poetry (including a 124-quatrain autobiography) and a useful family history, attending and transcribing sermons, amusing his nephew, and gradually getting on his brother's nerves.[22]

Uncle Benjamin stayed with the Franklins for four years, easily outlasting his welcome with his brother, if not with his nephew. Finally, he moved in with his own son Samuel, a cutler who had also immigrated to Boston. Years later, the younger Benjamin would write to his sister Jane and humorously recount the "disputes and misunderstandings" that grew between their father and uncle. The lesson his father drew was that visits from distant relatives "could not well be short enough for them to part good friends." In Poor Richard's almanac, Franklin would later put it more pithily: "Fish and guests stink after three days."[23]

EDUCATION

The plan for young Benjamin was to have him study for the ministry, Josiah's tenth son anointed as his tithe to the Lord. Uncle Benjamin was strongly supportive; among the many benefits of this plan was that it gave him something to do with his stash of secondhand sermons. For decades, he had scouted out the best preachers and transcribed their words in a neat shorthand of his own device. His nephew later noted with wry amusement that he "proposed to give me all his shorthand volumes, I suppose as a stock to set up with."

To prepare him for Harvard, Josiah sent his son, at age 8, to Boston Latin School, where Cotton Mather had studied and his son Samuel was then enrolled. Even though he was among the least privileged students, Franklin excelled in his first year, rising from the middle of the class to the very top, and then was jumped a grade ahead. Despite this success, Josiah abruptly changed his mind about sending him to Harvard. "My father," Franklin wrote, "burdened with a numerous family, was unable without inconvenience to support the expense of a college education."

This economic explanation is unsatisfying. The family was well-off enough, and there were fewer Franklin children being supported at home (only Benjamin and his two younger sisters) than had been the case for many years. There was no tuition at the Latin School, and as the top of his class he would easily have won a scholarship to Harvard. Of the forty-three students who entered the college when Franklin would have, only seven were from wealthy families; ten were sons of tradesmen, and four were orphans. The university at that time spent approximately 11 percent of its budget for financial aid, more than it does today.[24]

Most likely there was another factor. Josiah came to believe, no doubt correctly, that his youngest son was not suited for the clergy. Benjamin was skeptical, puckish, curious, irreverent, the type of person who would get a lifelong chuckle out of his uncle's notion that it would be useful for a new preacher to start his career with a cache of used sermons. Anecdotes about his youthful intellect and impish nature abound, but there are none that show him as pious or faithful.

Just the opposite. A tale related by his grandson, but not included in the autobiography, shows Franklin to be cheeky not only about religion but also about the wordiness in worship that was a hallmark of Puritan faith. "Dr. Franklin, when a child, found the long graces used by his father before and after meals very tedious," his grandson reported. "One day after the winter's provisions had been salted— 'I think, Father,' said Benjamin, 'if you were to say Grace over the whole cask—once for all—it would be a vast saving of time.' "[25]

So Benjamin was enrolled for a year at a writing and arithmetic academy two blocks away run by a mild but businesslike master named George Brownell. Franklin excelled in writing but failed math, a scholastic deficit he never fully remedied and that, combined with his lack of academic training in the field, would eventually condemn him to be merely the most ingenious scientist of his era rather than transcending into the pantheon of truly profound theorists such as Newton.

What would have happened if Franklin had, in fact, received a formal academic education and gone to Harvard? Some historians such as Arthur Tourtellot argue that he would have been stripped of his "spontaneity," "intuitive" literary style, "zest," "freshness," and the "unclutteredness" of his mind. And indeed, Harvard has been known to do that and worse to some of its charges.

But the evidence that Franklin would have so suffered is weak and does not do justice either to him or to Harvard. Given his skeptical turn of mind and allergy to authority, it is unlikely that Franklin would have become, as planned, a minister. Of the thirty-nine who were in what would have been his class, fewer than half eventually joined the clergy. His rebellious nature may even have been enhanced rather than repressed; the college administrators were at the time wrestling mightily with the excessive partying, eating, and drinking that was infecting the campus.

One aspect of Franklin's genius was the variety of his interests, from science to government to diplomacy to journalism, all of them approached from a very practical rather than theoretical angle. Had he gone to Harvard, this diversity in outlook need not have been lost, for the college under the liberal John Leverett was no longer under the firm control of the Puritan clergy. By the 1720s it offered famous courses in physics, geography, logic, and ethics as well as the classics and theology, and a telescope atop Massachusetts Hall made it a center for astronomy. Fortunately, Franklin acquired something that was perhaps just as enlightening as a Harvard education: the training and experiences of a publisher, printer, and newspaperman.

APPRENTICE

At age 10, with but two years of schooling, Franklin went to work full time in his father's candle and soap shop, replacing his older brother John, who had served his term as an apprentice and left to set up his own business in Rhode Island. It was not pleasant work—skimming rendered tallow from boiling cauldrons of fat was particularly noxious, and cutting wicks and filling molds was quite mindless—and Franklin made clear his distaste for it. More ominously, he expressed his "strong inclination for the sea," even though his brother Josiah Jr. had recently been lost to its depths.

Fearing that his son would "break loose and go to sea," Josiah took him on long walks through Boston to see other craftsmen, so that he could "observe my inclination and endeavor to fix it on some trade that would keep me on land." This instilled in Franklin a lifelong appreciation for craftsmen and tradesmen. His passing familiarity with an array of crafts also helped make him an accomplished tinkerer, which served him in good stead as an inventor.

Josiah eventually concluded that Benjamin would be best as a cutler, making knives and grinding blades. So he was, at least for a few days, apprenticed to Uncle Benjamin's son Samuel. But Samuel demanded an apprenticeship fee that struck Josiah as unreasonable, especially given the history of both hospitality and aggravation that existed between him and the elder Benjamin.[26]

Instead, almost by default rather than design, young Benjamin ended up apprenticed in 1718, at age 12, to his brother James, 21, who had recently returned from training in England to set up as a printer. At first, the willful young Benjamin balked at signing the indenture papers; he was a little older than usual for starting an apprenticeship, and his brother demanded a nine-year term instead of the typical seven years. Eventually, Benjamin signed on, though he was not destined to stay indentured until he was 21.

During his time in London, James saw how Grub Street balladeers would churn out odes and hawk them in the coffeehouses. So he promptly put Benjamin to work not only pushing type but also producing poetry. With encouragement from his uncle, young Franklin wrote two works based on news stories, both dealing with the sea: one about a family killed in a boating accident, and the other about the killing of the pirate known as Blackbeard. They were, as Franklin recalled, "wretched stuff," but they sold well, which "flattered my vanity."[27]

Herman Melville would one day write that Franklin was "everything but a poet." His father, no romantic, in fact preferred it that way, and he put an end to Benjamin's versifying. "My father discouraged me by ridiculing my performances and telling me verse-makers were generally beggars; so I escaped being a poet, most probably a very bad one."

When Franklin began his apprenticeship, Boston had only one newspaper: *The Boston News-Letter,* which had been launched in 1704 by a successful printer named John Campbell, who was also the town's postmaster. Then, as today, there was an advantage in the media business to controlling both content and distribution. Campbell was able to join forces with a network of fellow postmasters running from New Hampshire to Virginia. His books and papers were sent along the route for free—unlike those of other printers—and the postmasters in his network would send him a steady stream of news items. In addition, because he held an official position he could proclaim that his paper was "published by authority," an important certification at a time when the press did not pride itself on independence.

The link between being the postmaster and a newspaper publisher was so natural that when Campbell lost the former job, his successor as postmaster, William Brooker, assumed that he would also take over the newspaper. Campbell, however, kept hold of it, which prompted Brooker to launch, in December 1719, a rival: *The Boston Gazette*. He hired James Franklin, the cheapest of the town's printers, to produce it for him.

But after two years, James lost the contract to print the *Gazette*, and he did something quite audacious. He launched what was then the only truly independent newspaper in the colonies and the first with literary aspirations. His weekly *New England Courant* would very explicitly *not* be "published by authority."[28]

The *Courant* would be remembered by history mainly because it contained the first published prose of Benjamin Franklin. And James would become known for being the harsh and jealous master described in his brother's autobiography. In fairness, however, the *Courant* ought to be remembered on its own as America's first fiercely independent newspaper, a bold, antiestablishment journal that helped to create the nation's tradition of an irreverent press. "It was the first open effort to defy the norm," literary historian Perry Miller has written.[29]

Defying authority in Boston at that time meant defying the Mathers and the role of the Puritan clergy in secular life, a cause James took up on the first page of his paper's first edition. Unfortunately, the battle he chose was over inoculation for smallpox, and he happened to pick the wrong side.

Smallpox epidemics had devastated Massachusetts at regular intervals in the ninety years since its founding. A 1677 outbreak wiped out seven hundred people, 12 percent of the population. During the epidemic of 1702, during which three of his children were stricken but survived, Cotton Mather began studying the disease. A few years later, he was introduced to the practice of inoculation by his black slave, who had undergone the procedure in Africa and showed Mather his scar. Mather checked with other blacks in Boston and found that inoculation was a standard practice in parts of Africa.

Just before James Franklin's *Courant* made its debut in 1721, the HMS *Seahorse* arrived from the West Indies carrying what would become a new wave of smallpox. Within months, nine hundred of Boston's ten thousand inhabitants would be dead. Mather, trained as a physician before becoming a preacher, sent a letter to the ten practicing doctors in Boston (only one of whom had a medical degree) summarizing his knowledge of the African inoculation and urging that they adopt the practice. (Mather had evolved quite far from the superstitions that had led him to support Salem's witch hunts.)

Most of the doctors rejected the notion, and (with little justification other than a desire to prick at the pretensions of the preachers) so did James Franklin's new newspaper. The first issue of the *Courant* (August 7, 1721) contained an essay by a young friend of James's, John Checkley, a sassy Oxford-educated Anglican. He singled out for his sally the Puritan clergy, who "by teaching and practicing what's Orthodox, pray hard against sickness, yet preach up the Pox!" The issue also carried a diatribe by the town's only physician who actually had a medical degree, Dr. William Douglass, who dismissed inoculation as "the practice of Greek old women" and called Mather and his fellow ministerial proponents "six gentlemen of piety and learning profoundly ignorant of the matter." It was the first example, and a robust one at that, of a newspaper attacking the ruling establishment in America.[30]

Increase Mather, the family's aging patriarch, thundered, "I cannot but pity poor Franklin, who though but a young man, it may be speedily he must appear before the judgment seat of God." Cotton Mather, his son, wrote a letter to a rival paper denouncing the "notorious, scandalous paper called the *Courant,* full-freighted with nonsense, unmanliness, railery," and comparing its contributors to the Hell-Fire Club, a well-known clique of dapper young heretics in London. Cotton's cousin, a preacher named Thomas Walter, weighed in by writing a scathing piece entitled "The Anti-*Courant.*"

Knowing full well that this public spat would sell papers, and eager to profit from both sides of an argument, James Franklin quite happily took on the job of publishing and selling Thomas Walter's rebuttal. However, the escalating personal nature of the controversy began to unsettle him. After a few weeks, he announced in an editor's note that he had banned Checkley from his paper for letting the feud get too vindictive. Henceforth, he promised, the *Courant* would aim to be "innocently diverting" and would publish opinions on either side of the inoculation controversy as long as they were "free from malicious reflections."[31]

Benjamin Franklin managed to stay out of his brother's smallpox battle with the Mather family, and he never mentioned it in his autobiography or letters, a striking omission that suggests that he was not proud of the side the paper chose. He later became a fervent advocate of inoculation, painfully and poignantly espousing the cause right after his 4-year-old son, Francis, died of the pox in 1736. And he would, both as an aspiring boy of letters and as a striver who sought the patronage of influential elders, end up becoming Cotton Mather's admirer and, a few years later, his acquaintance.

BOOKS

The print trade was a natural calling for Franklin. "From a child I was fond of reading," he recalled, "and all the little money that came into my hands was ever laid out in books." Indeed, books were the most important formative influence in his life, and he was lucky to grow up in Boston, where libraries had been carefully nurtured since the *Arabella* brought fifty volumes along with the town's first settlers in 1630. By the time Franklin was born, Cotton Mather had built a private library of almost three thousand volumes rich in classical and scientific as well as theological works. This appreciation of books was one of the traits shared by the Puritanism of Mather and the Enlightenment of Locke, worlds that would combine in the character of Benjamin Franklin.[32]

Less than a mile from Mather's library was the small bookshelf of Josiah Franklin. Though certainly modest, it was still notable that an uneducated chandler would have one at all. Fifty years later, Franklin could still recall its titles: Plutarch's *Lives* ("which I read abundantly"), Daniel Defoe's *An Essay upon Projects,* Cotton Mather's *Bonifacius: Essays to Do Good,* and an assortment of "books in polemic divinity."

Once he began working in his brother's print shop, Franklin was able to sneak books from the apprentices who worked for booksellers, as long as he returned the volumes clean. "Often I sat up in my room reading the greatest part of the night, when the book was borrowed in the evening and to be returned early in the morning, lest it should be missed or wanted."

Franklin's favorite books were about voyages, spiritual as well as terrestrial, and the most notable of these was about both: John Bunyan's *Pilgrim's Progress,* the saga of the tenacious quest by a man named Christian to reach the Celestial City, which was published in 1678 and quickly became popular among Puritans and other dissenters. As important as its religious message, at least for Franklin, was the refreshingly clean and sparse prose style it offered in an age when writing had become clotted by the richness of the Restoration. "Honest John was the first that I know of," Franklin correctly noted, "who mixed narration and dialogue, a method of writing very engaging to the reader."

A central theme of Bunyan's book—and of the passage from Puritanism to Enlightenment, and of Franklin's life—was contained in its title: *progress,* the concept that individuals, and humanity in general, move forward and improve based on a steady increase of knowledge and the wisdom that comes from conquering adversity. Christian's famous opening phrase sets the tone: "As I walked through the wilderness of this world . . ." Even for the faithful, this progress was not solely the handiwork of the Lord but also the result of a human struggle, by individuals and communities, to triumph over obstacles.

Likewise, another Franklin favorite—and one must pause to marvel at a 12-year-old with such tastes in leisure pursuits—was Plutarch's *Lives,* which is also based on the premise that individual endeavor can change the course of history for the better. Plutarch's heroes, like Bunyan's Christian, are honorable men who believe that their personal strivings are intertwined with the progress of humanity. History is a tale, Franklin came to believe, not of immutable forces but of human endeavors.

This outlook clashed with some of the tenets of Calvinism, such as the essential depravity of man and the predestination of his soul, which Franklin would eventually abandon as he edged his way closer to the less daunting deism that became the creed of choice during the Enlightenment. Yet, there were many aspects of Puritanism that made a lasting impression, most notably the practical, sociable, community-oriented aspects of that religion.

These were expressed eloquently in a work that Franklin often cited as a key influence: *Bonifacius: Essays to Do Good,* one of the few gentle tracts of the more than four hundred written by Cotton Mather. "If I have been," Franklin wrote to Cotton Mather's son almost seventy years later, "a useful citizen, the public owes the advantage of it to that book." Franklin's first pen name, Silence Dogood, paid homage both to the book and to a famous sermon by Mather, "Silentiarius: The Silent Sufferer."

Mather's tract called on members of the community to form voluntary associations to benefit society, and he personally founded a neighborhood improvement group, known as Associated Families, which Benjamin's father joined. He also urged the creation of Young Men Associated clubs and of Reforming Societies for the Suppression of Disorders, which would seek to improve local laws, provide charity for the poor, and encourage religious behavior.[33]

Mather's ideas were influenced by Daniel Defoe's *An Essay upon Projects,* which was another favorite book of Franklin's. Published in 1697, it proposed for London many of the sort of community projects that Franklin would later launch in Philadelphia: fire insurance associations, voluntary seamen's societies to create pensions, schemes to provide welfare for the elderly and widows, academies to educate the children of the middle class, and (with just a touch of Defoe humor) institutions to house the mentally retarded paid for by a tax on authors because they happened to get a greater share of intelligence at birth just as the retarded happened to get less.[34]

Among Defoe's most progressive notions was that it was "barbarous" and "inhumane" to deny women equal education and rights, and *An Essay upon Projects* contains a diatribe against such sexism. Around that time, Franklin and "another bookish lad" named John Collins began engaging each other in debates as an intellectual sport. Their first topic was the education of women, with Collins opposing it. "I took the contrary side," Franklin recalled, not totally out of conviction but "perhaps a little for dispute sake."

As a result of his mock debates with Collins, Franklin began to tailor for himself a persona that was less contentious and confrontational, which made him seem endearing and charming as he grew older—or, to a small but vocal cadre of enemies, manipulative and conniving. Being "disputatious," he concluded, was "a very bad habit" because contradicting people produced "disgusts and perhaps enmities." Later in his life he would wryly say of disputing: "Persons of good sense, I have since observed, seldom fall into it, except lawyers, university men, and men of all sorts that have been bred at Edinburgh."

Instead, after stumbling across some rhetoric books that extolled Socrates' method of building an argument through gentle queries, he "dropped my abrupt contradiction" style of argument and "put on the humbler enquirer" of the Socratic method. By asking what seemed to be innocent questions, Franklin would draw people into making concessions that would gradually prove whatever point he was trying to assert. "I found this method the safest for myself and very embarrassing to those against whom I used it; therefore, I took a delight in it." Although he later abandoned the more annoying aspects of a Socratic approach, he continued to favor gentle indirection rather than confrontation in making his arguments.[35]

SILENCE DOGOOD

Part of his debate with Collins over the education of women was waged by exchanging letters, and his father happened to read them. Though Josiah did not take sides in the dispute (he achieved his own semblance of fairness by providing little formal education to any of his children of either sex), he did criticize his son for his weak and unpersuasive writing style. In reaction, the precocious young teen devised for himself a self-improvement course with the help of a volume of *The Spectator* that he found.

The Spectator, a London daily that flourished in 1711–12, featured deft essays by Joseph Addison and Richard Steele probing the vanities and values of contemporary life. The outlook was humanistic and enlightened, yet light. As Addison put it, "I shall endeavor to enliven Morality with Wit, and to temper Wit with Morality."

As part of his self-improvement course, Franklin read the essays, took brief notes, and laid them aside for a few days. Then he tried to recreate the essay in his own words, after which he compared his composition to the original. Sometimes he would jumble up the notes he took, so that he would have to figure out on his own the best order to build the essay's argument.

He turned some of the essays into poetry, which helped him (so he thought) expand his vocabulary by forcing him to search for words that had similar meanings but different rhythms and sounds. These, too, he turned back into essays after a few days, comparing them to see where he had diverged from the original. When he found his own version wanting, he would correct it. "But I sometimes had the pleasure of fancying that in certain particulars of small import I had been lucky enough to improve the method or the language, and this encouraged me to think that I might possibly in time come to be a tolerable English writer, of which I was extremely ambitious." [36]

More than making himself merely "tolerable" as a writer, he became the most popular writer in colonial America. His self-taught style, as befitting a protégé of Addison and Steele, featured a fun and conversational prose that was lacking in poetic flourish but powerful in its directness.

Thus was born Silence Dogood. James Franklin's *Courant*, which was modeled on *The Spectator*, featured sassy pseudonymous essays, and his print shop attracted a congregation of clever young contributors who liked to hang around and praise each other's prose. Benjamin was eager to become part of the crowd, but he knew that James, already jealous of his upstart young brother, was unlikely to encourage him. "Hearing their conversations, and their accounts of the approbation their papers were received with, I was excited to try my hand among them."

So one night, Franklin, disguising his handwriting, wrote an essay and slipped it under the printing house door. The cadre of Couranteers who gathered the next day lauded the anonymous submission, and Franklin had the "exquisite pleasure" of listening as they decided to feature it on the front page of the issue out the next Monday, April 2, 1722.

The literary character Franklin invented was a triumph of imagination. Silence Dogood was a slightly prudish widowed woman from a rural area, created by a spunky unmarried Boston teenager who had never spent a night outside of the city. Despite the uneven quality of the essays, Franklin's ability to speak convincingly as a woman was remarkable, and it showed both his creativity and his appreciation for the female mind.

The echoes of Addison are apparent from the outset. In Addison's first *Spectator* essay, he wrote, "I have observed that a reader seldom peruses a book with pleasure 'til he knows whether the writer of it be a black or a fair man, of a mild or choleric disposition, married or a bachelor." Franklin likewise began by justifying an autobiographical introduction from his fictitious narrator: "It is observed, that the generality of people, nowadays, are unwilling either to commend or dispraise what they read, until they are in some measure informed who or what the author of it is, whether he be poor or rich, old or young, a scholar or a leather apron man."

One reason the Silence Dogood essays are so historically notable is that they were among the first examples of what would become a quintessential American genre of humor: the wry, homespun mix of folksy tales and pointed observations that was perfected by such Franklin descendants as Mark Twain and Will Rogers. For example, in the second of the essays, Silence Dogood tells how the minister to whom she was apprenticed decided to make her his wife: "Having made several unsuccessful fruitless attempts on the more topping sort of our sex, and being tired with making troublesome journeys and visits to no purpose, he began unexpectedly to cast a loving eye upon me . . . There is certainly scarce any part of a man's life in which he appears more silly and ridiculous than when he makes his first onset in courtship."

Franklin's portrayal of Mrs. Dogood exhibits a literary dexterity that was quite subtle for a 16-year-old boy. "I could easily be persuaded to marry again," he had her declare. "I am courteous and affable, good humored (unless I am first provoked) and handsome, and sometimes witty." The flick of the word "sometimes" is particularly deft. In describing her beliefs and biases, Franklin had Mrs. Dogood assert an attitude that would, with his encouragement, become part of the emerging American character: "I am . . . a mortal enemy to arbitrary government and unlimited power. I am naturally very jealous for the rights and liberties of my country; and the least appearance of an encroachment on those invaluable privileges is apt to make my blood boil exceedingly. I have likewise a natural inclination to observe and reprove the faults of others, at which I have an excellent faculty." It was as good a description of the real Benjamin Franklin—and, indeed, of a typical American—as is likely to be found anywhere.[37]

Of the fourteen Dogood essays that Franklin wrote between April and October 1722, the one that stands out both as journalism and self-revelation is his attack on the college he never got to attend. Most of the classmates he had bested at Boston Latin had just entered Harvard, and Franklin could not refrain from lampooning them and their institution. The form he used was an allegorical narrative cast as a dream. In doing so, he drew on, and perhaps was mildly parodying, Bunyan's *Pilgrim's Progress,* also an allegorical journey set as a dream. Addison had used the form somewhat clumsily in an issue of *The Spectator* that Franklin read, which recounted the dream of a banker about an allegorical virgin named Public Credit.[38]

In the essay, Mrs. Dogood recounts falling asleep under an apple tree while she mulls over whether to send her son to Harvard. As she journeys in her dream toward this temple of learning, she makes a discovery about those who send sons there: "Most of them consulted their own purses instead of their children's capacities: so that I observed a great many, yea, the most part of those who were traveling thither were little better than Dunces and Blockheads." The gate of the temple, she finds, is guarded by "two sturdy porters named Riches and Poverty," and only those who meet the approval of the former could get in. Most of the students are content to dally with the figures called Idleness and Ignorance. "They learn little more than how to carry themselves handsomely, and enter a room genteelly (which might as well be acquired at a dancing school), and from thence they return, after abundance of trouble and charge, as great blockheads as ever, only more proud and self-conceited."

Picking up on the proposals of Mather and Defoe for voluntary civic associations, Franklin devoted two of his Silence Dogood essays to the topic of relief for single women. For widows like herself, Mrs. Dogood proposes an insurance scheme funded by subscriptions from married couples. The next essay extended the idea to spinsters. A "friendly society" would be formed that would guarantee £500 "in ready cash" to any member who reaches age 30 and is still not married. The money, Mrs. Dogood notes, would come with a condition: "No woman, who after claiming and receiving, has had the good fortune to marry, shall entertain any company [by praising] her husband above the space of one hour at a time upon pain of returning one half the money into the office for the first offense, and upon the second offense to return the remainder." In these essays, Franklin was being gently satirical rather than fully serious. But his interest in civic associations would later find more earnest expression, as we shall see, when he became established as a young tradesman in Philadelphia.

Franklin's vanity was further fed during that summer of 1722, when his brother was jailed for three weeks—without trial—by Massachusetts authorities for the "high affront" of questioning their competence in pursuing pirates. For three issues, Benjamin got to put out the paper.

He boasts in his autobiography that "I had the management of the paper, and I made bold to give our rulers some rubs in it, which my brother took very kindly, while others began to consider me in an unfavorable light as a young genius that had a turn for libeling and satire." In fact, other than a letter to the readers written from prison by James, nothing in Benjamin's three issues directly challenged the civil authorities. The closest he came was having Mrs. Dogood quote in full an essay from an English newspaper that defended free speech.

"Without freedom of thought there can be no such thing as wisdom," it declared, "and no such thing as public liberty without freedom of speech."[39]

The "rubs" that Franklin remembered came a week after his brother's return from prison. Writing as Silence Dogood, he unleashed a piercing attack on the civil authorities, perhaps the most biting of his entire career. The question that Mrs. Dogood posed was "Whether a Commonwealth suffers more by hypocritical pretenders to religion or by the openly profane?"

Unsurprisingly, Franklin's Mrs. Dogood argued that "some late thoughts of this nature have inclined me to think that the hypocrite is the most dangerous person of the two, especially if he sustains a post in the government." The piece attacked the link between the church and the state, which was the very foundation of the Puritan commonwealth. Governor Thomas Dudley, who moved from the ministry to the law, is cited (though not by name) as an example: "The most dangerous hypocrite in a Commonwealth is one who leaves the gospel for the sake of the law. A man compounded of law and gospel is able to cheat a whole country with his religion and then destroy them under color of law."[40]

By the fall of 1722, Franklin was running short of ideas for Silence Dogood. Worse yet, his brother was beginning to suspect the provenance of the pieces. In her thirteenth submission, Silence Dogood noted that she had overheard a conversation one night in which a gentleman had said, "Though I wrote in the character of a woman, he knew me to be a man; but, continued he, he has more need of endeavoring a reformation in himself than spending his wit in satirizing others." The next Dogood would be Franklin's last. When he revealed Mrs. Dogood's true identity, it raised his stature among the Couranteers but "did not quite please" James. "He thought, probably with reason, that it tended to make me too vain."

Silence Dogood had been able to get away with an attack on hypocrisy and religion, but when James penned a similar piece in January 1723, he landed in trouble yet again. "Of all knaves," he wrote, "the religious knave is the worst." Religion was important, he wrote, but, using words that would describe the lifelong attitude of his younger brother, he added, "too much of it is worse than none at all." The local authorities, noting "that the tendency of the said paper is to mock religion," promptly passed a resolution that required James to submit each issue to the authorities for approval before publication. James defied the order with relish.

The General Court responded by forbidding James Franklin from publishing the *Courant*. At a secret meeting in his shop, it was decided that the best way around the order was to continue to print the paper, but without James as its publisher. On Monday, February 11, 1723, there appeared atop the *Courant* the masthead: "Printed and sold by Benjamin Franklin."

Benjamin's *Courant* was more cautious than that of his brother. An editorial in his first issue denounced publications that were "hateful" and "malicious," and it declared that henceforth the *Courant* would be "designed purely for the diversion and merriment of the reader" and to "entertain the town with the most comical and diverting incidents of human life." The master of the paper, the editorial declared, would be the Roman god Janus, who could look two ways at once.[41]

The next few issues, however, hardly lived up to that billing. Most articles were slightly stale dispatches containing foreign news or old speeches. There was only one essay that was clearly written by Franklin, a wry musing on the folly of titles such as Viscount and Master. (His aversion to hereditary and aristocratic titles would be a theme throughout his life.) After a few weeks, James returned to the helm of the *Courant*, in fact if not officially, and he resumed treating Benjamin as an apprentice, subject to occasional beatings, rather than as a brother and fellow writer. Such treatment "demeaned me too much," Franklin recalled, and he became eager to move on. He had an urge for independence that he would help to make a hallmark of the American character.

THE RUNAWAY

Franklin managed his escape by taking advantage of a ruse his brother had contrived. When James had pretended to turn over the *Courant* to Benjamin, he signed an official discharge of his apprenticeship to make the transfer seem legitimate. But he then made Benjamin sign a new apprentice agreement that would be kept secret. A few months later, Benjamin decided to run away. He assumed, correctly, that his brother would realize that it was unwise to try to enforce the secret indenture.

Benjamin Franklin left behind a brother whose paper would slowly fail and whose reputation would eventually be reduced to a tarnished historical footnote. James was doomed by his brother's sharp pen to be remembered "for the blows his passion too often urged him to bestow upon me." Indeed, his significance in Franklin's life is described in a brusque footnote in the *Autobiography,* written during Franklin's time as a colonial agent fighting British rule: "I fancy his harsh and tyrannical treatment of me might be a means of impressing me with that aversion to arbitrary power that has stuck to me through my whole life."

James deserved better. If Franklin learned an "aversion to arbitrary power" from him, it was not merely because of his alleged tyrannical style but because he had set an example by challenging, with bravery and spunk, Boston's ruling elite. James was the first great fighter for an independent press in America, and he was the most important journalistic influence on his younger brother.

He was also an important literary influence. Silence Dogood may have been, in Benjamin's mind, modeled on Addison and Steele, but in fact she more closely resembled, in her down-home vernacular and common-touch perceptions, Abigail Afterwit, Jack Dulman, and the other pseudonymous characters that had been created for the *Courant* by James.

Benjamin's break with his brother was fortunate for his career. As great as it was to be raised in Boston, it would likely have become a constricting town for a free-spirited deist who had not attended Harvard. "I had already made myself a little obnoxious to the governing party," he later wrote, "and it was likely I might if I stayed soon bring myself into scrapes." His mockery of religion meant that he was pointed to on the streets "with horror by good people as an infidel or atheist." All in all, it was a good time for him to leave both his brother and Boston behind.[42]

It was a tradition among American pioneers, when their communities became too confining, to strike out for the frontier. But Franklin was a different type of American rebel. The wilderness did not beckon. Instead, he was enticed by the new commercial centers, New York and Philadelphia, that offered the chance to become a self-made success. John Winthrop may have led his Puritan band on an errand into the wilderness; Franklin, on the other hand, was part of a new breed leading an errand into the Market streets.

Afraid that his brother would try to detain him, Franklin had a friend secretly book him passage on a sloop for New York using the cover story that it was for a boy who needed to sneak away because he "had an intrigue with a girl of bad character" (or, as Franklin put it in an earlier draft, "had got a naughty girl with child"). Selling some of his books to pay for the fare, the 17-year-old Franklin set sail in a fair wind on the evening of Wednesday, September 25, 1723. The following Monday, the *New England Courant* carried a succinct, slightly sad little ad: "James Franklin, printer in Queen Street, wants a likely lad for an Apprentice."[43]

CHAPTER THREE

JOURNEYMAN

Philadelphia and London, 1723–1726

KEIMER'S SHOP

As a young apprentice, Franklin had read a book extolling vegetarianism. He embraced the diet, but not just for moral and health reasons. His main motive was financial: it enabled him to take the money his brother allotted him for food and save half for books. While his coworkers went off for hearty meals, Franklin ate biscuits and raisins and used the time for study, "in which I made the greater progress from that greater clearness of head and quicker apprehension which usually attend temperance in eating and drinking."[1]

But Franklin was a reasonable soul, so wedded to being rational that he became adroit at rationalizing. During his voyage from Boston to New York, when his boat lay becalmed off Block Island, the crew caught and cooked some cod. Franklin at first refused any, until the aroma from the frying pan became too enticing. With droll self-awareness, he later recalled what happened:

> I balanced some time between principle and inclination until I recollected that when the fish were opened, I saw smaller fish taken out of their stomachs. "Then," thought I, "if you eat one another, I don't see why we may not eat you." So I dined upon cod very heartily and have since continued to eat as other people, returning only now and then occasionally to a vegetable diet.

From this he drew a wry, perhaps even a bit cynical, lesson that he expressed as a maxim: "So convenient a thing it is to be a reasonable creature, since it enables one to find or make a reason for everything one has a mind to do."[2]

Franklin's rationalism would make him an exemplar of the Enlightenment, the age of reason that flourished in eighteenth-century Europe and America. He had little use for the fervor of the religious age into which he was born, nor for the sublime sentiments of the Romantic period that began budding near the end of his life. But like Voltaire, he was able to poke fun at his own efforts, and that of humanity in general, to be guided by reason. A recurring theme in his autobiography, as well as in his tales and almanacs, was his amusement at man's ability to rationalize what was convenient.

At 17, Franklin was physically striking: muscular, barrel-chested, open-faced, and almost six feet tall. He had the happy talent of being at ease in almost any company, from scrappy tradesmen to wealthy merchants, scholars to rogues. His most notable trait was a personal magnetism; he attracted people who wanted to help him. Never shy, and always eager to win friends and patrons, he gregariously exploited this charm.

On his runaway journey, for example, he met the sole printer in New York, William Bradford, who had published editorials supporting James Franklin's fight against the "oppressors and bigots" in Boston. Bradford had no job to offer, but he suggested that the young runaway continue on to Philadelphia and seek work with his son Andrew Bradford, who ran the family print shop and weekly newspaper there.

Franklin arrived at Philadelphia's Market Street wharf on a Sunday morning ten days after his departure from Boston. In his pocket he had nothing more than a Dutch dollar and about a shilling in copper, the latter of which he gave to the boatmen to pay for his passage. They tried to decline it, because Franklin had helped with the rowing, but he insisted. He also gave away two of the three puffy rolls he bought to a mother and child he had met on the journey. "A man [is] sometimes more generous when he has little money than when he has plenty," he later wrote, "perhaps through fear of being thought to have but little."[3]

From his first moments in Philadelphia, Franklin cared about such appearances. American individualists sometimes boast of not worrying about what others think of them. Franklin, more typically, nurtured his reputation, as a matter of both pride and utility, and he became the country's first unabashed public relations expert. "I took care not only to be in *reality* industrious and frugal," he later wrote, "but to avoid all *appearances* of the contrary" (his emphasis). Especially in his early years as a young tradesman, he was, in the words of the critic Jonathan Yardley, "a self-created and self-willed man who moved through life at a calculated pace toward calculated ends."[4]

With a population of two thousand, Philadelphia was then America's second-largest village after Boston. Envisioned by William Penn as a "green country town," it featured a well-planned grid of wide streets lined with brick houses. In addition to the original Quakers who had settled there fifty years earlier, the city named for brotherly love had attracted raucous and entrepreneurial German, Scotch, and Irish immigrants who turned it into a lively marketplace filled with shops and taverns. Though its economy was sputtering and most of its streets were dirty and unpaved, the tone set by both the Quakers and subsequent immigrants was appealing to Franklin. They tended to be diligent, unpretentious, friendly, and tolerant, especially compared to the Puritans of Boston.

The morning after his arrival, rested and better dressed, Franklin called on Andrew Bradford's shop. There he found not only the young printer but also his father, William, who had come from New York on horseback and made it there faster. Andrew had no immediate work for the runaway, so William brought him around to see the town's other printer, Samuel Keimer—a testament both to Franklin's charming ability to enlist patrons and to the peculiar admixture of cooperation and competition so often found among American tradesmen.

Keimer was a disheveled and quirky man with a motley printing operation. He asked Franklin a few questions, gave him a composing stick to assess his skills, and then promised to employ him as soon as he had more work. Not knowing that William was the father of his competitor, Keimer volubly described his plans for luring away most of Andrew Bradford's business. Franklin stood by silently, marveling at the elder Bradford's craftiness. After Bradford left, Franklin recalled, Keimer "was greatly surprised when I told him who the old man was."

Even after this inauspicious introduction, Franklin was able to get work from Keimer while he lodged with the younger Bradford. When Keimer finally insisted that he find living quarters that were less of a professional conflict, he fortuitously was able to rent a room from John Read, the father of the young girl who had been so amused by his appearance the day he straggled off the boat. "My chest and clothes being come by this time, I made rather a more respectable appearance in the eyes of Miss Read than I had done when she first happened to see me eating my roll in the street," he noted.[5]

Franklin thought Keimer an "odd fish," but he enjoyed having sport with him as they shared their love for philosophical debate. Franklin honed the Socratic method he found so useful for winning arguments without antagonizing opponents. He would ask Keimer questions that seemed innocent and tangential but eventually exposed his logical fallacies. Keimer, who was prone to embracing eclectic religious beliefs, was so impressed that he proposed they establish a sect together. Keimer would be in charge of the doctrines, such as not trimming one's beard, and Franklin would be in charge of defending them. Franklin agreed with one condition: that vegetarianism be part of the creed. The experiment ended after three months when Keimer, ravenous, gave in to temptation and ate an entire roast pig by himself one evening.

Franklin's magnetism attracted not only patrons but also friends. With his clever mind, disarming wit, and winning smile, he became a popular member of the town's coterie of young tradesmen. His clique included three young clerks: Charles Osborne, Joseph Watson, and James Ralph. Ralph was the most literary of the group, a poet convinced both of his own talent and of the need to be self-indulgent in order to be a great artist. Osborne, a critical lad, was jealous and invariably belittled Ralph's efforts. On one of their long walks by the river, during which the four friends read their work to one another, Ralph had a poem he knew Osborne would criticize. So he got Franklin to read the poem as if it were his own. Osborne, falling for the ruse, heaped praise on it, teaching Franklin a rule of human nature that served him well (with a few exceptions) throughout his career: people are more likely to admire your work if you're able to keep them from feeling jealous of you.[6]

AN UNRELIABLE PATRON

The most fateful patron Franklin befriended was Pennsylvania's effusive governor Sir William Keith, a well-meaning but feckless busybody. They met as a result of a passionate letter Franklin had written to a brother-in-law explaining why he was happy in Philadelphia and had no desire to return to Boston or let his parents know where he was. The relative showed the letter to Governor Keith, who expressed surprise that a missive so eloquent had been written by a lad so young. The governor, who realized that both of the established printers in his province were wretched, decided to seek out Franklin and encourage him.

When Governor Keith, dressed in all his finery, marched up the street to Keimer's print shop, the disheveled owner bustled out to greet him. To his surprise, Keith asked to see Franklin, whom he proceeded to lavish with compliments and an invitation to join him for a drink. Keimer, Franklin later noted, "stared like a pig poisoned."[7]

Over fine Madeira at a nearby tavern, Governor Keith offered to help Franklin set up on his own. He would use his influence, Keith promised, to get him the province's official business and would write Franklin's father a letter exhorting him to help finance his son. Keith followed up with invitations to dinner, further flattery, and continued encouragement. So, with a fulsome letter from Keith in hand and dreams of a familial reconciliation followed by fame and fortune, Franklin was ready to face his family again. He boarded a ship heading for Boston in April 1724.

It had been seven months since he had run away, and his parents were not even sure that he was still alive, so they were thrilled by his return and welcomed him warmly. Franklin had not, however, yet learned his lesson about the pitfalls of pride and of provoking jealousy.

He sauntered down to the print shop of his jilted brother James, proudly sporting a "genteel new suit," a fancy watch, and £5 of silver coins bulging his pocket. James looked him up and down, turned on his heels, and silently went back to work.

Franklin could not refrain from flaunting his new status. As James stewed, he regaled the shop's young journeymen with tales of his happy life in Philadelphia, spread his silver coins on the table for them to admire, and gave them money to buy drinks. James later told their mother he could never forget nor forgive the offense. "In this, however, he was mistaken," Franklin recalled.

His family's old antagonist Cotton Mather was more receptive, and instructive. He invited young Franklin over, chatted with him in his magnificent library, and let it be known that he forgave him for the barbs that had appeared in the *Courant*. As they were making their way out, they went through a narrow passage and Mather suddenly warned, "Stoop! Stoop!" Franklin, not understanding the exhortation, bumped his head on a low beam. As was his wont, Mather turned it into a homily: "Let this be a caution to you not always to hold your head so high. Stoop, young man, stoop—as you go through this world—and you'll miss many hard thumps." As Franklin later recalled to Mather's son, "This advice, thus beat into my head, has frequently been of use to me, and I often think of it when I see pride mortified and misfortunes brought upon people by carrying their heads too high." Although the lesson was a useful counterpoint to his showy visit to his brother's print shop, he failed to include it in his autobiography.[8]

Governor Keith's letter and proposal surprised Josiah Franklin. But after considering it for a few days, he decided it was imprudent to fund a rather rebellious runaway who was only 18. Though he was proud of the patronage his son had attracted and the industriousness he had shown, Josiah knew that Benjamin was still impudent.

Seeing no chance of a reconciliation between his two sons, Josiah did give his blessing for Benjamin to return to Philadelphia, with the exhortation "to behave respectfully to the people there . . . and avoid lampooning and libeling, to which he thought I had too much inclination." If he was able by "steady industry and prudent parsimony" to save almost enough to open his own shop by the time he was 21, Josiah promised he would help fund the rest.

Franklin's old friend John Collins, entranced by his tales, decided to leave Boston as well. But once in Philadelphia, the two teenagers had a falling-out. Collins, academically brighter than Franklin but less disciplined, soon took to drink. He borrowed money from Franklin and began to resent him. One day, when they were boating with friends on the Delaware, Collins refused to row his turn. Others in the boat were willing to let it pass, but not Franklin, who scuffled with him, grabbed him by the crotch, and threw him overboard. Each time Collins swam up to the boat, Franklin and the others would row it away a few feet more while insisting that he promise to take his turn at the oars. Proud and resentful, Collins never agreed, but they finally allowed him back in. He and Franklin barely spoke after that, and Collins ended up going to Barbados, never repaying the money he had borrowed.

In the course of a few months, Franklin had learned from four people—James Ralph, James Franklin, Cotton Mather, and John Collins—lessons about rivalry and resentments, pride and modesty. Throughout his life, he would occasionally make enemies, such as the Penn family, and jealous rivals, such as John Adams. But he did so less than most men, especially men so accomplished. A secret to being more revered than resented, he learned, was to display (at least when he could muster the discipline) a self-deprecating humor, unpretentious demeanor, and unaggressive style in conversation.[9]

Josiah Franklin's refusal to fund his son's printing venture did not dampen Governor Keith's enthusiasm. "Since he will not set you up, I will do it myself," he grandly promised. "I am resolved to have a good printer here." He asked Franklin for a list of what equipment was necessary—Franklin estimated it would cost about £100—and then suggested that Franklin should sail to London so that he could personally pick out the fonts and make contacts. Keith pledged letters of credit to pay for both the equipment and the voyage.[10]

The adventurous Franklin was thrilled. In the months leading up to his planned departure, he dined frequently with the governor.

Whenever he asked for the promised letters of credit, they were not ready, but Franklin felt no reason to worry.

At the time, Franklin was courting his landlady's daughter, Deborah Read. Despite his sexual appetites, he was practical about what he wanted in a wife. Deborah was rather plain, but she offered the prospect of comfort and domesticity. Franklin offered a lot as well, in addition to his husky good looks and genial charm. He had transformed himself from the bedraggled runaway she first spotted wandering up Market Street into one of the town's most promising and eligible young tradesmen, one who had found favor with the governor and popularity with his peers. Deborah's father had recently died, which put her mother into financial difficulty and made her open to the prospect of a good marriage for her daughter. Nevertheless, she was wary of allowing her to marry a suitor who was preparing to leave for London. She insisted that marriage wait until he returned.

LONDON

In November 1724, just over a year after arriving in Philadelphia, Franklin set sail for London. Traveling with him was the boy who had replaced Collins as his unreliable best friend, the aspiring poet James Ralph, who was leaving behind a wife and child. Franklin still had not received the letters of credit from Governor Keith, but he was assured that they would be sent on board in the final bag of dispatches.

Only after he arrived in London, on Christmas Eve, did Franklin discover the truth. The flighty governor had supplied no letters of credit nor recommendation. Franklin, puzzled, consulted a fellow passenger named Thomas Denham, a prominent Quaker merchant who had befriended him on the voyage. Denham explained to Franklin that Keith was incorrigibly capricious, and he "laughed at the idea of the Governor's giving me a letter of credit, having, as he said, no credit to give." For Franklin, it was an insight into human foibles rather than evil. "He wished to please everybody," Franklin later said of Keith, "and having little to give, he gave expectations."[11]

Taking Denham's advice, Franklin decided to make the best of his situation. London was enjoying a golden age of peace and prosperity, one particularly appealing to an intellectually ambitious young printer. Among those then brightening the world of London letters were Swift, Defoe, Pope, Richardson, Fielding, and Chesterfield.

With the dreamy wastrel Ralph under his wing, Franklin found cheap lodgings and a job at a famous printing house, Samuel Palmer's. Ralph tried to get work as an actor, then as a journalist or clerk. He failed on all fronts, borrowing money from Franklin all the while.

It was an odd-couple symbiosis of the type often found between ambitious, practical guys and their carefree, romantic pals: Franklin diligently made the money, Ralph made sure they spent it all on the theater and other amusements, including occasional "intrigues with low women." Ralph quickly forgot his own wife and child in Philadelphia, and Franklin followed suit by ignoring his engagement to Deborah and writing her only once.

The friendship exploded, not surprisingly, over a woman. Ralph fell in love with a pleasant but poor young milliner, moved in with her, then was finally motivated to find work as a teacher in a village school in Berkshire. He wrote Franklin often, sending installments of a bad epic poem along with requests that Franklin look after his girlfriend. That he did all too well. He lent her money, comforted her loneliness, and then ("being at the time under no religious restraint") tried to seduce her. Ralph returned in a fury, broke off their friendship, and declared that the transgression released him from the duty of paying back any debts, which amounted to £27.[12]

Franklin later concluded that the loss of money he was owed was balanced by the loss of the burden of having Ralph as a friend. A pattern was emerging. Beginning with Collins and Ralph, Franklin easily made casual friends, intellectual companions, useful patrons, flirty admirers, and circles of genial acquaintances, but he was less good at nurturing lasting bonds that involved deep personal commitments or emotional relationships, even within his own family.

CALVINISM AND DEISM

While at Palmer's, Franklin helped print an edition of William Wollaston's *The Religion of Nature Delineated,* an Enlightenment tract that argued that religious truths were to be gleaned through the study of science and nature rather than through divine revelation. With the intellectual spunk that comes from being youthful and untutored, Franklin decided that Wollaston was right in general but wrong in parts, and he set out his own thinking in a piece he wrote early in 1725 called "A Dissertation on Liberty and Necessity, Pleasure and Pain."

In it, Franklin strung together theological premises with logical syllogisms to get himself quite tangled up. For example: God is "all wise, all good, all powerful," he posited. Therefore, everything that exists or happens is with his consent. "What He consents to must be good, because He is good; therefore evil doth not exist."

Furthermore, happiness existed only as a contrast to unhappiness, and one could not exist without the other. Therefore, they balanced out: "Since pain naturally and infallibly produces a pleasure in proportion to it, every individual creature must, in any state of life, have an equal quantity of each." Along the way, Franklin disproved (to his own satisfaction at least) the concept of an immortal soul, the possibility of free will, and the fundamental Calvinist tenet that people are destined to be either saved or damned. "A creature can do nothing but what is good," he declared, and all "must be equally esteemed by the Creator." [13]

Franklin's "Dissertation" does not belong in the annals of sophisticated philosophy. Indeed, it was, as he later conceded, so shallow and unconvincing as to be embarrassing. He printed a hundred copies, called it an "erratum," and burned as many as he could retrieve.

In his defense, philosophers greater and more mature than Franklin have, over the centuries, gotten lost when trying to sort out the question of free will and reconcile it with that of an all-knowing God. And many of us can perhaps remember—or would cringe at being reminded of—our papers or freshmen dorm disquisitions from when we were 19. Yet even as he matured, Franklin would never develop into a rigorous, first-rank philosopher on the order of such contemporaries as Berkeley and Hume. Like Dr. Johnson, he was more comfortable exploring practical thoughts and real-life situations than metaphysical abstractions or deductive proofs.

The primary value of his "Dissertation" lies in what it reveals about Franklin's fitful willingness to abandon Puritan theology. As a young man, he had read John Locke, Lord Shaftesbury, Joseph Addison, and others who embraced the freethinking religion and Enlightenment philosophy of deism, which held that each individual could best discover the truth about God through reason and studying nature, rather than through blind faith in received doctrines and divine revelation. He also read more orthodox tracts that defended the dogmas of Calvinism against such heresies, but he found them less convincing. As he wrote in his autobiography, "The arguments of the deists which were quoted to be refuted appeared to me much stronger than the refutations."[14]

Nevertheless, he soon came to the conclusion that a simple and complacent deism had its own set of drawbacks. He had converted Collins and Ralph to deism, and they soon wronged him without moral compunction. Likewise, he came to worry that his own freethinking had caused him to be cavalier toward Deborah Read and others. In a classic maxim that typifies his pragmatic approach to religion, Franklin declared of deism, "I began to suspect that this doctrine, though it might be true, was not very useful."

Although divine revelation "had no weight with me," he decided that religious practices were beneficial because they encouraged good behavior and a moral society. So he began to embrace a morally fortified brand of deism that held God was best served by doing good works and helping other people.

It was a philosophy that led him to renounce much of the doctrine of the Puritans and other Calvinists, who preached that salvation came through God's grace alone and could not be earned by doing good deeds. That possibility, they believed, was lost when Adam rejected God's covenant of good works and it was replaced by a covenant of grace in which the saved were part of an elect predetermined by God. To a budding rationalist and pragmatist like Franklin, the covenant of grace seemed "unintelligible" and, even worse, "not beneficial."[15]

A PLAN FOR MORAL CONDUCT

After a year at Palmer's, Franklin got a better-paying job at a far larger printing house, John Watts's. There the pressmen drank pint after pint of watery beer throughout the day to keep them fortified. With his penchant for temperance and frugality, Franklin tried to convince his fellow workers that they could get their nourishment better by eating porringers of hot-water gruel with bread. Thus he became known as the "Water American," admired for his strength, clear head, and ability to lend them money when they had used up their weekly pay at the alehouses.

Despite his abstinence, the workers at Watts's insisted that he pay a five-shilling initiation fee used for drinks. When he was promoted from the pressroom to the composition room, he was called on to pay yet another initiation, but this time he refused. As a result, he was treated as an outcast and subjected to small mischiefs. Finally, after three weeks, he relented and paid up, "convinced of the folly of being on ill terms" with his workmates. He promptly regained his popularity, earning the reputation of "a pretty good riggite," someone whose jocularity and ability as a "verbal satirist" earned him respect.

One of the least shy men imaginable, Franklin was as sociable in London as he had been in Boston and Philadelphia. He frequented the roundtables hosted by minor literary luminaries of the day, and he sought out introductions to various interesting people. Among his earliest surviving letters is one he sent to Sir Hans Sloane, secretary of the Royal Society. Franklin wrote that he had brought from America a purse made of asbestos, and he wondered if Sloane might want to buy it. Sloane paid a call on Franklin, brought the lad back to his Bloomsbury Square home to show off his collection, and bought the purse for a handsome sum. Franklin also made a deal to borrow books from a neighborhood bookseller.

Ever since, as a young boy, he had invented some paddles and flippers to propel himself across Boston harbor, Franklin had been fascinated by swimming. He studied one of the first books on the subject, *The Art of Swimming*, written in 1696 by a Frenchman named Melchisedec Thevenot, which helped to popularize the breaststroke.

(The crawl did not catch on for more than another century.) Franklin perfected variations on the motions for swimming both on the surface and underwater, "aiming at the graceful and easy as well as the useful."

Among the friends he taught to swim was a fellow young printer named Wygate. One day, during a boat trip on the Thames with Wygate and others, Franklin decided to show off. He stripped, leaped into the river, and swam back and forth to the bank using a variety of strokes. One member of the party offered to fund a swim school for Franklin. Wygate, for his part, "grew more and more attached" to him, and he proposed that they travel around Europe together as journeymen printers and teachers. "I was once inclined to it," Franklin recalled, "but, mentioning it to my good friend Mr. Denham, with whom I often spent an hour when I had leisure, he dissuaded me from it, advising me to think only of returning to Pennsylvania, which he was now about to do."[16]

Denham, the Quaker merchant Franklin had met on the voyage over, was planning to open a general store once back in Philadelphia, and he offered to pay Franklin's passage if he would agree to sign on as his clerk at £50 a year. It was less than he was making in London, but it offered him the chance both to return to America and to become established as a merchant, a vocation more exalted than that of printer. Together they set sail in July 1726.

Franklin had been burned in the past by his attraction to romantic rogues (Keith, Collins, Ralph) of dubious character. Denham, on the other hand, was a man of integrity. He had left England years earlier deeply in debt, made a small fortune in America, and on his return to England threw a lavish dinner for his old creditors. After thanking them profusely, he told them all to look under their plates. There they discovered full repayment plus interest. Henceforth, Franklin would find himself more attracted to people who were practical and reliable rather than dreamy and romantic.

To perfect the art of becoming such a reliable person, Franklin wrote out a "Plan for Future Conduct" during his eleven-week voyage back to Philadelphia. It would be the first of many personal credos that laid out pragmatic rules for success and made him the patron saint of self-improvement guides. He lamented that because he had never outlined a design for how he should conduct himself, his life so far had been somewhat confused. "Let me, therefore, make some resolutions, and some form of action, that, henceforth, I may live in all respects like a rational creature." There were four rules:

1. It is necessary for me to be extremely frugal for some time, till I have paid what I owe.
2. To endeavor to speak truth in every instance; to give nobody expectations that are not likely to be answered, but aim at sincerity in every word and action—the most amiable excellence in a rational being.
3. To apply myself industriously to whatever business I take in hand, and not divert my mind from my business by any foolish project of suddenly growing rich; for industry and patience are the surest means of plenty.
4. I resolve to speak ill of no man whatever.[17]

Rule 1 he had already mastered. Rule 3 he likewise had little trouble following. As for 2 and 4, he would henceforth preach them diligently and generally make a show of practicing them, though he would sometimes be better at the show than the practicing.

On his voyage home, the 20-year-old Franklin indulged what would be a lifelong scientific curiosity. He experimented on the small crabs he found on some seaweed, calculated his distance from London based on the timing of a lunar eclipse, and studied the habits of dolphins and flying fish.

His journal of the voyage also reveals his talent for observing human nature. When he heard the tale of a former governor of the Isle of Wight who had been considered saintly yet was known to be a knave by the keeper of his castle, Franklin concluded that it was impossible for a dishonest person, no matter how cunning, to completely conceal his character. "Truth and sincerity have a certain distinguishing native luster about them which cannot be perfectly counterfeited; they are like fire and flame, that cannot be painted."

While gambling at checkers with some shipmates, he formulated an "infallible rule," which was that "if two persons equal in judgment play for a considerable sum, he that loves money most shall lose; his anxiety for the success of the game confounds him." The rule, he decided, applied to other battles; a person who is too fearful will end up performing defensively and thus fail to seize offensive advantages.

He also developed theories about the sociable yearnings of men, ones that applied particularly to himself. One of the passengers was caught cheating at cards, and the others sought to fine him. When the fellow resisted paying, they decided on an even tougher punishment: he would be ostracized and completely shunned until he relented. Finally the miscreant paid the fine in order to end his excommunication. Franklin concluded:

> Man is a sociable being, and it is, for aught I know, one of the worst punishments to be excluded from society. I have read abundance of fine things on the subject of solitude, and I know it is a common boast in the mouths of those that affect to be thought wise that they are never less alone than when alone. I acknowledge solitude an agreeable refreshment to a busy mind; but were these thinking people obliged to be always alone, I am apt to think they would quickly find their very being insupportable to them.

One of the fundamental sentiments of the Enlightenment was that there is a sociable affinity, based on the natural instinct of benevolence, among fellow humans, and Franklin was an exemplar of this outlook. The opening phrase of the passage—"Man is a sociable being"—would turn out to be a defining credo of his long life. Later in the voyage, they encountered another vessel. Franklin noted:

> There is really something strangely cheering to the spirits in the meeting of a ship at sea, containing a society of creatures of the same species and in the same circumstances with ourselves, after we had been long separated and excommunicated as it were from the rest of mankind. I saw so many human countenances and I could scarce refrain from that kind of laughter which proceeds from some degree of inward pleasure.

His greatest happiness, however, came when he finally glimpsed the American shore. "My eyes," he wrote, "were dimmed with the suffusion of two small drops of joy." With his deepened appreciation of community, his scientific curiosity, and his rules for leading a practical life, Franklin was ready to settle down and pursue success in the city that, more than Boston or London, he now realized was his true home.[18]

CHAPTER FOUR

PRINTER

Philadelphia, 1726–1732

A SHOP OF HIS OWN

Franklin was a natural shopkeeper: clever, charming, astute about human nature, and eager to succeed. He became, as he put it, "an expert at selling" when he and Denham opened a general store on Water Street shortly after their return to Philadelphia in late 1726. Denham served as both a mentor and a surrogate parent to the aspiring 20-year-old. "We lodged and boarded together; he counseled me as a father, having a sincere regard for me. I respected and loved him."[1]

But Franklin's dreams of becoming a prosperous merchant ended after a few months, when Denham took ill and later died. In his oral will, he forgave Franklin the £10 he still owed for his ocean passage, but he did not leave him the business they had built. With no money and few prospects, Franklin swallowed his pride and accepted an offer from the eccentric Keimer to come back to his print shop, this time as the manager.[2]

Because there was no foundry in America for casting type, Franklin contrived one of his own by using Keimer's letters to make lead molds. He thus became the first person in America to manufacture type. One of the most popular contemporary typefaces, a sans-serif font known as Franklin Gothic that is often used in newspaper headlines, was named after him in 1902.

When Keimer began to assert his power, the aversion to arbitrary authority that was part of Franklin's heritage and breeding flared. One day, there was a commotion outside of the shop, and Franklin poked his head out of the window to watch. Keimer, who was on the street below, shouted at him to mind his own business. The public nature of the rebuke was humiliating, and Franklin quit on the spot. But after a few days, Keimer came begging for him to return, and Franklin did. They each needed the other, at least for the time being.

Keimer had won the right to print a new issue of paper currency for the New Jersey assembly, and only Franklin had the skills to do the job properly. He contrived a copperplate press to make bills so ornate they could not easily be counterfeited, and together they traveled to Burlington. Once again, it was young Franklin, the willing and witty conversationalist, rather than his slovenly master, who befriended the dignitaries. "My mind, having been much more improved by reading than Keimer's, I suppose it was for that reason my conversation seemed more valued. They had me to their houses, introduced me to their friends, and showed me much civility."[3]

The relationship with Keimer was not destined to last. Franklin, ever striving and chafing, realized that he was being used. Keimer was paying him to train the four "cheap hands" who worked at the shop with the intention of laying him off once they were in shape. Franklin, in turn, was willing to use Keimer. He and one of those apprenticed hands, Hugh Meredith, made secret plans to open a competing print shop, funded by Meredith's father, once Meredith's servitude was completed. Though not an outright devious scheme, it did not fully comport with Franklin's high-minded pledge to "aim at sincerity in every word and action."

Meredith, 30, was fond of reading but also of alcohol. His father, a Welsh-bred farmer, took a liking to Franklin, especially because he had persuaded his son to abstain (at least temporarily) from drinking. He agreed to provide the funding necessary (£200) for the two young men to set up a partnership, Franklin's contribution being his own talent. They sent to London for equipment,* which arrived early in 1728,

---

* The fonts that Franklin ordered were those created in the early 1720s by the famed London type-maker William Caslon, and they are the model for the Adobe Caslon typeface used for the text in this book.

shortly after the New Jersey job was completed and Meredith's indenture had expired.

The two partners bid farewell to the hapless Keimer, leased a house on Market Street, set up shop, and promptly served their first customer, a farmer referred by a friend. "This country man's five shillings, being our first fruits and coming so seasonably, gave me more pleasure than any crown I have since earned."

Their business succeeded largely because of Franklin's diligence. When they were hired by a group of Quakers to print 178 pages of their history, the rest to be printed by Keimer, Franklin did not leave the shop each night until he had completed a four-page folio, often working past eleven. One night, just as he was finishing that day's sheet, the plate dropped and broke; Franklin stayed overnight to redo it. "This industry visible to our neighbors began to give us character and credit," Franklin noted. One of the town's prominent merchants told members of his club, "The industry of that Franklin is superior to anything I ever saw of the kind; I see him still at work when I go home from club, and he is at work again before his neighbors are out of bed."

Franklin became an apostle of being—and, just as important, of appearing to be—industrious. Even after he became successful, he made a show of personally carting the rolls of paper he bought in a wheelbarrow down the street to his shop, rather than having a hired hand do it.[4]

Meredith, on the other hand, was far from industrious, having taken again to drink. In addition, his father had paid only half of the money he had committed for their equipment, which prompted threatening letters from the suppliers. Franklin found two friends who were willing to finance him, but only if he dumped Meredith. Fortunately, Meredith realized that he was better off returning to farming. All ended well: Meredith let Franklin buy him out of their partnership, headed off to the Carolinas, and later wrote letters describing the countryside there, which Franklin published.

And so Franklin finally had a print shop of his own. More to the point, he had a career. Printing and its related endeavors—publisher, writer, newspaperman, postmaster—began to seem not merely a job but an interesting calling, both noble and fun. In his long life he would have many other careers: scientist, politician, statesman, diplomat. But henceforth he always identified himself the way he would do sixty years later in the opening words of his last will and testament: "I, Benjamin Franklin of Philadelphia, printer."[5]

THE JUNTO

Franklin was the consummate networker. He liked to mix his civic life with his social one, and he merrily leveraged both to further his business life. This approach was displayed when he formed a club of young workingmen in the fall of 1727, shortly after his return to Philadelphia, that was commonly called the Leather Apron Club and officially dubbed the Junto.

Franklin's small club was composed of enterprising tradesmen and artisans, rather than the social elite who had their own fancier gentlemen's clubs. At first, the members went to a local tavern for their Friday evening meetings, but soon they were able to rent a house of their own. There they discussed issues of the day, debated philosophical topics, devised schemes for self-improvement, and formed a network for the furtherance of their own careers.

The enterprise was typical of Franklin, who seemed ever eager to organize clubs and associations for mutual benefit, and it was also typically American. As the nation developed a shopkeeping middle class, its people balanced their individualist streaks with a propensity to form clubs, lodges, associations, and fraternal orders. Franklin epitomized this Rotarian urge and has remained, after more than two centuries, a symbol of it.

Franklin's Junto initially had twelve young members, among them his printing partner Hugh Meredith; George Webb, a witty but imprudent runaway Oxford student who was also apprenticed to Keimer; Thomas Godfrey, a glassworker and amateur mathematician; Joseph Breintnall, a scrivener and poetry lover; Robert Grace, a generous and pun-loving man with some family money; and William Coleman, a clear-headed and good-hearted clerk with exacting morals, who later became a distinguished merchant.

Besides being amiable club mates, the Junto members often proved helpful to one another personally and professionally. Godfrey boarded at Franklin's shop and his wife cooked for them. Breintnall was the friend who procured the Quaker printing commission. And Grace and Coleman funded Franklin when he broke with Meredith.

The tone Franklin set for Junto meetings was earnest. Initiates were required to stand, lay their hand on their breast, and answer properly four questions: Do you have disrespect for any current member? Do you love mankind in general regardless of religion or profession? Do you feel people should ever be punished because of their opinions or mode of worship? Do you love and pursue truth for its own sake?

Franklin was worried that his fondness for conversation and eagerness to impress made him prone to "prattling, punning and joking, which only made me acceptable to trifling company." Knowledge, he realized, "was obtained rather by the use of the ear than of the tongue." So in the Junto, he began to work on his use of silence and gentle dialogue.

One method, which he had developed during his mock debates with John Collins in Boston and then when discoursing with Keimer, was to pursue topics through soft, Socratic queries. That became the preferred style for Junto meetings. Discussions were to be conducted "without fondness for dispute or desire of victory." Franklin taught his friends to push their ideas through suggestions and questions, and to use (or at least feign) naïve curiosity to avoid contradicting people in a manner that could give offense. "All expressions of positiveness in opinion or of direct contradiction," he recalled, "were prohibited under small pecuniary penalties." It was a style he would urge on the Constitutional Convention sixty years later.

In a witty newspaper piece called "On Conversation," which he wrote shortly after forming the Junto, Franklin stressed the importance of deferring, or at least giving the appearance of deferring, to others. Otherwise, even the smartest comments would "occasion envy and disgust." His secret for how to win friends and influence people read like an early Dale Carnegie course: "Would you win the hearts of others, you must not seem to vie with them, but to admire them. Give them every opportunity of displaying their own qualifications, and when you have indulged their vanity, they will praise you in turn and prefer you above others . . . Such is the vanity of mankind that minding what others say is a much surer way of pleasing them than talking well ourselves."[6]

Franklin went on to catalog the most common conversational sins "which cause dislike," the greatest being "talking overmuch . . . which never fails to excite resentment." The only thing amusing about such people, he joked, was watching two of them meet: "The vexation they both feel is visible in their looks and gestures; you shall see them gape and stare and interrupt one another at every turn, and watch with utmost impatience for a cough or pause, when they may crowd a word in edgeways."

The other sins on his list were, in order: seeming uninterested, speaking too much about your own life, prying for personal secrets ("an unpardonable rudeness"), telling long and pointless stories ("old folks are most subject to this error, which is one chief reason their company is so often shunned"), contradicting or disputing someone directly, ridiculing or railing against things except in small witty doses ("it's like salt, a little of which in some cases gives relish, but if thrown on by handfuls spoils all"), and spreading scandal (though he would later write lighthearted defenses of gossip).

The older he got, the more Franklin learned (with a few notable lapses) to follow his own advice. He used silence wisely, employed an indirect style of persuasion, and feigned modesty and naïveté in disputes. "When another asserted something that I thought an error, I denied myself the pleasure of contradicting him." Instead, he would agree in parts and suggest his differences only indirectly. "For these fifty years past no one has ever heard a dogmatical expression escape me," he recalled when writing his autobiography. This velvet-tongued and sweetly passive style of circumspect argument would make him seem sage to some, insinuating and manipulative to others, but inflammatory to almost nobody. The method would also become, often with a nod to Franklin, a staple in modern management guides and self-improvement books.

Though the youngest member of the Junto, Franklin was, by dint of his intellectual charisma and conversational charm, not only its founder but its driving force. The topics discussed ranged from the social to the scientific and metaphysical. Most of them were earnest, some were quirky, and all were intriguing. Did importing indentured servants make America more prosperous? What made a piece of writing good? Why did condensation form on a cold mug? What accounted for happiness? What is wisdom? Is there a difference between knowledge and prudence? If a sovereign power deprives a citizen of his rights, is it justifiable for him to resist?

In addition to such topics of debate, Franklin laid out a guide for the type of conversational contributions each member could usefully make. There were twenty-four in all, and because their practicality is so revealing of Franklin's purposeful approach, they are worth excerpting at length:

1. Have you met with anything in the author you last read remarkable or suited to be communicated to the Junto? . . .

2. What new story have you lately heard agreeable for telling in conversation?

3. Hath any citizen in your knowledge failed in his business lately, and what have you heard of the cause?

4. Have you lately heard of any citizen's thriving well, and by what means?

5. Have you lately heard how any present rich man, here or elsewhere, got his estate?

6. Do you know of any fellow citizen who has lately done a worthy action deserving praise and imitation? Or who has committed an error proper for us to be warned against and avoid?

7. What unhappy effects of intemperance have you lately observed or heard? Of imprudence? Of passion? Or of any other vice or folly? . . .

12. Hath any deserving stranger arrived in town since last meeting that you heard of? And what have you heard of his character or merits? And whether you think it lies in the power of the Junto to oblige him or encourage him as he deserves? . . .

14. Have you lately observed any defect in the laws of your country of which it would be proper to move the legislature for an amendment?
15. Have you lately observed any encroachments on the just liberties of the people?
16. Has anybody attacked your reputation lately, and what can the Junto do toward securing it?
17. Is there any man whose friendship you want and which the Junto or any of them can procure for you? . . .
20. In what manner can the Junto or any of them assist you in any of your honorable designs? [7]

Franklin used the Junto as a launching pad for a variety of his public-service ideas. Early on, the group discussed whether Pennsylvania should increase its supply of paper currency, a proposal Franklin heartily favored because he thought it would benefit the economy and, of course, his own printing business. (Franklin and, by extension, the Junto were particularly fond of things that could help the public as well as themselves.) When the Junto moved into its own rented rooms, it created a library of books pooled from its members, which later formed the foundation for America's first subscription library. Out of the Junto also came Franklin's proposals for establishing a tax to pay for neighborhood constables, for creating a volunteer fire force, and for establishing the academy that later became the University of Pennsylvania.

Many of the rules and proposed queries for the Junto were similar to, though a bit less judgmental than, those that Cotton Mather had devised for his neighborhood benevolent societies a generation earlier in Boston. One of Mather's, for example, was: "Is there any particular person whose disorderly behavior may be so scandalous and so notorious that we may do well to send unto the said person our charitable admonitions?" Daniel Defoe's essay "Friendly Societies" and John Locke's "Rules of a Society which Met Once a Week for the Improvement of Useful Knowledge," both of which Franklin had read, also served as models. [8]

But, for the most part, with its earnest tenor and emphasis on self-improvement, the Junto was a product of Franklin's own persona and part of his imprint on the American personality. It flourished with him at the helm for thirty years. Although it operated in relative secrecy, so many people sought to join that Franklin empowered each member to form his own spinoff club. Four or five affiliates flourished, and the Junto served as an extension and amplification of Franklin's gregarious civic nature. Like Franklin himself, it was practical, industrious, inquiring, convivial, and middle-brow philosophical. It celebrated civic virtue, mutual benefits, the improvement of self and society, and the proposition that hardworking citizens could do well by doing good. It was, in short, Franklin writ public.

THE BUSY-BODY ESSAYS

Frugal and industrious, with a network of Junto members to steer business his way, Franklin was doing modestly well as one of three printers in a town that would naturally have supported only two. But he had learned from his apprentice days in Boston that true success would come if he had not only a printing operation but also his own content and distribution network. His competitor Andrew Bradford published the town's only newspaper, which was paltry but profitable, and that helped Bradford's printing business by giving him clout with the merchants and politicians. He also was the postmaster, which gave him some control over what papers got distributed plus first access to news from afar.

Franklin decided to take Bradford on, and over the next decade he would succeed by building a media conglomerate that included production capacity (printing operations, franchised printers in other cities), products (a newspaper, magazine, almanac), content (his own writings, his alter ego Poor Richard's, and those of his Junto), and distribution (eventually the whole of the colonial postal system).

First came the newspaper. Franklin decided to launch a competitor to Bradford's *American Weekly Mercury*, but he made the mistake of confiding his plan to George Webb, a fellow member of the Junto who was an apprentice at Keimer's print shop. Webb, to Franklin's dismay, told Keimer, who immediately launched a slapdash newspaper of his own, to which he gave the unwieldly name *The Universal Instructor in All Arts and Sciences, and Pennsylvania Gazette.* Franklin realized that it would be difficult to launch a third paper right away, and he did not have the funds. So he came up with a plan to first crush Keimer's paper by using the most powerful weapon at his disposal: the fact that he was the best writer in Philadelphia, and probably, at 23, the most amusing writer in all of America. (Carl Van Doren, a Franklin biographer and great literary critic of the 1930s, flatly declared of Franklin that in 1728, "he was the best writer in America." The closest rival for that title at the time would probably be the preacher Jonathan Edwards, who was certainly more intense and literary, though far less felicitous and amusing.)

In a competitive bank shot, Franklin decided to write a series of anonymous letters and essays, along the lines of the Silence Dogood pieces of his youth, for Bradford's *Mercury* to draw attention away from Keimer's new paper. The goal was to enliven, at least until Keimer was beaten, Bradford's dull paper, which in its ten years had never published any such features.

The first two pieces were attacks on poor Keimer, who was serializing entries from an encyclopedia. His initial installment included, innocently enough, an entry on abortion. Franklin pounced. Using the pen names "Martha Careful" and "Celia Shortface," he wrote letters to Bradford's paper feigning shock and indignation at Keimer's offense. As Miss Careful threatened, "If he proceeds farther to expose the secrets of our sex in that audacious manner [women would] run the hazard of taking him by the beard in the next place we meet him." Thus Franklin manufactured the first recorded abortion debate in America, not because he had any strong feelings on the issue, but because he knew it would help sell newspapers.

The next week Franklin launched a series of classic essays signed "Busy-Body," which Bradford published on his front page with a large byline. Franklin wrote at least four on his own and two others in part before turning the series over to fellow Junto member Joseph Breintnall. "By this means the attention of the public was fixed on that paper, and Keimer's proposals, which we burlesqued and ridiculed, were disregarded."[9]

The Busy-Body began by cleverly establishing the inadequacies of Bradford's paper ("frequently very dull") and declaring his intention to make it (at least temporarily) better. He would do so by being a scold and tattle, in the tradition of the character Isaac Bickerstaff that the English essayist Richard Steele had created, thus adding gossip columnist to the list of Franklin's American firsts. He readily admitted that much of this was "nobody's business," but "out of zeal for the public good," he volunteered "to take nobody's business wholly into my own hands." Some might find themselves offended, he warned. Yet, he pointed out what was, and is, the basic appeal of gossip: "As most people delight in censure when they themselves are not the objects of it, if any are offended at my publicly exposing their private vices, I promise they shall have the satisfaction, in a very little time, of seeing their good friends and neighbors in the same circumstances."

Keimer responded with a fusty admonition that the Busy-Body series might initially raise for readers of Bradford's paper the "expectation that they would now have some entertainment for their money," but they would soon feel "a secret grief to see the reputation of their neighbors blasted." When the Busy-Body merrily continued to publish his barbs, the excitable Keimer became more shrill. He responded with limp doggerel: "You hinted at me in your paper. Which now has made me draw my rapier. With scornful eye, I see your hate. And pity your unhappy fate." He paired this with a convoluted tale called "Hue and Cry after the Busy-Body," portraying Franklin and Breintnall as a two-headed monster, with Franklin described as "every Ape's epitome . . . as threadbare as his great coat, and skull as thick as his shoe soles."[10]

Keimer thus became one of Franklin's first outspoken foes. The betrayal, the press war, the dueling essays would all be repeated a decade later when Franklin and Bradford each decided to start magazines.

Sadly for those who enjoy titillation, the Busy-Body essays in fact failed to deliver much gossip. Instead, they tended to be clever tales with thinly disguised real-life counterparts (in one instance, a reader took the effort to publish a key to whom each character referred). Franklin employed what is now a standard disingenuous disclaimer:

"If any bad characters happen to be drawn in the course of these papers, they mean no particular person."

The final Busy-Body that was mainly written by Franklin made fun of treasure seekers who used divining rods and dug up the woods looking for buried pirate loot. "Men otherwise of very good sense have been drawn into this practice through an overweening desire of sudden wealth," he wrote, "while the rational and almost certain methods of acquiring riches by industry and frugality are neglected." The fable, an attack on the get-rich-quick schemes of the time, went on to preach Franklin's favorite theme: slow and steady diligence is the true way to wealth. He ended by quoting what his imaginary friend Agricola said on giving his son a parcel of land: "I assure thee I have found a considerable quantity of gold by digging there; thee mayst do the same. But thee must carefully observe this, Never to dig more than plow deep."

The essay had a second half that advocated more paper currency for Pennsylvania. Franklin wrote most of it, with a small section written by Breintnall. Franklin implied that those who opposed more paper currency were trying to protect their own financial interests, though he of course had his own financial interest in the approval of more printing work. He also launched the first of what would be many attacks on the province's Proprietors, the Penn family, and their appointed governor, by implying that they were trying to make the bulk of Pennsylvania's residents "their tenants and vassals." This ending was deleted in most editions of Bradford's newspaper, perhaps because Bradford was allied with the Penn family and their party.[11]

Another reason for pulling back the snide section on paper currency was that Franklin had produced a far more thoughtful essay on the subject, which he discussed in the Junto and published as a pamphlet the following week. "A Modest Enquiry into the Nature and Necessity of a Paper Currency" was Franklin's first serious analysis of public policy, and it holds up a lot better than his metaphysical musings on religion. Money was a concept he had a solid feel for, unlike theological abstractions.

Franklin argued that the lack of enough currency caused interest rates to rise, kept wages low, and increased dependence on imports. Creditors and big landowners opposed an increase in currency for selfish reasons, he charged, but "those who are lovers of trade and delight to see manufactures encouraged will be for having a large addition to our currency." Franklin's key insight was that hard currency, such as silver and gold, was not the true measure of a nation's wealth: "The riches of a country are to be valued by the quantity of labor its inhabitants are able to purchase, and not by the quantity of silver and gold they possess."

The essay was very popular, except among the wealthy, and it helped to persuade the legislature to adopt the proposed increase in paper currency. Although Bradford got the first commission to print some of the money, Franklin was given the next round of work. In the spirit of what Poor Richard would call "doing well by doing good," Franklin was not averse to mingling his private interests with his public ones. His friends in the legislature, "who considered I had been of some service, thought it fit to reward me by employing me in printing the money—a very profitable job and a great help to me. This was another advantage gained by my being able to write."[12]

THE PENNSYLVANIA GAZETTE

Franklin's scheme to put Keimer out of business, which was aided by the quirky printer's own incompetence and inability to ignore barbs, soon succeeded. He fell into debt, was briefly imprisoned, fled to Barbados, and as he was leaving sold his newspaper to Franklin. Jettisoning the serialized encyclopedia and part of the paper's unwieldy name, Franklin became the proud publisher of *The Pennsylvania Gazette* in October 1729. In his first letter to his readers, he announced that "there are many who have long desired to see a good newspaper in Pennsylvania," thus taking a poke at both Keimer and Bradford.[13]

There are many types of newspaper editors. Some are crusading ideologues who are blessed with strong opinions, partisan passions, or a desire to challenge authority. Benjamin's brother James was in this category. Some are the opposite: they like power and their proximity to it, and are comfortable with the established order and feel vested in it. Franklin's Philadelphia competitor Andrew Bradford was such.

And then there are those who are charmed and amused by the world and delight in charming and amusing others. They tend to be skeptical of both orthodoxies and heresies, and they are earnest in their desire to seek truth and promote public betterment (as well as sell papers). There fits Franklin. He was graced—and afflicted—with the trait so common to journalists, especially ones who have read Swift and Addison once too often, of wanting to participate in the world while also remaining a detached observer. As a journalist he could step out of a scene, even one that passionately engaged him, and comment on it, or on himself, with a droll irony. The depths of his beliefs were often concealed by his knack for engaging in a knowing wink.

Like most other newspapers of the time, Franklin's *Pennsylvania Gazette* was filled not only with short news items and reports on public events, but also with amusing essays and letters from readers. What made his paper a delight was its wealth of this type of correspondence, much of it written under pseudonyms by Franklin himself. This gimmick of writing as if from a reader gave Franklin more leeway to poke fun at rivals, revel in gossip, circumvent his personal pledge to speak ill of no one, and test-drive his evolving philosophies.

In a classic canny maneuver, Franklin corrected an early typo—he had reported that someone "died" at a restaurant when he meant to say "dined" at it—by composing a letter from a fictitious "J.T." who discoursed on other amusing misprints. For example, one edition of the Bible quoted David as saying he was "wonderfully mad" rather than "made," which caused an "ignorant preacher to harangue his audience for half an hour on the subject of spiritual madness." Franklin then went on (under the guise of J.T.) to praise Franklin's own paper, point out a similar typo made by his rival Bradford, criticize Bradford for being generally sloppier, and (with delicious irony) praise Franklin for not criticizing Bradford: "Your paper is most commonly very correct, and yet you were never known to triumph upon it by publicly ridiculing and exposing the continual blunders of your contemporary." Franklin even turned his false modesty into a maxim to forgive his typo: "Whoever accustoms himself to pass over in silence the faults of his neighbors shall meet with much better quarter from the world when he happens to fall into a mistake himself."[14]

The Franklin–Bradford newspaper war also included disputes over scoops and stolen stories. "When Mr. Bradford publishes after us," Franklin wrote in one editor's note, "and has occasion to take an Article or two out of the Gazette, which he is always welcome to do, he is desired not to date his paper a day before ours lest readers should imagine we take from him, which we always carefully avoid."

Their competition had been going on for a year when Franklin set out to win from Bradford the job of being the official printer for the Pennsylvania Assembly. He had already begun cultivating some of the members, especially those in the faction that resisted the power of the Penn family and its upper-crust supporters. After Bradford printed the governor's address to the Assembly in a "coarse and blundering manner," Franklin saw his opening. He printed the same message "elegantly and correctly," as he put it, and sent it to each of the members. "It strengthened the hands of our friends in the House," Franklin later recalled, "and they voted us their printers."[15]

Even as he became more political, Franklin resisted making his newspaper fiercely partisan. He expressed his credo as a publisher in a famous *Gazette* editorial "Apology for Printers," which remains one of the best and most forceful defenses of a free press.

The opinions people have, Franklin wrote, are "almost as various as their faces." The job of printers is to allow people to express these differing opinions. "There would be very little printed," he noted, if publishers produced only things that offended nobody. At stake was the virtue of free expression, and Franklin summed up the Enlightenment position in a sentence that is now framed on newsroom walls: "Printers are educated in the belief that when men differ in opinion, both sides ought equally to have the advantage of being heard by the public; and that when Truth and Error have fair play, the former is always an overmatch for the latter."

"It is unreasonable to imagine that printers approve of everything they print," he went on to argue. "It is likewise unreasonable what some assert, That printers ought not to print anything but what they approve; since . . . an end would thereby be put to free writing, and the world would afterwards have nothing to read but what happened to be the opinions of printers."

With a wry touch, he reminded his readers that publishers are in business both to make money and inform the public. "Hence they cheerfully service all contending writers that pay them well," even if they don't agree with the writers' opinions. "If all people of different opinions in this province would engage to give me as much for not printing things they don't like as I could get by printing them, I should probably live a very easy life; and if all printers everywhere were so dealt by, there would be very little printed."

It was not in Franklin's nature, however, to be dogmatic or extreme about any principle; he generally gravitated toward a sensible balance. The rights of printers, he realized, were balanced by their duty to be responsible. Thus, even though printers should be free to publish offensive opinions, they should generally exercise discretion. "I myself have constantly refused to print anything that might countenance vice or promote immorality, though . . . I might have got much money. I have also always refused to print such things as might do real injury to any person."

One such example involved a customer who asked the young printer to publish a piece in the *Gazette* that Franklin found "scurrilous and defamatory." In his effort to decide whether he should take the customer's money even though it violated his principles, Franklin subjected himself to the following test:

> To determine whether I should publish it or not, I went home in the evening, purchased a twopenny loaf at the baker's, and with the water from the pump made my supper; I then wrapped myself up in my great-coat, and laid down on the floor and slept till morning, when, on another loaf and a mug of water, I made my breakfast. From this regimen I feel no inconvenience whatever. Finding I can live in this manner, I have formed a determination never to prostitute my press to the purposes of corruption and abuse of this kind for the sake of gaining a more comfortable subsistence.

Franklin ended his "Apology for Printers" with a fable about a father and son traveling with a donkey. When the father rode and made his son walk, they were criticized by those they met; likewise, they were criticized when the son rode and made the father walk, or when they both rode the donkey, or when neither did. So finally, they decided to throw the donkey off a bridge. The moral, according to Franklin, was that it is foolish to try to avoid all criticism. Despite his "despair of pleasing everybody," Franklin concluded, "I shall not burn my press or melt my letters."[16]

Along with such high-minded principles, Franklin employed some more common strategies to push papers. One ever reliable method, which had particular appeal to the rather raunchy unmarried young publisher, was the time-honored truth that sex sells. Franklin's *Gazette* was spiced with little leering and titillating items. In the issue a week after his "Apology for Printers," for example, Franklin wrote about a husband who caught his wife in bed with a man named Stonecutter, tried to cut off the interloper's head with a knife, but only wounded him. Franklin ends with a smirking pun about castration: "Some people admire that when the person offended had so fair and suitable opportunity, it did not enter his head to turn St-n-c-tt-r himself."

The next issue had a similar short item about an amorous constable who had "made an agreement with a neighboring female to *watch* with her that night." The constable makes the mistake of climbing into the window of a different woman, whose husband was in another room. Reported Franklin: "The good woman perceiving presently by the extraordinary fondness of her bedfellow that it could not possibly be her husband, made so much disturbance as to wake the good man, who finding somebody had got into his place without his leave began to lay about him unmercifully."

And then there was the story of the sex-starved woman who wanted to divorce her husband because he could not satisfy her. She "at times industriously solicited most of the magistrates" to gain sympathy for her plight. After her husband was medically examined, however, she moved back in with him. "The report of the physicians (who in form examined his *abilities* and allowed him in every respect to be *sufficient*) gave her but small satisfaction," Franklin wrote. "Whether any experiments *more satisfactory* have been tried, we cannot say; but it seems she now declares it as her opinion that 'George is as good as de best.'" In another passing reference to sexual virility, which was also his first published notice of lightning, Franklin reported about a bolt that melted the pewter button on the pants of a young lad, adding: "'Tis well nothing else thereabouts was made of pewter."

Writing as "The Casuist," Franklin even helped to pioneer the genre of sexual and moral advice columns. (Although the literal definition of the word "casuistry" refers to the application of moral principles to everyday conduct, Franklin used it, with a touch of irony, in its more colloquial sense, which implies a slightly off-kilter or misleading application of those principles.) One letter from a reader, or from Franklin pretending to be a reader, posed the following dilemma: Suppose a person discovers that his wife has been seduced by his neighbor, and suppose he has reason to believe that if he reveals this to his neighbor's wife, then she might agree to have sex with him, "is he justifiable in doing it?" Franklin, writing as the Casuist, gave an earnest answer. If the questioner were a Christian, he would know that he should "return not evil for evil, but repay evil with good." And if he is not a Christian but instead "one who would make reason the rule of his actions," he would come to the same conclusion: "such practices can produce no good to society."[17]

Franklin also knew another maxim of journalism: crime stories sell, particularly when they are outlandish. In a report on the death of a young girl, for example, he provided the mix of reporting and outrage later perfected by racier tabloids. The case involved a couple who were charged with murdering the man's daughter from a previous marriage by neglecting her, forcing her "to lie and rot in her nastiness," giving her "her own excrements to eat," and "turning her out of doors." The child died, but a physician testified she would have died anyway from other ailments she had, so the judge sentenced the couple merely to be burned on the hand. Franklin raged at the "pathetic" ruling and delivered his own harsh verdict that the couple "had not only acted contrary to the particular law of all nations, but had even broken the universal law of nature."[18]

A third reliable method of selling papers was through a light and rather innocent willingness to gossip and scandalmonger. In his first Busy-Body essay for Bradford, Franklin had defended the value of nosiness and tattling. Now that he had his own paper, he made it clear that the *Gazette* was pleased, indeed proud, to continue this service. Using the same tone as the Busy-Body, Franklin wrote an anonymous letter to his paper defending gossip, backbiting, and censure "by showing its usefulness and the great good it does to society.

"It is frequently the means of preventing powerful, politic, ill-designing men from growing too popular," he wrote. "All-examining Censure, with her hundred eyes and her thousand tongues, soon discovers and as speedily divulges in all quarters every least crime or foible that is part of their true character. This clips the wings of their ambition." Gossip can also, he noted, promote virtue, as some people are motivated more by fear of public humiliation than they are by inner moral principles. " *'What will the world say of me if I act thus?'* is often a reflection strong enough to enable us to resist the most powerful temptation to vice or folly. This preserves the integrity of the wavering, the honesty of the covetous, the sanctity of some of the religious, and the chastity of all virgins."

It is amusing that Franklin, though he was willing to impugn the innate resolve of "all" virgins, protected himself by impugning only "some" religious people. In addition, he showed a somewhat cynical side by implying that most people act virtuously not because of an inner goodness, but because they are afraid of public censure.[19]

The following week Franklin defended the value of gossip in another letter, even more flavorful, purportedly penned by the aptly named Alice Addertongue. Franklin, who was then 26, had his fictional Alice identify herself, with an edge of irony, as a "young girl of about thirty-five." She lived at home with her mother and, she said, "find it my duty as well as inclination to exercise my talent at censure for the good of my country folks."

After taking a swipe at a "silly" piece in Bradford's *Mercury* that criticized women for being gossipy, Alice recounts how she once found herself at odds with her mother on this issue. "She argued that scandal spoiled all good conversation, and I insisted without it there could be no such thing." As a result, she was banished to the kitchen when visitors came for tea. While her mother engaged guests in high-minded discourse in the parlor, Alice regaled a few young friends with tales of a neighbor's intrigue with his maid. Hearing the laughter, her mother's friends began drifting from the parlor into the kitchen to partake in the gossip. Her mother finally joined them. "I have long thought that if you would make your paper a vehicle of scandal, you would *double the number of your subscribers.*"

Franklin's playful defenses of busybodies, among the most amusing pieces he ever wrote, set a lighthearted tone for his paper. Because of his gregarious personality and fascination with human nature, he appreciated tales about people's foibles and behavior, and he understood why others did as well. But he was, of course, only half-serious in his defense of gossip. The other part of his personality was more earnest: he continually resolved to speak ill of nobody. As a result, he toyed in the *Gazette* with the argument for gossip, but he did not really indulge in it much. For example, in one issue he noted that he had gotten a letter describing the disagreements and conduct of a certain couple, "but for charitable reasons the said letter is at present thought not fit to be published."[20]

Likewise, he was ambiguous when writing about drinking. He was a temperate man who nevertheless enjoyed the joviality of taverns. In one famous *Gazette* piece, destined to become a poster in countless pubs, he produced a "Drinker's Dictionary" listing 250 or so synonyms for being drunk: "Addled . . . afflicted . . . biggy . . . boozy . . . busky . . . buzzey . . . cherubimical . . . cracked . . . halfway to Concord . . ." Yet he also frightened readers with colorful news accounts of the deaths of drunks, and he wrote editorials on the "poisonous" effect of spirits. As a printer in London, he had lectured coworkers that strong drink made them less industrious; as an editor in Philadelphia, he continued this crusade.[21]

Franklin also perfected the art of poking fun at himself. He realized, as have subsequent American humorists, that a bit of wry self-deprecation could make him seem more endearing. In one small item in the *Gazette*, he recounted how "a certain printer" was walking along the wharf when he slipped and stuck his leg into a barrel of tar. His awkward escape resembled the saying about being "as nimble as a bee in a tarbarrel." Franklin ended the item with a little play on words: " 'Tis true he was no Honey Bee, nor yet a Humble Bee, but a Boo-bee he may be allowed to be, namely B.F."[22]

By the early 1730s, Franklin's business was thriving. He started building an extended little empire by sending his young workers, once they had served their time with him, to set up partnership shops in places ranging from Charleston to Hartford. He would supply the presses and part of the expenses, as well as some content for the publications, and in return take a portion of the revenue.

A PRACTICAL MARRIAGE

Now that he had established himself in business, Franklin found himself in want of a good wife. Bachelorhood was frowned on in colonial America, and Franklin had a sexual appetite that he knew required discipline. So he set out to find himself a mate, preferably one with a dowry attached.

Boarding at his house was a friend from the Junto, glazier and mathematician Thomas Godfrey, and his wife, who tended to their meals and homemaking. Mrs. Godfrey proposed a match with one of her nieces, whom Franklin found "very deserving," and a courtship ensued. Dowries being common, Franklin sought to negotiate his through Mrs. Godfrey: approximately £100, the amount he still owed on his printing business. When the girl's family replied that they could not spare that much, Franklin suggested rather unromantically that they could mortgage their home.

The girl's family promptly broke off the relationship, either out of outrage or (as Franklin suspected) in the hope that the courtship had gone so far that they would elope without a dowry. Resentful, Franklin refused to have anything more to do with the girl, even after Mrs. Godfrey suggested they were open to negotiations.

Not only did the courtship end, so did yet another Franklin friendship. Godfrey moved out, quit the Junto, and eventually turned over the printing of his little almanac to Franklin's competitor, Bradford. Years later, Franklin wrote dismissively about the man who once shared his house, club, and presumably affection. Godfrey "was not a pleasing companion, as like most great mathematicians I have met with he expected unusual precision in everything said, or was forever denying or distinguishing upon trifles to the disturbance of all conversation."

Franklin's annoyance also led him to satirize the situation in the *Gazette* not long thereafter, using the pseudonym Anthony Afterwit. The "honest tradesman" complains that when he was courting his wife, her father hinted that he could be in for a nice dowry, and he "formed several fine schemes" of how to spend the money. "When the old gentleman saw I was pretty well engaged, and that the match was too far gone to be easily broke off, he . . . forbid me the house and told his daughter that if she married me he would not give her a farthing." Afterwit, unlike the real Franklin, elopes. "I have since learned that there are old curmudgeons besides him who have this trick to marry their daughters and yet keep what they might well spare."

(The Anthony Afterwit essay had an interesting side effect. His fictional wife, Abigail Afterwit, was the name of a character that had been created almost a decade earlier by Franklin's estranged brother, James, in the *New England Courant*. James, who had since moved to Rhode Island, reprinted the Anthony Afterwit piece in his own paper along with a reply from a Patience Teacraft. Benjamin in turn reprinted the reply in his Philadelphia paper, and the following year he visited his brother for an emotional reconciliation. James's health was failing, and he begged his younger brother to look after his 10-year-old son. That Benjamin did, arranging for his education and taking him on as an apprentice. A dominant theme in Franklin's autobiography is that of making mistakes and then making amends, as if he were a moral bookkeeper balancing his accounts. Running away from his brother was, Franklin noted, "one of the first errata of my life." Helping James's son was the way to set the ledger back into balance. "Thus it was that I made my brother ample amends for the service I had deprived him of by leaving him so early.")

After his courtship of Mrs. Godfrey's niece was scuttled, Franklin scouted around for other possible brides, but he discovered that young printers were not valued enough to command a sure dowry. He could not expect money unless it was to marry a woman "I should not otherwise think agreeable." In his autobiography, which he began years later as a letter to the illegitimate son he fathered while looking for a wife, Franklin wrote a memorable line: "In the meantime, that hard-to-be-governed passion of youth had hurried me frequently into intrigues with low women that fell in my way, which were attended with some expense and great inconvenience."[23]

Deborah Read, the girl who had laughed at him when he first straggled into Philadelphia, was also in a rather desperate situation. After Franklin left her to live in London, she had received only one curt letter from him. So she made the mistake of marrying a charming but unreliable potter named John Rogers. He was unable to make a living, and Deborah soon heard rumors that he had abandoned a wife in England. So she moved back in with her mother, and Rogers stole a slave and absconded to the West Indies, leaving behind a load of debt. Although there were reports he had died there in a brawl, these were unconfirmed, which meant Deborah would have difficulty legally re-marrying. Bigamy was a crime punishable by thirty-nine lashes and life imprisonment.

Since the death of Deborah's father, her mother had been eking out a living by selling homemade medicines. An advertising bill, printed by Franklin, notes: "The widow Read . . . continues to make and sell her well-known ointment for the itch, with which she has cured abundance of people . . . It also kills or drives away all sorts of lice in once or twice using." Franklin frequently visited the Reads, advised them on business matters, and took pity on the dejected Deborah. He faulted himself for her plight, though Mrs. Read kindly took most of the blame for not having let them marry before he left for London. Fortunately for all, according to Franklin, "our mutual affection was revived."

Around that time, Franklin developed a method for making difficult decisions. "My way is to divide a sheet of paper by a line into two columns, writing over the one *Pro* and the other *Con*," he later recalled. Then he would list all the arguments on each side and weigh how important each was. "Where I find two, one on each side, that seem equal, I strike them both out; if I find a reason *pro* equal to some two reasons *con*, I strike out the three." By this bookkeeper's calculus, it became clear to him "where the balance lies."

However exactly he came to his decision, the balance of considerations eventually tipped toward Deborah, and in September 1730 they began living together as a married couple. There was no official ceremony. Instead, they entered into a type of common-law arrangement that served to protect them from charges of bigamy if Rogers unexpectedly reappeared. But he never did. Franklin viewed his union with Deborah, like his reconciliation with his brother, as an example of his rectifying an earlier error. "Thus I corrected that great erratum as well as I could," Franklin later wrote of his mistreatment of the younger Deborah.

Franklin is often described as (or accused of) being far more practical than romantic, a man of the head rather than heart. The tale of his common-law marriage to Deborah provides some support for this view. But it also illustrates some complexities of Franklin's character: his desire to tame his hard-to-govern passions by being practical, and the genuine fondness he felt for kindred companions. He was not given to starry-eyed soulful commitments or poetic love; instead, his emotional attachments tended to be the more prosaic bonds of affection that grew out of partnership, self-interest, collaboration, camaraderie, and good-humored kinship.

A wife who brought with her a dowry would have likely also brought expensive social airs and aspirations. Instead, Franklin found "a good and faithful helpmate" who was frugal and practical and devoid of pretensions, traits that he later noted were far more valuable to a rising tradesman. Their union remained mutually useful, if not deeply romantic, until Deborah's death forty-four years later. As Franklin would soon have Poor Richard pronounce in his almanac: "Keep your eyes wide open before marriage, half shut afterwards."[24]

WILLIAM

There was one major complication facing the new marriage. Around that time, Franklin fathered and took sole custody of an illegitimate son named William, which was probably the "great inconvenience" that he coldly wrote in his autobiography was the result of consorting with "low women."

The identity of William's mother is one of history's delicious mysteries, a source of speculation among scholars. Franklin never revealed the secret, nor did William, if he knew. In fact, even the date of his birth is unclear. Let's start there.

Most historians say that William was born sometime between April 12, 1730, and April 12, 1731. This is based on a letter Franklin wrote to his own mother on April 12, 1750, referring to William as "now 19 years of age, a tall, proper youth, and much of a beau."

Willard Sterne Randall in *A Little Revenge*, a fascinating but somewhat speculative account of Franklin's troubled relationship with his son, questions this. In September 1746, William left home with an ensign's commission on a military expedition to Canada, and Randall argues that he was unlikely to have been only 15 or 16. Perhaps, in writing his mother, Franklin was shaving a year or two off William's age to make him seem legitimate. Likewise, the meticulous Franklin scholar J. A. Leo Lemay, on his Web site detailing Franklin's life, surmises he was born in 1728 or 1729, as do some nineteenth-century biographers.

However, we know that before he was allowed to enlist, perhaps sometime in early 1746, William tried to run away to sea, and his father had to fetch him home from a ship in the harbor, which indicates that he indeed might have been not any older than 15 or 16 at the time (his father had considered running off to sea at age 12, and did run away to Philadelphia at 17). Sheila Skemp's comprehensive biography of William makes it seem quite logical that he embarked with the military at 16, well after he finished his schooling. In addition, William was responsible for the belief reported in a magazine that he was 82 when he died in 1813 (which would place his birth in late 1730 or early 1731).

On balance, because neither man ever denied William's illegitimacy, it makes sense to believe that Franklin was telling the truth to his mother when he referred to William's age, and it makes equal sense to believe that William was never (intentionally or not) misleading about his age. Based on these assumptions, it is likely that William was born around the time that Deborah began living with Franklin in late 1730.[25]

That being the case, might Deborah actually have been his mother, as some scholars speculate? Might the common-law marriage have been partly occasioned by her pregnancy, while William's origin was left murky in case Rogers reappeared and charged her with bigamy and adultery? As Carl Van Doren muses, "There was bound to be a scandal. But of course it would be less if the child appeared to be Franklin's and an unknown mother's. The lusty philosopher could take all the blame."

But this theory doesn't bear much scrutiny. If Deborah had been pregnant and given birth, there would surely be some friends and relatives, including her mother, who would have known. As H. W. Brands puts it, "Even after the passage of years precluded any further concerns about Rogers, Debbie declined to claim William as her own—an omission impossible to imagine in any mother, let alone one who had to watch from close at hand while her son spent his life labeled a bastard." On the contrary, she was openly hostile to him. According to a clerk who later worked for the Franklins, Deborah referred to William as "the greatest villain upon earth" and heaped upon him "invectives in the foulest terms I ever heard from a gentlewoman."[26]

During a heated election in 1764, William's paternity became an issue. One abusive pamphlet charged that he was the son of a prostitute named Barbara who was subsequently exploited by the Franklins as a maid until she died and was buried in an unmarked grave. Given the scurrilous nature of that campaign and the unlikelihood that any of the Franklins could have abided having William's real mother around as their maid, this also seems implausible.

The best explanation comes from a 1763 letter about William, rediscovered more than two centuries later, which was written by George Roberts, a prosperous Philadelphia merchant who was a close family friend. " 'Tis generally known here his birth is illegitimate and his mother not in good circumstances," Roberts wrote to a friend in London, "but the report of her begging bread in the streets of this city is without the least foundation in truth. I understand some small provision is made by him for her, but her being none of the most agreeable women prevents particular notice being shown, or the father and son acknowledging any connection with her." As Roberts was probably in a position to know, and as he had no ulterior motive, we are left with this as the likeliest scenario.[27]

A FRUGAL MATE

In his autobiography (which extols the virtues of "industry" and "frugality" a total of thirty-six times), Franklin wrote of his wife, "It was lucky for me that I had one as much disposed to industry and frugality as myself." He gives her even more credit in a letter written later, near the end of his life: "Frugality is an enriching virtue, a virtue I could never acquire in myself, but I was lucky enough to find it in a wife, who thereby became a fortune to me." For Franklin, this passed for true love. Deborah helped at the print shop, stitched pamphlets, and purchased rags for papermaking. At least initially, they had no servants, and Franklin ate his bread-and-milk porridge each morning from a twopenny bowl.

In later years, after a conflicted Franklin had developed some taste for finery while still clinging to his admiration for frugality, he wryly recounted a little lapse on Deborah's part that showed "how luxury will enter families and make a progress, in spite of principle." One day he arrived at breakfast to find it served in a china bowl with a silver spoon. Deborah had bought them at the "enormous sum" of 23 shillings, with "no other excuse or apology to make but that she thought her husband deserved a silver spoon and china bowl as well as any of his neighbors." With a droll mix of pride and disdain, Franklin recalled how, over many years, as their wealth grew, they ended up with china and furnishings worth several hundred pounds.

When the young Franklin heard that his little sister Jane was planning to marry, he wrote her a letter that reflected his view that a good wife should be frugal and industrious. He had thought about sending her a tea table, he said, but his practical nature got the better of him. "When I considered that the character of a good housewife was far preferable to that of being only a pretty gentlewoman, I concluded to send you a spinning-wheel." As Poor Richard would soon phrase it in his first almanac: "Many estates are spent in the getting/ Since women for tea forsook spinning and knitting."[28]

The virtue of frugality was also one of young Franklin's favorite themes in his newspaper writings. In Anthony Afterwit's letter, after complaining about having to elope with no dowry, he goes on to ridicule his wife for adopting the airs and spending habits of a gentlewoman. First she pays for a fancy mirror, which then requires a nice table under it, then a tea service, and then a clock. Facing mounting debts, Anthony decides to sell these things when his wife leaves town to visit relatives. To replace the fancy furniture, he buys a spinning wheel and some knitting needles. He asks the *Gazette* to publish the letter so that she will read it before she returns and thus be prepared. "If she can conform to this new scheme of living, we shall be the happiest couple perhaps in the province." And then, as a reward, he might let her have the nice mirror back.

Less sexist than most men of his day, Franklin also aimed his barbs at men. Afterwit's letter was answered two weeks later by one from another Franklin creation, Celia Single. With the delightful gossipy voice of his other female characters, such as Silence Dogood and Alice Addertongue, Single recounts a visit to a friend whose husband is trying to replicate Afterwit's approach. A raucous argument ensues. "There is neither sin nor shame in knitting a pair of stockings," the husband says. She replies, "There are poor women enough in town that can knit." Single finally leaves, "knowing that a man and his wife are apt to quarrel more violently when before strangers than when by themselves." She later hears that the knitting thread ended up in the fireplace.

Single (or rather Franklin) goes on to admonish Franklin for publishing more tales of self-indulgent women than men. "If I were disposed to be censorious, I could furnish you with instances enough," she says, then proceeds to rattle off a long list of men who waste their time playing pool, dice, or checkers and buying fancy clothes. Finally, Franklin has her cleverly poke at his veil of pseudonymity. "There are holes enough to be picked in your coat as well as others; and those who are affronted by the satires you may publish will not consider so much who wrote as who printed." [29]

On a more serious and less modern note, Franklin published, four weeks after he married, "Rules and Maxims for Promoting Matrimonial Happiness." He began with a paean to marriage, "the surest and most lasting foundation of comfort and love." However, the folly of some who enter into it often makes it "a state of the most exquisite wretchedness and misery." He apologized for aiming his advice at women, as men were in fact more faulty, "but the reason is because I esteem them better disposed to receive and practice it."

Among his rules: avoid all thoughts of managing your husband, never deceive him or make him uneasy, accept that he "is a man not an angel," "resolve every morning to be good-natured and cheerful," remember the word "obey" in your marriage vows, do not dispute with him, and "deny yourself the trivial satisfaction of having your own will." A woman's power and happiness, Franklin wrote, "has no other foundation than her husband's esteem and love." Therefore, a wife should "share and soothe his cares, and with the utmost diligence conceal his infirmities." And when it comes to sex: "Let the tenderness of your conjugal love be expressed with such decency, delicacy and prudence as that it may appear plainly and thoroughly distinct from the designing fondness of a harlot." [30]

Franklin's essays and fictional letters make it clear that he entered into his union with Deborah holding some traditional views on matrimony: wives should be supportive, households should be run frugally and industriously. Fortunately for him, Deborah tended to share those views. In general, she had plain tastes, a willingness to work, and a desire to please her spouse. Of course, as he might have pointed out, the same could be said of him at the time.

And so they settled into a partnership that was both more and less than a conventional marriage. A tireless collaborator both in the house and at work, Deborah handled most of the accounts and expanded their shop's inventory to include ointments made by her mother, crown soap made by Franklin's Boston relatives, coffee, tea, chocolate, saffron, cheese, fish, and various other sundries. She strained her eyes binding books and sewing clothes by candlelight. And though her spelling and choice of words reflected her lack of education—the sexton of the church was noted as the "seck stone" and one customer was called "Mary the Papist"—her copious entries in their shop book are a delightful record of the times.

Franklin's affection for her grew from his pride at her industry; many years later, when he was in London arguing before the House of Commons that unfair taxes would lead to boycotts of British manufacturers, he asserted that he had never been prouder than when he was a young tradesman and wore only clothes that had been made by his wife.

But Deborah was not merely a submissive or meek partner to the man she often addressed (as he did her) as "my dear child" and whom she sometimes publicly called "Pappy." She had a fierce temper, which Franklin invariably defended. "Don't you know that all wives are in the right?" he asked a nephew who was having a dispute with Deborah. Soon after their marriage, he wrote a piece called "A Scolding Wife," in which he defended assertive women by saying they tended to be "active in the business of the family, special good housewives, and very careful of their husband's interests."[31]

The only extant painting of Deborah makes her appear to be a sensible and determined women, plump and plain but not unattractive. In a letter he wrote her years later from London, he described a mug he was sending and compared it to her: "I fell in love with it at first sight, for I thought it looked like a fat, jolly dame, clean and tidy, with a neat blue and white calico gown on, good natured and lovely, and just put me in mind of—somebody."

It was a relationship that did not inspire great romantic verse, but it did produce an endearing ballad that he put into the mouth of Poor Richard. In it, Franklin paid tribute to "My Plain Country Joan" and blessed the day he made her his own. Among the lyrics:

> *Not a word of her shape, or her face, or her eyes,*
>   *Of flames or of darts shall you hear:*
> *Though I beauty admire, 'tis virtue I prize,*
>   *Which fades not in seventy years . . .*

In peace and good order my household she guides,
Right careful to save what I gain;
Yet cheerfully spends, and smiles on the friends
I've the pleasure to entertain . . .
The best have some faults, and so has my Joan,
But then they're exceedingly small,
And now, I'm used to 'em, they're so like my own.
I can scarcely feel them at all.

Over the years, Franklin would outgrow Deborah in many ways. Though they shared values, he was far more worldly and intellectual than she was, or ever wanted to be. There is some evidence that she may have been born in Birmingham and brought to America as a young child, but during her adult life she seems never to have spent a night away from Philadelphia, and she lived most of her life on Market Street within two blocks of the house where she was raised.

Franklin, on the other hand, loved to travel, and although he would, in later years, occasionally express some hope that she would accompany him, he knew that she was not so inclined. He seemed to sense that she would not be socially comfortable in his new realms. So, in this regard, they respected each other's independence, perhaps to a fault. For fifteen of the last seventeen years of Deborah's life, Franklin would be away, including when she died. Nevertheless, their mutual affection, respect, and loyalty—and their sense of partnership—would endure.[32]

FRANCIS

Two years into their marriage, in October 1732, Deborah gave birth to a son. Francis Folger Franklin, known as Franky, was doted on by both parents: he had his portrait painted when still a baby, and his father advertised for a tutor to teach both his children when Francis was 2 and William about 4. For the rest of his life, Franklin would marvel at the memory of how precocious, curious, and special Franky was.

These were, alas, destined to be only sorrowful memories. In one of the few searing tragedies of Franklin's life, Franky died of smallpox just after his fourth birthday. On his grave, Franklin chose a simple epitaph: "The delight of all who knew him."

The bitter irony was that Franklin had become a fervent advocate of smallpox vaccinations after they had been ridiculed in the *New England Courant* when Franklin worked there for his brother. In the years preceding Franky's birth, he had editorialized in the *Pennsylvania Gazette* in support of inoculations and published statistics showing how effective they were. In 1730, for example, he wrote an account of a Boston epidemic in which most people who had been vaccinated were spared.

He had planned to inoculate Franky, but he had delayed doing so because the boy had been ill with the flux. In a sad announcement that appeared in his paper a week after the boy's death, Franklin denied rumors that he died from being vaccinated. "I do hereby sincerely declare that he was not inoculated, but received the distemper in the common way of infection." He went on to declare his belief that inoculation was "a safe and beneficial practice."

The memory of Franky was one of the few things ever to cause Franklin painful reflections. When his sister Jane wrote to him in London years later with happy news about his grandsons, Franklin responded that it "brings often afresh to my mind the idea of my son Franky, though now dead thirty-six years, whom I have seldom since seen equaled in everything, and whom to this day I cannot think of without a sigh."[33]

Adding to the poignancy, Franklin had written for his paper, while Franky was still alive, an unusually deep rumination on "The Death of Infants," which was occasioned by the death of a neighbor's child. Drawing on his observations of the tiny Franky, he described the magical beauty of babies: "What curious joints and hinges on which limbs are moved to and fro! What an inconceivable variety of nerves, veins, arteries, fibers, and little invisible parts are found in every member! . . . What endless contrivances to secure life, to nourish nature, and to propagate the same to future animals!" How could it be, Franklin then asked, that "a good and merciful Creator should produce myriads of such exquisite machines to no other end or purpose but to be deposited in the dark chambers of the grave" before they were old enough to know good from evil or to serve their fellow man and their God? The answer, he admitted, was "beyond our mortal ken" to understand. "When nature gave us tears, she gave us leave to weep."[34]

DEFINING HIS GOD

When we last took Franklin's spiritual pulse in London, he had written his ill-conceived "Dissertation on Liberty and Necessity," which attacked the idea of free will and much of Calvinist theology, and then he had repudiated the pamphlet as an embarrassing "erratum." That left him in a religious quandary. He no longer believed in the received dogmas of his Puritan upbringing, which taught that man could achieve salvation only through God's grace rather than through good works. But he was uncomfortable embracing a simple and unenhanced version of deism, the Enlightenment-era creed that reason and the study of nature (instead of divine revelation) tell us all we can know about our Creator. The deists he knew, including his younger self, had turned out to be squirrelly in their morals.

On his return to Philadelphia, Franklin showed little interest in organized religion and even less in attending Sunday services. Still, he continued to hold some basic religious beliefs, among them "the existence of the Deity" and that "the most acceptable service of God was doing good to man." He was tolerant toward all sects, particularly those that worked to make the world a better place, and he made sure "to avoid all discourse that might tend to lessen the good opinion another might have of his own religion." Because he believed that churches were useful to the community, he paid his annual subscription to support the town's Presbyterian minister, the Rev. Jedediah Andrews.[35]

One day, Andrews prevailed on him to sample his Sunday sermons, which Franklin did for five weeks. Unfortunately, he found them "uninteresting and unedifying since not a single moral principle was inculcated or enforced, their aim seeming to be rather to make us good Presbyterians than good citizens." On his final visit, the reading from the Scripture (Philippians 4:8) related to virtue. It was a topic dear to Franklin's heart, and he hoped that Andrews would expound on the concept in his sermon. Instead, the minister focused only on dogma and doctrine, without offering any practical thoughts about virtue. Franklin was "disgusted," and he reverted to spending his Sundays reading and writing on his own.[36]

Franklin began to clarify his religious beliefs through a series of essays and letters. In them, he adopted a creed that would last the rest of his life: a virtuous, morally fortified, and pragmatic version of deism. Unlike most pure deists, he concluded that it was useful (and thus probably correct) to believe that a faith in God should inform our daily actions; but like other deists, his faith was devoid of sectarian dogma, burning spirituality, deep soul-searching, or a personal relationship to Christ.[37]

The first of these religious essays was a paper "for my own private use," written in November 1728, entitled "Articles of Belief and Acts of Religion." Unlike his London dissertation, which was clogged with convoluted imitations of analytic philosophy, it was elegant and sparse. He began with a simple affirmation: "I believe there is one Supreme most perfect being."[38]

It was an important statement, because some mushier deists shied even from going that far. As Diderot once quipped, a deist is someone who has not lived long enough to become an atheist. Franklin lived very long, and despite the suspicions of John Adams and others that he was a closet atheist, he repeatedly and indeed increasingly asserted his belief in a supreme God.

In the deist tradition, Franklin's Supreme Being was somewhat distant and uninvolved in our daily travails. "I imagine it great vanity in me to suppose that the Supremely Perfect does in the least regard such an inconsiderable nothing as man," he wrote. He added his belief that this "Infinite Father" was far above wanting our praise or prayers.

There is in all humans, however, a desire and a deeply felt duty to worship a more intimate God, Franklin surmised. Therefore, he wrote, the Supreme Being causes there to be lesser and more personal gods for mortal men to worship. Franklin thus has it both ways: combining the deist concept of God as a distant First Cause with the belief of other religions that worship a God who is directly involved in people's lives. The result is a Supreme Being that can be manifest in various ways, depending on the needs of different worshipers.

Some commentators, most notably A. Owen Aldridge, read this literally as Franklin's embracing some sort of polytheism, with a bevy of lesser gods overseeing various realms and planets. Occasionally throughout his life, Franklin would refer to "the gods," but these later references are quite casual and colloquial, and Franklin seems to be speaking more figuratively than literally in his 1728 paper. As Kerry Walters writes in *Benjamin Franklin and His Gods,* "It is an error to presume they point to a literal polytheism. Such a conclusion is as philosophically bizarre as it is textually unwarranted." (Given the difficulties Franklin sometimes seems to have in believing in one God, it seems unlikely he could find himself believing in many.)[39]

Franklin went on to outline how he viewed and worshiped his own personal God. This involved offering suitable prayers, and Franklin produced a whole liturgy that he had composed. It also required acting virtuously, and Franklin engaged in a moral calculus that was very pragmatic and even somewhat utilitarian: "I believe He is pleased and delights in the happiness of those He has created; and since without virtue man can have no happiness in this world, I firmly believe He delights to see me virtuous."

In a paper he subsequently read to his friends in the Junto, Franklin elaborated his religious beliefs by exploring the issue of "divine providence," the extent to which God gets involved in worldly matters. The Puritans believed in a detailed and intimate involvement, called "special providence," and regularly prayed to God for very specific intercessions. As Calvin himself put it, "Supposing that He remains tranquilly in heaven without caring for the world outrageously deprives God of all effective power." Most deists, on the other hand, believed in a "general providence," in which God expresses his will through the laws of nature he set in motion instead of by micromanaging our daily lives.

As was typical, Franklin sought a pragmatic resolution in his Junto talk, which he called "On the Providence of God in the Government of the World." He began by apologizing to "my intimate pot companions" for being rather "unqualified" to speak on spiritual matters. His study of nature, he said, convinced him that God created the universe and was infinitely wise, good, and powerful. He then explored four possibilities: (1) God predetermined and predestined everything that happens, eliminating all possibility of free will; (2) He left things to proceed according to natural laws and the free will of His creatures, and never interferes; (3) He predestined some things and left some things to free will, but still never interferes; (4) "He sometimes interferes by His particular providence and sets aside the effects which would otherwise have been produced by any of the above causes."[40]

Franklin ended up settling on the fourth option, but not because he could prove it; instead, it resulted from a process of elimination and a sense of which belief would be most useful for people to hold. Any of the first three options would mean that God is not infinitely powerful or good or wise. "We are then necessarily driven into the fourth supposition," he wrote. He admitted that many find it contradictory to believe both that God is infinitely powerful and that men have free will (it was the conundrum that stymied him in the London dissertation he wrote and then renounced). But if God is indeed all powerful, Franklin reasoned, he surely is able to find a way to give the creatures he made in his image some of his free will.

Franklin's conclusion had, as might be expected, practical consequences: people should love God and "pray to Him for His favor and protection." He did not, however, stray too far from deism; he placed little faith in the use of prayers for specific personal requests or miracles. In an irreverent letter he later wrote to his brother John, he calculated that 45 million prayers were offered in all of New England seeking victory over a fortified French garrison in Canada. "If you do not succeed, I fear I shall have but an indifferent opinion of Presbyterian prayers in such cases as long as I live. Indeed, in attacking strong towns I should have more dependence on *works* than on *faith.*"

Above all, Franklin's beliefs were driven by pragmatism. The final sentence of his Junto talk stressed that it was socially useful for people to believe in the version of divine providence and free will that he proposed: "This religion will be a powerful regulator of our actions, give

us peace and tranquility within our own minds, and render us benevolent, useful and beneficial to others."[41]

Not all of Franklin's religious musings were this earnest. Around
the time of his Junto paper, he wrote for his newspaper a tale called "A
Witch Trial at Mount Holly," which was a delightful parody of Puritan mystical beliefs clashing with scientific experimentation. The accused witches were to be subjected to two tests: weighed on a scale
against the Bible, and tossed in the river with hands and feet bound to
see if they floated. They agree to submit to these tests—on the condition that two of the accusers take the same test. With colorful details
of all the ridiculous pomp, Franklin described the process. The accused and accusers all succeed in outweighing the Bible. But both of
the accused and one of the accusers fail to sink in the river, thus indicating that they are witches. The more intelligent spectators conclude
from this that most people naturally float. The others are not so sure,
and they resolve to wait until summer when the experiment could be
tried with the subjects unclothed.[42]

Franklin's freethinking unnerved his family. When his parents
wrote of their concern over his "erroneous opinions," Franklin replied
with a letter that spelled out a religious philosophy, based on tolerance
and utility, that would last his life. It would be vain, he wrote, for any
person to insist that "all the doctrines he holds are true and all he rejects are false." The same could be said of the opinions of different religions as well. They should be evaluated, the young pragmatist said,
by their utility: "I think opinions should be judged by their influences
and effects; and if a man holds none that tend to make him less virtuous or more vicious, it may be concluded that he holds none that are
dangerous, which I hope is the case with me." He had little use for the
doctrinal distinctions his mother worried about. "I think vital religion
has always suffered when orthodoxy is more regarded than virtue. And
the Scripture assures me that at the last day we shall not be examined
by what we *thought*, but what we *did* . . . that we did good to our fellow creatures. See Matth 26." His parents, a bit more versed in the
Scripture, probably caught that he meant Matthew 25. They did,
nonetheless, eventually stop worrying about his heresies.[43]

THE MORAL PERFECTION PROJECT

Franklin's historical reputation has been largely shaped, for disciples and detractors alike, by his account in his autobiography of the famous project he launched to attain "moral perfection." This rather odd endeavor, which involved sequentially practicing a list of virtues, seems at once so earnest and mechanical that one cannot help either admiring him or ridiculing him. As the novelist D. H. Lawrence later sneered, "He made himself a list of virtues, which he trotted inside like a gray nag in a paddock."

So it's important to note the hints of irony and self-deprecation in his droll recollection, written when he was 79, of what he wryly dubbed "the bold and arduous project of arriving at moral perfection." His account has touches of the amused-by-his-younger-self tone to be found in the diverting little tales he wrote in France at the same time that he was writing this part of his autobiography. Yet it should also be noted that, as a young man, he seemed to approach his moral perfection program with an endearing sincerity, and even as an old man seemed proud of its worthiness.

Franklin began his quest around the time he ended his unsatisfactory visits to Presbyterian services and started spelling out his own religious creed. The endeavor was typically pragmatic. It contained no abstract philosophizing nor any reference to religious doctrines. As he later noted with pride, it was not merely an exhortation to be virtuous, it was also a practical guide on how to achieve that goal.

First he made a list of twelve virtues he thought desirable, and to each he appended a short definition:

Temperance: Eat not to dullness; drink not to elevation.

Silence: Speak not but what may benefit others or yourself; avoid trifling conversation.

Order: Let all your things have their places; let each part of your business have its time.

Resolution: Resolve to perform what you ought; perform without fail what you resolve.

Frugality: Make no expense but to do good to others or yourself; (i.e., waste nothing).

Industry: Lose no time; be always employed in something useful; cut off all unnecessary actions.

Sincerity: Use no hurtful deceit; think innocently and justly,
and, if you speak, speak accordingly.

Justice: Wrong none by doing injuries, or omitting the benefits
that are your duty.

Moderation: Avoid extremes; forbear resenting injuries so much
as you think they deserve.

Cleanliness: Tolerate no uncleanliness in body, clothes, or habi-
tation.

Tranquility: Be not disturbed at trifles, or at accidents common
or unavoidable.

Chastity: Rarely use venery but for health or offspring, never to
dullness, weakness, or the injury of your own or another's
peace or reputation.

A Quaker friend "kindly" informed him that he had left something
off: Franklin was often guilty of "pride," the friend said, citing many
examples, and could be "overbearing and rather insolent." So Franklin
added "humility" to be the thirteenth virtue on his list. "Imitate Jesus
and Socrates."[44]

The descriptions, such as the notably lenient one for chastity, were
rather revealing. So too was the endeavor itself. It was also, in its passion for self-improvement through diligent resolve, enchantingly
American.

Franklin's focus was on traits that could help him succeed in this
world, instead of ones that would exalt his soul for the hereafter.
"Franklin celebrated a characteristically bourgeois set of virtues,"
writes social theorist David Brooks. "These are not heroic virtues.
They don't fire the imagination or arouse the passions like the aristocratic love of honor. They are not particularly spiritual virtues. But
they are practical and they are democratic."

The set of virtues was also, as Edmund Morgan and others have pointed out, somewhat selfish. It did not include benevolence or charity, for example. But in fairness, we must remember that this was a young tradesman's plan for self-improvement, not a full-blown statement of his morality. Benevolence was and would continue to be a motivating ideal for him, and charity, as Morgan notes, "was actually the guiding principle of Franklin's life." The fundamental tenet of his morality, he repeatedly declared, was "The most acceptable service to God is doing good to man."[45]

Mastering all of these thirteen virtues at once was "a task of more difficulty than I had imagined," Franklin recalled. The problem was that "while my care was employed in guarding against one fault, I was often surprised by another." So he decided to tackle them like a person who, "having a garden to weed, does not attempt to eradicate all the bad herbs at once, which would exceed his reach and his strength, but works on one of the beds at a time."

On the pages of a little notebook, he made a chart with seven red columns for the days of the week and thirteen rows labeled with his virtues. Infractions were marked with a black spot. The first week he focused on temperance, trying to keep that line clear while not worrying about the other lines. With that virtue strengthened, he could turn his attention to the next one, silence, hoping that the temperance line would stay clear as well. In the course of the year, he would complete the thirteen-week cycle four times.

"I was surprised to find myself so much fuller of faults than I had imagined," he dryly noted. In fact, his notebook became filled with holes as he erased the marks in order to reuse the pages. So he transferred his charts to ivory tablets that could be more easily wiped clean.

His greatest difficulty was with the virtue of order. He was a sloppy man, and he eventually decided that he was so busy and had such a good memory that he didn't need to be too orderly. He likened himself to the hurried man who goes to have his ax polished but after a while loses patience and declares, "I think I like a speckled ax best." In addition, as he recounted with amusement, he developed another convenient rationalization: "Something that pretended to be reason was every now and then suggesting to me that such extreme nicety as I exacted of myself might be a kind of foppery in morals, which if it were known would make me ridiculous; that a perfect character might be attended with the inconvenience of being envied and hated."

Humility was also a problem. "I cannot boast of much success in acquiring the *reality* of this virtue, but I had a good deal with regard to the *appearance* of it," he wrote, echoing what he had said about how he had acquired the appearance of industry by carting his own paper through the streets of Philadelphia. "There is perhaps no one of our natural passions so hard to subdue as pride; disguise it, struggle with it, beat it down, stifle it, mortify it as much as one pleases, it is still alive and will every now and then peep out and show itself." This battle against pride would challenge—and amuse—him for the rest of his life. "You will see it perhaps often in this history. For even if I could conceive that I had completely overcome it, I would probably be proud of my humility."

Indeed, he would always indulge a bit of pride in discussing his moral perfection project. Fifty years later, as he flirted with the ladies of France, he would pull out the old ivory slates and show off his virtues, causing one French friend to exult at touching "this precious booklet."[46]

ENLIGHTENMENT CREED

This plan for pursuing virtue, combined with the religious outlook that he had simultaneously been formulating, laid the foundation for a lifelong creed. It was based on pragmatic humanism and a belief in a benevolent but distant deity who was best served by being benevolent to others. Franklin's ideas never ripened into a profound moral or religious philosophy. He focused on understanding virtue rather than God's grace, and he based his creed on rational utility rather than religious faith.

His outlook contained some vestiges of his Puritan upbringing, most notably an inclination toward frugality, lack of pretense, and a belief that God appreciates those who are industrious. But he detached these concepts from Puritan orthodoxy about the salvation of the elect and from other tenets that he did not consider useful in improving earthly conduct. His life shows, the Yale scholar A. Whitney Griswold has noted, "what Puritan habits detached from Puritan beliefs were capable of achieving."

He was also far less inward-looking than Cotton Mather or other Puritans. Indeed, he poked fun at professions of faith that served little worldly purpose. As A. Owen Aldridge writes, "The Puritans were known for their constant introspection, fretting about sins, real or imaginary, and agonizing about the uncertainty of their salvation. Absolutely none of this soul-searching appears in Franklin. One can scrutinize his work from first page to last without finding a single note of spiritual anxiety."[47]

Likewise, he had little use for the sentimental subjectivity of the Romantic era, with its emphasis on the emotional and inspirational, that began rising in Europe and then America during the later part of his life. As a result, he would be criticized by such Romantic exemplars as Keats, Carlyle, Emerson, Thoreau, Poe, and Melville.[48]

Instead, he fit squarely into the tradition—indeed, was the first great American exemplar—of the Enlightenment and its Age of Reason. That movement, which rose in Europe in the late seventeenth century, was defined by an emphasis on reason and observable experience, a mistrust of religious orthodoxy and traditional authority, and an optimism about education and progress. To this mix, Franklin added elements of his own pragmatism. He was able (as novelist John Updike and historian Henry Steele Commager, among others, have noted) to appreciate the energies inherent in Puritanism and to liberate them from rigid dogma so they could flower in the freethinking atmosphere of the Enlightenment.[49]

In his writings about religion over the next five decades, Franklin rarely displayed much fervor. This is largely because he felt it was futile to wrestle with theological questions about which he had no empirical evidence and thus no rational basis for forming an opinion. Thunderbolts from heaven were, for him, something to be captured by a kite string and studied.

As a result, he was a prophet of tolerance. Focusing on doctrinal disputes was divisive, he felt, and trying to ascertain divine certainties was beyond our mortal ken. Nor did he think that such endeavors were socially useful. The purpose of religion should be to make men better and to improve society, and any sect or creed that did so was fine with him. Describing his moral improvement project in his autobiography, he wrote, "There was in it no mark of any of the distinguishing tenets of any particular sect. I had purposely avoided them; for, being fully persuaded of the utility and excellency of my method, and that it might be serviceable to people in all religions, and intending some time or other to publish it, I would not have any thing in it that should prejudice any one, of any sect, against it."

This simplicity of Franklin's creed meant that it was sneered at by sophisticates and disqualified from inclusion in the canon of profound philosophy. Albert Smyth, who compiled volumes of Franklin's papers in the nineteenth century, proclaimed, "His philosophy never got beyond the homely maxims of worldly prudence." But Franklin freely admitted that his religious and moral views were not based on profound analysis or metaphysical thinking. As he declared to a friend later in life, "The great uncertainty I found in metaphysical reasonings disgusted me, and I quitted that kind of reading and study for others more satisfactory."

What he found more satisfactory—more than metaphysics or poetry or exalted romantic sentiments—was looking at things in a pragmatic and practical way. Did they have beneficial consequences? For him, there was a connection between civic virtue and religious virtue, between serving his fellow man and honoring God. He was unashamed by the simplicity of this creed, as he explained in a sweet letter to his wife. "God is very good to us," he wrote. "Let us . . . show our sense of His goodness to us by continuing to do good to our fellow creatures."[50]

POOR RICHARD AND THE WAY TO WEALTH

Poor Richard's Almanack, which Franklin began publishing at the end of 1732, combined the two goals of his doing-well-by-doing-good philosophy: the making of money and the promotion of virtue. It became, in the course of its twenty-five-year run, America's first great humor classic. The fictional Poor Richard Saunders and his nagging wife, Bridget (like their predecessors Silence Dogood, Anthony After-wit, and Alice Addertongue), helped to define what would become a dominant tradition in American folk humor: the naïvely wicked wit and homespun wisdom of down-home characters who seem to be charmingly innocent but are sharply pointed about the pretensions of the elite and the follies of everyday life. Poor Richard and other such characters "appear as disarming plain folk, the better to convey wicked insights," notes historian Alan Taylor. "A long line of humorists—from Davy Crockett and Mark Twain to Garrison Keillor—still re-work the prototypes created by Franklin."[51]

Almanacs were a sweet source of annual revenue for a printer, easily outselling even the Bible (because they had to be bought anew each year). Six were being published in Philadelphia at the time, two of which were printed by Franklin: Thomas Godfrey's and John Jerman's. But after falling out with Godfrey over his failed matchmak-ing and losing Jerman to his rival Andrew Bradford, Franklin found himself in the fall of 1732 with no almanac to help make his press profitable.

So he hastily assembled his own. In format and style, it was like other almanacs, most notably that of Titan Leeds, who was publish-ing, as his father had before him, Philadelphia's most popular version. The name Poor Richard, a slight oxymoron pun, echoed that of *Poor Robin's Almanack,* which had been published by Franklin's brother James. And Richard Saunders happened to be the real name of a noted almanac writer in England in the late seventeenth century.[52]

Franklin, however, added his own distinctive flair. He used his pseudonym to permit himself some ironic distance, and he ginned up a running feud with his rival Titan Leeds by predicting and later fabri-cating his death. As his ad in the *Pennsylvania Gazette* immodestly promised:

> Just published for 1733: *Poor Richard: An Almanack* containing the lunations, eclipses, planets motions and aspects, weather, sun and moon's rising and setting, highwater, etc. besides many pleasant and witty verses, jests and sayings, author's motive of writing, prediction of the death of his friend Mr. Titan Leeds . . . By Richard Saunders, philomath, printed and sold by B. Franklin, price 3s. 6d per dozen.[53]

Years later, Franklin would recall that he regarded his almanac as a "vehicle for conveying instruction among the common folk" and therefore filled it with proverbs that "inculcated industry and frugality as the means of procuring wealth and thereby securing virtue." At the time, however, he also had another motive, about which he was quite forthright. The beauty of inventing a fictional author was that he could poke fun at himself by admitting, only half in jest, through the pen of Poor Richard, that money was his main motivation. "I might in this place attempt to gain thy favor by declaring that I write almanacks with no other view than that of the public good; but in this I should not be sincere," Poor Richard began his first preface. "The plain truth of the matter is, I am excessive poor, and my wife . . . has threatened more than once to burn all my books and Rattling-Traps (as she calls my instruments) if I do not make some profitable use of them for the good of my family." [54]

Poor Richard went on to predict "the inexorable death" of his rival Titan Leeds, giving the exact day and hour. It was a prank borrowed from Jonathan Swift. Leeds fell into the trap, and in his own almanac for 1734 (written after the date of his predicted death) called Franklin a "conceited scribbler" who had "manifested himself a fool and a liar." Franklin, with his own printing press, had the luxury of reading Leeds before he published his own 1734 edition. In it, Poor Richard responded that all of these defamatory protestations indicate that the real Leeds must indeed be dead and his new almanac a hoax by someone else. "Mr. Leeds was too well bred to use any man so indecently and scurrilously, and moreover his esteem and affection for me was extraordinary."

In his almanac for 1735, Franklin again ridiculed his "deceased" rival's sharp responses—"Titan Leeds when living would not have used me so!"—and also caught Leeds in a language mishap. Leeds had declared it was "untrue" that he had himself predicted that he would "survive until" the date in question. Franklin retorted that if it were untrue that he survived until then, he must therefore be "really defunct and dead." " 'Tis plain to everyone that reads his last two almanacks," Poor Richard jibed, "no man living would or could write such stuff." [55]

Even after Leeds in fact did die in 1738, Franklin did not relent.

He printed a letter from Leeds's ghost admitting "that I did actually die at that time, precisely at the hour you mentioned, with a variation only of 5 minutes, 53 seconds." Franklin then had the ghost make a prediction about Poor Richard's other rival: John Jerman would convert to Catholicism in the coming year. Franklin kept up this jest for four years, even while he had, once again, the contract to print Jerman's almanac. Jerman's good humor finally ran out, and in 1743 he took his business back to Bradford. "The reader may expect a reply from me to R—— S——rs alias B—— F——ns way of proving me no Protestant," he wrote, adding that because "of that witty performance [he] shall not have the benefit of my almanack for this year."[56]

Franklin had fun hiding behind the veil of Poor Richard, but he also occasionally enjoyed poking through the veil. In 1736 he had Poor Richard deny rumors that he was just a fiction. He would not, he said, "have taken any notice of so idle a report if it had not been for the sake of my printer, to whom my enemies are pleased to ascribe my productions, and who it seems is as unwilling to father my offspring as I am to lose credit of it." The following year, Poor Richard blamed his printer (Franklin) for causing some mistakes in the weather forecasts by moving them around to fit in holidays. And in 1739, he lamented that his printer was pocketing his profits, but added, "I do not grudge it him; he is a man I have great regard for."

Richard and Bridget Saunders did, in many ways, reflect Benjamin and Deborah Franklin. In the almanac for 1738, Franklin had the fictional Bridget take a turn at writing the preface for Poor Richard. This was shortly after Deborah Franklin had bought her husband the china breakfast bowl, and it came at the time when Franklin's newspaper pieces were poking fun at the pretensions of wives who acquire a taste for fancy tea services. Bridget Saunders announced to the reader that year that she read the preface her husband had composed, discovered he had "been slinging some of his old skits at me," and tossed it away. "Cannot I have a little fault or two but all the country must see it in print! They have already been told at one time that I am proud, another time that I am loud, and that I have a new petticoat, and abundance of such kind of stuff. And now, forsooth! all the world must know that Poor Dick's wife has lately taken a fancy to drink a little tea now and then." Lest the connection be missed, she noted that the tea was "a present from the printer."[57]

Poor Richard's delightful annual prefaces never, alas, became as famous as the maxims and sayings that Franklin scattered in the margins of his almanacs each year, such as the most famous of all: "Early to bed and early to rise, makes a man healthy, wealthy and wise." Franklin would have been amused by how faithfully these were praised by subsequent advocates of self-improvement, and he would likely have been even more amused by the humorists who later poked fun at them. In a sketch with the ironic title "The Late Benjamin Franklin," Mark Twain jibed, "As if it were any object to a boy to be healthy and wealthy and wise on such terms. The sorrow that that maxim has cost me, through my parents, experimenting on me with it, tongue cannot tell. The legitimate result is my present state of general debility, indigence, and mental aberration. My parents used to have me up before nine o'clock in the morning sometimes when I was a boy. If they had let me take my natural rest where would I have been now? Keeping store, no doubt, and respected by all." Groucho Marx, in his memoirs, also picked up the theme: " 'Early to bed, early to rise, makes a man you-know-what.' This is a lot of hoopla. Most wealthy people I know like to sleep late, and will fire the help if they are disturbed before three in the afternoon . . . You don't see Marilyn Monroe getting up at six in the morning. The truth is, I don't see Marilyn Monroe getting up at any hour, more's the pity."[58]

Most of Poor Richard's sayings were not, in fact, totally original, as Franklin freely admitted. They "contained the wisdom of many ages and nations," he said in his autobiography, and he noted in the final edition "that not a tenth part of the wisdom was my own." Even a near version of his "early to bed and early to rise" maxim had appeared in a collection of English proverbs a century earlier.[59]

Franklin's talent was inventing a few new maxims and polishing up a lot of older ones to make them pithier. For example, the old English proverb "Fresh fish and new-come guests smell, but that they are three days old" Franklin made: "Fish and visitors stink in three days." Likewise, "A muffled cat is no good mouser" became "The cat in gloves catches no mice." He took the old saying "Many strokes fell great oaks" and gave it a sharper moral edge: "Little strokes fell great oaks." He also sharpened "Three may keep a secret if two of them are away" into "Three may keep a secret if two of them are dead." And the Scottish saying that "a listening damsel and a speaking castle shall never end with honor" was turned into "Neither a fortress nor a maidenhead will hold out long after they begin to parley."[60]

Even though most of the maxims were adopted from others, they offer insight into his notions of what was useful and amusing. Among the best are:

> He's a fool that makes his doctor his heir . . . Eat to live, and not live to eat . . . He that lies down with dogs shall rise up with fleas . . . Where there's marriage without love, there will be love without marriage . . . Necessity never made a good bargain . . . There's more old drunkards than old doctors . . . A good example is the best sermon . . . None preaches better than the ant, and she says nothing . . . A Penny saved is Twopence clear . . . When the well's dry we know the worth of water . . . The sleeping fox catches no poultry . . . The used key is always bright . . . He that lives on hope dies farting [he later wrote it as "dies fasting," and the early version may have been a misprint] . . . Diligence is the mother of good luck . . . He that pursues two hares at once does not catch one and lets the other go . . . Search others for their virtues, thy self for thy vices . . . Kings and bears often worry their keepers . . . Haste makes waste . . . Make haste slowly . . . He who multiplies riches multiplies cares . . . He's a fool that cannot conceal his wisdom . . . No gains without pains . . . Vice knows she's ugly, so puts on her mask . . . The most exquisite folly is made of wisdom spun too fine . . . Love your enemies, for they will tell you your faults . . . The sting of a reproach is the truth of it . . . There's a time to wink as well as to see . . . Genius without education is like silver in the mine . . . There was never a good knife made of bad steel . . . Half the truth is often a great lie . . . God helps them that help themselves.

What distinguished Franklin's almanac was its sly wit. As he was completing his 1738 edition, he wrote a letter in his newspaper, using the pen name "Philomath," that poked at his rivals by giving sarcastic advice about writing almanacs. A requisite talent, he said, "is a sort of gravity, which keeps a due medium between dullness and nonsense."

This is because "grave men are taken by the common people for wise men." In addition, the author "should write sentences and throw out hints that neither himself nor anybody else can understand." As examples, he cited some phrases used by Titan Leeds.[61]

In his final edition, completed while on his way to England in 1757, Franklin would sum things up with a fictional speech by an old man named Father Abraham who strings together all of Poor Richard's adages about the need for frugality and virtue. But Franklin's wry tone was, even then, still intact. Poor Richard, who is standing in the back of the crowd, reports at the end: "The people heard it, and approved the doctrine, and immediately practiced the contrary."[62]

All of this made Poor Richard a success and his creator wealthy. The almanac sold ten thousand copies a year, surpassing its Philadelphia rivals. John Peter Zenger, whose famous 1735 libel trial was covered by Franklin's paper, bought thirty-six dozen one year. James's widow sold about eighty dozen a year. Father Abraham's speech compiling Poor Richard's sayings was published as *The Way to Wealth* and became, for a time, the most famous book to come out of colonial America. Within forty years, it was reprinted in 145 editions and seven languages; the French one was entitled *La Science du Bonhomme Richard.* Through the present, it has gone through more than thirteen hundred editions.

Like Franklin's moral perfection project and *Autobiography,* the sayings of Poor Richard have been criticized for revealing the mind of a penny-saving prig. "It has taken me many years and countless smarts to get out of that barbed wire moral enclosure that Poor Richard rigged up," wrote D. H. Lawrence. But that misses the humor and irony, as well as the nice mix of cleverness and morality, that Franklin deftly brewed. It also mistakenly confuses Franklin with the characters he created. The real Franklin was not a moral prude, and he did not dedicate his life to accumulating wealth. "The general foible of mankind," he told a friend, is "in the pursuit of wealth to no end." His goal was to help aspiring tradesmen become more diligent, and thus more able to be useful and virtuous citizens.

Poor Richard's almanacs do provide some useful insights into Franklin, especially into his wit and outlook. But by half hiding behind a fictional cutout, Franklin once again followed his Junto rule of revealing his thinking only through indirection. In that, he was acting according to the advice he put in Poor Richard's mouth. "Let all men know thee, but no man know thee thoroughly: Men freely ford that see the shallows."[63]

CHAPTER FIVE

PUBLIC CITIZEN

Philadelphia, 1731–1748

ORGANIZATIONS FOR THE COMMON GOOD

The essence of Franklin is that he was a civic-minded man. He cared more about public behavior than inner piety, and he was more interested in building the City of Man than the City of God. The maxim he had proclaimed on his first trip back from London—"Man is a sociable being"—was reflected not only in his personal collegiality, but also in his belief that benevolence was the binding virtue of society. As Poor Richard put it, "He that drinks his cider alone, let him catch his horse alone."

This gregarious outlook would lead him, as a twentysomething printer during the 1730s, to use his Junto to launch a variety of community organizations, including a lending library, fire brigade, and night watchmen corps, and later a hospital, militia, and college. "The good men may do separately," he wrote, "is small compared with what they may do collectively."

Franklin picked up his penchant for forming do-good associations from Cotton Mather and others, but his organizational fervor and galvanizing personality made him the most influential force in instilling this as an enduring part of American life. "Americans of all ages, all stations in life, and all types of dispositions are forever forming associations," Tocqueville famously marveled. "Hospitals, prisons and schools take shape this way."

Tocqueville came to the conclusion that there was an inherent struggle in America between two opposing impulses: the spirit of rugged individualism versus the conflicting spirit of community and association building. Franklin would have disagreed. A fundamental aspect of Franklin's life, and of the American society he helped to create, was that individualism and communitarianism, so seemingly contradictory, were interwoven. The frontier attracted barn-raising pioneers who were ruggedly individualistic as well as fiercely supportive of their community. Franklin was the epitome of this admixture of self-reliance and civic involvement, and what he exemplified became part of the American character.[1]

Franklin's subscription library, which was the first of its type in America, began when he suggested to his Junto that each member bring books to the clubhouse so that the others could use them. It worked well enough, but money was needed to supplement and care for the collection. So he decided to recruit subscribers who would pay dues for the right to borrow books, most of which would be imported from London.

The Library Company of Philadelphia was incorporated in 1731, when Franklin was 27. Its motto, written by Franklin, reflected the connection he made between goodness and godliness: *Communiter Bona profundere Deum est* (To pour forth benefits for the common good is divine).

Raising funds was not easy. "So few were the readers at the time in Philadelphia and the majority of us so poor that I was not able with great industry to find more than fifty persons, mostly young tradesmen, willing to pay." In doing so, he learned one of his pragmatic lessons about jealousy and modesty: he found that people were reluctant to support a "proposer of any useful project that might be supposed to raise one's reputation." So he put himself "as much as I could out of sight" and gave credit for the idea to his friends. This method worked so well that "I ever after practiced it on such occasions." People will eventually give you the credit, he noted, if you don't try to claim it at the time. "The present little sacrifice of your vanity will afterwards be amply repaid."

The choice of books, recommended by learned Philadelphians such as James Logan, a wealthy fur trader and gentleman scholar whom Franklin got the chance to befriend for this purpose, reflected Franklin's practical nature. Of the first forty-five bought, there were nine on science, eight on history, and eight on politics; most of the rest were reference books. There were no novels, dramas, poetry, or great literature, other than two classics (Homer and Virgil).

Franklin spent an hour or two each day reading the books in the library, "and thus repaired in some degree the loss of the learned education my father once intended for me." His involvement also helped him climb socially: the Junto was composed mainly of poor tradesmen, but the Library Company allowed Franklin to elicit the patronage of some of the more distinguished gentlemen of the town and also begin a lifelong friendship with Peter Collinson, a London merchant who agreed to help acquire the books. Eventually, the idea of local subscription libraries caught on in the rest of the colonies, and so did the benefits. "These libraries have improved the general conversation of the Americans," Franklin later noted, and "made the common tradesmen and farmers as intelligent as most gentlemen from other countries." The Library Company thrives to this day. With 500,000 books and 160,000 manuscripts, it remains a significant historical repository and is the oldest cultural institution in the United States.[2]

Franklin often floated his ideas for civic improvements by writing under a pseudonym for his paper. Using the name Pennsylvanus, he wrote a description of the "brave men" who volunteer to fight fires, and suggested that those who didn't join them should help bear the expense of ladders, buckets, and pumps. A year later, in an essay he read to the Junto and subsequently published as a letter to his newspaper, he proposed the formation of a fire company. Again taking care not to claim credit, he pretended the letter was written by an old man (who, in declaring that "an ounce of prevention is worth a pound of cure," sounded quite like Poor Richard). Philadelphia had a lot of spirited volunteers, he noted, but they lacked "order and method." They should therefore consider following the example of Boston, he said, and organize into fire-fighting clubs with specific duties. Always a stickler for specifics, Franklin helpfully enumerated these duties in great detail: there should be wardens, who carry "a red staff of five feet," as well as axmen and hookmen and other specialties.

"This was much spoken of as a useful piece," Franklin recalled in his autobiography, so he set about organizing the Union Fire Company, which was incorporated in 1736. He was fastidious in detailing its rules and the fines that would be levied for infractions. This being a Franklin scheme, it included a social component as well; they met for dinner once a month "for a social evening together discussing and communicating such ideas as occurred to us on the subject of fires." So many people wanted to join that, like the Junto, it spawned sister fire companies around town.

Franklin remained actively involved in the Union Fire Company for years. In 1743, the *Gazette* carried a little notice: "Lost at the late fire on Water Street, two leather buckets, marked B. Franklin & Co. Whoever brings them to the printer hereof shall be satisfied for their trouble." Fifty years later, when he returned from Paris after the Revolution, he would gather the four remaining members of the company, along with their leather buckets, for meetings.[3]

Franklin also sought to improve the town's ineffective police forces. At the time, the ragtag groups of watchmen were managed by constables who either enlisted neighbors or dunned them a fee to avoid service. This resulted in roaming gangs that made a little money and, Franklin noted, spent most of the night getting drunk. Once again, Franklin suggested a solution in a paper he wrote for his Junto. It proposed that full-time watchmen be funded by a property tax levied according to the value of each home, and it included one of the first arguments in America for progressive taxation. It was unfair, he wrote, that "a poor widow housekeeper, all of whose property to be guarded by the watch did not perhaps exceed the value of fifty pounds, paid as much as the wealthiest merchant, who had thousands of pounds worth of goods in his stores."

Unlike the fire associations, these police patrols were conceived as a government function and needed Assembly approval. Consequently, they did not get formed until 1752, "when the members of our clubs were grown more in influence." By that time, Franklin was an assem-blyman, and he helped draft the detailed legislation on how the watchmen would be organized.[4]

THE FREEMASONS

One fraternal association, more exalted than the Junto, already existed in Philadelphia, and it seemed perfectly tailored to Franklin's aspirations: the Grand Lodge of Free and Accepted Masons. Free-masonry, a semisecret fraternal organization based on the ancient ritu-als and symbols of the stone-cutting guilds, had been founded in London in 1717, and its first Philadelphia lodge cropped up in 1727. Like Franklin, the Freemasons were dedicated to fellowship, civic works, and nonsectarian religious tolerance. They also represented, for Franklin, another step up the social ladder; many of the town's top merchants and lawyers were Freemasons.

Social mobility was not very common in the eighteenth century. But Franklin proudly made it his mission—indeed, helped it become part of America's mission—that a tradesman could rise in the world and stand before kings. This was not always easy, and at first he had trouble getting invited to join the Freemasons. So he began printing small, favorable notices about them in his newspaper. When that did not work, he tried a tougher tactic. In December 1730, he ran a long article that purported, based on the papers of a member who had just died, to uncover some of the secrets of the organization, including the fact that most of the secrets were just a hoax.

Within a few weeks, he was invited to join, after which the *Gazette* retracted its December article and printed some small, flattering no-tices. Franklin became a faithful Freemason. In 1732, he helped draft the bylaws of the Philadelphia lodge, and two years later became the Grand Master and printed its constitution.[5]

Franklin's fealty to the Freemasons embroiled him in a scandal that illustrated his aversion to confronting people. In the summer of 1737, a naïve apprentice named Daniel Rees wanted to join the group. A gang of rowdy acquaintances, not Freemasons, sought to have sport with him and concocted a ritual filled with weird oaths, purgatives, and butt kissing. When they told Franklin of their prank, he laughed and asked for a copy of the fake oaths. A few days later, the hooligans enacted another ceremony, where the hapless Rees was accidentally burned to death by a bowl of flaming brandy. Franklin was not involved, but he was called as a witness in the subsequent manslaughter trial. The newspaper printed by his rival Andrew Bradford, no friend of either Franklin or Freemasonry, charged that Franklin was indirectly responsible because he encouraged the tormentors.

Responding in his own paper, Franklin admitted that he initially laughed at the prank. "But when they came to those circumstances of their giving him a violent purge, leading him to kiss T's posteriors, and administering him the diabolical oath which R——n read to us, I grew indeed serious." His credibility, however, was not helped by the fact that he had asked to see the oath and then merrily showed it to friends.

News of the tragedy, and Franklin's involvement, was published in anti-Mason papers throughout the colonies, including the Boston *News Ledger*, and reached his parents. In a letter, he sought to allay his mother's concerns about the Freemasons. "They are in general a very harmless sort of people," he wrote, "and have no principles or practices that are inconsistent with religion or good manners." He did concede, however, that she had a right to be displeased that they did not admit women.[6]

THE GREAT AWAKENING

Although he was nondoctrinaire to the point of being little more than a deist, Franklin remained interested in religion, particularly its social effects. During the 1730s, he became enthralled by two preachers, the first an unorthodox freethinker like himself, the other an evangelical revivalist whose fiery conservatism ran counter to most of what Franklin believed.

Samuel Hemphill was a young preacher from Ireland who, in 1734, came to Philadelphia to work as a deputy at the Presbyterian church that Franklin had sporadically visited. More interested in preaching about morality than Calvinist doctrines, Hemphill started drawing large crowds, including a curious Franklin, who found "his sermons pleasing me, as they had little of the dogmatical kind, but inculcated strongly the practice of virtue." That dearth of dogma did not endear Hemphill to the church elders, however. Jedediah Andrews, the senior minister whose sermons had bored Franklin, complained that Hemphill had been imposed on his church and that "free thinkers, deists, and nothings, getting a scent of him, flocked to him." Soon Hemphill was brought before the synod on charges of heresy.

As the trial began, Franklin came to his defense with a deft article purporting to be a dialogue between two local Presbyterians. Mr. S., representing Franklin, listens as Mr. T. complains about how the "new-fangled preacher" talks too much about good works. "I do not love to hear so much of morality; I am sure it will carry no man to heaven."

Mr. S. rejoins that it is what "Christ and his Apostles used to preach." The Bible makes it clear, he says, that God would have us lead "virtuous, upright and good-doing lives."

But, asks Mr. T., isn't faith rather than virtue the path to salvation?

"Faith is recommended as a means of producing morality," Franklin's mouthpiece Mr. S. replies, adding heretically, "That from such faith alone salvation may be expected appears to me to be neither a Christian doctrine nor a reasonable one."

As a believer in tolerance, Franklin might have been expected to tolerate the Presbyterians' imposing whatever doctrine they wanted on their own preachers, but instead he had Mr. S. argue that they should not adhere to their orthodoxies. "No point of faith is so plain as that morality is our duty," Mr. S. concludes, echoing Franklin's core philosophy. "A virtuous heretic shall be saved before a wicked Christian."

It was a typical Franklin effort at persuasion: clever, indirect, and using fabricated characters to make his point. But when the synod unanimously censured and suspended Hemphill, Franklin shed his usual velvet gloves and, as he put it, "became his zealous partisan." He published an anonymous pamphlet (and, unlike his newspaper dialogue, made sure that the pamphlet remained anonymous) filled with uncharacteristic anger. Not only did he offer detailed theological rebuttals to each of the synod's charges, but he accused its members of "malice and envy."

Hemphill's accusers responded with their own pamphlet, which prompted Franklin to write another, even more vitriolic anonymous response that hurled phrases like "bigotry and prejudice" and "pious fraud." In a subsequent poem, he labeled Hemphill's critics "Rev. Asses."

It was a rare violation by Franklin of his Junto rule of avoiding direct contradiction or argumentation, one that was all the more odd because in the past he had cheerily forsaken any claim to care much about doctrinal disputes. His resentment of the entrenched, pious clerical establishment seemed to get the better of his temper.

Franklin's defense became more difficult when Hemphill was exposed as having plagiarized many of his sermons. Nevertheless, Franklin still stuck by him, explaining later that "I rather approved his giving us good sermons composed by others, than bad ones of his own manufacture, though the latter was the practice of our common teachers." In the end, Hemphill left town and Franklin quit the Presbyterian congregation for good.[7]

The Hemphill affair occurred just as an emotional tide of revivalism, known as the Great Awakening, began sweeping America. Fervent Protestant traditionalists, most notably Jonathan Edwards, were whipping congregants into spiritual frenzies and convulsive conversions with tales of fire and brimstone. As Edwards told his congregation in the most famous of his "terror" sermons, "Sinners in the Hands of an Angry God," the only thing that kept them from eternal damnation was the inexplicable grace of "the God that holds you over the pit of Hell, much as one holds a spider or some loathsome insect over fire."

Nothing could have been further from Franklin's theology. Indeed, Edwards and Franklin, the two preeminent Americans of their generation, can be viewed, Carl Van Doren noted, as "symbols of the hostile movements that strove for the mastery of their age." Edwards and the Great Awakeners sought to recommit America to the anguished spirituality of Puritanism, whereas Franklin sought to bring it into an Enlightenment era that exalted tolerance, individual merit, civic virtue, good deeds, and rationality.[8]

Thus, it might seem surprising, indeed somewhat odd, that Franklin became enthralled by George Whitefield, the most popular of the Great Awakening's roving preachers, who arrived in Philadelphia in 1739. The English evangelist had been an unhappy soul at Pembroke College, Oxford, and then had a "new birth" into Methodism and later Calvinism. He was doctrinally pure in his insistence that salvation came only through God's grace, but he was nevertheless deeply involved in charitable work, and his year-long tour through America was to raise money for an orphanage in Georgia. He raised more money than any other cleric of his time for philanthropies, which included schools, libraries, and almshouses across Europe and America. So perhaps it was not so surprising that Franklin took a liking to him though never embraced his theology.

Whitefield's nightly outdoor revival meetings in Philadelphia (by then America's largest town, with a population of thirteen thousand) drew huge crowds, and Franklin, sensing a great story, covered him lavishly in the *Pennsylvania Gazette*. "On Thursday," he reported, "the Rev. Mr. Whitefield began to preach from the Court House gallery in this city, about six at night, to nearly 6,000 people before him in the street, who stood in an awful silence to hear him." The crowds grew throughout his week-long visit, and Whitefield returned to the city three more times during his year-long American crusade.

Franklin was awed. He published accounts of Whitefield's appearances in forty-five weekly issues of his *Gazette,* and eight times he turned over his entire front page to reprints of the sermons. Franklin recounted in his autobiography, with a wryness born only after years of detachment, the enthusiasm that infected him at the time:

> I happened soon after to attend one of his sermons, in the course of which I perceived he intended to finish with a collection, and I silently resolved he should get nothing from me. I had in my pocket a handful of copper money, three or four silver dollars, and five pistoles in gold. As he proceeded I began to soften, and concluded to give the coppers. Another stroke of his oratory made me ashamed of that, and determined me to give the silver; and he finished so admirably, that I emptied my pocket wholly into the collector's dish, gold and all.

Franklin was also impressed with the transforming effect that Whitefield had on Philadelphia's citizenry. "Never did the people show so great a willingness to attend sermons," he reported in the *Gazette*. "Religion is become the subject of most conversation. No books are in request but those of piety."[9]

The financial implications of that last observation were not lost on Franklin. He met with Whitefield and arranged a deal to be the primary publisher of his sermons and journals, which no doubt added to his zeal to publicize him. After Whitefield's first visit, Franklin ran an advertisement soliciting orders for a series of Whitefield's sermons at two shillings a volume. A few months later, he ran a notice that he had received so many orders that those "who have paid or who bring the money in their hands will have the preference."

Thousands were sold, which helped to make Franklin rich and Whitefield famous. Franklin also published ten editions of Whitefield's journals, each five times more expensive than his almanac, and enlisted a sales force of eleven printers he knew throughout the colonies to make them bestsellers. His sister-in-law Anne Franklin of Newport took a shipment of 250. During 1739–41, more than half the books that Franklin printed were by or about Whitefield.

Some historians have consequently concluded that Franklin's passion for Whitefield was merely pecuniary. But that is too simplistic. As was often the case, Franklin was able to weave together seamlessly his financial interests with his civic desires and personal enthusiasms. He had a companionable personality, and he was genuinely attracted by Whitefield's mesmerizing charisma and charitable bent. He invited Whitefield to stay at his home, and when the preacher praised the invitation as being "for Christ's sake," Franklin corrected him: "Don't let me be mistaken; it was not for Christ's sake, but for your sake."

In addition, despite their theological differences, Franklin was attracted to Whitefield because he was shaking up the local establishment. Franklin's long-standing disdain for the religious elite led him to enjoy the discomfort and schisms caused by the intrusion of wildly popular itinerant preachers onto their turf. The tolerant Franklin was pleased that Whitefield's supporters had erected, with Franklin's financial support, a large new hall that, among other uses, could provide a pulpit to anyone of any belief, "so that even if the Mufti of Constantinople were to send a missionary to preach Mohammedanism to us, he would find a pulpit at his service."[10]

Franklin's populist delight at the discomfort of the elite was evident in the way he stoked up a controversy about a letter sent to the *Gazette* by some of the town's gentry, who wrote that Whitefield had not "met with great success among the better sort of people." The next week, using the pen name "Obadiah Plainman," Franklin ridiculed the use of the phrase "the better sort of people" and its implication that Whitefield's supporters were "the meaner sort, the mob or the rabble." Mr. Plainman said that he and his friends were proud to call themselves part of the rabble, but they hated it when people who styled themselves "better sort" used such terms and implied that common folks were "a stupid herd."

A haughty-sounding gentleman named Tom Trueman (or perhaps, given the name, Franklin pretending to be such a gentleman) wrote the next week to William Bradford's more upscale newspaper to deny that such offense was intended and to accuse Mr. Plainman of fancying himself a leader of the town's common folks. Franklin, again replying as Mr. Plainman, said he was merely "a poor ordinary" craftsman who, after his labors, "instead of going to the alehouse, I amuse myself with the books of the Library Company." As such, he rankled at those who proclaimed themselves to be of the better sort and "look on the rest of their fellow subjects with contempt." Though he was rising in the world in a way that would have allowed him, if he were so inclined, to put on aristocratic airs, Franklin was still allergic to snobbery and proud to be a Plainman defending the middling people.[11]

By the fall of 1740, Franklin showed signs of cooling slightly toward Whitefield, though not toward the profits that came from publishing him. The preacher's efforts to make him a "new born" believer in Calvinist orthodoxy wore thin, and valuable patrons among the Philadelphia gentry began to denounce the *Gazette*'s ardent flackery. In response to such criticism, Franklin printed an editorial denying (unconvincingly) any bias and restating his philosophy, first propounded in his 1731 "Apology for Printers," that "when truth has fair play, it will always prevail over falsehood." But he also included in the issue a letter from a preacher who criticized Whitefield's "enthusiastic ravings," and he subsequently published two pamphlets harshly attacking Whitefield as well as one giving Whitefield's response. The letters in Franklin's *Gazette*, 90 percent of which had been favorable to Whitefield in the first nine months of 1740, tipped mostly negative beginning in September, though the pieces written by Franklin remained positive.

Albeit with less ardor, Franklin continued to support Whitefield over the ensuing years, and they maintained an affectionate correspondence until the preacher's death in 1770. In his autobiography, written after Whitefield died, Franklin added a dose of ironic detachment to his warm recollections. He recounted one sermon he attended where, rather than being moved by Whitefield's words, Franklin spent the time calculating how far his voice carried. And as for Whitefield's effect on his spiritual life, Franklin wryly recalled, "He used, indeed, sometimes to pray for my conversion, but never had the satisfaction of believing that his prayers were heard."[12]

PUBLISHING WARS

As Franklin's publishing business grew, his competition with the town's other printer, Andrew Bradford, intensified. Throughout the early 1730s, they had poked fun at errors in each other's papers and sparred over such matters as the death of the aspiring young Freemason and the preachings of Samuel Hemphill. There was a political and social basis to the rivalry. The well-born Bradford and his *American Weekly Mercury* were aligned with Pennsylvania's "Proprietary faction," which supported the Penn family and their appointed governors. The leather-aproned Franklin and his *Pennsylvania Gazette* were more antiestablishment and tended to support the rights of the elected Assembly.

Their politics clashed during the 1733 reelection campaign of the Assembly's speaker, Andrew Hamilton, an anti-Proprietary leader who had helped Franklin wrest the government printing job from Bradford. Franklin admired Hamilton's antiaristocratic populism. "He was no friend to power," Franklin wrote. "He was the poor man's friend." Bradford, on the other hand, printed fervent attacks on Hamilton. Among them was an essay "On Infidelity," which was aimed at Hamilton but designed to wound Franklin as well. Another accused Hamilton of insulting the Penn family and abusing his power as head of the loan office.

Franklin came to Hamilton's defense with a dignified yet damning rebuttal. Cast as an account of a "Half-Hour's Conversation" with Hamilton, the piece skewered Bradford for sins ranging from malapropism (using "contemptibly" when he meant "contemptuously") to hiding behind the cloak of anonymity ("seeing it was commonly agreed to be wrote by nobody, he thought nobody should regard it"). Hamilton comes across as a polite Junto visitor with a touch of Poor Richard. "Throw enough dirt," he laments, "and some will stick."[13]

Hamilton won reelection, and in 1736 he got Franklin chosen as the clerk of the Assembly. Again, public service and private profit were combined. The clerkship, Franklin freely admitted, "gave me a better opportunity of keeping up an interest among the members, which secured to me the business of printing the votes, laws, paper money, and other occasional jobs for the public, that, on the whole, were very profitable."

It also taught him a useful trick for seducing opponents. After one rich and well-bred member spoke against him, Franklin decided to win him over:

> I did not, however, aim at gaining his favor by paying any servile respect to him, but, after some time, took this other method. Having heard that he had in his library a certain very scarce and curious book, I wrote a note to him, expressing my desire of perusing that book, and requesting he would do me the favor of lending it to me for a few days. He sent it immediately, and I returned it in about a week with another note, expressing strongly my sense of the favor. When we next met in the House, he spoke to me (which he had never done before), and with great civility; and he ever after manifested a readiness to serve me on all occasions, so that we became great friends, and our friendship continued to his death. This is another instance of the truth of an old maxim I had learned, which says, "He that has once done you a kindness will be more ready to do you another, than he whom you yourself have obliged."[14]

Franklin's competition with Bradford had one interesting aspect that might seem unusual but was, then as now, somewhat common. Even as they competed against each other in some areas, like modern media barons they cooperated in others. For example, in 1733, even as they were bitter opponents in the Hamilton election, they formed a joint venture to share the risk of publishing an expensive Psalm book. At Bradford's suggestion, Franklin handled the printing, Bradford supplied the paper, they split the costs, and each got half of the five hundred copies that were made.[15]

In his competition with Bradford, Franklin had one big disadvantage. Bradford was the postmaster of Philadelphia, and he used that position to deny Franklin the right, at least officially, to send his *Gazette* through the mail. Their ensuing struggle over the issue of open carriage was an early example of the tension that often still exists between those who create content and those who control distribution systems.

At one point, Franklin got Col. Alexander Spotswood, the postmaster for the colonies, to order Bradford to run an open system that would carry rival papers. But Bradford continued to make it difficult for Franklin's papers to get carriage, forcing Franklin to bribe the postal riders. Franklin worried not only about the expense but also about the public perception. Because Bradford controlled the Philadelphia post, Franklin wrote, "it was imagined he had better opportunities of obtaining news, [and] his paper was thought a better distributor of advertisements than mine."

Franklin was able to wrest the Philadelphia postmastership away when it was discovered that Bradford had been sloppy in his bookkeeping. Colonel Spotswood, with Franklin's encouragement, withdrew Bradford's commission in 1737 and offered the job to Franklin. "I accepted it readily," Franklin noted, "and found it of great advantage, for though the salary was small, it facilitated the correspondence that improved my newspaper, increased the number demanded, as well as the advertisements to be inserted, so that it came to afford me a very considerable income." Bradford's paper declined accordingly.

Instead of retaliating, Franklin allowed Bradford's *Mercury* to be carried through the mails along with the *Gazette* and others—at least initially. In his autobiography, Franklin congratulated himself for being so open. In fact, however, that policy lasted just two years. Because Bradford never settled the accounts from his tenure as Philadelphia postmaster, Spotswood sent Franklin an order to "commence suit against him" and "no longer suffer to be carried by the Post any of his newspapers."

Bradford had to resort to Franklin's old habit of bribing the postal riders to deliver his papers unofficially. Franklin knew this and tolerated it, just as Bradford had earlier tolerated it for Franklin. But even this partial indulgence by Franklin was not to last.[16]

In 1740, he and Bradford became involved in a race to start the first general-interest magazine in America. Franklin came up with the idea, but once again he was betrayed by a confidant, just as happened when he first planned to launch a newspaper. As a wiser Poor Richard would pointedly proclaim in his 1741 almanac, "If you would keep your secret from an enemy, tell it not to a friend."

This time the turncoat was a lawyer named John Webbe, who had contributed essays to the *Gazette* and had been chosen by Franklin to file the suit against Bradford that Colonel Spotswood ordered. Franklin described the magazine to Webbe and offered him the job of editor. But Webbe took the idea to Bradford and struck a better deal. On November 6, 1740, Bradford announced plans for *The American Magazine.* One week later, Franklin published his own plans for *The General Magazine.*

In his announcement, Franklin denounced Webbe's betrayal. "This Magazine . . . was long since projected," he wrote. "It would not, indeed, have been published quite so soon, were it not that a Person, to whom the scheme was communicated in confidence, has thought fit to advertise it in the last *Mercury* . . . and reap the Advantage of it wholly to himself." The ensuing spat led Franklin to ban completely Bradford's paper from the mails. It also turned the question of postal access into a public issue.

Webbe responded in the *Mercury* the next week with a sharp counterattack of his own. He particularly objected to one of Franklin's less endearing traits: his clever and often sly way of implying allegations rather than saying them outright. Franklin's indirection, "like the slyness of a pickpocket," was more "dastardly" than the audacity of a "direct liar," Webbe wrote. "The strokes being oblique and indirect, a man cannot so easily defend himself against them." Franklin liked to believe that his method of using indirect insinuation was less offensive than confrontational argument, but it sometimes led to even greater enmity and a reputation for crafty deceit.

Franklin did not respond. With an exquisite sense of how to goad Webbe and Bradford, he merely reprinted his original notice in his next issue of the *Gazette,* including the same allegation of Webbe's duplicity. This led Webbe to publish another screed in the *Mercury.* Once again, Franklin showed infuriating restraint: he did not respond, but again reprinted his original notice and allegation.

Webbe escalated the dispute in the December 4 *Mercury* with an allegation guaranteed to draw a response from Franklin. "Since my first letter," Webbe wrote, Franklin had "taken upon him to deprive the *Mercury* of the benefit of the Post." Franklin replied the following week with a somewhat disingenuous explanation. It had been a year, he said, since Bradford's *Mercury* had been barred free use of the mails. This had nothing to do with the dispute over the magazines. Instead, it was at the direct order of Colonel Spotswood. To prove his point, Franklin printed Spotswood's letter. He said that Bradford and Webbe knew this to be the case, Webbe in particular, as he had been the lawyer Franklin retained to file the suit.

Webbe replied by laying out the history of the postal practices. Yes, he conceded, Spotswood had ordered Franklin to stop carrying Bradford's paper. But, as Franklin well knew, the riders had continued to carry it unofficially. Moreover, Webbe charged, Franklin himself had confided to people that he permitted this arrangement because it helped assure that Bradford would take care not to print anything too harmful to Franklin. "He had declared," wrote Webbe, "that as he favored Mr. Bradford by permitting the Postman to distribute his Papers, he had him therefore under his thumb."

The public debate over postal practices quieted down as each side raced to put out its magazine. In the end, Bradford and Webbe won by three days. Their *American Magazine* came off the press February 13, 1741, and Franklin's *General Magazine* appeared on the 16th.

The word *magazine,* as then used, tended to mean a collection drawn from newspapers and other places. The contents of Franklin's, patterned after London's ten-year-old *Gentleman's Magazine,* were surprisingly dry: official proclamations, reports on government proceedings, discussion of paper currency issues, some smatterings of poetry, and a report about Whitefield's orphanage.

The formula failed. Bradford's magazine folded in three months, Franklin's in six. No memorable writing from Franklin came out of this process, except a poem he wrote parodying in Irish dialect one of the advertisements in Bradford's magazine. But the competition to launch the magazine did kindle Franklin's interest in the power of the postal system.[17]

SALLY FRANKLIN

In 1743, eleven years after the birth of their short-lived son, Franky, the Franklins had a baby girl. Named Sarah after Deborah's mother, and called Sally, she delighted and charmed both of her parents. When she was 4, Franklin wrote his mother that "your granddaughter is the greatest lover of her book and school of any child I ever knew." Two years later, he provided a similar report: "Sally grows a fine girl, and is extremely industrious with her needle and delights in her books. She is of most affectionate temper, and perfectly dutiful and obliging, to her parents and to all. Perhaps I flatter myself too much, but I have hopes that she will prove an ingenious, sensible, notable and worthy woman."

Franklin half-seriously pushed the notion that his young daughter might someday marry the son of William Strahan, a London printer who was one of his English correspondents. (In this he was not sexist: he also tried to fix up his son, William, and later his two grandsons with children of his English and French friends, all to no avail.) His descriptions of Sally in his letters to Strahan reveal both his affection for her and the traits he looked for in a daughter. "She discovers daily the seeds and tokens of industry and economy, and in short, of every female virtue," he wrote when she was 7. Six years later, he wrote,

"Sally is indeed a very good girl, affectionate, dutiful, and industrious, has one of the best hearts, and though not a wit, is for one of her years by no means deficient in understanding."

In one of his childhood debates with John Collins, Franklin had argued in favor of giving girls as well as boys an education, a case he reiterated as Silence Dogood. He practiced these preachings to some degree with Sally, with a predictable emphasis on practical subjects. He made sure she was taught reading, writing, and arithmetic. At her request, he got her French lessons, though her interest soon waned. He also insisted that she learn accounting; when a publishing partner he had in Charleston died and his wife had to take over the business, it reinforced in Franklin the practical view that girls should be taught accounting "as likely to be of more use to them and their children in case of widowhood than either music or dancing."

When Sally was only 8, Franklin imported from England a large shipment of books for her. The idea was that she would be in charge of selling them at his print shop, but presumably she might also learn something from them herself. Included in the order were three dozen manuals from the Winchester School, four dictionaries, and two dozen copies of a collection of "tales and fables with prudential maxims."

For the most part, however, Franklin urged Sally to perfect her domestic skills. One day, after watching as she tried unsuccessfully to sew a buttonhole, he arranged for his tailor to come give her lessons. She never got the formal academic training that he provided William. And when he drew up plans to establish an academy in Philadelphia, Sally was 6, but he made no provision for it to educate girls.[18]

With only one daughter (and an illegitimate stepson), Deborah's was an unusually small brood for a robust woman in colonial days; she was one of seven children, Franklin's father had seventeen in his two marriages, and the average family at the time had about eight. Franklin wrote glowingly of children and had Poor Richard sing praises to the look of a pregnant woman. In satires such as "Polly Baker" and serious essays such as "Observations on the Increase of Mankind," he extolled the benefits of fecundity. So the Franklins' paucity of children does not appear to reflect a deliberate decision; instead, it indicated either that they lacked abundant intimacy or found conceiving not always easy, or a combination of both. Whatever the cause, it would eventually give Franklin more leeway to retire from his business early to pursue scientific endeavors and far-flung diplomatic journeys. It also, perhaps, contributed to his lifelong practice of befriending younger people—women in particular—and forging relationships with them as if they were his children.[19]

POLLY BAKER

Franklin's attitudes toward women can be characterized as somewhat enlightened in the context of his time, but only somewhat. What is clear, however, is that he genuinely liked women, enjoyed their company and conversation, and was able to take them seriously as well as flirt with them. During Sally's early childhood, he wrote two famous essays that, in different ways, amusingly combined his lenient attitude toward unmarried sex with his appreciative attitude toward women.

"Advice to a Young Man on the Choice of a Mistress," written in 1745, is now quite famous, but it was suppressed by Franklin's grandson and other compilers of his papers throughout the nineteenth century as being too indecent to print. Franklin began the little essay by extolling marriage as being "the proper remedy" for sexual urges. But, if his reader "will not take this counsel" and yet still finds "sex inevitable," he advised that "in all your amours you should prefer old women to young ones."

Franklin then provided a saucy list of eight reasons: because they have more knowledge, they make better conversation; as they lose their looks, they learn a thousand useful services "to maintain their influence over men"; "there is no hazard of children"; they are more discreet; they age from the head down, so even after their face grows wrinkled their lower bodies stay firm, "so that covering all above with a basket, and regarding only what is below the girdle, it is impossible of two women to know an old one from a young one"; it is less sinful to debauch an older woman than a virgin; there is less guilt, because the older woman will be made happy whereas the younger one will be made miserable. Finally, Franklin produces the cheeky kicker to the piece: "Lastly, they are so grateful!!"[20]

"The Speech of Polly Baker" is a tale of sex and woe told from a woman's point of view, a literary device often used by Franklin with a dexterity that displayed his ability to appreciate the other sex. It purports to recount the speech of a young woman on trial for having a fifth illegitimate child. First published in London, it was then frequently reprinted in England and America without people's realizing that it was fiction. Thirty years would pass before Franklin revealed that he had written it as a hoax.

The light humor of the piece hides the fact that it is actually a sharp attack on hypocritical customs and unfair attitudes toward women and sex. Polly argues that she has been doing good by obeying God's injunction to be fruitful and multiply. "I have brought five fine children into the world, at the risk of my life; I have maintained them well by my own industry." Indeed, she complains, she could have maintained them a little better were it not for the fact that the court kept fining her. "Can it be a crime (in the nature of things I mean) to add to the number of the King's subjects in a new country that really wants people? I own it, I should think it a praiseworthy rather than a punishable action."

Franklin, who had fathered an illegitimate child but taken responsibility for it, is particularly scathing about the double standard that subjects Polly, but not the men who had sex with her, to humiliation. As Polly says, "I readily consented to the only proposal of marriage that ever was made me, which was when I was a virgin; but too easily confiding in the person's sincerity that made it, I unhappily lost my own honor by trusting his; for he got me with child, and then forsook me. That very person you all know; he is now become a magistrate of this county."

By doing her duty to bring children into the world, despite the fact that no one would marry her and despite the public disgrace, she argued that she deserved, "in my humble opinion, instead of a whipping, to have a statue erected to my memory." The court, Franklin wrote, was so moved by the speech that she was acquitted, and one of the judges married her the next day.[21]

THE AMERICAN PHILOSOPHICAL SOCIETY

Franklin was among the first to view the British settlements in America not only as separate colonies but also as part of a potentially unified nation. That was, in part, because he was far less parochial than most Americans. He had traveled from one colony to another, formed alliances with printers from Rhode Island to South Carolina, and gathered news for his paper and magazine by reading widely other American publications. Now, as the postmaster in Philadelphia, his connections to other colonies were easier, and his curiosity about them grew.

In a May 1743 circular, "A Proposal for Promoting Useful Knowledge Among the British Plantations in America," he proposed what was, in effect, an intercolonial Junto, to be called the American Philosophical Society. The idea had been discussed by the naturalist John Bartram, among others, but Franklin had the printing press, the inclination, and the postal contacts to pull it all together. It would be based in Philadelphia and include scientists and thinkers from other cities. They would share their studies by post, and abstracts would be sent to each member four times a year.

As with the detailed charter he created for the Junto, Franklin was very specific about the type of subjects to be explored, which were, unsurprisingly, more practical than purely theoretical: "newly discovered plants, herbs, trees, roots, their virtues, uses, etc.; . . . improvements of vegetable juices, such as ciders, wines, etc.; new methods of curing or preventing diseases; . . . improvements in any branch of mathematics . . . new arts, trades, and manufactures . . . surveys, maps and charts . . . methods of improving the breeds of animals . . . and all philosophical experiments that let light into the nature of things." Franklin volunteered to serve as secretary.

By the spring of 1744 the society began meeting regularly. The pedantic mathematician Thomas Godfrey was a member, indicating that his feud with Franklin over dowries and almanacs was over. One of the most important members was Cadwallader Colden, a scholar and official from New York whom Franklin had met on his travels the year before. They were to become lifelong friends and spur each other's scientific interests. Their club was not very active at first—Franklin complained that its members were "very idle gentlemen"—but it eventually grew into a learned society that thrives to this day.[22]

THE PENNSYLVANIA MILITIA

Most of the voluntary associations that Franklin had thus far formed—the Junto, library, philosophical society, even fire squad—had not usurped the core functions of government. (When he came up with a plan for a police patrol, he had suggested that the Assembly enact and control it.) But in 1747, he proposed something that was, though he may not have realized it, far more radical: a military force that would be independent of Pennsylvania's colonial government.

Franklin's plan for a volunteer Pennsylvania militia arose because of the feckless response by the colony's government to the ongoing threats from France and her Indian allies. Ever since 1689, the inter-mittent wars between Britain and France had been played out in America, with each side enlisting various Indian tribes and thuggish privateers to gain advantage. The latest American installment was known as King George's War (1744–48), which was an offshoot of Europe's War of Austrian Succession and a quaint British struggle with Spain known as the War of Jenkins's Ear (after a British smug-gler who had that body part removed by the Spanish). Among those Americans who marched off toward Canada to fight the French and Indians on behalf of the British in 1746 was William Franklin, then perhaps 16 or so, whose father realized it was futile to resist the wan-derlust he himself had felt at that age.

William never saw any action, but the war soon threatened the safety of Philadelphia when French and Spanish privateers began raiding towns along the Delaware River. The Assembly, dominated by pacifist Quakers, dithered and failed to authorize any defenses. Frank-lin was appalled by the unwillingness of the various groups in the colony—Quakers and Anglicans and Presbyterians, city and country folks—to work together. So in November 1747, he stepped into the breach by writing a vibrant pamphlet entitled "Plain Truth," signed by "a Tradesman of Philadelphia."

His description of the havoc that a privateer raid might wreak sounded like a Great Awakening terror sermon:

> On the first alarm, terror will spread over all . . . The man that has a wife and children will find them hanging on his neck, beseeching him with tears to quit the city . . . Sacking the city will be the first, and burning it, in all probability, the last act of the enemy . . . Confined to your houses, you will have nothing to trust but the enemy's mercy . . . Who can, without the utmost horror, conceive the miseries of the latter when your persons, fortunes, wives and daughters shall be subject to the wanton and unbridled rage, rapine and lust.

With a small pun on the word "Friends," Franklin first blamed the Quakers of the Assembly: "Should we entreat them to consider, if not as Friends, at least as legislators, that protection is as truly due from the government to the people." If their pacifist principles prevent them from acting, he said, they should step aside. He then turned on the "great and rich men" of the Proprietary faction, who were refusing to act because of their "envy and resentment" toward the Assembly.

So who could save the colony? Here came Franklin's great rallying cry for the new American middle class. "We, the middling people," he wrote proudly, using the phrase twice in the pamphlet. "The trades-men, shopkeepers and farmers of this province and city!"

He then proceeded to spin an image that would end up applying to much of his work over the ensuing years. "At present we are like sepa-rate filaments of flax before the thread is formed, without strength be-cause without connection," he declared. "But Union would make us strong."

Of particular note was his populist insistence that there be no class distinctions. The militia would be organized by geographic area in-stead of social strata. "This," he said, "is intended to prevent people's sorting themselves into companies according to their ranks in life, their quality or station. It is designed to mix the great and the small together . . . There should be no distinction from circumstance, but all be on the level." In another radically democratic approach, Franklin proposed that each of the new militia companies elect its own officers rather than have them appointed by the governor or Crown.

Franklin concluded with an offer to draw up proposals for a militia if his plea was well received. It was. "The pamphlet had a sudden and surprising effect," he later wrote. So, a week later, in an annotated article in his newspaper, he presented his plans for a militia, filled with his typical detailed description of its organization, training, and rules. Even though he was never an avid or effective public orator, he agreed to address a crowd of his fellow middling people at a sail-making loft and then, two days later, spoke to a more upscale audience of "gentlemen, merchants and others" at the New Hall that had been built for Whitefield.[23]

Soon some ten thousand men from all over the colony had signed up and formed themselves into more than one hundred companies. Franklin's local company in Philadelphia elected him their colonel, but he declined the post by saying he was "unfit." Instead, he served as a "common soldier" and regularly took his turn patrolling the batteries he had helped build along the Delaware River banks. He also amused himself by designing an array of insignia and mottos for the various companies.

To furnish the Militia Association with cannons and equipment, Franklin organized a lottery that raised £3,000. The artillery had to be purchased from New York, and Franklin led a delegation to convince Gov. George Clinton to approve the sale. As Franklin recounted with some amusement:

> He at first refused us peremptorily; but at dinner with his council, where there was great drinking of Madeira wine, as the custom of that place then was, he softened by degrees, and said he would lend us six. After a few more bumpers he advanced to ten; and at length he very good-naturedly conceded eighteen. They were fine cannon, eighteen-pounders, with their carriages, which we soon transported and mounted on our battery.

Franklin did not quite realize how radical it was for a private association to take over from the government the right to create and control a military force. His charter, both in its spirit and wording, faintly foreshadowed a declaration that would come three decades later. "Being thus unprotected by the government under which we live," he wrote, "we do hereby, for our mutual defense and security, and for the security of our wives, children and estates . . . form ourselves into an Association."

Thomas Penn, the colony's Proprietor, understood the implications of Franklin's actions. "This association is founded on a contempt to government," he wrote the clerk of the governor's council, "a part little less than treason." In a subsequent letter, he called Franklin "a sort of tribune of the people," and lamented: "He is a dangerous man and I should be very glad [if] he inhabited any other country, as I believe him of a very uneasy spirit."

By the summer of 1748, the threat of war had passed and the Militia Association disbanded, without any attempt by Franklin to capitalize on his new power and popularity. But the lessons he learned stayed with him. He realized that the colonists might have to fend for themselves instead of relying on their British governors, that the powerful elites deserved no deference, and that "we the middling people" of workers and tradesmen should be the proud sinews of the new land. It also reinforced his core belief that people, and perhaps someday colonies, could accomplish more when they joined together rather than remained separate filaments of flax, when they formed unions rather than stood alone.[24]

RETIREMENT

Franklin's print shop had by then grown into a successful, vertically integrated media conglomerate. He had a printing press, publishing house, newspaper, an almanac series, and partial control of the postal system. The successful books he had printed ranged from Bibles and psalters to Samuel Richardson's novel *Pamela*, a tale whose mix of raciness and moralism probably appealed to him. (Franklin's 1744 reprint of *Pamela* was the first novel published in America.) He also had built a network of profitable partnerships and franchises from Newport and New York to Charleston and Antigua. Money flowed in, much of which he invested, quite wisely, in Philadelphia property. "I experienced," he recalled, "the truth of the observation, that after getting the first £100, it is more easy to get the second."

Accumulating money, however, was not Franklin's goal. Despite the pecuniary spirit of Poor Richard's sayings and the penny-saving reputation they later earned Franklin, he did not have the soul of an acquisitive capitalist. "I would rather have it said," he wrote his mother, " 'He lived usefully,' than, 'He died rich.' "

So, in 1748 at age 42—which would turn out to be precisely the midpoint of his life—he retired and turned over the operation of his printing business to his foreman, David Hall. The detailed partnership deal Franklin drew up would leave him rich enough by most people's standards: it provided him with half of the shop's profits for the next eighteen years, which would amount to about £650 annually. Back then, when a common clerk made about £25 a year, that was enough to keep him quite comfortable. He saw no reason to keep plying his trade to make even more. Now he would have, he wrote Cadwallader Colden, "leisure to read, study, make experiments, and converse at large with such ingenious and worthy men as are pleased to honor me with their friendship."[25]

Up until then, Franklin had proudly considered himself a leather-apron man and common tradesman, devoid and even contemptuous of aristocratic pretenses. Likewise, that is how he would portray himself again in the late 1760s, when his antagonism to British authority grew (and his hopes for high patronage posts were dashed), and that is how he would cast himself in his autobiography, which he began writing in 1771. It was also the role he would play later in life as a revolutionary patriot, fur-capped envoy, and fervent foe of hereditary honors and privileges.

However, on his retirement, and intermittently over the next decade or so, he would occasionally fancy himself a refined gentleman. In his groundbreaking study *The Radicalism of the American Revolution,* historian Gordon Wood calls him "one of the most aristocratic of the founding fathers." That assessment is perhaps a bit too sweeping or stretches the definition of aristocrat, for even during the years right after his retirement Franklin eschewed most elitist pretensions and remained populist in most of his local politics. But his retirement did indeed usher in a period in his life when he had aspirations to be, if not part of the aristocracy, at least, as Wood says, "a gentleman philosopher and public official" with a veneer of "enlightened gentility."[26]

Franklin's ambivalent flirtation with a new social status was captured on canvas when Robert Feke, a popular self-taught painter from Boston, arrived in Philadelphia that year. He produced the earliest known portrait of Franklin (now at Harvard's Fogg Art Museum), and it shows him garbed as a gentleman with a velvet coat, ruffled shirt, and wig. Yet, compared to Feke's other subjects that year, Franklin had himself portrayed in a rather simple way, devoid of social ostentation. "He is represented in an almost painfully plain and unpretentious manner," notes art historian Wayne Craven, an expert on colonial portraiture. "Franklin's plainness is not accidental: both the portrait painter and his subject would have agreed that this was the most appropriate way to represent a member of colonial mercantile society who was successful, but not actually wealthy."

Franklin was not aspiring, by his retirement, to become merely an idle gentleman of leisure. He left his print shop because he was, in fact, eager to focus his undiminished ambition on other pursuits that beckoned: first science, then politics, then diplomacy and statecraft. As Poor Richard said in his almanac that year, "Lost time is never found again."[27]

CHAPTER SIX

SCIENTIST AND INVENTOR

Philadelphia, 1744–1751

STOVES, STORMS, AND CATHETERS

Even when he was young, Franklin's intellectual curiosity and his Enlightenment-era awe at the orderliness of the universe attracted him to science. During his voyage home from England at age 20, he had studied dolphins and calculated his location by analyzing a lunar eclipse, and in Philadelphia he had used his newspaper, almanac, the Junto, and the philosophical society to discuss natural phenomena. His scientific interests would continue throughout his life, with research into the Gulf Stream, meteorology, the earth's magnetism, and refrigeration.

His most intense immersion into science was during the 1740s, and it reached a peak in the years right after he retired from business in 1748. He had neither the academic training nor the grounding in math to be a great theorist, and his pursuit of what he called his "scientific amusements" caused some to dismiss him as a mere tinkerer. But during his life he was celebrated as the most famous scientist alive, and recent academic studies have restored his place in the scientific pantheon. As Harvard professor Dudley Herschbach declares, "His work on electricity was recognized as ushering in a scientific revolution comparable to those wrought by Newton in the previous century or by Watson and Crick in ours."[1]

Franklin's scientific inquiries were driven, primarily, by pure curiosity and the thrill of discovery. Indeed, there was joy in his antic curiosity, whether it was using electricity jolts to cook turkeys or whiling away his time as Assembly clerk by constructing complex "magic squares" of numbers where the rows, columns, and diagonals all added up to the same sum.

Unlike in some of his other pursuits, he was not driven by pecuniary motives; he declined to patent his famous inventions, and he took pleasure in freely sharing his findings. Nor was he motivated merely by his quest for the practical. He acknowledged that his magic squares were "incapable of useful application," and his initial interest in electricity was prompted more by fascination than a quest for utility.

He did, however, always keep in mind the goal of making science useful, just as Poor Richard's wife had made sure that he did something practical with all his old "rattling traps." In general, he would begin a scientific inquiry driven by pure intellectual curiosity and then seek a practical application for it.

Franklin's study of how dark fabrics absorb heat better than bright ones is an example of this approach. These experiments (which were begun in the 1730s with his Junto colleague Joseph Breintnall, based on the theories of Isaac Newton and Robert Boyle) included putting cloth patches of different colors on snow and determining how much the sun heated each by measuring the melting. Later, in describing the experiments, he turned his mind to the practical consequences, among them that "black clothes are not so fit to wear in a hot sunny climate" and that the walls of fruit sheds should be painted black. In reporting these conclusions, he famously noted: "What signifies philosophy that does not apply to some use?"[2]

A far more significant instance of Franklin's application of scientific theory for practical purpose was his invention, in the early 1740s, of a wood-burning stove that could be built into fireplaces to maximize heat while minimizing smoke and drafts. Using his knowledge of convection and heat transfer, Franklin came up with an ingenious (and probably too complex) design.

The stove was constructed so that heat and smoke from the fire rose to warm an iron plate on top, then were carried by convection down a channel that led under the wall of the hearth and finally up through the chimney. In the process, the fire heated an inner metal chamber that drew clean cool air up from the basement, warmed it, and let it out through louvers into the room. That was the theory.

In 1744, he had a fellow Junto member who was an ironworker manufacture the new stove, and he got two of his brothers and several other friends to market them throughout the northeast. The promotional pamphlet Franklin wrote was filled with both science and salesmanship. He explained in detail how warm air expands to take up more space than cold, how it is lighter, and how heat radiates whereas smoke is carried only by air. He then included testimonials about his new design and touted that it minimized cold drafts and smoke, thus reducing the chance of fevers and coughs. It would also save on fuel, he advertised.

The new Pennsylvania Fireplaces, as he called them, were initially somewhat popular, at £5 apiece, and papers around the colonies were filled with testimonials. "They ought to be called, both in justice and gratitude, Mr. Franklin's stoves," declared one letter writer in the *Boston Evening Post.* "I believe all who have experienced the comfort and benefit of them will join with me that the author of this happy invention merits a statue."

The governor of Pennsylvania was among the enthusiastic, and he offered Franklin what could have been a lucrative patent. "But I declined it," Franklin noted in his autobiography. "As we enjoy great advantages from the invention of others, we should be glad of an opportunity to serve others by any invention of ours, and this we should do freely and generously." It was a noble and sincere sentiment.

An exhaustive study by one scholar shows that Franklin's design eventually proved less practical and popular than he hoped. Unless the chimney and lower channels were hot, there was not enough convection to keep the smoke from being forced back into the room. That made getting started a problem. Sales tapered off, manufacturing ceased within two decades, and most models were modified by their owners to eliminate the back channel and chamber. Throughout the rest of his life, Franklin would refine his theories about chimney and fireplace designs. But what is today commonly known as the Franklin Stove is a far simpler contraption than what he originally envisioned.[3]

Franklin also combined science and mechanical practicality by devising the first urinary catheter used in America, which was a modification of a European invention. His brother John in Boston was gravely ill and wrote Franklin of his desire for a flexible tube to help him urinate. Franklin came up with a design, and instead of simply describing it he went to a Philadelphia silversmith and oversaw its construction. The tube was thin enough to be flexible, and Franklin included a wire that could be stuck inside to stiffen it while it was inserted and then be gradually withdrawn as the tube reached the point where it needed to bend. His catheter also had a screw component that allowed it to be inserted by turning, and he made it collapsible so that it would be easier to withdraw. "Experience is necessary for the right using of all new tools or instruments, and that will perhaps suggest some improvements," Franklin told his brother.

The study of nature also continued to interest Franklin. Among his most noteworthy discoveries was that the big East Coast storms known as northeasters, whose winds come from the northeast, actually move in the opposite direction from their winds, traveling up the coast from the south. On the evening of October 21, 1743, Franklin looked forward to observing a lunar eclipse he knew was to occur at 8:30. A violent storm, however, hit Philadelphia and blackened the sky. Over the next few weeks, he read accounts of how the storm caused damage from Virginia to Boston. "But what surprised me," he later told his friend Jared Eliot, "was to find in the Boston newspapers an account of the observation of that eclipse." So Franklin wrote his brother in Boston, who confirmed that the storm did not hit until an hour after the eclipse was finished. Further inquiries into the timing of this and other storms up and down the coast led him to "the very singular opinion," he told Eliot, "that, though the course of the wind is from the northeast to the southwest, yet the course of the storm is from the southwest to the northeast." He further surmised, correctly, that rising air heated in the south created low-pressure systems that drew winds from the north. More than 150 years later, the great scholar William Morris Davis proclaimed, "With this began the science of weather prediction."[4]

Dozens of other scientific phenomena also engaged Franklin's interest during this period. For example, he exchanged letters with his friend Cadwallader Colden on comets, the circulation of blood, perspiration, inertia, and the earth's rotation. But it was a parlor-trick show in 1743 that launched him on what would be by far his most celebrated scientific endeavor.

ELECTRICITY

On a visit to Boston in the summer of 1743, Franklin happened to be entertained one evening by a traveling scientific showman from Scotland named Dr. Archibald Spencer. (In his autobiography, Franklin gets the name and year wrong, saying it was a Dr. Spence in 1746.) Spencer specialized in amazing demonstrations that verged on amusement shows. He depicted Newton's theories of light and displayed a machine that measured blood flow, both interests of Franklin's. But more important, he performed electricity tricks, such as creating static electricity by rubbing a glass tube and drawing sparks from the feet of a boy hanging by silk cords from the ceiling. "Being on a subject quite new to me," Franklin recalled, "they equally surprised and pleased me."

In the previous century, Galileo and Newton had demystified gravity. But that other great force of the universe, electricity, was understood little better than it had been by the ancients. There were people, such as Dr. Spencer, who played with it to perform spectacles. The Abbé Nollet, court scientist to France's King Louis XV, had linked 180 soldiers and then 700 monks and made them jump in unison for the court's amusement by sending through them a jolt of static electricity. But Franklin was the perfect person to turn electricity from a parlor trick into a science. That task demanded not a mathematical or theoretical scholar, but instead a clever and ingenious person who had the curiosity to perform practical experiments, plus enough mechanical talent and time to tinker with a lot of contraptions.

A few months after Franklin returned to Philadelphia, Dr. Spencer came to town. Franklin acted as his agent, advertised his lectures, and sold tickets from his shop. His Library Company also received, early in 1747, a long glass tube for generating static electricity, along with papers describing some experiments, from its agent in London, Peter Collinson. In his letter thanking Collinson, Franklin was effusive in describing the fun he was having with the device: "I never was before engaged in any study that so totally engrossed my attention." He commissioned a local glassblower and silversmith to make more such gadgets, and he enlisted his Junto friends to join in the experimenting.[5]

Franklin's first serious experiments involved collecting an electric charge and then studying its properties. He had his friends draw charges from the spinning glass tube and then touch each other to see if sparks flew. The result was the discovery that electricity was "not *created* by the friction, but *collected* only." In other words, a charge could be drawn into person A and out of person B, and the electric fluid would flow back if the two people touched each other.

To explain what he meant, he invented some new terms in a letter to Collinson. "We say B is electrised *positively;* A *negatively:* or rather

B is electrised *plus* and A *minus*." He apologized to the Englishman for the new coinage: "These terms we may use until your philosophers give us better."

In fact, these terms devised by Franklin are the ones we still use today, along with other neologisms that he coined to describe his findings: battery, charged, neutral, condense, and conductor. Part of Franklin's importance as a scientist was the clear writing he employed. "He has written equally for the uninitiated as well as the philosopher," the early nineteenth-century English chemist Sir Humphry Davy noted, "and he has rendered his details as amusing as well as perspicuous."

Until then, electricity had been thought to involve two types of fluids, called vitreous and resinous, that could be created independently. Franklin's discovery that the generation of a positive charge was accompanied by the generation of an equal negative charge became known as the conservation of charge and the single-fluid theory of electricity. The concepts reflected Franklin's bookkeeper mentality, which was first expressed in his London "Dissertation" positing that pleasure and pain are always in balance.

It was a breakthrough of historic proportions. "As a broad generalization that has withstood the test of 200 years of fruitful application," Harvard professor I. Bernard Cohen has pronounced, "Franklin's law of conservation of charge must be considered to be of the same fundamental importance to physical science as Newton's law of conservation of momentum."

Franklin also discovered an attribute of electrical charges—"the wonderful effects of points"—that would soon lead to his most famous practical application. He electrified a small iron ball and dangled a cork next to it, which was repelled based on the strength of the ball's charge. When he brought the tip of a pointed piece of metal near the ball, it drew away the charge. But a blunt piece of metal did not draw a charge or spark as easily, and if it was insulated instead of grounded, did not draw a charge at all.

Franklin continued his experiments by capturing and storing electric charges in a primitive form of capacitor called, after the Dutch town where it was invented, a Leyden jar. These jars had a metal foil on the outside; on the inside, separated from the foil by the glass insulation, was lead or water or metal that could be charged up through a wire. Franklin showed that when the inside of the jar was charged, the outside foil had an equal and opposite charge.

Also, by pouring out the water and metal inside a charged Leyden jar and not being able to elicit a spark, he found that the charge did not actually reside in them; instead, he correctly concluded, it was the glass itself that held the charge. So he lined up a series of glass plates flanked by metal, charged them up, wired them together, and created (and gave a name to) a new device: "what we called an electrical battery."[6]

Electricity also energized his antic sense of fun. He created a charged metal spider that leaped around like a real one, he electrified the iron fence around his house to produce sparks that amused visitors, and he rigged a picture of King George II to produce a "high-treason" shock when someone touched his gilded crown. "If a ring of persons take the shock among them," Franklin joked, "the experiment is called The Conspirators." Friends flocked to see his shows, and he reinforced his reputation for playfulness. (In one of the weirder scenes in Thomas Pynchon's novel *Mason & Dixon*, Franklin lines up some young men in a tavern to jolt them from his battery, shouting "All hold hands, Line of Fops.")

As the summer of 1749 approached and the rising humidity made experiments more difficult, Franklin decided to suspend them until the fall. Although his findings were of great historical significance, he had yet to put them to practical use. He lamented to Collinson that he was "chagrined a little that we have hitherto been able to discover nothing in the way of use to mankind." Indeed, after many revised theories and a couple of painful shocks that knocked him senseless, the only "use discovered of electricity," said the man who was always trying to tackle his own pride, was that "it may help make a vain man humble."

The end of the experimenting season gave an occasion for a "party of pleasure" on the banks of the river. Franklin described it in a letter to Collinson: "A turkey is to be killed for our dinners by the electrical shock; and roasted by the electrical jack, before a fire kindled by the electrified bottle; while the healths of all the famous electricians in England, France and Germany are to be drank in electrified bumpers, under the discharge of guns from the electrical battery."

The frivolity went well. Though turkeys proved harder to kill than chickens, Franklin and friends finally succeeded by linking together a big battery. "The birds killed in this manner eat uncommonly tender," he wrote, thus becoming a culinary pioneer of fried turkey. As for doing something more practical, there would be time for that in the fall.[7]

SNATCHING LIGHTNING FROM THE SKY

In the journal he kept for his experiments, Franklin noted in November 1749 some intriguing similarities between electrical sparks and lightning. He listed twelve of them, including "1. Giving light. 2. Color of the light. 3. Crooked directions. 4. Swift motion. 5. Being conducted by metals. 6. Crack or noise in exploding . . . 9. Destroying animals . . . 12. Sulpherous smell."

More important, he made a connection between this surmise about lightning and his earlier experiments on the power of pointed metal objects to draw off electrical charges. "Electrical fluid is attracted by points. We do not know whether this property is in lightning. But since they agree in all particulars wherein we can already compare them, is it not probable they agree likewise in this?" To which he added a momentous rallying cry: *"Let the experiment be made."*

For centuries, the devastating scourge of lightning had generally been considered a supernatural phenomenon or expression of God's will. At the approach of a storm, church bells were rung to ward off the bolts. "The tones of the consecrated metal repel the demon and avert storm and lightning," declared St. Thomas Aquinas. But even the most religiously faithful were likely to have noticed this was not very effective. During one thirty-five-year period in Germany alone during the mid-1700s, 386 churches were struck and more than one hundred bell ringers killed. In Venice, some three thousand people were killed when tons of gunpowder stored in a church was hit. As Franklin later recalled to Harvard professor John Winthrop, "The lightning seems to strike steeples of choice and at the very time the bells are ringing; yet still they continue to bless the new bells and jangle the old ones whenever it thunders. One would think it was now time to try some other trick."[8]

Many scientists, including Newton, had noted the apparent connection between lightning and electricity. But no one had declared "Let the experiment be made," nor laid out a methodical test, nor thought of the practicality of tying this all in with the power of pointed metal rods.

Franklin first sketched out his theories about lightning in April 1749, just before his end-of-season turkey fry. The water vapors in a cloud can be electrically charged, he surmised, and the positive ones will separate from the negative ones. When such "electrified clouds pass over," he added, "high trees, lofty towers, spires, masts of ships . . . draw the electrical fire and the whole cloud discharges." It was not a bad guess, and it led to some practical advice: "Dangerous therefore it is to take shelter under a tree during a thunder gust." It also led to the most famous of all his experiments.[9]

Before he tried to conduct his proposed experiments himself, Franklin described them in two famous letters to Collinson in 1750, which were presented to the Royal Society in London and then widely published. The essential idea was to use a tall metal rod to draw some of the electrical charge from a cloud, just as he had used a needle to draw off the charge of an iron ball in his lab. He detailed his proposed experiment:

> On the top of some high tower or steeple, place a kind of sentry box big enough to contain a man and an electrical stand. From the middle of the stand, let an iron rod rise . . . upright 20 or 30 feet, pointed very sharp at the end. If the electrical stand be kept clean and dry, a man standing on it when such clouds are passing low might be electrified and afford sparks, the rod drawing fire to him from the cloud. If any danger to the man be apprehended (though I think there would be none) let him stand on the floor of his box, and now and then bring near to the rod the loop of a wire that has one end fastened to the leads; he holding it by a wax handle [i.e., insulating him from it]. So the sparks, if the rod is electrified, will strike from the rod to the wire and not affect him.

Franklin's one mistake was thinking that there would be no danger, as at least one European experimenter fatally discovered. His suggestion of using a wire held with an insulating wax handle was a smarter approach.

If his suppositions held true, Franklin wrote in another letter to Collinson, then lightning rods could tame one of the greatest natural dangers people faced. "Houses, ships and even towns and churches may be effectually secured from the stroke of lightning by their means," he predicted. "The electrical fire would, I think, be drawn out of a cloud silently." He wasn't certain, however. "This may seem whimsical, but let it pass for the present until I send the experiments at large."[10]

Franklin's letters were excerpted in London by *The Gentleman's Magazine* in 1750 and then published as an eighty-six-page booklet the following year. More significant, they were translated into French in early 1752 and became a sensation. King Louis XV asked that the lab tests be performed for him, which they were in February by three Frenchmen who had translated Franklin's experiments, led by the naturalists Comte de Buffon and Thomas-François D'Alibard. The king was so excited that he encouraged the group to try Franklin's proposed lightning rod experiment. As a letter to London's Royal Society noted, "These applauses of his Majesty having excited in Messieurs de Buffon, D'Alibard and de Lor a desire of verifying the conjectures of Mr. Franklin upon the analogy of thunder and electricity, they prepared themselves for making the experiment."

In the village of Marly on the northern outskirts of Paris, the Frenchmen constructed a sentry box with a 40-foot iron rod and dragooned a retired soldier to play Prometheus. On May 10, 1752, just after 2 in the afternoon, a storm cloud passed over and the soldier was able to draw sparks as Franklin had predicted. An excited local prior grabbed the insulated wire and repeated the experiment six times, shocking himself once but surviving to celebrate the success. Within weeks it was replicated dozens of times across France. "M. Franklin's idea has ceased to be a conjecture," D'Alibard reported to the French Royal Academy. "Here it has become a reality."

Though he did not yet know it, Franklin had become an international sensation. An ecstatic Collinson wrote from London that "the Grand Monarch of France strictly commands" that his scientists convey "compliments in an express manner to Mr. Franklin of Philadelphia for the useful discoveries in electricity and application of the pointed rods to prevent the terrible effects of thunderstorms."[11]

The following month, before word of the French success reached America, Franklin came up with his own ingenious way to conduct the experiment, according to accounts later written by himself and his friend the scientist Joseph Priestley. He had been waiting for the steeple of Philadelphia's Christ Church to be finished, so he could use its high vantage point. Impatient, he struck on the idea of using instead a kite, a toy he had enjoyed flying and experimenting with since his boyhood days in Boston. To do the experiment in some secrecy, he enlisted his son, William, to help fly the silk kite. A sharp wire protruded from its top and a key was attached near the base of the wet string, so that a wire could be brought near it in an effort to draw sparks.

Clouds passed over to no effect. Franklin began to despair when he suddenly saw some of the strands of the string stiffen. Putting his knuckle to the key, he was able to draw sparks (and, notably, to survive). He proceeded to collect some of the charge in a Leyden jar and found it had the same qualities as electricity produced in a lab. "Thereby the sameness of electrical matter with that of lightning," he reported in a letter the following October, was "completely demonstrated."

Franklin and his kite were destined to be celebrated not just in the annals of science but also in popular lore. Benjamin West's famous 1805 painting, *Franklin Drawing Electricity from the Sky*, mistakenly shows him as a wrinkled sage rather than a lively 46-year-old, and an equally famous nineteenth-century Currier and Ives print shows William as a little boy rather than a man of about 21.

Even among scientific historians, there is some mystery about Franklin's celebrated kite flying. Although it supposedly took place in June 1752, before word had reached him of the French tests a few weeks earlier, Franklin made no public declaration of it for months. He did not mention it in the letters he wrote Collinson that summer, and he apparently did not tell his friend Ebenezer Kinnersley, who was lecturing on electricity in Philadelphia at the time. Nor did he publicly report his kite experiment even when word reached him, probably in late July or August, of the French success. His *Pennsylvania Gazette* for August 27, 1752, reprinted a letter about the French experiments, but it made no mention that Franklin and his son had already privately confirmed the results.

The first public report came in October, four months after the fact, in a letter Franklin wrote to Collinson and printed in his *Pennsylvania Gazette.* "As frequent mention is made in the public papers from Europe of the success of the Philadelphia Experiment for drawing the electric fire from the clouds," he wrote, "it may be agreeable to the curious to be informed that the same experiment has succeeded in Philadelphia, though made in a different and more easy manner." He went on to describe the details of constructing the kite and other apparatus, but in an oddly impersonal way, never using the first person to say explicitly that he and his son had carried it out themselves. He ended by expressing pleasure that the success of his experiments in France had prompted the installation of lightning rods there, and he made a point of noting that "we had before placed them upon our academy and state house spires." The same issue of the paper advertised the new edition of *Poor Richard's Almanack,* with an account of "how to secure houses, etc., from lightning."

A more colorful and personal account of the kite flying, including the details about William's involvement, appeared in Joseph Priestley's *The History and Present State of Electricity,* first published in 1767. "It occurred to him that, by means of a common kite, he could have a readier and better access to the regions of thunder than by any spire whatever," Priestley wrote of Franklin, and "he took the opportunity of the first approaching thunder storm to take a walk into a field, in which there was a shed convenient for his purpose." Priestley, a noted English scientist, based his account on information directly from Franklin, whom he first met in London in 1766. Franklin supplied Priestley with scientific material and vetted the manuscript, which ends with the flat declaration: "This happened in June 1752, a month after the electricians in France had verified the same theory, but before he had heard of anything they had done."[12]

The delay by Franklin in reporting his kite experiment has led some historians to wonder if he truly did it that summer, and one recent book even charges that his claim was a "hoax." Once again, the meticulous I. Bernard Cohen has done an exhaustive job of historical sleuthing. Drawing on letters, reports, and the fact that lightning rods were erected in Philadelphia that summer, he concludes after forty pages of analysis that "there is no reason to doubt that Franklin had conceived and executed the kite experiment before hearing the news of the French performance." He goes on to say that it was performed "not only by Franklin but by others," and he adds that "we may with confidence conclude that Franklin performed the lightning kite experiment in June 1752, and that soon after, in late June or July 1752, it was in Philadelphia that the first lightning rods ever to be erected were put in service."[13]

Indeed, it is unreasonable, I think, to believe that Franklin fabricated the June date or other facts of his kite experiment. There is no case of his ever embellishing his scientific achievements, and his description and the account by Priestley contain enough specific color and detail to be convincing. Had he wanted to embellish, Franklin could have claimed that he flew his kite before the French scientists carried out their version of his experiment; instead, he generously admitted that the French scientists were the first to prove his theory. And Franklin's son, with whom he later had a vicious falling-out, never contradicted the well-told tale of the kite.

So why did he delay reporting what may be his most famous scientific feat? There are many explanations. Franklin almost never printed immediate accounts of his experiments in his newspaper, or elsewhere. He usually waited, as he likely did in this case, to prepare a full account rather than a quick announcement. These often took him a while to write out and then recopy; he did not publicly report his 1748 experiments, for example, until his letter to Collinson in April 1749, and there was a similar delay in conveying his results for the following year.

He also may have feared being ridiculed if his initial findings turned out to be wrong. Priestley, in his history of electricity, cited such worries as being the reason Franklin flew his kite secretly. Indeed, even as the experiments were being carried out that summer, many scientists and commentators, including the Abbé Nollet, were calling them foolish. He thus may have been waiting, as Cohen speculates, to repeat and perfect the experiments. Another possibility, suggested by Van Doren, is that he wanted the revelation to coincide with the publication of the article about lightning rods in his new almanac edition that October.[14]

Whatever his reason for delaying the report of his experiment, Franklin was prompted that summer to convince the citizens of Philadelphia to erect at least two grounded lightning rods on high buildings, which were apparently the first in the world to be used for protection. That September, he also erected a rod on his own house with an ingenious device to warn of the approaching of a storm. The rod, which he described in a letter to Collinson, was grounded by a wire connected to the pump of a well, but he left a six-inch gap in the wire as it passed by his bedroom door. In the gap were a ball and two bells that would ring when a storm cloud electrified the rod. It was a typical combination of amusement, research, and practicality. He used it to draw charges for his experiments, but the gap was small enough to allow the safe discharge if lightning actually struck. Deborah, however, was less amused. Years later, when Franklin was living in London, he responded to her complaint by instructing her, "if the ringing frightens you," to close the bell gap with a metal wire so the rod would protect the house silently.

In some circles, especially religious ones, Franklin's findings stirred controversy. The Abbé Nollet, jealous, continued to denigrate his ideas and claimed that the lightning rod was an offense to God. "He speaks as if he thought it presumption in man to propose guarding himself against the thunders of Heaven!" Franklin wrote a friend. "Surely the thunder of Heaven is no more supernatural than the rain, hail or sunshine of Heaven, against the inconvenience of which we guard by roofs and shades without scruple."

Most of the world soon agreed, and lightning rods began sprouting across Europe and the colonies. Franklin was suddenly a famous man. Harvard and Yale gave him honorary degrees in the summer of 1753, and London's Royal Society made him the first person living outside of Britain to receive its prestigious gold Copley Medal. His reply to the Society was typically witty: "I know not whether any of your learned body have attained the ancient boasted art of multiplying gold; but you have certainly found the art of making it infinitely more valuable."[15]

A PLACE IN THE PANTHEON

In describing to Collinson how metal points draw off electrical charges, Franklin ventured some theories on the underlying physics. But he admitted that he had "some doubts" about these conjectures, and he added his opinion that learning *how* nature acted was more important than knowing the theoretical reasons *why:* "Nor is it much importance to us to know the manner in which nature executes her laws; it is enough if we know the laws themselves. It is of real use to know that china left in the air unsupported will fall and break; but how it comes to fall and why it breaks are matters of speculation. It is a pleasure indeed to know them, but we can preserve our china without it."

This attitude, and his lack of grounding in theoretical math and physics, is why Franklin, ingenious as he was, was no Galileo or Newton. He was a practical experimenter more than a systematic theorist. As with his moral and religious philosophy, Franklin's scientific work was distinguished less for its abstract theoretical sophistication than for its focus on finding out facts and putting them to use.

Still, we should not minimize the theoretical importance of his discoveries. He was one of the foremost scientists of his age, and he conceived and proved one of the most fundamental concepts about nature: that electricity is a single fluid. "The service which the one-fluid theory has rendered to the science of electricity," wrote the great nineteenth-century British physicist J. J. Thompson, who discovered the electron 150 years after Franklin's experiments, "can hardly be overestimated." He also came up with the distinction between insulators and conductors, the idea of electrical grounding, and the concepts of capacitors and batteries. As Van Doren notes, "He found electricity a curiosity and left it a science."

Nor should we underestimate the practical significance of proving that lightning, once a deadly mystery, was a form of electricity that could be tamed. Few scientific discoveries have been of such immediate service to humanity. The great German philosopher Immanuel Kant called him the "new Prometheus" for stealing the fire of heaven. He quickly became not only the most celebrated scientist in America and Europe, but also a popular hero. In solving one of the universe's greatest mysteries, he had conquered one of nature's most terrifying dangers.

But as much as he loved his scientific pursuits, Franklin felt that they were no more worthy than endeavors in the field of public affairs. Around this time, his friend the politician and naturalist Cadwallader Colden also retired and declared his intention to devote himself full time to "philosophical amusements," the term used in the eighteenth century for scientific experiments. "Let not your love of philosophical amusements have more than its due weight with you," Franklin urged in response. "Had Newton been pilot but of a single common ship, the finest of his discoveries would scarce have excused or atoned for his abandoning the helm one hour in time of danger; how much less if she had carried the fate of the Commonwealth."

So Franklin would soon apply his scientific style of reasoning—experimental, pragmatic—not only to nature but also to public affairs. These political pursuits would be enhanced by the fame he had gained as a scientist. The scientist and statesman would henceforth be interwoven, each strand reinforcing the other, until it could be said of him, in the two-part epigram that the French statesman Turgot composed, "He snatched lightning from the sky and the scepter from tyrants."[16]

CHAPTER SEVEN

POLITICIAN

Philadelphia, 1749–1756

THE ACADEMY AND THE HOSPITAL

The ingenious lad who did not get to go to Harvard, who skewered that college's pretensions with ill-disguised envy as a teenage essayist, and whose thirst for knowledge had made him the best self-taught writer and scientist of his times had for years nurtured the dream of starting a college of his own. He had discussed the idea in his Junto back in 1743, and after his retirement he became further motivated by the joy he found in science and reading. So in 1749 he published a pamphlet on "Proposals Relating to the Education of Youth in Pennsylvania" that described, with his usual indulgence in detail, why an academy was needed, what it should teach, and how the funds might be raised.

This was not to be a religiously affiliated, elite bastion like the four colleges (Harvard, William & Mary, Yale, and Princeton) that already existed in the colonies. The focus, as to be expected from Franklin, would be on practical instruction, such as writing, arithmetic, accounting, oratory, history, and business skills, with "regard being had to the several professions for which they are intended." Earthly virtues should be instilled; students would live "plainly, temperately and frugally" and be "frequently exercised in running, leaping, wrestling and swimming."

Franklin's plan was that of an educational reformer taking on the rigid classicists. The new academy should not, he felt, train scholars merely to glorify God or to seek learning for its own sake. Instead, what should be cultivated was "an inclination joined with an ability to serve mankind, one's country, friends and family." That, Franklin declared in conclusion, "should indeed be the great *aim* and *end* of all learning."

The pamphlet was crammed with footnotes citing ancient scholars and his own experience on everything from swimming to writing style. Like any good Enlightenment thinker, Franklin loved order and precise procedures. He had displayed this penchant by outlining, in the most minute detail imaginable, his rules for running the Junto, Masonic lodge, library, American Philosophical Society, fire corps, constable patrol, and militia. His proposal for the academy was an extreme example, crammed with exhaustive procedures on the best ways to teach everything from pronunciation to military history.

Franklin quickly raised £2,000 in donations (though not the £5,000 he recalled in his autobiography), drew up a constitution that was as detailed as his original proposal, and was elected president of the board. He also happened to be on the board of the Great Hall that had been built for the Rev. Whitefield, which had fallen into disuse as religious revivalism waned. He was thus able to negotiate a deal to have the new academy take over the building, divide it into floors and classrooms, and leave some space available for visiting preachers and a free school for poor children.

The academy opened in January 1751 as the first nonsectarian college in America (by 1791 it came to be known as the University of Pennsylvania). Franklin's reformist instincts were thwarted at times. Most of the trustees were from the wealthy Anglican establishment, and they voted over his objection to choose as the school's rector the Latin rather than English master. William Smith, a flighty minister from Scotland whom Franklin had befriended, was made the provost, but he and Franklin soon had a bitter falling-out over politics. Nonetheless, Franklin remained a trustee for the rest of his life and considered the college one of his proudest achievements.[1]

Soon after the college opened, Franklin moved on to his next project, raising money for a hospital. The public appeal he published in the

Gazette, which vividly described the moral duty people have to help the sick, contained the typical Franklin ringing refrain: "The good particular men may do separately in relieving the sick is small compared with what they may do collectively."

Raising money was difficult, so he concocted a clever scheme: he got the Assembly to agree that, if £2,000 could be raised privately, it would be matched by £2,000 from the public purse. The plan, Franklin recalled, gave people "an additional motive to give, since every man's donation would be doubled." Political opponents would later criticize Franklin for being too conniving, but he took great joy in this example of his cleverness. "I do not remember any of my political maneuvers the success of which gave me at the time more pleasure, or that in after thinking about it I more easily excused myself for having made use of cunning."[2]

AN AMERICAN POLITICAL PHILOSOPHY

By coming up with what is now known as the matching grant, Franklin showed how government and private initiative could be woven together, which remains to this day a very American approach. He believed in volunteerism and limited government, but also that there was a legitimate role for government in fostering the common good. By working through public-private partnerships, he felt, governments could have the best impact while avoiding the imposition of too much authority from above.

There were other streaks of conservatism, albeit what would now be labeled compassionate conservatism, in Franklin's political style. He believed very much in order, and it would end up taking a lot to radicalize him into an American revolutionary. Though charitable and very much a civic activist, he was wary of the unintended consequences of too much social engineering.

This was reflected in a ruminative letter on human nature he sent to his London friend Peter Collinson. "Whenever we attempt to mend the scheme of providence," Franklin wrote, "we had need be very circumspect lest we do more harm than good." Perhaps even welfare for the poor was an example. He asked whether "the laws peculiar to England which compel the rich to maintain the poor have not given the latter a dependence." It was "godlike" and laudable, he added, "to relieve the misfortunes of our fellow creatures," but might it not in the end "provide encouragements for laziness"? He added a cautionary tale about the New Englanders who decided to get rid of blackbirds that were eating the corn crop. The result was that the worms the blackbirds used to eat proliferated and destroyed the grass and grain crops.

But these were questions more than assertions. In his political philosophy, as in his religion and science, Franklin was generally nonideological, indeed allergic to anything smacking of dogma. Instead, he was, as in most aspects of his life, interested in finding out what worked. As one writer noted, he exemplified the Enlightenment's "regard for reason and nature, its social consciousness, its progressivism, its tolerance, its cosmopolitanism, and its bland philanthropy." He had an empirical temperament that was generally averse to sweeping passions, and he espoused a kindly humanism that emphasized the somewhat sentimental (but still quite real) earthly goal of "doing good" for his fellow man.[3]

What made him a bit of a rebel, and later much more of one, was his inbred resistance to establishment authority. Not awed by rank, he was eager to avoid importing to America the rigid class structure of England. Instead, even as a retired would-be gentleman, he continued in his writings and letters to extol the diligence of the middling class of tradesmen, shopkeepers, and leather-aprons.

Out of this arose a vision of America as a nation where people, whatever their birth or social class, could rise (as he did) to wealth and status based on their willingness to be industrious and cultivate their virtues. In this regard, his ideal was more egalitarian and democratic than even Thomas Jefferson's view of a "natural aristocracy," which sought to pluck selected men with promising "virtues and talents" and groom them to be part of a new leadership elite. Franklin's own idea was more expansive: he believed in encouraging and providing opportunities for all people to succeed based on their diligence, hard work, virtue, and ambition. His proposals for what became the University of Pennsylvania (in contrast to Jefferson's for the University of Virginia) were aimed not at filtering a new elite but at encouraging and enriching all "aspiring" young men.

Franklin's political attitudes, along with his religious and scientific ones, fit together into a rather coherent outlook. But just as he was not a profound religious or scientific theorist—no Aquinas or Newton—neither was he a profound political philosopher on the order of a Locke or even a Jefferson. His strength as a political thinker, as in other fields, was more practical than abstract.

This was evident in one of his most important political tracts, "Observations Concerning the Increase of Mankind," which he wrote in 1751. The abundance of unsettled land in America, he said, led to a faster population growth. This was not a philosophical surmise but an empirical calculation. He observed that the colonists were only half as likely as the English to remain unmarried, that they married younger (around age 20), and that they averaged twice as many children (approximately eight). Thus, he concluded, America's population would double every twenty years and surpass that of England in one hundred years.

He turned out to be right. America's population surpassed that of England by 1851, and kept doubling every two decades until the frontier ran out at the end of that century. Adam Smith cited Franklin's tract in his 1776 classic, *The Wealth of Nations,* and Thomas Malthus, famous for his gloomy views on overpopulation and inevitable poverty, also used Franklin's calculations.

Franklin, however, was no Malthusian pessimist. He believed that, at least in America, increased productivity would keep ahead of population growth, thus making everyone better off as the country grew. In fact, he predicted (also correctly) that what would restrain America's population growth in the future was likely to be wealth rather than poverty, because richer people tended to be more "cautious" about getting married and having children.

Franklin's most influential argument—one that would play a significant role in the struggles ahead—was against the prevailing British mercantilist desire to restrain manufacturing in America. Parliament had just passed a bill prohibiting ironworks in America, and it held fast to an economic system based on using the colonies as a source of raw materials and a market for finished products.

Franklin countered that America's abundance of open land would preclude the development of a large pool of cheap urban labor. "The danger, therefore, of these colonies interfering with their Mother Country in trades that depend on labor, manufactures, etc., is too remote to require the attention of Great Britain." Britain would soon be unable to supply all of America's needs. "Therefore Britain should not too much restrain manufactures in her colonies. A wise and good mother will not do it. To distress is to weaken, and weakening the children weakens the whole family."[4]

The seriousness of this tract on imperial affairs was balanced by a satirical one he wrote around the same time. Britain had been expelling convicts to America, which it justified as a way to help the colonies grow. Writing as Americanus in the *Gazette*, Franklin sarcastically noted that "such a tender parental concern in our Mother Country for the welfare of her children calls aloud for the highest returns of gratitude." So he proposed that America ship a boatload of rattlesnakes back to England. Perhaps the change of climate might tame them, which is what the British had claimed would happen to the convicts. Even if not, the British would get the better deal, "for the rattlesnake gives warning before he attempts his mischief, which the convict does not."[5]

SLAVERY AND RACE

One great moral issue historians must wrestle with when assessing America's Founders is slavery, and Franklin was wrestling with it as well. Slaves made up about 6 percent of Philadelphia's population at the time, and Franklin had facilitated the buying and selling of them through ads in his newspaper. "A likely Negro woman to be sold. Enquire at the Widow Read's," read one such ad on behalf of his mother-in-law. Another offered for sale "a likely young Negro fellow" and ended with the phrase "enquire of the printer hereof." He personally owned a slave couple, but in 1751 he decided to sell them because, as he told his mother, he did not like having "Negro servants" and he found them uneconomical. Nevertheless, he would later, at times, have a slave as a personal servant.

In "Observations on the Increase of Mankind," he attacked slavery on economic grounds. Comparing the costs and benefits of owning a slave, he concluded that it made no sense. "The introduction of slaves," he wrote, was one of the things that "diminish a nation." But he mainly focused on the ill effects to the owners rather than the immorality done to the slaves. "The whites who have slaves, not laboring, are enfeebled," he said. "Slaves also pejorate the families that use them; white children become proud, disgusted with labor."

The tract was, in fact, quite prejudiced in places. He decried German immigration, and he urged that America be settled mainly by whites of English descent. "The number of purely white people in the world is proportionally very small," he wrote. "Why increase the sons of Africa by planting them in America, where we have so fair an opportunity, by excluding all blacks and tawneys, of increasing the lovely white and red? But perhaps I am partial to the complexion of my country, for such kind of partiality is natural to mankind."

As the final sentence indicates, he was beginning to reexamine his "partiality" to his own race. In the first edition of "Observations," he remarked on "almost every slave being by nature a thief." When he reprinted it eighteen years later, he changed it to say that they became thieves "from the nature of slavery." He also omitted the entire section about the desirability of keeping America mainly white.[6]

What helped shift his attitude was another of his philanthropic endeavors. In the late 1750s, he became active in an organization that established schools for black children in Philadelphia and then elsewhere in America. After visiting the Philadelphia school in 1763, he would write a reflective letter about his previous prejudices:

> I was on the whole much pleased, and from what I then saw have conceived a higher opinion of the natural capacities of the black race than I had ever before entertained. Their apprehension seems as quick, their memory as strong, and their docility in every respect equal to that of white children. You will wonder perhaps that I should ever doubt it, and I will not undertake to justify all my prejudices.[7]

In his later life, as we shall see, he became one of America's most active abolitionists, one who denounced slavery on moral grounds and helped advance the rights of blacks.

As indicated by the phrase he used in "Observations" about increasing "the lovely white and red" faces in America, Franklin's feelings about the Indians were generally positive. He marveled, in a letter to Collinson, that the simplicity of the Indians' wilderness life had a romantic appeal. "They have never shown any inclination to change their manner of life for ours," he wrote. "When an Indian child has been brought up among us, taught our language and habituated to our customs, yet if he goes to see his relations and make one Indian ramble with them, there is no persuading him ever to return."

White people also sometimes feel this preference for the Indians' way of living, Franklin noted. When white children were captured and raised by Indians, then later returned to white society, "in a short time they become disgusted with our manner of life, and the care and pains that are necessary to support it, and take the first good opportunity of escaping again into the woods."

He also told the story of some Massachusetts commissioners who invited the Indians to send a dozen of their youth to study free at Harvard. The Indians replied that they had sent some of their young braves to study there years earlier, but on their return "they were absolutely good for nothing, being neither acquainted with the true methods for killing deer, catching beaver, or surprising an enemy." They offered instead to educate a dozen or so white children in the ways of the Indians "and make men of them."[8]

ASSEMBLYMAN, INDIAN DIPLOMAT, AND POSTMASTER

Serving as clerk of the Pennsylvania Assembly, as he had since 1736, frustrated Franklin. Unable to take part in the debates, he amused himself by concocting his numerical magic squares. So when one of the members from Philadelphia died in 1751, Franklin readily accepted election to the seat (and passed on the clerkship to his unemployed son, William). "I conceived my becoming a member would enlarge my powers of doing good," he recalled, but then admitted: "I would not, however, insinuate that my ambition was not flattered."[9]

Thus began Franklin's career in politics, which would last for most of thirty-seven years until his retirement as president of the Pennsylvania Executive Council. As a private citizen, he had proposed various civic improvement schemes, such as the library, fire corps, and police patrol. Now, as a member of the Assembly, he could do even more to be, as he put it, "a great promoter of useful projects."

The quintessence of these was his effort to sweep, pave, and light the city streets. The endeavor began when he became bothered by the dust in front of his house, which faced the farmers' market. So he found "a poor industrious man" who was willing to sweep the block for a monthly fee and then wrote a paper that described all the benefits of hiring him. Houses on the block would remain cleaner, he noted, and shops would attract more customers. He sent the paper around to his neighbors, who all agreed to contribute a portion of the street sweeper's pay each month. The beauty of the scheme was that it opened the way for grander civic improvements. "This raised a general desire to have all the streets paved," Franklin recalled, "and made the people more willing to submit to a tax for that purpose."

As a result, Franklin was able to draw up a bill in the Assembly to pay for street paving, and he accompanied it with a proposal to install street lamps in front of each house. With his love of science and detail, Franklin even worked on a design for the lamps. The globes imported from London, he noticed, did not have a vent on the bottom to allow air in, which meant the smoke collected and darkened the glass. Franklin invented a new model with vents and a chimney, so that the lamp remained clean and bright. He also designed the style of lamp, common today, that had four flat panes of glass rather than one globe, making it easier to repair if broken. "Some may think these trifling matters not worth minding," Franklin said, but they should remember that "human felicity is produced . . . by little advantages that occur every day."[10]

There were, of course, more momentous issues to debate. The Assembly was dominated by Quakers, who were generally pacifist and frugal. They were often at odds with the family of the Proprietors, led by the great William Penn's not-so-great son Thomas, who didn't help relations when he married an Anglican and drifted away from the Quaker faith. The main concerns of the Proprietors were getting more land from the Indians and making sure that their property remained exempt from taxation.

(Pennsylvania was a Proprietary colony, which meant that it was governed by a private family that owned most of the unsettled land. In 1681, Charles II granted such a charter to William Penn, in repayment of a debt. A majority of the colonies started out as Proprietary ones, but by the 1720s most had become Royal colonies directly ruled by the king and his ministers. Only Pennsylvania, Maryland, and Delaware remained under their Proprietors until the Revolution.)

Two big issues faced Pennsylvania at the time: forging good relations with the Indians and protecting the colony from the French. These were related, because alliances with the Indians became all the more important whenever the recurring wars with the French flared up.

Remaining on good terms with the Indians required significant sums of money for gifts, and colonial defense was also costly. This led to complex political struggles in Pennsylvania. The Quakers opposed military spending on principle, and the Penns (acting through a series of appointed lackey governors) opposed anything that would cost them much money or subject their lands to taxes.

Franklin had been instrumental in finessing these issues in 1747, when he formed the voluntary militia. But by the early 1750s, tensions with France over control of the Ohio valley were rising again and would soon erupt into the French and Indian War (an offshoot of what was known in Europe as the Seven Years' War). The situation would lead Franklin to take two momentous initiatives that were to shape not only his political career but also the destiny of America:

- He became an increasingly fervent opponent of the Proprietors, and eventually of the British, as they stubbornly asserted their right to control the taxes and government of the colony, a stance that reflected his anti-authoritarian and populist sentiments.

- He became a leader of the effort to get the colonies, heretofore truculently independent of one another, to join together
  and unite for common purposes, which reflected his penchant
  for forging associations, his nonparochial view of America,
  and his belief that people could accomplish more when they
  worked together than when they stood separately.

The process began in 1753, when Franklin was appointed one of
three commissioners from Pennsylvania to attend a summit conference with a congregation of Indian leaders at Carlisle, halfway between Philadelphia and the Ohio River. The goal was to secure the
allegiance of the Delaware Indians, who were angry with the Penns
for cheating them in what was known as the "Walking Purchase." (An
old deed had given the Penns a tract of Indian land that was defined as
what a man could walk in a day and a half, and Thomas Penn had
hired three fleet runners to sprint for thirty-six hours, thus claiming
far more land than intended.) Allied on the side of the Pennsylvanians
were the Six Nations of the Iroquois confederacy, which included the
Mohawk and Seneca tribes.

More than a hundred Indians came to the Carlisle conference.
After the Pennsylvanians presented the traditional string of wampum,
in this case, a whopping £800 worth of gifts,* the Iroquois chief
Scaroyady proposed a peace plan. The white settlers should pull back
to the east of the Appalachians, and their traders should be regulated
to operate honestly and sell the Indians more ammunition and less
rum. They also wanted assurances that the English would help defend
them from the French, who were militarizing the Ohio valley.

The Pennsylvanians ended up pledging little more than a stricter
regulation of their traders, which eventually caused the Delaware to
drift over to the French side. On the last night, Franklin saw a fright-
ening display of the dangers of rum. The Pennsylvanians had refused
to offer the Indians any until the summit was over, and when the ban
was lifted, a bacchanal erupted. As Franklin described the scene:

---

* Roughly equivalent to $128,000 in 2002 dollars. See page 507 for currency equiva-
lents.

They had made a great bonfire in the middle of the square. They were all drunk, men and women, quarreling and fighting. Their dark-colored bodies, half naked, seen only by the gloomy light of the bonfire, running after and beating one another with firebrands, accompanied by their horrid yellings, formed a scene the most resembling our ideas of hell that could well be imagined.

Franklin and his fellow commissioners wrote an angry report de-crying the white traders who regularly sold rum to the Indians. By doing so they threatened to "to keep these poor Indians continually under the force of liquor" and "entirely estrange the affections of the Indians from the English."[11]

Upon his return, Franklin learned that he had been appointed by the British government to share, along with William Hunter of Virginia, the top post office job in America, known as the Deputy Postmaster for the Colonies. He had been eagerly seeking the position for two years and had even authorized Collinson to spend up to £300 lobbying on his behalf in London. "However," Franklin joked, "the less it costs the better, as it is for life only, which is an uncertain tenure."

His quest was driven by his usual mix of motives: control of the post would allow him to invigorate the American Philosophical Society, improve his publishing network by placing friends and relatives in postal jobs across America, and perhaps make some money. He installed his son as Philadelphia's postmaster, and he later gave jobs in various towns to his brothers Peter and John, John's stepson, his sister Jane's son, two of Deborah's relatives, and his New York printing partner James Parker.

Franklin drew up typically detailed procedures for running the service more efficiently, established the first home-delivery system and dead letter office, and took frequent inspection tours. Within a year, he had cut to one day the delivery time of a letter from New York to Philadelphia. The reforms were costly, and he and Hunter incurred £900 in debt over their first four years. But then they started turning a profit, earning at least £300 a year apiece.

By 1774, when the British fired him for his rebellious political stances, he would be making more than £700 a year. But an even greater benefit of the job, both to him and history, was that it fur-

thered Franklin's conception of the disparate American colonies as a
potentially unified nation with shared interests and needs.[12]

THE ALBANY PLAN FOR
AN AMERICAN UNION

The summit of Pennsylvanians and Indians at Carlisle had done
nothing to deter the French. Their goal was to confine the British settlers to the East Coast by building a series of forts along the Ohio
River that would create a French arc from Canada to Louisiana. In response, Virginia's governor sent a promising young soldier named
George Washington to the Ohio valley in late 1753 to demand that
the French vacate. He failed, but his vivid account of the mission
made him a hero and a colonel. The following spring, he began a series
of haphazard raids against the French forts that would grow into a
full-scale war.

Britain's ministers had been wary of encouraging too much cooperation among their colonies, but the French threat now made it necessary. The Board of Trade in London thus asked each colony to send
delegates to a conference in Albany, New York, in June 1754. They
would have two missions: meeting with the Iroquois confederation to
reaffirm their allegiance and discussing among themselves ways to
create a more unified colonial defense.

Cooperation among the colonies did not come naturally. Some of
their assemblies declined the invitation, and most of the seven that accepted instructed their delegates to avoid any plan for colonial confederation. Franklin, on the other hand, was always eager to foster more
unity. "It would be a very strange thing," he had written his friend
James Parker in 1751, "if six nations of ignorant savages [the Iroquois]
could be capable of forming a scheme for such a union . . . and yet that
a like union should be impracticable for ten or a dozen English
colonies, to whom it is more necessary."

In his letter to Parker, Franklin sketched out a structure for colonial cooperation: there should be, he said, a General Council with delegates from all the colonies, in rough proportion to the amount each
paid in taxes to the general treasury, and a governor appointed by the

king. The meeting sites should rotate among the various colonial capitals, so delegates could better understand the rest of America, and money would be raised by a tax on liquor. Typically, he felt the council should arise voluntarily rather than being imposed by London. The best way to get it going, he thought, was to pick a handful of smart men to visit influential people throughout the colonies and enlist support. "Reasonable, sensible men can always make a reasonable scheme appear such to other reasonable men."

When news of Washington's defeats reached Philadelphia in May 1754, just before the Albany conference, Franklin wrote an editorial in the *Gazette*. He blamed the French success "on the present disunited state of the British colonies." Next to the article he printed the first and most famous editorial cartoon in American history: a snake cut into pieces, labeled with names of the colonies, with the caption: "Join, or Die."[13]

Franklin was one of the four commissioners (along with the Proprietor's private secretary, Richard Peters, Thomas Penn's nephew John, and Assembly Speaker Isaac Norris) chosen to represent Pennsylvania at the Albany Conference. The Assembly, to his regret, had gone on record against "propositions for a union of the colonies," but Franklin was undeterred. He carried with him, as he left Philadelphia, a paper he had written called "Short Hints towards a Scheme for Uniting the Northern Colonies." It had one modification from the union plan that he had described in his earlier letter to James Parker: because the colonial assemblies seemed recalcitrant, perhaps it would be best, if and when the commissioners in Albany adopted such a plan, to send it back to London "and an act of Parliament obtained for establishing it."

On a stopover in New York, Franklin shared with friends the plan he had drafted. In the meantime, Peters and others went shopping for the £500 of wampum the Assembly had authorized as gifts for the Indians: blankets, ribbons, gunpowder, guns, vermilion for face paint, kettles, and cloth. Then, on June 9, they left on a well-laden sloop for Albany with "a pipe of the oldest and best Madeira wine to be got."[14]

Before the Indians arrived, the twenty-four colonial commissioners gathered for their own discussions. New York governor James De-

Lancey proposed a plan to build two western forts, but it stalled because the delegates could not agree to share the costs. So a motion was passed, likely at Franklin's instigation, that a committee be appointed "to prepare and receive plans or schemes for the union of the colonies." Franklin was one of seven named to the committee, which offered a perfect venue for him to gather support for the plan he had in his pocket.

In the meantime, the Indians arrived led by the Mohawk chief Tiyanoga, also known as Hendrick Peters. He was scornful. The Six Nations had been neglected, he said, "and when you neglect business, the French take advantage of it." In another tirade he added, "Look at the French! They are men, they are fortifying everywhere. But, we are ashamed to say it, you are all like women."

After a week of discussions, the commissioners made a series of promises to the Indians: There would be more consultation on settlements and trade routes, certain land sales would be investigated, and laws would be passed to restrict the rum trade. The Indians, with little choice, accepted the presents and declared their covenant chain with the English to be "solemnly renewed." Franklin was not impressed. "We brightened the chain with them," he wrote Peter Collinson, "but in my opinion no assistance is to be expected from them in any dispute with the French until by a complete union among ourselves we are able to support them in case they should be attacked."

In his effort to forge such a union at Albany, Franklin's key ally was a wealthy Massachusetts shipping merchant named Thomas Hutchinson. (Remember the name; he was later to become a fateful foe.) The plan that their committee approved was based on the one Franklin had written. There would be a national congress composed of representatives selected by each state roughly in proportion to their population and wealth. The executive would be a "President General" appointed by the king.

At its core was a somewhat new concept that became known as federalism. A "General Government" would handle matters such as national defense and westward expansion, but each colony would keep its own constitution and local governing power. Though he was sometimes dismissed as more of a practitioner than a visionary, Franklin in Albany had helped to devise a federal concept—orderly, balanced, and enlightened—that would eventually form the basis for a unified American nation.

On July 10, more than a week after the Indians had left Albany, the full group of commissioners finally voted on the plan. Some New York delegates opposed it, as did Isaac Norris, the Quaker leader of Pennsylvania's Assembly, but it nevertheless passed rather easily. Only a few revisions had been made to the scheme sketched out in the "Short Hints" that Franklin had carried with him to Albany, and he accepted them in the spirit of compromise. "When one has so many different people with different opinions to deal with in a new affair," he explained to his friend Cadwallader Colden, "one is obliged sometimes to give up some smaller points in order to obtain greater." It was a sentiment he would express in similar words when he became the key conciliator at the Constitutional Convention thirty-three years later.

The commissioners decided that the plan should be sent both to the colonial assemblies and to Parliament for approval, and Franklin promptly launched a public campaign on its behalf. This included a spirited exchange of open letters with Massachusetts governor William Shirley, who argued that the king rather than the colonial assemblies should choose the federal congress. Franklin replied with a principle that would be at the heart of the struggles ahead: "It is supposed an undoubted right of Englishmen not to be taxed but by their own consent given through their representatives."

It was to no avail. The Albany Plan was rejected by all of the colonial assemblies for usurping too much of their power, and it was shelved in London for giving too much power to voters and encouraging a dangerous unity among the colonies. "The assemblies did not adopt it as they all thought there was too much *prerogative* in it," Franklin recalled, "and in England it was judged to have too much of the *democratic*."

Looking back on it near the end of his life, Franklin was convinced that the acceptance of his Albany Plan could have prevented the Revolution and created a harmonious empire. "The colonies so united would have been sufficiently strong to have defended themselves," he reasoned. "There would then have been no need of troops from England; of course the subsequent pretence for taxing America, and the bloody contest it occasioned, would have been avoided."

On that score he was probably mistaken. Further conflicts over Britain's right to tax her colonies and keep them subservient were almost inevitable. But for the next two decades, Franklin would struggle to find a harmonious solution even as he became more convinced of the need for the colonies to unite.[15]

CATHERINE RAY

After the Albany Conference, Franklin embarked on a tour of his postal realms that culminated in a visit to Boston. He had not been back there since before his mother's death two years earlier, and he spent time with his sprawling family, arranging jobs and apprenticeships. While staying with his brother John, he met an entrancing young woman who became the first intriguing example of his many amorous and romantic—but probably never consummated—flirtations.

Catherine Ray was a lively and fresh 23-year-old from Block Island, whose sister was married to John Franklin's stepson. Franklin, then 48, was immediately both charmed and charming. She was a great talker; so too was Franklin, when he wanted to flatter, and he was also a great listener. They played a game where he tried to guess her thoughts; she called him a conjurer and relished his attention. She made sugarplums; he insisted they were the best he'd ever eaten.

When it came time, after a week, for her to leave Boston to visit another sister in Newport, he decided to accompany her. Along the way, their poorly shod horses had trouble on the icy hills; they got caught in cold rains and on one occasion took a wrong turn. But they would recall, years later, the fun they had talking for hours, exploring ideas, gently flirting. After two days with her family in Newport, he saw her off on the boat to Block Island. "I stood on the shore," he wrote her shortly afterward, "and looked after you, until I could no longer distinguish you, even with my glass."

He left for Philadelphia slowly and with reluctance, loitering on the way for weeks. When he finally arrived home, there was a letter from her. Over the next few months he would write her six times, and through the course of their lives more than forty letters would pass between them. Franklin didn't save most of her letters, perhaps out of prudence, but the correspondence that does survive reveals a remarkable friendship and provides insights into Franklin's relations with women.

From reading their letters, and reading between the lines, one gets the impression that Franklin made a few playful advances that Caty gently deflected, and he seemed to respect her all the more for it. "I write this during a Northeaster storm of snow," he said in the first one he sent after their meeting. "The snowy fleeces which are pure as your virgin innocence, white as your lovely bosom—and as cold." In a letter a few months later, he spoke of life, math, and the role of "multiplication" in marriage, adding roguishly: "I would gladly have taught you that myself, but you thought it was time enough, and wouldn't learn."

Nevertheless, Caty's letters to him were filled with ardor. "Absence rather increases than lessens my affections," she wrote. "Love me one thousandth part so well as I do you." She was soulful and tearful in her letters, which conveyed her affection for him yet also described the men who were courting her. She begged him to destroy them after he had finished reading them. "I have said a thousand things that nothing should have tempted me to say."

Franklin reassured her that he would be discreet. "You may write freely everything you think fit, without the least apprehension of any person's seeing your letters but myself," he promised. "I know very well that the most innocent expressions of warm friendship . . . between persons of different sexes are liable to be misinterpreted by suspicious minds." That, he explained, was why he was being circumspect in his own letters. "Though you say more, I say less than I think."

And so we are left with a set of surviving letters that are filled with nothing more than tantalizing flirtations. She sent him some sugarplums that she had marked with (one assumes) a kiss. "They are every one sweetened as you used to like," she said. He replied, "The plums came safe, and were so sweet from the cause you mentioned that I could scarce taste the sugar." He spoke of the "pleasures of life" and noted that "I still have them all in my power." She wrote of spinning a long strand of thread, and he replied, "I wish I had hold of one end of it, to pull you to me."

How did his loyal and patient wife, Deborah, fit into this type of long-distance flirtation? Oddly enough, he seemed to use her as a shield, both with Caty and the other young women he later toyed with, to keep his relationships just on the safe side of propriety. He invariably invoked Deborah's name and praised her virtues in almost every letter he wrote to Caty. It was as if he wanted Caty to keep her ardor in perspective and to realize that, though his affection was real, his flirtations were merely playful. Or, perhaps, once his sexual advances had been rebuffed, he wanted to show (or to pretend) that they had not been serious. "I almost forgot I had a home," he wrote to Caty in describing his trip back from their first encounter. But soon he began "to think of and wish for home, and as I drew nearer I found the attraction stronger and stronger." So he sped ever faster, he wrote, "to my own house and to the arms of my good old wife and children, where I remain, thanks to God."

Later that fall, he was even more explicit in reminding Caty that he was a married man. When she sent him a present of cheese, he replied, "Mrs. Franklin was very proud that a young lady should have so much regard for her old husband as to send such a present. We talk of you every time it comes to table." Indeed, there was an interesting aspect to this and subsequent letters he wrote to her: they revealed less about the nature of his relationship with Caty than about the relationship, less passionate but deeply comfortable, that he had with his wife. As he told Caty, "She is sure you are a sensible girl and . . . talks of bequeathing me to you as a legacy. But I ought to wish you a better, and hope she will live these hundred years; for we are grown old together, and if she has any faults I am so used to them that I don't perceive them . . . Let us join in wishing the old lady a long life and happy."

Instead of merely continuing their flirtation, Franklin also began to provide Caty with paternal exhortations about duty and virtue. "Be a good girl," he urged, "until you get a good husband; then stay at home, and nurse the children, and live like a Christian." He hoped that when he next visited her, he would find her surrounded by "plump, juicy, blushing pretty little rogues, like their mama." And so it happened. The next time they met, she was married to William Greene, a future governor of Rhode Island, with whom she would have six children.[16]

So what are we to make of their relationship? Clearly, there were sweet hints of romantic attraction. But unless Franklin was dissembling in his letters in order to protect her reputation (and his), the joy came from fun fancies rather than physical realities. It was probably typical of the many flirtations he would have with younger women over the years: slightly naughty in a playful way, flattering to both parties, filled with intimations of intimacy, engaging both the heart and the mind. Despite a reputation for lecherousness that he did little to dispel, there is no evidence of any serious sexual affair he had after his marriage to Deborah.

Claude-Anne Lopez, a former editor of the Franklin Papers project at Yale, has spent years researching his private life. Her analysis of the type of relationships he had with women such as Catherine Ray seems both astute and credible:

> A romance? Yes, but a romance in the Franklinian manner, somewhat risqué, somewhat avuncular, taking a bold step forward and an ironic step backward, implying that he is tempted as a man but respectful as a friend. Of all shades of feeling, this one, the one the French call *amité amoureuse*—a little beyond the platonic but short of the grand passion—is perhaps the most exquisite.[17]

Franklin only occasionally forged intimate bonds with his male friends, who tended to be either intellectual companions or jovial club colleagues. But he relished being with women, and he formed deep and lasting relationships with many. For him, such relationships were not a sport or trifling amusement, despite how they might appear, but a pleasure to be savored and respected. Throughout his life, Franklin would lose many male friends, but he never lost a female one, including Caty Ray. As he would tell her thirty-five years later, just a year before he died, "Among the felicities of my life I reckon your friendship."[18]

SUPPLYING GENERAL BRADDOCK

When he returned to Philadelphia in early 1755 after his dalliance with Caty Ray, Franklin was able, for the moment, to forge a workable relationship with most of the political leaders there. The Proprietors had appointed a new governor, Robert Hunter Morris, and Franklin assured him that he would have a comfortable tenure "if you will only take care not to enter into any dispute with the Assembly." Morris responded half-jokingly. "You know I love disputing," he said. "It is one of my greatest pleasures." Nevertheless, he promised to "if possible avoid them."

Franklin likewise worked hard to avoid disputes with the new governor, especially when it involved the issue of protecting Pennsylvania's frontier. So he was pleased when the British decided to send Gen. Edward Braddock to America with the mission of pushing the French out of the Ohio valley, and he supported Governor Morris's request that the Assembly appropriate funds to supply the troops.

Once again, the members insisted that the Proprietors' estates be taxed. Franklin proposed some clever schemes involving loans and excise taxes designed to break the impasse, but he was not able to resolve the issue right away. So he took on the mission of finding other ways to make sure that Braddock got the necessary supplies.

A delegation of three governors—Morris of Pennsylvania, Shirley of Massachusetts, and DeLancey of New York—had been chosen to meet with the general on his arrival in Virginia. The Pennsylvania Assembly wanted Franklin to be part of the delegation, as did his friend Governor Shirley, and Franklin was eager to be involved. So he joined the group wearing his postmaster hat, ostensibly to help arrange ways to facilitate Braddock's communications. Along the way, he impressed his fellow delegation members with his scientific curiosity. Encountering a small whirlwind, Franklin rode his horse into it, studied its effects, and even tried to break it up with his whip.[19]

General Braddock was brimming with arrogance. "I see nothing that can obstruct my march to Niagara," he crowed. Franklin cautioned that he should be wary of Indian ambushes. Replied Braddock:

"These savages may be a formidable enemy to your raw American militia, but upon the king's regular and disciplined troops, sir, it is impossible they would make any impression." As Franklin later recalled, "He had too much self-confidence."

What he lacked, besides humility, were supplies. Because the Americans had come up with only a fraction of the horses and wagons promised, he declared his intention to return home. Franklin interceded. Pennsylvanians would rally to his cause, he said. The general promptly designated Franklin to be in charge of procuring the equipment.

The broadsides that Franklin wrote advertising Braddock's need to hire horses and wagons played on fear, self-interest, and patriotism. The general had proposed to seize the horses and compel Americans into service, he said, but had been prevailed on instead to try "fair and equitable means." The terms were good, Franklin argued: "The hire of these wagons and horses will amount to upwards of £30,000, which will be paid you in silver and gold and the King's money." As an inducement, he assured the farmers that "the service will be light and easy." Finally came a threat that if voluntary offers did not come, "your loyalty will be strongly suspected," "violent measures will probably be used," and a "Hussar with a body of soldiers will immediately enter the province."

Franklin acted selflessly, indeed remarkably so. When the farmers said they were unwilling to trust the financial pledges of an unknown general, Franklin gave his personal bond that they would receive full payment. His son, William, helped him sign up the farmers, and within two weeks they had procured 259 horses and 150 wagons.[20]

General Braddock was thrilled with Franklin's performance, and the Assembly profusely commended him as well. But Governor Morris, not heeding Franklin's advice to avoid disputes, could not resist attacking the Assembly for being of little help. This upset Franklin, but he still tried to be a conciliator. "I am heartily sick of our present situation: I like neither the governor's conduct nor the Assembly's," he wrote his London friend Collinson, "and having some share in the confidence of both, I have endeavored to reconcile them, but in vain."

Ever collegial, Franklin was able to remain on good personal terms with the governor for the time being. "You must go home with me and spend the evening," Morris said one day on meeting him on the street. "I am to have some company that you will like." One guest told the tale of Sancho Panza, who, when offered a government, requested that his subjects be blacks so that he could sell them if they gave him trouble. "Why do you continue to side with these damned Quakers?" he asked Franklin. "Had not you better sell them? The Proprietors would give you a good price." Franklin replied, "The governor has not yet *blacked* them enough."

Though everyone laughed, the fissures were deepening. By attempting to blacken the reputation of the Assembly, Franklin later wrote, Morris had "negrofied himself." Morris likewise had begun to distrust Franklin. In a letter to Proprietor Thomas Penn, he charged that Franklin was "as much a favorer of the unreasonable claims of American assemblies as any man whatever." [21]

In the meantime, Braddock was confidently marching west. Most Philadelphians were sure that he would prevail, and they even launched a collection to buy fireworks to celebrate. Franklin, more cautious, refused to contribute. "The events of war are subject to great uncertainty," he warned.

His worries were warranted. The British army was ambushed and routed, and Braddock was killed along with two-thirds of his soldiers. "Who would have thought it?" Braddock whispered to an aide just before he died. Among the few survivors was the American colonel George Washington, who had two horses shot out from under him and four bullets pierce his clothing.

Adding to Franklin's distress was the financial exposure he faced because of the loans he had personally guaranteed. These "amounted to near £20,000, which to pay would have ruined me," he recalled. Just as the farmers began to sue him, Massachusetts governor Shirley, now the general of the British troops, came to his rescue and ordered that the farmers be paid from the army's funds.

Braddock's disaster increased the threat from the French and Indians, and it deepened the political rift in Philadelphia. The Assembly quickly passed a bill appropriating £50,000 for defense, but again it insisted a tax be placed on all lands, "those of the proprietors not excepted." Governor Morris rejected it, demanding that the word "not" be changed to "only."

Franklin was furious. No longer casting himself as a mediator, he wrote the reply that the Assembly sent to Morris. He called the governor a "hateful instrument of reducing a free people to the abject state of vassalage," and he accused Proprietor Thomas Penn of "taking advantage of public calamity" and trying "to force down their throats laws of imposition abhorrent to common justice and common reason."

Franklin became particularly enraged when he learned that Morris was required by a secret clause in his commission as governor to reject any tax on the Proprietary estates. In another message from the Assembly a week later, responding to Morris's objection to the use of the word "vassalage," Franklin wrote of Penn: "Our lord would have us defend his estate at our own expense! This is not merely vassalage, it is worse than any vassalage we have heard of; it is something we have no adequate name for; it is even more slavish than slavery itself." In a subsequent message, he added what would become a revolutionary cry: "Those who would give up essential liberty to purchase a little temporary safety deserve neither liberty nor safety."

In the end, a series of patchwork compromises was reached. The Proprietors, on gauging the Assembly's anger, agreed to a voluntary contribution of £5,000 to supplement whatever the Assembly raised. Although that defused the immediate crisis, the principle remained unresolved. More significant, for himself and for history, Franklin had abandoned his long-standing aversion to dispute. Henceforth he would become an increasingly fervent foe of the Proprietors.[22]

COLONEL FRANKLIN OF THE MILITIA

The issue of how to pay for frontier defense had been settled, for the time being, by the uneasy compromises between the Assembly and the Proprietors. To Franklin fell the task of figuring out how to spend the money and raise a militia. He pushed through a bill to create a force that was purely voluntary, thus securing the support of the Quakers, and then published an imaginary discourse designed to rally support for the plan. One character, objecting to the idea that the

Quakers did not have to join, declares, "Hang me if I'll fight to save the Quakers." Replies his friend: "That is to say you won't pump ship, because it will save the rats as well as yourself."

Franklin's plan was modeled on the Association Militia he had organized in 1747, but this time it would be under the aegis of the government. Once again, he spelled out at length the details of training, organization, and election of officers. In one letter he also came up with a very specific scheme for using dogs as scouts. "They should be large, strong and fierce," he wrote, "and every dog led in a slip strong to prevent them tiring themselves by running out and in and discovering the party by barking at squirrels."

Governor Morris grudgingly accepted Franklin's militia bill, though he disliked the provisions making it voluntary and allowing the democratic election of officers. Even more distressing was that Franklin had become the de facto leader and most powerful man in the colony. "Since Mr. Franklin has put himself at the head of the Assembly," Morris warned Penn, his followers "are using every means in their power, even while their country is invaded, to wrest the government out of your hands." For his part, Franklin had developed a burning contempt for Morris. "This man is half a madman," he wrote the Assembly's lobbyist in London.[23]

The Proprietors' fears were not calmed when Franklin donned a military uniform and, along with his son, headed to the frontier to oversee the construction of a line of stockades. He spent the week of his fiftieth birthday, in January 1756, camping at the Lehigh Gap and dining on the provisions that his dutiful wife had sent. "We have enjoyed your roast beef and this day began on the roast veal," he wrote her. "Citizens that have their dinners hot know nothing of good eating; we find it in much greater perfection when the kitchen is four score miles from the dining room."

Franklin enjoyed his stint as a frontier commander. Among his clever accomplishments was devising a reliable method for getting the five hundred soldiers under his command to attend worship services: he assigned to the militia's chaplain the task of doling out the daily allotments of rum right after his services. "Never were prayers more generally and punctually attended." He also found time to observe and record, in his wry way, the customs of the local Moravians, who believed in arranged marriages. "I objected if the matches were not made by the mutual choice of the parties, some of them may chance to be very unhappy," Franklin recounted. " 'And so they may,' answered my informer, 'if you let the parties choose for themselves,' which indeed I could not deny."[24]

After seven weeks on the frontier, Franklin returned to Philadelphia. Despite the worries of the Proprietors and their governor, he had little desire to play the hero on horseback or parlay his popularity into political power. Indeed, he hurried his return so that he arrived late at night to avoid the triumphant welcome that his supporters had planned.

He did not, however, decline when the militia's Philadelphia regiment elected him their colonel. Governor Morris, who had reluctantly sought Franklin's help during the crisis, balked at approving the selection. But he had little choice, as Franklin's militia bill called for the democratic selection of officers, and after a few weeks he grudgingly assented.

Throughout his life, Franklin would find himself torn (and amused) by the conflict between his professed desire to acquire the virtue of humility and his natural thirst for acclaim. His tenure as a colonel was no exception. He could not refrain from indulging his vanity by scheduling a grand public review of his troops. More than a thousand marched past his Market Street house with great pomp and ceremony. Each company arrived to the sounds of fifes and oboes, showed off their freshly painted cannons, and then fired off a volley to herald the arrival of the next company. The shots, he later noted wryly, "shook down and broke several glasses of my electrical apparatus."

When he left a few weeks later on a postal inspection trip, "the officers of my regiment took it into their heads that it would be proper for them to escort me out of town." They drew their swords and accompanied him to the ferry, which infuriated Thomas Penn when he read of it in London. "This silly affair," Franklin noted, "greatly increased his rancor against me . . . and he instanced this parade with my officers as a proof of my having an intention to take the government of the province out of his hands by force." Franklin was likewise "chagrined" by the display, or at least so he said in retrospect. "I had not been previously acquainted with the project or I should have prevented it, being naturally averse to the assuming of state on any occasion."

In fairness to Franklin, he was never the type of person who liked to revel in public ceremony or the pomposity and perks of power. When Penn and his allies sought to neutralize him by forming rival militias in Philadelphia and then convincing the king's ministers to nullify his militia act, Franklin responded by readily surrendering his commission. In a reflective letter to his friend Peter Collinson, he admitted that he enjoyed the public affection but realized that he should not allow it to go to his head. "The people happen to love me," he wrote, but then added, "Forgive your friend a little vanity, as it's only between ourselves . . . You are now ready to tell me that popular favor is a most uncertain thing. You are right. I blush at having valued myself so much upon it." [25]

A NEW MISSION

Franklin's days as a dexterous politician, one who was willing and able to seek pragmatic compromises in times of crisis, were temporarily over. At the height of earlier tensions, he had enjoyed occasional amiable consultations and social interactions with Governor Morris, but that was no longer the case. Morris and others in the Proprietary faction were doing whatever they could to humiliate him, and for a while he talked of moving to Connecticut or even out west to help start a colony in the Ohio region.

So his postal inspection trip to Virginia was a welcome respite, one he extended for as long as possible. From Williamsburg he wrote to his wife that he was "as gay as a bird, not beginning yet to long for home, the worry of perpetual business being fresh in my memory." He met with Colonel Washington and other acquaintances, marveled at the size of the peaches, accepted an honorary degree from William & Mary, and rode through the countryside inspecting postal accounts at a leisurely pace.

When he finally returned home after more than a month, the atmosphere of Philadelphia was even more polarized. The Proprietors' secretary, Richard Peters, conspired with William Smith, whom Franklin had recruited to run the Pennsylvania Academy, to oust him from the presidency of that board. Smith had been writing harsh attacks on Franklin, and the two men stopped speaking to each other, another in the line of rifts he had with male friends.

Late that summer of 1756, there was a brief period of hope for restored civility when a professional military man, William Denny, replaced Morris as governor. All sides hastened to greet and embrace him. At his festive inaugural dinner, he took Franklin aside to a private room and tried to cultivate him. Drinking liberally from a decanter of Madeira, Denny profusely flattered Franklin, which was a smart approach, and then tried to bribe him with financial promises, which wasn't. If Franklin's opposition abated, Denny promised, he could "depend on adequate acknowledgments and recompenses." Franklin replied that "my circumstances, thanks to God, were such as to make proprietary favors unnecessary to me."

Denny was less fastidious about financial inducements. Like his predecessor, he confronted the Assembly by rejecting bills that taxed the Proprietary estates, but he later reversed himself, without permission from the Penns, on being offered a generous salary by the Assembly.

The Assembly, in the meantime, decided that the obstinacy of the Proprietors could no longer be tolerated. In January 1757, the members voted to send Franklin to London as their agent. His goal, at least initially, would be to lobby the Proprietors to be more accommodating to the Assembly over taxation and other matters, and then, if that failed, to take up the Assembly's cause with the British government.

Peters, the Proprietors' secretary, was worried. "B.F.'s view is to effect a change of government," he wrote Penn in London, "and considering the popularity of his character and the reputation gained by his electricity discoveries, which will introduce him into all sorts of company, he may prove a dangerous enemy." Penn was more sanguine. "Mr. Franklin's popularity is nothing here," he replied. "He will be looked upon coldly by great people."

In fact, Peters and Penn would both turn out to be right. Franklin set sail in June 1757 with the firm belief that the colonists should forge a closer union among themselves and be accorded their full rights and liberties as subjects of the British Crown. But he held these views as a proud and loyal Englishman, one who sought to strengthen his majesty's empire rather than seek independence for the American colonies. Only much later, after he was indeed looked on coldly by great people in London, would Franklin prove a dangerous enemy to the imperial cause.[26]

CHAPTER EIGHT

TROUBLED WATERS

London, 1757–1762

MRS. STEVENSON'S LODGER

As he crossed the Atlantic in the summer of 1757, Franklin noticed something about the other ships in the convoy. Most roiled the water with large wakes. One day, however, the ocean behind two of them was oddly tranquil. Ever inquisitive, he asked about the phenomenon. "The cooks," he was told, "have been emptying their greasy water through the scuppers, which has greased the sides of those ships."

The explanation did not satisfy Franklin. Instead, he recalled reading about how Pliny the Elder, the first-century Roman senator and scientist, had calmed agitated water by pouring oil on it. In the ensuing years, Franklin would engage in a variety of oil-and-water experiments, and he even devised a parlor trick where he stilled waves by touching them with a cane that contained a hidden cruet of oil. The metaphor, though obvious, is too good to resist: Franklin, by nature, liked to find ingenious ways to calm turbulent waters. But during his time as a diplomat in England, this instinct would fail him.[1]

Also during the crossing, his ship narrowly avoided being wrecked on the Scilly Isles when it sought to evade French privateers in the fog. Franklin described his grateful reaction in a letter home to his wife. "Were I a Roman Catholic, perhaps I should on this occasion vow to build a chapel to some saint," he wrote. "But as I am not, if I were to vow at all, it should be to build a *lighthouse*." Franklin always took pride in his instinct for practical solutions, but that too would fail him in England.[2]

Franklin's return to London at age 51 came almost thirty-three years after his first visit there as a teenage printer. His mission as Pennsylvania's agent was to mix lobbying with deft diplomacy. Unfortunately, his usual observational skills, his sense of practicality and prudence, and his soothing temperament and cool head would be overwhelmed by frustration and then bitterness. Yet, even as his diplomatic mission foundered, there would be aspects of his life in London—the company of cosmopolitan intellectuals who doted on him, the creation of a contented home life similar to his in Philadelphia—that would make it hard for him to tear himself away. He initially thought his work would be done in five months, but he ended up staying more than five years, and then, after a brief interlude back home, another ten.

Franklin arrived in London in July accompanied by his son, William, then about 26, and two slaves who had been their household servants. They were met by his longtime pen pal Peter Collinson, the London Quaker merchant and botanist, who had helped procure books for the Junto's first library and later published Franklin's letters on electricity. Collinson put Franklin up at his stately home just north of London and immediately invited over others, such as the printer William Strahan, who were likewise delighted finally to meet in person the now-legendary man they had known only through years of correspondence.[3]

After a few days, Franklin found lodgings (including a room for his electricity experiments) in a cozy but convenient four-story row house on Craven Street, nestled between the Strand and the Thames River just off what is now Trafalgar Square, a short walk from the ministries of Whitehall. His landlady was a sensible and unpretentious middle-aged widow named Margaret Stevenson. With her he would form a familial relationship, at once both curious and mundane, that replicated the marriage of comforting convenience that he enjoyed with Deborah in Philadelphia. His London friends often treated Franklin and Mrs. Stevenson as a couple, inviting them together to dinners and inquiring after them both in letters. Though it is possible that their relationship had some sexual aspect, there was no particular passion, and it provoked very little gossip or scandal in London.[4]

More complex was his relation with her daughter Mary, known as Polly. She was a lively and endearing 18-year-old with the sort of inquisitive intellect that Franklin loved in women. In some respects, Polly served as the London counterpart to his daughter, Sally. He treated her in an avuncular, and sometimes even paternal, manner, instructing her on life and morals as well as science and education. But she was also an English version of Caty Ray, a pretty young woman of playful demeanor and lively mind. His letters to her were flirtatious at times, and he flattered her with the focused attention that he lavished on women he liked.

Franklin spent hours talking to Polly, whose eager curiosity enchanted him, and then, when she went to live with an aunt in the country, carried on an astonishing correspondence. During his years in London, he wrote to her far more often than he wrote to his family. Some of the letters were flirtatious. "Not a day passes in which I do not think of you," he wrote less than a year after their first meeting. She sent him little gifts. "I have received the garters you have so kindly knit for me," he said in one letter. "They are of the only sort that I can wear, having worn none of any kind for 20 years, until you began to supply me . . . Be assured that I shall think as often of you in the wearing as you did of me in the making."

As with Caty Ray, his relationship with Polly was an engagement of the mind as much as the heart. He wrote to her at great length and in sophisticated detail about how barometers work, colors absorb heat, electricity is conducted, waterspouts are formed, and the moon affects tidal flows. Eight of these letters were later included in a revised edition of his electricity papers.

He also worked with Polly to come up with what was essentially a correspondence course to teach her a variety of subjects. "Our easiest method of proceeding, I think, will be for you to read some books I may recommend to you," he suggested. "Those will furnish matter for your letters to me and, in consequence, of mine also to you." Such intellectual tutoring was, for him, the ultimate way to flatter a young woman. As he ended one letter to her, "After writing six folio pages of philosophy to a young girl, is it necessary to finish such a letter with a compliment? Is not such a letter of itself a compliment? Does it not say, She has a mind thirsty after knowledge and capable of receiving it?"[5]

His one concern was that Polly would take her studies *too* seriously. Even though he appreciated her mind, Franklin flinched when she hinted at her desire to devote herself to learning at the expense of getting married and raising a family. So he provided her with some paternal prodding. In response to her suggestion that she might "live single" the rest of her life, he lectured her about the "duty" of a woman to raise a family:

> There is, however, a prudent moderation to be used in studies of this kind. The knowledge of nature may be ornamental, and it may be useful, but if to attain an eminence in that we neglect the knowledge and practice of essential duties, we deserve reprehension. For there is no rank in natural knowledge of equal dignity and importance with that of being a good parent, a good child, a good husband, or wife.

Polly took the injunction to heart. "Thank you my dear preceptor for your indulgence in satisfying my curiosity," she replied. "As my greatest ambition is to render myself amiable in your eyes, I will be careful never to transgress the bounds of moderation you prescribe." And then, over the next few weeks, they proceeded to engage in an extensive colloquy, filled with both factual research and various theories, of how the tides affect the flow of water at the mouth of a river.[6]

Polly would eventually marry, have three children, and then become widowed, but through it all she remained extraordinarily close to Franklin. As he would write to her in 1783, near the end of his life, "Our friendship has been all clear sunshine, without the least cloud in its hemisphere." And she would be at his bedside when he died, thirty-three years after their first meeting.[7]

Margaret and Polly Stevenson provided a replica of the family he left in Philadelphia, just as comfortable and more intellectually stimulating. So what did this mean for his real family? Franklin's English friend William Strahan expressed concern. He wrote Deborah to try to persuade her to join her husband in London. The opposite of the peripatetic Franklin, she had no desire to travel and was deeply afraid of the sea. Strahan assured her that no one had ever been killed crossing from Philadelphia to London, not mentioning that this statistic ignored that many had been killed on similar routes. The trip would also be a great experience for Sally, Strahan went on to urge.

That was the sweet part of the letter, the carrots designed to entice. But it was followed, almost rudely, by some jarringly presumptuous advice, which was courteously cloaked but contained barely concealed warnings that reflected Strahan's knowledge of Franklin's nature: "Now madam, as I know the ladies here consider him in exactly the same light I do, upon my word I think that you should come over with all convenient speed to look after your interest; not but that I think him as faithful to his Joan [Franklin's poetic nickname for Deborah] as any man breathing, but who knows what repeated and strong temptation may in time, and while he at so great a distance from you, accomplish." In case Deborah missed the point, Strahan dropped a poison-tinged reassurance at the very end of his letter: "I cannot take my leave of you without informing you that Mr. F. has the good fortune to lodge with a very discreet gentlewoman who is particularly careful of him, who attended him during a very severe cold with an assiduity, concern and tenderness which, perhaps, only yourself could equal; so that I don't think you could have a better substitute until you come over to take him under your own protection."[8]

Franklin was fond of Deborah, relied on her, and respected her solid and simple manner, but he knew that she would be out of place in this more sophisticated London world. So he seemed somewhat ambivalent about the prospect of enticing her to England—and typically realistic about the likelihood. "[Strahan] has offered to lay me a considerable wager that a letter he wrote to you will bring you immediately over here," he wrote. "I tell him I will not pick his pocket, for I am sure there is no inducement strong enough to prevail with you to cross the seas." When she replied that she would indeed be staying in Philadelphia, Franklin showed little grief. "Your answer to Mr. Strahan was just what it should be; I was very much pleased with it. He fancied his rhetoric and art would certainly bring you over."

In his letters home, Franklin walked a fine line of assuring Deborah that he was well looked after, but also reassuring her that he missed her love. After falling ill a few months after his arrival, he wrote, "I have made your compliments to Mrs. Stevenson. She is indeed very obliging, takes great care of my health, and is very diligent when I am in any way indisposed; but yet I have a thousand times wished you with me, and my little Sally . . . There is a great difference in sickness between being nursed with that tender attention which proceeds from sincere love."

Accompanying the letter was an assortment of gifts, some of which, he told her, were chosen by Mrs. Stevenson. The shipment included china, four of London's "newest but ugliest" silver salt ladles, "a little instrument to core apples, another to make little turnips out of great ones," a basket for Sally from Mrs. Stevenson, garters for Deborah that had been knit by Polly ("who favored me with a pair of the same kind"), carpets, blankets, tablecloths, gown fabric chosen for Deborah by Mrs. Stevenson, candle snuffers, and enough other items to assuage any guilt.[9]

Deborah was generally sanguine about the women in Franklin's life. She supplied him with all the news and gossip from home, including the latest she had heard from Caty Ray asking for advice about (of all things) her love life. "I am glad to hear that Miss Ray is well, and that you correspond," Franklin replied, though he urged her not to "be forward in giving advice in such cases."

Their correspondence, for the most part, contained little of the emotional or intellectual content to be found in the letters Franklin exchanged with Polly or Caty Ray or later with his female friends in Paris. Nor did he discourse much with her on political matters, the way he did with his sister Jane Mecom. Although his letters conveyed what seems to be a sincere fondness for Deborah and for the practical nature of their partnership, there were no signs of the more profound partnership that is so evident, for example, in John Adams's correspondence with his wife, Abigail.

Eventually, as Franklin's mission stretched on, Deborah's letters to him would become more bereft and self-pitying, especially after her mother died in a horrible kitchen fire in 1760. Shortly after, she wrote in her awkward way about her loneliness and her worries about rumors she had heard about him and other women. Franklin's reply, though reassuring, was phrased in a coolly abstract manner. "I am concerned that so much trouble should be given you by idle reports," he wrote. "Be satisfied, my dear, that while I have my senses, and God vouchsafes me his protection, I shall do nothing unworthy the character of an honest man, and one that loves his family."[10]

FRANKLIN'S LONDON WORLD

With 750,000 inhabitants and growing rapidly, London in the 1750s was the largest city in Europe and second only to Beijing (pop: 900,000) in the world. It was cramped and dirty, filled with disease and prostitutes and crime, and had long been stratified into an upper class of titled aristocrats and a lower class of impoverished workers who struggled with starvation. Yet it was also vibrant and cosmopolitan, and by the 1750s it had an emerging middle class of merchants and industrialists as well as a growing coffeehouse society of intellectuals, writers, scientists, and artists. Although Philadelphia was the largest city in America, it was a tiny village by comparison, with only 23,000 inhabitants (about the size of Franklin, Wisconsin, or Franklin, Massachusetts, today).

In the cosmopolitan mix of old and new classes that made up London, Franklin quickly found favor among the intellectual and literary set. But despite his reputation for social climbing, he showed little inclination to court the members of the Tory aristocracy, and the feeling was mutual. He liked to be among people with lively minds and simple virtues, and he had an inbred aversion to powerful establishments and idle elites. One of his first visits was to the press where he had once worked. There he bought buckets of beer and drank toasts to the "success of printing."

Strahan and Collinson formed the nucleus of a new set of friends that replicated for Franklin his old Junto but with more sophistication and distinction. He had been corresponding with Strahan, a printer and part-owner of the London *Chronicle,* since 1743, when Strahan provided a letter of recommendation for his apprentice, David Hall, whom Franklin hired and later made his partner. They had exchanged more than sixty letters before they even met, and when they finally did, Strahan was smitten by the larger-than-life Franklin. "I never saw a man who was, in every respect, so perfectly agreeable to me," he wrote Deborah Franklin. "Some are amiable in one view, some in another, he in all."

Collinson, the merchant with whom he had corresponded about electricity, introduced Franklin to the Royal Society, which had already elected him its first American member a year before he arrived. Through Collinson he met Dr. John Fothergill, one of London's foremost physicians, who became his doctor and helped advise him on dealing with the Penns, and also Sir John Pringle, a crusty Scottish professor of moral philosophy and later royal physician, who became his traveling companion. Collinson also brought him into the Honest Whigs, a discussion club of pro-American liberal intellectuals. Among its members, Franklin befriended Joseph Priestley, who wrote the history of electricity that secured Franklin's reputation and went on to isolate oxygen, and Jonathan Shipley, the Bishop of St. Asaph, at whose home Franklin would write much of his autobiography.[11]

Franklin also got in touch with the wayward friend of his youth, James Ralph, who had been his companion on his earlier trip to London, during which they had a falling-out over money and a woman. Ralph's character hadn't changed much. Franklin carried from Philadelphia a letter to Ralph written by the daughter he had abandoned, who was now the mother of ten children. But Ralph didn't want his own English wife and daughter to learn of his connections to America, so he refused to write back. He merely told Franklin to pass along his "great affection." Franklin had little to do with Ralph after that.[12]

For the fashionable gentlemen of the aristocracy, elegant eating and gambling clubs, such as White's and later Brookes's and Boodle's, were starting to spring up in St. James's. For the burgeoning new class of writers, journalists, professionals, and intellectuals whose company Franklin preferred, there were the coffeehouses. London had more than five hundred at the time. They contained newspapers and periodicals for the patrons to read and tables around which discussion clubs could be formed. Fellows of the Royal Society tended to meet at the

Grecian coffeehouse in the Strand, just a short walk from Craven Street. The Club of Honest Whigs met on alternate Thursdays at St. Paul's coffeehouse. Others, such as the Massachusetts and Pennsylvania coffeehouses, provided an American connection. Franklin, always fond of clubs and the occasional glass of Madeira, frequented these and others.[13]

And thus he created an embracing new set of friends and hangouts that replicated the joys of the Junto and provided him with a modest power base among the city's intellectuals. But it was, as Thomas Penn had predicted, a somewhat limited power base. The Proprietor had reassured his own allies, after Franklin's appointment, that he might find favor among those who cared about his scientific experiments, but these middle-class Whiggish intellectuals were not the ones who would decide Pennsylvania's fate. "There are very few of any consequence that have heard of his electrical experiments, those matters being attended to by a particular set of people," Penn wrote. "But it is quite another sort of people who are to determine the dispute between us." Indeed it was.[14]

BATTLING THE PENNS

Franklin came to London not only as a loyalist to the Crown but as an enthusiast for the empire, of which he felt that America was an integral part. But he soon found out that he labored under a misconception. He believed that His Majesty's subjects who happened to live in the colonies were not second-class citizens. Instead, he felt they should have all the rights of any British subject, including that of electing assemblies with legislative and tax-writing powers similar to those of Parliament. The Penns might not see it that way, but certainly the enlightened British ministers would, he believed, help him pressure the Penns to revise their autocratic ways.

That is why it was a rude surprise to Franklin when, shortly after his arrival, he met Lord Granville, the president of the Privy Council, the group of top ministers who acted for the king. "You Americans have wrong ideas of the nature of your constitution," Lord Granville said. The instructions given to colonial governors were "the law of the land," and colonial legislatures had no right to ignore them. Franklin replied that "this was new doctrine to me." The colonial charters specified that the laws were to be made by the colonial assemblies, he argued; although the governors could veto them, they could not dictate them. "He assured me that I was totally mistaken," recalled Franklin, who was so alarmed that he wrote the conversation down verbatim as soon as he returned to Craven Street.[15]

Franklin's interpretation had merit. Years earlier, Parliament had rejected a clause that would give the power of law to governors' instructions. But the rebuke from Granville, who happened to be an in-law of the Penns, served as a warning that the Proprietors' interpretation had support in court circles.

A few days later, in August 1757, Franklin began a series of meetings with the primary Proprietor, Thomas Penn, and his brother Richard. He was already acquainted with Thomas, who had lived for a while in Philadelphia and even had bookplates printed at Franklin's shop (though Franklin's account books show he did not pay all of his bills). Initially, the sessions were cordial; both sides proclaimed their desire to be reasonable. But as Franklin later noted, "I suppose each party had its own idea of what should be meant by *reasonable*."[16]

The Penns asked for the Assembly's case in writing, which Franklin produced in two days. Entitled "Heads of Complaint," Franklin's memo demanded that the appointed governor be allowed "use of his best discretion," and it called the Proprietors' demand to be exempt from the taxes that helped defend their land "unjust and cruel." More provocative than its substance was the informal style Franklin used; he did not address the paper to the Penns directly or use their correct title of "True and Absolute Proprietaries."

Offended by the snub, the Penns advised Franklin that he should henceforth deal only through their lawyer, Ferdinand John Paris. Franklin refused. He considered Paris a "proud, angry man," who had developed a "mortal enmity" toward him. The impasse served the Proprietors' ends; for a year they avoided giving any response while waiting for legal rulings from the government's lawyers.[17]

Franklin's famous ability to be calm and congenial abandoned him at a rancorous meeting with Thomas Penn in January 1758. At issue was Penn's right to veto the Assembly's appointment of a set of commissioners to deal with the Indians. But Franklin used the meeting to assert the broader claim that the Assembly had powers in Pennsylvania comparable to those that Parliament had in Britain. He argued that Penn's revered father, William Penn, had expressly given such rights to Pennsylvania's Assembly in his 1701 "Charter of Privileges" granted to the colonists.

Thomas replied that the royal charter held by his father did not give him the power to make such a grant. "If my father granted privileges he was not by the royal charter empowered to grant," Penn said, "nothing can be claimed by such a grant."

Franklin replied, "If then your father had no right to grant the privileges he pretended to grant, and published all over Europe as granted, those who came to settle in the province . . . were deceived, cheated and betrayed."

"The royal charter was no secret," Penn responded. "If they were deceived, it was their own fault."

Franklin was not entirely correct. William Penn's 1701 charter in fact declared that the Pennsylvania Assembly would have the "power and privileges of an assembly, according to the rights of the free-born subjects of England, and as is usual in any of the King's Plantations in America," and thus was subject to some interpretation. Franklin was nevertheless furious. In a vivid description of the row, written to Assembly Speaker Isaac Norris, Franklin used words that would later, when the letter leaked public, destroy any chance he had to be an effective lobbyist with the Proprietors: "[Penn spoke] with a kind of triumphing, laughing insolence, such as a low jockey might do when a purchaser complained that he had cheated him in a horse. I was astonished to see him thus meanly give up his father's character, and conceived at that moment a more cordial and thorough contempt for him than I have ever before felt for any man living."

Franklin found his face growing warm, his temper starting to rise. So he was careful to say little that would betray his emotions. "I made no other answer," he recalled, "than that the poor people were no lawyers themselves, and confiding in his father, did not think it necessary to consult any."[18]

The venomous meeting was a turning point in Franklin's mission. Penn refused any further personal negotiations, described Franklin as looking like a "malicious villain," and declared that "from this time I will not have any conversation with him on any pretence." Whenever they subsequently ran into one another, Franklin reported, "there appears in his wretched countenance a strange mixture of hatred, anger, fear and vexation."

Abandoning his usual pragmatism, Franklin began to vent his anger to allies back in Pennsylvania. "My patience with the Proprietors is almost, though not quite, spent," he wrote his Pennsylvania ally Joseph Galloway. He was, along with his son, preparing to publish a history of the Pennsylvania disputes, one "in which the Proprietors will be gibbeted up as they deserve, to rot and stink in the nostrils of posterity."[19]

Franklin's ability to act as an agent was thus pretty much over, at least for the time being. He was nevertheless still able to provide his Philadelphia friends with inside intelligence, such as advance word that the Penns were planning to fire Gov. William Denny, who had violated his instructions by allowing a compromise that taxed the Proprietary estates. "It was to have been kept a secret from me," he wrote Deborah, adding with a bit of Poor Richard's wit: "So you may make a secret of it too, if you please, and oblige all your friends with it."

He also was effective, as he had been since a teenager, at using the press to wage a propaganda campaign. Writing anonymously in Strahan's paper, the London *Chronicle,* he decried the actions of the Penns as being contrary to the interests of Britain. A letter signed by William Franklin, but clearly written with the help of his father, attacked the Penns more personally, and it was reprinted in a book on the history of Pennsylvania that Franklin helped compile.[20]

As the summer of 1758 approached, Franklin faced two choices: he could return home to his family, as planned, but his mission would have been a failure. Or he could, instead, spend his time traveling through England and enjoying the acclaim he found among his intellectual admirers.

There is no sign that Franklin found it a difficult decision. "I have no prospect of returning until next Spring," he reported to Deborah rather coolly that June. He would spend the summer, he reported, wandering the countryside. "I depend chiefly on these intended journeys for the establishment of my health." As for Deborah's complaints about her own health, Franklin was only mildly solicitous: "It gives me concern to receive such frequent accounts of your being indisposed; but we both of us grow in years, and must expect our constitutions, though tolerably good in themselves, will by degrees give way to the infirmities of age."

His letters remained, as always, kindly and chatty but hardly romantic. They tended to be paternalistic, perhaps a bit condescending at times, and they were certainly not as intellectually engaging as those to his sister Jane Mecom or Polly Stevenson. But they do convey some genuine fondness and even devotion. He appreciated Deborah's sensible practicality and the accommodating nature of their partnership. And for the most part, she seemed accepting of the arrangement they had made long ago and generally content about staying ensconced in her comfortable home and familiar neighborhood, rather than having to follow him on his far-flung travels. Their correspondence contained, until near the end, only occasional reproaches from either side, and he dutifully provided gossip, instructions about how to dismantle his lightning rod bells, and some old-fashioned advice about women and politics. "You are very prudent not to engage in party disputes," he wrote at one point. "Women should never meddle in them except in endeavors to reconcile their husbands, brothers and friends, who happen to be on contrary sides. If your sex can keep cool, you may be a means of cooling ours the sooner."

Franklin was likewise solicitous, but again only mildly so, about the daughter he had left behind. He expressed his happiness at receiving a portrait of Sally, and he sent her a white hat and cloak, some sundries, and a buckle made of French paste stones. "They cost three guineas, and are said to be cheap at that price," he wrote. If he felt the tug of his family, it was not particularly strong, because he had a mirror one in London. As he noted in a cavalier postscript to a rambling letter to Deborah that June, "Mrs. Stevenson and her daughter desire me to present their respects."[21]

WILLIAM AND THE FAMILY TREE

William Franklin, perhaps in reaction to being referred to regularly by his family's enemies as a base-born bastard, had a yearning for social status that was far greater than his father's. Among the most thumbed of his books was one titled *The True Conduct of Persons of Quality,* and in London he liked to frequent the fashionable homes of the young earls and dukes instead of the coffeehouses and intellectual salons favored by his father. Both in his social world and in his legal studies at the Inns of Court, where his father enrolled him, William would eventually be tugged toward a more Tory and loyalist outlook. But the change would be gradual, fitful, and filled with personal conflicts.

Before leaving Philadelphia, William had been courting a well-born young debutante named Elizabeth Graeme. Her father, Dr. Thomas Graeme, a physician and member of the Governor's Council, owned a grand home on Society Hill and a three-hundred-acre country estate considered the finest in the Philadelphia area. Her mother was the stepdaughter of Benjamin Franklin's unreliable patron Governor Keith. The relationship between the Graemes and the Franklins was strained; Dr. Graeme had felt insulted when the elder Franklin did not initially enlist him to run the staff of the new Philadelphia Hospital, and he was a close friend of the Penn family in its struggle with the Assembly.

Nevertheless, with the grudging assent of Dr. Graeme, the relationship had progressed to the point where Elizabeth tentatively accepted William's offer of marriage. She was 18, he close to ten years older. It came with a stipulation: William would withdraw from any involvement in politics. She refused, however, to accompany him to London or to marry him before he left. They would, both agreed, await his return to be married.

Once in England, William's ardor for her apparently cooled far more than his ardor for politics. After a short note on his arrival, he did not write her again for five months. Gone were the flowery clichés he had once penned about their love, replaced instead with descriptions of the joy of "this bewitching country." Worse yet, he proudly sent her the political screed he had signed in the London *Chronicle* attacking the Proprietors, and he went so far as to solicit her opinion of how the article was received back in Philadelphia.

Thus ended the relationship. She waited months before sending a cold and bitter response, which labeled him "a collection of party malice." The next day he replied, through a mutual friend, that the fault lay with her fickleness and he would be glad to see her find happiness with another man. For his part, William was finding his own happiness, both with the fashionable ladies of London and, too much his father's son, occasionally with prostitutes and other women of low repute.[22]

Benjamin Franklin, who had mixed emotions about the relationship, seemed unfazed by the breakup. His own hope was that his son would marry Polly Stevenson. There was little chance of that, as William's social aspirations were higher than those of his father. Indeed, William was developing social and financial airs that had begun to worry Franklin. So he began an effort, which would later become a theme in the section of his autobiography that was written ostensibly as a letter to his son, to restrain William from putting on upper-class pretensions. It would ultimately prove futile and become, as much as politics, a cause of their estrangement.

Years earlier, Franklin had warned William not to expect much of an inheritance. "I have assured him that I intend to spend what little I have myself," he wrote his own mother. Once in England, Franklin kept a meticulous account of all of William's expenses—including meals, lodging, clothing, and books—with the understanding that they were advances that must someday be repaid. By 1758, even as he was pampering himself a bit with a carriage at Pennsylvania's expense, Franklin was warning his son to be more frugal on meals and to avoid becoming attached to a high style of London living. William, who was traveling with friends in the south of England, was cowed. "I am extremely obliged to you for your care in supplying me with money," he wrote, adding that he had changed his lodgings for something "much for the worse, though cheaper."[23]

As part of his effort to keep his son rooted in his "middling" heritage, Franklin took him on a genealogical excursion during the summer of 1758. They traveled to Ecton, about sixty miles northwest of London, where generations of Franklins had lived before Josiah had migrated to America. Still living nearby was Franklin's first cousin Mary Franklin Fisher, daughter of Josiah's brother Thomas. She was "weak with age," Franklin noted, but "seems to have been a very smart, sensible woman."

At the parish church, the Franklins uncovered two hundred years of birth, marriage, and death records of their family. The rector's wife entertained them with stories of Franklin's uncle Thomas, whose life bore some resemblance to that of his nephew. As Franklin reported to Deborah:

> [Thomas Franklin was] a very leading man in all county affairs, and much employed in public business. He set on foot a subscription for erecting chimes in their steeple, and completed it, and we heard them play. He found out an easy method of saving their village meadows from being drowned, as they used to be sometimes by the river, which method is still in being . . . His advice and opinion were sought for on all occasions, by all sorts of people, and he was looked upon, she said, by some, as something of a conjuror. He died just four years before I was born, on the same day of the same month."

Franklin may have noted that the description "conjuror" was the same that Caty Ray had once used about him. And William, impressed by the coincidence of dates, surmised that a "transmigration" had occurred.

At the cemetery, as William copied data from the gravestones, Franklin's servant, Peter, used a hard brush to scour off the moss. Franklin's account of the scene is a reminder that, as enlightened as he would eventually become, he had brought with him to England two slaves. He viewed them, however, more as old family servants than as property. When one of them left soon after they arrived in England, Franklin did not try to force his return, as British law would have allowed. His response to Deborah, when she asked about their welfare later, is revealing:

> Peter continues with me, and behaves as well as I can expect in a country where there are many occasions of spoiling servants, if they are

ever so good. He has as few faults as most of them, [but I see them] with only one eye and hear with only one ear; so we rub on pretty comfortably. King, that you enquire after, is not with us. He ran away from our house, near two years ago, while we were absent in the country; but was soon found in Suffolk, where he had been taken in the service of a lady that was very fond of the merit of making him a Christian and contributing to his education and improvement.[24]

As he felt about Peter, so too he felt about slavery for the time being: he saw the faults with only one eye, heard them with only one ear, and rubbed along pretty comfortably, though increasingly less so. The evolution of his views on slavery and race was indeed continuing. He would soon be elected to the board of an English charitable group, the Associates of Dr. Bray, dedicated to building schools for blacks in the colonies.

With William in tow, Franklin spent that spring and summer of 1758 wandering England to soak up the hospitality and acclaim of his intellectual admirers. On a visit to Cambridge University, he conducted a series of experiments on evaporation with the renowned chemist John Hadley. Franklin had previously studied how liquids produce different refrigeration effects based on how quickly they evaporate. With Hadley he experimented using ether, which evaporates very quickly. In a 65-degree room, they repeatedly coated a thermometer bulb with ether and used a bellows to evaporate it. "We continued this operation, one of us wetting the ball, and another of the company blowing on it with the bellows to quicken the evaporation, the mercury sinking all the time until it came down to 7, which is 25 degrees below the freezing point," Franklin wrote. "From this experiment one may see the possibility of freezing a man to death on a warm summer's day." He also speculated, correctly, that summer breezes do not by themselves cool people; instead, the cooling effect comes from the increased evaporation of human perspiration caused by the breeze.

His study of heat and refrigeration, though not as seminal as his work on electricity, continued throughout his life. In addition to his evaporation experiments, they included further studies of how different colors absorb heat from light, how materials such as metal that conduct electricity are also good at transmitting heat, and how to better design stoves. As usual, his strength was devising not abstract theories but practical applications that could improve everyday life.[25]

His visit to Cambridge made such an impression that he was invited back later that summer to view the university's commencement. "My vanity was not a little gratified by the particular regard shown me," he admitted to Deborah. But that regard was not awaiting him when he returned to London in the fall.[26]

THE PENNS RESPOND

In November 1758, more than a year after Franklin had submitted his "Heads of Complaint," the Penns finally responded. Snubbing Franklin, they had their lawyer, Ferdinand Paris, write directly to the Pennsylvania Assembly, with a copy to Franklin, and then followed with a letter of their own to the Assembly.

On the issue of the Assembly's power, the Proprietors held firm: their instructions to their governors were inviolable, and the charter "gives the power to make laws to the Proprietary." The Assembly could provide only "advice and consent." On the issue of taxation, however, the Penns held open the possibility of some compromise. "They are very ready to have the annual income of their estate inquired into," Paris wrote, and consider some contributions based on what "is in its nature taxable."

The murky response, which offered no concrete assurances of any real money, prompted Franklin to write seeking clarification. But a key aspect of the Proprietors' position was that they would not deal with him anymore. Paris pointedly told the Assembly that they had not chosen a "person of candor" to be their agent. And the Penns, in their own letter, said that further negotiations would require "a very different representation." To emphasize the point, Paris visited Franklin personally to deliver the Penns' message that "we do not think it necessary to keep up a correspondence with a gentleman who acknowledges he is not empowered to conclude proper measures." Franklin "answered not a word," Paris reported, and "looked as if much disappointed."

"Thus a final end is put to all further negotiation between them and me," Franklin wrote Assembly Speaker Norris. His mission stymied, he could have returned home and let others work out the details of a compromise on taxation. So he made a halfhearted offer to resign. "The House will see," he wrote Norris, "that if they propose to continue treating with the Proprietors, it will be necessary to recall me and appoint another person or persons for that service who are likely to be more acceptable or more pliant than I am, or, as the Proprietors express it, persons of candor."

But Franklin did not recommend this approach. His usual pragmatic instincts fell prey to sentiments he had once tried to train himself to avoid, such as bitterness, wounded pride, emotionalism, and political fervor. He proposed, instead, a radically different alternative: attempting to take Pennsylvania away from the Penns and turning it into a Crown colony under the king and his ministers. "If the House, grown at length sensible of the dangers to the liberties of the people necessarily arising from such growing power and property in one family with such principles, shall think it expedient to have the government and property in different hands, and for that purpose shall desire that the Crown would take the province into its immediate care, I believe that point might without much difficulty be carried." With some eagerness he concluded, "In that I think I could still do service."[27]

There was no reason to believe that England's ministers would meddle with the Proprietary charter or strike a blow for democracy in the colonies. So why did Franklin fixate on an ill-considered, and ill-fated, crusade to turn Pennsylvania into a royal colony? Part of the problem was that his animosity toward the Penns had blurred his peripheral vision. To the Yale historian Edmund Morgan, this "prolonged fit of political blindness" seems surprising, even puzzling. "Franklin's preoccupation, not to say obsession, with the Proprietary prerogatives not only wasted his immense talents but obscured his vision and his perceptions of what was politically feasible," he writes.

Yet Franklin's actions can be explained, at least partly, by his enthusiasm for the glory of the king's growing empire. "Once we fully accept the fact that Franklin between 1760 and 1764 was an enthusiastic and unabashed royalist who did not and could not foresee the breakup of the Empire, then much of the surprise, confusion and mystery of his behavior in these years falls away," argues Brown University professor Gordon Wood.[28]

Others in America were quicker than Franklin to realize that it was the prevailing attitude among most British leaders, and not merely the Proprietors, that the colonies ought to be subservient both politically and economically. Franklin's allies in the Pennsylvania Assembly, however, shared his belief that the struggle was with the Proprietors, and they agreed he should stay to fight them. So, with no personal desire to leave England, he launched assaults against the Penns on three fronts.

The first involved the Penns' handling of Indian affairs. Franklin had long been sympathetic to the rights of the Indians, especially the Delawares, who felt that the Penns had cheated them of land. In the fall of 1758, he submitted a brief on the Delawares' behalf to the Privy Council. In it, he echoed his use of the phrase "low jockey" that he knew had already enraged the Penns. The Penns, he wrote, had extended their holdings "by such arts of jockeyship [that] gave the Indians the worst of opinions of the English." Little came of Franklin's advocacy, but he helped publicize the case to score propaganda points against the way the Penns managed their colony.[29]

Franklin's second line of attack involved a libel case the Pennsylvania Assembly had won against William Smith, the provost of the Academy who had become Franklin's political adversary. When Smith appealed to the Privy Council in London for a reversal, Franklin turned the case into a larger struggle on behalf of the Assembly's rights. Ferdinand Paris represented Smith, arguing that "the Assembly of Pennsylvania was not a Parliament nor had anything near so much power as the House of Commons had." In June 1759, the Privy Council ruled against Franklin. On a narrow point, it noted that the Assembly in question had adjourned and a new one been voted in, so the current Assembly had no case. More ominously, it noted that "inferior assemblies" like those in the colonies "must not be compared in power or privileges to the House of Commons."[30]

On the third issue Franklin was somewhat more successful. It involved the case of Gov. William Denny, who had violated his instruction in a number of cases by approving bills that taxed the Proprietors' estates. The Penns, alleging with some evidence that Denny had been bribed, not only recalled him but also appealed to the Privy Council to have the bills nullified.

An initial advisory opinion by the Board of Trade went against Franklin and the Assembly. But something surprising happened when the Privy Council heard the appeal. Lord Mansfield, a member of the Council, beckoned Franklin to join him in the clerk's office while the lawyers were arguing. Was he really of the opinion that the taxes could be levied in such a way that did not injure the Penn estates?

"Certainly," Franklin replied.

"Then," said Lord Mansfield, "you can have little objection to enter into an engagement to assure that point."

"None at all," said Franklin.

Thus a compromise was reached. Franklin agreed that the Assembly's tax bill would exclude the "unsurveyed wastelands" belonging to the Proprietors and would tax unsettled land at a rate "no higher than similar land owned by others." By reverting to his old pragmatism, Franklin had won a partial victory. But the compromise did not settle permanently the issue of the Assembly's power, nor did it restore harmony between it and the Proprietors.[31]

The compromise also did nothing to further Franklin's crusade to strip the Penns of their proprietorship of Pennsylvania. Quite the contrary. In all of its rulings, the Privy Council showed no inclination to alter the charter of the Proprietors, nor had Franklin succeeded in whipping up any public support for such a course. Once again, he faced a situation in which there was little more he could achieve in England and no real reason he could not return home. Yet once again, Franklin felt no inclination to leave.

"DENSEST HAPPINESS"

Among Franklin's greatest joys were his summer travels. In 1759, he and William went to Scotland, their path paved with introductions to the intellectual elite from William Strahan and John Pringle, both Edinburgh natives. He stayed at the manor of Sir Alexander Dick, a renowned physician and scientist, and there met the greats of the

Scottish Enlightenment: the economist Adam Smith, the philosopher David Hume, and the jurist and historian Lord Kames.

One night at dinner, Franklin regaled the guests with one of his best literary hoaxes, a biblical chapter he fabricated called the Parable against Persecution. It told of Abraham giving food and shelter to a 198-year-old man, then throwing him out when he said he did not believe in Abraham's God. The parable concluded:

> And at midnight God called upon Abraham, saying, Abraham where is the stranger?
>
> And Abraham answered and said, Lord, he would not worship thee; neither would he call upon thy name. Therefore have I driven him out before my face into the wilderness.
>
> And God said, Have I borne with him these hundred ninety and eight years, and nourished him, and clothed him, notwithstanding his rebellion against me, and couldst thou not, that art thyself a sinner, bear with him one night?[32]

The guests, charmed by Franklin and his philosophy of tolerance, asked him to send them copies, which he did. It was also at this time that Franklin wrote Hume about the tale of the dispute over a Maypole, which involved a Lord Mareschal who had been asked to opine on whether all forms of damnation were for eternity. Franklin compared it to the plight of a mayor in a Puritan Massachusetts village who was called on to resolve a dispute between those who wanted to erect a Maypole and others who considered it blasphemous:

> He heard their altercation with great patience, and then gravely determined thus: You that are for having no Maypole shall have no Maypole; and you that are for having a Maypole shall have a Maypole. Get about your business and let me hear no more of this quarrel. So methinks Lord Mareschal might say: You that are for no more damnation than is proportioned to your offenses, have my consent that it may be so; and you that are for being damned eternally, G——d eternally d——n you all, and let me hear no more of your disputes.[33]

David Hume was the greatest British philosopher of his era and one of the most important logical and analytic thinkers of all time. He had already written the two seminal tracts, *A Treatise of Human Nature* and *Essays Concerning Human Understanding*, that are now considered among the most important works in the development of empirical thought, placing him in the pantheon with Locke and Berkeley. When Franklin met him, he was completing the six-volume *History of England* that would make him rich and famous.

Franklin assiduously courted him and helped convert him to the colonial cause. "I am not a little pleased to hear of your change of sentiments in some particulars relating to America," Franklin subsequently wrote him, adding as flattery, "I know no one that has it more in his power to rectify" the British misunderstandings. Of one of Hume's essays favoring free trade with the colonies, Franklin enthused that it would have "a good effect in promoting a certain interest too little thought of by selfish man . . . I mean the interest of humanity, or common good of mankind."

Franklin and Hume also shared an interest in language. When Hume berated him for coining new words, Franklin agreed to quit using the terms "colonize" and "unshakeable." But he lamented that "I cannot but wish the usage of our tongue permitted making new words when we want them." For example, Franklin argued, the word "inaccessible" was not nearly as good as coining a new word such as "uncomeatable." Hume's response to this suggestion is unknown, but it did nothing to diminish his ardent admiration for his new friend. "America has sent us many good things, gold, silver, sugar, tobacco, indigo," he wrote back. "But you are the first philosopher, and indeed the first great man of letters, for whom we are beholden to her."[34]

During his visit to Scotland, Franklin also became friends with Henry Home, Lord Kames, whose interests ranged from farming and science to literary criticism and history. Among the things they discussed on their horseback rides through the countryside was the need for Britain to keep control of Canada, which had been wrested from the French earlier that year when an Anglo-American force captured Quebec in one of the decisive battles of the French and Indian War. Franklin pushed the case "not merely as I am a colonist, but as I am a Briton." As he wrote Kames soon after his departure, "The future grandeur and stability of the British Empire lie in America." For all his problems with the Penns, he had not yet turned into a rebel.

The visit to Scotland was capped by Franklin's acceptance of an honorary doctorate from the University of St. Andrews. As the crimson silk and white satin robe was draped over his shoulder, Franklin was read a citation praising "the rectitude of his morals and sweetness of his life and conversation." It added, "By his ingenious inventions and successful experiments, with which he has enriched the science of natural philosophy and more especially of electricity which heretofore was little known, [he has] acquired so much praise throughout the world as to deserve the greatest honors in the Republic of Letters." Thereafter, he was often referred to, even by himself, as Dr. Franklin.

The time he spent in Scotland, he wrote Lord Kames on his way home, "was six weeks of the densest happiness I have met with in any part of my life." This was, perhaps, a small exaggeration. But it helped explain why he was not hurrying back to Philadelphia.[35]

Indeed, by early 1760, Franklin was beginning to harbor some hope that Deborah and Sally would join him in England. His dream, now that he realized William was unlikely to marry Polly Stevenson, was another middle-class union: to have Sally marry William Strahan's son Billy. It was a match he had fantasized about when Sally was a mere toddler and Strahan was someone he knew only through his letters. Although arranged marriages were no longer prevalent, they were not uncommon, and Strahan proposed in writing a plan to unite their children. Franklin passed it along to Deborah tentatively, assuming that it was unlikely to entice her over:

> I received the enclosed some time since from Mr. Strahan. I afterwards spent an evening in conversation with him on the subject. He was very urgent with me to stay in England and prevail with you to move hither with Sally. He proposed several advantageous schemes to me which appeared reasonably founded. His family is a very agreeable one; Mrs. Strahan a sensible and good woman, the children of amiable characters and particularly the young man, who is sober, ingenious and industrious, and a desirable person.
>
> In point of circumstances there can be no objection, Mr. Strahan being in so thriving a way as to lay up a thousand pounds every year

from the profits of his business, after maintaining his family and paying all charges . . . I gave him, however, two reasons why I could not think of removing hither. One my affection to Pennsylvania, and long established friendships and other connections there. The other your invincible aversion to crossing the seas.

Sally was almost 17, and the union held out the promise of a comfortable life in a smart and fun circle. But Franklin left the decision up to his wife. "I thanked him for the regard shown us in the proposal, but gave him no expectation that I should forward the letters," he wrote. "So you are at liberty to answer or not as you think proper." There is no indication that Deborah was tempted in the least.[36]

As for William, Franklin was not only a bad matchmaker, he was an even worse role model. Around this time, probably in February 1760, William followed in his father's steps by siring an illegitimate son, William Temple Franklin, known as Temple. His mother was apparently a woman of the streets who (like William's own mother) seems never to have been heard from again. William accepted paternity, but instead of promptly finding a wife and taking him home (as his own father had done), he sent the child to be raised secretly by a foster family.[37]

Temple would eventually become a treasured grandchild to Benjamin Franklin, who oversaw his education and then brought him under his wing as a personal secretary. Later, when his grandfather and father were on opposite sides during the Revolutionary War, Temple would become a pawn in a heart-wrenching struggle for his loyalty and devotion, one that Benjamin Franklin would win at great personal cost. But for the time being, he was kept out of sight while William enjoyed the social whirl of London and more excursions with his celebrated father.

The most memorable was a trip to the continent in the summer of 1761. Because Britain was still at war with France, they traveled instead to Holland and Flanders. Franklin noted with pleasure that the observance of religion there was not as strict as in America, especially when it came to observing Sundays as the Sabbath. "In the afternoon, both high and low went to the play or the opera, where there was plenty of singing, fiddling and dancing," he reported to a Connecticut friend. "I looked around for God's judgments but saw no signs of them." He concluded, with a touch of amusement, that this provided evidence that the Lord did not care so much about preventing pleasure on the Sabbath as the strict Puritans would have people believe. The happiness and prosperity in Flanders, he wrote, "would almost make one suspect that the Deity is not so angry at that offense as a New England justice."

Franklin's fame as a scientist meant that he was celebrated wherever he went. In Brussels, Prince Charles of Lorrains showed them the equipment he had bought to replicate Franklin's electricity experiments. And in Leyden, a meeting of the world's two great electricians occurred: Franklin spent time with Pieter van Musschenbroek, inventor of the Leyden jar. The professor said he was about to publish a book that would make use of a letter Franklin had sent him about electricity, but alas, he died just two weeks after the Franklins left.[38]

CANADA AND EMPIRE

Franklin cut short his trip to the continent to come back to London to attend the coronation of King George III in September 1761. Still very much a proud British royalist, he harbored high hopes for the new king and fancied that he might protect the colonies from the tyranny of the Proprietors.

In America, the French and Indian War had pretty much ended, with England and her colonies capturing control of Canada and many of the Caribbean sugar islands belonging to France and Spain. In Europe, however, the broader struggle between Britain and France, known as the Seven Years' War, would not be resolved until a Treaty of Paris was signed in 1763. Franklin's ardor for the expansion of the king's empire led him to continue his crusade to convince Britain to keep control of Canada, rather than cede it back to France in return for some Caribbean islands as part of a negotiated settlement. In an anonymous article in Strahan's London *Chronicle,* he used his old trick of parody and produced ten facetious reasons why Canada *should* be restored to France. Among them:

   We should restore Canada because an uninterrupted trade with the
Indians throughout a vast country, where the communication by water
is so easy, would increase our commerce, already too great . . .
   We should restore it lest, through a greater plenty of beaver, broad-
brimmed hats become cheaper to that unmannerly sect, the Quakers.
   We should restore Canada that we may soon have another war, and
another opportunity of spending two or three millions a year in America, there being great danger of our growing too rich.

On a far more serious note, he produced a fifty-eight-page pamphlet entitled "The Interest of Great Britain Considered with Regard
to Her Colonies," in which he argued that keeping control of Canada
would benefit the British Empire and help protect its American
colonies from constant harassment by the French and their Indian allies. "To leave the French in possession of Canada when it is in our
power to remove them," he wrote, "seems neither safe nor prudent."

The pamphlet dwelled in great detail on the issue of Canada, but it
also raised an even more important topic: the relationship between
Britain and her colonies. Franklin wrote as a man who was still a loyal,
indeed an ardent, supporter of the empire, "happy as we now are under
the best of Kings." The inhabitants of the colonies, he argued, were
"anxious for the glory of her crown, the extent of her power and commerce, the welfare and future repose of the whole British people." The
best way to assure continued harmony, he wrote, was to provide safe
and abundant land so that the colonies could expand.

Franklin had a theory about the underlying cause of the growing
friction between Britain and her colonies, one that he first expressed
nine years earlier in his "Observations Concerning the Increase of
Mankind." The conflicts, he believed, grew from the attitude of the
British mercantilists, who had something in common with the Proprietors: they viewed the colonies as a market to be exploited. Consequently, they opposed the development of manufacturing in the
colonies as well as greater rights of self-government. In the pamphlet,
he noted his fear that this attitude could even provoke "the future independence of our colonies."

The best way to make America prosperous without turning it into
a manufacturing center, Franklin said, was to keep Canada and thus

assure there was always an abundance of land for the colonists to set-tle. "No man who can have a piece of land of his own, sufficient by his labor to subsist his family in plenty, is poor enough to be a manufac-turer and work for a master," he wrote. "Hence while there is enough land in America for our people, there can never be manufacturers of any amount or value." An expanding America would thus always pro-vide a market for British goods.

He also argued that, as long as Britain avoided "tyranny and op-pression," there was no danger of the colonies rebelling. "While the government is mild and just, while important civil and religious rights are secure, such subjects will be dutiful and obedient." Then he pro-vided a metaphor that drew from his studies of turbulent waters: "The waves do not rise, but when the winds blow."

Britain would therefore be best served, he concluded, by treating the people of the colonies as full citizens of the empire, with the same liberties and rights and economic aspirations. He would, in the end, fail to sell the British ministry on this expansive vision of imperial har-mony. But he and others who argued for Britain's retention of Canada did prevail.[39]

BITTERSWEET FAREWELL

In the summer of 1762, five years after his arrival, Franklin finally decided it was time to return home. He was torn. He loved his life in England, both the acclaim (he had just been awarded an honorary doctorate at Oxford) and the friends and surrogate family he had made.

But the decision was made a bit easier because he assumed that he would soon be back. "The attraction of *reason* is at present for the other side of the water, but that of *inclination* will be for this side," he wrote Strahan. "You know which usually prevails." Indeed, his inclina-tion to be in England would prevail again within two years. He was, however, too optimistic about both his personal and public life when he added, "I shall probably make but this one vibration and settle here forever. Nothing will prevent it if I can, as I hope I can, prevail with Mrs. F. to accompany me."[40]

William was ready to return as well, and he needed a job. He had applied for appointment as deputy secretary of North Carolina and inquired about opportunities in the customs service and the Caribbean. But luck and good connections ended up producing something surprisingly better. The royal governor of New Jersey had just been recalled, and his presumed replacement decided to decline the post. Acting quietly to avoid alerting the Penns, William successfully lobbied for the job with the help of his father's friend John Pringle, who was the doctor and close adviser of the new prime minister, Lord Bute. When news of the pending appointment became public, the Penns surreptitiously tried to derail it by spreading word that he was a bastard, but to no avail.

William's appointment was partly an attempt by Bute and others to assure the loyalty of William's famous father, but there is no sign that the elder Franklin did much to help his son. Years later, Franklin would tell his friends in France that he had tried to dissuade his son from pursuing the post, or any appointed patronage position, by telling him of the time as a child when he had paid too much for a whistle. "Think of what the whistle may one day cost you," he said to William. "Why not become a joiner or a wheelwright, if the estate I leave you is not enough? The man who lives by his labor is at least free." William, however, had become infatuated with the title "excellency" as a way to emerge from his father's shadow.[41]

In possession of a public job, William was in need of a wife. So, at the same time he was securing his appointment, he was making plans to marry a sweet and well-born planter's daughter, Elizabeth Downes, a fixture of high Tory society whom he had met at the balls of London. His father had trouble extinguishing all hope that William would marry Polly Stevenson, but he finally gave his "consent and approbation" to the marriage.

In a letter to his sister Jane, Franklin professed to be pleased by William's new appointment and even more by his marriage. "The lady is of so amiable a character that the latter gives me more pleasure than the former, though I have no doubt but that he will make as good a governor as husband, for he has good principles and good dispositions, and I think is not deficient in good understanding." Yet Franklin, usually so fond of younger ladies and surrogate family members, did not warm up to Elizabeth, and never would.

Franklin was, in fact, unenthusiastic about, perhaps even bothered by, his son's successes. William's marriage to an upper-class woman was a declaration of independence, and his appointment as governor meant he was no longer subservient to his father. Indeed, it meant that William, then about 31, would have a station in life higher than his father's, one that would likely reinforce his son's unattractive tendency to adopt elitist airs and pretenses.

A cloud was coming over the horizon, and there was no lightning rod to defuse its emotional charge. The first signs of the tension that would develop between father and son came when Franklin decided to sail from England without him on August 24, 1762—the very day the news of William's pending appointment appeared in the papers and less than two weeks before his scheduled wedding. On September 4, William married Elizabeth Downes at the fashionable St. George's Church on Hanover Square, without his father in attendance. A few days later, he went to St. James's Palace, where he kissed the ring of young King George III and received his royal commission. His father, who had rushed back to London from Flanders a year earlier to witness George III's coronation, was not there. Then William and Elizabeth sailed for New Jersey, leaving William's secret son, Temple, behind in England.

With the cool detachment he could display toward his family, Franklin never expressed any sorrow or apologies for missing these momentous events in his son's life. In his parting letter to Polly Stevenson, on the other hand, he expressed great emotion and regret that she had not become his daughter-in-law. Writing from a "wretched inn" in Portsmouth, using the third person, he lamented that he "once flattered himself" that she "might become his own in the tender relation of a child, but can now entertain such pleasing hopes no more." Yet, though his son had not married her, Franklin promised that his paternal love would be undiminished. With more emotion than he ever used in his letters to his real daughter, he bid Polly farewell. "Adieu, my dearest child: I will call you so. Why should I not call you so, since I love you with all the tenderness, all the fondness of a father?"[42]

Franklin's mission to London had produced mixed results. The dispute over taxing the Proprietors had reached a compromise for the moment, and the end of the French and Indian War had calmed the larger disagreements over raising funds for colonial defense. Unresolved, however, was the underlying question of colonial governance. For Franklin, who saw himself equally as a Briton and an American, the answer was obvious. The powers of the colonial assemblies should evolve to mirror those of Parliament, and Englishmen on either side of the ocean should enjoy the same liberties. After five years in England, however, he had begun to realize that the Penns were not the only ones who saw things differently.

On his voyage home, Franklin resumed his study of the calming effect of oil on water, this time with more disturbing metaphorical implications. The lanterns aboard his ship had a thick layer of oil that floated atop a layer of water. The surface was always calm and flat, so viewed from above, it would seem that the oil had stilled the roiling water. But when the lantern was viewed from the side, so that both layers could be seen, it became evident that, as Franklin recorded, "the water under the oil was in great commotion." Even though oil could give the appearance of stilling turbulence, the water beneath the surface was still "rising and falling in irregular waves." This underlying turbulence, Franklin realized, was not something that could easily be calmed, even by the most judicious application of oil.[43]

CHAPTER NINE

HOME LEAVE

Philadelphia, 1763–1764

THE PERIPATETIC POSTMASTER

When William Franklin arrived in Philadelphia in February 1763, three months after his father's arrival, any tension between the two men quickly dissipated. He and his new wife stayed four days at Franklin's house, recovering from their frightful winter crossing, and then father and son set off for New Jersey. The local gentry came out in sleighs to escort them to Perth Amboy, a tiny village of two hundred homes, during a driving snowstorm. After William took his oath of office there, they traveled to repeat the ceremony in the colony's other capital, Burlington, where the festivities concluded "with bonfires, ringing of bells, firing of guns."

In Philadelphia, Franklin's enemies were appalled that his son had won a royal appointment. But Proprietor Thomas Penn, writing from London, suggested it might have a calming effect. "I am told you will find Mr. Franklin more tractable, and I believe we shall," he said. "His son must obey instructions, and what he is ordered to do the father cannot well oppose in Pennsylvania."[1]

That would turn out to be wishful thinking, because Franklin (at least for the time being) saw a distinction between instructions issued by the Proprietor and those issued by the king. Nevertheless, his first year back in America would be a peaceful one. He was, indeed, far more tractable about Pennsylvania politics—partly because he was less engaged by politics, and partly because he was less engaged by life in Pennsylvania. Always invigorated by travel and the pursuit of diverse interests, and clearly not wedded to the hearth and home he had forsaken for five years, Franklin left in April on a seven-month, 1,780-mile postal inspection tour that took him from Virginia to New Hampshire.

In Virginia, he performed one of those acts of quiet generosity that led him to have, even in controversial times, more loyal friends than enemies. His partner as colonial postmaster, William Hunter, had died, leaving a destitute illegitimate son. Franklin was asked by one of Hunter's friends to take care of the boy and oversee his education. It was a difficult assignment, and Franklin expressed some reluctance. "Like other older men, I begin in most things to consult my ease," he noted. "But I shall with pleasure undertake the charge you propose to me." With both an illegitimate son and grandson of his own, he was sensitive to the situation, and he noted that Hunter would have done the same for him.[2]

Franklin hoped that Hunter's death would mean that, after twenty-four years of service, he would become the sole postmaster in the colonies, as his original commission stipulated. That was not to be. Despite Franklin's ardent appeal to his superiors in London, Virginia's governor was able to secure the appointment of his secretary, John Foxcroft, as Franklin's new partner. Franklin's more collegial nature returned to the fore, and he forged a friendship with Foxcroft on his visit to Virginia. There was much work to be done. With Canada now part of the British Empire, they set up a system for extending mail delivery to Montreal. They also arranged for packet ships to the West Indies and for postal riders to travel at night. A letter sent from Philadelphia to Boston could receive a reply within six days, and a round-trip to New York could be done within twenty-four hours, a service that seems remarkable even now.

Foxcroft joined Franklin on a brief visit to Philadelphia, and then they left for New York and a tour of the northern post offices. Franklin ardently wanted Deborah to come. If she could learn to share his love for travel and curiosity about the world, he felt, she might even agree to accompany him to London someday. Not surprisingly, she again refused to be uprooted; she was as independent in her own way as he was in his. But their relationship was close enough that he gave her permission to open any mail he got from England, "as it must give you pleasure to see that people who knew me there so long and so intimately retain so sincere of a regard for me." There was more than vanity involved: the letters might, he hoped, soften her resistance to visiting England.[3]

In Deborah's stead, he took their daughter, Sally, then 19, on his tour. It would serve as her coming-out party. In New Jersey they stayed with William and Elizabeth, who took them to formal parties as well as pleasant excursions to the countryside. They then traveled by boat to Newport, where Sally had the pleasure (and it did indeed turn out to be that) of meeting her father's long-ago flirtation Caty, now Catherine Ray Greene, a married mother of two girls. (Never one to forget the women who had become parts of his extended family, he also exchanged letters with Polly Stevenson on the trip, noting that "the tender filial regard you constantly express for your old friend is particularly engaging.")[4]

Franklin dislocated his shoulder falling from his carriage, and Sally was willing to linger in Newport so that she and Caty could nurse him. But he was eager to press on to Boston. They stayed there for two months, Franklin living with his sister Jane Mecom and Sally with her cousins, who owned a harpsichord. "I would not have her lose her practice," Franklin explained to Jane, adding sweetly, "and then I shall be more with my dear sister."

During much of his stay in Boston, Franklin was confined to the house. He had suffered another fall, on a short trip to New Hampshire, and once again dislocated his shoulder. With most of his Boston relatives now dead, and his own stamina at age 57 diminished, his letters turned more reflective and less flirtatious. "I am not yet able to travel rough roads," he lamented to Caty. Nevertheless, he still harbored hopes of traveling to England again. "No friend can wish me more in England than I do myself," he wrote Strahan. "But before I go, everything I am concerned in must be settled here as to make another return to America unnecessary."[5]

When he got back to Philadelphia in November, he would find it harder than ever to settle affairs in a way that would allow him a sedentary retirement in England. More ferocious political turmoil, and four more crossings of the Atlantic, lay ahead. Franklin's seven-month tour of the colonies, along with the time he had spent in England, put him in a unique position to play a role in the coming storms. As a publishing magnate and then as a postmaster, he was one of the few to view America as a whole. To him, the colonies were not merely disparate entities. They were a new world with common interests and ideals.

During his postal trip, Franklin made plans and issued instructions for the construction of a new three-story brick home on Market Street, just steps from the spot where Deborah had first spotted him as a runaway lad. Since their common-law marriage in 1730, they had lived in at least six rented houses, but never one that they owned. Now, for the first time, they would have room to enjoy all the finery they had acquired since Deborah had bought him his first china breakfast bowl: the armonica and harpsichord, the stove and scientific equipment, the library and lace curtains.

Was Franklin becoming domesticated? In some ways, despite his love of travel and sometimes distant relationship to his own household, the aging runaway had always been a rather domestic soul, wherever he had lived. He loved his Junto and clubs, his regular routine, and the surrogate domestic arrangements he had made in England. He had also remained somewhat solicitous, even caring, about his wife and daughter, as well as his relatives, even as he indulged his wanderlust. Whether his new house was intended for his own enjoyment or mainly for that of his family was unclear, perhaps even to himself, but his love of projects led him to be deeply involved in all the details, down to the quality of the doorknobs and hinges.

Despite what he had written Strahan, the conflict about which side of the ocean he would inhabit was still unresolved. Deborah, for sure, still had no desire to live more than a few hundred yards from where she had been raised. "My mother is so averse to going to sea that I believe my father will never be induced to see England again," William wrote in his own letter to Strahan. "He is now building a house to live in himself." Franklin had also flirted with the idea of getting a land grant in Ohio, looking west rather than east. By late in 1763, he was confessing to Strahan that he was baffled about where he would spend his remaining years: "We shall see in a little time how things will turn out."[6]

THE PAXTON BOYS

Franklin's future plans would depend, in part, on the conduct of Pennsylvania's new governor, John Penn, who was a nephew of Proprietor Thomas Penn and had been a delegate with Franklin to the Albany Conference. Franklin was hopeful. "He is civil," he wrote to Collinson, "so I think we shall have no personal difference, at least I will give him no occasion."

The first issue that Penn and the Pennsylvania Assembly faced was frontier defense. The British victory in the French and Indian War had not fully secured peace with all of the Indians, and settlers in the west were being plagued by raids led by the Ottawa chief known as Pontiac. By the fall of 1763, the fighting had subsided, but not the resentments of many of Pennsylvania's rough-hewn backwoodsmen.

These erupted on December 14, when a mob of more than fifty frontiersmen from around the town of Paxton murdered six unarmed Indians, all of them peaceful, converted Christians. Two weeks later, an even larger mob slaughtered fourteen more Indians who had been harbored for their safety in a nearby workhouse.

The "Paxton Boys," as the growing mob of frontiersmen came to be called, declared that their next stop was Philadelphia, where more than 140 other peaceful Indians were being sheltered. They threatened to kill not only the Indians but also any whites who protected them, including prominent Quakers. This provoked some Quakers to set aside pacifism and take up arms, and it led others to flee the city.

The uprising threatened to become the most serious crisis Pennsylvania had ever faced, a full-fledged social and religious civil war. On one side were the frontiersmen, mainly Presbyterians, plus their working-class sympathizers in town, including many German Lutherans and Scots-Irish Presbyterians. On the other side were Philadelphia's old-line Quakers, with their pacifist proclivities and desire to

trade with the Indians. The Quakers, despite being now easily out-
numbered by the new German immigrants, dominated the Assembly
and repeatedly resisted spending much for frontier defense. For a
change, Philadelphia's upper-class Anglican merchants, who tended
to support the Proprietors in their fights with the Assembly, found
themselves allied with the Quakers, at least temporarily.

A virulent pamphlet war ensued. Philadelphia's Presbyterians, supporting their backwoods brethren, assailed the Quakers for coddling
the Indians and refusing to allow the frontiersmen the proper representation in the Assembly that was decreed in the charter. Franklin responded with his own pamphlet in late January 1764. Entitled "A
Narrative of the Late Massacres in Lancaster County," it was among
the most emotional pieces he ever wrote.

He began his screed with poignant profiles of each of the Indians
killed, which stressed their gentle personalities and used their English
names. "These poor, defenseless creatures were immediately fired
upon, stabbed and hatcheted to death!" he wrote, describing the massacre in gory detail. The eldest Indian was "cut to pieces in his bed,"
the others "scalped and otherwise horribly mangled."

Franklin went on to describe the second massacre two weeks later
in even more horrid terms:

> Being without the least weapon for defense, they divided into their
> little families, the children clinging to their parents. They fell on their
> knees, protested their innocence, declared their love to the English, and
> that, in their whole lives, they had never done them injury; and in this
> posture they all received the hatchet! Men, women and little children—
> were every one inhumanly murdered!—in cold blood!

To the Paxton Boys, all Indians were alike and there was no need to
treat them as individuals. "Whoever proclaimed war," their spokesman declared, "with part of a nation, and not with the whole?" Franklin, on the other hand, used his pamphlet to denounce prejudice and
make the case for individual tolerance that was at the core of his political creed. "If an Indian injures me, does it follow that I may revenge
that injury on all Indians?" he asked. "The only crime of these poor
wretches seems to have been that they had a reddish brown skin and

black hair." It was immoral, he argued, to punish an individual as revenge for what others of his race, tribe, or group may have done. "Should any man with a freckled face and red hair kill a wife or child of mine, [by this reasoning] it would be right for me to revenge it by killing all the freckled red-haired men, women and children I could afterwards anywhere meet."

To reinforce his point, he provided historical examples of how various other people—Jews, Muslims, Moors, blacks, and Indians—had all shown a greater morality and tolerance in similar situations. It was necessary, Franklin concluded, for the entire province to stand up to the Paxton Boys as they prepared to march on Philadelphia and to bring them to justice. Ignoring the slight inconsistency in his argument, he warned of the collective guilt all whites would otherwise share: "The guilt will lie on the whole land till justice is done on the murderers."[7]

The pamphlet would later damage Franklin politically, for it reflected his underlying prejudice against the German settlers as well as his lifelong distaste for Presbyterian-Calvinist dogma. He showed little sympathy for the grievances of the frontiersmen, calling them "barbarous men" who had acted "to the eternal disgrace of their country and color." Though a populist in many ways, he was wary of the rabble. His outlook, as usual, was from the perspective of a new middle class: distrustful both of the unwashed mob and of the entrenched elites.

On Saturday, February 4, a week or so after Franklin's pamphlet was published, Gov. John Penn called a mass meeting on the State House grounds as the Paxton Boys headed toward the city. At first he took a strong stand. He ordered the arrest of the mob leaders, deployed British troops, and asked the crowd to join the militia companies that Franklin and others were organizing. Even many Quakers took up arms, though most of the town's Presbyterians refused.

At midnight on Sunday, the mob of 250 reached Germantown, just north of the city. Church bells pealed alarms, and amid the chaos a surprising alliance was formed. Governor Penn, Franklin wrote a friend, "did me the honor, on an alarm, to run to my house at midnight, with his counselors at his heels, for advice, and made it his headquarters for some time." Penn went so far as to offer Franklin control of the militia, but Franklin prudently declined. "I chose to carry a musket and strengthen his authority by setting an example of obedience to his orders."[8]

Franklin and others, including many Quakers, wanted the governor to order an attack. Instead, Penn decided to send a delegation of seven city leaders, including Franklin, to meet with the Paxton Boys. "The fighting face we put on and the reasonings we used with the insurgents," Franklin later recalled, "restored quiet to the city." The mob agreed to disperse if they could send some of their leaders into town to present their grievances.

As the tension with the Paxton Boys receded, the antagonism between Franklin and Penn resumed. Franklin took a hard line. He wanted the governor and Assembly, acting jointly, to confront the Paxton delegation together and hold them accountable for the massacres. The governor, however, realized the political advantage he could gain by forging an alliance with the Presbyterians and Germans who sympathized with the frontiersmen (and who were offended by the harsh slurs Franklin had written about them). So he met with the Paxton delegation in private, listened to them courteously, and agreed not to press charges against them. He also, at their suggestion, instituted a policy of offering a bounty for any Indian scalps, male or female.

Franklin was livid. "These things bring him and his government into sudden contempt," he wrote a friend. "All regard for him in the Assembly is lost. All hopes of happiness under a Proprietary government are at an end." The feeling was mutual. In a letter to his uncle, the Proprietor Thomas Penn, Gov. John Penn wrote an equally strong condemnation of Franklin: "There will never be any prospect of ease and happiness while that villain has the liberty of spreading about the poison of that inveterate malice and ill nature which is deeply implanted in his own black heart."

A darkness had indeed begun to infect Franklin's usually optimistic heart. Feeling confined by Philadelphia and its foul politics, restless at home, and finding few scientific or professional diversions, he lost some of his amused, wry demeanor. His letters contained harsh rather than humorous assessments of politics and even gloomier personal passages. To the medical doctor John Fothergill, a Quaker friend living in London, Franklin wrote, "Do you please yourself with the fancy that you are doing good? You are mistaken. Half the lives you save are not worth saving, as being useless; and almost the other half ought not to be saved, as being mischievous."[9]

FIGHTING THE PROPRIETORS AGAIN

And so the fights between governor and Assembly resumed, more heated than ever. They clashed over control of militia appointments, a lighthouse, and, of course, taxes. When the Assembly passed a bill taxing the Proprietors' estates, which followed the general outline but not the precise formula of the Privy Council compromise, Franklin wrote a message from the Assembly to the governor warning that the consequences of vetoing the bill "will undoubtedly add to that load of obloquy and guilt the Proprietary family is already burdened with and bring their government into (if possible) still greater contempt." The governor vetoed it.[10]

At stake was not just principle but power. Franklin realized that the Proprietary party now had strong support from the frontiersmen and their Scots-Irish and German kinsmen. That reignited his resolve to continue pursuing, against all odds, his dream of convincing the British to revoke the Proprietors' charter and make Pennsylvania a Crown colony.

Most people in Pennsylvania still did not share his fervor for a royal rather than Proprietary government. The members of Philadelphia's merchant aristocracy were friends with the Penns. The Presbyterian frontiersmen and ethnic working class had forged a new alliance after the Paxton Boys affair, plus they feared a royal takeover would bring the official establishment of the Church of England, which their dissenting families had fled. Even many prominent Quakers such as Isaac Norris and Israel Pemberton, who tended to be Franklin's allies, were leery of a new charter that might remove some of the religious liberties that the late William Penn had secured long ago. With his stubborn crusade, Franklin was succeeding in dividing his friends and uniting his enemies.

Likewise, in London there was no more support for a royal takeover than there had been when Franklin began his crusade as an agent there. Lord Hyde, Franklin's boss at the British postal department, wrote that even those royal ministers who might like to "get their hands on" the colony were not willing to take on the Penn family. He publicly warned Franklin, a royal appointee, that "all officers of the crown are expected to assist government." Franklin made a little joke of the warning, noting that he would "not be Hyde-bound."[11]

Nevertheless, Franklin still enjoyed effective control of the Assembly, and in March 1764 he pushed through a series of twenty-six resolutions—a "necklace of resolves," he called them—calling for the end of Proprietary government. The Proprietors, he wrote, had acted in ways that were "tyrannical and inhuman." They had used the Indian threat "to extort privileges from the people . . . with the knife of savages at their throat." The final resolution declared that the Assembly would consult citizens as to whether a "humble address" should be sent to the king "praying that he would be graciously pleased to take the people of this province under his immediate protection and government."

The result was a petition drive asking for the ouster of the Proprietors. Franklin printed copies in English and German, and even created a slightly different version for the Quaker community, but his supporters could garner merely thirty-five hundred signers. Opponents of the change were eventually able to come up with fifteen thousand on their own petitions.

Once again, a pamphlet war broke out. Franklin's contribution, "Cool Thoughts on the Present Situation," was more heated than its title implied. He was not, at least for now, detached enough to employ his old tools of humor, satire, indirection, and gentle wryness in argument. His pamphlet attacked the Proprietors for truckling to the Paxton Boys and for being unable to manage the colony. "Religion has happily nothing to do with our present differences, though great pains is taken to lug it into the squabble," he wrote, not altogether correctly.

In any case, he continued, the Crown rather than the Proprietors was most likely to protect religious liberties.

Franklin's newest opponent was John Dickinson, a young lawyer who was the son-in-law of the great Quaker eminence, Isaac Norris. Dickinson had been a friend of Franklin's and no great fan of the Proprietors, but he rationally argued that the safeguards of the Penn charter should not be lightly abandoned, nor should it be assumed that the royal ministers would be more enlightened than the Proprietors. Norris, unwilling to be caught in the crossfire, feigned sickness and resigned as Assembly speaker in May. Franklin was elected to the post.

Franklin also faced a more vitriolic older opponent: Chief Justice William Allen, who had also once been a friend but whose ardent support of the Proprietors had long ago led to a bitter break. When Allen returned from a trip to England in August, Franklin paid him a visit as "an overture." In front of other guests, Allen denounced his assault on the Proprietors. A switch to a royal government, he said, would cost Pennsylvania £100,000, and it had no support in London.

As the October 1 Assembly elections neared, the pamphlet war turned vicious as Franklin's foes sought to thwart his bid for reelection. One anonymous offering, entitled "What is Sauce for a Goose is also Sauce for a Gander," raked up every possible allegation against Franklin—most notably, that his son, William, was the bastard child of a "kitchen wench" named Barbara. It also reprinted, and embellished a bit, various anti-German passages Franklin had written earlier. And it accused him, falsely but vociferously, of buying honorary degrees, seeking a royal governorship for himself, and stealing his electricity experiments from other scientists.

Another broadside painted him as an excitable lecher:

> Franklin, though plagued with fumbling age,
> Needs nothing to excite him,
> But is too ready to engage,
> When younger arms invite him.[12]

Modern election campaigns are often criticized for being negative, and today's press is slammed for being scurrilous. But the most brutal of modern attack ads pale in comparison to the barrage of pamphlets in the 1764 Assembly election. Pennsylvania survived them, as did Franklin, and American democracy learned that it could thrive in an atmosphere of unrestrained, even intemperate, free expression. As the election of 1764 showed, American democracy was built on a foundation of unbridled free speech. In the centuries since then, the nations that have thrived have been those, like America, that are most comfortable with the cacophony, and even occasional messiness, that comes from robust discourse.

Election Day was as wild as the pamphlets. Throngs of voters clogged the State House steps throughout the day of October 1, and the lines remained long well past midnight. Franklin's supporters were able to force the polls to stay open until dawn as they roused anyone they could find who had not yet voted. It was a tactical mistake. The Proprietary party sent workers up to Germantown to round up even more supporters. Franklin finished thirteenth out of fourteen candidates vying for the eight seats in Philadelphia.

His faction, however, kept control of the Assembly, which promptly voted to submit to the British ministers the petition against the Proprietors. And as a consolation prize that was perhaps better than a victory, it voted 19–11 to send Franklin back to England as an agent to present it.

That prompted a new flurry of pamphlets. Dickinson declared that Franklin would be ineffectual because he was hated by the Penns, disdained by the king's ministers, and "extremely disagreeable to a very great number of the serious and reputable inhabitants" of Pennsylvania. Chief Justice Allen labeled him "the most unpopular and odious name in the province . . . delirious with rage, disappointment and malice." But now that he was heading back to England, Franklin's even temper started to return. "I am now to take leave (perhaps a last leave) of the country I love," he wrote in response. "I wish every kind of prosperity to my friends, and I forgive my enemies."[13]

Once again, his wife declined to accompany him to England. Nor would she permit him to take their daughter. So why was he so willing to leave home again? Partly because he missed London, and partly because he felt depressed and confined by Philadelphia.

There was also a loftier reason. Franklin had been developing a vision of an American future that went beyond even wresting Pennsylvania from the Proprietors. It involved a greater union among the colonies, along the lines of his Albany Plan, and a more equal relationship between the colonies and the mother country as part of a greater British Empire. That could include, he suggested, representation in Parliament. Responding to reports that Britain might propose taxes on the colonies, he wrote to Richard Jackson, whom he had left behind in London as Pennsylvania's other agent, a suggested response: "If you choose to tax us, give us members in your legislature, and let us be one people."

As he prepared to leave for England in November 1764, Franklin wrote a letter to his daughter. It included paternal exhortations to be "dutiful and tender towards your good mama" and typical Franklin advice, such as "to acquire those useful accomplishments arithmetic and bookkeeping." But it also contained a more serious note. "I have many enemies," he said. "Your slightest indiscretions will be magnified into crimes, in order the more sensibly to wound and afflict me. It is therefore the more necessary for you to be extremely circumspect in all your behavior that no advantage may be given to their malevolence."

He also had many supporters. More than three hundred cheered him as he left Philadelphia for his ship. Cannons were fired as a send-off, and a song was sung to the tune of "God Save the King," with the new ending "Franklin on thee we fix / God save us all." He told some friends that he expected to be gone only a few months, others that he might never return. It is not clear which prediction, if either, he truly believed, but as it turned out, neither proved correct.[14]

CHAPTER TEN

AGENT PROVOCATEUR

London, 1765–1770

AN EXTENDED FAMILY

Mrs. Stevenson was out when Franklin arrived, unannounced, at his old home on Craven Street, and her maid did not know where to find her. "So I sat me down and waited her return," Franklin recalled in a letter to her daughter, Polly. "She was a good deal surprised to find me in her parlor." Surprised, perhaps, but prepared. His rooms had been left vacant, for his English friends and surrogate family had no doubt he would someday return.[1]

It would be just a short visit, he led his real wife, and perhaps even himself, to believe. He wanted to be back home by the end of the summer, he wrote Deborah soon after his arrival. "A few months, I hope, will finish affairs here to my wish, and bring me to that retirement and repose with my little family." She had heard that many times before. He would, in fact, never see her again. Despite her pleas and declining health, he would continue his increasingly futile mission for more than ten years, right up to the eve of the Revolution.

That mission involved complex balancing acts that would test all of Franklin's wiles. On the one hand, he was still a committed royalist who wanted to stay in favor with the king's ministers in order to wrest Pennsylvania from the hated Penns. He also had personal motives: protecting his postmastership, perhaps achieving an even higher appointment, and pursuing his dream of a land grant. On the other hand, once it became clear that the British government had little sympathy for colonial rights, he would have to scramble to reestablish his reputation as an American patriot.[2]

In the meantime, Franklin had the pleasure of settling back into the life he loved in London. Sir John Pringle, the distinguished physician, had become his best friend. They played chess, made the rounds to their regular coffeehouse clubs, and soon got into the habit of taking summer trips together. The great Samuel Johnson biographer James Boswell was another acquaintance. After dropping in on one of their chess games, Boswell noted in his journal that Pringle had "a peculiar sour manner," but that Franklin was, as always, "all jollity and pleasantry." Franklin and Mrs. Stevenson resumed their relationship of domestic convenience, and Polly, still living with an aunt in the countryside, remained an object of Franklin's paternal affection and intellectual flirtation.

He picked Polly as his first potential convert to a new phonetic alphabet that he had invented in a quixotic quest to simplify English spelling. It is easy to see why it did not catch on. "Kansider chis alfabet, and giv mi instanses af syts Inlis uyrds and saunds az iu mee hink kannat perfektlyi bi eksprest byi it," went one of his more comprehensible sentences. After a long reply that is near impossible to translate, in which she halfheartedly says the alphabet "myit bi uv syrvis," she lapses into standard English to conclude, "With ease & with sincerity, I can in the old way subscribe myself . . ."

It was a measure of their intellectual bonding that Polly would indulge this linguistic fantasy as faithfully as she did. Franklin's phonetic reform showed little of his usual regard for utility, and it took his passion for social improvement to radical extremes. It required the invention of six new letters for which there were no printing fonts, and it dropped six other letters that Franklin considered superfluous. Answering Polly's many objections, he insisted that the difficulty in learning the new spellings would be overcome by the logic behind them, and he dismissed her concerns that the words would be divorced from their etymological roots and thus lose their power. But he soon gave up the endeavor. Years later, he turned his scheme over to Noah Webster. The famed lexicographer reprinted Franklin's letters to

Polly in his 1789 book *Dissertations on the English Language* (which he dedicated to Franklin) and called the project "deeply interesting," but added, "Whether it will be defeated by insolence and prejudice remains for my countrymen to determine."[3]

Franklin brought his grandson, Temple, the illegitimate son of his own illegitimate son, out of anonymity and into his odd domestic orbit on Craven Street. The relationship was weird, even by Franklin family standards. The boy, who was 4 when Franklin reestablished contact, had been cared for by a series of women who sent itemized bills for his expenses (haircuts, inoculations, clothes) to Mrs. Stevenson, who then sought reimbursement from William in New Jersey. In all of his letters to Deborah at the time, filled with details of various friends and acquaintances, Franklin never mentioned Temple. But by the time the boy turned 9, William was asking, in a quite cowardly way, whether his son could be brought to live with him in America. "He might then take his proper name and be introduced as the son of a poor relation, for whom I stood Godfather and intended to bring up as my own."

Foreshadowing a later struggle for the boy's allegiance, Franklin instead took him under his own wing. On Craven Street he was known merely as "William Temple," and Franklin enrolled him in a school run by William Strahan's brother-in-law, an eccentric educator who shared Franklin's passion for spelling reform. Even though Temple became part of the extended Stevenson family, they pretended (at least publicly) to be unaware of his exact provenance.

(As late as 1774, in a letter describing a wedding in which he was an usher, Polly would refer to him as "Mr. Temple, a young gentleman who is at school here and is under the care of Dr. Franklin." Not until later, after Franklin and his grandson returned to America and Temple took up his true last name, did Polly confess that she suspected all along that there was some relationship. "I rejoiced to hear he has the addition of Franklin [to his name], which I always knew he had some right to.")[4]

THE STAMP ACT OF 1765

Back in Philadelphia, Franklin was still seen as a "tribune of the people" and a defender of their rights. When word finally reached there in March 1765 of his safe arrival in London, bells were rung "almost all night," his supporters "ran about like mad men," and copious quantities of "libations" were drunk to his health. But their joy would be fleeting. Franklin was about to become embroiled in a controversy over the notorious Stamp Act, which would require a tax stamp on every newspaper, book, almanac, legal document, and deck of cards.[5]

It was the first time that Parliament had proposed a major internal tax on the colonies. Franklin believed that Parliament had the right to impose external taxes, such as duties and tariffs, to regulate trade. But he thought it unwise, perhaps even unconstitutional, for Parliament to levy an internal tax on people who had no representation in that assembly. Nevertheless, he did not fight the Stamp Act proposal with much vigor. Instead, he tried to play conciliator.

He and a small group of colonial agents met in February 1765 with George Grenville, the prime minister, who explained that the high cost of the Indian wars made some tax on the colonies necessary. What was a better way to levy it? Franklin argued that it should be done in the "usual constitutional way," which meant by a request from the king to the various colonial legislatures, who alone had the power to tax their own inhabitants. Would Franklin and his fellow agents, Grenville asked, be able to commit that the colonies would agree to the proper amount and how to apportion it among themselves? Franklin and the others admitted that they could make no firm commitment.

Franklin offered another alternative a few days later. It stemmed from his long-standing desire, both as a rather sophisticated economic theorist and as a printer, to have more paper currency circulating in America. Parliament, he proposed, could authorize new bills of credit that would be issued to borrowers at 6 percent interest. These paper bills would serve as legal tender and circulate like currency, thus increasing America's money supply, and Britain would collect the interest instead of levying direct internal taxes. "It will operate as a general tax on the colonies, and yet not an unpleasing one," said Franklin. "The rich, who handle most money, would in reality pay most of the tax." Grenville was, in Franklin's words, "besotted with his stamp scheme," and dismissed the idea. This may have been fortunate for Franklin, as he later heard that even his friends in Philadelphia disliked his paper credit idea as well.[6]

When the Stamp Act passed in March, Franklin made the mistake of taking a pragmatic attitude. He recommended that his good friend John Hughes be appointed the collection officer in Pennsylvania. "Your undertaking to execute it may make you unpopular for a time, but your acting with coolness and steadiness and with every circumstance in your power of favor to the people will by degrees reconcile them," he mistakenly argued in a letter to Hughes. "In the meantime, a firm loyalty to the Crown and faithful adherence to the government of this nation will always be the wisest course for you and I to take, whatever may be the madness of the populace." In his desire to remain on decent terms with the royal ministers, Franklin badly underestimated the madness of the populace back home.

Thomas Penn, on the other hand, played the situation cleverly. He refused to offer his own candidate for stamp collector, saying that if he did so "the people might suppose we were consenting to the laying this load upon them." John Dickinson, Franklin's young adversary as the leader of the Proprietary party in the Assembly, drew up a declaration of grievances against the Stamp Act that resoundingly passed.[7]

It was one of Franklin's worst political misjudgments. His hatred of the Penns blinded him to the fact that most of his fellow Pennsylvanians hated taxes imposed from London more. "I took every step in my power to prevent the passing of the Stamp Act," he claimed unconvincingly to his Philadelphia friend Charles Thomson, "but the tide was too strong against us." He then went on to argue the case for pragmatism: "We might well have hindered the sun's setting. That we could not do. But since it is down, my friend, and it may be long before it rises again, let us make as good a night of it as we can. We may still light candles."

The letter, which became public, was a public relations disaster for Franklin. Thomson replied that Philadelphians, rather than being willing to light candles, were ready to launch "the works of darkness." By September, it was clear that this could include mob violence. "A sort of frenzy or madness has got such hold of the people of all ranks that I fancy some lives will be lost before this fire is put out," a frightened Hughes wrote the man who had gotten him what had become an unenviable job.[8]

Franklin's printing partner, David Hall, sent a similar warning. "The spirit of the people is so violently against everyone they think has the least concern with the Stamp law," he wrote. Angry Philadelphians had "imbibed the notion that you had a hand in the framing of it, which has occasioned you many enemies." He added that he would be afraid for Franklin's safety if he were to return. A cartoon printed in Philadelphia showed the devil whispering in Franklin's ear: "Thee shall be agent, Ben, for all my dominions."[9]

The frenzy climaxed one evening in late September 1765 when a mob gathered at a Philadelphia coffeehouse. Leaders of the rabble accused Franklin of advocating the Stamp Act, and they set out to level his new home, along with those of Hughes and other Franklin supporters. "If I live until tomorrow morning, I shall give you a farther account," Hughes wrote in a log he later sent Franklin.

Deborah dispatched their daughter to New Jersey for safety. But ever the homebound stalwart, she refused to flee. Her cousin Josiah Davenport arrived with more than twenty friends to help defend her. Her account of that night, while harrowing, is also a testament to her strength. She described it in a letter to her husband:

> Toward night I said he [cousin Davenport] should fetch a gun or two, as we had none. I sent to ask my brother to come and bring his gun. Also we made one room the magazine. I ordered some sort of defense upstairs as I could manage myself. I said when I was advised to remove that I was very sure you had done nothing to hurt anybody, nor I had not given any offense to any person at all. Nor would I be made uneasy by anybody. Nor would I stir.

Franklin's house and his wife were saved when a group of supporters, dubbed the White Oak Boys, gathered a force to confront the mob. If Franklin's house was destroyed, they declared, so too would be the homes of anyone involved. Finally, the mob dispersed. "I honor much the spirit and courage you showed," he wrote Deborah after hearing of her ordeal. "The woman deserves a good house that is determined to defend it."[10]

The Stamp Act crisis sparked a radical transformation in American affairs. A new group of colonial leaders, who bristled at being subservient to England, were coming to the fore, especially in Virginia and Massachusetts. Even though most Americans harbored few separatist or nationalist sentiments until 1775, the clash between imperial control and colonial rights was erupting on a variety of fronts. Young Patrick Henry, 29, rose in Virginia's House of Burgesses to decry taxation without representation. "Caesar had his Brutus, Charles the First his Cromwell, and George the Third . . ." He was interrupted by shouts of "Treason!" before he could finish, but it was clear that some colonists were becoming deadly serious. Soon he would find an ally in Thomas Jefferson. In Boston, a group that would take the name the Sons of Liberty met at a distillery and attacked the homes of the Massachusetts tax commissioner and Gov. Thomas Hutchinson. Among the rising patriots there who would eventually become rebels were a young merchant named John Hancock, a fiery agitator named Samuel Adams, and his sour lawyer cousin John Adams.

For the first time since the Albany Conference of 1754, leaders from different parts of America were galvanized into thinking as a collective unit. A congress of nine colonies, including Pennsylvania, was held in New York in October. Not only did it urge the repeal of the Stamp Act, it denied the right of Parliament to levy internal taxes on the colonies. The motto they adopted was the one Franklin had written as a cartoon caption more than a decade earlier, as he sought to rally unity at Albany: "Join, or Die."

From his distance in London, Franklin was slow to join the frenzy. "The rashness of the Assembly in Virginia is amazing," he wrote Hughes. "I hope, however, that ours will keep within the bounds of prudence and moderation." For the time being, he was still more in sympathy with Governor Hutchinson of Massachusetts, later a great enemy. Both were reasonable men appalled by mob rule, and in this case threatened by it. "When you and I were at Albany ten years ago,"

Hutchinson wrote him, "we did not propose a union for such purposes as these."[11]

Franklin's moderation was due in part to his temperament, his love of Britain, and his dreams of a harmonious empire. It was in his nature to be a smooth operator rather than a revolutionary. He liked witty discussion over Madeira, and he hated disorder and mob behavior. The fine wines and meals contributed not only to his gout, but also to his blurred vision about the animosity that was building back home. Perhaps more important, he was making one last attempt to turn Pennsylvania into a royal rather than Proprietary colony.

It was always an unlikely quest, now all the more so because of the turmoil over the Stamp Act, which made royal rule less popular in Pennsylvania and made colonial pleadings less popular in London. In November 1765, a year after Franklin's arrival and just as he was absorbing the damage done to his reputation by his waffling over the Stamp Act, the Privy Council officially deferred action on the anti-Penn petition he had brought. Franklin initially believed (or at least publicly professed) that this was merely a temporary setback. But he soon came to realize that Thomas Penn was correct when he wrote to his nephew, Gov. John Penn, that the action meant the issue was dead "forever."[12]

SPIN CYCLE

By the end of 1765, with his reputation as a defender of colonial rights in tatters because of his equivocation over the Stamp Act, Franklin faced one of the great challenges in the annals of political damage control. He began with a letter-writing campaign. To his partner David Hall and others, he strongly denied that he had ever supported the act. He also had prominent London Quakers write on his behalf. "I can safely aver that Benjamin Franklin did all in his power to prevent the Stamp Act from passing," John Fothergill wrote a Philadelphia friend. "He asserted the rights and privileges of America with the utmost firmness." Hall reprinted the letter in the *Pennsylvania Gazette*.

Franklin felt the best way to force repeal, one that appealed to his

Poor Richard penchant for frugality and self-reliance, was for Americans to boycott British imports and refrain from transactions that would require use of the stamps. This approach would also rally British tradesmen and manufacturers, hurt by the loss of exports, to the cause of repeal. Writing anonymously as "Homespun" in a British paper, he ridiculed the notion that Americans could not get by without such British imports as tea. If need be, they would make tea from corn. "Its green ears roasted are a delicacy beyond expression."[13]

Franklin's two sardonic essays signed Homespun were among at least thirteen attacks on the Stamp Act that he published in a three-month period. In one hoax, signed "A Traveler," he claimed that America had no need of British wool because "the very tails of the American sheep are so laden with wool that each has a car or wagon on four little wheels to support and keep it from trailing on the ground." Writing as "Pacificus Secundus," he resorted to his old tactic of scathing satire by pretending to support the idea that military rule be imposed in the colonies. It would take only fifty thousand British soldiers at a cost of merely £12 million a year. "It may be objected that by ruining our colonies, killing one half the people, and driving the rest over the mountains, we may deprive ourselves of their custom for our manufacturers; but a moment's consideration will satisfy us that since we have lost so much of our European trade, it can be only the demand in America that keeps up and has of late so greatly enhanced the price of those manufacturers, and therefore a stop put to that demand will be an advantage to all of us, as we may thereafter buy our own goods cheaper." The only downside for England, he noted, was that "multitudes of our poor may starve for want of employment."[14]

(As has been frequently noted, Franklin often wrote anonymously or using a pseudonym, beginning as a young teen when he wrote as Silence Dogood and then as the Busy-Body, Alice Addertongue, Poor Richard, Homespun, and others. Sometimes, he was trying to be truly anonymous; at other times, he was wearing only a thin mask. This practice was not unusual, indeed it was quite common, among writers of the eighteenth century, including such Franklin heroes as Addison, Steele, and Defoe. "Scarce one part in ten of the valuable books which are published are with the author's name," Addison once declared, with a bit of exaggeration. At the time, writing anonymously was considered cleverer, less vulgar, and less likely to lead to libel or sedition charges. Gentlemen sometimes thought it was beneath their stature to have their names on pamphlets and press pieces. The practice also assured that dissenting political and religious writings were rebutted on their merits rather than by personal attacks.)[15]

Franklin also produced a political cartoon, a counterpart to his "Join, or Die," that showed a bloodied and dismembered British Empire, its limbs labeled with the names of colonies. The motto underneath, "Give a Penny to Belisarius," referred to the Roman general who oppressed his provinces and died in poverty. He had the cartoon printed on note cards, hired a man to hand them out in front of Parliament, and sent one to his sister Jane Mecom. "The moral," he told her, "is that the colonies may be ruined, but that Britain would thereby be maimed." Enforcing the Stamp Act, he warned one British minister, would end up "creating a deep-rooted aversion between the two countries and laying the foundation of a future total separation."[16]

Still a loyal Briton, Franklin was eager to prevent such a split. His preferred solution was colonial representation in Parliament. In a set of notes he prepared for his meetings with ministers, Franklin jotted down the argument: "Representation useful two ways. It brings information and knowledge to the great council. It conveys back to the remote parts of the empire the reasons of public conduct . . . It will forever preserve the union which otherwise may be various ways broken."

But he also warned that the time to seize that opportunity was passing. "The time has been when the colonies would have esteemed it a great advantage as well as honor to them to be permitted to send members to Parliament," he wrote a friend in January 1766. "The time is now come when they are indifferent about it, and will probably not ask it, though they might accept it if offered them; and the time will come when they will certainly refuse it."

Short of representation in Parliament, Franklin wrote, "the next best thing" would be the traditional method of requesting funds to be appropriated by each of the colonial legislatures. In the notes he wrote for his conversation with ministers, he suggested a third alternative that would be a step toward independence for the colonies: "empowering them to send delegates from each Assembly to a common council." In other words, the American colonies would form their own federal legislature rather than be subject to the laws of Parliament. The only thing that would then unite the two parts of the British Empire would be loyalty to the king. It derived from the plan he had proposed more than a decade earlier; next to this idea in his notes he wrote the phrase "Albany Plan."[17]

On February 13, 1766, Franklin got the chance to present his case directly to Parliament. His dramatic appearance was a masterpiece of both lobbying and theater, helpfully choreographed by his supporters in that body. In one afternoon of highly charged testimony, he would turn himself into the foremost spokesman for the American cause and brilliantly restore his reputation back home.

Many of the 174 questions directed at him were scripted in advance by leaders of the new Whig ministry of Lord Rockingham, which was sympathetic to the colonies and was looking for a way out of the Stamp Act debacle. Others were more hostile. Through it all, Franklin was cogent and calm. The questioning was begun by a member whose manufacturing business had been hurt by the breakdown in trade, who asked Franklin whether the Americans already paid taxes voluntarily to Britain. "Certainly many, and very heavy taxes," he replied, and he went on to recount their history in detail (though leaving out some of the disputes over taxing of Proprietary lands).

An adversary broke in. "Are not the colonies," he asked, "very able to pay the Stamp duty?" Replied Franklin: "There is not gold and silver enough in the colonies to pay the stamp duty for one year."

Grenville, who had proposed the act, defended it by asking whether Franklin didn't agree that the colonies should pay for the defense provided them by royal forces. The Americans, Franklin countered, had defended themselves, and by doing so had defended British interests as well. "The colonies raised, clothed and paid, during the last war, near 25,000 men and spent many millions," he explained, adding that only a small portion had been reimbursed.

The larger issue, Franklin stressed, was how to promote harmony within the British Empire. Before the Stamp Act was imposed, asked a supporter named Grey Cooper, "What was the temper of America towards Great Britain?"

Franklin: The best in the world. They submitted willingly to the government of the Crown, and paid, in all their courts, obedience to the acts of Parliament . . . They cost you nothing in forts, citadels, garrisons or armies to keep them in subjection. They were governed by this country at the expense of only a little pen, ink and paper. They were led by a thread. They had not only a respect but an affection for Great Britain; for its laws, its customs and manners, and even a fondness for its fashions, which greatly increased the commerce.

Cooper: And what is their temper now?

Franklin: Oh, very much altered.

Cooper: In what light did the people of America used to consider the Parliament?

Franklin: They considered the Parliament as the great bulwark and security of their liberties.

Cooper: And have they not still the same respect?

Franklin: No, it is greatly lessened.

Once again, Franklin emphasized a distinction between external and internal taxes. "I have never heard any objection to the right of laying duties to regulate commerce. But a right to lay internal taxes was never supposed to be in Parliament, as we are not represented there."

Would America submit to a compromise? No, said Franklin, it was a matter of principle. So only military force could compel them to pay the Stamp Tax?

"I do not see how a military force could be applied to that purpose," Franklin answered.

Question: Why may it not?

Franklin: Suppose a military force is sent into America. They will find nobody in arms. What are they then to do? They cannot force a man to take stamps who chooses to do without them. They will not find a rebellion; they may indeed make one.

The finale came when supporters of the Stamp Act tried to dismiss the distinction between external and internal taxes. If the colonies successfully opposed an internal tax, might they later start opposing tariffs and other external taxes?

"They never have hitherto," replied Franklin. "Many arguments have lately been used here to show them that there is no difference . . . At present they do not reason so. But in time they may possibly be convinced by these arguments."

It was a dramatic ending, and a foreboding one. In making a distinction between internal taxes and external tariffs, Franklin was again taking a stance more moderate and pragmatic than some emerging American leaders, including most members of the Massachusetts Assembly, who rankled at the prospect of heavy import duties levied by London. But the Boston Tea Party was still almost eight years in the future. On both sides of the Atlantic, there was great rejoicing when Parliament promptly repealed the Stamp Act, even though it laid the ground for future conflict by adding a Declaratory Act stating that Parliament had the right "in all cases whatsoever" to enact laws for the colonies.[18]

Franklin had displayed, with steely words cloaked in velvet, both reason and resolve. For a generally reluctant public speaker, it was the longest sustained oratorical performance of his life. He made his case less through eloquence than through a persuasive persistence in focusing the debate on the realities that existed in America. Even one of his diehard opponents told him afterward, Franklin recorded, "that he liked me from that day for the spirit I showed in defense of my country." Famed in Britain as a writer and scientist, he was now widely recognized as America's most effective spokesman. He also became, in effect, the ambassador for America in general; besides representing Pennsylvania, he was soon named the agent for Georgia, and then New Jersey and Massachusetts.

In Philadelphia, his reputation was fully restored. His friend William Strahan helped assure that by sending a transcript of the testimony back to David Hall for publication there. "To this examination," Strahan wrote, "more than to anything else, you are indebted to the speedy and total repeal of this odious law." Salutes were fired from a barge christened *The Franklin,* and at the taverns there were free drinks and presents to all those who arrived with news of the triumph from England. "Your enemies at last began to be ashamed of their base insinuations and to acknowledge that the colonies are under obligation to you," Charles Thomson wrote.[19]

SALLY AND RICHARD BACHE

The battle served to remind Franklin about the virtues of the wife he had left back home, or at least to feel guiltier about his neglect of her. Deborah's frugality and self-reliance were symbols of America's ability to sacrifice rather than submit to an unfair tax. Now that it was repealed, Franklin rewarded her with a shipment of gifts: fourteen yards of Pompadour satin (he noted that it "cost eleven shillings a yard"), two dozen gloves, a silk negligee and petticoat for Sally, a Turkish rug, cheeses, a corkscrew, and some tablecloths and curtains, which he politely informed her had been selected by Mrs. Stevenson. In the letter accompanying the gifts, he wrote:

> My Dear Child,
>   As the Stamp Act is at length repealed, I am willing you should have a new gown, which you may suppose I did not send sooner as I knew you would not like to be finer than your neighbors, unless in a gown of your own spinning. Had the trade between the two countries totally ceased, it was a comfort to me to recollect that I had once been clothed from head to foot in woolen and linen of my wife's manufacture, that I was never prouder of any dress in my life, and that she and her daughter might do it again if necessary.

Perhaps, he jovially noted, some of the cheese would be left for him to enjoy by the time he got home. But even though he had turned 60 during the repeal battle and his work in England seemed done, Franklin was not ready to return. Instead, he made plans to spend the summer of 1766 visiting Germany with his friend the physician Sir John Pringle.[20]

Deborah's letters to her husband, awkward though they were, convey both her strength and her loneliness: "I partake of none of the diversions. I stay at home and flatter myself that the next packet will bring me a letter from you." She coped with his absence and the political tensions by cleaning the house, she said, and she tried hard (perhaps on his instructions) not to bother him with her worries about political matters. "I have wrote several letters to you one almost every day but then I could not forbear saying something to you about public affairs then I would destroy it and then begin again and burn it again and so on." Describing their newly completed house, she reported that she had not yet hung his pictures because she feared driving nails into the wall without his approval. "There is great odds between a man's being at home and abroad as everybody is afraid that they shall do wrong so every thing is left undone."

His letters, in return, were generally businesslike, focusing mainly on the details of the house. "I could have wished to have been present at the finishing of the kitchen," he wrote. "I think you will scarce know how to work it, the several contrivances to carry off steam and smell and smoke not being fully explained to you." He issued detailed instructions for how to paint each room and occasionally made tantalizing references to his eventual homecoming: "If that iron [furnace] is not set, let it alone till my return, when I shall bring a more convenient copper one."[21]

At the end of 1766, his printing partnership with David Hall expired after eighteen years. The end came with a bit of acrimony. Hall had become less ardent about using the pages of the *Pennsylvania Gazette* to attack the Proprietors, and two of Franklin's friends helped fund a new printer and paper to take up the cause. Hall considered this a breach of the spirit of their partnership agreement, even though it had expired. "Though you are not absolutely prohibited from being any farther concerned in the printing business in this place, yet so much is plainly implied," he wrote plaintively.

Franklin replied from London that the new rival print shop had been "set on foot without my knowledge or participation, and the first notice I had of it was by reading the advertisement in your paper." He professed his deep affection for Hall and said he had no disagreements with his politics or editorial policies, even if some of his political allies felt otherwise. "I never thought you of any party, and as you never blamed me for the side I took in public affairs, so I never censured you for not taking the same, believing as I do that every man has and ought to enjoy a perfect liberty of judging for himself in such matters."

Still, he felt compelled to add that their original agreement did not in fact prevent him from competing now that it had expired: "I could not possibly foresee 18 years beforehand that I should at the end of that term be so rich as to live without business." Then he added a veiled threat, wrapped in a promise, by saying that he had been offered a chance to become a partner in the rival business but would refrain from doing so as long as Hall provided some more of what Franklin thought he was owed. "I hope I shall have no occasion to do it," he said of the possibility that he would join with Hall's rival. "I know there must be a very great sum due to me from our customers, and I hope much more of it will be recovered by you for me than you apprehend." If so, Franklin promised, that money along with his other income would allow him to stay retired. "My circumstances will be sufficiently affluent, especially as I am not inclined to much expense. In this case I have no purpose of being again concerned in printing."[22]

The expiration of the partnership meant that Franklin would lose about £650 in income a year, which stoked his sense of economy. His life in London was a middle-class mix of frugality and indulgence. Although he did not entertain or live in the grand style that might be expected of someone of his stature, he liked to travel, and his accounts show that he ordered top-quality beer for his home at 30 shillings a barrel (a sharp contrast to his first stay in London, when he preached the virtues of bread and water over beer). His efforts at economy were mainly directed at his wife. In June of 1767 he wrote her:

> A great source of our income is cut off, and if I should lose the post office, which . . . is far from being unlikely, we should be reduced to our rents and interests of money for a subsistence, which will by no means afford the chargeable housekeepings and entertainments we have been used to. For my own part I live here as frugally as possible not to be destitute of the comforts of life, making no dinners for anybody and contenting myself with a single dish when I dine at home; and yet such is the dearness of living here that my expenses amaze me. I see too by the sums you have received in my absence that yours are very great, and I am very sensible that your situation naturally brings you a great many

visitors, which occasion an expense not easily to be avoided . . . But when people's incomes are lessened, if they cannot proportionally lessen their outgoings they must come to poverty.[23]

What made the letter particularly cold was that it was written in response to the news that their daughter had fallen in love and hoped for his approval to marry. Sally had grown into a distinguished fixture in Philadelphia society, attending all the balls and even riding in the carriage of Franklin's adversary Governor Penn. But she fell in love with a man who seemed to be of questionable character and financial security.

Richard Bache, the suitor in question, had emigrated from England to work as an importer and marine insurance broker with his brother in New York, and then he headed to Philadelphia to open a dry goods store on Chestnut Street. Charming to women but hapless in business, Bache had been engaged to Sally's best friend, Margaret Ross. When Margaret became fatally ill, she made a deathbed request for Sally to take care of Bache for her, and Sally was quite willing to oblige.[24]

For Deborah, deciding what to do in her husband's absence was an overwhelming responsibility. "I am obliged to be father and mother," she wrote Franklin, with a tinge of accusation. "I hope I act to your satisfaction, I do so according to my best judgment."

Surely, this should have precipitated Franklin's return. He remained, however, distant from his family. The only time he had hastened home to Philadelphia was when his son was planning to marry—in London. "As I am in doubt whether I shall be able to return this summer," he wrote Deborah, "I would not occasion a delay in her happiness if you thought the match a proper one." Permitting himself to be indulgent from afar, he sent Sally two summer hats with the letter.

A few weeks later, he sent his long sermon about saving money. "Do not make an expensive feasting wedding," he wrote Deborah, "but conduct everything with frugality and economy, which our circumstances really now require." She should make clear to Bache, he added, that they would provide a nice but not excessive dowry:

I hope his expectations are not great of any fortune to be had with our daughter before our death. I can only say that if he proves a good husband to her, and a good son to me, he shall find me as good a father as I can be. But at present I suppose you would agree with me that we cannot do more than fit her out handsomely in clothes and furniture not exceeding in the whole five hundred pounds of value.[25]

Then came more disturbing news. At Franklin's request, William checked into Bache's financial situation and discovered it was in shambles. Worse yet, he learned that Margaret Ross's father had previously found the same thing and denied them permission to marry. "Mr. Bache had often attempted to deceive him [Ross] about his circumstances," William reported. "In short, he is a mere fortune hunter who wants to better his circumstances by marrying into a family that will support him." He ended the letter with a request: "Do burn this." Franklin didn't.

So the marriage was put on hold, and Bache tried to explain himself to Franklin in a letter. It was true, he admitted, that he had suffered a severe financial reversal, but he claimed it was not his fault. He had unfairly been left holding the bills for a merchant ship that suffered in the Stamp Act boycott.[26]

"I love my daughter perhaps as well as ever a parent did a child," Franklin replied with perhaps some exaggeration. "But I have told you before that my estate is small, scarce a sufficiency for the support of me and my wife . . . Unless you can convince her friends of the probability of your being able to maintain her properly, I hope you will not persist in a proceeding that may be attended with ruinous consequences to you both." Franklin wrote Deborah the same day to say that he assumed Bache would now back off. "The misfortune that has lately happened to his affairs," said Franklin, "will probably induce him to forbear entering hastily" into a marriage. He suggested that Sally might, instead, want to visit England, where she could meet other men, such as William Strahan's son.[27]

Though Franklin's sentiments were clear, his letters did not outright forbid his daughter from getting married. Perhaps he felt that, because he was unwilling to come home to deal with the matter, he had neither the moral right nor practical ability to issue any decrees.

Detached from his family by distance, he also remained rather emotionally detached.

Further complicating the odd family dynamics, Mrs. Stevenson decided to weigh in. Having lived with Franklin, she felt herself to be Deborah's soul mate, and she wrote to share her sympathy. Franklin, she reported, was in a foul humor. Stung by his temper, she consoled herself by buying some silk and making a petticoat for his daughter, even though she had never met her. Indeed, she confided, she was so excited by the possible wedding that she had wanted to buy even more gifts, but Franklin had forbidden it. She longed for the opportunity to sit down and chat, she told Deborah. "I truly think your expectations of seeing Mr. Franklin from time to time has been too much for a tender affectionate wife to bear."[28]

Ignoring the family drama back in Philadelphia, Franklin escaped in August 1767 for a summer vacation to France. "I have stayed too long in London this summer, and now sensibly feel the want of my usual journey to preserve my health," he wrote Deborah. His mood was so sour that, on the way, he "engaged in perpetual disputes with the innkeepers," he told Polly. He and his traveling companion, John Pringle, were upset that their carriage was rigged in such a way that they had little view of the countryside. The coachman's explanation of the rationale, Franklin groused, "made me, as upon a hundred other occasions, almost wish that mankind had never been endowed with a reasoning faculty, since they know so little how to make use of it."

When they got to Paris, however, things improved. He was intrigued by how the ladies there applied their rouge, which he chose to share in great detail in a letter to Polly rather than to his own daughter. "Cut a hole of three inches in diameter in a piece of paper, place it on the side of your face in such a manner as that the top of the hole may be just under your eye; then with a brush dipped in the color paint face and paper together, so when the paper is taken off there will remain a round patch of red."[29]

Franklin was feted as a celebrity in France, where electrical experimenters were known as *franklinistes,* and he and Pringle were invited to Versailles to attend a grand *couvert* (public supper) with King Louis XV and Queen Marie. "He spoke to both of us very graciously and cheerfully," Franklin reported to Polly. Despite his travails with England's ministers, however, he stressed he was still loyal "in thinking my own King and Queen the very best in the world and the most amiable."

Versailles was magnificent but negligently maintained, he noted, "with its shabby half brick walls and broken windows." Paris, on the other hand, had some pristine qualities that appealed to his affection for civic improvement schemes. The streets were swept daily so they were "fit to walk in," unlike those of London, and the water was made "as pure as that of the best spring by filtering it through cisterns filled with sand." While his daughter was preparing for a wedding without him, Franklin was getting new tailored clothes and "a little bag wig" that made him look "twenty years younger," he told Polly. The trip had done so much to invigorate his health, he joked, that "I was once very near to making love to my friend's wife."[30]

On his return from France, Franklin promptly wrote charming letters to Polly and others, but only a short note home. He seemed miffed that the letters from Philadelphia carried little news of his daughter, other than that she was "disappointed" that her marriage plans were put in limbo. He assured Deborah that he had been "extremely hearty and well ever since my return," and then deigned to inquire about his daughter's welfare.

By that time, though he did not know it, Sally and Richard had already gone ahead and gotten married. In October 1767, as recorded in the *Pennsylvania Chronicle* (the new rival to Franklin's old *Gazette*), "Mr. Richard Bache, of this city, merchant, was married to Miss Sally Franklin, the only daughter of the celebrated Doctor Franklin, a young lady of distinguished merit. The next day all the shipping in the harbor displayed their colors on this happy occasion."[31]

There is no sign that Franklin ever expressed regret for missing the wedding of his only daughter. In December, his sister Jane Mecom wrote to offer congratulations on the "marriage of your beloved daughter to a worthy gentleman whom she loves and is the only one that can make her happy." Franklin replied the following February in a cool manner: "She has pleased herself and her mother, and I hope she will do well; but I think they should have seen some better prospect than they have, before they married, how the family was to be maintained."[32]

In his occasional letters over the next few months, Franklin would send his love to Deborah and Sally, but he never made any overtures to Bache. Finally, in August 1768, Franklin wrote Bache admitting him into the family. "Loving son," he began promisingly, before turning a bit cool. "I thought the step you had taken, to engage yourself in the charge of a family while your affairs bore so unpromising an aspect with regard to the probable means of maintaining it, a very rash and precipitate one." This was why, Franklin explained, he had not answered Bache's earlier letters. "I could say nothing agreeable: I did not choose to write what I thought, being unwilling to give pain where I could not give pleasure." But at the end of the one-paragraph letter, Franklin softened somewhat. "Time has made me easier," he said. "My best wishes attend you, and that if you prove a good husband and son, you will find me an affectionate father." In a one-sentence postscript, he gave his love to Sally and noted that he was sending her a new watch.

Deborah was thrilled. In a note she sent when forwarding Franklin's letter to Bache, who was visiting Boston, she wrote, "Mr. Bache (or my son Bache), I give you joy: although there are no fine speeches as some would make, your father (or so I will call him) and you, I hope, will have many happy days together."[33]

Deborah got even better news from Franklin at the beginning of 1769. His health was very good, he wrote, but "I know that according to the course of nature I cannot at most continue much longer." He had just turned 63. Therefore, he was "indulging myself in no future prospect except one, that of returning to Philadelphia, there to spend the evening of my life with my friends and family." Sally and her husband came back from Boston hoping to find Franklin there. But he was still not ready, despite what he had written, to return.

Nor did he return that spring when he learned that Deborah had suffered a small stroke. "These are bad symptoms in advanced life and augur danger," her doctor wrote to Franklin. He consulted his traveling companion, John Pringle, who was physician to the queen, and forwarded his advice to Deborah. For once expressing slight impatience with her wayward husband, she disparaged the advice and said that her condition was largely caused by "dissatisfied distress" brought on by his prolonged absence: "I was only unable to bear any more and so I fell and could not get up again."

Even good news could not yet entice him back to Philadelphia. When he heard that Sally was pregnant that summer, he conveyed his affection by sending a little luxury: six caudle cups, which were used by pregnant women to share a brew of wine, bread, and spice. Sally missed no opportunity for seeking his affection. The child, born in August 1769, was named Benjamin Franklin Bache. Franklin would turn out to be closer to his grandchildren than his children; Benny Bache, like his cousin Temple, would eventually become part of his retinue. In the meantime, he sent his best wishes and instructions to make sure that Benny was inoculated for smallpox.[34]

THE SURROGATE FAMILY

In his family life, as in the rest of his personal life, Franklin clearly did not look for deep commitments. He did, however, have a need for domestic comfort and intellectual stimulation. That is what he found with his surrogate family in London. On Craven Street there was a cleverness and spirit that was absent on Market Street. His landlady, Mrs. Stevenson, was livelier than Deborah, her daughter, Polly, a bit smarter than Sally. And in September 1769, just after Franklin returned from France, Polly found a suitor who was more distinguished than Bache.

William Hewson was a good catch for Polly, who by then was 30 and still unmarried. He was on the verge of what would be a prominent career as a medical researcher and lecturer. "He must be clever because he thinks as *we* do," Polly gushed in a letter from the country home where she was staying. "I should not have you or my mother surprised if I should run off with this young man; to be sure it would be an imprudent step at the discreet age of 30."

Amid these half-jokes, Polly played coy with Franklin by confessing (or feigning) her lack of enthusiasm for marrying Hewson. "He may be too young," she told her older admirer. She was filled with happiness, she added, but she couldn't be sure whether "this flight might be owing to this new acquaintance or to the joy of hearing my old one [meaning Franklin, who had been in Paris] is returned to this country."

Franklin's reply, written the very next day, contained more flirtations than felicitations. "If the truth were known, I have reason to be jealous of this insinuating handsome young physician." He would flatter his vanity, he said, and "turn a deaf ear to reason" by deciding "to suppose you were in spirits because of my safe return."

For almost a year, Polly held off getting married because Franklin refused to advise her to accept Hewson's proposal. Finally, in May 1770, Franklin wrote that he had no objections. It was hardly an overwhelming endorsement. "I am sure you are a much better judge in this affair of your own than I can possibly be," he said, adding that the match appeared "a rational one." As for her worry that she would not bring much of a financial dowry, Franklin could not resist noting that "I should think you a fortune sufficient for me without a shilling."[35]

Although he had missed the weddings of both his own children, this was one Franklin made sure not to miss. Even though it was held in midsummer, when he usually traveled abroad, he was there to walk Polly down the aisle and play the role of her father. A few weeks later, he professed to be pleased that she was happy, but he confessed that he was "now and then in low spirits" at the prospect of having lost her friendship. Fortunately for all, it was not to be. He became close to the new couple, and he and Polly would exchange more than 130 more letters during their lifelong friendship.

Indeed, a few months after their wedding, Polly and William Hewson came to stay with Franklin while Mrs. Stevenson spent one of her long weekends visiting friends in the country. Together they published a fake newspaper to mark the occasion. *The Craven Street Gazette* for Saturday, September 22, 1770, reported on the departure of "Queen Margaret" and Franklin's ensuing grumpiness. "The GREAT person (so called from his enormous size) . . . could hardly be comforted this morning, though the new ministry promised him roasted shoulder of mutton and potatoes for his dinner." Franklin, it was reported, was also miffed that Queen Margaret had taken the keys to a closet so that he could not find his ruffled shirts, which prevented him from going to St. James's Palace for Coronation Day. "Great clamors were made on this occasion against her Majesty . . . The shirts were afterwards found, tho' too late, in another place."

For four days, the newspaper poked fun at various Franklin foibles: how he violated his sermons about saving fuel by making a fire in his bedroom when everyone else was out, how he vowed to fix the front door but gave up because he was unable to decide whether it required buying a new lock or a new key, and how he pledged to go to church on Sunday. "It is now found by sad experience that good resolutions are easier made than executed," Sunday's edition reported. "Notwithstanding yesterday's solemn Order of Council, nobody went to church today. It seems the GREAT person's broad-built bulk lay so long abed that breakfast was not over until it was too late." The moral of the tale could have been written by Poor Richard: "It seems a vain thing to hope reformation from the example of our great folks."

One particularly intriguing entry seems to refer to a woman living nearby with whom Franklin had an unrequited flirtation. That Sunday, Franklin pretended to visit her: "Dr. Fatsides made 469 turns in his dining room, as the exact distance of a visit to the lovely Lady Barwell, whom he did not find at home, so there was no struggle for and against a kiss, and he sat down to dream in his easy chair that he had it without any trouble." By the third day of Mrs. Stevenson's absence, the *Gazette* was reporting that Dr. Fatsides "begins to wish for her Majesty's return."

That final edition contained one of Franklin's inimitable letters to the editor, signed with the pseudonym "Indignation," decrying the food and conditions. Referring to Polly and her husband, it railed: "If these nefarious wretches continue in power another week, the nation will be ruined—undone!—totally undone if the Queen does not return; or (which is better) turn them all out and appoint me and my friends to succeed them." It was answered by "A Hater of Scandal," who wrote that the surly Franklin had been offered a wonderful dinner of beef ribs and had rejected it, saying "that beef does not with him perspire well, but makes his back itch, to his no small vexation now that he hath lost the little Chinese ivory hand at the end of the stick, commonly called a scratchback, presented to him by Her Majesty."[36]

Franklin was able to indulge on Craven Street the many eccentricities he had developed. One of these was taking hour-long "air baths" early each morning, during which he would open his windows and "sit in my chamber without any clothes whatever." Another was engaging in little flirtations. The famous painter Charles Willson Peale recounted how he once visited Craven Street unannounced and found "the Doctor was seated with a young lady on his knee." The lady in question was probably Polly, though the sketch Peale later made of the scene is ambiguous.[37]

Eventually, Polly and William Hewson moved into Craven Street and brought with them Hewson's skeletons, "prepared fetuses," and other tools for his medical research. Later, Franklin and Mrs. Stevenson moved a few doors away. Their odd relationship was reflected in a crotchety letter Franklin wrote her during one of her regular escapes to visit friends in the country. Reminding her of Poor Richard's adage that guests become tiresome after three days, he urged her to return on the next stagecoach. But lest she think he was too dependent on her, he spelled out his contentment at being alone. "I find such a satisfaction in being a little more my own master, going anywhere and doing anything just when and how I please," he claimed. "This happiness however is perhaps too great to be conferred on any but Saints and holy hermits. Sinners like me, I might have said us, are condemned to live together and tease one another."[38]

HILLSBOROUGH AND THE TOWNSHEND DUTIES

In his dramatic testimony arguing for repeal of the Stamp Act, Franklin made a serious misjudgment: he said that Americans recognized Parliament's right to impose external taxes, such as tariffs and export duties, just not internal taxes that were collected on transactions inside the country. He repeated the argument in April 1767, writing as "A Friend to Both Countries" and then as "Benevolus" in a London paper. In an effort to soothe troubled relations, he recounted all the times that Americans had been very accommodating in helping to raise money for the defense of the empire. "The colonies submit to pay all external taxes laid upon them by way of duty on merchandise imported into their country and never disputed the authority of Parliament to lay such duties," he wrote.[39]

Charles Townshend, the new chancellor of the exchequer, had been among those who grilled Franklin in Parliament about his acceptance of external but not internal taxes. The distinction was complete "nonsense," Townshend felt, but he decided to pretend to please the colonies—or call their bluff—by adopting it. In a brilliant speech that earned him the nickname "Champagne Charlie" because it was delivered while he was half-drunk, he laid out a plan for import duties on glass, paper, china, paint colors, and tea. Making matters worse, part of the money raised would be used to pay royal governors, thus freeing them from dependence on colonial legislatures.

Once again, as with the passage of the Stamp Act, Franklin expressed little concern when the Townshend duties passed in June 1767, and he did not realize how far he lagged behind the growing radicalism in parts of the colonies. Outrage at the new duties grew particularly strong in the port city of Boston, where the Sons of Liberty, led by Samuel Adams, effectively roused sentiments with dances around a "Liberty Tree" near the common. Adams got the Massachusetts Assembly to draft a circular letter to the rest of the colonies that petitioned for repeal of the act. The British ministry demanded that the letter be rescinded and sent troops to Boston after the Assembly refused.

When reports of American anger reached him in London, Franklin remained rather moderate and wrote a series of essays calling for "civility and good manners" on both sides. To friends in Philadelphia, he expressed his disapproval of the radicalism growing in Boston; in articles published in England, he tried hard—indeed, too hard—to pull off an adroit feat of ambidexterity.

His juggling act was reflected in a long, anonymous essay he wrote in January 1768 for the London *Chronicle,* called "Causes of the American Discontents." Written from the perspective of an Englishman, it explained the Americans' belief that their own legislatures should control all revenue measures, and it added in a squirrelly manner, "I do not undertake here to support these opinions." His goal, he averred, was to let people "know what ideas the Americans have." In doing so, Franklin tried to have it both ways: he warned that America's fury at being taxed by Parliament could tear apart the empire, then pretended to lament these "wild ravings" as something "I do not pretend to support." [40]

His reaction was similar when he read a set of anonymous articles, published in Philadelphia, called "Letters from a Farmer in Pennsylvania." At the time, Franklin did not know that they were written by John Dickinson, his adversary in Philadelphia's battles over the Proprietors. Dickinson's letters conceded that Parliament had a right to regulate trade, but he argued that it could not use that right to raise revenues from the colonies without their consent. Franklin arranged to have the letters published as a pamphlet in London in May 1768 and wrote an introduction. But he refrained from fully endorsing their arguments. "How far these sentiments are right or wrong I do not pretend at present to judge."

By then, Franklin had begun to realize that his distinction between external and internal taxes was probably unworkable. "The more I have thought and read on the subject," he wrote William in March, "the more I find myself confirmed in my opinion that no middle doctrine can be well maintained." There were only two alternatives: "that Parliament has a power to make *all* laws for us, or that it has the power to make *no laws* for us." He was beginning to lean toward the latter, but he admitted that he was unsure. [41]

Franklin's inelegant dance around the issue of parliamentary power during the first half of 1768 caused his contemporaries (as well as subsequent historians) to come to different conclusions about what he really believed or what games he was playing. In fact, there were many factors jangling in his mind: he sincerely hoped that moderation and reason would lead to a restoration of harmony between Britain and the colonies; he wanted to make one last attempt to wrest Pennsylvania from the Proprietors; and he was still pursuing land deals that required the favor of the British government. Above all, as he admitted in some letters, his views were in flux and he was still trying to make up his mind.

There was one other complicating factor. His desire to help resolve the disputes, combined with his ambition, led him to hope that he might be appointed an official in the British ministry overseeing colonial affairs. Lord Hillsborough had just been named secretary of state of that ministry, and Franklin thought (incorrectly) that he might turn out to be friendly to the colonies. "I do not think this nobleman in general an enemy to America," he wrote a friend in January. In a letter to his son, Franklin admitted the more personal ambition. "I am told there is talk of getting me appointed undersecretary to Lord Hillsborough," he said. His chances, he admitted, were slim: "It is a settled point here that I am too much of an American."

That was the crux of Franklin's dilemma. He had rendered himself suspect, he noted in a letter to a friend, "in England of being too much of an American, and in America of being too much of an Englishman." With his dreams for a harmonious and growing British Empire, he still hoped that he could be both. "Being born and bred in one of the countries and having lived long and made many agreeable connections in the other, I wish all prosperity to both," he proclaimed. Thus, he was intrigued, even hopeful, about securing a government job in which he could try to hold the two parts of the empire together.[42]

When Hillsborough consolidated his power by becoming the head of the board of trade as well as colonial secretary, Franklin won support from other British ministers who felt that giving him a government post would provide some balance. Most notable was Lord North, who had become chancellor of the exchequer after Townshend's death. Franklin met with him in June and professed to have plans to return to America. He added, however, that "I should stay with pleasure if I could any ways be useful to government." North took the hint, and he began trying to line up backing for his appointment.

It was not to be. Franklin's hope of joining the British government ended abruptly when he had a long and contentious meeting with Lord Hillsborough in August 1768. Hillsborough declared that he had no intention of appointing Franklin and would instead choose as his deputy John Pownall, a loyal bureaucrat. Franklin was dismayed. Pownall "seems to have a strong bias against us," he wrote Joseph Galloway, his ally in the Pennsylvania Assembly. Adding injury to insult, Hillsborough also rejected once and for all any further consideration of the petition to remove Pennsylvania from Proprietary rule. With two of his main goals dashed, Franklin was ready to abandon his moderation in the colonies' battles with Parliament. The turning point had been reached.[43]

THE AMERICAN PATRIOT

With the situation clarified in his own mind, Franklin took up his pen to wage an essay war against Hillsborough and the Townshend duties. Most of his articles were anonymous, but this time he did little to disguise his authorship. He even signed one of them, with clear frankness, "Francis Lynn." Relations between Britain and America had been amicable, he argued, "until the idea of taxing us by the power of Parliament unfortunately entered the heads of your ministers." He claimed that the colonies had no desire to rebel against the king, but misguided ministers were likely "to convert millions of the King's loyal subjects into rebels for the sake of establishing a newly-claimed power in Parliament to tax a distant people." Something must be done. "Is there not one wise and good man to be found in Britain who can propose some conciliating measure that may prevent this mischief?" In another piece, written as if from a concerned Englishman, he proposed seven "queries" to be considered "by those gentlemen who are for vigorous measures with the Americans." Among them: "Why must they be stripped of their property without their consent?" As for Hillsborough personally, Franklin labeled him "our new Haman."[44]

His opponents returned the fire. One article signed by "Machiavel" in the *Gazetteer* called it a "burlesque on patriotism" that so many Americans were "filling newspapers and consecrating trees to liberty" with lamentations about being taxed while at the same time surreptitiously recommending their friends for appointments and "trying to obtain offices" for themselves. Machiavel provided a list of fifteen such hypocrites, with Franklin the postmaster at the top. Franklin responded (anonymously) that the Americans were attacking Parliament, not the king. "Being loyal subjects to their sovereign, the Americans think they have as good a right to enjoy offices under him in America as a Scotchman has in Scotland or an Englishman in England."

Throughout 1769, Franklin became increasingly worried that the situation would lead to a rupture. America could not be subjugated by British troops, he argued, and it soon would be strong enough to win its own independence. If that happened, Britain would be sorry that it missed the opportunity to create a system of imperial harmony. To make his point, he published a parable in January 1770 about a young lion cub and a large English dog traveling together on a ship. The dog picked on the lion cub and "frequently took its food by force." But the lion grew and eventually became stronger than the dog. One day, in response to all the insults, it smashed the dog with "a stunning blow," leaving the dog "regretting that he had not rather secured its friendship than provoked its enmity." The parable was "humbly inscribed" to Lord Hillsborough.[45]

Many in Parliament were seeking a compromise. One proposal was to remove most of the Townshend duties, leaving only the one on tea as a way to assert the principle that Parliament retained the right to regulate trade and tariffs. It was the type of pragmatic solution that in earlier days would have appealed to Franklin. But he was now in no mood for moderation. "It is not the sum paid in that duty on tea that is complained of as a burden, but the principle of the act," he wrote Strahan. A partial repeal "may inflame matters still more" and lead to "some mad action" and an escalation that "will thus go on to complete the separation."[46]

Separatist sentiments were, in fact, already being inflamed, especially in Boston. On March 5, 1770, a young apprentice insulted one of the redcoats sent to enforce the Townshend duties, a fight broke out, bells rang, and a swarm of armed and angry Bostonians came out in force. "Fire and be damned," the crowd taunted. The British soldiers did. Five Americans ended up dead in what soon became known as the Boston Massacre.

Parliament went ahead with the partial repeal of the Townshend duties that month, leaving a duty on tea. In a letter to his Philadelphia friend Charles Thomson, which was promptly published throughout the colonies, Franklin urged a continued boycott of all British manufactured goods. America, he argued, must be "steady and persevere in our resolutions."

Franklin had finally caught up with the more ardent patriotism spreading through the colonies, most notably Massachusetts. Writing to Samuel Cooper, a Boston minister, he declared that Parliament had no authority to tax the colonies or order British troops there: "In truth they have no such right, and their claim is founded only on usurpation."

Still, like many Americans, he was not yet willing to advocate a total break with Britain. The solution, he felt, was a new arrangement in which the colonial assemblies would remain loyal to the king but no longer be subservient to Britain's Parliament. As he told Cooper, "Let us therefore hold fast our loyalty to our King (who has the best disposition toward us, and has a family interest in our prosperity) as that steady loyalty is the most probable means of securing us from the arbitrary power of a corrupt Parliament that does not like us and conceives itself to have an interest in keeping us down and fleecing us." It was an elegant formula for commonwealth governance. Alas, it was based on the unproven assumption that the king would be more sympathetic to colonial rights than was Parliament.[47]

Franklin's letter to Cooper, widely published, helped to secure him an appointment by the Massachusetts lower house to be its agent in London as well. In January 1771, he paid a call on Lord Hillsborough to present those new credentials. Although the minister was dressing for court, he cheerfully had Franklin admitted to his chambers. But when Franklin mentioned his new appointment, Hillsborough sneered. "I must set you right there, Mr. Franklin. You are not agent."

"I do not understand your lordship," replied Franklin. "I have the appointment in my pocket."

Hillsborough maintained that Massachusetts governor Hutchinson had vetoed the bill appointing Franklin.

"There was no such bill," said Franklin. "It is a vote of the House."

"The House of Representatives has no right to appoint an agent," Hillsborough angrily retorted. "We shall take no notice of agents but such as are appointed by Acts of Assembly to which the governor gives his assent."

Hillsborough's argument was clearly specious. Franklin had, of course, been appointed as the agent of the Pennsylvania Assembly without the consent of the Penn family's governors there. The minister was trying to eliminate the right of the people to choose their own agents in London, and Franklin was appalled. "I cannot conceive, my lord, why the consent of the *governor* should be thought necessary to the appointment of an agent for the *people*."

The discussion went downhill from there. Hillsborough, turning pale, launched into a tirade about how his "firmness" was necessary to bring order to the rebellious colonials. To which Franklin added a personal insult: "It is, I believe, of no great importance whether the appointment is acknowledged or not, for I have not the least conception that an agent *at present* can be of any use to any of the colonies. I shall therefore give your lordship no farther trouble." At that point, Franklin abruptly departed and went home to write down a transcript of the discussion.[48]

Hillsborough "took great offense at some of my last words, which he calls extremely rude and abusive," Franklin reported to Samuel Cooper in Boston. "I find that he did not mistake me."

Initially, Franklin pretended to be unconcerned about Hillsborough's enmity. "He is not a whit better liked by his colleagues in the ministry than he is by me," Franklin claimed in his letter to Cooper. In another letter, he described Hillsborough as "proud, supercilious, extremely conceited of his political knowledge and abilities (such as they are), fond of everyone that can stoop to flatter him, and inimical to all that dare tell him disagreeable truths." The only reason he remained in power, Franklin surmised, was that the other ministers had "difficulty of knowing how to dispose of or what to do with a man of his wrong-headed bustling energy."

Nevertheless, it soon became clear that the showdown with Hillsborough depressed Franklin. His friend Strahan noticed that he had become "very reserved, which adds greatly to his natural inactivity and there is no getting him to take part in anything." It also made him far more pessimistic about the eventual outcome of America's growing tensions with Britain. One could see in Parliament's actions "the seeds sown of a total disunion of the two countries," he reported to the Massachusetts Committee on Correspondence, which brought out the more radical side of him. "The bloody struggle will end in absolute slavery to America, or ruin to Britain by the loss of her colonies."[49]

Despite such pessimistic feelings, Franklin still hoped for a reconciliation. He urged the Massachusetts Assembly to avoid passing an "open denial and resistance" to Parliament's authority and instead adopt a strategy designed "gradually to wear off the assumed authority of Parliament over America." He even went so far as to advise Cooper that it might "be prudent in us to indulge the Mother Country in this concern for her own honor." And he continued to urge a policy of loyalty to the Crown, if not to Parliament.

This led some of his enemies to accuse him of being too conciliatory. "The Dr. is not the dupe but the instrument of Lord Hillsborough's treachery," the ambitious Virginian Arthur Lee wrote to his friend Samuel Adams. Lee went on to accuse Franklin of wanting to cling to his postmastership and keep his son in office. All of this explained, he said, "the temporizing conduct he has always held in American affairs."

Lee had his own motives: he wanted Franklin's job as agent in London. But Franklin still had the support of most Massachusetts patriots, including (at least for the time being) Samuel Adams. Adams ignored Lee's letter, allowed it to leak, and Franklin's friends in Boston, including Thomas Cushing and Samuel Cooper, assured him of their support. Lee's attack, Cooper wrote, served to "confirm the opinion of your importance, while it shows the baseness of its author." But it also highlighted the difficulty that Franklin faced in attempting, as he had during the Stamp Act crisis, to be both a loyal Briton and an American patriot.[50]

CHAPTER ELEVEN

REBEL

London, 1771–1775

THE VACATIONS OF 1771

As the summer of 1771 approached, Franklin decided to forsake the world of public affairs for the time being. He had been stymied, at least for the moment, in all of his political missions: the fight against the Proprietors and then Parliament, his pursuit of a land grant and a royal appointment. But he was still not ready to return home. So, instead, he escaped the pressures of politics in the manner he loved best, by taking an extended series of trips that lasted until the end of the year: to England's industrial midland and north in May, to a friend's estate in southern England in June and again in August, and then to Ireland and Scotland in the fall.

On his rambles in May, Franklin visited the village of Clapham, where there was a large pond. It was a windy day and the water was rough, so he decided to test his theories about the calming effect of oil. Using just a teaspoon, he watched in amazement as it "produced an instant calm" that extended gradually to make a "quarter of the pond, perhaps half an acre, as smooth as a looking glass."

Although Franklin would continue to study the effect of oil on water seriously, he also found ways to have fun by turning it into a conjuring trick. "After this, I contrived to take with me, whenever I went into the country, a little oil in the upper hollow joint of my bamboo cane," he wrote. On a visit to the house of Lord Shelburne, he was walking by a stream with a group of friends, including the great actor David Garrick and the visiting French philosopher the Abbé Morellet, and told them he could still the waves. He walked upstream, waved his cane three times, and the surface of the stream calmed. Only later did he show off his cane and explain the magic.[1]

His tour of midland and north England in the company of two fellow scientists gave Franklin the chance to study the Industrial Revolution that was booming there. He visited an iron and tin factory in Rotherham, the metal casting shops of Birmingham, and a silk mill in Derby where 63,700 reels were turning constantly "and the twist process is tended by children of about 5 to 7 years old." In Manchester, he "embarked in a luxurious horse-drawn boat" owned by the Duke of Bridgewater that, befitting the peer's name, took him onto an aqueduct that crossed a river before ending in a coal mine. Near Leeds they called on the scientist Joseph Priestley, "who made some very pretty electrical experiments" for them and then described the various gases he had been discovering.

Franklin had denounced England's mercantile trading laws, which were designed to suppress manufacturing in her colonies, by arguing (a bit disingenuously) that she would never have to fear that America would become an industrial competitor. In his letters from his tour in 1771, however, he sent detailed advice about creating silk, clothing, and metal industries that would make the colonies self-sufficient. He had become "more and more convinced," he wrote his Massachusetts friend Thomas Cushing, of the "impossibility" that England would be able to keep up with America's growing demand for clothing. "Necessity therefore, as well as prudence, will soon induce us to seek resources in our own industry."

Franklin returned to London briefly in early June "in time to be at Court for the King's birthday," he wrote Deborah. Despite his disagreements with Parliament's taxation policies, he was still a loyal supporter of George III. "While we are declining the usurped authority of Parliament," he wrote Cushing that week, "I wish to see a steady dutiful attachment to the King and his family maintained among us."[2]

After a fortnight in London, Franklin headed to the south of England, where he visited his friend Jonathan Shipley at his Tudor manor in Twyford, just outside Winchester. Shipley was an Anglican bishop in Wales, but he spent most of his time in Twyford with his wife and five spirited daughters. It was such a delightful visit (Franklin might well have defined delight as an intellectually stimulating country house filled with five spirited young women) that he lamented that he had to leave after a week to attend to the correspondence that had been piling up in London. In his thank-you note to the Shipleys, which included a present of dried apples from America, Franklin complained that he had to "breathe with reluctance the smoke of London" and said he hoped to get back to the "sweet air of Twyford" for a longer visit later that summer.[3]

THE AUTOBIOGRAPHY

Franklin, at 65, had begun to think about family matters more. He felt affection for all of his kin, despite the fact—or perhaps, as he himself speculated, because of the fact—that he continued to live far away from them. In a long letter to his sole surviving sibling, Jane Mecom, that summer, he praised her for getting along well with her Philadelphia in-laws and, in a telling passage, reflected on how much easier it was for relatives to remain friendly from afar. "Our father, who was a very wise man, used to say nothing was more common than for those who loved one another at a distance to find many causes of dislike when they came together." A good example, he noted, was the relationship their father had with his brother Benjamin. "Though I was a child I still remember how affectionate their correspondence was" while Benjamin remained in England. But when Uncle Benjamin moved to Boston, they began to engage in "disputes and misunderstandings."

Franklin also wrote Jane about Sally Franklin, a 16-year-old who had joined his surrogate family on Craven Street. Sally was the only child of a second cousin who had continued the Franklin family's textile dyeing business in Leicestershire. Accompanying the letter was a detailed family tree showing how they were all descendants of Thomas Franklin of Ecton and noting that Sally was the last in England to bear the family name.

His interest in family was further piqued when he happened to visit one of his favorite used-book shops in London. The dealer showed him a collection of old political pamphlets that were filled with annotations. Franklin was amazed to discover that they had belonged to his Uncle Benjamin. "I suppose he parted with them when he left England," Franklin wrote in a letter to another cousin. He promptly bought them.[4]

So, in late July, when he was finally free to return to Twyford for a longer stay with the Shipleys, he was in a reflective mood. His career was at an impasse, and the history of his family was on his mind. Thus, the stage was set for the first installment of the most enduring of his literary efforts, *The Autobiography of Benjamin Franklin*.

"Dear son," he began, casting his account as a letter to William, whom he had not seen for seven years. The epistolary guise gave him the opportunity to be chatty and casual in his prose. He pretended, at least initially, that this was merely a personal communication rather than a work of literature. "I used to write more methodically," he said in a paragraph he inserted into the text after rereading some of the rambling genealogical digressions he had composed on the first day. "But one does not dress for private company as for a public ball."

Was the autobiography really just for the private company of his son? No. It was clear from the outset that Franklin was writing for public consumption as well. The family information that would most interest his son was omitted completely: the identity and description of William's own mother. Nor did Franklin write the letter on regular stationery; instead, he used the left half of large folio sheets, leaving the right half blank for revisions and additions.

At the beginning of his second day of writing, he stopped to make an outline of his entire career, showing his intention to construct a full memoir. Also, that second morning, he used the blank right-hand columns of his first pages to insert a long section justifying the "vanity" of his decision to "indulge the inclination so natural in old men to be talking of themselves." His goal, he declared, was to describe how he rose from obscurity to prominence and to provide some useful hints about how he succeeded, expressing hope that others might find them suitable to be imitated.

This was obviously directed at an audience beyond that of his son, who was already 40 and the governor of New Jersey. There was, however, a subtext directed at him: William had taken on airs since becoming a governor, and he was far more enamored of the aristocracy and establishment than his father. The autobiography would be a reminder of their humble origins and a paean to hard work, thrift, shopkeeping values, and the role of an industrious middle class that resisted rather than emulated the pretensions of the well-born elite.

For almost three weeks, Franklin wrote by day and then read aloud portions to the Shipleys in the evening. Because the work was cast as a letter, and because it was read aloud, Franklin's prose took on the voice of a lovable old raconteur. Lacking in literary flair, with nary a metaphor nor poetic flourish, the narrative flowed as a string of wry anecdotes and instructive lessons. Occasionally, when he found himself writing with too much pride about an event, he would revise it by adding a self-deprecating comment or ironic aside, just as would a good after-dinner storyteller.

The result was one of Franklin's most delightful literary creations: the portrait he painted of his younger self. The novelist John Updike has memorably called it an "elastically insouciant work, full of cheerful contradictions and humorous twists—a fond look back upon an earlier self, giving an intensely ambitious young man the benefit of the older man's relaxation."

With a mix of wry detachment and amused self-awareness, Franklin was able to keep his creation at a bit of a distance, to be modestly revealing but never deeply so. Amid all the enlightening anecdotes, he included few intimations of inner torment, no struggles of the soul or reflections of the deeper spirit. More pregnant than profound, his recollections provide a cheerful look at a simple approach to life that only hints at the deeper meanings he found in serving his fellow man and thus his God. What he wrote had little pretension other than pretending to poke fun at all pretensions. It was the work of a gregarious man who loved to recount stories, turn them into down-home parables that could lead to a better life, and delve into the shallows of simple lessons.

To some, this simplicity is its failing. The great literary critic Charles Angoff declares that "it is lacking in almost everything necessary to a really great work of *belles lettres:* grace of expression, charm of personality, and intellectual flight." But surely it is unfair to say that it lacks charm of personality, and as the historian Henry Steele Commager points out, its "artless simplicity, lucidity, homely idiom, freshness and humor have commended it anew to each generation of readers." Indeed, read with an unjaundiced eye, it is a pure delight as well as an archetype of homespun American literature. And it was destined to become, through hundreds of editions published in almost every language, the world's most popular autobiography.

In this age of instant memoirs, it is important to note that Franklin was producing something relatively new for his time. St. Augustine's *Confessions* had mainly been about his religious conversion, and Rousseau's *Confessions* had not yet been published. "There had been almost no famous autobiographies before Franklin, and he had no models," writes Carl Van Doren. That is not entirely true. Among those who had already published some form of autobiography were Benvenuto Cellini, Lord Herbert of Cherbury, and Bishop Gilbert Burnet. But Van Doren is correct when he says that Franklin "wrote for a middle class which had few historians. His book was the first masterpiece of autobiography by a self-made man." The closest model that he had, in terms of narrative style, was one of his favorite books, John Bunyan's allegorical dream, *A Pilgrim's Progress.* But Franklin's was the story of a very real pilgrim, albeit a lapsed one, in a very real world.

By the time he had to leave Twyford in mid-August, he had finished the first of four installments in what would later become known as the *Autobiography.* It took him through his years as a young printer engaged in civic endeavors and ended with the founding of the Philadelphia library and its offshoots in 1731. Only in his last lines did he let a note of politics creep in. "These libraries," he noted, "have made the common tradesmen and farmers as intelligent as most gentlemen from other countries, and perhaps have contributed in some degree to the stand so generally made throughout the colonies in defense of their privileges." It would be thirteen years before, at the urging of friends, he would pick up that part of the tale.[5]

Always eager to create a family wherever he could find one, Franklin took the Shipley's youngest daughter, Kitty, 11, under his wing and brought her in his coach back to London, where she was going to school. Along the way, they chatted about the type of man each of the Shipley daughters would marry. Kitty felt all of her sisters deserved a very rich merchant or aristocrat. As for herself, Kitty coquettishly allowed, "I like an old man, indeed I do, and somehow or another all the old men take to me." Perhaps she should marry a younger man, Franklin suggested, "and let him grow old upon your hands, because you'll like him better and better every year as he grows older." Kitty replied that she would prefer to marry someone already older, "and then you know I may be a rich young widow."

Another lifelong flirtation was born. He had his wife send over a squirrel from Philadelphia as a pet for all the Shipley girls. When the creature met an untimely end a year later in the jaws of a dog, Franklin composed a flowery epitaph and then added a simpler one that would become famous: "Here Skugg/Lies snug/As a bug/In a rug." His affection for Kitty would be immortalized fifteen years later when Franklin, then 80, wrote for her a little essay on "The Art of Procuring Pleasant Dreams."

On his last evening at Twyford, the Shipleys had insisted on throwing a birthday party, in absentia, for his Philadelphia grandson, 2-year-old Benjamin Franklin Bache. "That he may be as good as his grandfather," Mrs. Shipley said in her toast. Franklin responded that he hoped that Benny would, in fact, turn out much better. To which Bishop Shipley added, "We will compound the matter and be contented if he should not prove *quite* so good."[6]

The odd thing about all this affection for Benny was that Franklin had never met him, nor showed much of an inclination to do so. He had not even met the boy's father. But at that moment, Richard Bache was arriving in England on a mission to find his famous father-in-law. Bache appeared unannounced on Craven Street, where Mrs. Stevenson joyously greeted him. Franklin, however, had already departed, after little more than a week in London, for another extended vacation.

IRELAND AND SCOTLAND

Traveling with Richard Jackson, Pennsylvania's other agent in England, Franklin left in late August 1771 for three months in Ireland and Scotland, hoping to see if the relationship those countries were trying to forge within the British Empire might serve as a model for America. There were some promising signs. When they visited the Irish Parliament, Jackson was accorded the right to sit in the chamber because he was a member of England's Parliament. On seeing the famous Franklin, the Speaker proposed that, because he represented American legislatures, he should be accorded such a privilege as well. "The whole House gave a loud, unanimous Aye," Franklin reported to Cushing. "I esteemed it a mark of respect for our country."

On the other hand, much of what he saw in Ireland distressed him. England severely regulated Irish trade, and absentee English landlords exploited Irish tenant farmers. "They live in wretched hovels of mud and straw, are clothed in rags, and subsist chiefly on potatoes," he noted. His shock at the disparity between rich and poor made him all the more proud that America was building a vibrant middle class. The strength of America, he wrote, was its proud freeholders and tradesmen, who had the right to vote on public affairs and ample opportunity to feed and clothe their families.[7]

While in Dublin, Franklin happened to run into his nemesis, Lord Hillsborough, whose family estate was in northern Ireland. Surprisingly, Hillsborough insisted that he and Jackson stop by on their way to Scotland. Franklin was conflicted. "As it might afford an opportunity of saying something on American affairs," he wrote one friend, "I concluded to comply with his invitation." But he subsequently wrote his son that he had "determined not to go." As it turned out, Jackson insisted on going, and Franklin could not find another coach so had to follow along.

It was an astonishingly friendly visit. At Hillsborough's house, Franklin was "detained by a thousand civilities" for almost a week. The minister "seemed attentive to everything that might make my stay in his house agreeable." That even included "putting his own cloak about my shoulders when I went out, that I might not take cold."

In discussing Ireland's poverty, Hillsborough blamed it on England for restraining manufacturing there. Wasn't the same true, Franklin asked, about England's policy toward America? To Franklin's pleasure, Hillsborough responded that "America ought not to be restrained in manufacturing." He even suggested a subsidy for American silk industries and winemaking. He would be pleased to hear Franklin's "opinion and advice" on that, as well as on how to form a government for Newfoundland. Would Franklin consider these issues and when he returned to London "favor him with my sentiments?"

"Does not all this seem extraordinary to you?" he wrote his son. In a letter to Thomas Cushing, he suggested there might be a more cynical explanation. Hillsborough's behavior might be "meant only, by patting and stroking the horse, to make him more patient when the reins are drawn tighter and the spurs set deeper into his sides." Or, perhaps "he apprehended an approaching storm and was desirous of lessening beforehand the number of enemies he had so imprudently created."[8]

Franklin arrived, through storms and floods, in Edinburgh late on a Saturday and spent one night "lodged miserably" at an inn. "But that excellent Christian, David Hume, agreeable to the precepts of the gospel, has received the stranger and I now live with him," Franklin reported the next day. His old friend Hume had built a new house, and he took pride that the sheep's head soup made by his cook was the best in Europe. The talk at the table was also enviable: philosophy (Hume had recently befriended Rousseau in Paris), history, and the plight of the American colonies.

After ten days, Franklin traveled west toward Glasgow to see Lord Kames, his other favorite Scottish philosopher. Kames was also a great botanist who cultivated arbors of diverse trees; the ones Franklin planted on his visit are alive today. On his way back to Edinburgh, Franklin stopped at the Carron iron works, where James Watt was developing the steam engine, so that he could continue his study of industrialization. Among the ordnance they saw being cast, some of which would be used against the colonies in a few years, were cannons that weighed up to thirty-two tons.

Back at Hume's house in Edinburgh, Franklin spent another few days enjoying the intellectual circle there. He met with Adam Smith, who reportedly showed him some early chapters of the *Wealth of Nations* that he was then writing. Perhaps suspecting that they would never see their American friend again, Hume hosted a farewell dinner that included a variety of Franklin's favorite Scottish academics and writers, including Lord Kames.[9]

MEETING BACHE

Franklin had planned to stay longer with Hume, but two letters caught up with him while he was there. One was from his son-in-law, Richard Bache. Having missed Franklin in London, he wrote, he had gone to visit his own parents in Preston, a city in the north of England near Manchester. The other was from Polly. "Mr. Bache is at Preston, where he will wait with the pleasing expectation of seeing you on your return. We were all very much pleased with him." So Franklin hastened his departure for London and decided to visit his new in-law on the way.

Sally Franklin Bache, not surprisingly, was fretting back in Philadelphia about how her husband and father would get along. "If it should not be as cordial as I could wish," she wrote Richard, "I know when you consider it is my father, your goodness to and affection for me will make you try a little to gain his esteem and friendship." As it turned out, her fears were unfounded. "I can," Bache joyously wrote Deborah, "with great satisfaction, tell you that he received me with open arms and with a degree of affection I did not expect." He was particularly pleased that everyone told him he looked like Franklin, a revelation in those pre-Freudian times that was not seen as a reflection of Sally's taste in a husband. "I should be glad to be like him in any respect," Bache enthused.

Indeed, the old charmer wowed everyone in Bache's family, particularly his mother, Mary Bache, a "stately" and "serious" widow of 68, who had borne twenty children. During the visit, she stayed up until midnight talking to Franklin. A few weeks later, Franklin sent her a thank-you note with some oysters and (his vanity not fully conquered) a portrait of himself. Mrs. Bache carried it back and forth from the parlor to the dining room so she could view it all the time. "It is so like the original you cannot imagine with what pleasure we look at it, as we can perceive in it the likeness of my son as well as yourself." [10]

Bache traveled back to London with Franklin, stayed with him for a while on Craven Street, and tried hard to please. "His behavior here has been agreeable to me," Franklin told Deborah. But his affection did not extend to offering Bache the help he sought in winning a public appointment, such as customs inspector. "I am of the opinion that almost any profession a man has been educated in is preferable to an office held . . . subject to the caprices of superiors." Instead, he advised Bache to go home, become a merchant "selling only for ready cash," and to "always be close" to his wife. This advice, it must be remembered, came from a man who had lived across an ocean from his wife for much of fifteen years and had been clinging to his appointment as a royal postmaster.

As for Sally, he advised that she should learn accounting (always a theme) and help her husband out. "In keeping a store, if it be where you dwell, you can be serviceable to him as your mother was to me; for you are not deficient in that capacity, and I hope are not too proud." The Baches, ever mindful, would end up living in Deborah's house, opening a store in one of Franklin's Market Street buildings, and advertising "for cash only" a variety of silks and textiles for sale. When this dry goods shop turned out to be, as Bache complained to Franklin, a "sorry concern," he converted it to a "wine and grocery business," which also fared poorly. It was not the status or situation a woman of Sally's education and Bache's ambition felt was their due, but they followed Franklin's injunction to be not too proud. [11]

Deborah wrote Franklin so often about their grandson Benny that one can detect a note of caution creeping into his responses: "I can see you are quite in love with him, and your happiness wrapped up in his." He praised her for not stepping in during an argument when Sally was trying to discipline Benny: "I feared, from your fondness of him, that he would be too much humored, and perhaps spoiled."

He felt differently, however, about spoiling Polly Stevenson's new son, William Hewson, who had been born that spring. "Pray let him have everything he likes," he had written to Polly. "It gives [children] a pleasant air and . . . the face is ever after the handsomer for it." In the same letter, he responded sanguinely to Polly's teasing news that her mother had a new male friend. "I have been used to rivals," replied Franklin, "and scarce ever had a friend or a mistress in my whole life that other people did not like as well as myself."

Within two years, Billy Hewson had become Franklin's surrogate grandson. Responding to yet another letter from his wife describing their own grandson, Franklin wrote: "In return for your history of your *grandson*, I must give you a little of the history of my *godson*. He is now 21 months old, very strong and healthy, begins to speak a little, and even to sing. He was with us a few days last week, grew fond of me, and would not be contented to sit down to breakfast without coming to call Pa." He did deign to add, however, that watching Billy "makes me long to be at home to play with Ben."[12]

MORE SCIENCE AND INVENTION

When he poured the teaspoon of oil on the pond in Clapham and noted that it spread for a half acre, Franklin had come close to a discovery that would not be made for another century: determining the size of a molecule. If he had taken the volume of the teaspoon of oil (2 cubic centimeters) and divided it by the half-acre area it covered (2,000 square meters), he would have arrived at a ballpark figure (10^{-7} centimeters) for the thickness of an oil molecule. As Charles Tanford noted in his wonderful book, *Ben Franklin Stilled the Waves*, "Franklin had actually correctly determined the scale of magnitude of molecular dimensions, the first person ever to do so, but he did not recognize it."

Franklin was always better at practical applications than theoretical analysis. Rather than speculate about the size of molecules, he looked for uses for his oil-and-water experiments. Might it be possible to save ships from dangerous waves by dumping oil into the ocean? With three friends from the Royal Academy, he went to Portsmouth to see. "The experiment," Franklin reported, "had not the success we wished." The surface ripples were smoothed, but not the force of the underlying surges (another metaphor, perhaps). His report on his failed experiment was deemed useful enough, however, to be published in the *Philosophical Transactions* of the Royal Society.[13]

Throughout his time in England, whenever he could escape the demands of politics, he continued his scientific inquiries. After he wired some lightning rods on St. Paul's Cathedral, the keepers of the royal munitions asked him to propose ways to protect their buildings from lightning as well. This again embroiled Franklin in a dispute over whether lightning rods should have pointed or rounded tops; Franklin insisted on pointed ones, but (perhaps for political reasons) King George changed them to rounded ones after the American Revolution. Franklin also devised a system of hot-water pipes to keep the House of Commons warm.

Other excursions into science and invention during his years in London included:

- *The Cause of Colds:* Although germs and viruses had yet to be discovered, Franklin was one of the first to argue that colds and flu "may possibly be spread by contagion" rather than cold air. "Traveling in our severe winters, I have often suffered cold sometimes to the extremity only short of freezing, but this did not make me catch cold," he wrote the Philadelphia physician Benjamin Rush in 1773. "People often catch cold from one another when shut up together in close rooms, coaches, etc., and when sitting near and conversing so as to breathe in each other's transpiration." The best defense was fresh air. Throughout his life, Franklin liked good ventilation and open windows, even in the midst of winter.[14]

- *The Study of Exercise:* One way to prevent colds, he argued, was regular exercise. The best way to measure exercise, he argued, was not by its duration but "by the degree of warmth it produces in the body." This was one of the first theories linking exercise to calories of heat. For example, he explained, walking a mile up and down stairs produced five times more body warmth than walking a mile on a level surface. When swinging weights, Franklin calculated that this raised his pulse from 60 to 100 beats per minute. Again, he rightly calculated that body "warmth generally increases with quickness of pulse."[15]

- *Lead Poisoning:* As a printer, Franklin had noticed that the handling of hot lead type often caused a stiffness or paralysis. He also noticed that people in certain trades were prone to a severe illness called "dry belly ache." A friend added a clue by noting that people who drank rum from stills that used metal coils also got the disease. Acting as an epidemiologist, Franklin became one of the first to discover the cause of this malady. "It affects among tradesmen those that use lead, however different their trades, as glazers, type-founders, plumbers, potters, white-lead makers and painters." He suggested, among other things, that the coils of stills should be made of pure tin, instead of pewter that includes lead.[16]
- *Ships in Canals:* When visiting Holland, Franklin and his friend Sir John Pringle, president of the Royal Society, were told that ships passing through shallow canals went more slowly than those in deeper canals. This was because, Franklin surmised, each time a boat moved one length of distance, it would have to displace an amount of water equal to the space that her hull took up under the water. That water would then have to pass alongside or underneath the boat. If the passage underneath was constrained by being shallow, more water would have to rush past the sides of the boat, thus slowing her down. Here was a scientific theory that had enormous practical importance. So Franklin reacted accordingly. "I determined to make an experiment of this," he wrote Pringle. He built a fourteen-foot wooden trough that was six inches wide and deep, and in it he put a little boat that was tugged by a silk thread. The thread was placed over a pulley and pulled by the weight of a small coin. He repeatedly timed how fast the toy boat moved when the water was at various depths. The results showed that it took 20 percent more power or time to move a boat through a shallow canal than a deeper one.[17]
- *The Saltiness of Oceans:* At the time, the prevailing opinion about why the oceans were salty was that they had originally been filled with fresh water, but over the eons they accumu-

lated the salts and minerals that were dumped into them by rivers. Franklin surmised, in a letter to his brother Peter, that there was just as much evidence for the other hypothesis: "All the water on this globe was originally salt, and the fresh water we find in springs and rivers is the produce of distillation." As it turns out, Franklin was incorrect in this case. The oceans, over the centuries, have been getting saltier.[18]

- *The Armonica:* Among the most amusing of his inventions was a musical instrument he called the armonica. It was based on the common practice of bored dinner guests, and some musicians, of producing a resonant tone by moving a wet finger around the rim of a glass. Franklin attended a concert in England of music performed on wineglasses, and in 1761 he perfected the idea by taking thirty-seven glass bowls of different sizes and attaching them to a spindle. He rigged up a foot pedal and flywheel to spin the contraption, which allowed him to produce various tones by pressing on the glass pieces with his wet fingers. In a letter to an Italian electrician, Franklin described the new instrument in minute detail. "It is an instrument," he said, "that seems peculiarly adapted to Italian music, especially that of the soft and plaintive kind." Franklin's armonica was quite a rage for a while. Marie Antoinette took lessons on it, Mozart and Beethoven wrote pieces for it, and its haunting tones became popular at weddings. But it tended to produce melancholia, perhaps from lead poisoning, and it eventually went out of fashion.[19]

SOCIAL PHILOSOPHY

Over the years, Franklin had been developing a social outlook that, in its mixture of liberal, populist, and conservative ideas, would become one archetype of American middle-class philosophy. He exalted hard work, individual enterprise, frugality, and self-reliance. On the other hand, he also pushed for civic cooperation, social compassion, and voluntary community improvement schemes. He was equally distrustful of the elite and the rabble, of ceding power to a well-born establishment or to an unruly mob. With his shopkeeper's values, he cringed at class warfare. Bred into his bones was a belief in social mobility and the bootstrap values of rising through hard work.

His innate conservatism about government intervention and welfare was evident in the series of questions he had posed to Peter Collinson in 1753 (see pp. 148–49). Back then, he had asked whether laws "which compel the rich to maintain the poor have not given the latter a dependence" and "provide encouragements for laziness."[20]

To Collinson these points were raised as questions. But in his essays in the late 1760s and early 1770s, Franklin asserted his conservatism more forcefully. Most notable was an anonymous piece entitled "On the Laboring Poor," which he signed "Medius," from the Latin word for "middle," and published in *The Gentleman's Magazine* in 1768. In the essay, he chastised writers who stirred up the rabble by claiming that the poor were oppressed by the rich. "Will you admit a word or two on the other side of the question?" he asked. The condition of the poor in England was the best in Europe, he argued. Why? Because in England there was legislation to help support the poor. "This law was not made by the poor. The legislators were men of fortune . . . They voluntarily subjected their own estates, and the estates of others, to a payment of a tax for the maintenance of the poor."

These laws were compassionate. But he warned that they could have unintended consequences and promote laziness: "I fear the giving mankind a dependence on anything for support in age or sickness, besides industry and frugality during youth and health, tends to flatter our natural indolence, to encourage idleness and prodigality, and thereby to promote and increase poverty, the very evil it was intended to cure."

Not only did he warn against welfare dependency, but he offered his own version of the trickle-down theory of economics. The more money made by the rich and by all of society, the more money that would make its way down to the poor. "The rich do not work for one another . . . Everything that they or their families use and consume is the produce of the laboring poor." The rich spend their money in ways that enrich the laboring poor: clothing and furniture and dwellings. "Our laboring poor receive annually the whole of the clear revenues of

the nation." He also debunked the idea of imposing a higher mini-
mum wage: "A law might be made to raise their wages; but if our manufactures are too dear, they might not vend abroad." [21]

His economic conservatism was balanced, however, by his fundamental moral belief that actions should be judged by how much they
benefit the common good. Policies that encouraged hard work were
good, but not because they led to great accumulations of private
wealth; they were good because they increased the total well-being of
a community and the dignity of every aspiring individual. People who
acquired more wealth than they needed had a duty to help others and
to create civic institutions that promoted the success of others. "His
ideal was of a prosperous middle class whose members lived simple
lives of democratic equality," writes James Campbell. "Those who met
with greater economic success in life were responsible to help those in
genuine need; but those who from lack of virtue failed to pull their
own weight could expect no help from society." [22]

To this philosophical mix Franklin added an increasingly fervent
advocacy of the traditional English liberal values of individual rights
and liberties. He had not yet, however, completed his evolution on the
great moral question of slavery. As an agent for some of the colonies,
including Georgia, he found himself awkwardly and unconvincingly
defending America against British attacks that slavery made a mockery of the colonists' demands for liberty.

In 1770, he published anonymously a "Conversation on Slavery" in
which the American participant tries to defend himself against
charges of hypocrisy. Only "one family in a hundred" in America has
slaves, and of those, "many treat their slaves with great humanity." He
also argued that the condition of the "working poor" in England
"seems something a little like slavery." At one point, the speaker's argument even lapses into racism: "Perhaps you imagine the Negroes to
be a mild tempered, tractable kind of people. Some of them are indeed
so. But the majority are of a plotting disposition, dark, sullen, malicious, revengeful and cruel in the highest degree." [23]

In his desire to defend America at all costs, Franklin had produced
what was one of the worst arguments he ever wrote. Even his facts
were wrong. The proportion of slave-owning families in America was

not one in a hundred, but close to one in nine (47,664 families out of a total 410,636 American families owned slaves in 1790). Making his argument morally as well as factually weak was the fact that, even as he tried to argue that slave owning was an aberration, Franklin's own family was among those who still kept slaves. Although the two slaves who had accompanied him on his first trip to England were no longer with him, one or two continued to be part of Deborah's Philadelphia household.[24]

His views, however, were still evolving. Two years after he wrote the "Conversation," Franklin began corresponding with the ardent Philadelphia abolitionist Anthony Benezet. He used some of Benezet's arguments in a 1772 piece he wrote for the London *Chronicle* in which he decried, using stronger language than ever, the "constant butchery of the human species by this pestilent detestable traffic in the bodies and souls of men." He even edged closer to Benezet's argument that slavery itself—not merely the importation of new slaves—had to be abolished. "I am glad to hear that the disposition against keeping Negroes grows more general in North America," he wrote Benezet. "I hope in time it will be taken into consideration and suppressed by the legislature."

Franklin wrote in a similar vein to his friend the Philadelphia physician Benjamin Rush. "I hope in time that the friends to liberty and humanity will get the better of a practice that has so long disgraced our nation and religion." Yet it is important to note that, both to Benezet and to Rush, Franklin included the same qualifying phrase: "in time." For Franklin, support for complete abolition of slave ownership (rather than merely ending the importation of slaves) would come only in time, only after the Revolution.[25]

DEFEATING HILLSBOROUGH

Lord Hillsborough's solicitous warmth in Ireland, which had so baffled Franklin, soon dissipated. "When I had been a little while returned to London," Franklin wrote his son, "I waited on him to thank him for his civilities in Ireland." The porter informed Franklin that the minister was "not at home." Franklin left his card and returned another day to hear the same response, even though Franklin knew Hillsborough was indeed receiving guests that day. He tried the next week, then the next, to no avail. "The last time was on a levee day, when a number of carriages were at his door. My coachman, driving up, alighted and was opening the coach door when the porter, seeing me, came out and surlily chid the coachman for opening the door before he had enquired whether my lord was at home; and then, turning to me, said: 'My lord is not at home.' I have never since been nigh him, and we have only abused one another at a distance."

Hillsborough "threw me away as an orange that would yield no juice and therefore not worth more squeezing," Franklin complained. Again he considered returning to Philadelphia. "I grow homesick," he wrote William. But there was still one factor that kept him from leaving England in fury. Against all odds, he remained hopeful that he could secure for himself (and friends, family, and partners) a western land grant along the Ohio.[26]

To that end, he had been involved with a variety of partnerships, including ones called the Illinois Company and then the Indiana Company, that had failed to win support in London. In the summer of 1769, Franklin helped organize a consortium so powerful that he was convinced it would be able to outmaneuver Lord Hillsborough. The Grand Ohio Company, as it was named, included a collection of some of London's richest and most prominent names, most notably Thomas and Richard Walpole. For a while, it seemed the group, known as the Walpole Company, was destined for success. But in the summer of 1770, Hillsborough managed to have the scheme tabled for more study.

The Walpole group, however, was able to keep its prospects alive by spreading around ownership shares to an array of top ministers, including the lord chancellor and the president of the Privy Council. By the spring of 1772, Hillsborough could delay the matter no longer. Even the king let Hillsborough know that he expected the matter to be considered. In April, the board of trade sent the land application to the Privy Council with a recommendation that it be denied. But the Privy Council, two months later, held its own hearing, attended by Franklin, Walpole, and many of their influential shareholders. Hillsborough threatened to resign if it was approved, a prospect that likely hurt his case because many on the council were eager, in Franklin's words, "to mortify him." And they did. The grant was approved, and Hillsborough resigned.

Franklin and friends would never end up getting their land grant; the growing tensions between Britain and the colonies intervened. "The affair of the grant goes on but slowly," he wrote a friend the following year. "I begin to be a little of the sailor's mind when they were handing a cable out of a store into a ship, and one of them said: ' 'Tis a long, heavy cable. I wish we could see the end of it.' 'Damn me,' says another, 'if I believe it has any end; somebody has cut it off.' "

Still, Franklin had succeeded in ousting his nemesis. "At length we have gotten rid of Lord Hillsborough," he exulted to William. Hillsborough, in turn, called Franklin "one of the most mischievous men in England." Yet, in that odd way they had of cloaking their enmity in occasional bouts of feigned cordiality, the two men made peace when they happened upon each other at Oxford the following summer. Hillsborough made a point of bowing and complimenting Franklin. "In return for this extravagance," Franklin reported to William, "I complimented him on his son's performance in the theatre, though indeed it was but indifferent; so that account was settled. For as people say when they are angry: 'If he strikes me, I'll strike him again'; I sometimes think it might be right to say: 'If he flatters me, I'll flatter him again.' "[27]

THE HUTCHINSON LETTERS

"There has lately fallen into my hands part of a correspondence that I have reason to believe laid the foundation of most if not all our present grievances." With these fateful words, written to his Massachusetts supporter Thomas Cushing in December 1772, Franklin stirred up a tempest that would lead to his final break with Britain. Enclosed was a batch of letters, six of them written by Massachusetts governor Thomas Hutchinson, a Boston merchant from an old Puritan family, who had once been Franklin's friend when they had put together the Albany Plan for colonial union in 1754. The letters had been given to Franklin surreptitiously by an unnamed member of Parliament, and he forwarded them to Cushing with the injunction that they not be made public.

Hutchinson's letters were filled with advice on how to subdue colonial unrest. "There must be an abridgment of what are called English liberties," he had written. When they were published in Boston (John and Samuel Adams, with the acquiescence of Thomas Cushing, made sure that they were, despite Franklin's request that they not be), they stoked the growing fury of the radical patriots there.

This was the opposite of what Franklin had intended. His aim was to calm the rebellious sentiments by privately showing Cushing and a few other leaders that England's misguided policies had been caused by bad advice from people such as Hutchinson more than by unreasonable hatred for America. The letters, he believed, might even promote a "tendency . . . towards a reconciliation," which is what, he later claimed, "I earnestly wished."[28]

Indeed, most of Franklin's missives in early 1773 were designed to decrease tensions. "I hope that great care will be taken to keep our people quiet," he wrote Cushing in March, "since nothing is more wished for by our enemies than that by insurrections we would give a good pretence for increasing the military among us and putting us under more severe restraints." When the Massachusetts Assembly passed a resolution declaring that it was not subservient to Parliament, Franklin similarly urged the English to refrain from overreacting. "In my opinion, it would be better and more prudent to take no notice of it," he wrote Colonial Secretary Lord Dartmouth, who had replaced Hillsborough. "It is words only."[29]

To make his point without stirring up more animosity, Franklin reverted to his youthful love of satire in two anonymous propaganda pieces he wrote for the English papers in September 1773. The first was entitled "Rules by Which a Great Empire May be Reduced to a Small One." Noting that "an ancient sage" (it was the Greek admiral and ruler Themistocles) had once boasted that he knew how to turn a little city into a great one, the essay listed twenty ways to do the reverse to an empire. Among them:

In the first place, gentlemen, you are to consider that a great empire, like a great cake, is most easily diminished at the edges.

Take special care the provinces are never incorporated with the Mother Country, that they do not enjoy the same common rights, the same privileges in commerce, and that they are governed by severer laws, all of your enacting, without allowing them any share in the choice of legislators.

However peaceably your colonies have submitted to your government, shown their affection to your interest, and patiently borne their grievances, you are to suppose them always inclined to revolt, and treat them accordingly. Quarter troops among them, who by their insolence may provoke the rising of mobs . . . Like the husband who uses his wife ill from suspicion, you may in time convert your suspicions into realities.

Whenever the injured come to the capital with complaints . . . punish such suitors with long delay, enormous expense, and a final judgment in favor of the oppressor.

Resolve to harass them with novel taxes. They will probably complain to your Parliaments that they are taxed by a body in which they have no representative, and that this is contrary to common right . . . Let the Parliaments flout their claims . . . and treat the petitioners with utmost contempt.

The list, reflecting the indignities that had been perpetrated on America, went on at length: send them "prodigals" and "petty-fogging lawyers" to govern them, "perplex their commerce with infinite regulations," appoint "insolent" tax collectors, and garrison your troops in their homes rather than on the frontier where they can be of use. If you follow these rules for diminishing your colonies, the essay concluded, you will "get rid of the trouble of governing them." It was signed "Q.E.D.," the initials for the Latin phrase *quod erat demonstrandum* (which was to be demonstrated), used at the end of a philosophical argument to note the proposition was proved.[30]

Two weeks later, Franklin published an even broader parody of

Britain's treatment of America, "An Edict by the King of Prussia." A thinly disguised hoax, it purported to be a declaration issued by King Frederick II. Whereas the Germans had long ago created the first settlements in England and had lately protected it in the war against France, they had decided "that a revenue should be raised from said colonies in Britain." So Prussia was levying 4.5 percent duties on all English imports and exports, and it was prohibiting the creation of any further manufacturing plants in England. The edict added that the felons in German jails "shall be emptied out" and sent to England "for the better peopling of that country." Lest anyone be so thick as to miss the point, it concluded by noting that all of these measures should be considered "just and reasonable" in England because they were "copied" from the rules imposed by the British Parliament on the American colonies.[31]

When his "Edict" appeared, Franklin had the pleasure of being a guest at the country estate of Lord Le Despencer, who, as postmaster general of Britain, was Franklin's boss and had become his friend. Le Despencer was, in Van Doren's words, a "seasoned old sinner" who had restored a former abbey where he gathered dissolute friends for, as rumor had it, blasphemous rites and an occasional orgy. Franklin befriended him in 1772, when Le Despencer had become a bit more respectable, and helped him compile a simplified and deistic version of the Book of Common Prayer. (In his reformist zeal, Franklin had recently written a "more concise" version of the Lord's Prayer as well.)

Franklin was chatting in the breakfast parlor with Le Despencer and others when a guest "came running in to us out of breath" with the morning papers and exclaimed, "Here's the King of Prussia claiming a right to this kingdom!" Franklin feigned innocence as the story was read aloud.

"Damn his impudence," one of those present proclaimed.

But as the reading neared its end, another guest began to sense the hoax. "I'll be hanged if this is not some of your American jokes upon us," he said to Franklin. The reading, Franklin noted, "ended with abundance of laughing and a general verdict that it was a fair hit."

Franklin proudly described the parodies in a letter to William. He preferred the one on "Rules," he said, because of the "quantity and variety of the matter contained and a kind of spirited ending of each paragraph," but others preferred the "Edict." He boasted, "I am not suspected as the author, except by one or two friends, and have heard the latter ['Edict'] spoken of in the highest terms as the keenest and severest piece that has appeared here for a long time."

His letter to William, however, was not wholly jovial. Slowly, inevitably, a rift was widening between the increasingly radical American agent and the royal governor with upper-class friends and aspirations. "Parliament has no right to make any law whatever binding on the colonies," Franklin argued in the letter. "I know your sentiments differ from mine on these subjects. You are a thorough government man."[32]

IN THE COCKPIT

"I want much to hear how that tea is received," Franklin worriedly wrote a friend in late 1773. Parliament had added to the indignity of its continued tariff on tea by passing new regulations that gave the corrupt East India Company a virtual monopoly over the trade. Franklin urged calm, but the radicals of Boston, led by Sam Adams and the Sons of Liberty, did not. On December 16, 1773, after a mass rally in the Old South Church, some fifty patriots disguised as Mohawk Indians went down to the wharves and dumped 342 chests of tea worth £10,000 into the sea.

Franklin was shocked by "the act of violent injustice on our part." His sympathies for the colonial cause were not enough to overcome his basic conservatism about rabble rule. The shareholders of the East India Company "are not our adversaries," he declared. It was wrong "to destroy private property."[33]

As Boston was having its tea party, England was being roiled by recriminations from the release of the purloined Hutchinson letters. Franklin had expressed surprise that "my name has not been heard" in connection with the affair and added his "wish it may continue unknown." But in December, two men engaged in an inconclusive duel in Hyde Park after one accused the other of leaking the letters. When a rematch seemed imminent, Franklin felt he had to step forward. "I alone am the person who obtained and transmitted to Boston the letters in question," he wrote in a letter to the London *Chronicle* on Christmas Day. But he did not apologize. These were not "private letters between friends," he claimed, but were "written by public officers to persons in public station." They were designed to "incense the Mother Country against her colonies."[34]

Franklin's role in publicizing purloined copies gave ammunition to those in Britain who saw him as a troublemaker. In early January, he was summoned to appear before the Privy Council in a famed room known as the Cockpit, because cockfights had been held there during the time of Henry VIII. The ostensible reason was to hear testimony on a petition from the Massachusetts Assembly to remove Hutchinson from the governorship. The questioning, however, quickly focused on whether the letters from Hutchinson, which had been presented as evidence by Franklin, were private and how they were obtained.

Franklin was surprised to find at the hearing the solicitor general, Alexander Wedderburn, a nasty and ambitious prosecutor who had voted against the repeal of the Stamp Act and possessed (in the words of his prime minister Lord North) "an accommodating conscience." It was clear that the political issue of the petition against Hutchinson was being turned into a legal case against Franklin for making his letters public. The government, Wedderburn said pointedly, had "the right of inquiring how they were obtained."

"I thought this had been a matter of politics and not of law," Franklin told the committee, "and I have not brought any counsel."

"Dr. Franklin may have the assistance of counsel, or go on without it, as he shall choose," said one of the lords on the council.

"I desire to have counsel," Franklin replied. Asked how long he needed to prepare his case, Franklin answered, "Three weeks."

It was not a fun three weeks for Franklin. News of the Boston Tea Party reached England, further undermining sympathy for the American cause. He was called "an incendiary" and, he noted, "the papers were filled with invectives against me." There were even hints that he might be jailed. His fellow shareholders in the Walpole group expressed fear that his involvement would hurt their case for a land grant, so he wrote them that "I do therefore desire that you will strike

1

Franklin's birthplace on Milk Street in Boston,
across from the Old South Church.

Deborah Franklin, circa 1759,
by Benjamin Wilson.

2

William Franklin, circa 1790,
by Mather Brown.

3

Sarah "Sally" Franklin Bache, 1793, by John Hoppner.

4

Jean-Antoine Houdon's famous bust of Franklin.

5

Francis Folger Franklin, circa 1736, who died of smallpox at age 4.

6

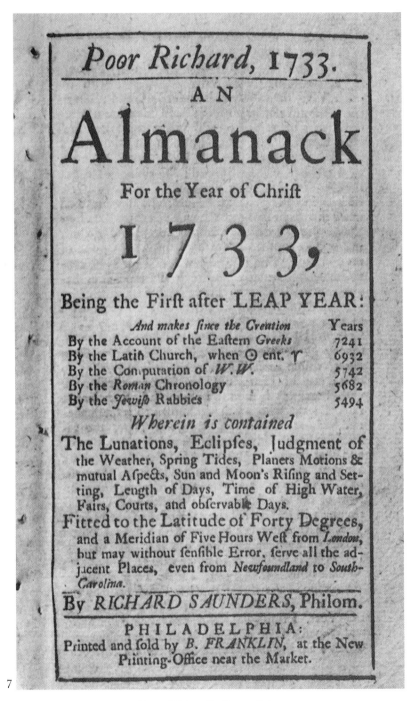

Poor Richard, 1733.

A N
Almanack

For the Year of Chrift

1733,

Being the Firft after LEAP YEAR:

And makes fince the Creation	Years
By the Account of the Eaftern *Greeks*	7241
By the Latin Church, when ☉ ent. ♈	6932
By the Computation of *W. W.*	5742
By the *Roman* Chronology	5682
By the *Jewiſh* Rabbies	5494

Wherein is contained

The Lunations, Eclipfes, Judgment of the Weather, Spring Tides, Planets Motions & mutual Afpects, Sun and Moon's Rifing and Setting, Length of Days, Time of High Water, Fairs, Courts, and obfervable Days.
Fitted to the Latitude of Forty Degrees, and a Meridian of Five Hours Weft from *London,* but may without fenfible Error, ferve all the adjacent Places, even from *Newfoundland* to *South-Carolina.*

By RICHARD SAUNDERS, Philom.

PHILADELPHIA:
Printed and fold by B. *FRANKLIN,* at the New Printing-Office near the Market.

7

Poor Richard's first edition.

8

Benjamin Franklin Drawing Electricity from the Sky,
by Benajmin West, circa 1817.

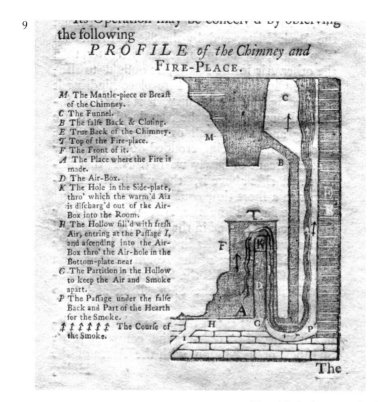

Its Operation may be conceiv'd by obferving the following

PROFILE of the Chimney and FIRE-PLACE.

M The Mantle-piece or Breaft of the Chimney.

C The Funnel.

B The falfe Back & Clofing.

E True Back of the Chimney.

T Top of the Fire-place.

F The Front of it.

A The Place where the Fire is made.

D The Air-Box.

K The Hole in the Side-plate, thro' which the warm'd Air is difcharg'd out of the Air-Box into the Room.

H The Hollow fill'd with frefh Air, entring at the Paffage *I*, and afcending into the Air-Box thro' the Air-hole in the Bottom-plate near

G The Partition in the Hollow to keep the Air and Smoke apart.

P The Paffage under the falfe Back and Part of the Hearth for the Smoke.

↟ ↟ ↟ ↟ ↟ The Courfe of the Smoke.

The

Franklin's diagram for his stove, 1744.

The glass armonica, Franklin's musical invention.

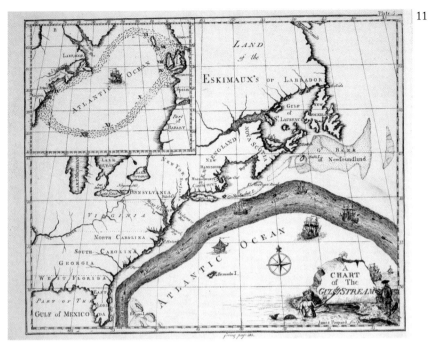

A chart of the Gulf Stream based on Franklin's notes.

12

Franklin's battery of Leyden jars.

13

Franklin's machine for
collecting static electricity.

The first portrait of Franklin, as a simple gentleman,
by Robert Feke, 1748.

15

Franklin's foe, Thomas Penn,
Pennsylvania's Proprietor.

The Pennsylvania Statehouse, 1778.   16

17

Franklin's house on Craven Street, London.

Franklin's friend William Strahan, by Joshua Reynolds.

18

19

JOIN, or DIE.

America's first political cartoon, produced by Franklin.

20

Franklin in London, studying under the gaze of Newton, by David Martin, 1766.

21

Charles Willson Peale made this sketch after walking in on Franklin kissing a girl, perhaps Polly Stevenson, on Craven Street.

Franklin standing silent as he is humiliated in London's cockpit in 1774.

22

A Declaration by the Representatives of the UNITED STATES OF AMERICA, in General Congress assembled.

When in the course of human events it becomes necessary for one people to dissolve the political bands which have connected them with another, and to assume among the powers of the earth the separate and equal station to which the laws of nature & of nature's god entitle them, a decent respect to the opinions of mankind requires that they should declare the causes which impel them to the separation.

We hold these truths to be self-evident; that all men are created equal, that they are endowed by their creator with inherent & inalienable rights; that among these are life, liberty, & the pursuit of happiness; that to secure these rights, governments are instituted among men, deriving their just powers from the consent of the governed; that whenever any form of government shall become destructive of these ends, it is the right of the people to alter

Edits by Franklin and Adams of Jefferson's rough draft of the Declaration of Independence; Franklin's heavy backslashes change "sacred and undeniable" to "self-evident."

Congress debates the Declaration, with Franklin dozing, center.

The famous portrait by Siffrèd Duplessis, 1778.

VIR

Engraving based on the portrait, circa 1778, by Rosalie Filleul, one of Franklin's lady friends in Paris, who wrote that she would "look forward to kissing" him, and was later guillotined during the French Revolution.

Franklin and the ladies of Paris.

28

A view of Passy.

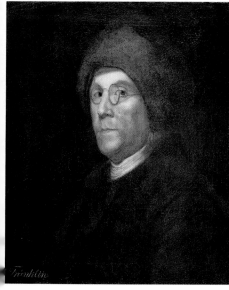

29

Franklin in his famous marten fur cap.

30

Engraving of Madame Helvetius.

The American negotiators at the peace talks with Britain in Paris, in an unfinished painting by Benjamin West, 1783: Temple Franklin, Henry Laurens, Benjamin Franklin, John Adams, John Jay.

A mural in the U.S. Capitol of Franklin under his Mulberry tree during the Constitutional Convention, with Alexander Hamilton, James Wilson, and James Madison.

my name out of the list of your Associates." (The letter, it should be noted, was cleverly phrased so that he did not, in fact, actually resign; he remained a secret shareholder without voting rights.)[35]

When the Privy Council reconvened in the Cockpit on January 29, 1774, the showdown made the original use of that room seem tame. "All the courtiers were invited," Franklin noted, "as to an entertainment." The packed crowd of councilors and spectators ranged from the Archbishop of Canterbury to the revenge-hungry Lord Hillsborough, with but a few friends of Franklin—including Edmund Burke, Lord Le Despencer, and Joseph Priestley—there to lend him moral support. Franklin later said it was like a "bull baiting."

Wedderburn, that man of sharp tongue, was both clever and brutal in his hour-long tirade. He called Franklin the "prime conductor"—an allusion to his electric fame—of the agitation against the British government. Instead of focusing on the merits of the Massachusetts petition, he homed in on the purloined letters. "Private correspondence has hitherto been held sacred," he raged. "He has forfeited all the respect of societies and of men." With a zinging wit, he added, "He will henceforth call it a libel to be called a man of letters." In addition to wit there was ample invective. Burke called Wedderburn's attack a "furious Phillipic," and another spectator called it "a torrent of virulent abuse."

Amid his fury, Wedderburn scored some valid points. Ridiculing Franklin's argument that Hutchinson's desire to keep the letters secret was an admission he had something to hide, the solicitor correctly noted that Franklin had kept his own involvement in the affair secret for almost a year. "He kept himself concealed until he nearly occasioned the murder" of an innocent man, he said, referring to the duel in Hyde Park. Pounding the council table until (according to Jeremy Bentham) it "groaned under the assault," Wedderburn accused Franklin of wanting to be governor himself.

The crowd cheered and jeered, but Franklin betrayed not the slightest emotion as he stood at the edge of the room wearing a plain suit made of blue Manchester velvet. Edward Bancroft, a friend of Franklin's (who later spied on him in Paris), described his behavior: "The Doctor was dressed in a full suit of spotted Manchester velvet, and stood conspicuously erect, without the smallest movement of any part of his body. The muscles of his face had been previously composed as to afford a placid tranquil expression of countenance, and he did not suffer the slightest alteration of it to appear."

At the finale of his speech, Wedderburn called Franklin forward as a witness and declared, "I am ready to examine him." The official records of the proceedings notes, "Dr. Franklin being present remained silent, but declared by his counsel that he did not choose to be examined." Silence had often been his best weapon, making him seem wise or benign or serene. On this occasion, it made him look stronger than his powerful adversaries, contemptuous rather than contrite, condescending rather than cowed.[36]

The Privy Council, as expected, rejected the Massachusetts petition against Hutchinson, calling it "groundless, vexatious and scandalous." The next day, Franklin was informed by letter that his old friend Lord Le Despencer "found it necessary" to remove him from his job as American postmaster. This infuriated him, for he was proud of having made the colonial system efficient and profitable, and he wrote a terse note to William suggesting that he leave his governorship and become a farmer. "It is an honester and more honorable, because a more independent, employment." To his sister Jane, he was more ruminative: "I am deprived of my office. Don't let this give you any uneasiness. You and I have almost finished the journey of life; we are now but a little way from home, and have enough in our pocket to pay the post chaises."[37]

Fearing that he might be arrested or his papers confiscated, Franklin slipped down to the Thames near Craven Street a few days after the Cockpit hearing. Carrying a trunk of his papers, he took a boat upriver to a friend's house in Chelsea, where he laid low for a few days. When the danger passed, he returned to Craven Street and resumed receiving guests. "I do not find that I have lost a single friend on the occasion," he noted. "All have visited me repeatedly with affectionate assurances of unaltered respect." At their request, he wrote a very long and detailed account of the Hutchinson affair, but then did not publish it, noting that "such censures I have generally passed over in silence."[38]

He did, however, continue his torrent of anonymous publications. Indulging an atypical but, given the circumstances, understandable desire to be boastful, he wrote a semianonymous piece (signed *Homo Trium Literarum,* a "Man of Letters," the insulting pun Wedderburn had hurled at him) that declared that "the admirers of Dr. Franklin in England are much shocked at Mr. Wedderburn's calling him a thief." He noted that the French, in the preface to his scientific papers just published there, also called him a thief: "To steal from the Heaven its sacred fire he taught." In an unsigned description of the Cockpit hearings, published in a Boston paper, he claimed of himself that "the Doctor came by these letters honorably, his intention in sending them was virtuous: to lessen the breach between Britain and the colonies."[39]

His satires and sarcasm became ever more biting. In one essay, written after General Gage had been sent to replace Hutchinson as governor in Massachusetts, he suggested that Britain "without delay introduce into North America a government absolutely and entirely military." That would "so intimidate the Americans" that they would happily submit to all taxes. "When the colonists are drained of their last shilling," he added, "they should be sold to the best bidder," such as Spain or France. In another piece, he proposed a policy for General Gage to assure that more rebels did not arise in America: "all the males there be castrated." For good measure, the "ringleaders" such as John Hancock and Sam Adams "should be shaved quite close." Among the side benefits, he added, were that it would be useful to the opera and it would reduce the number of people emigrating from Britain to America.[40]

Once again, the question arose: Why not finally head home? His wife was near death, he was a political outcast. Once again, he resolved to do so. As soon as he settled the post office accounts, he told friends; by May, he promised Richard Bache. And once again, he ended up not returning. For the rest of 1774, Franklin stayed in England with little to do, no official business to conduct, no ministers to lobby. Even the king found it curious.

"Where is Dr. Franklin?" His Majesty asked Lord Dartmouth that summer.

"I believe, sir, he is in town. He was going to America, but I fancy he is not gone."

"I heard," said the king, "he was going to Switzerland."

"I think," Lord Dartmouth replied, "there has been such a report."

In fact, he had stayed close to Craven Street, venturing out rarely, seeing mainly close friends. As he would write to his sister in September, "I have seen no minister since January, nor had the least communication with them."[41]

THE BREACH WITH WILLIAM

The impending clash between Britain and America inevitably foreshadowed a personal one between Franklin and his loyalist son. Tormented about the former prospect, Franklin remained callous about the latter.

William, on the other hand, agonized mightily as he tried to balance his duties as a son with those of being the royal governor of New Jersey. In his letters to his father after the Cockpit fight, he hoped to curry favor by flattering him, reassuring him, and cajoling him to come home. "Your popularity in this country, whatever it may be on the other side, is greatly beyond what it ever was," William wrote in May. "You may depend when you return here on being received with every mark of regard and affection." He made clear, however, that he had no intention of resigning his governorship, despite his father's occasional suggestions that he do so.

Caught in the middle was the printer William Strahan, one of Franklin's closest friends in England, who had become a confidant of the younger Franklin as well. He urged William to be his own man, to stick to loyalist positions, and to let the ministers know that he would not let his father's views interfere with his allegiance to the government he served.

William heeded the advice. Shortly after writing the solicitous letter to his father, he wrote one to Lord Dartmouth, the colonial secretary. "His Majesty may be assured that I will omit nothing in my power to keep this province quiet," he promised. Then he added pointedly, "No attachment or connections shall ever make me swerve from the duty of my station." Translation: his loyalty to his father would not tug him away from his loyalty to Britain. Lord Dartmouth promptly responded with reassurances: "I should do injustice to my own sentiments of your character and conduct in supposing you could be induced by any consideration whatever to swerve from the duty you owe the King."

William went further than merely offering professions of fealty. He opened what he called a "secret and confidential" correspondence with Lord Dartmouth that provided information about American sentiments. Support was growing throughout the colonies to aid Massachusetts, he warned, in reaction to the British decision to blockade Boston's port. A meeting of colonial delegates, which would become known as the First Continental Congress, had been scheduled for Philadelphia in September. William made clear which side he was on. The proposed gathering, he declared, was "absurd if not unconstitutional," and he doubted that it would lead to a mass boycott of British goods.[42]

His father disagreed on all counts. He had been recommending a continental congress for more than a year, he felt strongly that it should call for a boycott, and he was confident that it would. In that case, he wrote gleefully to William, "the present ministry will certainly be knocked up." He also chided William for clinging to his governorship and, typically, cast the issue in pecuniary as well as political terms. By remaining dependent on the salary of a governor, said Franklin, he would never be able to pay off the debts he owed his father. In addition, the changing political climate meant "you will find yourself in no comfortable situation and perhaps wish you had soon disengaged yourself." It was signed, simply, "B. Franklin."[43]

Even though he knew his letters were being opened and read by British authorities, Franklin forcefully urged his American supporters to take a firm stand. The Continental Congress, he wrote, must vote "immediately to stop all commerce with this country, both exports and imports . . . until you have obtained redress." At stake was "no less than whether Americans, and their endless generations, shall enjoy the common rights of mankind or be worse than eastern slaves."

In those days, when it could take up to two months for the mail to be delivered overseas, there were a lot of crossed letters. William continued to try to convince his father that a continental congress was a bad idea. "There is no foreseeing the consequences that may result from such a Congress." Instead, Bostonians should make restitution for the tea they destroyed, and then "they might get their port opened in a few months."

Franklin had actually expressed, a few months earlier, similar sentiments about how Bostonians would be prudent to pay restitution for their tea party. "Such a step will remove much of the prejudice now entertained against us," he had written Cushing in March. It infuriated him, however, to be given such a lecture by his son, and in September he wrote a crushing response rebutting William point by point. Britain had "extorted many thousands of pounds" from the colonies unconstitutionally. "Of this money they ought to make restitution." The argument ended in insult: "But you, who are a thorough courtier, see everything with government eyes."

Franklin wrote his son again in October, making many of the same arguments and then turning personal: he pointedly noted that his son was behind in paying back the money he had loaned him over the years and would not likely be able to do so if he remained a royal governor.[44]

For a while there was no answer. Then, on Christmas eve of 1774, William sent his father a letter of brutal sadness and pain. Deborah had died, with Franklin not there.

"I came here on Thursday last to attend the funeral of my poor old mother, who died Monday," he began, referring to his stepmother.

Franklin's dutiful and long-suffering wife had been pining away since her stroke five years earlier. "I find myself growing very feeble very fast," she had written in 1772. For most of 1774, she had been too weak to write at all. Oblivious, Franklin had continued to send off short notes to her, some paternalistic and others businesslike, that contained breezy references to his own health, greetings from the Stevenson family, and admonitions for not writing him.

"A very respectable number of the inhabitants were at the funeral," William continued. Clearly wanting his father to feel guilty, he described his last visit with Deborah that October. "She told me that she never expected to see you unless you returned this winter, that she was sure she would not live until next summer. I heartily wish you had happened to have come over in the fall, as I think her disappointment preyed a good deal on her spirits."

At the end of the letter, William turned plaintive as he beseeched his father to leave England. "You are looked upon with an evil eye in that country, and are in no small danger of being brought into trouble for your political conduct," William warned. "You had certainly better return while you are able to bear the fatigues of the voyage to a country where the people revere you." He also ached to see his own son, Temple, now 14, and he begged Franklin to bring him to America. "I hope to see you and him in the spring and that you will spend some time with me."[45]

THE HOWE–CHATHAM SECRET TALKS

As his wife was dying that December, Franklin was enjoying a flirtatious series of chess matches with a fashionable woman he had just met in London. But the games were not merely social. They were part of a secret last-ditch effort by some members of Britain's Whig opposition to stave off a revolution by the colonies.

The process had begun in August, when he received a request to call on Lord Chatham, formerly William Pitt the Elder, who had served two stints as prime minister and been known as "the Great Commoner" until unwisely accepting a peerage as the Earl of Chatham. The great Whig orator was a steadfast supporter of America. By 1774, he was ailing and out of government, but he had decided to reengage in public affairs as an outspoken opponent of Lord North and his policy of colonial repression.

Lord Chatham received Franklin warmly, professed full support for the resistance by the colonies to British taxation, and said he "hoped they would continue firm." Franklin responded by urging Chatham to join with other Whig "Wise Men" to oust the "present set of bungling ministers" and form a government that would restore the "union and harmony between Britain and her colonies."

That was not likely, Chatham said. There were too many in England who felt that there could be no further concessions because "America aimed at setting up for itself an independent state."

"America did not aim at independence," Franklin claimed. "I assured him that, having more than once traveled almost from one end of the continent to the other, and kept a great variety of company, eating, drinking and conversing with them freely, I never had heard in any conversation, from any person drunk or sober, the least expression of a wish for separation."

Franklin was not being fully forthright. It had been ten years since he had traveled in America, and he knew full well that a small but growing number of radical colonists, drunk and sober, desired independence. He had even begun entertaining that possibility himself. Josiah Quincy Jr., a zealous Boston patriot and son of an old Franklin friend, visited him that fall and reported that they had discussed "total emancipation" of the colonies as an increasingly likely outcome.[46]

The next act in the drama began with a curious invitation from a well-connected society matron who let it be known that she wanted to play chess with Franklin. The woman in question was Caroline Howe, the sister of Adm. Richard Howe and Gen. William Howe. They would eventually end up the commanders of England's naval and land forces during the Revolution, but at the time they were both somewhat sympathetic to the American cause. (Their sister was the widow of a distant cousin, Richard Howe, and thus known as Mrs. Howe.)[47]

When Franklin called on Mrs. Howe in early December, he found her "of very sensible conversation and pleasing behavior." They enjoyed a few games and Franklin "most readily" accepted an invitation to play again a few days later. This time, the conversation wandered. They discussed her interest in math, which Franklin noted was "a little unusual in ladies," and then Mrs. Howe turned to politics.

"What is to be done," she asked, "about this dispute between Great Britain and her colonies?"

"They should kiss and be friends," replied Franklin.

"I have often said that I wished the government would employ you to settle the dispute," she said. "I am sure nobody could do it so well. Don't you think that the thing is practicable?"

"Undoubtedly, madam, if the parties are disposed to reconciliation," he responded. "The two countries really have no clashing interests." It was a matter that "reasonable people might settle in half an hour." He added, however, that "the ministers will never think of employing me in that good work; they choose rather to abuse me."

"Aye," she agreed, "they have behaved shamefully to you. And indeed some of them are now ashamed of it themselves."

Later that same evening, Franklin dined with two old friends, the Quakers John Fothergill and David Barclay, who made the same plea that he act as a mediator. "Put pen to paper," they urged him, and draft a plan for reconciliation.

And so he did. His "Hints for a Conversation" included seventeen points, among them: Massachusetts would pay for the destroyed tea, the tea duties would be repealed, the regulations on colonial manufacturing would be reconsidered, all money raised by trade duties would go to the colonial treasuries, no troops would be stationed in a colony without the approval of its legislature, and all powers of taxation would reside with the colonial legislatures rather than Parliament. His friends asked permission to show the list to some "moderate ministers," and Franklin agreed.

These private negotiations were interrupted in mid-December, when Franklin finally received the resolutions that had been approved by the First Continental Congress. At its meeting in Philadelphia, which lasted until late October, the rump assembly had reasserted America's loyalty to the Crown—but not to Parliament. In addition, it voted a boycott of British goods if Parliament did not repeal its coercive acts.

Many of the colonial agents in London refused to have anything to do with the resolutions when they arrived. So Franklin and the other agents from Massachusetts took it upon themselves to deliver them to Lord Dartmouth, who "told us it was a decent and proper petition and cheerfully undertook to present it to his Majesty."

On Christmas day, Franklin visited Mrs. Howe for another chess match. As soon as he arrived, she mentioned that her brother, Admiral Lord Richard Howe, wanted to meet him. "Will you give me leave to send for him?" she asked.

Franklin readily agreed, and soon he was listening as Lord Howe showered him with compliments. "No man could do more towards reconciling our differences," the admiral told him. He asked Franklin to offer some suggestions, which he would then communicate to the proper ministers.

Franklin, wary of being caught in the middle, noted that the Continental Congress had made clear what the colonies wanted. But he agreed to another secret session a week later, again under the guise of visiting Mrs. Howe to play chess.

This time, the meeting was not quite as cordial. Lord Howe asked Franklin if he thought it might be useful for England to send an emissary to America to seek an accommodation. It might "be of great use," Franklin responded, as long as the person was one of "rank and dignity."

Mrs. Howe interjected by nominating her brother for such a role, subtly noting that there was talk of sending over their other brother, the army general, on a less peaceful mission. "I wish, brother, you were to be sent thither on such a service," she said. "I should like that much better than General Howe's going to command the army there."

"I think, madam," Franklin said pointedly, "they ought to provide for General Howe some more honorable employment."

Lord Howe then pulled out a piece of paper and asked if Franklin knew anything about it. It was a copy of the "Hints for a Conversation" that he had prepared. Franklin said that his role in drawing up the paper was supposed to be a secret, but he readily owned up to having been the originator. Howe replied that he "was rather sorry" to find that the propositions were Franklin's, because there was no likelihood that the ministers would accept them. He urged Franklin to reconsider the proposals and come up with a new plan "that would be acceptable." Mrs. Howe could recopy it in her own hand, so that the authorship would be kept secret. If Franklin did so, Lord Howe hinted, he could "expect any reward in the power of the government to bestow."

Franklin bristled at the implied bribe. "This to me was what the French call 'spitting in the soup,' " he later noted. Nevertheless, Franklin found himself trusting Lord Howe and decided to play along. "I liked his manner," he noted, "and found myself disposed to place great confidence in him."

The paper he sent to Mrs. Howe the next day made no substantive concessions. Instead, it merely restated the American position and declared them necessary "to cement a cordial union." Although the talks with Howe continued fitfully through February, fueled mainly by the admiral's ambition to be chosen as an envoy, they never moved much closer to a solution.

In the meantime, Franklin was engaged in a variety of other back-channel talks and negotiations, most notably with Lord Chatham. The former prime minister invited him to his country house to show him a series of proposals he planned to put before Parliament, and then visited him for two hours on Craven Street for further discussions. Lord Chatham's presence at Franklin's humble boarding-house—his coach waiting very visibly in the narrow street outside the door—caused quite a stir in the neighborhood. "Such a visit from so great a man, on so important a business, flattered not a little my vanity," Franklin admitted. It was particularly savory because it fell precisely on the first anniversary of his humiliation in the Cockpit.

The compromise that Chatham proposed, as the two men sat together in the tiny parlor of Mrs. Stevenson's house, would permit Parliament to regulate imperial trade and to send troops to America. But only the colonial legislatures would have the right to impose taxes, and the Continental Congress would be given official and permanent standing. Although Franklin did not approve of all its particulars, he readily agreed to lend his support by being present when Chatham presented the plan to the House of Lords on February 1.

Chatham gave an eloquent explanation of his proposals, and Lord Dartmouth responded for the government by saying they were of "such weight and magnitude as to require much consideration." For a moment, Franklin felt that all of his back-channel talks and lobbying might be bearing fruit.

Then Lord Sandwich, who as first lord of the admiralty had taken a hard line on colonial affairs, took the floor. In a "petulant, vehement speech," he attacked Chatham's bill and then turned his aim on Franklin. He could not believe, he said, that the plan came from the pen of an English peer. Instead, it appeared to him the work of some American. As Franklin recounted the scene: "Turning his face to me,

[he] said he fancied he had in his eye the person who drew it up, one of the bitterest and most mischievous enemies this country had ever known. This drew the eyes of many lords upon me; but . . . I kept my countenance as immovable as if my features had been made of wood."

Chatham replied that the plan was his own, but he was not ashamed to have consulted "a person so perfectly acquainted with the whole of American affairs as the gentleman alluded to and so injuriously reflected on." He then proceeded to heap praise on Franklin as a person "whom all Europe held in high estimation for his knowledge and wisdom and ranked with our Boyles and Newtons; who was an honor not to the English nation only but to human nature." Franklin later wrote to his son, with perhaps a bit of feigned humility, "I found it harder to stand this extravagant compliment than the preceding equally extravagant abuse." [48]

But Chatham was not only out of power, he was out of touch. Lord Dartmouth quickly abandoned his initial openness and agreed with Lord Sandwich that the bill should be rejected immediately, which it was. "Chatham's bill," Franklin wrote to a Philadelphia friend, "was treated with as much contempt as they could have shown to a ballad offered by a drunken porter." [49]

For the next few weeks, Franklin engaged in a flurry of further meetings designed to salvage some compromise. But by early March 1775, as he finally prepared to leave England, his patience had run out. He drew up an insolent petition to Lord Dartmouth demanding British reparations for the blockade of Boston Harbor. When he showed it to his friend and land deal partner Thomas Walpole, "he looked at it and me several times alternately, as if he apprehended me a little out of my senses." Franklin returned to his senses and decided not to submit the petition.

Instead, he played a small role in one of the final and most eloquent pleas for peace. He spent the afternoon of March 19 with the great Whig orator and philosopher Edmund Burke. Three days later, Burke rose in Parliament to give his famous but futile "On Conciliation with America" speech. "A great empire and little minds go ill together," he proclaimed.

By then, Franklin was already on the Philadelphia packet ship heading west from Portsmouth. He had spent his last day in London with his old friend and scientific partner Joseph Priestley. People who did not know Franklin, Priestley wrote, sometimes found him reserved, even cold. But that day, as they discussed the looming war and read from the newspapers, he grew very emotional. For a while, the tears in his eyes made it impossible for him to read.[50]

CHAPTER TWELVE

INDEPENDENCE

Philadelphia, 1775–1776

CHOOSING SIDES

Just as his son, William, had helped him with his famed kite-flying experiment, now William's son, Temple, lent a hand as he lowered the homemade thermometer into the ocean. Three or four times a day, they would take the temperature and record it on a chart. Franklin had learned from his Nantucket cousin, the whaling captain Timothy Folger, about the course of the Gulf Stream. During the latter half of his six-week voyage home, after writing a detailed account of his futile negotiations, Franklin turned his attention to studying it. The maps he published and the temperature measurements he made are included on the NASA Web site, which notes how remarkably similar they are to the infrared data gathered by modern satellites.[1]

The voyage was notably calm, but in America the long-brewing storm had begun. On the night of April 18, 1775, while Franklin was in midocean, a contingent of British redcoats headed north from Boston to arrest the tea party planners Samuel Adams and John Hancock and capture the munitions stockpiled by their supporters. Paul Revere spread the alarm, as did others less famously. When the redcoats reached Lexington, seventy American "minutemen" were there to meet them.

"Disperse, ye rebels," the British major ordered. At first they did. Then a shot was fired. In the ensuing skirmish, eight Americans were killed. The victorious redcoats marched on to Concord, where, as Emerson put it, "the embattled farmers stood, and fired the shot heard round the world." (Somehow, the poor Lexington fighters lost out in Emerson's poetic version of history, just as William Dawes and other messengers got slighted in Longfellow's "Paul Revere's Ride.") On their day-long retreat back to Boston, more than 250 redcoats were killed or wounded by American militiamen.

When Franklin landed in Philadelphia with his 15-year-old grandson on May 5, delegates were beginning to gather there for the Second Continental Congress. Bells were rung to celebrate his arrival. "Dr. Franklin is highly pleased to find us arming and preparing for the worst events," wrote one reporter. "He thinks nothing else can save us from the most abject slavery."

America was indeed arming and preparing. Among those arriving in Philadelphia that week, with his uniform packed and ready, was Franklin's old military comrade, George Washington, who had become a plantation squire in Virginia after the French and Indian War. Close to a thousand militiamen on horse and foot met him at the outskirts of Philadelphia, and a military band played patriotic songs as his carriage rode into town. Yet there was still no consensus, except among the radical patriots in the Massachusetts delegation, about whether the war that had just erupted should be waged for independence or merely for the assertion of American rights within a British Empire that could still be preserved. For that question to be resolved would take another year, though not for Franklin.

Franklin was selected a member of the Congress the day after his arrival. Nearing 70, he was by far the oldest. Most of the sixty-two others who convened in the Pennsylvania statehouse—such as Thomas Jefferson and Patrick Henry from Virginia and John Adams and John Hancock from Massachusetts—had not even been born when Franklin first went to work there more than forty years earlier.

Franklin moved to the house on Market Street that he had designed but never known, the one where Deborah had been living without him for the past ten years. His daughter, Sally, took care of his housekeeping needs, her husband, Richard Bache, remained dutiful, and their two children, Ben and Will, provided amusement. "Will has got a little gun, marches with it, and whistles at the same time by way of fife," Franklin wrote.[2]

For the time being, Franklin kept quiet about whether or not he favored independence, and he avoided the taverns where the other delegates spent the evenings debating the topic. He diligently attended sessions and committee meetings, said little, and then went home to dine with his family. Beginning what would become a long and conflicted association with Franklin, the loquacious and ambitious John Adams complained that the older man was treated with reverence even as he was "sitting in silence, a great part of the time fast asleep in his chair."

Many of the younger, hotter-tempered delegates had never witnessed Franklin's artifice of silence, his trick of seeming sage by saying nothing. They knew him by reputation as the man who had successfully argued in Parliament against the Stamp Act, not realizing that oratory did not come naturally to him. So rumors began to circulate. What was his game? Was he a secret loyalist?

Among the suspicious was William Bradford, who had taken over the printing business and newspaper of his father, Franklin's first patron and later competitor. Some of the delegates, he confided to the young James Madison, "begin to entertain a great suspicion that Dr. Franklin came rather as a spy than as a friend, and that he means to discover our weak side and make his peace with the ministers."[3]

In fact, Franklin was biding his time through much of May because there were two people, both very close to him, whom he first wanted to convert to the American rebel cause. One was Joseph Galloway, his old ally in the struggle against the Penns, who had acted as his lieutenant and surrogate for ten years in the Pennsylvania Assembly. During the First Continental Congress, Galloway had proposed the creation of an American congress that would have power parallel to that of Parliament, with both loyal to the king. It was a plan for an imperial union along the lines that Franklin had supported at the Albany Conference and later, but the Congress peremptorily rejected it. Sulking, Galloway had declined an appointment to the Second Continental Congress.

By early 1775, Franklin had come to believe it was too late for a plan like Galloway's to work. Nevertheless, he tried to persuade Galloway to join him as a member of the new Congress. It was wrong to quit public life, he wrote, "at a time when your abilities are so much wanted." Initially, he also gave Galloway no more clue than he had given others about where he stood on the question of independence. "People seemed at a loss what party he would take," Galloway later recalled.[4]

The other person Franklin hoped to convert to the revolutionary cause was someone even closer to him.

THE SUMMIT AT TREVOSE

New Jersey governor William Franklin, still loyal to the British ministry and embroiled in disputes with his own legislature, read of his father's return to Philadelphia in the papers. It was, he wrote Strahan, "quite unexpected news to me." He was eager to meet with his father and to reclaim his son, Temple. First, however, he had to endure a special session of the New Jersey legislature he had called for May 15. Shortly after it ended in rancor, the three generations of Franklins— father and son and a poor grandson caught in the middle—were finally reunited.[5]

Franklin and his son chose a neutral venue for their summit: Trevose, the grand fieldstone manor house of Joseph Galloway in Bucks County, just north of Philadelphia. Surprisingly, given the intensely emotional nature of the meeting, neither they nor Galloway apparently ever wrote about it. The only source for what transpired is, ironically, the diary of Thomas Hutchinson, the Massachusetts governor whose letters Franklin had purloined; in his diary, Hutchinson recorded an account of the meeting Galloway gave three years later, when both men were exiled loyalists in England.

The evening started awkwardly, with embraces and then small talk. At one point, William pulled Galloway aside to say that he had avoided, until now, seriously talking politics with his father. But after a while, "the glass having gone around freely" and much Madeira consumed, they confronted their political disagreements. "Well, Mr. Galloway," Franklin asked his longtime ally, "you are really of the mind that I ought to promote a reconciliation?"

Galloway was indeed of such a mind, but Franklin would hear none of it. He had brought with him the long letter he had written to William during his Atlantic crossing, which detailed his futile attempts at negotiating a reconciliation. Although Galloway had already heard portions of it, Franklin again read most of it aloud and told of the abuse he had suffered. Galloway volleyed with his own horror stories about how anonymous radicals had sent him a noose for proposing a plan to save the British union. A revolution, he stressed, would be suicidal.

William argued that it was best for them all to remain neutral, but his father was not moved. As Hutchinson later recorded, he "opened himself and declared in favor of measures for attaining to independence" and "exclaimed against the corruption and dissipation of the kingdom." William responded with anger, but also with a touch of concern for his father's safety. If he intended "to set the colonies in flame," William hoped, he should "take care to run away by the light of it."[6]

So William rode back to New Jersey, defeated and dejected, to resume his duties as royal governor. With him was his son, Temple. The one issue that Benjamin and William had settled at Trevose was that the boy would spend the summer in New Jersey, then return to Philadelphia to be enrolled in the college his grandfather had founded there. William had hoped to send him to King's College (now Columbia) in New York, but Benjamin scuttled that plan because it had become a hotbed of English loyalism. Temple was soon to be caught in a tug-of-war between two men who vied for his loyalty. He eagerly sought to please them both, but he was fated to find that impossible.

FRANKLIN THE REBEL

It is hard to pinpoint precisely when America crossed the threshold of deciding that complete independence from Britain was necessary and desirable. It is even difficult to determine when that tipping point came for specific individuals. Franklin, who for ten years had juggled hope and despair that a breach could be avoided, made his own private declaration to his family during their summit at Trevose. By early July 1775, precisely a year before his fellow American patriots made their own stance official, he was ready to come out publicly.

There were many specific events that pushed Franklin across the line to rebellion: personal slights, dashed hopes, betrayals, and the accretion of hostile British acts. But it is also important to take note of the core causes of Franklin's evolution and, by extension, that of a people he had come to exemplify.

When Englishmen such as his father had immigrated to a new land, they had bred a new type of people. As Franklin repeatedly stressed in his letters to his son, America should not replicate the rigid ruling hierarchies of the Old World, the aristocratic structures and feudal social orders based on birth rather than merit. Instead, its strength would be its creation of a proud middling people, a class of frugal and industrious shopkeepers and tradesmen who were assertive of their rights and proud of their status.

Like many of these new Americans, Franklin chafed at authority, which is why he had run away from his brother's print shop in Boston. He was not awed by established elites, whether they be the Mathers or the Penns or the peers in the House of Lords. He was cheeky in his writings and rebellious in his manner. And he had imbibed the philosophy of the new Enlightenment thinkers, who believed that liberty and tolerance were the foundation for a civil society.

For a long time he had cherished a vision of imperial harmony in which Britain and America could both flourish in one great expanding empire. But he felt that it would work only if Britain stopped subjugating Americans through mercantile trading rules and taxes imposed from afar. Once it was clear that Britain remained intent on subordinating its colonies, the only course left was independence.

The bloody Battle of Bunker Hill and the burning of Charleston, both in June 1775, further inflamed the hostility that Franklin and his fellow patriots felt toward the British. Nevertheless, most members of the Continental Congress were not quite as far down the road to revolution. Many colonial legislatures, including Pennsylvania's, had instructed their delegates to resist any calls for independence. The captain of the cautious camp was Franklin's long-time adversary John Dickinson, who still refrained from erecting a lightning rod on his house.

On July 5, Dickinson pushed through the Congress one last appeal to the king, which became known as the Olive Branch Petition. Blaming the troubles on the perfidies of "irksome" and "delusive" ministers, it "beseeched" the king to come to America's rescue. The Congress also passed a Declaration of the Causes and Necessity for Taking Up Arms, in which it proclaimed "that we mean not to dissolve that union which has so long and so happily subsisted between us, and which we sincerely wish to see restored."

Like the other delegates, Franklin agreed for the sake of consensus to sign the Olive Branch Petition. But he made his own rebellious sentiments public the same day. The outlet he chose was quite odd: a letter to his long-time London friend and fellow printer, William Strahan. No longer addressing him as "dear Straney," he wrote in cold and calculated fury:

> Mr. Strahan,
> You are a Member of Parliament, and one of that Majority which has doomed my country to destruction. You have begun to burn our towns, and murder our people. Look upon your hands! They are stained with the blood of your relations! You and I were long friends: You are now my enemy, and I am, Yours,
> B. Franklin.

What made the famous letter especially odd was that Franklin allowed it to be circulated and publicized—but he never sent it. Instead, it was merely an artifice for making his sentiments clear to his fellow Americans.

In fact, Franklin wrote Strahan a much mellower letter two days later, which he actually sent. "Words and arguments are now of no use," he said in tones more sorrowful than angry. "All tends to a separation." Just as he had not mailed the angrier version, Franklin did not keep a copy of the milder letter in his papers.[7]

(Franklin ended up remaining close friends with Strahan, who four years earlier had declared that "though we differ we do not disagree." The very day Franklin wrote his unsent note, Strahan wrote one from London lamenting the possibility that the looming war would lead to "the ultimate ruin of the whole of the most glorious fabric of civil and religious government that ever existed." They continued to correspond throughout 1775, with Strahan begging Franklin to return to England "with proposals of accommodation." Franklin responded in October by suggesting that Strahan "send us over fair proposals of peace, if you choose it, and nobody will be more ready than myself to promote their acceptation: for I make it a rule not to mix personal resentments with public business." He signed the letter, as Strahan had signed his, "your affectionate and humble servant." A year later, when he arrived in Paris as an American envoy, Franklin would receive a gift of Stilton cheese that Strahan sent over from London.)[8]

Franklin wrote his two other close British friends on July 7 as well. To Bishop Shipley, he railed against England's tactics of stirring up slaves and Indians against the colonists, and then he apologized for the angry tone of his letter. "If a temper naturally cool and phlegmatic can, in old age, which often cools the warmest, be thus heated, you will judge by that of the general temper here, which is now little short of madness."[9]

To Joseph Priestley, he lamented that the Olive Branch Petition was destined to be rejected. "We have carried another humble petition to the crown, to give Britain one more chance, one opportunity more of recovering the friendship of the colonies; which however I think she has not sense enough to embrace, and so I conclude she has lost them for ever." The letter to Priestley also offered a glimpse into Franklin's workday and the mood of relative frugality in the colonies:

> My time was never more fully employed. In the morning at 6, I am at the committee of safety, appointed by the assembly to put the province in a state of defense; which committee holds till near 9, when I am at the congress, and that sits till after 4 in the afternoon . . . Great frugality and great industry are now become fashionable here: Gentlemen who used to entertain with two or three courses, pride themselves

now in treating with simple beef and pudding. By these means, and the stoppage of our consumptive trade with Britain, we shall be better able to pay our voluntary taxes for the support of our troops.[10]

Liberated by his private break with his son and his public break with Strahan, Franklin became one of the most ardent opponents of Britain in the Continental Congress. He served on a committee to draft a declaration to be issued by General Washington, and the result was so strong that the Congress was afraid to pass or publish it. The document clearly came from Franklin's pen. It contained phrases he had used before to refute Britain's claims of having funded the defense of the colonies ("groundless assertions and malicious calumnies"), and it even concluded by seriously comparing the American-British relationship to the one between Britain and Saxony ("her mother country"), a comparison he had earlier made facetiously in his parody "An Edict by the King of Prussia." In an even more strongly worded preamble to a congressional resolution on privateering that he drafted but never submitted, Franklin accused Britain of "the practice of every injustice which avarice could dictate or rapacity execute" and of "open robbery, declaring by a solemn act of Parliament that all our estates are theirs."[11]

No longer was there any doubt, even among his detractors, where Franklin stood. Ever eager, like many Virginians, to hear about Franklin, Madison wrote to Bradford to see if the rumors of his ambivalence persisted. "Has anything further been whispered relative to the conduct of Dr. Franklin?" Bradford confessed that opinions had changed. "The suspicions against Dr. Franklin have died away. Whatever was his design at coming over here, I believe he has now chosen his side and favors our cause."

Likewise, John Adams reported to his wife, Abigail, that Franklin was now squarely in their revolutionary camp. "He does not hesitate at our boldest measures, but rather seems to think us too irresolute." The jealous orator could not suppress a slight resentment that the British believed that American opposition was "wholly owing" to Franklin, "and I suppose their scribblers will attribute the temper and proceedings of this Congress to him."[12]

FRANKLIN'S FIRST ARTICLES OF CONFEDERATION PLAN

For the colonies to cross the threshold of rebellion, they needed to begin conceiving of themselves as a new nation. To become independent of Britain, they had to become less independent of each other. As one of the most traveled and least parochial of colonial leaders, Franklin had long espoused some form of confederation, beginning with his Albany Plan of 1754.

That plan, which was never adopted, envisioned an intercolonial Congress that would be loyal to the king. Now, in 1775, Franklin put forth the idea again, but with one big difference: although his plan allowed for the possibility that the new confederation would remain part of the king's empire, it was designed to work even if the empire broke apart.

The Articles of Confederation and Perpetual Union that he presented to the Congress on July 21, like his Albany Plan, contained the seeds of the great conceptual breakthrough that would eventually define America's federal system: a division of powers between a central government and those of the states. Franklin, however, was ahead of his time. His proposed central government was very powerful, indeed more powerful than the one eventually created by the actual Articles of Confederation that the Congress began to draft the following year.

Much of the wording in Franklin's proposal was drawn from New England confederation plans that stretched back to one forged by settlements in Massachusetts and Connecticut in 1643. But the scope and powers went far beyond anything previously proposed. "The Name of the Confederacy shall henceforth be The United Colonies of North America," Franklin's detailed thirteen articles began. "The said United Colonies hereby severally enter into a firm League of Friendship with each other, binding on themselves and their posterity, for their common defense against their enemies, for the security of their liberties and properties, the safety of their persons and families, and their mutual and general welfare."[13]

Under Franklin's proposal, the Congress would have only a single chamber, in which there would be proportional representation from each state based on population. It would have the power to levy taxes, make war, manage the military, enter into foreign alliances, settle disputes between colonies, form new colonies, issue a unified currency, establish a postal system, regulate commerce, and enact laws "necessary to the general welfare." Franklin also proposed that, instead of a single president, the Congress appoint a twelve-person "executive council" whose members would serve for staggered three-year terms.

Franklin included an escape provision: in the event that Britain accepted all of America's demands and made financial reparation for all of the damage it had done, the union could be dissolved. Otherwise, "this confederation is to be perpetual."

As Franklin fully realized, this pretty much amounted to a declaration of independence from Britain and a declaration of dependence by the colonies on each other, neither of which had widespread support yet. So he read his proposal into the record but did not force a vote on it. He was content to wait for history, and the rest of the Continental Congress, to catch up with him.

By late August, when it was time for Temple to return from New Jersey to Philadelphia, William tentatively suggested that he could accompany the boy there. Franklin, uncomfortable at the prospect of his loyalist son arriving in town while the rebellious Congress was in session, decided instead to fetch Temple himself.[14]

Temple was lanky, fun-loving, and as disorganized as most 15-year-olds. Much correspondence was spent reuniting him with personal items he had left in the wrong place. As his stepmother noted, "You are extremely unlucky in your clothes." William tried hard to keep up the pretense of family harmony and included kind words about Franklin in all his letters to Temple. He also tried to keep up with Temple's frequent requests for more money; in the tug-of-war for his affections, the lad got fewer lectures about frugality than other members of his family had.

Once again, Franklin surrounded himself with the sort of domestic menagerie he found so comfortable: his daughter and her husband, their two children (Benny, 6, and William, 2), Temple, and eventually Jane Mecom, his sole surviving sibling. In none of the letters we have from that time is Deborah mentioned; life on Market Street seemed to go along without her.

For the time being, Franklin was able to close out his accounts, literally and symbolically, with his counterpart family back in London. He sent Mrs. Stevenson a £1,000 payment for his back rent, and stiffly warned her to invest it in a piece of land instead of stocks. "Britain having begun a war with us, which I apprehend is not likely soon to be ended," he wrote, "there is great probability of these stocks falling headlong."

For her part, Mrs. Stevenson sunk into "weak spirits" pining for his return. "Without the animating hope of spending the remainder of life with you," a friend of hers wrote Franklin, "she would be very wretched indeed." In his jovial way, Franklin once again proposed an arranged marriage, this time between his grandson Benny and Polly Stevenson's daughter, Elizabeth Hewson.[15]

A TRIP TO CAMBRIDGE

Franklin had been serving his country, as it headed toward revolution, in roles befitting a man of his age: diplomat, elder statesman, sage, and dozing delegate. But he still had the inclination and talent for hands-on management, organizing things and making them happen in a practical way.

He was the obvious choice to chair a committee to figure out how to replace the British-run postal system and then become, as he did in July, America's new postmaster general. The job paid a handsome £1,000 per year, but Franklin's patriotism overwhelmed his frugality: he donated the salary to care for wounded soldiers. "Men can be as diligent with us from zeal for the public good as with you for thousands per annum," he wrote Priestley. "Such is the difference between uncorrupted new states and corrupted old ones." His penchant for nepotism, however, remained intact. Richard Bache became the financial comptroller of the new system.

Franklin was also put in charge of establishing a system of paper currency, one of his long-standing passions. As usual, he immersed himself in many of the details. Using his botanical knowledge of the vein structures of different types of leaves, he personally drew the leaf designs for the various notes to make them harder to counterfeit. Once again, Bache benefited: he was one of those Franklin selected to oversee the printing.

Franklin's other assignments included heading up the effort to collect lead for munitions, devising ways to manufacture gunpowder, and serving on committees to deal with the Indians and to promote trade with Britain's enemies. In addition, he was made president of Pennsylvania's own defense committee. In that capacity, he oversaw construction of a secret system of underwater obstructions to prevent enemy warships from navigating the Delaware River and wrote detailed proposals, filled with historical precedents, for using pikes and even bows and arrows (reminiscent of the suggestions he had made in 1755 for using dogs) to compensate for the colonial shortage of gunpowder. The idea of using arrows might seem quirky, but he justified it in a letter to Gen. Charles Lee in New York. Among the reasons he offered: "A man may shoot as truly with a bow as with a common musket . . . He can discharge four arrows in the same time of charging and discharging one bullet . . . A flight of arrows, seen coming upon them, terrifies and disturbs the enemies' attention to their business . . . An arrow striking in any part of a man puts him hors du combat till it is extracted."[16]

Given his age and physical infirmities, Franklin might have been expected to contribute his expertise from the comfort of Philadelphia. But among his attributes was a willingness, indeed an eagerness, to be involved in practical details rather than detached theorizing. He was also, both as a teen and as a septuagenarian, revitalized by travel. Thus, he would find himself embarked on missions for the Congress in October 1775 and the following March.

The October trip came in response to an appeal from General Washington, who had taken command of the motley Massachusetts militias and was struggling to make them, along with various undisciplined backwoodsmen who had arrived from other colonies, into the nucleus of a true continental army. With little equipment and declining morale, it was questionable whether he could hold his troops together through the winter. So the Congress appointed a committee to look into the situation, which was about all it could do, and Franklin agreed to serve as its head.

On the eve of his departure, Franklin wrote two of his British friends to emphasize that America was determined to prevail. "If you flatter yourselves with beating us into submission, you know neither the people nor the country," he told David Hartley. To Joseph Priestley, he provided a bit of math for one of their friends to ponder: "Britain, at the expense of three millions, has killed 150 Yankees this campaign, which is £20,000 a head . . . During the same time, 60,000 children have been born in America. From these data his mathematical head will easily calculate the time and expense necessary to kill us all."[17]

Franklin and his two fellow committee members met with General Washington in Cambridge for a week. Discipline was a big problem, and Franklin approached it in his usual meticulous manner by drawing up (as he had done two decades earlier for Pennsylvania's militia) incredibly detailed methods and procedures. His list of prescribed punishments, for example, included between twenty and thirty-nine lashes for sentries caught sleeping, a fine of a month's pay for an officer absent without leave, seven days' confinement with only bread and water for an enlisted man absent without leave, and the death penalty for mutiny. The rations for each man were spelled out in similar detail: a pound of beef or salt fish per day, a pound of bread, a pint of milk, a quart of beer or cider, and so on, down to the amount of soap and candles.[18]

As they were preparing to leave, Washington asked the committee to stress to the Congress "the necessity of having money constantly and regularly sent." That was the colonies' greatest challenge, and Franklin provided a typical take on how raising £1.2 million a year could be accomplished merely through more frugality. "If 500,000 families will each spend a shilling a week less," he explained to Bache, "they may pay the whole sum without otherwise feeling it. Forbearing to drink tea saves three-fourths of the money, and 500,000 women doing each threepence worth of spinning or knitting in a week will pay the rest." For his own part, Franklin forked over his postmaster's salary plus £100 that Mrs. Stevenson had helped raise in London for the American wounded. He also collected from the Massachusetts Assembly the money it owed him for his services as their London agent, and that he kept.[19]

At a dinner during the trip, he met John Adams's wife, Abigail, who was later to be disparaging about Franklin but on that night was charmed. Her description in a letter to her husband shows that she had a good insight into his demeanor, though not his religious convictions:

> I found him social but not talkative, and when he spoke something useful dropped from his tongue. He was grave, yet pleasant and affable. You know I make some pretensions to physiognomy, and I thought I could read into his countenance the virtues of his heart; among which patriotism shone in its full luster, and with that is blended every virtue of a Christian: for a true patriot must be a religious man.[20]

On his way back to Philadelphia, Franklin stopped in Rhode Island to meet his sister Jane Mecom. She had fled British-occupied Boston and taken refuge with Franklin's old friend Catherine Ray Greene and her husband. Caty's house now included dozens of refugee relatives and friends, and Franklin worried that Jane "must be a great burden to that hospitable house." In fact, as Claude-Anne Lopez notes, "Jane and Caty, a generation apart in age, a world in circumstances and temperament, had a marvelous rapport." Just as Franklin was wont to find surrogate daughters for himself, Jane took to treating Caty as one. ("Would to God I had such a one!" she wrote Caty, even though Jane in fact had a daughter of her own from whom she was estranged.)[21]

Franklin reciprocated. When he picked up Jane, he convinced Caty's 10-year-old son, Ray, to come with them back to Philadelphia and enroll with Temple at the college there. The carriage ride through Connecticut and New Jersey was a delight for Jane. "My dear brother's conversation was more than the equivalent of all the fine weather imaginable," she reported to Caty. The good feelings were so strong that they were able to overcome any political tensions when they made a brief stop at the governor's mansion in Perth Amboy to call on William.

It would turn out to be the last time Franklin would see his son other than a final tense meeting in England ten years later. But neither man knew that at the time, and they kept the meeting short. "We would willingly have detained them longer," William's wife wrote Temple, "but Papa was anxious to get home."[22]

Back in Philadelphia, a group of Marine units were being organized to try to capture British arms shipments. Franklin noticed that one of their drummers had painted a rattlesnake on his drum emblazoned with the words "Don't tread on me." In an anonymous article, filled with bold humor and a touch of venom, Franklin suggested that this should be the symbol and motto of America's fight. The rattlesnake, Franklin noted, had no eyelids, and "may therefore be esteemed an emblem of vigilance." It also never initiated an attack nor surrendered once engaged, and "is therefore an emblem of magnanimity and true courage." As for the rattles, the snake on the drum had thirteen of them, "exactly the number of the colonies united in America; and I recollected too that this was the only part of the snake which increased in number." Christopher Gadsen, a delegate to the Congress from South Carolina, picked up the suggestion in Franklin's article and subsequently designed a yellow flag with a rattlesnake emblazoned "Don't Tread on Me." It was flown in early 1776 by America's first Marine units and later by many other militias.[23]

CANADA

Undertaking a mission to the Boston area in autumn was understandable: it was an easy enough trip to the town of his birth. The Congress's decision to send him on his second mission, and his willingness to agree, was less explicable. In March 1776, Franklin, now 70, embarked on a brutal trip to Quebec.

A combined American force, led in part by the still-patriotic Benedict Arnold, had invaded Canada with the goal of preventing Britain from launching an expedition down the Hudson and splitting the colonies. Trapped and under siege, the American forces had spent the winter freezing and begging the Congress for reinforcements. Once more, the Congress responded by appointing a committee, again with Franklin at the head.

On their first day of travel, Franklin and his fellow commissioners passed just north of Perth Amboy, where William kept up the pretense of governing even though local rebels restricted his movements. Franklin did not visit. His son was now an enemy. Indeed, William showed where his loyalties now were: he sent back to London all the information he had been able to gather on his father's mission. "Dr. Franklin," he noted, planned to "prevail on the Canadians to enter into the Confederacy with the other colonies." Yet, in his letters to Temple, William poured out his sorrow and fears. Was the old man healthy enough to survive the journey? Was there a way to dissuade him from going? "Nothing ever gave me more pain than his undertaking that journey."

By the time he reached Saratoga, where they paused to wait for the ice on the lakes to clear, Franklin realized that he in fact might not survive. "I have undertaken a fatigue that at my time of life may prove too much for me," he wrote Josiah Quincy. "So I sit down to write to a few friends by way of farewell." But he soldiered on and, after an arduous month of travel that included time spent sleeping on the floors of abandoned houses, finally reached Montreal. Along the way, he picked up a soft marten fur cap that he would later make famous when, as an envoy in Paris, he wore it as part of his pose as a simple frontier sage.[24]

Despite the disarray of his forces, Benedict Arnold hosted Franklin and his fellow commissioners at a grand supper graced by a profusion of young French ladies. Alas, Franklin was in no shape to enjoy it. "I suffered much from a number of large boils," he later wrote. "In Canada, my legs swelled and I apprehended a dropsy."

The military situation was equally bad. America's besieged army had expected the committee to bring needed funds, and there was great discouragement when they discovered this was not the case. Franklin's delegation hoped, on the other hand, that it would be able to raise funds from the local Canadians, but that proved impossible. Franklin personally provided £353 in gold from his own pocket to Arnold, a nice gesture that bought him some affection while doing little to solve the situation.

Franklin had been instructed to try to entice Quebec into joining the American rebellion, but he decided not to even try. "Until the arrival of money, it seems improper to propose the federal union of this province with the others," he reported, "as the few friends we have here will scarce venture to exert themselves in promoting it until they see our credit recovered and a sufficient army arrived."

When reports came that more British ships were on their way, the Canadians became even less hospitable. The committee reached what was an inevitable conclusion: "If money cannot be had to support your army here with honor, so as to be respected instead of being hated by the people, we repeat it as our firm and unanimous opinion that it is better immediately to withdraw."

Exhausted and feeling defeated, Franklin spent the month of May struggling to make it back to Philadelphia. "I find I grow daily more feeble," he wrote. When he arrived home, his gout was so bad that he could not leave his house for days. It seemed he had performed his last mission for his country.

But his strength gradually returned, spurred by a visit from General Washington and by some tidings of a big event that was about to occur. His poor health, he wrote Washington on June 21, "has kept me from Congress and company almost ever since you left us, so that I know little of what has passed there except that a Declaration of Independence is preparing."[25]

THE PATH TO THE DECLARATION

Until 1776, most colonial leaders believed—or politely pretended to believe—that America's dispute was with the king's misguided ministers, not with the king himself nor the Crown in concept. To declare independence, they had to convince their countrymen, and themselves, to take the daunting leap of abandoning this distinction. One thing that helped them do so was the publication, in January of that year, of an anonymous forty-seven-page pamphlet entitled *Common Sense.*

In prose that drew its power, as Franklin's often did, from being unadorned, the author argued that there was no "natural or religious reason [for] the distinction of men into kings and subjects." Hereditary rule was a historic abomination. "Of more worth is one honest man to society and in the sight of God, than all the crowned ruffians that ever lived." Thus, there was only one path for Americans: "Every thing that is right or natural pleads for separation."

Within weeks of its appearance in Philadelphia, the pamphlet sold an astonishing 120,000 copies. Many thought Franklin the author, for it reflected his blunt sentiments about the corruption of hereditary power. In fact, Franklin's hand was more indirect: the real author was a cheeky young Quaker from London named Thomas Paine, who had failed as a corset maker, been fired as a tax clerk, and then gained an introduction to Franklin, who, not surprisingly, took a liking to him. When Paine decided he wanted to immigrate to America and become a writer, Franklin procured him passage and wrote to Richard Bache in 1774 asking him to help get Paine a job. Soon he was working for a Philadelphia printer and honing his skills as an essayist. When Paine showed him the manuscript for *Common Sense,* Franklin offered his wholehearted support along with a few suggested revisions.[26]

Paine's pamphlet galvanized the forces favoring outright revolution. Cautious colonial legislatures became less so, revising their instructions to their delegates so that they now were permitted to consider the question of independence. On June 7, as Franklin recuperated, Virginia's Richard Henry Lee, brother of his once and future rival Arthur Lee, put the motion on the table, to wit: "These United Colonies are, and of right ought to be, free and independent states."

Although the Congress put off a vote on the motion for a few weeks, it took one immediate step toward independence that affected the Franklins personally: ordering the removal of all royal governments in the colonies. Patriotic new provincial congresses asserted themselves, and the one in New Jersey, on June 15, 1776, declared that Gov. William Franklin was "an enemy of the liberties of this country." In deference to the fact that he was a Franklin, the order for William's arrest did suggest that he be handled "with all the delicacy and tenderness which the nature of the business can possibly admit."

William was in no mood for delicacy or tenderness. The speech he made at his trial on June 21 was so defiant that one of the judges described it as "every way worthy of his exalted birth," referring to his illegitimacy rather than to his famous paternity. For his part, the elder

Franklin was not acting particularly paternal. His letter to Washington that noted the preparation of a declaration of independence was written on the same day that his son was being tried, but Franklin didn't mention it. Nor did he say or do anything to help his son when the Continental Congress, three days later, voted to have him imprisoned in Connecticut.

Thus, the words that William wrote on the eve of his confinement to his own son, who was now firmly ensconced in his grandfather's custody, read so painfully generous: "God bless you, my dear boy; be dutiful and attentive to your grandfather, to whom you owe great obligation." Then he concluded with a bit of forced optimism: "If we survive the present storm, we may all meet and enjoy the sweets of peace with the greater relish." [27]

They would, in fact, survive the storm, and indeed all meet again, but never to relish the sweets of peace together. The wounds of 1776 would prove too deep.

EDITING JEFFERSON

As the Congress prepared to vote on the question of independence, it appointed a committee for what, in hindsight, would turn out to be a momentous task, but one that at the time did not seem so important: drafting a declaration that explained the decision. It included Franklin, of course, and Thomas Jefferson and John Adams, as well as Connecticut merchant Roger Sherman and New York lawyer Robert Livingston. [28]

How was it that Jefferson, at 33, got the honor of drafting the document? His name was listed first on the committee, signifying that he was the chairman, because he had gotten the most votes and because he was from Virginia, the colony that had proposed the resolution. His four colleagues had other committee assignments that they considered to be more important, and none of them realized that the document would eventually become viewed as a text akin to scripture.

For his part, Adams mistakenly thought he had already secured his place in history by writing the preamble to a May 10 resolution that called for the dismantling of royal authority in the colonies, which he proclaimed incorrectly would be regarded by historians as "the most important resolution that ever was taken in America." Years later, in his pompous way, he would claim that Jefferson wanted him to be the declaration's writer, but that he had convinced the younger man to do the honors, arguing: "Reason first, you are a Virginian, and a Virginian ought to appear at the head of this business. Reason second, I am obnoxious, suspected, and unpopular. You are very much otherwise. Reason third, you can write ten times better than I can." Jefferson's recollection was quite different. The committee "unanimously pressed on myself alone to make the draught," he later wrote.[29]

As for Franklin, he was still laid up in bed with boils and gout when the committee first met. Besides, he later told Jefferson, "I have made it a rule, whenever in my power, to avoid becoming the draughtsman of papers to be reviewed by a public body."

And thus it was that Jefferson had the glorious honor of composing, on a little lap desk he had designed, some of the most famous phrases in history while sitting alone in a second-floor room of a home on Market Street just a block from Franklin's home. "When in the course of human events . . ." he famously began. Significantly, what followed was an attack not on the British government (i.e., the ministers) but on the British state incarnate (i.e., the king). "To attack the king was," historian Pauline Maier notes, "a constitutional form. It was the way Englishmen announced revolution."[30]

The document Jefferson drafted was in some ways similar to what Franklin would have written. It contained a highly specific bill of particulars against the British, and it recounted, as Franklin had often done, the details of America's attempts to be conciliatory despite England's repeated intransigence. Indeed, Jefferson's words echoed some of the language that Franklin had used earlier that year in a draft resolution that he never published:

> Whereas, whenever kings, instead of protecting the lives and properties of their subjects, as is their bounden duty, do endeavor to perpetrate the destruction of either, they thereby cease to be kings, become tyrants, and dissolve all ties of allegiance between themselves and their people; we hereby further solemnly declare, that whenever it shall appear clearly to us, that the King's troops and ships now in America, or

hereafter to be brought there, do, *by his Majesty's orders,* destroy any town or the inhabitants of any town or place in America, or that the savages have been by the same orders hired to assassinate our poor out-settlers and their families, we will from that time renounce all allegiance to Great Britain, so long as that kingdom shall submit to him, or any of his descendants, as its sovereign.[31]

Jefferson's writing style, however, was different from Franklin's. It was graced with rolling cadences and mellifluous phrases, soaring in their poetry and powerful despite their polish. In addition, Jefferson drew on a depth of philosophy not found in Franklin. He echoed both the language and grand theories of English and Scottish Enlighten-ment thinkers, most notably the concept of natural rights propounded by John Locke, whose *Second Treatise on Government* he had read at least three times. And he built his case, in a manner more sophisti-cated than Franklin would have, on a contract between government and the governed that was founded on the consent of the people.

Jefferson also, it should be noted, borrowed freely from the phras-ings of others, including the resounding Declaration of Rights in the new Virginia constitution that had just been drafted by his fellow planter George Mason, in a manner that today might subject him to questions of plagiarism but back then was considered not only proper but learned. Indeed, when the cranky John Adams, jealous of the ac-claim that Jefferson had gotten, did point out years later that there were no new ideas in the Declaration and that many of the phrases had been lifted from others, Jefferson retorted: "I did not consider it as any part of my charge to invent new ideas altogether and to offer no sentiment which had ever been expressed before."[32]

When he had finished a draft and incorporated some changes from Adams, Jefferson sent it to Franklin on the morning of Friday, June 21. "Will Doctor Franklin be so good as to peruse it," he wrote in his cover note, "and suggest such alterations as his more enlarged view of the subject will dictate?"[33] People were much more polite to editors back then.

Franklin made only a few changes, some of which can be viewed written in his own hand on what Jefferson referred to as the "rough draft" of the Declaration. (This remarkable document is at the Library of Congress and on its Web site.) The most important of his edits was small but resounding. He crossed out, using the heavy backslashes that he often employed, the last three words of Jefferson's phrase "We hold these truths to be sacred and undeniable" and changed them to the words now enshrined in history: "We hold these truths to be self-evident."[34]

The idea of "self-evident" truths was one that drew less on John Locke, who was Jefferson's favored philosopher, than on the scientific determinism espoused by Isaac Newton and on the analytic empiricism of Franklin's close friend David Hume. In what became known as "Hume's fork," the great Scottish philosopher, along with Leibniz and others, had developed a theory that distinguished between synthetic truths that describe matters of fact (such as "London is bigger than Philadelphia") and analytic truths that are self-evident by virtue of reason and definition ("The angles of a triangle equal 180 degrees"; "All bachelors are unmarried"). By using the word "sacred," Jefferson had asserted, intentionally or not, that the principle in question—the equality of men and their endowment by their creator with inalienable rights—was an assertion of religion. Franklin's edit turned it instead into an assertion of rationality.

Franklin's other edits were less felicitous. He changed Jefferson's "reduce them to arbitrary power" to "reduce them under absolute despotism," and he took out the literary flourish in Jefferson's "invade and deluge us in blood" to make it more sparse: "invade and destroy us." And a few of his changes seem somewhat pedantic. "Amount of their salaries" became "amount and payment of their salaries."[35]

On July 2, the Continental Congress finally took the momentous step of voting for independence. Pennsylvania was one of the last states to hold out; until June, its legislature had instructed its delegates to "utterly reject" any actions "that may cause or lead to a separation from our Mother Country." But under pressure from a more radical rump legislature, the instructions were changed. Led by Franklin, Pennsylvania's delegation, with conservative John Dickinson abstaining, joined the rest of the colonies in voting for independence.

As soon as the vote was completed, the Congress formed itself into a committee of the whole to consider Jefferson's draft Declaration. They were not so light in their editing as Franklin had been. Large sections were eviscerated, most notably the one that criticized the king for perpetuating the slave trade. The Congress also, to its credit, cut by more than half the draft's final five paragraphs, in which Jefferson had begun to ramble in a way that detracted from the document's power.[36]

Jefferson was distraught. "I was sitting by Dr. Franklin," he recalled, "who perceived that I was not insensible to these mutilations." But the process (in addition to in fact improving the great document) had the delightful consequence of eliciting from Franklin, who sought to console Jefferson, one of his most famous little tales. When he was a young printer, a friend starting out in the hat-making business wanted a sign for his shop. As Franklin recounted:

> He composed it in these words, "John Thompson, hatter, makes and sells hats for ready money," with a figure of a hat subjoined. But he thought he would submit it to his friends for their amendments. The first he showed it to thought the word "Hatter" tautologous, because followed by the words "makes hats," which showed he was a hatter. It was struck out. The next observed that the word "makes" might as well be omitted, because his customers would not care who made the hats . . . He struck it out. A third said he thought the words "for ready money" were useless, as it was not the custom of the place to sell on credit. Everyone who purchased expected to pay. They were parted with; and the inscription now stood, "John Thompson sells hats." "Sells hats!" says his next friend; "why, nobody will expect you to give them away. What then is the use of that word?" It was stricken out, and "hats" followed, the rather as there was one painted on the board. So his inscription was reduced ultimately to "John Thompson," with the figure of a hat subjoined."[37]

At the official signing of the parchment copy on August 2, John Hancock, the president of the Congress, penned his name with his famous flourish. "There must be no pulling different ways," he declared. "We must all hang together." According to the early American historian Jared Sparks, Franklin replied: "Yes, we must, indeed, all hang together, or most assuredly we shall all hang separately." Their lives, as well as their sacred honor, had been put on the line.[38]

CONSTITUTIONAL IDEAS

Having declared the collective colonies a new nation, the Second Continental Congress now needed to create, from scratch, a new system of government. So it began work on what would become the Articles of Confederation. The document was not completed until late 1777, and it would take another four years before all the colonies ratified it, but the basic principles were decided during the weeks following the declaration of independence.

In the Articles of Confederation plan he had submitted a year earlier, Franklin proposed a strong central government run by a popularly elected congress based on proportional representation. By temperament and upbringing, he was among the most democratic of the colonial leaders. Most of his ideas did not prevail in the new Articles, but the arguments he made in the debate—and in the concurrent meetings at which the Pennsylvania Assembly wrote a new constitution for that state—were eventually to prove influential.

One of the core issues, then and throughout American history, was whether they were creating a confederacy of sovereign states or a single unified nation. More specifically: Should each state have one vote in Congress, or should representation be in proportion to population? Franklin, not surprisingly, favored the latter, not merely because he was from a big state, but also because he felt that the power of the national congress should come from the people and not from the states. In addition, giving small states the same representation as large ones would be unfair. "A confederation upon such iniquitous principles will never last long," he correctly predicted.

As the argument got heated, Franklin attempted to add some levity. The smaller states had argued that they would be overwhelmed by the larger ones if there was proportional representation. Franklin replied that some Scots had said, at the time of the union with England, that they would meet Jonah's fate of being swallowed by a whale, but so many Scots ended up being part of the government "that it was found, in the event, that Jonah had swallowed the whale." Jefferson noted that the Congress laughed heartily enough to regain its humor. Nevertheless, it voted to keep the system of one vote per state.

Franklin initially threatened to persuade Pennsylvania not to join the confederation, but he eventually backed down.

Another issue was whether slaves should be counted as part of a state's population for the purpose of assessing its tax liability. No, argued one South Carolina delegate, slaves were not population but property, more akin to sheep than to people. This drew a rebuke from Franklin: "There is some difference between them and sheep: Sheep will never make any insurrections."[39]

At the same time the Congress was debating the new Articles, Pennsylvania was holding its own state constitutional convention, conveniently in the same building. Franklin was unanimously chosen as its president, and his main contribution was to push for a legislature composed of only one house. The idea of balancing the power of a directly elected legislature with an indirectly chosen "upper" house, he contended, was a vestige of the aristocratic and elitist system against which America was rebelling. Franklin likened a legislature with two branches to "the fabled" snake with two heads: "She was going to a brook to drink, and in her way was to pass through a hedge, a twig of which opposed her direct course; one head chose to go on the right side of the twig, the other on the left; so that time was spent in the contest, and, before the decision was completed, the poor snake died with thirst." His fingerprints were also visible in the list of qualifications that Pennsylvania's officeholders must meet: unlike in other states, they did not have to own property, but they should have a "firm adherence to justice, moderation, temperance, industry and frugality."

Franklin's preference for a unicameral legislature would eventually be discarded both by Pennsylvania and the United States, but it was greeted with great acclaim in France, which implemented it (with dubious results) after its own revolution. Another ultrademocratic proposal Franklin made to the Pennsylvania convention was that the state's Declaration of Rights discourage large holdings of property or concentrations of wealth as "a danger to the happiness of mankind." That also ended up being too radical for the convention.

In his spare time, Franklin served on a variety of congressional committees. He helped design, for example, the Great Seal of the new nation, working once again with Jefferson and Adams. Jefferson proposed a scene of the children of Israel being led through the wilderness, and Adams suggested a depiction of Hercules. Franklin's proposal was to have the motto *E Pluribus Unum* on the front and an ornate scene on the reverse of Pharaoh being engulfed by the Red Sea with the phrase "Rebellion to Tyrants is obedience to God." Jefferson then embraced Franklin's plan, and much of it was adopted by the Congress.[40]

MEETING LORD HOWE AGAIN

Franklin's negotiations in London with Adm. Richard Howe—the ones that began under the cover of chess matches at Howe's sister's house at the end of 1774—had ended in failure, but they did not destroy the respect the two men felt for each other. What particularly frustrated Lord Howe was that the impasse had dashed his dream of being designated a peace envoy to the colonies. By July 1776, the admiral was commander of all British forces in America, with his brother, Gen. William Howe, in charge of the ground troops. In addition, he had gotten his wish of being commissioned to try to negotiate a reconciliation. He carried with him a detailed proposal that offered a truce, pardons for the rebel leaders (with John Adams secretly exempted), and promises of rewards for any American who helped restore peace.

Because the British did not recognize the Continental Congress as a legitimate body, Lord Howe was unsure where to direct his proposals. So when he reached Sandy Hook, New Jersey, he sent a letter to Franklin, whom he addressed as "my worthy friend." He had "hopes of being serviceable," Howe declared, "in promoting the establishment of lasting peace and union with the colonies."[41]

Franklin had the letter read to the Congress and was granted permission to reply, which he did on July 30. It was an adroit and eloquent response, one that made clear America's determination to remain independent yet set in motion a fascinating final attempt to avert an all-out revolution.

"I received safe the letters your Lordship so kindly forwarded to me, and beg you to accept my thanks," Franklin began with requisite civility. But his letter quickly turned heated, even resurrecting the phrase "deluge us in blood" that he had edited out of Jefferson's draft of the Declaration:

> Directing pardons to be offered to the colonies, who are the very parties injured, expresses indeed that opinion of our ignorance, baseness and insensibility which your uninformed and proud nation has long been pleased to entertain of us; but it can have no other effect than that of increasing our resentments. It is impossible we should think of submission to a government that has with the most wanton barbarity and cruelty burnt our defenseless towns in the midst of winter, excited the savages to massacre our peaceful farmers, and our slaves to murder their masters, and is even now bringing foreign mercenaries to deluge our settlements with blood.

Skillfully, however, Franklin included in his letter more than mere fury. With great sorrow and poignancy, he went on to recall how they had worked together to prevent an irreparable breach. "Long did I endeavor, with unfeigned and unwearied zeal, to preserve from breaking that fine and noble china vase, the British empire; for I knew that, being once broken, the separate parts could not retain even their share of the strength or value that existed in the whole," he wrote. "Your Lordship may possibly remember the tears of joy that wet my cheek when, at your good sister's in London, you once gave me expectations that a reconciliation might soon take place."

Perhaps, Franklin intimated, peace talks could be useful. It was not likely. It would require that Howe be willing to treat Britain and America "as distinct states." Franklin said he doubted that Howe had such authority. But if Britain wanted to make peace with an independent America, Franklin offered, "I think a treaty for that purpose is not yet quite impracticable." He ended on a graceful personal note, declaring "the well-founded esteem and, permit me to say, affection which I shall always have for your Lordship."[42]

Howe was understandably taken aback by the terms of Franklin's response. The messenger who delivered it reported the "surprise" on his face and his comment that "his old friend had expressed himself very warmly." When the messenger asked if he wanted to send a reply, "he declined, saying the doctor had grown too warm, and if he expressed his sentiments fully to him, he should only give him pain, which he wished to avoid."

Howe waited two weeks, as the British outmaneuvered General Washington's forces on Long Island, before sending a carefully worded and exceedingly polite response to his "worthy friend." In it, the admiral admitted that he did not have the authority "to negotiate a reunion with America under any other description than as subject to the crown of Great Britain." Nevertheless, he said, a peace was possible under terms that the Congress had laid out in its Olive Branch Petition to the king a year earlier, which included all of the colonial demands for autonomy yet still preserved some form of union under the Crown. Although he had refrained from being explicit "in my public declaration," he now made clear that the peace he envisioned would be "of mutual interest to both countries." In other words, America would be treated as a separate country within the framework of the empire.[43]

This was what Franklin had envisioned for years. Yet it was, after July 4, likely too late. Franklin now felt so. Even more fervently, John Adams and others in his radical faction felt that way. So there was much discussion and dissent within the Congress about whether Franklin should even keep the correspondence alive. Howe forced the issue by paroling a captured American general and sending him to Philadelphia with an invitation for the Congress to send an unofficial delegation for talks before "a decisive blow was struck."

Three members—Franklin, Adams, and Edward Rutledge of South Carolina—were appointed to meet with Howe to hear what he had to say. The inclusion of Adams (who had warned the Congress that, in his biographer David McCullough's words, Howe's messenger was "a decoy duck sent to seduce Congress into renunciation of independence") was a safeguard that Franklin would not revert to his old peace-seeking habits.

With perhaps a hint of irony, Franklin proposed that the meeting could take place in the governor's mansion at Perth Amboy, which had lately been vacated by his captive son, or alternatively on Staten Island. Howe chose the latter. On the way there, the committee spent the night in New Brunswick, where the inn was so full that Franklin and Adams were forced to share a bed. The result was a somewhat farcical night, recorded by Adams in his diary, which gave a delightful glimpse at Franklin's personality and the odd-couple relationship he had over the years with Adams.

Adams was suffering from a cold, and as they went to bed he shut the small window in their room. "Oh!" said Franklin. "Don't shut the window. We shall be suffocated."

Adams replied that he was afraid of the evening air.

"The air within this chamber will soon be, and is indeed now, worse than that outdoors," Franklin replied. "Come! Open the window and come to bed, and I will convince you. I believe you are not acquainted with my theory of colds."

Adams reopened the window and "leaped into bed," a sight that must have been worth beholding. Yes, he said, he had read Franklin's letters (see p. 264) arguing that nobody got colds from cold air, but the theory was inconsistent with his own experience. Would Franklin please explain?

Adams, with a touch of wryness unusual for him, recorded: "The Doctor then began a harangue, upon air and cold and respiration and perspiration, with which I was so much amused that I soon fell asleep, and left him and his philosophy together." In addition to winning the argument over leaving open the window, it should be noted that Franklin, perhaps as a result, did not catch Adams's cold.[44]

When Howe sent a barge to ferry the American delegation to Staten Island, he instructed his officer to stay behind as a hostage. Franklin and his committee brought the officer with them as a gesture of confidence in Howe's honor. Although Howe marched his guests past a double line of menacing Hessian mercenaries, the three-hour meeting on September 11 was cordial, and the Americans were treated to a feast of good claret, ham, tongue, and mutton.

Howe pledged that the colonies could have what they had requested in the Olive Branch Petition: control over their own legislation and taxes, and "a revisal of any of the plantation laws by which the colonists may be aggrieved." The British, he said, were still kindly disposed toward the Americans: "When an American falls, England feels it." He felt the same, even more strongly. If America fell, he said, "I should feel and lament it like the loss of a brother."

Adams recorded Franklin's retort: "Dr. Franklin, with an easy air and collected countenance, a bow, a smile and all that naiveté which sometimes appeared in his conversation and is often observed in his writings, replied, 'My Lord, we will do our utmost endeavors to save your Lordship that mortification.' "

The dispute that was causing this horrible war, Howe insisted, was merely about the method Britain should use in raising taxes from America. Franklin replied, "That we never refused, upon requisition."

America offered other sources of strength to the empire, Howe continued, including "her men." Franklin, whose writings on population growth Howe knew well, agreed. "We have a pretty considerable manufactury of men."

Why then, Howe asked, was it not possible "to put a stop to these ruinous extremities?"

Because, Franklin replied, it was too late for any peace that required a return to allegiance to the king. "Forces have been sent out and towns have been burnt," he said. "We cannot now expect happiness under the domination of Great Britain. All former attachments have been obliterated." Adams, likewise, "mentioned warmly his own determination not to depart from the idea of independency."

The Americans suggested that Howe send home for authority to negotiate with them as an independent nation. That was a "vain" hope, replied Howe.

"Well, my Lord," said Franklin, "as America is to expect nothing but upon unconditional submission . . ."

Howe interrupted. He was not demanding submission. But it was clear, he acknowledged, that no accommodation was possible, at least for now, and he apologized that "the gentlemen had the trouble of coming so far to so little purpose." [45]

TO FRANCE, WITH TEMPLE AND BENNY

Within two weeks of his return from meeting Lord Howe, Franklin was chosen, by a congressional committee acting in great secrecy, to embark on the most dangerous, complex, and fascinating of all his public missions. He was to cross the Atlantic yet again to become an envoy in Paris, with the goal of cajoling from France, now enjoying a rare peace with Britain, the aid and alliance without which it was unlikely that America could prevail.

It was an odd appointment. Elderly and ailing, Franklin was now happily ensconced, finally, in a family nest that actually included members of his own brood. But there was a certain logic, from the Congress's perspective, to the choice. Though he had visited there only twice, he was the most famous and revered American in France. In addition, as a member of the Congress's Committee of Secret Correspondence, Franklin had held confidential talks over the past year with a variety of French intermediaries. Among them was Julien de Bonvouloir, an agent personally approved by the new king, Louis XVI. Franklin met with him three times in December 1775, and came away with the impression, though Bonvouloir was scrupulously circumspect, that France would be willing to support, at least secretly, the American rebellion.[46]

Two other commissioners were also chosen for the mission to France: Silas Deane, a merchant and congressional delegate from Connecticut who had already been sent to Paris in March 1776, and Thomas Jefferson. When Jefferson begged off for family reasons, his place was given to the cantankerous Virginian Arthur Lee, who had taken over Franklin's duties as a colonial agent in London.

Franklin professed to accept the assignment reluctantly. "I am old and good for nothing," he said to his friend Benjamin Rush, who was sitting next to him in the Congress. "But as the storekeepers say of their remnants of cloth, I am but a fag end, and you may have me for what you are pleased to give."[47]

Yet, knowing Franklin—with his love for travel, attraction to new experiences, taste for Europe, and (perhaps) his proclivity to run away from awkward situations—it is likely that he welcomed the assignment, and there is some evidence that he sought it. During the Secret Committee's deliberations the previous month, he had written a "Sketch of Propositions for Peace" with England, which the committee ended up not using. In his draft, Franklin noted his own inclination for going back to England:

Having such propositions to make, or any powers to treat of peace, will furnish a pretence for B.F.'s going to England, where he has many friends and acquaintances, particularly among the best writers and ablest speakers in both Houses of Parliament; he thinks he shall be able when there, if the terms are not accepted, to work up such a division of sentiments in the nation as to greatly weaken its exertions against the United States.[48]

His meeting with Lord Howe, which occurred after he had drafted this memo, made a mission to England less enticing, especially compared to the possibilities of Paris. From his previous visits he knew that he would love Paris, and it would certainly be safer than remaining in America with the outcome of war so unclear (Howe was edging closer to Philadelphia at the time). A few of Franklin's enemies, including the British ambassador to Paris and some American loyalists, thought he was finding a pretense to flee the danger. Even his friend Edmund Burke, the pro-American philosopher and member of Parliament, thought so. "I will never believe," he said, "that he is going to conclude a long life, which has brightened every hour it continued, with so foul and dishonorable flight."[49]

Such suspicions were probably too harsh. If personal safety were his prime concern, a wartime crossing of an ocean controlled by the enemy's navy at age 70 while plagued with gout and kidney stones was not the most logical course. As with all of Franklin's decisions about crossing the Atlantic, this one involved many conflicting emotions and desires. But surely the opportunity to serve his country in a task for which there was no American better equipped, and the chance to live and be feted in Paris, were simple enough reasons to explain his decision. As he prepared for his departure, he withdrew more than £3,000 from his bank account and lent it to the Congress for prosecuting the war.

His grandson Temple had been spending the summer taking care of his forlorn stepmother in New Jersey. The arrest of her husband had left Elizabeth Franklin, who was fragile in the best of times, completely distraught. "I can do nothing but sigh and cry," she wrote her sister-in-law Sally Bache in July. "My hand shakes to such a degree that I can scarcely hold a pen." In pleading with Temple to come stay with her, she complained of the "unruly soldiers" who surrounded her mansion. "They have been extremely rude, insolent and abusive to me and have terrified me almost out of my senses." They even, she added, tried to steal Temple's pet dog.[50]

Temple arrived at his stepmother's house at the end of July, typically forgetting some of his clothes on the way. ("There seems to be," his grandfather wrote, "a kind of fatality attending the conveyance of your things between Amboy and Philadelphia.") The elder Franklin sent along some money for Elizabeth, but she begged for something more. Couldn't he "sign a parole" so that William would be permitted to return to his family? "Consider, my Dear and Honored Sir, that I am now pleading the cause of your son and my beloved husband." Franklin refused, and he dismissed her pitiful complaints about her plight by noting that others were suffering far worse at the hands of the British. Nor did he make any effort to see her when he passed through Amboy on his way to meet Lord Howe. Ever since her marriage to his son, he had shown little desire to befriend her, visit her, or correspond with her, much less engage in any of the flatteries he usually lavished on younger women.[51]

Temple was more sympathetic. In early September, he made plans to travel to Connecticut so he could visit his captive father and bring him a letter from Elizabeth. But Franklin forbade him to go, saying that it was important for him to resume his studies in Philadelphia soon. Temple kept pushing. He had no secret information, just a letter he wanted to deliver. His grandfather remained unmoved. "You are mistaken in imagining that I am apprehensive of your carrying dangerous intelligence to your father," he chided. "You would have been more in the right if you could have suspected me of a little tender concern for your welfare." If Elizabeth wanted to write her husband, he added, she could do so in care of the Connecticut governor, and he even included some franked stationery for that purpose.

Franklin, in fact, realized that his grandson had other motives—one bad, the other honorable—for wanting to go see his father: "I rather think the project takes its rise from your own inclination to ramble and disinclination for returning to college, joined with a desire I do not blame of seeing a father you have so much reason to love."

Not blaming him for wanting to see his father? Saying he had so much reason to love him? For Franklin, such sentiments with regard to William were somewhat surprising, even poignant. They did, however, come in a letter that had denied William's son the right to visit him.[52]

The dispute became moot less than a week later. Careful about keeping the news of his appointment as envoy to France secret, Franklin was cryptic. "I hope you will return hither immediately and your mother will make no objections to it," he wrote. "Something offering here that will be much to your advantage."

In deciding to take Temple to France, Franklin never consulted with Elizabeth, who would die a year later without seeing her husband or stepson again. Nor did he inform William, who did not learn until later of the departure of his sole son, a lad he had gotten to know for only a year. It is a testament to the powerful personal force exerted by Benjamin Franklin, a man so often callous about the feelings of his family, that William was so pitifully accepting of the situation. "If the old gentleman has taken the boy with him," he wrote to his forlorn wife, "I hope it is only to put him in some foreign university."[53]

Franklin also decided to take along his other grandson, Benny Bache. So it was an odd trio that set sail on October 27, 1776, aboard a cramped but speedy American warship aptly named *Reprisal:* a restless old man about to turn 71, plagued by poor health but still ambitious and adventurous, heading for a friendless land from whence he was convinced he would never return, accompanied by a high-spirited, frivolous lad of about 17 and a brooding, eager-to-please child who had just turned 7. The experience in Europe would be good for his grandchildren, he hoped, and their presence would be comforting to him. Two years later, writing of Temple but using words that applied to both boys, Franklin explained one reason he wanted them along: "If I die, I have a child to close my eyes."[54]

CHAPTER THIRTEEN

COURTIER

Paris, 1776–1778

THE WORLD'S MOST FAMOUS AMERICAN

The rough winter crossing aboard the *Reprisal*, though a fast thirty days, "almost demolished me," Franklin later recalled. The salt beef brought back his boils and rashes, the other food was too tough for his old teeth, and the small frigate pitched so violently that he barely slept. So, on sighting the coast of Brittany, an exhausted Franklin, unwilling to wait for winds to take him closer to Paris, had a fishing boat ferry him and his two bewildered grandchildren to the tiny village of Auray. Until he could get to Paris by coach, he wrote John Hancock, he would avoid taking "a public character" and try to keep a low profile, "thinking it prudent first to know whether the court is ready and willing to receive ministers publicly from the Congress."[1]

France was not a place, however, where the world's most famous American would find, nor truly seek, anonymity. When his carriage reached Nantes, the city feted him at a hastily arranged grand ball, where Franklin reigned as a celebrity philosopher-statesman and Temple marveled at the height of the women's ornately adorned coiffures. After seeing Franklin's soft fur cap, the ladies of Nantes began wearing wigs that imitated it, a style that became known as the *coiffure à la Franklin*.

To the French, this lightning-defying scientist and tribune of liberty who had unexpectedly appeared on their shores was a symbol both of the virtuous frontier freedom romanticized by Rousseau and of the Enlightenment's reasoned wisdom championed by Voltaire. For more than eight years he would play his roles to the hilt. In a clever and deliberate manner, leavened by the wit and joie de vivre the French so adored, he would cast the American cause, through his own personification of it, as that of the natural state fighting the corrupted one, the enlightened state fighting the irrational old order.

Into his hands, almost as much as those of Washington and others, had been placed the fate of the Revolution. Unless he could secure the support of France—its aid, its recognition, its navy—America would find it difficult to prevail. Already the greatest American scientist and writer of his time, he would display a dexterity that would make him the greatest American diplomat of all times. He played to the romance as well as the reason that entranced France's *philosophes*, to the fascination with America's freedom that captivated its public, and to the cold calculation of national interest that moved its ministers.

With its 440-year tradition of regular wars with England, France was a ripe potential ally, especially because it yearned to avenge the loss it suffered in the most recent American outcropping of these struggles, the Seven Years' War. Just before he left, Franklin learned that France had agreed to send some aid to the American rebels secretly through a cutout commercial entity.

But convincing France to do more was not going to be easy. The nation was now financially strapped, ostensibly at peace with Britain, and understandably cautious about betting big on a country that, after Washington's precipitous retreat from Long Island, looked like a loser. In addition, neither Louis XVI nor his ministers were instinctive champions of America's desire, which might prove contagious, to cast off hereditary monarchs.

Among Franklin's cards was his fame, and he was among a long line of statesmen, from Richelieu to Metternich to Kissinger, to realize that with celebrity came cachet, and with that came influence. His lightning theories had been proved in France in 1752, his collected works published there in 1773, and a new edition of Poor Richard's *The Way to Wealth,* entitled *La Science du Bonhomme Richard,* was published soon after his arrival and reprinted four times in two years. His fame was so great that people lined the streets hoping to get a glimpse of his entry into Paris on December 21, 1776.

Within weeks, all of fashionable Paris seemed to desire some display of his benign countenance. Medallions were struck in various sizes, engravings and portraits were hung in homes, and his likeness graced snuffboxes and signet rings. "The numbers sold are incredible," he wrote his daughter, Sally. "These, with the pictures, busts and prints (of which copies upon copies are spread everywhere), have made your father's face as well known as that of the moon." The fad went so far as to mildly annoy, though still amuse, the king himself. He gave the Comtesse Diane de Polignac, who had bored him often with her praise of Franklin, a Sèvres porcelain chamber pot with his cameo embossed inside.[2]

"His reputation was more universal than that of Leibniz, Frederick or Voltaire, and his character more loved and esteemed," John Adams would recall many years later, after his own jealousy of Franklin's fame had somewhat subsided. "There was scarcely a peasant or a citizen, a valet de chambre, coachman or footman, a lady's chambermaid or a scullion in the kitchen who was not familiar with Franklin's name."[3]

The French even tried to claim him as one of their own. He always assumed, as noted at the beginning of this book, that his surname came from the class of landowning English freemen known as franklins, and he was almost surely correct. But the *Gazette* of Amiens reported that the name Franquelin was common in the province of Picardie, from which many families had emigrated to England.

Various groups of French philosophers, in addition to the disciples of Voltaire and Rousseau, also made intellectual claims on him. Most notable were the physiocrats, who pioneered the field of economics and developed the doctrine of laissez-faire. The group became for him a new Junto, and he wrote essays for their monthly journal.

One of the most famous physiocrats, Pierre-Samuel Du Pont de Nemours (who emigrated in 1799 and with his son founded the DuPont chemical company), described his friend Franklin in almost mythic terms. "His eyes reveal a perfect equanimity," he wrote, "and his lips the smile of an unalterable serenity." Others were awed by the fact that he dressed so plainly and wore no wig. "Everything in him announced the simplicity and the innocence of primitive morals," marveled one Parisian, who added the perfect French compliment about his love of silence: "He knew how to be impolite without being rude."

His taciturnity and unadorned dress led many to mistake him for a Quaker. One French cleric reported shortly after Franklin's arrival, "This Quaker wears the full dress of his sect. He has a handsome physiognomy, glasses always on his eyes, very little hair, a fur cap, which he always wears." It was an impression he did little to correct, for Franklin knew that fascination about the Quakers was fashionable in France. Voltaire had famously extolled their peaceful simplicity in four of his "Letters on England," and as Carl Van Doren has noted, "Paris admired the sect for its gentle and resolute merits."[4]

Franklin was well aware of, and amused by, the image he created for himself. Picture me, he wrote a friend, "very plainly dressed, wearing my thin gray straight hair that peeps out under my only coiffure, a fine fur cap, which comes down to my forehead almost to my spectacles. Think how this must appear among the powdered heads of Paris." It was a very different image from the one he had adopted, and wrote Polly about, during his first visit in 1767, when he bought "a little bag wig" and had his tailor "transform me into a Frenchman."[5]

Indeed, his new rustic look was partly a pose, the clever creation of America's first great image-maker and public relations master. He wore his soft marten fur cap, the one he had picked up on his trip to Canada, during most of his social outings, including when he was received at the famous literary salon of Madame du Deffand shortly after his arrival, and it became a feature in the portraits and medallions of him. The cap, like that worn by Rousseau, served as his badge of homespun purity and New World virtue, just as his ever-present spectacles (also featured in portraits) became an emblem of wisdom. It helped him play the part that Paris imagined for him: that of the noble frontier philosopher and simple backwoods sage—even though he had lived most of his life on Market Street and Craven Street.

Franklin reciprocated France's adoration. "I find them a most amiable nation to live with," he wrote Josiah Quincy. "The Spaniards are by common opinion supposed to be cruel, the English proud, the Scotch insolent, the Dutch avaricious, etc., but I think the French have no national vice ascribed to them. They have some frivolities, but they are harmless." As he put it to a Boston relative, "This is the civilest nation upon earth."[6]

FRANKLIN'S COURT AT PASSY

In England, Franklin had set up a cozy household with a surrogate family. In France, he quickly assembled not merely a household but a miniature court. It was situated, both figuratively and geographically, between the salons of Paris and the palace at Versailles, and it would grow to include not only the requisite new family but also a visiting cast of fellow commissioners, deputies, spies, intellectuals, courtiers, and flirtatious female admirers.

The village of Passy, where Franklin reigned over this coterie, was a collection of villas and chateaux about three miles from the center of Paris on the edge of the Bois de Boulogne. One of the finest of these estates was owned by Jacques-Donatien Leray de Chaumont, a nouveau riche merchant who had made a fortune trading in the East Indies and was now motivated—by sincere sympathies as well as the prospect of profit—to associate himself with the American cause. He offered, initially at no rent, rooms and board to Franklin and his crowd, and his Passy compound became America's first foreign embassy.

It was an idyllic arrangement for Franklin. He had a "fine house" and a "large garden to walk in" as well as an "abundance of acquaintances," he wrote to Mrs. Stevenson. The only thing missing was "that order and economy in my family that reigned in it when under your direction," he added, giving only the slightest hint that he might like her to come over and be his household partner again. But it was not a suggestion that he pushed, for he found himself quite comfortable with a new set of domestic and female companions. "I never remember to have seen my grandfather in better health," Temple wrote Sally. "The air of Passy and the warm bath three times a week have made quite a young man out of him. His pleasing gaiety makes everybody in love with him, especially the ladies, who permit him always to kiss them."

Chaumont's main house (on which Franklin erected a lightning rod) was set amid chains of pavilions, formal gardens, stately terraces, and an octagonal pond that overlooked the Seine. Dinners, served at 2 P.M., were seven-course extravaganzas, and Franklin built a wine collection that soon included more than one thousand bottles of Bordeaux, champagne, and sherry. The witty Madame Chaumont served as hostess, and her eldest daughter became Franklin's "ma femme." He also took a fancy to the teenage daughter of the seigneur of the village, whom he referred to wishfully as his "mistress." (When she ended up marrying the Marquis de Tonnerre, Madame Chaumont punned, "All the rods of Mr. Franklin could not prevent the lightning [in French, *tonnerre*] from falling on Mademoiselle.")

Through his trading companies, Chaumont procured supplies for the American cause, including saltpeter and uniforms. Because he emulated Poor Richard's injunction to do well by doing good, many questioned his motives. "He would grasp, if he could, the commerce of the thirteen colonies for himself alone," wrote one newspaper.[7]

Chaumont also served as Franklin's publicist. He commissioned the great Italian sculptor Giovanni Battista Nini to produce a series of Franklin medallions and the king's portraitist Joseph-Siffrèd Duplessis to do a majestic oil painting of him. Franklin's favorite, the Duplessis now hangs in a room atop the grand stairway of New York's Metropolitan Museum (others by Duplessis are in Washington's National Portrait Gallery and elsewhere).

Benny was placed in a nearby boarding school, where he quickly mastered French; he came to dine, occasionally with some American classmates, with his grandfather every Sunday. Jonathan Williams, a grandnephew, arrived from England and for a while was entrusted to oversee commercial transactions. Temple served as Franklin's very loyal aide, though not a great one; he became a bit of a playboy who had yet to master most of his grandfather's thirteen virtues.

Franklin, who was kept busy wrestling with the complexities of arms shipments and commercial transactions, would need whatever loyalty and family support he could muster, as he would find himself working alongside one co-commissioner who was corrupt, another who hated everyone, a secretary who was a spy, a cook who was an embezzler, and a landlord who hoped to be a profiteer.

Of the motley lot, the corrupt commissioner, who was in fact quite congenial and not all that dishonest, was Franklin's favorite. Silas Deane of Connecticut had arrived in France in July 1776, five months before Franklin, and helped arrange France's first secret shipment of aid. In that endeavor, he worked with a most unlikely middleman: Pierre-Augustin Caron de Beaumarchais, a diplomatic dabbler, would-be profiteer, and the world-famous dramatist who had just written *The Barber of Seville* and was soon to write *The Marriage of Figaro*. Like Beaumarchais, Deane seemed to have sticky fingers and inscrutable accounting methods. He would be recalled in a year to face, and fail, a congressional audit. But Franklin remained friendly throughout.

The great antagonist amid this menagerie, to Deane and then to Franklin, was the third American commissioner, Arthur Lee of Virginia. He was suspicious of all around him to the point of paranoia, a trait only partly vindicated by the fact that he was right in many cases. He had been jealous of Franklin since serving with him as a colonial agent in London (and being part of a rival land scheme syndicate). Along with his brothers, William Lee and Richard Henry Lee, he was behind many of the rumors casting doubts on Franklin's loyalty and character.

As soon as he had succeeded in exposing, with some justification, Deane's dubious transactions, Lee embarked on a campaign, with no justification, to cast doubt on Franklin. "I am more and more satisfied that the old doctor is concerned in the plunder," he wrote his brother. He later noted, this time with a bit more justification, that Franklin was "more devoted to pleasure than would become even a young man in his station."[8]

Having once thought Franklin too soft on England, Lee now thought him too soft on France. He was also convinced that nearly everyone at Passy was a spy or a crook, and he fretted over every detail down to the color of the uniforms being sent to America and the fact that Deane had gotten rooms closer to Franklin's.

On rare occasions, Lee and Franklin put aside their animosity as they discussed their common cause. One evening at Passy, Franklin regaled him at length with the grand tale of July 1776, all of which Lee, who had been in London at the time, recorded reverentially in his diary. It was "a miracle in human affairs," Franklin recounted, one that would result in "the greatest revolution the world ever saw."

By early 1778, however, Lee and Franklin would barely be speaking to each other. "I have a right to know your reasons for treating me thus," Lee wrote, after a barrage of his resentful letters had gone unanswered. Franklin let loose with the angriest words he is known to have ever written:

> Sir: It is true I have omitted answering some of your letters. I do not like to answer angry letters. I hate disputes. I am old, cannot have long to live, have much to do and no time for altercation. If I have often received and borne your magisterial snubbings and rebukes without reply, ascribe it to the right causes, my concern for the honor & success of our mission, which would be hurt by our quarrelling, my love of peace, my respect for your good qualities, and my pity of your sick mind, which is forever tormenting itself, with its jealousies, suspicions & fancies that others mean you ill, wrong you, or fail in respect for you. If you do not cure your self of this temper it will end in insanity, of which it is the symptomatic forerunner, as I have seen in several instances. God preserve you from so terrible an evil: and for His sake pray suffer me to live in quiet.

As with his other famous angry letter, the one calling his friend Strahan an enemy, Franklin did not send this one. Although he meant every word of it, he was generally averse to altercations, and was now, as he noted, too old for them. Instead, on the following day, he wrote Lee a slightly milder response. In the revised version, he again admitted that he had not answered some of Lee's letters, "particularly your angry ones in which you with very magisterial airs schooled and documented me as if I had been one of your domestics." Instead, he had burned these letters, he said, because "I saw in the strongest light the importance of our living in a decent civility towards each other." He complained to Deane, "I bear all his rebukes with patience for the good of the service, but it goes a little hard on me."[9]

Lee attracted like-minded visitors who proved equally annoying.

His brother William had been sent as envoy to Austria but, not being received there, ended up in Paris. So, too, did Ralph Izard, a wealthy and jealous South Carolina planter, who came after finding himself unwelcome as an envoy in Tuscany. When Izard took the side of the Lees, Franklin retaliated with an anonymous satire, "The Petition of the Letter Z, Commonly called Ezzard, Zed, or Izard." In it the letter Z complains about being "placed at the tail end of the alphabet" and "totally excluded from the word WISE."[10]

BANCROFT THE SPY

Arthur Lee was particularly vituperative toward Edward Bancroft, the secretary of the American delegation. Bancroft was an intriguing character in all senses of those two words. Born in Massachusetts in 1744, he had been tutored as a young man by Silas Deane and then went to work at age 19 on a plantation in Guiana, where he wrote about tropical plants and patented a textile dye made from a native black oak bark. In 1767, at age 23, he moved to London, where he became a physician and stock speculator. There he befriended Franklin, who sponsored his election to the Royal Society and paid him to gather intelligence on British leaders. When Deane was preparing to leave for France in March 1776, he was instructed by Franklin to "procure a meeting with Mr. Bancroft by writing a letter to him, under cover to Mr. Griffiths at Turnham Green near London, and desiring him to come over to you." Bancroft arrived in Paris in July, just as Deane did, and began working for his former tutor.[11]

When Franklin arrived later that year, he made Bancroft the secretary of the delegation. What he did not know (and what historians were only to discover a century later by turning up secret documents in London archives) was that Bancroft had recently begun working as a highly active British secret agent.

The British Secret Service, which was spending close to £200,000 per year by 1777 to gather intelligence, was run by a quick-witted man named William Eden, later Lord Auckland. Overseeing his operations in France was a New Hampshire native, Paul Wentworth, who had moved to London in the 1760s and made money by speculating in stocks and buying land in the West Indies and South America, including the plantation in Guiana where Bancroft had worked as a young medical researcher.

Wentworth in turn recruited Bancroft to be one of his many spies in Paris, and in December 1776 they entered into a formal agreement, using the flimsy code name "Dr. Edward Edwards" for Bancroft. "Dr. Edwards engages to correspond with P. Wentworth to communicate to him whatever may come to his knowledge in the following subjects," the memo began. It then went on for ten paragraphs to detail the information that Bancroft would provide. This included:

> The progress of the treaty with France and of the assistance expected . . . The same with Spain and of every other court in Europe . . . The means of obtaining credit, effect and money and the channels and agents used . . . Franklin's and Deane's correspondence with Congress in secret . . . Descriptions of the ships and cargoes, the time of sailing and the ports bound to . . . The intelligence that may arrive from America.

Every week, the genial and urbane Bancroft would provide his secret reports by writing between the lines of fake love letters in an invisible ink. The British spymasters had a special chemical wash that could make the writing visible. Bancroft would put the letters in a bottle with a string attached and, at 9:30 every Tuesday evening, drop it in the hollow of a tree near the south terrace of the Tuileries Gardens, where it would be picked up by a messenger from the British embassy. The instructions for the drop were explicit: "The bottle to be sealed and tied by the neck with a common twine, about half a yard in length, the other end of which to be fastened to a peg of wood . . . the peg into the ground on the west side." For these services he was initially paid £500 annually, but he performed so well that his stipend rose to £1,000, which was on top of the £1,000 per year he was making as secretary to Franklin's American delegation. He also made a lot of money on the side by using his inside information to speculate in the stock markets.[12]

The hundreds of secret reports that Bancroft sent to the British were filled with sensitive information on the transactions of the

Americans in Passy, the discussion they held with French ministers, the schedules of arms shipments being sent to America, and other military matters. He told, for example, of Lafayette's departure for America in April 1777, listed the French officers accompanying him, and revealed that he was leaving from the Spanish port of San Sebastian and heading "directly to Port Royal South Carolina." He also warned that the French were "ordering eight to ten ships of war to protect the trade of the colonies near the coast of France and to remove the British cruisers," and in September 1777 added that "four ships of war are sailed from Toulons to join the Brest fleet." The following year, in April 1778, he sent word that the French Admiral Count d'Estaing was sailing from Toulon to join the American war effort "and commands a fleet of 17 ships of the line and frigates to destroy or secure the English fleet." In his letter the next week, he revealed that "the Brest fleet is nearly ready" and noted the possibility that "Count Broglio [a noted French marshal] is to conduct an invasion of England."[13]

Franklin and Deane trusted Bancroft so fully that they often had him travel secretly to London to gather intelligence there. He would use these trips to convey some of his most sensitive espionage to the British, and then return with information that seemed valuable but was in fact planted by his spymasters. The British were so intent on keeping his cover that on one trip to London, in March 1777, they pretended to arrest him and briefly imprison him for being an American agent. "Dr. Bancroft is arrested in London for corresponding with and assisting us," a distraught Deane informed the Congress, and he added, "I feel more for Dr. Bancroft than I can express." In what seemed a nice miracle, Bancroft was released from prison within weeks and allowed to go back to work in Passy.[14]

Arthur Lee soon became suspicious of his loyalties. "The notorious character of Dr. Bancroft as a stock-jobber is perfectly known to you," he wrote Franklin and Adams after learning that he was being sent on yet another secret mission to London in February 1779. "His living in open defiance of decency and religion you are no strangers to; nor to his enmity against me." More seriously, Lee cited material that indicated Bancroft was a spy: "I have evidence in my possession that makes me consider Dr. Bancroft as a criminal with regard to the United States."

Because he was paranoid about almost everyone, Lee's suspicions were generally ignored. He was not, however, paranoid enough to realize that his own private secretary was also a spy. Among the papers buried in the British Library are secret transcripts of more than a dozen of Lee's most sensitive letters as well as a memo informing the head of the spy service that their agent "stole Lee's journal and copied the information."[15]

Through it all, Franklin remained sanguine about the possibility of spies in his midst, even though, shortly after his arrival, he had been warned to be wary by a Philadelphia woman then living in Paris. "You are surrounded with spies who watch your every movement," she wrote. With an eye more to extolling his virtues than addressing the problem, he sent what became a famous response:

> I have long observed one rule which prevents any inconveniences from such practices. It is simply this: to be concerned in no affairs I should blush to have made public, and to do nothing but what spies may see and welcome. When a man's actions are just and honorable, the more they are known, the more his reputation is increased and established. If I was sure, therefore, that my valet de place was a spy, as he probably is, I think I should probably not discharge him for that, if in other respects I liked him.[16]

On one level, Franklin's answer was naïve, for Bancroft's treachery led to ships being endangered. (As it turned out, there is no direct evidence that any were consequently lost: Lafayette sailed safely, the British were not able to act quickly enough to block d'Estaing's passage through the Straits of Gibraltar, and Broglio did not invade England.) On another level, however, Franklin was shrewd, for he would end up using his assumption that there were spies in his midst to play the English off against the French when serious negotiations began.

REALISM AND IDEALISM

France's foreign minister, the Comte de Vergennes, was a dowdy professional diplomat, portly and lacking in pretense, but in the words of Susan Mary Alsop, whose book *Yankees at the Court* is a delightful portrayal of the period, "he was a human and affectionate man and a shrewd judge of character." He would, indeed, be both affectionate and shrewd in his dealings with Franklin. He was never fully accepted socially at the court of Louis XVI because his wife was bourgeois, but he admired those sensible middle-class qualities in her and presumably found them agreeable in Franklin as well.[17]

Vergennes was very much a realist in his view of international relations, an outlook he summarized pithily in 1774, when he declared that "the influence of every power is measured by the opinion one has of its intrinsic force." He was also ardently anti-British, which helped make him sympathetic to the American cause.

In the spring of 1776, just before Franklin's arrival, Vergennes had composed for the king a set of proposals that argued in unvarnished terms what France's policy should be: "England is the natural enemy of France; and she is an avid enemy, ambitious, unjust, brimming with bad faith; the permanent and cherished object of her policy is the humiliation and ruin of France." America, he said, needed French support to prevail. It was in France's interest, economically and politically, to try to cripple England by embracing the new nation. He presented these proposals to Louis XVI and his cabinet—which included the comptroller of finances, Anne-Robert-Jacques Turgot, who was to become Franklin's friend and fan—in the gold-gilded Council Chamber of Versailles.

Turgot and the other ministers were worried about France's tight finances and lack of preparedness, so they urged caution. The king approved a compromise: France would lend some support to America, but only secretly. Vergennes's letters on the subject, it was decided, would be dictated to his 15-year-old son, whose handwriting would not be identifiable if they fell into the wrong hands.[18]

Franklin first met Vergennes later that year, on December 28, 1776, at a secret session in Paris, just days after his arrival. With Deane and Lee at his side, Franklin pushed forcefully, and perhaps a bit too quickly, for a French alliance. The foreign minister complimented Franklin on his knowledge and wit, but he made no commitments other than to say that he would consider a memo on the subject if Franklin wished to write one. In his notes that evening, he described Franklin as "intelligent but circumspect," and in a letter to his ambassador in London he noted, "His conversation is gentle and honest, he appears to be a man of much talent."[19]

Franklin accepted Vergennes's suggestion that he write a memo, and in it he emphasized the realistic balance-of-power calculus that he knew the French minister would appreciate. If France and her ally Spain joined the American cause, Britain would lose her colonies, her possessions in the West Indies, and the "commerce that has rendered her so opulent," thus reducing her to a "state of weakness and humiliation." America would be willing to "guarantee in the firmest manner" that France and Spain could keep any of the West Indian islands Britain lost. But if France balked, then America might be "reduced to the necessity of ending the war by an accommodation" with Britain. "Delay may be attended with fatal consequences."[20]

But Franklin realized that appealing to a cold calculus of interests was only part of the equation. Better than most other diplomats in the nation's history, he understood that America's strength in world affairs would come from a unique mix that included idealism as well as realism. When woven together, as they would later be in policies ranging from the Monroe Doctrine to the Marshall Plan, they were the warp and woof of a resilient foreign policy. "America's great historical moments," writes historian Bernard Bailyn, "have occurred when realism and idealism have been combined, and no one knew this better than Franklin."[21]

As he would prove in France, Franklin not only knew how to play a calculated balance-of-power game like the best practitioner of realpolitik, but he also knew how to play with his other hand the rousing chords of America's exceptionalism, the sense that America stood apart from the rest of the world because of its virtuous nature. Both the hard power that came from its strategic might and the soft power that flowed from the appeal of its ideals and culture would, he realized, be equally important in assuring its influence. In his diplomacy, as in his personal business, he was "a man who believed in the power of reason and the reality of virtue," declared the writer and mathematician Condorcet, who became one of his best French friends.

So, after writing Vergennes a memo infused with classic diplomatic realism, Franklin settled down in Passy to pursue the gambit of drawing power from America's idealism. He arranged for the inspiring documents coming out of America—including the constitution he had written for Pennsylvania—to be translated and published as a way of winning hearts and minds in France and elsewhere. "All Europe is for us," he wrote the Committee of Secret Correspondence in a letter that explained his rationale for publishing those documents. Then he went on to give a classic formulation of the lure of America's ideals: "Tyranny is so generally established in the rest of the world that the prospect of an asylum in America for those who love liberty gives general joy, and our cause is esteemed the cause of all mankind." He ended by echoing the shining "city upon a hill" metaphor used by the great American exceptionalists from John Winthrop to Ronald Reagan. "We are fighting for the dignity and happiness of human nature," he proclaimed. "Glorious it is for the Americans to be called by Providence to this post of honor." A few weeks later, he wrote in a similar vein to a Boston friend, concluding, "It is a common observation here that our cause is the cause of all mankind, and that we are fighting for their liberty in defending our own."[22]

Franklin's public diplomacy strategy puzzled Vergennes. "I really do not know what Franklin has come to do here," he wrote. "At the beginning we thought he had all sorts of projects, but all of a sudden he has shut himself up in sanctuary with the *philosophes*." The French minister rejected America's proposal for an immediate alliance, deflected requests for further meetings, and kept his distance from Franklin for a few months, waiting to see how the war evolved. He did, however, quietly offer some aid: France would make another secret loan to America and allow its ports to be used by American merchant ships.

Franklin also waged his public relations campaign, as he had in England, with some anonymous pieces in the press. The most powerful was a brutal parody, along the lines of "An Edict by the King of Prussia," that he wrote shortly after his first meeting with Vergennes. It purported to be a letter to the commander of the Hessian troops in America from a German count who got paid a bounty for the death of each of the soldiers he sent over. Because Britain had decided not to pay for any wounded soldiers, only for those who died, the count encouraged his commander to make sure that as many died as possible:

> I do not mean by this that you should assassinate them; we should be humane, my dear Baron, but you may insinuate to the surgeons with entire propriety that a crippled man is a reproach to their profession, and that there is no wiser course than to let every one of them die when he ceases to be fit to fight . . . You will therefore promise promotion to all who expose themselves; you will exhort them to seek glory in the midst of dangers.

He also used his wit to parry the propaganda reports being spread by the British ambassador, Lord Stormont. Asked about one of these reports, Franklin retorted, "It is not a truth; it is only a Stormont." After that, he and fashionable Paris began using the ambassador's name as a verb, "stormonter," a weak pun on the French verb *mentir*, meaning "to lie."[23]

Wild rumors began to circulate about Franklin's various strategies and schemes in France. One British spy (not Bancroft) reported that Franklin was preparing "a great number of reflecting mirrors" that would be placed on the Calais coast to focus the heat from the sun on the British navy, thus destroying it. That would be followed by an electric shock sent over a cross-channel chain that would disrupt the entire British island. The New Jersey *Gazette* went further: Franklin was inventing an electrical apparatus that could shift landmasses and a method of using oil that could still the waves in one place while stirring up tempests in another.[24]

Alas, what he was actually doing was more mundane, such as coping with European supplicants who sought commissions to serve as officers in the American army. His collected letters are clogged with requests, more than four hundred in all, some valiant and others vain. "Not a day passes in which I have not a number of soliciting visits, besides letters," he complained. "You can have no conception how I am harassed." There was the mother who offered up three of her flock of sons, the Dutch surgeon who wanted to study bodies that had been blown apart, and the Benedictine monk who promised to pray for America if it would pay off his gambling debts. Franklin's favorite was a less than effusive recommendation he received from a mother, which began: "Sir, If in your America one knows the secret of how to reform a detestable subject who has been the cross of his family . . ."

The case of one such supplicant showed how Franklin's difficulty in saying no made him an easy mark. An Irishman living in Paris named William Parsons wrote Franklin a pitiful letter describing his unfortunate plight and begging for a commission to join the American army. Franklin did not offer him a recommendation, but he did lend him fifteen guineas, which Parsons then absconded with to England, leaving his poor wife behind. When the wife wrote Franklin a sad letter accusing him of causing her husband to leave, Franklin denied that he had given him any encouragement, wrote off the fifteen-guinea loan, and sent along another guinea to help the wife buy food. For the next three months, she peppered him with pleas for even more relief.

Not all the supplicants were vagabonds. Franklin was able to find, among those seeking commissions, a few great officers to recommend: the Marquis de Lafayette, Baron von Steuben (whose rank in the Prussian army Franklin inflated in his eagerness to get General Washington to take him), and Count Pulaski, a famed Polish fighter who became a heroic brigadier general for America. Nevertheless, Washington quickly grew testy about the number of aspiring officers Franklin was sending his way. "Our corps being already formed and fully officered," he wrote, "every new arrival is only a source of embarrassment to Congress and myself and of disappointment and chagrin to the gentlemen who come over."

So Franklin tried as best he could to reject most of the commission seekers or provide them only with letters that used such phrases as "goes over at his own expense, contrary to my advice." To cope with the constant flood of requests, or perhaps merely to make fun of them, Franklin even composed a form letter which he had printed up. "The bearer of this, who is going to America, presses me to give him a letter of recommendation, though I know nothing of him, not even his name," it read. "I must refer you to himself for his character and merits, with which he is certainly better acquainted than I can possibly be."[25]

In September 1777, Franklin and his fellow commissioners went to press Vergennes again for French recognition and, as if to conceal the weakness of their position, to request seven times more aid than had already been given. It was an inauspicious meeting for two reasons. Before it even happened, the spying Bancroft had leaked details of the planned request to Ambassador Stormont, who protested it to Vergennes, who then chided the Americans for being so unguarded. In addition, shortly after the meeting, news arrived that British General Howe had captured Philadelphia.

Howe's success was a personal blow for Franklin. His house on Market Street was commandeered by a British captain named John André, who, as the Baches took refuge in the countryside, stole his electrical equipment, books, musical instruments, and an elegant portrait of him that had been painted by Benjamin Wilson in 1759. (It was returned from England in 1906 and now hangs on the second floor of the White House.)

For America, it threatened to be an even worse blow. Howe was in Philadelphia and General Burgoyne was heading down the Hudson; if and when the two British armies linked, New England would be cut off from the rest of the colonies.

Nonetheless, Franklin kept his equanimity. Told of Howe's triumph, he replied, "You mistake the matter. Instead of Howe taking Philadelphia, Philadelphia has taken Howe." On one level it seemed a flippant bon mot. On another, it was a shrewd assessment. If Burgoyne was slowed in his move down the Hudson, and if Howe did not press northward to reinforce him, both could end up isolated.

Arthur Lee wanted to use America's precarious position to present an ultimatum to the French: either they join America in a military alliance immediately or else America would be forced to reconcile with Britain. "Dr. Franklin was of a different position," Lee recorded in his journal. "The effect of such a declaration," Franklin argued, "might make them abandon us in despair or anger." He felt that America would eventually gain a position that would make it in France's own interest to want an alliance.

He was right. Shortly before noon on December 4, a messenger from America galloped into the courtyard of Passy bearing a message from the front. Franklin asked if, as he had already heard, Philadelphia had fallen. "Yes, sir," said the messenger. Franklin turned his back.

"But, sir, I have greater news than that," said the messenger. "General Burgoyne and his whole army are prisoners!" Burgoyne had been defeated at the Battle of Saratoga, and now Howe was indeed isolated.[26]

The very dramatic dramatist Beaumarchais, who happened to be at Passy at the time, was eager to use the inside news to speculate in the stock markets; he raced back to Paris at such a high speed that his cabriolet overturned, fracturing his arm. Bancroft also immediately scurried off, heading for London to consult with his spymasters (he would also have speculated, but the news reached London before he did).

Franklin, far calmer than his odd friends, wrote up a news release filled with little details and large exaggerations: "Mail arrived from Philadelphia at Dr. Franklin's house in Passy after 34 days. On October 14th General Burgoyne was forced to lay down his arms, 9200 men killed or taken prisoner . . . General Howe is in Philadelphia, where he is imprisoned. All communication with his fleet is cut off."

Howe was not in fact trapped, nor was America on the verge of victory. Still, the British surrender at Saratoga was a great turning point on the battlefield and—because Franklin knew that power on the battlefield correlated to power at the bargaining table—it was a great turning point for his diplomatic efforts. The note he wrote to Vergennes that afternoon was more restrained than his news release. "We have the honor to acquaint your Excellency," it began, "with advice of the total reduction of the force under General Burgoyne."

Two days later, Louis XVI from his chamber at Versailles put his royal assent on a gilt-edged paper, prepared for him by Vergennes, that invited the Americans to resubmit their request for a formal alliance. In delivering the message, Vergennes's secretary added that "it could be done none too soon."[27]

THE TREATIES OF FRIENDSHIP AND ALLIANCE

After a full year of deflecting requests for an alliance, the French were suddenly impatient as 1777 drew to a close. They were prodded not only by America's success at Saratoga and the completion of their own naval rearmament program, but also by a new gambit by Franklin. He began to play the French and British off against one another and to let each side discover—and here is where he relied on the spies he knew were in his midst—how eager the other side was for a deal.

Franklin wrote a renewed proposal for a French-American alliance on December 7, Temple delivered it the next day, and within a week the three American commissioners were meeting with Vergennes. The French quickly agreed to full recognition of America and treaties of trade and alliance. There was one caveat: France needed the approval of Spain, as the two countries had pledged in the Bourbon family pact of 1761 to act in concert. Vergennes sent his courier to Madrid and promised the Americans they would have a response in three weeks.

In the meantime, the British sent to Paris the most trusted envoy they could muster, Paul Wentworth, their able spymaster. At the time, Wentworth was angry with his secret agent Bancroft for sending inside information to his stock speculating partner before sending it to Wentworth, who also was a speculator. King George III, upset by the bad news that his spies were giving him, denounced them all as untrustworthy stock manipulators, but he reluctantly approved Wentworth's secret peace mission.

Wentworth arrived in Paris in mid-December, just as the Americans were meeting with Vergennes, and sent a missive to Silas Deane that was worthy of a British spy: a gentleman who wished to meet him, it said, could be found the next morning in a coach at a specified place on the road to Passy, or later at an exhibition in the Luxembourg Gallery, or at the public baths on the Seine, where Deane would find a note giving the room number to use. Deane sent a reply worthy of an American: he would be in his office, where he would be happy to see anyone who wanted to come by.[28]

At dinner with Deane, Wentworth proposed a plan for reconciliation between Britain and her colonies. America would have its own Congress, would be subject to Parliament only in matters of foreign policy and trade, and all the offensive acts passed since 1763 would be repealed. He also offered personal inducements—knighthoods, peerages, jobs, money—to Deane or any American who helped secure such a peace.

Franklin at first refused to meet with Wentworth. But then word came of Spain's answer to France's proposal for an alliance with America. Somewhat surprisingly, the Spanish king had rejected the plan and declared that Spain saw no reason to recognize America. It would now be up to France to act alone, if it so chose.

So, during the first week of 1778, Franklin applied pressure. He let word leak to the press that British emissaries were in town and that they might reach a pact with the Americans if the French did not do so promptly. Such a pact, the stories went, might even include American support for Britain's efforts to capture France's islands in the West Indies. He also agreed to meet with Wentworth on January 6, though he made him promise not to offer any personal bribes.

Wentworth's report back to London was written in the clumsy code that might be expected from an agent who had tried to set up a secret rendezvous in a bathhouse: "I called on 72 [Franklin] yesterday, and found him very busy with his nephew [either Jonathan Williams or, more likely, Temple] who was directed to leave the room, and we remained together two hours before 51 [Deane] joined us, when the conversation ceased." Wentworth added that he had offered to Franklin an unsigned letter that spoke of the possibility of "unqualified 107," which was the code he used for independence. "[Franklin] said it was a very interesting, sensible letter," Wentworth reported, "and applauded the candor, good sense and benevolent spirit of it." Then he added the kicker: "Pity it did not come a little sooner."

Not quite sure who was spying on whom, Franklin pursued the cleverly naïve approach he had described a year earlier. It was in his interest that the British discover (as they did through their spy Bancroft) how close the Americans were to a deal with France. And it was in his interest that the French discover (as they did through their own constant surveillance of Wentworth) that the Americans were having discussions with a British emissary. Everything he said to Wentworth he was happy to have the French overhear. As Yale historian Jonathan Dull has noted, "The ineptitude of the British government presented Franklin with a chance to play one of his best diplomatic roles: the innocent who may not be so innocent as he pretends."[29]

Indeed, Franklin's meeting with Wentworth seemed to prod the French. Two days later, Vergennes's secretary called on the Americans. He had only one question: "What is necessary to be done to give such satisfaction to the American commissioners as to engage them not to listen to any proposition from England for a new connection with that country?" Thanks to Franklin's maneuvers as well as the victory of Saratoga, the French now wanted an alliance as eagerly as America did.

Franklin personally wrote out the answer: "The commissioners have long since proposed a treaty of amity and commerce which is not yet concluded. The immediate conclusion of that treaty will remove the uncertainty they are under with regard to it and give them such a reliance on the friendship of France as to reject firmly all propositions made to them of peace from England which have not for their basis the entire freedom and independence of America."

That was all the French now needed to hear. Franklin was told that the king would assent to the treaties—one on friendship and trade, the other creating a military alliance—even without the participation of Spain. France made one stipulation: America could not make peace with Britain in the future without France's consent. And so the treaties of friendship and alliance were won.

The treaties had an important aspect: they did not violate the idealistic view, held by Franklin and others, that America, in its virgin purity, should avoid becoming entangled in foreign alliances or European spheres of influence. The commercial rights that the Americans granted were mutual, nonexclusive, and permitted a system of open and free trade with other nations. "No monopoly of our trade was granted," Franklin pointed out in a letter to the Congress. "None are given to France but what we are at liberty to grant to any other nation."[30]

The American commissioners met in Paris on February 5, 1778, for the signing of the treaty. Vergennes's secretary had a cold, however, so the ceremony was put off for a day. At both gatherings, Franklin appeared without his usual brown coat. Instead, he wore a suit of blue Manchester velvet that was faded and a bit worn. Silas Deane, finding this puzzling, asked why. "To give it a little revenge," Franklin answered. "I wore this coat the day Wedderburn abused me at Whitehall." It had been four years since his humiliation in the Cockpit, and he had saved the suit for such an occasion.[31]

Standing near Franklin, ready to assist, was his supposedly loyal secretary, Edward Bancroft. The British spy took the document, made a copy, hired a special messenger, and got it to the ministers in London within forty-two hours. He had already, two weeks earlier, written coded letters in invisible ink that provided the outline of what the treaty would contain plus the intelligence that a French convoy of three ships and two war frigates was preparing to leave Quiberon to bring the document back to an anxious American Congress. He also sent word that "we have just received a letter from the Prussian ministry to say that the King of Prussia will immediately follow France in acknowledging the independency of America."

Years later, when he was haggling with the British over back pay, Bancroft wrote a secret memo telling the foreign secretary that this was "information for which many individuals here would, for purposes of speculation, have given me more than all that I have received from the government." In fact, Bancroft had indeed used this information to make money speculating on the markets. He had sent £420 to his stock partner in England, the Philadelphia-born merchant Samuel Wharton, and provided him word of the impending treaties so that it could be used to short stocks. "The bulls in the alley are likely to be left in the lurch," he wrote in one secret missive to Wharton, using invisible ink. That letter was intercepted by the English spy service, but others made it through to Wharton and also to their other partner, the British banker Thomas Walpole. Bancroft ended up making £1,000 in the transactions.[32]

Louis XVI made the Franco-American treaties official by receiving the three commissioners at Versailles on March 20. Crowds gathered at the palace gates to catch a glimpse of the famous American, and they shouted "Vive Franklin" as his coach passed through the gold-crested gates.

Among those in the courtyard were, according to Susan Mary Alsop, the "officious porters" who rented out to visitors the ceremonial swords that were generally required for admission to the palace. The other American commissioners each wore one, along with the other items of official court dress. But not Franklin. Seeing no reason to abandon the simple style that had served him well, he dressed in a plain brown suit with his famous spectacles as his only adornment. He did not wear a sword and, when he discovered that the wig he had bought for the occasion did not sit well on his head, decided to forsake it as well. "I should have taken him for a big farmer," wrote one female observer, "so great was his contrast with the other diplomats, who were all powdered, in full dress, and splashed all over with gold and ribbons."

His one fashion concession to the occasion was that he did not wear his fur cap but instead carried a hat of pure white under his arm. "Is that white hat a symbol of liberty?" asked Madame du Deffand, the old aristocrat at whose salon Franklin had worn his fur cap. Whether or not he meant it to be, white hats for men were soon in vogue in Paris, as everything else Franklin wore was wont to become.

When Franklin was ushered into the king's bedchamber at noon, after the official levee, Louis XVI was in a posture of prayer. "I hope that this will be for the good of both nations," he said, giving a royal imprimatur to America's status as an independent nation. On a personal note, he added, "I am very satisfied with your conduct since you arrived in my kingdom."

After a midafternoon dinner hosted by Vergennes, Franklin had the honor, if not pleasure, of being allowed to stand next to the queen, the famously haughty Marie-Antoinette, as she played at the gambling tables. Alone among the throng at Versailles, she seemed to have little appreciation for the man who, she had been told, had once been "a printer's foreman." As she noted dismissively, a man of that background would never have been able to rise so high in Europe. Franklin would have proudly agreed.[33]

Franklin's diplomatic triumph would help seal the course of the Revolution. It would also alter the world's balances of power, not just between France and England, but also—though France certainly did not intend it to—between republicanism and monarchy.

"Franklin had won," writes Carl Van Doren, "a diplomatic campaign equal in results to Saratoga." The Yale historian Edmund Morgan goes even further, calling it "the greatest diplomatic victory the United States has ever achieved." With the possible exception of the creation of the NATO alliance, that assessment may be true, though it partly points up the paucity of American successes over the years at bargaining tables, whether in Versailles after World War I or in Paris at the end of the Vietnam War. At the very least, it can be said that Franklin's triumph permitted America the possibility of an outright victory in its war for independence while conceding no lasting entanglements that would encumber it as a new nation.

Before word of the treaty reached Philadelphia, the Congress had been debating whether to consider the new peace offers that had arrived from Britain. Now, after only two days of deliberation, it decided instead to ratify the alliance with France. "You cannot conceive what joy the treaties with France have diffused among all true Americans," Franklin's friend Samuel Cooper wrote from Massachusetts.[34]

CHAPTER FOURTEEN

BON VIVANT

Paris, 1778–1785

JOHN ADAMS

In April 1778, shortly after the American treaties with France had been signed, John Adams arrived in Paris to replace the recalled Silas Deane as one of the three American commissioners. The French were not thrilled by the switch. "Mr. Deane," reported Edward Bancroft to his spymasters in London, "is highly esteemed here and his successor J. Adams is much distrusted." Bancroft reported that Adams was also unhappy. "Adams is heartily disappointed to find everything done and talks of returning."

When they served together in the Congress, Adams had initially distrusted Franklin, then gone through a blender of emotions: bemusement, resentment, admiration, and jealousy. On their trip to negotiate with Lord Howe on Staten Island (when they shared a bed and open window), he had found Franklin both amusing and annoying. So, when he arrived in Paris, it was probably inevitable that he and Franklin would, as they did, enjoy and suffer a complex mix of disdain and grudging admiration for one another.

Some have found the relationship baffling: Did Adams resent or respect Franklin? Did Franklin find Adams maddening or solid? Did they like or dislike each other? The answer, which is not all that baffling because it is often true of the relationship between two great and strong people, is that they felt all of these conflicting emotions about each other, and more.

They were both very smart, but otherwise they had quite different personalities. Adams was unbending and outspoken and argumentative, Franklin charming and taciturn and flirtatious. Adams was rigid in his personal morality and lifestyle, Franklin famously playful. Adams learned French by poring over grammar books and memorizing a collection of funeral orations; Franklin (who cared little about the grammar) learned the language by lounging on the pillows of his female friends and writing them amusing little tales. Adams felt comfortable confronting people, whereas Franklin preferred to seduce them, and the same was true of the way they dealt with nations.

Adams, who was 42 when he arrived, was thirty years younger than Franklin and about five years younger than Franklin's son, William. More sensitive to insults, real and imagined, Adams came to feel more strongly about Franklin than vice versa. At times, he was driven almost to distraction by Franklin's insouciance and self-indulgence. "He envied—and suspected—people with no rough edges, people who moved easily in the finer circles," Berkeley historian Robert Middlekauff writes of Adams in his textured study *Benjamin Franklin and His Enemies*. He was "incapable of the easy gesture, and incapable too of the small hypocrisies that carry other men through life." David McCullough, in his masterly biography of Adams, is more sympathetic and balanced about him, but he too conveys the rich complexity of his attitudes toward Franklin.[1]

Most of Adams's resentments were occasioned by ill-disguised jealousy at being overshadowed. Franklin had "a monopoly of reputation here and an indecency in displaying it," Adams complained to a friend after a few months in Paris. But in reading some of the unkind things he had to say about Franklin, it is important to note that at one time or another, Adams hurled a few nasty adjectives at just about everyone he met. (For instance, he once described George Washington as a "muttonhead.") Despite their personal friction, Adams and Franklin were bound together by their shared patriotism and their ardor for America's independence.

Franklin took Adams under his wing at Passy, enrolled 10-year-old John Quincy Adams at Benny Bache's boarding school, and took his new colleague on all of his social and cultural rounds, including his grand embrace of Voltaire at the Académie. On Adams's first day at Passy, Franklin brought him along to dine at the home of Jacques Turgot, the former finance minister, and then on subsequent days to the salons of the various women whose seductive styles entranced Franklin and appalled Adams.

Even more appalling to the puritanical Adams was Franklin's living and work style. He was disturbed by what he assumed to be the cost of the luxurious accommodations at Passy, then even more upset when he learned that the ambitious Chaumont was charging them no rent. Soon after his arrival, Adams vented in his diary about the difficulty of getting Franklin to focus on work:

> I found out that the business of our commission would never be done unless I did it . . . The life of Dr. Franklin was a scene of continual dissipation . . . It was late when he breakfasted, and as soon as breakfast was over, a crowd of carriages came to his levee . . . some philosophers, academicians, and economists; some of his small tribe of humble friends in the literary way whom he employed to translate some of his ancient compositions, such as his Bonhomme Richard and for what I know his Polly Baker, etc., but by far the greater part were women and children, come to have the honor to see the great Franklin, and to have the pleasure of telling stories about his simplicity, his bald head . . .
>
> He was invited to dine every day and never declined unless we had invited company to dine with us. I was always invited with him, till I found it necessary to send apologies, that I might have some time to study the French language and do the business of the mission. Mr. Franklin kept a horn book always in his pocket in which he minuted all his invitations to dinner, and Mr. Lee said it was the only thing in which he was punctual . . . In these agreeable and important occupations and amusements the afternoon and evening was spent, and he came home at all hours from nine to twelve o'clock at night.[2]

One of Franklin's French friends put a more positive spin on his work habits: "He would eat, sleep, work whenever he saw fit, according to his needs, so that there never was a more leisurely man, though he certainly handled a tremendous amount of business." These two descriptions of Franklin's style reveal not just differing views about him but also differing views about work. Franklin was always industrious, and in America he famously believed in also giving the *appearance* of being industrious. But in France, where the appearance of pleasure was more valued, Franklin knew how to adopt the style. As Claude-Anne Lopez notes, "In colonial America it was sinful to look idle, in France it was vulgar to look busy."[3]

One day, a Frenchman asked Adams whether he was surprised that Franklin never attended any religious services. "No," Adams replied laughing, "because Mr. Franklin has no . . ." Adams did not finish the sentence for fear of seeming too blasphemous.

"Mr. Franklin adores only great nature," said the Frenchman, "which has interested a great many people of both sexes in his favor."

"Yes," replied Adams, "all the atheists, deists and libertines, as well as all the philosophers and ladies, are in his train."

"Yes," the Frenchman continued, "he is celebrated as the great philosopher and the great legislator of America."

Adams was unable to control his resentment. "He is a great philosopher, but as a legislator of America he has done very little," he told the Frenchman. "It is universally believed in France, England and all Europe that his electric wand has accomplished all this revolution, but nothing is more groundless . . . He did not even make the constitution of Pennsylvania, bad as it is." (Adams, who was not as much of a democrat as Franklin and believed in checks on the power of the people, strongly objected to the unicameral legislature.)[4]

After a few years, Franklin would tire of Adams and declare that he was "sometimes, and in some things, absolutely out of his senses." But for the time being, he found Adams tolerable, at times even admirable. And he was happy to make him part of his social set, despite Adams's minimal enthusiasm for such frivolities.[5]

VOLTAIRE

The *philosophes* of France were, like Franklin, eager to engage in the real world rather than lose themselves in abstruse metaphysics. Their secular version of the Bible was the *Encyclopédie* compiled by Diderot, which included articles by Turgot on economics, Montesquieu on politics, Rousseau on the arts, Condorcet on sciences, and Helvétius on man. Reigning as their king and god—or perhaps neither, as he was skeptical of both—was Voltaire, a man who contributed anonymously to the *Encyclopédie* but prominently to the intellectual life of France.

Voltaire and Franklin were, at least in the mind of the French public, soul mates. Both were aging embodiments of the wit and reason of the Enlightenment, playful yet pointed parodists, debunkers of orthodoxy and pretense, disciples of deism, tribunes of tolerance, and apostles of revolution. So it was inevitable not only that the two sages would meet but also that their meetings would, even more than the one between Franklin and the king himself, capture the public imagination.[6]

By early 1778, Voltaire was 84 and ailing, and there had even been stories that he had died. (His retort, even better than Mark Twain's similar one, was that the reports were true, only premature.) In February, Franklin paid a ceremonial visit to his home and asked him to give his blessing to 7-year-old Benny Bache. As twenty awed disciples watched and shed "tears of tenderness," Voltaire put his hands on the boy's head and pronounced in English, "God and Liberty." According to Condorcet, one of the witnesses, he added, "This is the only appropriate benediction for the grandson of Monsieur Franklin."

Some derided the rather histrionic display. One of Paris's more caustic papers accused them of "playing out a scene" of "puerile adulation," and when former Massachusetts governor Hutchinson heard of the "God and Liberty" benediction, he remarked that it was "difficult to say which of those words had been most used to bad purposes." Mainly, however, the encounter was reverentially publicized throughout Europe.[7]

Franklin and Voltaire staged an even more dramatic meeting at the Académie Royale on April 29 of that year. Franklin was dressed with trademark simplicity: plain coat, no wig, and no adornments other than his spectacles. Voltaire, who would die within a month, was gaunt and frail. The crowd demanded that they give each other a French embrace, an act that evoked, in the words of Condorcet, such "noisy acclamation one would have said it was Solon who embraced

Sophocles." The comparison to the great Greek philosophers, one famous for his laws and the other for his literature, was proclaimed throughout Europe, as eyewitness John Adams reported with his typical mix of awe and resentment:

> There was a general cry that M. Voltaire and M. Franklin should be introduced to each other. This was no satisfaction; there must be something more. Neither of our philosophers seemed to divine what was wished or expected; they however took each other by the hand. But this was not enough. The clamor continued until the explanation came out: Il faut s'embrasser à la française. The two aged actors upon this great theater of philosophy and frivolity then embraced each other by hugging one another in their arms and kissing each other's cheeks, and then the tumult subsided. And the cry immediately spread through the kingdom, and I suppose all over Europe: Qu'il est charmant de voir embrasser Solon et Sophocles.[8]

The Académie served as one of Franklin's bases among the intellectual elite of Paris. Another was a remarkable Masonic lodge known, in honor of the muses, as the Lodge of the Nine Sisters. Freemasonry in France was evolving from being just a set of businessmen's social clubs, which is what it mainly was in America, and was becoming part of the movement led by the *philosophes* and other freethinkers who challenged the orthodoxies of both the church and the monarchy. Claude-Adrien Helvétius, a very freethinking *philosophe*, had first envisioned a superlodge in Paris that would be filled with the greatest writers and artists. When he died, his widow, Madame Helvétius (about whom we will soon hear a lot more), helped fund its creation in 1776.

Franklin and Voltaire joined the Lodge of the Nine Sisters in April 1778, the same month as their public meeting at the Académie. The lodge provided Franklin with influential supporters and enjoyable evenings. But it was risky. Both the king and the clerics were wary of the renegade lodge—and of Franklin's membership in it.

The controversy surrounding the lodge was heightened when, in November 1778, it held a memorial service for Voltaire, who, on his deathbed a few months earlier, had waved off priests seeking to give him last rites. Some friends, such as Condorcet and Diderot, thought it wise to avoid the ceremony. But Franklin not only attended, he took part in it.

The hall was draped in black, lit only dimly by candles. There were songs, speeches, and poems attacking the clergy and absolutism in all forms. Voltaire's niece presented a bust by Houdon. (Houdon, a member, also did a bust of Franklin for the lodge, which is now in the Philadelphia Museum of Art.) Then a flame of light revealed a grand painting of the apotheosis of Voltaire emerging from his tomb to be presented in heaven by the goddesses of Truth and Benevolence. Franklin took the Masonic wreath from his head and solemnly laid it at the foot of the painting. Everyone then adjourned to the banquet room, where the first toast included a tribute to Franklin—"the captive thunder dying at his feet"—and to America.

Louis XVI, though a Mason himself, was annoyed by the spectacle and worked through the other Masonic lodges to have the Nine Sisters expelled. After months of controversy, the situation was resolved when the Nine Sisters reorganized itself and Franklin took over as its Venerable, or Grand Master. During the ensuing years, Franklin would induct many Americans into the lodge, including his grandson Temple, the spy Edward Bancroft, and the naval warrior John Paul Jones. He also helped create from within the lodge a group somewhat akin to his American Philosophical Society, known as the Société Apollonienne.[9]

MADAME BRILLON

As fascinating as the freemasons and *philosophes* were, it was not for his male friends that Franklin was famous in France. Among his many reputations was that of a legendary and lecherous old lover who had many mistresses among the ladies of Paris. The reality, truth be told, was somewhat less titillating. His famed female friends were mistresses only of his mind and soul. Yet that hardly made their relationships less interesting.

The first of these was with a talented and high-strung neighbor in Passy, Madame Brillon de Jouy, an accomplished musician who was noted for her performances on the harpsichord and the new pianos that were becoming fashionable in France. When she first met Franklin in the spring of 1777, she worried that she had been too shy to make a good impression. So the next day she asked a mutual friend to send her some of the Scottish melodies she knew Franklin loved. "I would try to play them and compose some in the same style!" she wrote. "I do wish to provide the great man with some moments of relaxation from his occupations, and also to have the pleasure of seeing him."

Thus began their intense companionship, which soon became sexually charged and the fodder for much gossip. Adams and others were shocked by what Madame Brillon called her "sweet habit of sitting on your lap" and by stories of their late nights spent together. "I am certain you have been kissing my wife," her husband once wrote Franklin.

Yet Monsieur Brillon added in his letter, "My dear Doctor, let me kiss you back in return." Franklin's relationship with Madame Brillon, like so many of his others with distinguished ladies, was complex and never fully consummated. It was, as Claude-Anne Lopez has ably described, an *amité amoureuse* in which Franklin had to settle for playing the role of "Cher Papa," an oddly flirtatious father.[10]

Madame Brillon, who was 33 when she met Franklin, was buffeted by conflicting passions and variable moods. Her husband, twenty-four years her senior (but fourteen years younger than Franklin), was wealthy, doting, and unfaithful. She had two daughters with beautiful singing voices and lived in one of the most elegant estates in Passy, yet she was prone to fits of depression and self-pity. Although she spoke no English, she and Franklin exchanged more than 130 letters during their eight-year relationship, and she was able not only to enchant him but also to manipulate him.

She did so by composing and playing music for him, creating a salon around him, and writing him flattering letters in French and in the third person. "It is," she declared, "a real source of joy for her to think that she can sometimes amuse Mr. Franklin, whom she loves and esteems as he deserves." When the Americans won the Battle of Saratoga, she composed a triumphal overture entitled "Marche des Insurgents" (which is still sometimes performed) and played it for him in a private concert. They also flirted over the chessboard. "She is still a little miffed," Madame Brillon teasingly wrote of herself, "about the six games of chess he won so inhumanly and she warns him she will spare nothing to get her revenge."[11]

By March 1778, after months of just music and chess, Franklin was ready for something more. So he shocked her with some of his libertine theology and challenged her to save his soul. "You were kind enough," she wrote, now comfortable in the first person, "to entrust me with your conversion." Her propositions were promising, even suggestive. "I know my penitent's weak spot, I shall tolerate it! As long as he loves God, America, and me above all things, I absolve him of all of his sins, present, past and *future*."

Madame Brillon went on to describe the seven cardinal sins, merrily noting that he had conquered well the first six, ranging from pride to sloth. When she got to the seventh, the sin of lust, she became a bit coy: "The seventh—I shall not name it. All great men are tainted with it . . . You have loved, my dear brother; you have been kind and lovable; you have been loved in return! What is so damnable about that?"

"She promises to lead me to heaven along a road so delicious," Franklin exulted in his reply to her. "I am in raptures when I think of being absolved of the *future* sins." Turning to the Ten Commandments, he argued that there were actually two others that should be included: to multiply and fill the earth, and to love one another. He had always obeyed those two very well, he argued, and should not that "compensate for my having so often failed to respect one of the ten? I mean the one which forbids us to covet thy neighbor's wife, a commandment which (I confess) I have consistently violated."[12]

Alas, Madame Brillon took that cue to beat a hasty retreat. "I dare not decide the question without consulting that neighbor whose wife you covet," she wrote, referring to her husband. There was, she explained, a double standard she must obey. "You are a man, I am a woman, and while we might think along the same lines, we must speak and act differently. Perhaps there is no great harm in a man having desires and yielding to them; a woman may have desires, but she must not yield."

Little did she know that her own husband was engaging in this double standard. Once again, it was John Adams who recorded the situation in shocked detail after Franklin took him to dine with "a large company of both sexes" at the Brillons. Madame Brillon struck Adams as "one of the most beautiful women of France," her husband as "a rough kind of country squire." Among the crowd was a "very plain and clumsy" woman. "I afterwards learned both from Dr. Franklin and his grandson," Adams noted, "that this woman was the amie of Mr. Brillon." He also surmised, this time incorrectly, that Madame Brillon was having an affair with another neighbor. "I was astonished that these people could live together in such apparent friendship and indeed without cutting each other's throats. But I did not know the world."

A year later, Madame Brillon found out about her husband's affair with this "clumsy" young woman, Mademoiselle Jupin, who was the governess of the Brillon girls. She banished the young woman from the house, and then began to fear that she might take a job as Franklin's housekeeper. After Franklin assured her, in a closed-door session at his office, that he had no intention of hiring the woman, Madame Brillon wrote him a relieved letter. "My soul is calmer, my dear Papa, since it has unburdened itself into yours, since it does not fear anymore that Mlle J—— might settle down with you and be your torment."[13]

Even before this fit of jealousy, Madame Brillon had begun a crusade to stop Franklin from turning his attentions to other women, despite being unwilling to satisfy his ardor. "When you scatter your friendship, as you have done, my friendship does not diminish, but from now on I shall try to be somewhat sterner to your faults," she threatened.

In a forceful yet seductive reply, Franklin argued that she had no right to be so possessive. "You renounce and totally exclude all that might be of the flesh in our affection, allowing me only some kisses, civil and honest, such as you might grant your little cousins," he chided. "What am I receiving that is so special as to prevent me from giving the same to others?"

He included in the letter a proposed nine-article treaty of "peace, friendship and love" between the two of them. It began with articles that she would accept, followed by ones declaring pretty much the opposite that he would accept. The former included one saying that "Mr.

F. shall come to her whenever she sends for him" and another saying that he would "stay with her as long as she pleases." His stipulations, on the other hand, included one saying that "he will go away from Madame B's whenever he pleases," and another that "he will stay away as long as he pleases." The final article of the treaty was one on his side: "That he will love any other woman as far as he finds her amiable." He added, however, that he was "without much hope" that she would agree to this final provision, and in any event "I despair of finding any other woman that I could love with equal tenderness."[14]

In describing his sexual desires, Franklin could be quite salacious. "My poor little boy, whom you ought to have cherished, instead of being fat and jolly like those in your elegant drawings, is thin and starved for want of the nourishment that you inhumanely deny him." Madame Brillon continued the colloquy by calling him an Epicurean, who "wants a fat chubby love," and herself a Platonist, who "tries to blunt his little arrows." In another suggestive letter, he told a fable about a man who refused to lend out his horses to a friend. He was not like that. "You know that I am ready to sacrifice my beautiful big horses."

After dozens of such sensuous parries and thrusts had passed between them, at least on paper, Madame Brillon ended up rejecting once and for all his desires for a more corporeal love. In return, she also abandoned her attempt to prevent him from seeking it elsewhere. "Platonism may not be the gayest sect, but it is a convenient defense for the fair sex," she wrote. "Hence, the lady, who finds it congenial, advises the gentleman to fatten up his favorite at other tables than hers, which will always offer too meager a diet for his greedy appetites."[15]

The letter, which concluded with an invitation for tea the next day, did not end their relationship. Instead, it took on another form: Madame Brillon declared that she would henceforth like to play the role of an adoring daughter, and she assigned to him the role of a loving father.

> It is to her father that this tender and loving daughter is speaking; I had a father once, the best of men, he was my first, my closest friend. I lost him too soon! You have often asked me: "Couldn't I take the place of those you regret?" And you have told me about the humane custom

of certain savages who adopt their prisoners of war and put them in the place of their own dead relatives. You have taken in my heart the place of that father.

Franklin, either out of desire or necessity, formally agreed. "I accept with infinite pleasure, my dear friend, the proposal you make, with such kindness, of adopting me as your father," he wrote. Then he turned philosophical. It was, as he had said of Benny and Temple, important for him, now that he was separated from his own "affectionate daughter" in Philadelphia, to have always some child with him "to take care of me during my life and tenderly close my eyelids when I must take my last rest." He would work hard, he promised, to play the role properly. "I love you as a father, with all my heart. It is true that I sometimes suspect that heart of wanting to go further, but I try to conceal it from myself."[16]

The transformation of their relationship evoked from Franklin one of his most wistful and self-revealing little tales, *The Ephemera,* written to her after a stroll in the garden. (The theme came from an article he had printed in the *Pennsylvania Gazette* fifty years earlier.) He had happened to overhear, he wrote, a lament by one of the tiny short-lived flies who realized that his seven hours on this planet were nearing an end.

> I have seen generations born, flourish and expire. My present friends are the children and grandchildren of the friends of my youth, who are now, alas, no more! And I must soon follow them; for by the course of nature, though still in health, I cannot expect to live above seven or eight minutes longer. What now avails all my toil and labor in amassing honey-dew on this leaf, which I cannot live to enjoy! . . .
>
> My Friends would comfort me with the idea of a name they say I shall leave behind me; and they tell me I have lived long enough, to nature and to glory. But what will fame be to an Ephemere who no longer exists? . . .
>
> To me, after all my eager pursuits, no solid pleasures now remain, but the reflection of a long life spent in meaning well, the sensible conversation of a few good Lady-Ephemeres, and now and then a kind smile and a tune from the ever-amiable BRILLANTE. [In the original French version, the final words more clearly refer to the recipient: "toujours amiable Brillon."][17]

Throughout his remaining years in France, and even in letters after his return to America, Franklin would stay emotionally attached to Madame Brillon. Their new arrangement still allowed him such liberties as playing chess with a mutual friend, late into the night, in her bathroom, while she soaked in her tub and watched. But it was, as bathtub chess games go, rather innocent; the tub was covered, as was the style, by a wooden plank. "I'm afraid that we may have made you very uncomfortable by keeping you so long in the bath," he apologized the next day, adding a wry little promise: "Never again will I consent to start a chess game with the neighbor in your bathing room. Can you forgive me this indiscretion?" She certainly could. "No, my good papa, you did not do me any ill yesterday," she replied. "I get so much pleasure from seeing you that it made up for the little fatigue of having come out of the bath a little too late."

Having forsaken the possibility of an earthly romance, they amused themselves by promising themselves one in heaven. "I give you my word," she teased him at one point, "that I will become your wife in paradise on the condition that you will not make too many conquests among the heavenly maidens while you are waiting for me. I want a faithful husband when I take one for eternity."

More than almost anyone, she could articulate what made him so charming to women, "that gaiety and that gallantry that cause all women to love you, because you love them all." With both insight and affection, she declared, "You combine the kindest heart with the soundest moral teaching, a lively imagination, and that droll roguishness which shows that the wisest of men allows his wisdom to be perpetually broken against the rocks of femininity."[18]

In the ensuing years, Franklin would help guide Madame Brillon through her bouts of depression, and he would try, as we shall see, to encourage a marriage between Temple and either of her daughters. But increasingly, by 1779, he was turning more of his attention toward another woman, one with an even more fascinating household, who lived in the neighboring village of Auteuil.

MADAME HELVÉTIUS

Anne-Catherine de Ligniville d'Autricourt was born to one of the great aristocratic families of Lorraine, but she was the tenth of twenty children and thus lacked a dowry. So when she was 15 and of marriageable age, she was sent off to a convent. As it turned out, she certainly did not have the temperament for a cloistered life nor, for that matter, the funds. At age 30, her pension ran out and so did she, to Paris, where she was taken in by a kindly aunt who had left her husband, become a novelist, and created a salon filled with bright and slightly bohemian intellectuals.

There Anne-Catherine's vivacity and beauty attracted many suitors, most notably the economist Turgot, eight years her junior, who would later become France's comptroller and a friend of Franklin. Turgot was engaging but not wealthy enough, so she instead married someone more established, Claude-Adrien Helvétius.

Helvétius was one of France's fifty or so Farmers General, a royal-chartered group with the very lucrative assignment of collecting taxes and holding leases. Once he had made his fortune, Helvétius set out to satisfy his social and intellectual aspirations. So the rich financier married the poor aristocrat and became, as mentioned above, a noted philosopher who helped plan the Nine Sisters Masonic Lodge. His great work, *De l'Esprit* (1758), was a controversial espousal of godless hedonism, which argued that the love of pleasure motivated human activity. Around him he gathered the stars of the Enlightenment, including Diderot, Condorcet, Hume on his occasional visits from Edinburgh, and Turgot, still in favor though spurned as a suitor.

When Helvétius died in 1771, five years before Franklin's arrival, his widow Anne-Catherine, now Madame Helvétius, married off their two daughters to men of their own choosing, gave each of them one of the family chateaux, and bought a rambling farm in Auteuil near Passy. She was lively, outgoing and, as befitted her aristocratic birth but impoverished upbringing, somewhat of a free-spirited bohemian who enjoyed projecting an earthy aura. There is an oft-repeated remark that has been attributed to many but was likely first famously uttered by the writer Fontenelle, who was in his late nineties when he frequented her salon. Beholding Madame Helvétius in one of her more casual states of undress, he proclaimed, "Oh, to be seventy again!"

At Auteuil she cultivated a free-spirited garden that was devoid of all French formality, a collection of ducks and dogs that formed a noisy and motley menagerie, and a salon that displayed many of the same attributes. Friends brought her rare plants, unusual pets, and provocative ideas, and she nurtured them all at what became jokingly known as "l'Académie d'Auteuil."[19]

Living with Madame Helvétius were two priests and one acolyte:

- The Abbé André Morellet, a noted political economist and contributor to the *Encyclopédie*, in his late forties who had first befriended Franklin in 1772 at the English house party where he played the trick of stilling the waves with his magic cane, and who shared his love for fine wine, song, economic theories, and practical inventions.
- The Abbé Martin Lefebvre de la Roche, in his late thirties, a former Benedictine whom (in Morellet's words) "Helvétius had after a fashion secularized."
- Pierre-Jean-Georges Cabanis, a bachelor poet in his early twenties, who translated Homer, studied medicine, wrote a book on hospitals, and revered Franklin, whose tales and anecdotes he faithfully recorded.

"We discoursed of morality, of politics, and of philosophy," la Roche recalled. "Notre Dame d'Auteuil excited your coquetry, and the Abbé Morellet wrangled over the cream and ushered his arguments to prove what we did not believe."[20]

It was Turgot, still smitten by Madame Helvétius, who first brought Franklin to visit her in 1778, when she was nearly 60 but still both lively and beautiful. Her domestic menagerie, filled with banter and intellectual irreverence, was perfectly tailored to Franklin's tastes, and shortly thereafter he wrote her a letter in which he described her electromagnetism:

I have in my way been trying to form some hypothesis to account for your having so many friends and of such various kinds. I see that statesmen, philosophers, historians, poets and men of learning of all sorts attach themselves to you as straws to a fine piece of amber . . . We find in your sweet society that charming benevolence, that amiable attention to oblige, that disposition to please and be pleased, which we do not always find in the society of one another . . . In your company, we are not only pleased with you, but better pleased with one another and with ourselves.[21]

Not surprisingly, John Adams was shocked by both Madame Helvétius and her household when Franklin brought him for a visit. The two abbots, he sniped, "I suppose have as much power to pardon a sin as they have to commit one." Of the moral "absurdities" at the house he commented, "No kind of republican government can ever exist with such national manners." His wife, Abigail, was even more horrified when she visited later, and she described Madame Helvétius with a delightfully vicious pen:

> Her hair was frizzled; over it she had a small straw hat, with a dirty gauze handkerchief behind . . . She carried on the chief of the conversation at dinner, frequently locking her hand into the Doctor's, and sometimes spreading her arms upon the arms of both the gentlemen's chairs, then throwing her arms carelessly upon the Doctor's neck . . . I was highly disgusted, and never wish for an acquaintance with ladies of this cast. After dinner, she threw herself on a settee, where she showed more than her feet. She had a little lap-dog, who was, next to the doctor, her favorite. This she kissed, and when he wet the floor she wiped it up with her shirt.[22]

Franklin did more than flirt with Madame Helvétius; by September 1779, he was ardently proposing marriage in a way that was more than half-serious but retained enough ironic detachment to preserve their dignities. "If that Lady likes to pass her days with him, he in turn would like to pass his nights with her," he wrote through Cabanis, using the third person. "As he has already given her many of his days, though he has so few left to give, she appears ungrateful never to have given him a single one of her nights, which steadily pass as a pure loss, without giving happiness to anyone except Poupon [her dog]."[23]

She led him on lightly. "I hoped that after putting such pretty things on paper," she scrawled, "you would come and tell me some." He continued his quest in a clever, yet still humorously detached, fashion by composing for her two little tales. The first was written in the voice of the flies living in his apartment. They complain about the dangers they faced from the spiders at Passy and thank her for making him clean out their webs. "There only remains one thing for us to wish," they conclude. "It is to see both of you forming at last but one ménage."[24]

Turgot, now more jealous than amused by Franklin, counseled her to decline his marriage proposals, which she did. Franklin nevertheless renewed his suit with one of his most famous tales, "The Elysian Fields," in which he recounted a dream about going to heaven and discussing the matter with her late husband and his late wife, who had themselves married. Praising Madame Helvétius's looks over those of his departed wife, he suggested they take revenge:

> Vexed by your barbarous resolution, announced so. positively last evening, to remain single all your life in respect to your dear husband, I went home, fell on my bed, and, believing myself dead, found myself in the Elysian Fields . . . [M. Helvétius] received me with great courtesy, having known me for some time, he said, by the reputation I had there. He asked me a thousand things about the war, and about the present state of religion, liberty, and the government in France. You ask nothing then of your dear friend Madame H——; nevertheless she still loves you excessively and I was at her place but an hour ago.
>
> Ah! said he, you make me remember my former felicity.—But it is necessary to forget it in order to be happy here. During several of the early years, I thought only of her. Finally I am consoled. I have taken another wife. The most like her that I could find. She is not, it is true, so completely beautiful, but she has as much good sense, a little more of Spirit, and she loves me infinitely. Her continual study is to please me; and she has actually gone to hunt the best Nectar and the best Ambrosia in order to regale me this evening; remain with me and you will see her.
>
> . . . At these words the new Madame H—— entered with the Nectar: at which instant I recognized her to be Madame F——, my old American friend. I reclaimed to her. But she told me coldly, "I have been your good wife forty-nine years and four months, nearly a half century; be content with that. Here I have formed a new connection, which will endure to eternity."

Offended by this refusal of my Eurydice, I suddenly decided to leave these ungrateful spirits, to return to the good earth, to see again the sunshine and you. Here I am! Let us revenge ourselves.[25]

Beneath the frivolity lurked a sincere desire—his friends thought so, as did his friendly rival Turgot—yet it was expressed with a flair that made it seem safe and clever. Always uncomfortable with deep emotional bonds, Franklin performed the perfect distancing trick. Instead of conducting his suit in secret, which would have given it a dangerous seriousness, he took it public by publishing the story on his private press a few months later. By doing so, he put his heart out for all to see, and there it could dance safely in the realm between sincerity and self-deprecating playfulness. "Franklin somehow never committed himself wholly in love," notes Claude-Anne Lopez. "A part of him was always holding back and watching the proceedings with irony."

It was all too much, both the seriousness and the public playfulness, for Madame Helvétius. She fled in June 1780 to spend the summer in Tours with the hope, according to a letter Turgot wrote a mutual friend, "that she may forget, if possible, all the turmoil that has tormented her." He added that the vacation was best "not only for her own tranquility, but also to reestablish it in that other head [i.e., Franklin's] that has agitated so ill-advisedly."[26]

As for Franklin, the deft dance of half-serious flirtations, unrequited though they were, had a rejuvenating effect on his body and spirit. "I do not find that I grow any older," he wrote a friend that spring. "Being arrived at 70, and considering that by traveling further in the same road I should probably be led to the grave, I stopped short, turned about, and walked back again; which having done these four years, you may now call me 66."[27]

THE BAGATELLES

One product of Franklin's flirtations at Passy and Auteuil was the collection of fables and tales—such as "The Ephemera," "The Flies," and "The Elysian Fields," mentioned above—that he wrote to amuse his friends. He called them bagatelles, the French term for a sprightly little musical piece, and he published many of them on the private press he installed at Passy. They were similar to little stories he had written in the past, such as "The Trial of Polly Baker," but the dozen or so written in Passy have a slight French accent to them.

They have been the subject of much critical fawning. "Franklin's bagatelles combine delight with moral truth," declares Alfred Owen Aldridge. "They are among the world's masterpieces of light literature." Not exactly. Their value lies more in the glimpse they give into Franklin's personality than in their literary merit, which is somewhat slight. They are jeux d'esprit, as fun as a five-finger exercise. Most display Franklin's typical wry self-awareness, though some are a bit heavy-handed in their attempt to teach a moral lesson.[28]

The most amusing is "Dialogue between the Gout and Mr. Franklin," a precursor to the old Alka Seltzer commercial in which a man is berated by his stomach. When he was bedridden by the malady in October 1780, Madame Brillon wrote him a poem, "Le Sage et la Goutte," that implied that his malady was caused by his love for "one pretty mistress, sometimes two, three, four." Among the lines:

> "Moderation, dear Doctor," said the Gout,
> "Is no virtue for which you stand out.
> You like food, you like ladies' sweet talk,
> You play chess when you should walk."

Franklin replied one midnight with a long and rollicking dialogue in which the gout chided him for his indulgences and also, because Franklin liked to be instructive, prescribed a course of exercise and fresh air:

MR. F.: Eh! oh! eh! What have I done to merit these cruel sufferings?

THE GOUT: Many things; you have ate and drank too freely, and too much indulged those legs of yours in their indolence.

MR. F.: Who is it that accuses me?

THE GOUT: It is I, even I, the Gout.

MR. F.: What! my enemy in person?

THE GOUT: No, not your enemy.

MR. F.: I repeat it, my enemy; for you would not only torment my body to death, but ruin my good name; you reproach me as a glutton and a tippler; now all the world, that knows me, will allow that I am neither the one nor the other.

THE GOUT: The world may think as it pleases; it is always very complaisant to itself, and sometimes to its friends; but I very well know that the quantity of meat and drink proper for a man who takes a reasonable degree of exercise, would be too much for another who never takes any . . .

If your situation in life is a sedentary one, your amusements, your recreation, at least, should be active. You ought to walk or ride; or, if the weather prevents that, play at billiards. But let us examine your course of life. While the mornings are long, and you have leisure to go abroad, what do you do? Why, instead of gaining an appetite for breakfast by salutary exercise, you amuse yourself with books, pamphlets, or newspapers, which commonly are not worth the reading. Yet you eat an inordinate breakfast, four dishes of tea with cream, and one or two buttered toasts, with slices of hung beef, which I fancy are not things the most easily digested.

Immediately afterwards you sit down to write at your desk, or converse with persons who apply to you on business. Thus the time passes till one, without any kind of bodily exercise. But all this I could pardon, in regard, as you say, to your sedentary condition. But what is your practice after dinner? Walking in the beautiful gardens of those friends with whom you have dined would be the choice of men of sense; yours is to be fixed down to chess, where you are found engaged for two or three hours!

. . . You know M. Brillon's gardens, and what fine walks they contain; you know the handsome flight of an hundred steps which lead from the terrace above to the lawn below. You have been in the practice of visiting this amiable family twice a week, after dinner, and it is a maxim of your own, that "a man may take as much exercise in walking a mile up and down stairs, as in ten on level ground." What an opportunity was here for you to have had exercise in both these ways! Did you embrace it, and how often?

MR. F.: I cannot immediately answer that question.

THE GOUT: I will do it for you; not once.[29]

He sent the bagatelle to Madame Brillon along with a letter that, in a cheeky way, rebutted her poem's contention "that mistresses have had a share in producing this painful malady." As he pointed out, "When I was a young man and enjoyed more of the favors of the fair sex than I do at present, I had no gout. Hence, if the ladies of Passy had shown more of that Christian charity that I have so often recommended to you in vain, I should not be suffering from the gout right now." Sex had become, by then, a topic of banter rather than of tension for them. "I will do my best for you, in a spirit of Christian charity," she wrote back, "but to the exclusion of *your* brand of Christian charity."

Franklin used his bagatelles as a way to improve his language skills; he would translate them back and forth, show them to friends like the Abbé de la Roche, and then incorporate corrections. He wrote his famous story about paying too much for a whistle as a child, for example, in two columns, the left in French and the right in English, with space in the margins for revisions. Because Madame Brillon spoke no English, Franklin sent her the French versions of his writings, often showing her the corrections others had made.

She was looser about grammar than about morals. "The corrector of your French spoiled your work," she said of the edits la Roche made to the gout dialogue. "Leave your works as they are, use words that say things, and laugh at grammarians, who by their purity weaken all your sentences." For example, Franklin often coined new French words, such as "indulger" (meaning "to indulge"), which his friends would then revise. Madame Brillon, however, found these neologisms charming. "A few purists might quibble with us, because those birds weigh words on a scale of cold erudition," she wrote, but "since you seem to express yourself more forcefully than a grammarian, my judgment goes in your favor."[30]

Franklin found it particularly difficult to master the language's masculine and feminine distinctions, and he even jokingly put the word "masculines" in the feminine form, and "feminines" in the masculine when complaining about the need to look such things up in the dictionary. "For sixty years now [since age 16], masculine and feminine things—and I am not talking about modes and tenses—have been giving me a lot of trouble," he noted wryly. "It will make me all the happier to go to paradise where, they say, all such distinctions will be abolished."

So how good was Franklin's French? By 1780, he was speaking and writing with great flourish and gusto, though not always with proper pronunciation and grammar. That approach appealed to most of his friends there, particularly the women, but not surprisingly, it offended John Adams. "Dr. Franklin is reported to speak French very well, but I find upon attending to him critically that he does not speak it grammatically," Adams chided. "He acknowledged to me that he was wholly inattentive to grammar. His pronunciation, too, upon which the French gentlemen and ladies complimented him very highly, and which he seemed to think pretty well, I soon found out was very inaccurate."[31]

The bagatelle that most enchanted his French friends, entitled "Conte," was a parable about religious tolerance. A French officer who is about to die recounts a dream in which he arrives at the gates of heaven and watches St. Peter ask people about their religion. The first replies that he is a Catholic, and St. Peter says, "Take your place there among the Catholics." A similar procedure follows for an Anglican and a Quaker. When the officer confesses that he has no religion, St. Peter is indulgent: "You can come in anyway; just find a place for yourself wherever you can." (Franklin seems to have revised the manuscript a few times to make his point about tolerance clear, and in one version expressed it more forcefully as: "Enter anyway and take any place you wish.")[32]

The tale echoed many of Franklin's previous light writings advocating religious tolerance. Although Franklin's belief in a benevolent God was becoming stronger as he grew older, the French intellectuals admired the fact that he did not embrace any religious sect. "Our freethinkers have adroitly sounded him on his religion," one acquaintance wrote, "and they maintain that they have discovered he is one of their own, that is that he had none at all."[33]

CHESS AND FARTS

One of Franklin's famous passions was chess, as evidenced by the late-night match he played in Madame Brillon's bathroom. He saw the game as a metaphor for both diplomacy and life, a point that he made explicit in a bagatelle he wrote in 1779 on "The Morals of Chess," which was based on an essay he had drafted in 1732 for his Philadelphia Junto. "The game of chess is not merely an idle amusement," he began. "Several very valuable qualities of the mind, useful in the course of human life, are to be acquired or strengthened by it. For life is a kind of chess, in which we have often points to gain and competitors or adversaries to contend with."

Chess, he said, taught foresight, circumspection, caution, and the importance of not being discouraged. There was also an important etiquette to be practiced: never hurry your opponent, do not try to deceive by pretending to have made a bad move, and never gloat in victory: "Moderate your desire of victory over your adversary, and be pleased with the one over yourself." There were even times when it was prudent to let an opponent retract a bad move: "You may indeed happen to lose the game to your opponent, but you will win what is better, his esteem." [34]

During one of Franklin's late-night chess matches in Passy, a messenger arrived with an important set of dispatches from America. Franklin waved him off until the game was finished. Another time, he was playing with his equal, the Duchess of Bourbon, who made a move that inadvertently exposed her king. Ignoring the rules of the game, he promptly captured it. "Ah," said the duchess, "we do not take Kings so." Replied Franklin in a famous quip: "We do in America." [35]

One night in Passy he was absorbed in a game when the candles flickered out. Refusing to quit, he sent his opponent to find more. The man quickly returned with a surprised look and the news that it was already light outside. Franklin threw open the shutters. "You are right, it is daytime," he said. "Let's go to bed."

The incident was the inspiration for a bagatelle he wrote about his surprise at discovering that the sun rose and poured forth light at 6 in the morning. By this stage in his life, it should be noted, he no longer shared Poor Richard's belief in being early to bed and early to rise. He declared that this discovery would surprise his readers, "who with me have never seen any signs of sunshine before noon." This led him to conclude that if people would simply get up much earlier, they could save a lot of money on candles. He even included some pseudo-scientific calculations of what could be saved by this "Economical Project" if during the summer months Parisians would shift their sleeping time seven hours earlier: close to 97 million livres, "an immense sum that the city of Paris might save every year by the economy of using sunshine instead of candles."

Franklin concluded by bestowing the idea on the public without any request for royalty or reward. "I expect only to have the honor of it," he declared. He ended up with far more honor than he could have imagined: most histories of the invention of Daylight Savings Time credit the idea to this essay by Franklin, even though he wrote it mockingly and did not come up with the idea of actually shifting clocks by an hour during the summer.[36]

The essay, which parodied both human habits and scientific treatises, reflected (as did his writings as a youth) the influence of Jonathan Swift. "It was the type of irony Swift would have written in place of 'A Modest Proposal' if he had spent five years in the company of Mmes. Helvétius and Brillon," notes Alfred Owen Aldridge.[37]

A similar scientific spoof, even more fun and famous (or perhaps notorious), was the mock proposal he made to the Royal Academy of Brussels that they study the causes and cures of farting. Noting that the academy's leaders, in soliciting questions to study, claimed to "esteem utility," he suggested a "serious enquiry" that would be worthy of "this enlightened age":

> It is universally well known that in digesting our common food, there is created or produced in the bowels of human creatures a great quantity of wind. That the permitting this air to escape and mix with the atmosphere is usually offensive to the company from the fetid smell that accompanies it. That all well-bred people therefore, to avoid giving such offense, forcibly restrain the efforts of nature to discharge that wind. That so retained contrary to nature, it not only gives frequently great present pain, but occasions future diseases . . .

> Were it not for the odiously offensive smell accompanying such escapes, polite people would probably be under no more restraint in discharging such wind in company than they are in spitting or in blowing their noses. My Prize Question therefore should be, To discover some drug wholesome and not disagreeable, to be mixed with our common food or sauces, that shall render the natural discharges of wind from our bodies, not only inoffensive, but agreeable as perfumes.

With a pretense of scientific seriousness, Franklin proceeded to explain how different foods and minerals change the odor of farts. Might not a mineral such as lime work to make the smell pleasant? "This is worth the experiment!" There would be "immortal honor" attached to whoever made the discovery, he argued, for it would be far more "useful [than] those discoveries in science that have heretofore made philosophers famous." All the works of Aristotle and Newton, he noted, do little to help those plagued by gas. "What comfort can the vortices of Descartes give to a man who has whirlwinds in his bowels!" The invention of a fart perfume would allow hosts to pass wind freely with the comfort that it would give pleasure to their guests. Compared to this luxury, he said with a bad pun, previous discoveries "are, all together, scarcely worth a Fart-hing."

Although he printed this farce privately at his press in Passy, Franklin apparently had qualms and never released it publicly. He did, however, send it to friends, and he noted in particular that it might be of interest to one of them, the famous chemist and gas specialist Joseph Priestley, "who is apt to give himself airs."[38]

Yet another delightful essay of mock science was written as a letter to the Abbé Morellet. It celebrated the wonders of wine and the glories of the human elbow:

> We hear of the conversion of water into wine at the marriage in Cana as a miracle. But this conversion is, through the goodness of God, made every day before our eyes. Behold the rain which descends from heaven upon our vineyards; there it enters the roots of the vines, to be changed into wine; a constant proof that God loves us, and loves to see us happy. The miracle in question was performed only to hasten the operation.

As for the human elbow, Franklin explained, it was important that it be located at the right place, otherwise it would be hard to drink wine. If Providence had placed the elbow too low on the arm, it would be hard for the forearm to reach the mouth. Likewise, if the elbow had been placed too high, the forearm would overshoot the mouth. "But by the actual situation, we are enabled to drink at our ease, the glass going exactly to the mouth. Let us, then, with glass in hand, adore this benevolent wisdom; let us adore and drink!"[39]

FAMILY MATTERS

Where did this new circle of ersatz family members leave Franklin's actual family? At a distance. His daughter, Sally, who adored him, wrote of her diligence in restoring their house in Philadelphia after the British had withdrawn in May 1778. But whereas the letters from his French lady friends began "Cher Papa," most of those from his real daughter began more stiffly, with "Dear and honored sir." His replies, addressed to "Dear Sally" and occasionally "My Dear Child," often expressed delight about the exploits of his grandchildren. But sometimes even his compliments were freighted with exhortations. "If you knew how happy your letters make me," he lectured at one point, "I think you would write oftener."

In early 1779, Sally wrote of the high price of goods in America and how she was busy spinning her own tablecloths. Unfortunately, however, she made the mistake of adding that she had been invited to a ball in honor of General Washington and had sent to France for pins, lace, and feathers so she could look fashionable. "There never was so much dressing and pleasure going on," she exulted to her father, and she added that she hoped he would send her some accessories so that she could take pride in showing off his taste.

At the time, Franklin was writing his sweet bagatelles to his French friends and promising Polly Stevenson a pair of diamond earrings if one of his lottery tickets won. But he responded with dismay at Sally's plea for a few luxuries. "Your sending for long black pins, and lace, and feathers! disgusted me as much as if you had put salt in my strawberries," he chided. "The spinning, I see, is laid aside, and you are to be dressed for the ball! You seem not to know, my dear daughter, that, of all the dear things in this world, idleness is the dearest." He sent her some of the items she had requested "that are useful and necessary," but added a dose of homespun advice, with just a touch of his humor, about the frivolous fineries. "If you wear your cambric ruffles as I do, and take care not to mend the holes, they will come in time to be lace; and feathers, my dear girl, may be had in America from every cock's tail." [40]

Clearly hurt, she replied with a detailed description of how industrious and frugal she was being, and she tried to work back into his graces by sending over some homespun American silk for him to present from her to Queen Marie-Antoinette. Knowing her father's desire to promote the local silk industry, she noted, "It will show what can be sent from America."

It was a sweet gesture, with all the elements—industriousness, selflessness, promotion of American products, gratitude toward France—that should have appealed to Franklin. Alas, the silk was stained by salt water on the way over and, worse yet, her father scoffed at the entire scheme. "I wonder how, having yourself scarce shoes to your feet, it would come into your head to give clothes to a Queen," he wrote back. "I shall see if the stains can be covered by dyeing it and make summer suits of it for myself, Temple and Benny." He did, however, end on a kinder and gentler note. "All the things you order will be sent, for you continue to be a good girl, and spin and knit your family stockings." [41]

Franklin's heart proved far softer when it came to news about his grandchildren. In late 1779, Sally had a fourth child and, in hopes of pleasing Franklin, baptized the boy Louis, after the French king. The name was so unusual in America that people had to inquire whether the child was a boy or girl. When her son Willy recited the Lord's Prayer after a nightmare and addressed it to Hercules, she asked her father for his advice: "Whether it is best to instruct him in a little religion or let him pray a little longer to Hercules?" Franklin replied, with a hint of humor, that she should teach him "to direct his worship more properly, for the deity of Hercules is now quite out of fashion." Sally complied. A little later she wrote that Willy was learning his Bible well and that he had "an extraordinary memory" for all literature. "He has learned the speech of Anthony over Caesar's body, which he can scarcely speak without tears." Her daughter, Elizabeth, she added, was fond of looking at the picture of her grandfather "and has frequently tried to tempt you to walk out of the frame to play with her with a piece of apple pie, the thing of all others she likes best."[42]

Sally also found a project that enabled her to earn Franklin's unvarnished approval. With Washington's army suffering in tattered uniforms in December 1779, she rallied the women of Philadelphia to raise donations, buy cloth, and sew more than two thousand shirts for the beleaguered troops. "I am very busily employed in cutting out and making shirts . . . for our brave soldiers," she reported. When Washington tried to pay cash for even more shirts, the ladies refused it and kept working for free. "I hope you will approve of what we have done," she wrote, clearly fishing for an expression of praise. Franklin, of course, did approve. He wrote back commending her for her "amor patrie," and he had an account of her activities published in France.[43]

Her son Benny also felt the vagaries of Franklin's affection, even though the boy had been snatched from the bosom of the Bache family to accompany him to Europe. After two years at a boarding school near Passy, where he saw his grandfather but once a week, the quiet 9-year-old was packed off to an academy in Geneva, where he would not see him for more than four years. Despite his love of the French, Franklin felt that a Catholic monarchy was not the best place to educate his grandson, he wrote Sally, "as I intend him for a Presbyterian as well as a Republican."[44]

Benny was taken to Geneva by a French diplomat, Philibert Cramer, who was a publisher of Voltaire. Hungry as ever for affection and a father figure, Benny latched on to Cramer, who died suddenly a few months later. So he lived for a while with Cramer's widow, Catherine, and then was left in the charge of Gabriel Louis de Marignac, a former poet and military officer who ran the academy.

Horribly lonely, Benny begged that his brother William, or his former Passy classmate John Quincy Adams, be sent to join him. At the very least, could he please have a picture of Franklin and some news?

Franklin, ever willing to send out his portrait, obliged with one, along with the news of Sally's success in supplying shirts to Washington's troops. "Be diligent in your studies that you also may be qualified to do service to your country and be worthy of so good a mother," he wrote. He also sent word that four of Benny's former Passy schoolmates had died of smallpox, and he should be thankful he had been inoculated as a child. Yet even his expressions of affection contained a note of contingency. "I shall always love you very much if you continue to be a good boy," he closed one letter.[45]

Benny did well his first year and even won the school prize for translating Latin into French. Franklin sent him some money so that he could host the celebration the prizewinner traditionally gave for his classmates. He also asked Polly Stevenson, still in London, to pick out some books for Benny in English, as he was showing signs of losing that language. Polly, knowing how to flatter her friend, picked out a book that included mentions of Franklin.[46]

But Benny eventually fell into the funk of a depressed adolescent, perhaps because Franklin never visited, nor did Temple, nor was he brought back to Passy for vacations. He turned shy and indolent, reported Madame Cramer, who continued to keep an eye on him. "He has an excellent heart; he is sensible, reasonable, he is serious, but he has neither gaiety nor vivacity; he is cold, he has few needs, no fantasies." He didn't play cards, never got in fights, and showed no signs that he would ever display "great talents" or "passions." (In this prediction she was wrong, for in later life Benny would become a crusading newspaper editor.) When she reminded Benny that he had won the Latin prize and was clearly capable of being a good student, "he answered coldly that it had been sheer luck," she wrote Franklin. And when she offered to request for him a larger allowance from his grandfather, he showed no interest.

Benny's parents became worried, and Richard Bache timidly suggested that perhaps Franklin could find time to go see him. "It would give us pleasure to hear that you had found leisure enough to visit him at Geneva," Bache wrote, noting that "the journey might conduce to your health." But it was a tentative suggestion made almost apologetically. "I suspect your time has been more importantly employed," he quickly added. Madame Cramer, for her part, suggested that at the very least he could write Benny more frequently.[47]

Franklin did not find time to travel to Geneva, but he did compose for him one of his didactic little essays that proclaimed the virtues of education and diligence. Those who study hard, he wrote, "live comfortably in good houses," whereas those who are idle and neglect their schoolwork "are poor and dirty and ragged and ignorant and vicious and live in miserable cabins and garrets." Franklin liked the lesson so much that he made a copy and sent it to Sally, who gushed that "Willy shall get it by heart." Benny, on the other hand, did not even acknowledge receiving it. So Franklin sent him another copy and ordered him to translate it into French and send it back to assure he understood it.[48]

Finally, Benny found a friend who brought him out of his torpor: Samuel Johonnot, the grandson of Franklin's Boston friend the Rev. Samuel Cooper. A "turbulent and factious" lad, he was expelled from the school in Passy, and Franklin arranged to send him to the Geneva academy. He was a smart student, placing first in the class and spurring Benny to come in a respectable third.

Socially, Johonnot's effect on Benny was even more pronounced. He began to develop more of his family's rebellious streak. At one point, a cat killed one of their pet guinea pigs, and they resolved to kill a cat, any cat, in revenge, which they did. Benny went to his first dance, which unnerved him so much that he was relieved when a fire across the street brought it to an abrupt end, but then he went to another dance and a third, where he enjoyed himself thoroughly. He wrote to his grandfather that he was now having fun, told of his butterfly-hunting and grape-harvesting expeditions, and was even so bold to hint that he would, after all, like a larger allowance. That, and a watch, "a good golden one." It would be practical, he assured his grandfather, and he promised to take good care of it.

Franklin responded the way he had to Sally's request for lace and feathers: "I cannot afford to give gold watches to children," he wrote. "You should not tease me for expensive things that can be of little or no service to you." He was also appalled when young Johonnot asked that he and Benny be allowed to come back to Paris. That elicited another stern admonition sent to Johonnot but directed at both boys: "It is time for you to think of establishing a character for manly steadiness."[49]

It was an injunction that should have been addressed to his other grandson, Temple, who had gone to France to continue his own education but had neither enrolled in a college nor taken a course. Temple's work for the American delegation was competent enough, but he spent most of his time hunting, riding, partying, and chasing women. Hoping to help him settle down with both a dowry and a job, Franklin proposed a marriage between his roguish grandson and the Brillons' elder daughter, Cunégonde.

This was nothing new. An incorrigible but never successful matchmaker, Franklin was incessantly trying, usually with ironic half-seriousness, to marry off his children and grandchildren to those of his friends. This time, however, he was wholly serious, indeed earnestly plaintive. His letter making the formal proposal, awkwardly written in a French that was uncorrected by his friends, declared that Madame Brillon was a daughter to him and expressed hope that her daughter would become one as well. He said that Temple, whom the Brillons called Franklinet, had agreed to the proposal, especially after Franklin promised to "remain in France until the end of my days" if the marriage took place. After repeating his desire to have children nearby "to close my eyes when I die," he went on to extol the virtues of Temple, "who has no vices" and "has what it takes to become, in time, a distinguished man."

Knowing Temple well, the Brillons may not have fully agreed with that assessment. They certainly did not agree to the marriage proposal. The main excuse they gave was that Temple was not a Catholic. That gave Franklin an opening to write, as he had often done before, about the need for religious tolerance and how all religions had at their core the same basic principles. (Among the five he listed in his letter was his own oft-stated religious credo, "The best service to God is doing good to men.")

Madame Brillon agreed, in her reply, that "there is only one religion and one morality." Nevertheless, she and her husband refused to assent to the marriage. "We are obliged to submit to the customs of our country," she said. M. Brillon was looking to retire from his posi-

tion as a tax receiver-general and wanted a son-in-law who could succeed him. "This position is the most important of our assets," she
wrote, ignoring that she had frequently complained to Franklin that
she was trapped in an arranged marriage made for financial reasons.
"It calls for a man who knows the laws and customs of our country, a
man of our religion."

Franklin realized that M. Brillon's objections might be caused by
something more than merely Temple's religion. "There may be other
objections he has not communicated to me," he wrote Madame Brillon, "and I ought not give him trouble." For his part, Temple embarked
on a year-long series of affairs with women high and low, including a
French countess and an Italian, until suddenly falling in love, albeit
briefly, with the Brillons' younger daughter, who was only 15. This
time M. Brillon seemed ready to approve of the alliance, and even offered a job and dowry, but the fickle Temple had already moved on to
other women, including a married mistress who would, eventually,
end up making him the third generation of Franklins to bear an illegitimate son.[50]

CHAPTER FIFTEEN

PEACEMAKER

Paris, 1778–1785

MINISTER PLENIPOTENTIARY

By the summer of 1778, it had become clear to all three American commissioners that there should be only one person in charge. Not only was it difficult for the three of them to agree on policies, Franklin told the Congress, but it was now even difficult for them to work in the same house together. Even their servants were quarreling. In addition, the French had appointed a minister plenipotentiary to America, and protocol demanded that the new nation reciprocate with an appointee of similar rank. Arthur Lee nominated himself and conspired with his brothers to win the prize. John Adams more graciously suggested to friends that Franklin, despite his work habits and softness toward France, would be best. Franklin did not overtly push for the job, but he did strongly ask the Congress, in July 1778, to "separate us."

The French did Franklin's lobbying for him. They let it be known that he was their choice, and the Congress complied in September by electing him the sole minister plenipotentiary. The vote was 12–1, the dissenting state being Pennsylvania, where his enemies questioned his loyalty and that of his grandson Temple, the son of an imprisoned loyalist governor.[1]

Word of his appointment did not reach Paris until February 1779, for the war and the winter hindered the passage of American ships.

When it did, Arthur Lee sulked and refused to hand over his papers to Franklin. As for Adams, his biographer David McCullough writes, "The new arrangement was exactly what Adams had recommended and the news was to leave him feeling more miserable than ever." He soon left Paris, at least for the time being, to make his way back to Massachusetts.

Franklin was suffering from the gout and could not immediately present his new credentials, but in late March he paid a call on the king and his ministers. Mindful of Adams's hurt feelings, Franklin worked to keep their relationship cordial. He wrote Adams a polite and amusing letter in which he described his rounds at Versailles and complained that "the fatigue however was a little too much for my feet and disabled me for near another week." In his own letters, Adams kept up a collegial façade, and he even expressed some support for Franklin's deep fealty to the French, despite his own doubts about the wisdom of becoming too aligned with them. "I am much pleased with your reception at court in the new character," he replied, "and I do not doubt that your opinion of the good will of this court to the United States is just."

Adams's fragile equanimity was shaken, however, when Franklin and the French decided to commandeer the ship that was supposed to take him home and assign it to be part of the fleet that John Paul Jones planned to use against the British (of which more below). Well aware that Adams was impatiently waiting at the port of Nantes to set sail, Franklin was apologetic, and he even got the powerful French naval minister Antoine de Sartine to write a letter explaining the decision. Another ship would be assigned to take him home as soon as feasible, Franklin promised, and it would allow Adams the benefit of traveling with the new French minister to the United States.

Adams pretended to be understanding: "The public service must not be obstructed for the private convenience of an individual, and the honor of a passage with the new Ambassador should be a compensation to me for the loss of the prospect of so speedy a return home." Showing just a touch of the polite hypocrisy that he was generally famed for lacking, Adams even went so far as to ask Franklin to "oblige me much by making my compliments [to] Madame Brillon and Madame Helvétius, ladies for whose characters I have a great respect."

But as he brooded in port, Adams became increasingly bitter. After dining with Jones, he declared that the captain was a man of "eccentricities and irregularities," and he grew furious at the thought that Jones and Franklin were conspiring to delay his trip home. "It is decreed that I shall endure all sorts of mortifications," he wrote in his diary. "Do I see that these people despise me, or do I see that they dread me?" Inevitably, he began to ascribe dark motives to Franklin. Simmering in self-importance, Adams began to suspect that Franklin was hindering his return because he feared the "dangerous truths" he might reveal. "Does the Old Conjurer dread my voice in Congress?" Adams wrote in his diary. "He had some reason, for he has often heard it there, a terror to evil doers."

Franklin was blithely oblivious of Adams's dark suspicions, and he carried on trying to be cordial in his letters. "I shall take care to present your respects to the good ladies you mention," he cheerfully promised. He even agreed, after three strident requests from Adams, that the new ship might go directly to Boston, rather than accommodating the French minister by going to Philadelphia first. But it was to no avail. New specters of distrust had infected Adams's mind, and they were destined to haunt his relationship with Franklin when he returned the following year.[2]

While Adams simmered, Arthur Lee and his brothers declared open war on Franklin back in America. Lee circulated a letter accusing Franklin of "weaving little plots" and "sowing pernicious dissension," and he also made sure that the Congress saw the flurry of accusatory letters to Franklin, questioning his honor, that he and Ralph Izard had written earlier that year.

Warned by his son-in-law, Richard Bache, of all these intrigues, Franklin was able to dismiss the resentments of the Lees. "My too great reputation," he wrote, "grieve those unhappy gentlemen, unhappy in their tempers and in the dark, uncomfortable passions of jealousy, anger, suspicion, envy and malice."

He was, however, far more wounded by Bache's reports that Lee and his allies were attacking Temple, for he loved his grandson with a blindness that was unusual for him. "Izard, Lees & company," Bache wrote, "lay some stress upon your employing as a private secretary your grandson whom they hold unfit to be trusted because of his father's principles." Then he added ominously, "They have had some thoughts of bringing a motion to have him removed." In a separate note, Sally Bache confided that her husband had been afraid to inform Franklin of this campaign against Temple because he knew it would upset him.

It certainly did. "Methinks it is rather some merit that I have rescued a valuable young man from the danger of being a Tory," he wrote Richard. Then he let loose a cry of anger at the thought that Temple might be recalled:

> It is enough that I have lost my *son;* would they add my *grandson!* An old man of seventy, I undertook a winter voyage at the command of the Congress, and for the public service, with no other attendant to take care of me. I am continued here in a foreign country, where, if I am sick, his filial attention comforts me, and if I die, I have a child to close my eyes and take care of my remains.

In a letter to Sally at the same time, he repeated these sentiments and added that trying to deprive him of Temple would be cruel but futile. "I should not part with the child, but with the employment," he threatened. "But I am confident that, whatever may be proposed by weak or malicious people, the Congress is too wise and too good to think of treating me in that manner." The Congress was indeed supportive. There was no serious effort to have Temple dismissed, and he remained the secretary to the American delegation.[3]

Temple was about 19 at the time, still a roguish lad who worked hard but had earned the deep respect of few besides his grandfather. As the controversy swirled around him in the summer of 1779, he decided to prove his mettle by taking part in an audacious mission with Lafayette to launch a surprise attack on Britain itself.

The French general, less than three years older than Temple, had recently returned from serving under George Washington. By this time, the Revolution had reached an unsteady stalemate, with British troops under Sir Henry Clinton still ensconced in New York but doing little for the time being other than conducting hit-and-run raids. So Lafayette, on arriving back in Paris, hatched his audacious plan to attack the British mainland, and he shared it with Franklin and the French military. "I admire much the activity of your genius," Franklin wrote. "It is certain that the coasts of England and Scotland are extremely open and defenseless." He conceded that he did not know enough about military strategy to "presume upon advising it." But he could give encouragement. "Many instances of history prove that in war, attempts thought to be impossible do often, for that very reason, become possible and practicable because nobody expects them."

Lafayette was eager to have Temple at his side. "We will be always together during the campaign, which I do assure you gives me great pleasure," he wrote the young man. For his part, Temple, ever the dandy, fretted about his rank, his title, his commission, and his uniform. He wanted to be commissioned as an officer rather than merely as a volunteer, and he insisted on the right to wear the epaulettes of an officer, even though Lafayette advised against it. Just as all these issues were being settled, the land invasion was called off by the French military.

Franklin professed to be disappointed. "I flattered myself," he wrote Lafayette, "that he might possibly catch from you some tincture of those engaging manners that make you so much the delight of all that know you." Once again, Temple's chance to make a name for himself on his own was scuttled.[4]

JOHN PAUL JONES

One component of the proposed invasion of Britain did proceed, and it inserted a colorful character into Franklin's life. When Lafayette was first planning his mission, Franklin told him that "much will depend on a prudent and brave sea commander who knows the coasts." They settled instead for a commander who was, as Franklin was already well aware, more brave than prudent: John Paul Jones.

Born John Paul, the son of a Scottish landscape designer, he had shipped off to sea at age 13, served as the first mate of a slave vessel, and soon commanded his own merchant ship. But the hotheaded captain, who throughout his career was prone to provoking mutinies, got into trouble by flogging a crew member who later died and then, after being exonerated, running his sword through yet another crew member who was threatening an insurrection. So he fled to Virginia, changed his last name to Jones, and at the beginning of the Revolution won a commission in America's motley navy of ex-privateers and adventurers. By 1778, he was making his reputation by conducting daring attacks along the English and Scottish coasts.

On one of these raids, Jones decided to kidnap a Scottish earl, but the man was away taking the waters down in Bath, so the crew instead forced his wife to hand over the family silver. In a fit of noble guilt, Jones decided to buy the booty from his crew so that he could return it to the family, and he wrote a flowery letter to the earl declaring his intention, copies of which he circulated to various friends, including Franklin, who had by then assumed the difficult task of acting as his American overseer as well as his occasional host in Passy. Franklin tried to help Jones resolve the problem, but it led to such a convoluted exchange of letters with the outraged earl and his baffled wife that the silver was not returned until after the end of the war.

Franklin decided that the impetuous captain would do more good, or less harm, if he focused his raids on the Channel Islands instead. "The Jersey privateers do us a great deal of mischief," he wrote to Jones in May 1778. "It has been mentioned to me that your small vessel, commanded by so brave an officer, might render great service by following them where greater ships dare not venture." He added that the suggestion came "from high authority," meaning the great French naval minister Antoine Sartine.[5]

Jones, not so easily managed, replied that his ship, *Ranger,* was too "crank and slow," and it would require promises of great reward for him to convince his men to undertake more missions. But he knew how to flatter Franklin: he sent him a copy of his battle journals, which Franklin read avidly. So, without permission from his fellow commissioners or from France, Franklin decided that Jones should be given command of a ship that had just been built for the Americans in Amsterdam. Alas, the nervous Dutch, who were trying to remain neutral, scuttled the plan, especially after the British, who had learned of it through their spy Bancroft, applied pressure.

Franklin was finally able to help secure for Jones, in February 1779, an old forty-gun man-of-war named the *Duras*, which Jones promptly rechristened the *Bonhomme Richard* in his patron's honor. Jones was so thrilled that he paid a visit to Passy that month to thank Franklin and his landlord Chaumont, who had helped supply Jones with uniforms and funds. There was perhaps another reason for the visit: Jones may have been having an illicit affair with Madame de Chaumont.[6]

During this stay, an incident occurred that, as played out in subsequent letters, resembled a French farce. A wizened old woman, who was the wife of the Chaumonts' gardener, alleged that Jones tried to rape her. Franklin made a passing allusion to the alleged incident in a postscript to a subsequent letter, and Jones mistakenly assumed that "the mystery you so delicately mention" referred to the controversy that surrounded his killing of the rebellious crew member years earlier. So he provided a long and anguished account of that old travail.

Confused and somewhat amused by Jones's detailed explanation of impaling the mutineer, Franklin replied that he had never heard that story and informed Jones that the "mystery" he alluded to referred, instead, to an allegation made by the gardener's wife that Jones had "attempted to ravish her" in the bushes of the estate at "about 7 o'clock the evening before your departure." The woman had recounted the horror in great detail, "some of which are not fit for me to write," and three of her sons had declared that they "were determined to kill you." But Jones should not worry: everyone at Passy found the tale to be the subject of great merriment. It "occasioned some laughing," wrote Franklin, "the old woman being one of the grossest, coarsest, dirtiest and ugliest that one may find in a thousand." Madame Chaumont, whose own familiarity with Jones's sexual appetites did not prevent her from a great display of French insouciance, declared that "it gave a high idea of the strength of appetite and courage of the Americans."

They all ended up concluding, Franklin assured Jones, that it must have been a case of mistaken identity. As part of the Mardi Gras festivities, a chamber girl had apparently dressed up in one of his uniforms and, so they surmised, attacked the gardener's wife as a prank. It seems quite implausible that the gardener's wife, even in the dimness of early evening, could have been so easily fooled—not even their friend Beaumarchais would have attempted such a cross-dressing rape scene in *The Marriage of Figaro*—but the explanation was satisfactory enough that the event was not mentioned in subsequent letters.[7]

All of this occurred just as Franklin was helping to plan the proposed sneak attack on Britain by Jones and Lafayette, who had both arrived at Passy and were spending hours warily assessing one another under Franklin's worried eye. Both officers were proud, and they were soon struggling over matters large and small, ranging from who would be in charge of various aspects of the invasion to whether their men would eat at the same tables. Franklin resorted to his most indirect manner in trying to soothe Jones. "It has been observed that joint expeditions of land and sea forces often miscarry through jealousies and misunderstandings between the officers of different corps," he pointed out. Then, saying almost the opposite of what he truly felt, he added, "Knowing you both as I do and your just manner of thinking on these occasions, I am confident nothing of the kind can happen between you." But Franklin made it clear that he was concerned, quite understandably, about Jones's temperament. "A cool, prudent conduct" was necessary, he cautioned. Jones must remember that Lafayette was the ranking officer, and it would be "a kind of trial of your abilities and of your fitness in temper and disposition for acting in concert with others."

In his formal set of instructions to Jones, Franklin was even more explicit in ordering him to show restraint, especially in light of his crew's previous plundering of the Scottish earl's silver. "Although the English have wantonly burnt many defenseless towns in America, you are not to follow this example, unless where a reasonable ransom is refused; in which case your own generous feelings, as well as this instruction, will induce you to give timely notice of your intention, so that sick and ancient persons, women and children, may be first removed." Replied Jones, "Your liberal and noble minded instructions would make a coward brave."[8]

When Lafayette's part of the mission was scrapped, Franklin and the French decided that Jones should proceed with a purely naval attack, which he did in September 1779. The result was the fabled sea battle between the *Bonhomme Richard* and the much better-equipped *Serapis*. When the British captain, after applying a fierce pounding, asked him to surrender, Jones replied, at least according to legend, "I have not yet begun to fight!" As Jones put it in his vivid and detailed account of the battle to Franklin, "I answered him in the most determined negative."

Jones was able to lash the *Bonhomme Richard* into a death grip with the *Serapis*, and his men scrambled up the masts to lob grenades into the ammunition holds of the enemy ship. After a three-hour battle, in which half of his three hundred crew members were killed or wounded, Jones captured control of the *Serapis* just before the *Bonhomme Richard* sank. "The scene was dreadful beyond the reach of language," he wrote Franklin. "Humanity cannot but recoil and lament that war should be capable of producing such fatal consequences."

Franklin took great pride in Jones's success, and they became even closer friends. "Scarce anything was talked of at Paris and Versailles but your cool conduct and persevering bravery during that terrible conflict," he replied. He helped to get Jones, who was desperately eager to gain social respect, initiated into the Nine Sisters Masonic Lodge, and he accompanied him on a triumphal visit to the king at Versailles. Franklin even got embroiled in Jones's lengthy and bitter disputes with the insubordinate Pierre Landais, captain of the *Alliance*, which was supposed to be part of Jones's fleet. Landais had failed to come to the rescue during the battle with the *Serapis*, and in fact had actually fired on the *Bonhomme Richard*. For the next two years, Franklin and Jones fought with Landais, who was supported by Arthur Lee, over who should be the captain of the *Alliance*. When Landais finally commandeered the vessel and sailed away, a beleaguered Franklin decided it was best to let others sort it all out. He had other things in France to deal with.[9]

FRIEND OF THE COURT

The absence of John Adams from Paris, so pleasing both to Franklin and the French court, was too good to last. He had left, in a mood even more sour than usual, after Franklin was made the sole minister to France, but he had been home only a few months when the Congress decided to send him back to Paris. His new official mission was to negotiate a peace accord with the British, if and when the time ever became ripe. As the time was not, in fact, ripe for such talks, Adams contented himself by meddling in Franklin's duties.

This thoroughly annoyed the French foreign minister Vergennes. When Adams proposed, on his arrival in February 1780, to make public his authority to negotiate with the British, Vergennes invoked the American promise not to act independently of France. He should say and do nothing. "Above all," Vergennes sternly instructed him, "take the necessary precautions that the object of your commission remain unknown to the Court of London." [10]

Franklin was also annoyed. Adams's return threatened to disrupt his careful cultivation of the French court, and it reminded him of the attacks on his reputation that had long been waged by the Adams and Lee family factions in the Congress. In a ruminative mood, he wrote Washington a letter that ostensibly offered reassurance about the general's reputation but clearly reflected his worries about his own. "I must soon quit the scene," Franklin wrote, in an unusually introspective way, referring not to his post in France but his life in this world. Washington's own great reputation in France, he said, was "free from those little shades that the jealousy and envy of a man's countrymen and contemporaries are ever endeavoring to cast over living merit." It was clear that he was trying to reassure not only Washington but also himself that history would ignore "the feeble voice of those groveling passions." [11]

More specifically, Franklin sought to explain, to himself and his friends (and also to history), why Adams rather than he had been chosen to negotiate any potential peace with Britain. Just as Adams was arriving, Franklin wrote a letter to his old friend David Hartley, a member of Parliament with whom he had previously discussed prisoner exchanges and peace feelers. Hartley had proposed a ten-year truce between Britain and America. Franklin replied that it was his "private opinion" that a truce might make sense, but he noted that "neither you nor I are at present authorized" to negotiate such matters.

That authority now resided with Adams, and Franklin put his own spin on the Congress's choice: "If the Congress have therefore entrusted to others rather than to me the negotiations for peace, when such shall be set on foot, as has been reported, it is perhaps because they may have heard of a very singular opinion of mine, that there hardly ever existed such a thing as a bad peace, or a good war, and that I might therefore easily be induced to make improper concessions."[12]

Franklin had indeed often used the phrase about there being no such thing as a bad peace or a good war, and he would repeat it to dozens of other friends after the Revolution ended. It is sometimes used as an antiwar slogan and cited to cast Franklin as one of history's noble pacifists. But that is misleading. Throughout his life, Franklin supported wars when he felt they were warranted; he had helped form militias in Philadelphia and raised supplies for the battles with the French and Indians. Though he had initially worked to avert the Revolution, he supported it strongly when he decided that independence was inevitable. The sentiments in his letter were aimed both at Hartley and at history. He wanted to explain why he had not been chosen as a peace negotiator. Perhaps more intriguing, he also wanted to let his friends in Britain know that he could eventually provide a good channel, better than Adams, if the talks ever began.[13]

In the meantime, Franklin was ardently committed to the French alliance, more so than most of his American colleagues. This led to a great public rift with Adams after his return in early 1780. Previously, the tension between the two men had been based more on their differences in personality and style, but this one was caused by a fundamental disagreement over policy: whether or not America should show gratitude, allegiance, and fealty to France.

In the early days of the Revolution, both men shared a somewhat isolationist or exceptionalist view, one that has since been a thread throughout American history: the United States should never be a supplicant in seeking support from other nations, and it should be coy and cautious about entering into entangling foreign alliances. Even after he began his love affair with France in 1777, Franklin restated this principle. "I have never yet changed the opinion I gave in Congress that a virgin state should preserve the virgin character, and

not go about suitoring for alliances," he assured Arthur Lee. In negotiating the alliance with France, he had successfully resisted making
any concessions that would give a monopoly over American trade or
favors.

Once the treaties were signed in early 1778, however, Franklin became a strong believer in showing gratitude and loyalty. In the words
of diplomatic historian Gerald Stourzh, he "extolled the magnanimity
and generosity of France in terms which at times touch on the slightly
ridiculous." America's fealty to France, in Franklin's view, was based on
idealism as well as realism, and he described it in moral terms rather
than merely in the cold calculus of commercial advantages and European power balances. "This is really a generous nation, fond of glory,
and particularly that of protecting the oppressed," he declared of
France in a letter to the Congress. "Telling them their *commerce* will be
advantaged by our success, and that it is their *interest* to help us, seems
as much to say, 'help us and we shall not be obliged to you.' Such indis-
creet and improper language has been sometimes held here by some of
our people, and produced no good effects." [14]

Adams, on the other hand, was much more of a cold realist. He
felt that France had supported America because of its own national
interests—weakening Britain, gaining a lucrative new trading relationship—and neither side owed the other any moral gratitude.
France, he correctly predicted, would help America only up to a point;
it wanted the new nation to break with Britain but not to become so
strong that it no longer needed France's support. Franklin showed too
much subservience to the court, Adams felt, and on his return in 1780
he forcefully propounded this view. "We ought to be cautious," Adams
wrote the Congress in April, "how we magnify our ideas and exagger-
ate our expressions of the generosity and magnanimity of any of those
powers."

Vergennes, not surprisingly, was eager to deal only with Franklin,
and by the end of July 1780 he had exchanged enough strained correspondence with Adams—on everything from American currency
revaluation to the deployment of the French navy—that he felt justified in sending him a stinging letter that managed to be both formally
diplomatic and undiplomatic at the same time. On behalf of the

court of Louis XVI, he declared, "The King did not stand in need of your solicitations to direct his attentions to the interests of the United States." In other words, France would not deal with Adams any longer.[15]

Vergennes informed Franklin of this decision and sent him copies of all his testy correspondence with Adams, with the request that Franklin "lay the whole before Congress." In his reply, Franklin was exceedingly candid with Vergennes, indeed dangerously so, in revealing his own frustration with Adams. "It was from his particular indiscretion alone, and not from any instructions received by him, that he has given such just cause of displeasure." Franklin went on to explicitly distance himself from Adams's activities. "He has never yet communicated to me more of his business in Europe than I have seen in the newspapers," Franklin told Vergennes. "I live upon terms of civility with him, not of intimacy." He concluded by promising to send the Congress the offending Adams correspondence that Vergennes had supplied.

Although Franklin could have, and perhaps should have, dispatched the letters without comment, he took the opportunity to write ("with reluctance") a letter of his own to the Congress that detailed his disagreement with Adams. Their dispute was partly due to a difference in style. Adams believed in blunt assertions of American interests, whereas Franklin favored suasion and diplomatic charm. But the dispute was also caused by a fundamental difference in philosophy. Adams believed that America's foreign policy should be based on realism; Franklin believed that it should also include an element of idealism, both as a moral duty and as a component of America's national interests. As Franklin put it in his letter:

> Mr. Adams . . . thinks, as he tells me himself, that America has been too free in expressions of gratitude to France; for that she is more obliged to us than we to her; and that we should show spirit in our applications. I apprehend that he mistakes his ground, and that this Court is to be treated with decency and delicacy. The King, a young and virtuous prince, has, I am persuaded, a pleasure in reflecting on the generous benevolence of the action in assisting an oppressed people, and proposes it as a part of the glory of his reign. I think it right to increase this

pleasure by our thankful acknowledgments, and that such an expression
of gratitude is not only our duty, but our interest.[16]

With the British not yet ready to deal with him and the French no
longer willing to deal with him, Adams once again left Paris feeling
resentful. And Franklin once again tried to keep their disagreements
from becoming personal. He wrote to Adams in Holland, where he
had gone to try to elicit a loan for America, and commiserated about
the difficulties of that task. "I have long been humiliated," he said,
"with the idea of our running from court to court begging for money
and friendship." And in a subsequent letter complaining about how
long France was taking to answer his own requests, Franklin wryly
wrote Adams: "I have, however, two of the Christian graces, faith and
hope. But my faith is only that of which the apostle speaks, the evidence of things not seen." If their mutual endeavors failed, he added,
"I shall be ready to break, run away, or go to prison with you, as it shall
please God."[17]

America's need for more money had indeed become quite desperate by the end of 1780. Earlier in the year, the British commander Sir
Henry Clinton had sailed south from New York, with General Cornwallis as his deputy, to launch an attack on Charleston, South Carolina. It succeeded in May, and Cornwallis set up a British command
there after Clinton returned to New York. Also that summer, the troubled American general Benedict Arnold had turned coat in a way that
made his name synonymous with treachery. "Our present situation,"
Washington wrote Franklin in October of that year, "makes one of two
things essential to us: a peace, or the most vigorous aid of our allies,
particularly in the article of money."

Franklin thus resorted to all of his wiles—personal pleadings
mixed with appeals to idealism and national interests—in his application to Vergennes in February 1781. "I am grown old," he said, adding
that his illness made it probable that he would soon retire. "The present conjuncture is critical." If more money did not come soon, the
Congress could lose its influence, the new government would be still-
born, and England would recover control over America. That, he
warned, would tilt the balance of power in a way that "will enable

them to become the Terror of Europe and to exercise with impunity that insolence which is so natural to their nation."[18]

His request was audacious: 25 million livres.* In the end, France agreed to provide 6 million, which was a great victory for Franklin and enough money to keep American hopes alive.

Franklin, however, was disheartened. Back home, his enemies were being as vindictive as ever. "The political salvation of America depends upon the recalling of Dr. Franklin," Ralph Izard wrote Richard Lee. Even Vergennes expressed some doubts that made their way back to the Congress. "Although I have a high esteem for M. Franklin," he wrote to his minister in Philadelphia, "I am nevertheless obliged to concede that his age and his love of tranquility produce an apathy incompatible with the affairs in his charge." Izard pushed a recall vote that was supported by the Lee–Adams faction. Although Franklin easily survived, the Congress did decide to send a special envoy to take over the work of handling future financial transactions.

So, in March, after receiving word of France's new loan, Franklin informed the Congress that he was ready to resign. "I have passed my 75th year," he wrote, adding that he was plagued by gout and weakness. "I do not know that my mental faculties are impaired; perhaps I shall be the last to discover that." Having served in public life for fifty years, he had received "honor sufficient to satisfy any reasonable ambition, and I have no other left but that of repose, which I hope Congress will grant me."

He included one personal request: that the members find a job for his grandson Temple, who had passed up the chance to study law so that he could serve his country in Paris. "If they shall think fit to employ him as a secretary to their minister at any European court, I am

---

* This is the rough equivalent of $130 million in purchasing power in 2002 U.S. dollars. In 1780, there were about 23.5 livres to the British pound, and £1 in 1780 had the same purchasing power as £83 in 2002. Although the American Congress had begun issuing paper currency denominated in dollars by 1780, the states continued to issue their own currencies, often in pounds. Rapid changes in the value of all American currencies during the Revolution made them difficult to compare to European currencies. By 1786, an ounce of gold cost $19 or £4.2, making £1 worth $4.52, which became the semiofficial exchange rate in 1790. See page 507 for more currency conversion data.[19]

persuaded they will have reason to be satisfied with his conduct, and I shall be thankful for his appointment as a favor to me." [20]

PEACE COMMISSIONER

The Congress refused Franklin's offer to resign. Instead, in what came as a pleasant surprise, he was not only kept on as minister to France, he was also given an additional role: one of the five commissioners to handle the peace negotiations with Britain if and when the time came for an end to the war. The others were John Adams (who originally had been designated the sole negotiator and was at the time still in Holland), Thomas Jefferson (who again declined the overseas assignment for personal reasons), South Carolina planter-merchant Henry Laurens (who was captured at sea by the British and imprisoned in the Tower of London), and New York lawyer John Jay.

Franklin's selection was controversial, and it came partly because of pressure from Vergennes. Despite his doubts about Franklin's energy, the French minister instructed his envoy in Philadelphia to lobby on his behalf and inform the Congress that his conduct "is as zealous and patriotic as it is wise and circumspect." Vergennes also asked the Congress to require that the new delegation take no steps without France's approval. The Congress complied by giving its commissioners strict instructions "to make the most candid and confidential communications upon all subjects to the ministers of our generous ally, the King of France; to undertake nothing in the negotiations for peace or truce without their knowledge and concurrence." [21]

Adams was appalled at being so shackled to France's will, and he called the instructions "shameful." Jay agreed, declaring that by "casting herself into the arms of the King of France" America would not "advance either her interest or her reputation." Franklin, on the other hand, was pleased with the instructions to follow France's guidance. "I have had so much experience of his majesty's goodness to us," he wrote the Congress, "and of the sincerity of this upright and able minister [Vergennes], that I cannot but think the confidence well and judiciously placed and that it will have happy effects." [22]

He was heartened as well by a personal triumph. Over the objections of even such friends as Silas Deane, he was able to get Temple appointed as the secretary to the new delegation. The honor of his new appointment, and the rejection of his resignation, rejuvenated him. "I call this continuance an honor," he wrote a friend, "and I really esteem it to be greater than my first appointment, when I consider that all the interest of my enemies . . . were not sufficient to prevent it."

He even wrote another friendly letter to Adams, whose own commission to negotiate with Britain had been diluted by the addition of the new delegation. Their mutual appointments, Franklin told Adams, were a great honor, but he wryly lamented that they were likely to be criticized for whatever they accomplished. "I have never known a peace made, even the most advantageous, that was not censured as inadequate," he said. " 'Blessed are the peacemakers' is, I suppose, to be understood in the other world, for in this they are frequently cursed."[23]

As a master of the relationship between power and diplomacy, Franklin knew that it would be impossible to win at the negotiating table what was unwinnable on the battlefield. He had been able to negotiate an alliance with France only after America had won the Battle of Saratoga in 1777; he would be able to negotiate a suitable peace with Britain only after America and its French allies won an even more decisive victory.

That problem was solved in October 1781. The British general Lord Cornwallis had marched north from Charleston, seeking to engage General Washington's forces, and had taken his stand at Yorktown, Virginia. France's support proved critical: Lafayette moved to Cornwallis's southern flank to prevent a retreat, a French fleet arrived at the mouth of the Chesapeake to preclude an escape by sea, French artillery arrived from Rhode Island, and nine thousand French soldiers joined eleven thousand Americans under General Washington's command. Two four-hundred-man columns, one French and the other American, began the allied assault and bombardment, which continued day and night with such intensity that when Cornwallis sent out a drummer on October 17 to signal his willingness to surrender, it took a while for him to get noticed. It had been four years since the battle of Saratoga, six and a half since Lexington and Concord. On November 19, word of the allied triumph at Yorktown reached Vergennes, who sent a note to Franklin that he reprinted on his press at Passy and distributed the following dawn.

Although the war seemed effectively over, Franklin was cautious. Until the present ministry resigned, there was always the chance that Britain would renew the struggle. "I remember that, when I was a boxing boy, it was allowed, even after an adversary said he had enough, to give him a rising blow," he wrote Robert Morris, the American finance minister. "Let ours be a douser."[24]

Lord North's government finally collapsed in March 1782, replaced by one headed by Lord Rockingham. Peace talks between America and Britain could now begin. Franklin, it so happened, was the only one of the five American commissioners who was then in Paris. So, for the next few months, until Jay and then Adams finally arrived, he would handle the negotiations on his own. In doing so, he would face two complicating factors:

- America had pledged to coordinate its diplomacy with France and her allies, rather than negotiate with London separately. But the British wanted direct talks leading to a separate peace with America. Franklin, on the surface, would initially insist on acting in concert with the French. But behind the scenes, he would arrange for private and direct peace negotiations with the British.
- The Rockingham government had two rival ministers, Foreign Secretary Charles Fox and Colonial Secretary Lord Shelburne, each of whom sent their own negotiators to Paris. Franklin would maneuver to ensure that Shelburne's envoy, whom he liked better and found more malleable, was given a commission to negotiate with the Americans.

THE NEGOTIATIONS BEGIN

"Great affairs sometimes take their rise from small circumstances," Franklin recorded in the journal he began of the 1782 peace negotiations. In this case, it was a chance meeting between his old flame Madame Brillon and an Englishman named Lord Cholmondeley, who was a friend of Shelburne. Madame Brillon sent Cholmondeley to call on Franklin in Passy, and through him Franklin sent his regards to the new colonial secretary. Franklin had known and liked Shelburne since at least 1766, when he lobbied him about getting a western land grant and made occasional visits to his grand country manor in Wiltshire. Madame Helvétius also played a small role; Shelburne had just sent her some gooseberry bushes, and Franklin wrote politely that they had arrived "in excellent order."[25]

Shelburne responded by dispatching Richard Oswald, a retired one-eyed London merchant and former slave trader who had once lived in America, to begin negotiating with Franklin. Oswald arrived on April 15 and immediately tried to convince Franklin that America could get a quicker and better deal if it negotiated independently of the French. Franklin was not yet willing. "I let him know," he wrote, "that America would not treat but in concert with France." Instead, he took Oswald to Versailles the next day to meet with Vergennes, who proposed to host a general peace conference of all the warring parties in Paris.[26]

On the way back from Versailles, Oswald argued again for a separate peace. Once the issue of American independence was settled by negotiations, he said, it should not be held up while matters relating only to France and Spain (including the ownership of Gibraltar) were still being disputed. He added an implicit threat: if France became involved and made too many demands, England would continue the war and finance it by stopping payment on its public debt.

The issue of independence, Franklin pointedly replied, had already been settled back in 1776. Britain should simply acknowledge it, rather than offer to negotiate it. As for reneging on their debt in order to renew the war, Franklin made no reply. "I did not desire to discourage their stopping payment, which I considered as cutting the throat of their public credit," he wrote in his journal. "Such menaces were besides an encouragement with me, remembering the old adage that *they who threaten are afraid.*"

Instead, Franklin suggested that Britain consider offering reparations to America, especially to "those who had suffered by the scalping and burning parties" that England had enlisted the Indians to wage. "Nothing could have a greater tendency to conciliate," he said, and that would lead to the renewal of commerce that Britain both needed and desired.

He even suggested a specific reparations proposal: Britain should offer to cede control of Canada. The money Britain could make from the Canadian fur trade, after all, was tiny compared to what it would save by not having to defend Canada. It was also far less than Britain could make through the renewed commerce with America that would flow from a friendly settlement. In addition, the money that America made from selling open land in Canada could be used to compensate the patriots whose homes had been destroyed by British troops and also the British loyalists whose estates had been confiscated by the Americans.

Behind France's back, Franklin was playing a wily balance-of-power game. He knew that France, despite her enmity toward Britain, did not want it to cede control of Canada to America. That would make America's borders more secure, reduce its tensions with Britain, and lessen its need for a friendship with France. If England continued to hold Canada, Franklin explained to Oswald, it "would necessarily oblige us to cultivate and strengthen our union with France." In his report to Vergennes about his conversation with Oswald, Franklin did not mention that he had suggested the ceding of Canada. It was the first small indication that Franklin, despite his insistence that he would work hand in glove with the French, would be willing to act unilaterally when warranted.

As usual, Franklin was speaking from notes he had prepared, and Oswald "begged" to be trusted with them so he could show them to Shelburne. After some hesitation, Franklin agreed. Oswald was charmed by Franklin's trust, and Franklin found Oswald to be sensible and devoid of guile. "We parted exceeding good friends," he noted.

Franklin had one regret about the paper he entrusted to Oswald: its hint that compensation might be due to the British loyalists in America whose property had been confiscated. So he published on his Passy press, and sent to Adams and others, a fake issue of a Boston newspaper that purported to describe, in gruesome detail, the horrors that the British had perpetrated on innocent Americans. His goal was to emphasize that no sympathy was due the British loyalists, and that it was the Americans who deserved compensation. The fake edition was cleverly convincing. It featured a description of a shipment of American scalps purportedly sent by the Seneca Indians to England and a letter that he pretended was from John Paul Jones. To make it more realistic, he even included fake little ads about a new brick house for sale in south Boston and a missing bay mare in Salem.[27]

Britain agreed to Vergennes's proposal for an all-parties peace conference, but that meant sending a new envoy, one who represented the foreign secretary Charles Fox rather than the colonial secretary Shelburne. The new envoy's name was not auspicious: Thomas Grenville, the son of the despised George Grenville who had imposed the Stamp Act back in 1765. But Fox, who had long been sympathetic to the American side, assured Franklin that the young Grenville, a mere 27, was to be trusted. "I know your liberality of mind too well to be afraid that any prejudices against Mr. Grenville's *name* may prevent you from esteeming those excellent qualities of heart and head which belong to him, or from giving the fullest credit to the sincerity of his wishes for peace."[28]

When Grenville arrived in early May, Franklin immediately took him to Versailles, where the young Englishman made the mistake of suggesting to Vergennes that if "England gave America independence," France should give back some of the Caribbean islands it had conquered and a peace could be quickly settled.

With the hint of a smile, Vergennes turned on the novice English diplomat and belittled his offer of independence. "America," he said, "did not ask it of you. There is Mr. Franklin. He will answer you as to that point."

"To be sure," said Franklin, "we do not consider ourselves as under any necessity of bargaining for such a thing that is our own and which we have bought at the expense of much blood and treasure."

Like Oswald, Grenville hoped to be able to convince Franklin to negotiate a separate peace with Britain rather than remain linked to France's demands as well. To that end, he visited Passy a few days later and warned that France "might insist on" provisions that were not related to the treaty she had made with America. If that happened, America should not feel obligated by that treaty to "continue the war to obtain such points for her."

As he had done with Oswald, Franklin refused to make such a concession. "I gave a little more of my sentiments on the general subject of benefits, obligations and gratitude," Franklin noted. People who wanted to get out of obligations often "became ingenious in finding out reasons and arguments" to do so, but America would not follow that route. Even if a person borrows money from another and then repays it, he still owes gratitude: "He has discharged the money debt, but the obligation remains."

This was stretching the idea of gratitude rather far, replied Grenville, for France was the party that actually benefited from America's separation from Britain. Franklin insisted that he felt so strongly about the "generous and noble manner" in which France had supported America that "I could never suffer myself to think of such reasonings for lessening the obligations."[29]

Grenville further annoyed Franklin by trying to hide the fact that his commission gave him the authority to negotiate only with France and not directly with the United States, which Britain did not yet recognize as an independent country. Franklin confronted him on this point at the beginning of June. Why did his commission not explicitly authorize him, Franklin asked, to deal directly with the United States? As Franklin reported to Adams the next day, "He could not explain this to my satisfaction, but said he believed the omission was occasioned by their copying an old commission." That, of course, did not convince Franklin. He insisted that Grenville get a new commission before any negotiation could begin. This was not merely a nicety of protocol, as Franklin well knew. He was insisting that the British tacitly accept America's independence as a precondition for talks. "I imagine there is a reluctance in their King to take this first step," he wrote Adams, "as the giving such a commission would itself be a kind of acknowledgment of our independence."[30]

Franklin was willing to work in concert with France, but he had no intention of allowing Britain to insist that France negotiate on America's behalf. Vergennes agreed. "They want to treat with us for you. But this the King [of France] will not agree to. He thinks it not consistent with the dignity of your state. You will treat for yourselves." All that was necessary, Vergennes added, was "that the treaties go hand in hand and are signed the same day."

Wittingly or not, Vergennes had given Franklin tacit permission to begin separate discussions with the British. Because the British were very eager to have such talks, and because there were two British negotiators vying to conduct them, Franklin had a lot of leverage. When Grenville returned to Passy at the beginning of June to argue once again for direct talks, this time Franklin decided "to evade the discussion" rather than reject the idea.

"If Spain and Holland and even if France should insist on unreasonable terms," Grenville asked, "can it be right that America should be dragged on in a war for their interests only?"

It was "unnecessary to enter at present into considerations of that kind," Franklin replied. "If any of the other powers should make extravagant demands," he continued enticingly, "it would then be time enough to consider what our obligations were."

Because Grenville was so eager to get direct talks underway, he was willing to tell Franklin, confidentially, that he was "instructed to acknowledge the independence of America previous to the commencement of the treaty." Oswald was also eager for direct talks to begin, and he came to Passy two days later to hint that he would be willing to serve as Britain's negotiator if Franklin preferred. He was coy. He was not trying to supplant Grenville, he insisted, for he was old and had no need for further glory. But it was clear to Franklin that he was now in the happy position of having a choice between two hungry suitors.

Oswald was more sophisticated than Grenville, and he was able to appear both more eager and more threatening. Peace was "absolutely necessary" for Britain, he confided. "Our enemies may now do what they please with us; they have the ball at their foot." On the other hand, there were those back in London who were "a little too much elated" by Britain's recent victory over the French navy in a major battle in the West Indies. If he and Franklin did not act soon, they might prevail in prolonging the war. There had even been serious discussions, Oswald warned, of ways to finance further fighting by canceling debt payment only on bonds of more than £1,000, which would not upset most of the population.

Franklin noted that he viewed this "as a kind of intimidation." Yet Oswald was able to soften Franklin through flattery. "He repeatedly mentioned the great esteem the ministers had for me," Franklin recorded. "They depended on me for the means of extricating the nation from its present desperate situation; that perhaps no single man had ever in his hands an opportunity of doing so much good as I had at present."

Oswald further endeared himself to Franklin by seeming to agree with him privately on what should be in a treaty. When Franklin railed against the idea of paying compensation to loyalists whose estates had been confiscated, saying that such a demand would elicit a contrary one from America demanding reparations for all the towns the British had burned, Oswald confidentially said that he personally felt the same. He also said that he agreed with Franklin that Britain should cede Canada to America. It was as if he were competing with young Grenville in an audition for the job of being Britain's negotiator and trying to win Franklin's recommendation.

Indeed, oddly enough, he was. He showed Franklin a memo that Shelburne had written that offered to give Oswald, if Franklin wished it, a commission to be the special negotiator with America. Shelburne wrote that he was willing to give Oswald any authority "which Dr. Franklin and he may judge conducive to a final settlement of things between Great Britain and America." That way, Shelburne's memo added, Britain could forge a peace with America "in a very different manner from the peace between Great Britain and France, who have always been at enmity with each other."

Oswald coyly noted that Grenville was "a very sensible young gentleman," and he was perfectly willing to leave it to him to conduct the negotiations in concert with France. However, if Franklin thought it would be "useful" to have Oswald deal directly with the Americans, he was "content to give his time and service."

Franklin was happy to accept. Oswald's "knowledge of America," he noted, meant that he would be better than Grenville "in persuading the ministry to things reasonable." Franklin asked Oswald whether he would prefer to negotiate with all the countries, including France, or to negotiate with America alone. Oswald's answer, obviously, was the latter. "He said he did not choose to be concerned in treating with the foreign powers," Franklin noted. "If he accepted any commission, it should be that of treating with America." Franklin agreed to write Shelburne secretly recommending that course.[31]

Partly, Franklin was motivated by his affection for Oswald, who was his age, and his lack of affection for the younger Grenville, who had annoyed Franklin by leaking to the London *Evening Post* an inaccurate account of one of their meetings. "Mr. Oswald, an old man, seems now to have no desire but that of being useful in doing good," Franklin noted. "Mr. Grenville, a young man, naturally desirous of acquiring a reputation, seems to aim at that of being an able negotiator." Franklin, though still ambitious at 76, now believed in the moderating effects of old age.

Although Franklin had made a great show of insisting that the French be involved in all negotiations, he had come to believe that it was now in America's interest to have its own separate and private channel with Britain. So, when he went to Versailles in mid-June, a week after his momentous meeting with Oswald, he was less candid than usual with Vergennes. "We spoke of all [Britain's] attempts to separate us, and the prudence of holding together and treating in concert," he recorded. This time, however, he held back some information. He did not detail Oswald's offer to have a private negotiating channel or his suggestion that Britain cede Canada to America.

Nor was Franklin fully candid with the Congress, which had instructed its peace commissioners, with Franklin's approval, not to do anything without France's full knowledge and support. In a letter in late June to Robert Livingston, the new American foreign secretary, Franklin reported that Britain had sent over two envoys, Oswald and Grenville, and he claimed that he had rejected their attempts to split America from France. "They had at first some hopes of getting the belligerent powers to treat separately, one after another, but finding that impracticable, they have, after several messages sent to and fro, come to a resolution of treating with all together for a general peace."

The very next day, however, he reiterated his desire for a separate channel in a letter he wrote for Oswald to give to Shelburne: "I cannot but hope that it is still intended to vest you with [authority] respecting the treaty with America."

Britain was likewise engaging in back-channel intrigue. In addition to holding informal discussions with the French, it sent envoys directly to the Congress trying to urge members to accept some form of dominion status for America that would permit separate parliaments loyal to a common king. When Franklin heard of these overtures, he wrote another letter to Livingston warning that they must be forcefully resisted. "The King hates us most cordially," he declared. If he were allowed "any degree of power or government" over America, "it will soon be extended by corruption, artifice, and force, until we are reduced to absolute subjection." [32]

FRANKLIN'S PEACE PLAN

At the beginning of July, the negotiating situation was simplified by the death of Lord Rockingham. Shelburne took over as prime minister, Fox resigned as foreign secretary, and Grenville was recalled. The time was right for Franklin to make an informal, but precise, peace offer to Oswald, which he did on July 10.

His proposal was divided into two parts, "necessary" provisions and "advisable" ones. Four fell into the former category: independence for America that was "full and complete in every sense," the removal of all British troops, secure boundaries, and fishing rights off the Canadian coast. In the advisable category were four suggested provisions: payment of reparations for the destruction in America, an acknowledgment of British guilt, a free trade agreement, and the ceding of Canada to the United States.

Oswald immediately sent Shelburne all the details, but Franklin kept the proposals private and never recorded them. Nor did he consult with, or even inform, Vergennes about the offer he had made to Oswald. [33]

Thus, with clear vision and a bit of conniving, Franklin had set the stage for the final negotiations that would end the Revolutionary War.

Shelburne promptly informed Oswald that the suggestions were "un-equivocal proofs of Dr. Franklin's sincerity." Britain was willing, he said, to affirm America's independence as a preliminary to negotia-tions, and it should "be done decidedly so as to avoid future risks of enmity." If America would drop the "advisable" provisions, Shelburne said, and "those called necessary alone retained as the ground of dis-cussion," then he was confident that a treaty could be "speedily con-cluded." Although it would take a few more months, that is in essence what happened.[34]

The final resolution was delayed, however, when Franklin was struck by "cruel gout" and kidney stones, which incapacitated him for much of August and September. John Jay, who had finally arrived in Paris, took over as the lead negotiator. The flinty New Yorker objected that the wording of Oswald's commission, which authorized him to negotiate "with the said colonies and plantations," was not much bet-ter than Grenville's had been, and he demanded that Oswald get a clear statement that he was dealing with an independent nation before talks proceeded further.

When Jay and Franklin went to call on Vergennes, the French minister advised that it did not seem necessary to insist that Oswald's commission contain a clear declaration of America's sovereignty. Franklin, who likewise gave his opinion that Oswald's commission "would do," was thrilled by Vergennes's tacit approval for the British-American negotiations to proceed, which he interpreted as a magnan-imous and supportive gesture showing France's "gracious goodwill."

Jay's interpretation, more sinister but more correct, was that Ver-gennes did not want Britain to recognize American independence ex-cept as part of a comprehensive peace settlement involving France and Spain. "This Court chooses to postpone an acknowledgment of our independence by Britain," Jay reported to the Congress, "in order to keep us under their direction" until all the demands of France and Spain were met. "I ought to add that Dr. Franklin does not see the conduct of this Court in the light I do."[35]

Jay's skepticism about France's motives led to a heated argument with Franklin when they returned to Passy from Versailles that evening. Jay was especially angry, he told Franklin, that Vergennes had brought up Spain's desire to claim some of the land between the Allegheny Mountains and the Mississippi River. Franklin fully agreed that Spain should not be permitted to "coop us up," but he gave Jay one of his gentle lectures about the wisdom of assuming that a friend like France was acting in good faith until there was hard evidence to the contrary. France was not trying to hold up negotiations, as Jay kept angrily insisting; instead, Franklin argued, Vergennes had shown a willingness to speed them along by not objecting to the wording of Oswald's commission.

But Jay's suspicions were reinforced when he learned that Vergennes had sent a deputy on a secret mission to London. Trusting neither the French nor Franklin, Jay joined in the back-channel fandango by dispatching a secret envoy of his own to London. What made this especially intriguing was that the man he sent was Benjamin Vaughan, Franklin's longtime friend and publisher, who had come to Paris to visit Franklin and do what he could to promote peace.

Jay asked Vaughan to tell Lord Shelburne that Oswald's commission needed to state unambiguously that he was to negotiate with "the United States." Such an explicit acknowledgment of American independence at the outset, Jay promised, would help "cut the cords" that bound America to France. Shelburne, eager to conclude a peace before his government toppled, was willing to go far enough to satisfy Jay. In mid-September his cabinet granted Oswald a new commission "to treat with the commissioners appointed by the colonies under the title of 13 united states," and it reaffirmed that American independence could be acknowledged as a preliminary to further discussions.

So, on October 5, with Jay and Franklin both satisfied and back in harmony, official negotiations began. Oswald presented his formal new commission, and Jay presented a proposed treaty that was very similar to the one Franklin had informally offered in July. The only addition to Franklin's four "necessary" points was a provision that was sure to please Britain, though not France or Spain: that both Britain and America would have free navigation rights on the Mississippi.

Their momentum, however, was slowed for a few weeks after Britain succeeded in beating back a French-Spanish attack on Gibraltar, thus emboldening their ministers. To stiffen Oswald's backbone,

Shelburne sent over Henry Strachey, a cabinet officer who had served as Admiral Howe's secretary. Just as he arrived, so did John Adams, yet again, to assume his role as a member of the American delegation.

Adams was as blunt as ever, filled with suspicions and doubting everyone's character but his own. Even Lafayette, who had become Franklin's close confidant, was immediately slammed by Adams as a "mongrel character" of "unlimited ambition" who was "panting for glory." Adams also displayed, in a public and undiplomatic way, his personal distrust of Vergennes by not calling on him for almost three weeks, until the minister "caused him to be reminded of" his duty to do so. (Vergennes, who was as smooth as Adams was rough, baffled the wary Adams by laying on a lavish dinner and plying him with fine wines and Madeira.) [36]

Adams likewise initially balked at paying a courtesy call on Franklin, who was pretty much confined to Passy with the gout and kidney stones, even though they had managed to exchange civil letters during Adams's mission in Holland. "He could not bear to go near him," Matthew Ridley, an American merchant in Paris, recorded in his diary. Ridley, who was a friend of both men, finally convinced Adams that it was necessary.

Adams felt particularly spiteful because he had recently learned about the letter Franklin had written to the Congress, at the behest of Vergennes, which had led to his earlier recall. Franklin had been motivated by "base jealousy" and "sordid envy," Adams told a friend. That was a complete misreading of Franklin, who had acted more out of annoyance than jealousy and whose occasional vices did not include an excess of envy.

Whatever the cause, Adams was filled with anger by the time he arrived back in Paris. "That I have no friendship for Franklin I avow," he wrote. "That I am incapable of having any with a man of his moral sentiments I avow." In his diary, Adams had even more to say: "Franklin's cunning will be to divide us. To this end he will provoke, he will insinuate, he will intrigue, he will maneuver." [37]

So it was a great testament to Franklin's charm that, as it turned out, he got along rather well with Adams once they settled down to work. When Adams bluntly told him, during the visit he finally made to Passy, that he agreed with Jay's tougher attitude toward France, "the Doctor heard me patiently, but said nothing." And at a meeting of the three commissioners the next day, Franklin serenely agreed with Adams and Jay that it made sense to meet with the British negotiators without coordinating with the French. Turning to Jay he said, "I am of your opinion and will go on with these gentlemen in the business without consulting this [France's] Court."

Franklin's willingness to negotiate without consulting France was not new; he had begun pursuing that approach before Jay and Adams arrived in Paris. But he made it seem that he was doing it partly in deference to the views of his two fellow commissioners, which served to soften Adams's attitude. Franklin "has gone on with us in entire harmony and unanimity," Adams happily recorded in his diary, "and has been able and useful, both by his sagacity and his reputation, in the whole negotiation."

For his part, Franklin continued to feel the same mixture of admiration and annoyance toward Adams that he had long held. As he would put it to Livingston a few months later, once the negotiations were over, "He means well for his country, is always an honest man, often a wise one, but sometimes and in some things, absolutely out of his senses."[38]

On October 30, Adams's forty-seventh birthday, the American negotiators and their British counterparts launched an intense week of negotiations, which started at eleven each morning and continued through late suppers most evenings. The British readily accepted the four "necessary points" that Franklin had proposed back in July, but not the "advisable points," such as the ceding of Canada. The main disputes they faced that week were:

- Fishing rights off Newfoundland: This was a major issue for Adams, who, as David McCullough points out, was eloquent in his sermons on "New England's ancient stake in the sacred codfish." Franklin was likewise firm on the point, and he provided an economic argument: the money that Americans made from fishing would be spent on British manufactures once friendship was restored. "Are you afraid there is not fish enough," he asked, "or that we should catch too many?" The British conceded the point, to the dismay of France, which was hoping to win special fishing rights of its own. (When Franklin was accused by his enemies in America of favoring the French position and opposing a demand for American fishing rights, he wrote Jay and Adams asking them to attest to his firmness; Jay graciously complied, and Adams did so more grudgingly.) [39]

- Prewar debts still owed by Americans to British merchants: Franklin and Jay felt they should be renounced, because Britain had taken or destroyed so much American property. Adams, however, insisted that such debts be honored, and his view prevailed.

- The western boundary: With his lifelong vision of American expansion, Franklin insisted that no other nation should have rights to the land between the Alleghenies and the Mississippi. As Jay recorded, "He has invariably declared it to be his opinion that we should insist on the Mississippi as our Western boundary." Again, this is not something that France or Spain would have supported at a general peace conference. But Britain was happy to accept the river as the western boundary along with free navigation rights for both nations.

- Compensation for the British loyalists in America whose estates had been confiscated: This was the most contentious issue, and Franklin made it even more so. He justified his implacable stance on moral grounds. The loyalists had helped cause the war, and their losses were far less than those suffered by American patriots whose property had been destroyed by the British. But his stubbornness also had a personal component. Among the most visible loyalists were his former friend Joseph Galloway and, more notably, his estranged son, William. Franklin's anger toward his son, and his desire to prove it publicly, had a major impact on his attitude toward the loyalist claims, and it added a painful personal poignancy to the final weeks of negotiations.

William, who had been released from his Connecticut captivity through a prisoner exchange in September 1778, had been living in British-occupied New York, where he served as the president of the Board of Associated Loyalists. In that capacity, he had encouraged a series of small but brutal raids on American forces. One of these resulted in the lynching murder of an American captain, and General Washington had responded by threatening to hang one of his British prisoners, a young and very well-connected officer named Charles Asgill, if the perpetrators were not brought to justice.

Asgill's friends and family used their great influence to try to save his life, and Shelburne sent a personal appeal to Franklin to intercede. Franklin sharply refused. Washington's aim was "to obtain the punishment of a deliberate murderer," he replied. "If the English refuse to deliver up or punish this murderer, it is saying that they choose to preserve him rather than Captain Asgill. It seems to me therefore that the application should be made to the English ministers." [40]

The issue became more personal for Franklin when a British court-martial acquitted the accused British soldier on the grounds that he was merely following orders. That prompted outraged Americans to demand the arrest of the person who had issued those orders: William Franklin. So, in August 1782, twenty years after his arrival in America as New Jersey governor, William prudently fled back to London, where he arrived in late September, just as his father's final round of peace negotiations with Oswald were beginning.

The meddlesome Vaughan further complicated matters by urging Shelburne to be solicitous toward William. He informed the prime minister that Temple Franklin had, when Vaughan discussed it with him in Passy, "intimated hopes to see something done for his father," and Vaughan later added his own belief, very mistaken, that doing so would have a "seasonable effect" on Benjamin Franklin's disposition toward Britain. So Shelburne met with William and promised to do all he could to help both him and the loyalists. Franklin was chagrined when he learned of all this, and was especially angry when he discovered that Vaughan's misguided interference had come at the behest of young Temple, who had interceded on his father's behalf without telling his grandfather. [41]

Franklin expressed his sentiments, as he often did, in a short fable. There was once, he wrote, a great lion, king of the forest, who "had among his subjects a body of faithful dogs." But the lion king, "influenced by evil counselors," went to war with them. "A few of them, of a mongrel race, derived from a mixture of wolves and foxes, corrupted by royal promises of great rewards, deserted the honest dogs and joined their enemies." When the dogs won their freedom, the wolves and foxes of the king's council gathered to argue for compensation to the mongrels who had remained loyal. But a horse arose, "with a boldness and freedom that became the nobleness of his nature," and argued that any reward for fratricide was unjust and would lead only to further wars. "The council had sense enough," Franklin concluded, "to resolve that the demand be rejected."[42]

In the final days of the negotiations, Franklin became even more obdurate against any compensation for the loyalists, even as Adams and Jay showed some willingness to compromise on the issue. In the past, Adams had accused Franklin of being untrustworthy because of his supposed sympathy toward his loyalist son. Now he was baffled that Franklin was being so belligerent in the other direction. "Dr. Franklin is very staunch against the Tories," he noted in his diary, "more decided on this point than Mr. Jay or myself."

Given the influence of the loyalist emigrants now living in Britain, Shelburne knew that his ministry might fall if he did nothing to satisfy their claims. His negotiators pushed until the very last day, but Franklin threatened to scuttle the entire treaty over this point. He pulled from his pocket a paper that resurrected his own demand that Britain, if it wanted any recompense for the loyalists' estates, must pay for all of the American towns destroyed, goods taken, cargo captured, villages burned, and even his own looted library in Philadelphia.

The British were forced to relent. After hearing Franklin's diatribe, they retired to an adjacent room, huddled, and returned to say they would accept instead a somewhat meaningless promise that the Congress would "earnestly recommend" to the individual states that they make whatever restitution each of them saw fit for the loyalists' estates confiscated there. The Americans knew that the states would end up doing little, so they agreed, but Franklin still insisted on one caveat, aimed at William: the recommendation would not apply to loyalists who had "borne arms against the said United States."

The next morning, November 30, 1782, the American negotiators, along with their secretary, Temple Franklin, met with the British in Oswald's suite at the Grand Hotel Muscovite to sign the provisional treaty that, in effect, ended the Revolutionary War. In a nod to the obligations owed France, the pact would not become formally binding "until terms of a peace shall be agreed upon between Great Britain and France." That would take another nine months. But the treaty had an immediate and irrevocable import that was contained in its opening line, which declared the United States "to be free, sovereign and independent."

That afternoon, the American negotiators all went to Passy, where Franklin hosted a celebratory dinner. Even John Adams was feeling mellower, at least for the time being. He conceded to his friend Matthew Ridley that Franklin had "behaved well and nobly."[43]

PLACATING THE FRENCH

To Franklin fell the difficult duty of explaining to Vergennes why the Americans had breached their obligations to France, and their instructions from the Congress, by agreeing to a treaty without consulting him. After sending Vergennes a copy of the signed accord, which he stressed was provisional, Franklin called on him at Versailles the following week. The French minister remarked, coolly but politely, that "proceeding in this abrupt signature of the articles" was not "agreeable to the [French] King" and that the Americans "had not been particularly civil." Nevertheless, Vergennes did allow that the Americans had done well by themselves, and he noted that "our conversation was amicable."

Only when Franklin followed up with a brash request for yet another French loan, along with the information that he was transmitting the peace accord to the Congress, did Vergennes take the opportunity to protest officially. It was lacking in propriety, he wrote Franklin, for him "to hold out a certain hope of peace to America without even informing yourself on the state of negotiation on our part." America was under an obligation not to consider ratifying any peace until France had also come to terms with Britain. "You have all your life performed your duties," Vergennes continued. "I pray you to consider how you propose to fulfill those which are due to the King."[44]

Franklin's response, which has been called "a diplomatic master-piece" and "one of the most famous of all diplomatic letters," combined a few dignified expressions of contrition with appeals to France's national interest. "Nothing has been agreed in the preliminaries contrary to the interests of France," he noted, not entirely correctly, "and no peace is to take place between us and England until you have concluded yours." Using a French word that roughly translates as "propriety," Franklin sought to minimize the American transgression:

> In not consulting you before they were signed, we have been guilty of neglecting a point of *bienséance*. But, as this was not from want of respect for the King, whom we all love and honor, we hope it will be excused, and that the great work, which has hitherto been so happily conducted, is so nearly brought to perfection, and is so glorious to his reign, will not be ruined by a single indiscretion of ours.

He went on, undaunted, to press his case for another loan. "Certainly the whole edifice sinks to the ground immediately if you refuse on that account to give us any further assistance." With that came both a plea and an implied threat: making a public issue of the transgression, he warned, could hurt the mutual interests of both countries. "The English, I just now learn, flatter themselves they have already divided us. I hope this little misunderstanding will therefore be kept a secret, and that they will find themselves totally mistaken."[45]

Vergennes was stunned by Franklin's letter, a copy of which he sent to his ambassador in Philadelphia. "You may imagine my astonishment," he wrote. "I think it proper that the most influential members of Congress should be informed of the very irregular conduct of their commissioners in regard to us." He did not blame Franklin personally, except to say that "he has yielded too easily to the bias of his colleagues." Vergennes went on to lament, correctly, that the new nation was not one that would enter into entangling alliances. "We shall be but poorly paid for all that we have done for the United States," he complained, "and for securing to them a national existence."

There was little Vergennes could do. Forcing a showdown, as Franklin had subtly warned, would drive the Americans into an even faster and closer alliance with Britain. So, reluctantly, he let the matter drop, instructed his envoy not to file an official protest with the Congress, and even agreed to supply yet another French loan.[46]

"Two great diplomatic duelists had formally crossed swords," Carl Van Doren noted, "and the philosopher had exquisitely disarmed the minister." Yes, but perhaps a better analogy would be to Franklin's own favorite game of chess. From his opening gambit that led to America's treaty of alliance with France to the endgame that produced a peace with England while preserving French friendship, Franklin mastered a three-dimensional game against two aggressive players by exhibiting great patience when the pieces were not properly aligned and carefully exploiting strategic advantages when they were.[47]

Franklin had been instrumental in shaping the three great documents of the war: the Declaration of Independence, the alliance with France, and the treaty with England. Now he turned his thoughts to peace. "All wars are follies, very expensive, and very mischievous ones," he wrote Polly Stevenson. "When will mankind be convinced of this, and agree to settle their differences by arbitration? Were they to do it, even by the cast of a die, it would be better than by fighting and destroying each other." To Joseph Banks, one of the many old friends from England he wrote in celebration, he asserted yet again his famous, albeit somewhat misleading, credo: "There never was a good war or a bad peace."[48]

BENNY AND TEMPLE

Rather than return home immediately, Franklin decided to relish his newly earned peace and leisure by enjoying the friends, family, and intellectual pursuits available to him in the idyllic setting of Passy. His grandson Benny had been languishing at his school in Geneva, which had recently been thrown into political turmoil over plans to give full

voting rights to all citizens. Now that his diplomatic duties had subsided, Franklin decided to permit Benny to come back to Passy for a
vacation during the summer of 1783, his first since leaving four years
earlier.[49]

Reunited at last with the grandfather he was so eager to impress,
Benny was completely charmed. Franklin was "very different from
other old persons," he told a visitor, "for they are fretful and complaining and dissatisfied, and my grandpapa is laughing and cheerful like a
young person." Their new proximity also warmed Franklin. Benny
was "so well grown," he wrote the boy's parents, "and so much improved in his learning and behavior." To Polly Stevenson he wrote,
"He gains every day upon my affections."

That summer, during which Benny turned 14, his grandfather took
him to the Seine for swimming lessons, and his cousin Temple taught
him fencing and dancing. Temple also impressed him by pretending to
kill a mouse with helium, then reviving him, then killing him for good
with an electric spark from one of Franklin's batteries. "I am sure my
cousin would pass for a conjurer in America," Benny wrote his parents.[50]

Benny had been sickly and depressed at school, Franklin learned,
and the political situation in Geneva remained volatile. So he decided
that the boy need not return, even though he had left his clothes and
books there. He had earlier considered sending Benny to school in
England under the care of Polly Stevenson, who had been excited by
the prospect. Now, worried that Benny was losing his command of
English, he raised the possibility with Polly more seriously. "Would
that still be convenient to you?" he asked. "He is docile and of gentle
manners, ready to receive and follow good advice, and will set no bad
example to your *other* children." Polly was wary but willing. "I fear he
will think us so unpolished he will scarcely be able to endure us," she
replied, "but if English cordiality will make amends for French refine-
ment, we may have some chance of making him happy."[51]

Franklin, who had grown ever more fond of Benny, instead decided that he should stay in Passy. "He showed such an unwillingness
to leave me, and Temple such a fondness for retaining him, that I concluded to keep him," Franklin explained to Polly in a letter at the end
of 1783. "He behaves very well, and we love him very much."

Perhaps, with his felicity in language, Benny could become a diplomat, Franklin thought. That would require, however, getting him a public appointment, something that was proving difficult for Temple. He had once told Richard Bache, just as he had told his son, William, and many others, that it was demeaning to be dependent on a government appointment. Now he expressed the same sentiment to Richard again, this time in a letter about his son Benny: "I have determined to give him a trade that he may have something to depend on, and not be obliged to ask favors or offices of anybody."[52]

The trade Franklin chose was the obvious one. His private little printing press at Passy was busy that autumn turning out editions of his bagatelles, so he was delighted when the boy eagerly started to work there. A master founder was hired to teach him how to cast type, and by spring Franklin had persuaded François Didot, the greatest and most artistic printer in France, to take him on as a student. Benny was destined to follow in Franklin's footsteps, not only as a printer but also eventually as a newspaper editor.

As for Temple, Franklin was reduced to asking for favors and offices. As he was enjoying the sweet summer of 1783, he wrote to Foreign Secretary Livingston yet another plaintive plea on poor Temple's behalf:

> He has now gone through an apprenticeship of near seven years in the ministerial business, and is very capable of serving the States in that line, as possessing all the requisites of knowledge, zeal, activity, language, and address . . . But it is not my custom to solicit employments for myself, or any of my family, and I shall not do it in this case. I only hope, that if he is not to be employed in your new arrangement, I may be informed of it as soon as possible, that, while I have strength left for it, I may accompany him in a tour to Italy, returning through Germany, which I think he may make to more advantage with me than alone, and which I have long promised to afford him, as a reward for his faithful service, and his tender filial attachment to me.

Temple did not get a ministerial posting, nor did his grandfather take him on a grand tour. Instead, he emulated his grandfather (and father) in a less laudable way than Benny. After failing to marry either of the Brillons' daughters, Temple became involved with a married woman who lived near Passy, Blanchette Caillot, whose husband was a successful actor. With her he fathered an illegitimate son, Theodore. In a cruel irony, the child died from smallpox, the disease that had taken the only legitimate son among three generations of Franklins.

Theodore Franklin, the illegitimate son of the illegitimate son of Franklin's own illegitimate son, was, albeit briefly, the last male-line descendant of Benjamin Franklin, who would in the end leave no family line bearing his name.[53]

BALLOON MANIA

Among the diversions Benny enjoyed with his grandfather in the summer and fall of 1783 were the grand spectacles of the first balloon flights. The age of air travel began in June when two brothers, Joseph and Etienne Montgolfier, launched an unmanned hot-air balloon near Lyons that rose to a height of six thousand feet. The Franklins were not there, but they did witness in late August the first unmanned flight using hydrogen. A scientist named Jacques Charles launched a twelve-foot-diameter silk balloon filled with hydrogen produced by pouring oil of vitriol over fiery iron filings. With great fanfare, it took off from Paris in front of fifty thousand spectators and floated for more than forty-five minutes before landing in a village more than fifteen miles away. "The country people who saw it fall were frightened," Franklin wrote Sir Joseph Banks, president of the Royal Society, "and attacked it with stones and knives so that it was much mangled."

The race was then on to produce the first *manned* flight, and it was won on November 21 by the Montgolfiers with their hot-air model. As a huge crowd cheered and countless women fainted, the balloon took off with two champagne-toting noblemen, who initially found themselves snared by some tree branches. "I was then in great pain for the men, thinking them in danger of being thrown out or burnt," Franklin reported. But soon they were free and gliding their way over the Seine, and after twenty minutes they landed on the other side and popped their corks in triumph. Franklin was among the distinguished scientists who signed the official certification of the historic flight the following evening, when the Montgolfiers called on him at Passy.

The Montgolfiers believed that the lift was caused not just by hot air but also by smoke, so they instructed their "aeronauts" to ply the fire with wet straw and wool. Franklin, however, was more partial to Charles's "inflammable air" model using hydrogen, and he helped to finance the first manned flight in such a balloon. It took place ten days later. As Franklin watched from his carriage parked near the Tuileries Gardens (his gout preventing him from joining the throng on the wet grass), Charles and a partner flew for more than two hours and landed safely twenty-seven miles away. Once again, Franklin provided a report to the Royal Society through Banks: "I had a pocket glass, with which I followed it until I lost sight, first of the men, then of the car, and when I last saw the balloon it appeared no bigger than a walnut."

Ever since the days of his electricity experiments, Franklin believed that science should be pursued initially for pure fascination and curiosity, and then practical uses would eventually flow from what was discovered. At first, he was reluctant to guess what practical use might come of balloons, but he was convinced that experimenting with them would someday, as he told Banks, "pave the way to some discoveries in natural philosophy of which at present we have no conception." There could be, he noted in another letter, "important consequences that no one can foresee." More famous was his pithier expression of the same sentiment, made in response to a spectator who asked what use this new balloon thing could be. "What is the use," he replied, "of a new-born baby?"[54]

Because the English saw no utility in ballooning and because they were a bit too proud to follow the French, they did not join in the excitement. "I see an inclination in the more respectable part of the Royal Society to guard against the Ballomania [until] some experiment likely to prove beneficial either to society or science is proposed," Banks wrote. Franklin scoffed at this attitude. "It does not seem to me a good reason to decline prosecuting a new experiment which apparently increases the power of man over matter until we can see to what use that power may be applied," he replied. "When we have learned to manage it, we may hope some time or other to find uses for it, as men have done for magnetism and electricity, of which the first experiments were mere matters of amusement." By early the following year, he had come up with one possibility for a practical use: balloons might serve as a way to wage war, or even better, as a way to preserve peace. "Convincing sovereigns of the folly of wars may perhaps be one effect, since it will be impracticable for the most potent of them to guard his dominions," he wrote to his friend Jan Ingenhousz, the Dutch scientist and physician.

Mainly, however, Franklin contented himself with enjoying the craze and all the entertainments surrounding it. Exhibition flights of fanciful balloons, decorated and gilded in glorious patterns, became the rage in Paris that season, and they even influenced hats and hairstyles, fashions and dances. Temple Franklin and Benny Bache produced their own miniature models. And Franklin wrote one of his typical parodies, which, like many of his early ones, used the anonymous voice of a fictional woman. "If you want to fill your balloons with an element ten times lighter than inflammable air," she wrote to one of the newspapers, "you can find a great quantity of it, and ready made, in the promises of lovers and of courtiers."[55]

EMINENCE GRISE

Even as he indulged in the frivolities of prerevolutionary Paris, Franklin focused much of his writing on his egalitarian, antielitist ideas for building a new American society based on middle-class virtues. His daughter, Sally, sent him newspaper clippings about the formation of a hereditary order of merit called the Society of the Cincinnati, which was headed by General Washington and open to distinguished officers of the American army who would pass the title down to their eldest sons. Franklin, replying at the beginning of 1784, ridiculed the concept. The Chinese were right, he said, to honor the parents of people who earned distinction, for they had some role in it. But honoring a worthy person's descendants, who had nothing to do with achieving the merit, "is not only groundless and absurd but often hurtful to that posterity." Any form of hereditary aristocracy or nobility was, he declared, "in direct opposition to the solemnly declared sense of their country."

He also, in the letter, ridiculed the symbol of the new Cincinnati order, a bald eagle, which had also been selected as a national symbol. That provoked one of Franklin's most famous riffs about America's values and the question of a national bird:

> I wish the bald eagle had not been chosen as the representative of our country; he is a bird of bad moral character, he does not get his living honestly; you may have seen him perched on some dead tree, near the river where, too lazy to fish for himself, he watches the labors of the fishing-hawk . . . The turkey is, in comparison, a much more respectable bird, and a true original native of America . . . He is (though a little vain and silly, it is true, but not the worse emblem for that) a bird of courage, and would not hesitate to attack a grenadier of the British guards.[56]

Franklin heard so frequently from people who wanted to emigrate to America that in early 1784 he printed a pamphlet, in French and English, designed to encourage the more industrious of them while discouraging those who sought a life of upper-class leisure. His essay, "Information to Those Who Would Remove to America," is one of the clearest expressions of his belief that American society should be based on the virtues of the middle (or "mediocre," as he sometimes called them, meaning it as a word of praise) classes, of which he still considered himself a part.

There were few people in America either as poor or as rich as those in Europe, he said. "It is rather a general happy mediocrity that prevails." Instead of rich proprietors and struggling tenants, "most people cultivate their own lands" or follow some craft or trade. Franklin was particularly harsh on those who sought hereditary privilege or who had "no other quality to recommend him but his birth." In America, he said, "people do not enquire of a stranger, What is he? but, What can he do?" Reflecting his own pride in discovering that he had hardworking forebears rather than aristocratic ones, he said that a true American "would think himself more obliged to a genealogist who could prove for him that his ancestors and relations for ten generations had been ploughmen, smiths, carpenters, turners, weavers, tanners or even shoemakers, and consequently that they were useful members of society, than if he could only prove that they were Gentlemen, doing nothing of value but living idly on the labor of others."

America was creating a society, Franklin proclaimed, where a "mere man of Quality" who does not want to work would be "despised and disregarded," while anyone who has a useful skill would be honored. All of this made for a better moral clime. "The almost general mediocrity of fortune that prevails in America, obliging its people to follow some business for subsistence, those vices that arise usually from idleness are in a great measure prevented," he concluded. "Industry and constant employment are great preservatives of morals and virtue." He purported to be describing the way America was, but he was also subtly prescribing what he wanted it to become. All in all, it was his best paean to the middle-class values he represented and helped to make integral to the new nation's character.[57]

Franklin's affection for the middle class and its virtues of hard work and frugality meant that his social theories tended to be a blend of conservatism (as we have seen, he was dubious of generous welfare laws that led to dependency among the poor) and populism (he was opposed to the privileges of inheritance and to wealth idly gained through ownership of large estates). In 1784, he expanded on these ideas by questioning the morality of excess personal luxuries.

"I have not," he lamented to Benjamin Vaughan, "thought of a remedy for luxury." On the one hand, the desire for luxury spurred people to work hard. He recalled how his wife had once given a fancy hat to a country girl, and soon all the other girls in the village were working hard spinning mittens in order to earn money to buy fancy hats. This appealed to his utilitarian sentiments: "Not only the girls were made happier by having fine caps, but the Philadelphians by the supply of warm mittens." However, too much time spent seeking luxuries was wasteful and "a public evil." So he suggested that America should impose heavy duties on the importation of frivolous fineries.[58]

His antipathy to excess wealth also led him to defend high taxes, especially on luxuries. A person had a "natural right" to all he earned that was necessary to support himself and his family, he wrote finance minister Robert Morris, "but all property superfluous to such purposes is the property of the public, who by their laws have created it." Likewise, to Vaughan, he argued that cruel criminal laws had been wrought by those who sought to protect excess ownership of property.

"Superfluous property is the creature of society," he said. "Simple and mild laws were sufficient to guard the property that was merely necessary."[59]

To some of his contemporaries, both rich and poor, Franklin's social philosophy seemed an odd mix of conservative and radical beliefs. In fact, however, it formed a very coherent leather-apron outlook. Unlike many subsequent revolutions, the American was not a radical rebellion by an oppressed proletariat. Instead, it was led largely by propertied and shopkeeping citizens whose rather bourgeois rallying cry was "No taxation without representation." Franklin's blend of beliefs would become part of the outlook of much of America's middle class: its faith in the virtues of hard work and frugality, its benevolent belief in voluntary associations to help others, its conservative opposition to handouts that led to laziness and dependency, and its slightly ambivalent resentment of unnecessary luxury, hereditary privileges, and an idle landowning leisure class.

The end of the war permitted the resumption of amiable correspondence with old friends in England, most notably his fellow printer William Strahan, to whom he had written the famous but unsent letter nine years earlier declaring "You are now my enemy." By 1780, he had mellowed enough to draft a letter signed "Your formerly affectionate friend," which he then changed to "Your long affectionate humble servant." By 1784, he was signing himself "Most affectionately."

Once again, they debated Franklin's theories that top government officials should serve without pay and that England's society and government were inherently corrupt. Now, however, the tone was bantering as Franklin suggested that the Americans, who "have some remains of affection" for the British, perhaps should help govern *them*. "If you have not sense and virtue enough left to govern yourselves," he wrote, "dissolve your present old crazy constitution and send members to Congress." Lest Strahan not realize he was joking, Franklin confessed, "You will say my advice smells of Madeira. You are right. This foolish letter is mere chitchat between ourselves over the second bottle."[60]

Franklin also spent the early summer of 1784 adding more to his memoirs. He had written about 40 percent of what would become his famous *Autobiography* at Bishop Shipley's in Twyford in 1771. Now he responded to a request from Vaughan, who said that Franklin's story would help to explain the "manners of a rising people," and in Passy wrote what would become another 10 percent of that work. His focus at the time was on the need to build a new American character, and most of the section he wrote in 1784 was devoted to an explanation of the famous self-improvement project in which he sought to train himself in the thirteen virtues ranging from frugality and industry to temperance and humility.

His Passy friends were especially thrilled by the tale of the slate booklet Franklin used to record his efforts at acquiring these virtues. Franklin, who still had not fully acquired all aspects of humility, proudly showed off the tablets to Cabanis, the young physician who lived with Madame Helvétius. "We touched this precious booklet," Cabanis exulted in his journal. "We held it in our hands. Here was, in a way, the chronological story of Franklin's soul!" [61]

In his spare time, Franklin perfected one of his most famous and useful inventions: bifocal glasses. Writing to a friend in August 1784, he announced himself "happy in the invention of Double Spectacles, which, serving for distant objects as well as near ones, make my eyes as useful to me as ever they were." A few months later, in response to a request for more information about "your invention," Franklin provided details:

> The same convexity of glass through which a man sees clearest and best at the distance proper for reading is not the best for greater distances. I therefore had formerly two pair of spectacles, which I shifted occasionally, as in traveling I sometimes read, and often wanted to regard the prospects. Finding this change troublesome, and not always sufficiently ready, I had the glasses cut and half of each kind associated in the same circle. By this means, as I wear my spectacles constantly, I have only to move my eyes up or down, as I want to see distinctly far or near, the proper glasses being always ready. [62]

A portrait by Charles Willson Peale, done in 1785, shows him wearing his new spectacles.

Because of his renown both as a scientist and a rationalist, Franklin was appointed by the king in 1784 to a commission to investigate the theories of Friedrich Anton Mesmer, whose advocacy of a new method of healing led to the new word "mesmerize." (Another member of Franklin's commission, Dr. Joseph-Ignace Guillotin, would also have his name turned into a neologism during the French Revolution.) A flamboyant healer from Vienna, Mesmer believed that maladies were caused by the artificial disruption of a universal fluid emitted by heavenly bodies and they could be cured by the techniques of animal magnetism he had discovered. His treatment involved putting patients around huge oak tubs filled with glass and iron filings while a healer, carrying an iron wand, magnetized and mesmerized them. In a sign that the Enlightenment was losing its grip, Mesmerism became wildly popular in Paris, replacing ballooning as the fad of the moment, with adherents that included Lafayette, Temple Franklin, and Queen Marie-Antoinette.

Many of the commission's meetings were held in Passy, where Franklin himself, in the name of science, submitted to the treatments. In his diary, 14-year-old Benny recorded one session where Mesmer's disciples, "after having magnetized many sick persons . . . are gone into the garden to magnetize some trees." It was clear that the power of suggestion could produce some strange effects. The commissioners, however, decided that "our role was to keep cool, rational and open-minded." So they blindfolded the patients, not letting them know whether or not they were being treated by Mesmer's doctors. "We discovered we could influence them ourselves so that their answers were the same, whether they had been magnetized or not." They concluded that Mesmer was a fraud and what was at work was, at they put it in their report, "the power of imagination." An unpublished annex to the report did note that the treatment was powerful at sexually stimulating young women when "titillations delicieuses" were applied.

Franklin wrote to Temple, who was no longer a disciple of Mesmer, that the report had roundly debunked the theories. "Some think it will put an end to Mesmerism," he said, "but there is a wonderful deal of credulity in the world, and deceptions as absurd have supported themselves for ages."[63]

FINALE

One source of despair for Franklin was that, in negotiating treaties with other European nations, he had to work with John Adams again. He was worried, he told one friend, about "what will be the offspring of a coalition between my ignorance and his positiveness." Adams's brief period of mellowness had lasted for only a few months after the signing of the provisional peace with Britain, and he subsequently resumed his backbiting. Franklin was an "unintelligible politician," Adams wrote Robert Livingston. "If this gentleman and the marble Mercury in the garden of Versailles were in nomination for an embassy, I would not hesitate to give my vote for the statue, upon the principle that it would do no harm."

So Franklin was thrilled when Thomas Jefferson, who had twice resisted congressional commissions to join Franklin and Adams as a minister in Paris, finally relented and arrived there in August 1784. Jefferson was everything that Adams was not: diplomatic and charming, partial to France, secure rather than jealous, a lover of women and social gaiety with no Puritan prudishness. He was also a philosopher, inventor, and scientist whose Enlightenment curiosity meshed perfectly with Franklin's.

To make matters even better, Jefferson was fully aware of the darkness that infected Adams. James Madison had written him to complain that Adams's letters were "a display of his vanity, his prejudice against the French court and his venom against Dr. Franklin." Jefferson replied, "He hates Franklin, he hates Jay, he hates the French, he hates the English. To whom will he adhere?"

Jefferson shared Franklin's belief that idealism and realism should both play a role in foreign policy. "The best interest of nations, like men, was to follow the dictates of conscience," he declared. And unlike Adams, he completely revered Franklin. "More respect and veneration attached to the character of Dr. Franklin in France than to that of any other person, foreign or native," he wrote, and he proclaimed Franklin "the greatest man and ornament of the age." When word spread, a few months later, that he was being tapped to replace Franklin, Jefferson gave his famed reply: "No one can replace him, Sir, I am only his successor."[64]

Jefferson dined often with Franklin, played chess with him, and listened to his lectures about the loyalty America owed France. His calming presence even helped Franklin and Adams get along better, and the three men who had worked together on the Declaration now worked together at Passy almost every day throughout September preparing for new European treaties and commercial pacts. There was, in fact, a lot that the three patriots could agree on. They shared a faith in free trade, open covenants, and the need to end the mercantilist system of repressive commercial arrangements and restrictive spheres of influence. As Adams, with uncharacteristic generosity, noted, "We proceeded with wonderful harmony, good humor and unanimity."

For both men and nations, it was a season of reconciliation. If Franklin could repair his relationship with Adams, there was even hope that he could do so with his son. "Dear and honored father," William wrote from England that summer. "Ever since the termination of the unhappy contest between Great Britain and America, I have been anxious to write to you, and to endeavor to revive that affectionate intercourse and connection which, until the commencement of the late troubles, had been the pride and happiness of my life."

It was a noble, gracious, and plaintive gesture from a son who, through it all, had never said anything bad about his estranged father nor stopped loving him. But William was still a Franklin, and he could not bring himself to admit that he had been in the wrong, nor to apologize. "If I have been mistaken, I cannot help it. It is an error of judgment that the maturest reflection I am capable of cannot rectify; and I verily believe were the same circumstances to occur again tomorrow, my conduct would be exactly similar to what it was." He offered to come to Paris if his father did not want to come to England so they could settle their issues with "a personal interview."[65]

Franklin's response revealed his pain, but it also offered some hints of hope. He began by saying he was "glad to find that you desire to revive the affectionate intercourse," and he even brought himself to add, "it will be agreeable to me." Yet he immediately segued from love to anger:

> Indeed nothing has ever hurt me so much and affected me with such keen sensations as to find myself deserted in my old age by my only son; and not only deserted, but to find him taking up arms against me, in a cause, wherein my good fame, fortune and life were all at stake. You conceived, you say, that your duty to your King and regard for your country required this. I ought not to blame you for differing in sentiment with me in public affairs. We are men, all subject to errors. Our opinions are not in our own power; they are formed and governed much by circumstances, that are often as inexplicable as they are irresistible. Your situation was such that few would have censured your remaining neuter, *though there are natural duties which precede political ones* [emphasis is Franklin's].

Then he caught himself. "This is a disagreeable subject," he wrote. "I drop it." It would not be convenient, he added, to "have you come here at the present." Instead, Temple would be sent to London to act as an intermediary. "You may confide to your son the family affairs you wish to confer upon with me." Then, a bit condescendingly, he added, "I trust you will prudently avoid introducing him to company that it may be improper for him to be seen with." Temple may have been William's son, but Franklin made it clear who controlled him.[66]

At 24, Temple had little of his grandfather's wisdom but possessed a lot more of the normal emotions that bind families, even estranged ones. He had long been hoping, he wrote a London friend, to return there to "embrace my father." On his visit to England, he nevertheless was careful to show fealty to his grandfather, even asking for permission before accompanying his father on a trip to the seashore.

After a few weeks, Franklin began to fear that Temple might be forsaking him for his father, and he chided him for not writing enough. "I have waited with impatience the arrival of every post. But not a word." Among other things, Franklin complained, this was embarrassing him with those who kept asking whether he had heard from Temple: "Judge what I must feel, what they must think, and tell me what I am to think of such neglect." Of all the members of his family, Temple alone could cause such jealousy and possessiveness.

For his part, Temple was thoroughly enjoying himself. He was treated as a celebrity prince: feted by the Royal Society, the Lord Mayor, and various ladies who held teas in his honor. He had his portrait painted by Gilbert Stuart, and a friend gave him a list of the best bootmakers and tailors, adding, "And when lewd, go to the following safe girls who I think are quite handsome."[67]

Temple was not able to resolve the issues dividing his father and grandfather, but he was able to accomplish another part of his mission: enticing Polly Stevenson to come to Passy. Now 45, she had been widowed for a decade, and her mother, Franklin's longtime landlady and companion, had died a year earlier. (She "loved you with the most ardent affection," Polly had written when conveying the sad news.) Franklin had written Polly that she must come see him soon, for he was now like a building that required "so many repairs that in a little time the Owner will find it cheaper to pull it down and build a new one." By the end of the summer of 1784, his letters had become even more plaintive. "Come, my dear friend, live with me while I stay here, and go with me, if I do go, to America."[68]

In early December 1784, many people converged on Passy and provided for Franklin, during his final winter in France, a most satisfying version of the hybrid families, real and adopted, he so loved to assemble around him. There to pamper him were Temple and Benny, Polly and her three children, Thomas Jefferson and other great minds, plus Mesdames Brillon and Helvétius along with their wonderful retinues. "For a fragile moment," note Claude-Anne Lopez and Eugenia Herbert, "his various 'families' were almost in perfect poise, drawing closer in a network of good will of which he was the center."[69]

Polly was amused by Temple on first seeing him again in London after ten years, and she joked with Franklin about how he had tried to keep the boy's lineage secret back then. "We see a strong resemblance of you, and indeed saw it when we did not think ourselves at liberty to say we did, as we pretended to be as ignorant as you supposed we were, or chose that we should be." That gave her an opportunity to chide them both a bit: "I believe you may have been handsomer than your grandson is, but then you never were so genteel."

But close familiarity with Temple did not, except in his grandfather's case, necessarily breed fondness, and Polly became somewhat disenchanted with him after their arrival in Passy. "He has such a love of dress," she wrote a relative, "and is so absorbed in self-importance and so engaged in the pursuit of pleasure that he is not an amiable or respectable character."

Benny, on the other hand, with the benefit of his Geneva education and natural eagerness to please, struck Polly as "sensible and manly in his manner without the slightest tincture of the coxcomb." He wore his hair like an English lad rather than a French fop, and "with the simplicity of his dress retains a lovely simplicity of character." Temple might look more like Franklin, but Benny—who swam in the Seine, flew kites with a passion, took Polly on tours of Paris, and yet was ever diligent in his printing work—resembled him more "in mind."[70]

ADIEU

There were times, indeed many of them, when Franklin wrote of his inclination not to disrupt this little paradise, but instead to remain in France and die among those who so loved and pleased him. His gout and his kidney stones made the prospect of an ocean voyage something to dread, while the embers of his passions for the ladies of Paris were something he could still savor. In May 1785, he wrote a friend recalling one of his favorite old drinking songs:

> *May I govern my Passions with an absolute sway,*
> *Grow wiser and better as my Strength wears away,*
> *Without Gout or Stone, by a gentle Decay.*

"But what signifies our wishing?" he asked. "I have sung that wishing song a thousand times, when I was young, and now find, at fourscore, that the three contraries have befallen me, being subject to the gout and the stone, and not being yet master of all my passions."

Nevertheless, when word reached him that month that the Congress had at long last accepted his resignation and that Temple was not being offered an overseas assignment, Franklin decided it was time to go home. From Passy he wrote Polly, who had returned to England, begging her to accompany him. He had taken the liberty of reserving a spacious cabin for her whole family. "You may never have so good an opportunity." For the time being at least, she decided to stay in England.

He sent word of his travel plans to his sister Jane and explained, "I have continued to work until late in the day; 'tis time I should go home, and go to bed." Such metaphors had begun to creep into his writing, and he expanded on them to his friend David Hartley, who had helped him during his many negotiations. "We were long fellow laborers in the best of all works, the work of peace," he wrote. "I leave you still in the field, but having finished my day's work, I am going home *to go to bed*! Wish me a good night's rest, as I do you a pleasant evening. Adieu!"[71]

The farewells at Passy were dramatic and tearful. "Every day of my life I shall remember that a great man, a sage, has wanted to be my friend," Madame Brillon wrote after their final meeting. "If it ever pleases you to remember the woman who loved you the most, think of me."

Madame Helvétius was not to be outdone. "Come back, my dear friend, come back to us," she wrote in a letter dispatched to catch up with him as he boarded his boat. To each of his friends went a gift that was to become a relic: Cabanis got the hollow cane that magically stilled the waves, the Abbé Morellet a tool chest and armchair, and his landlord Chaumont a table that could be ingeniously raised and lowered. (He also gave Chaumont a bill for the improvements he had made to his apartments, including installing a lightning rod and fixing the chimney "to cure it of its intolerable malady of smoke.")

To ease his travel to the port of Le Havre, Queen Marie-Antoinette sent her personal enclosed litter borne by surefooted Spanish mules. Her husband, King Louis XVI, sent a miniature portrait of himself surrounded by 408 small diamonds. Franklin also exchanged gifts with Vergennes, who noted to an aide that "the United States will never have a more zealous and more useful servant than M. Franklin."[72]

On the day he left Passy, July 12, Benny recorded in his diary, "A mournful silence reigned around him, broken only by a few sobs."

Jefferson had come to see him off, and he later recalled: "The ladies smothered him with embraces, and on his introducing me as his successor, I told him I wished he would transfer these privileges to me, but he answered, 'You are too young a man.' "[73]

Franklin's plan was to cross the English Channel and then determine whether he felt he could endure an ocean crossing. If not, he would ferry back to Le Havre, and the Queen's litter, which waited there for word, would carry him back to Passy.

As usual, however, travel was a tonic rather than travail for Franklin, and he turned out to be the only passenger not to get sick during the rough channel crossing. When they arrived in Southampton, he and his party went to visit a hot saltwater spa where, he noted in his journal, he bathed in the springs "and, floating on my back, fell asleep, and slept near an hour by my watch, without sinking or turning!"[74]

There was one last dramatic scene to be played out, one last emotional moment, before he could set sail on his eighth and final crossing of the Atlantic. For four days he stayed at the Star Inn in Southampton, so that he could receive some of his old English friends and bid them a final farewell. Bishop Shipley came, along with his daughter Kitty. So did Benjamin Vaughan, his back-channel missions for Jay and Temple forgiven, who was preparing to publish a new edition of his friend's writings. There were grand dinners and celebrations, which he described in his journal as "very affectionate."

But the main person who had come to see him at the Star Inn got only a brusque mention in his journal. "Met my son, who arrived from London the evening before," Franklin noted. There was no reconciliation, no recorded tears or affection, just a cold negotiation over debts and property.

Franklin had regained full control over Temple by then, and he drove a hard bargain on his grandson's behalf. He insisted that William sell his New Jersey farm to Temple for less than he had paid, and he applied against the purchase price the decades of debts, carefully recorded, that William still owed him. He also took title to all of William's land claims in New York. Having taken William's son from him, he was now extracting his wealth and his connections to America.

This final reunion of three generations of Franklin men, so fraught with father-son tensions, ended so coldly that none of them ever saw fit to discuss it. Franklin's journal offers not a word of detail, nor is there any record of his ever writing or telling about it. He and his son never corresponded again. William wrote a letter to his half-sister, Sally, four days later, but amazingly, he rambled on about her children and a portrait he was trying to send her without ever describing the climactic scene. The closest he came, at the end of the long letter, was to lament, in discussing how everyone would soon be in Philadelphia, that "my fate has thrown me on a different side of the globe." Even decades later, after his father and grandfather had both died and he finally got around to producing a collection of his grandfather's life and works, Temple provided only a desultory and unrevealing phrase noting that at Southampton, Franklin "had the satisfaction of seeing his son, the former Governor of New Jersey."[75]

William was not invited to the farewell party aboard his father's vessel on the evening of July 27. Fully revitalized by travel and showing no remorse over the cool parting with his son, Franklin stayed up with his friends until 4 A.M. When he awoke late that morning, his friends were gone, his two grandsons were with him, and his ship was already under sail for home.

CHAPTER SIXTEEN

SAGE

Philadelphia, 1785–1790

HOME AT LAST

On this, his final voyage across the ocean, Franklin felt no need to study, or even to mention, the calming effect of oil on troubled waters. Nor, despite his many promises to friends, did he bring himself to work on his memoirs, which he had begun as a letter to the "dear son" he had just forsaken.

Instead, he indulged the passion that both relaxed and invigorated his mind: scientific inquiries awash with experimental details and practical consequences. The result was a forty-page gusher of observations and theories on a wide variety of maritime topics, replete with charts and drawings and data tables. At one point he paused, admitted that "the garrulity of an old man has got hold of me," and then sailed forth. "I think I might as well now, once and for all, empty my nautical budget."

That budget was a full one: theories, illustrated with diagrams, on how to design hulls to minimize their resistance to wind as well as water; descriptions of his old experiments, along with proposals for new ones, on the effects of air currents on objects of various shapes; how to rig up sliced playing cards to gauge the effects of wind; how to translate that experiment into one using sails and booms; ways to use pulleys to prevent anchor cables from breaking; an analysis of how ships fill with water after a leak; proposals for compartmentalizing hulls the way the Chinese did; tales from history about endangered ships that sank and those that survived, with speculations as to why; learned comparisons of Eskimo kayaks, Chinese rowboats, Indian canoes, Bermuda sloops, and Pacific island proas; proposals for building water propellers and air propellers; and more, much more, for page after page, diagram after diagram.

He also turned his attention to the Gulf Stream again, this time devising an experiment to test whether it extended to the depths or was more like a warm river flowing near the surface of the ocean. An empty bottle with a cork in its mouth was lowered to thirty-five fathoms, at which point the water pressure pushed the cork in and allowed the bottle to fill. The water gathered from that depth was six degrees cooler than that on the surface. A similar experiment using a keg with two valves found the water on the bottom, even at only eighteen fathoms, to be twelve degrees cooler than the water at the surface. He provided temperature charts and maps, along with the suggestion that a "thermometer may be a useful instrument to a navigator," that could help captains catch a ride on the Gulf Stream going eastbound and avoid it westbound, thus potentially saving a week or more of travel.[1]

In addition, Franklin wrote papers, equally long and filled with experimental findings, on how to cure smoky chimneys and how to build better stoves. From a modern vantage these treatises might seem obsessive in their immersion into details, but it must be remembered that they addressed one of the most serious issues of the time: the choking soot that plagued most homes and cities. It was, altogether, his most prodigious scientific outpouring since his electricity experiments of 1752. And like those previous studies, the ones he produced during his ocean crossing of 1785 showed his unique appreciation—that of an ingenious man if not a genius—for combining scientific theory, technical invention, clever experiments, and practical utility.[2]

When Franklin and his two grandchildren arrived at Philadelphia's Market Street wharf in September 1785, sixty-two years after he had first straggled ashore there as a 17-year-old runaway, "we were received by a crowd of people with huzzas and accompanied with acclamations quite to my door." Cannons boomed, bells rang, Sally embraced him, and tears ran down Temple's cheeks. Long worried about the damage the Lees and Adamses may have done to his reputation, Franklin was much relieved. "The affectionate welcome I meet with from my fellow citizens is far beyond my expectation," he proudly wrote John Jay.[3]

Gathered around him now at his Market Street home, even more than at Passy, would be that glorious assembly of family both real and adopted he always relished. There was his ever-dutiful daughter, Sally, who would play the role of his housekeeper, and her husband, Richard Bache, never successful but always accommodating. In addition to Benny and Willy, there were now four new Bache children—"four little prattlers who cling about the knees of their grandpapa and afford me great pleasure"—with another soon on the way. And within a year, Polly Stevenson would make good on her promise to come over, along with her three children. "As to my domestic circumstances," Franklin wrote Bishop Shipley, "they are at present as happy as I could wish them. I am surrounded by my offspring, a dutiful and affectionate daughter in my house, with six grandchildren."[4]

Benny enrolled at the Philadelphia Academy his grandfather had founded (by then renamed the University of the State of Pennsylvania), and on his graduation in 1787 became a full-time printer. Franklin was delighted, almost too much so. He built Benny a shop, helped him choose and cast fonts, and suggested books for him to publish. His knack for creating bestsellers like Poor Richard's almanacs, however, had given way to a desire for more edifying and educational tomes, and Benny eventually began to squirm, just a bit, at his hovering presence. Yet he loyally served as Franklin's secretary and scrivener.

Temple tried to turn himself into a gentleman farmer on the New Jersey estate that had just been wrested from his father, but he was temperamentally unsuited to caring much about crops and herds. In an ill-conceived attempt to create a showcase chateau, he pestered his French friends to send him specimen deer (American venison he declared tasteless), hunting dogs, and costumes for his workers. After the deer kept dying en route, Temple reverted to his urban dandy ways and spent most of his time on the party circuit in Philadelphia, while his grandfather, the only person to dote on him, continued his futile efforts to win him a ministerial appointment.

Though less mobile than before, Franklin was as clubbable as he had been as a young tradesman, and the few surviving members of his old associations resumed their gatherings, often at his house. There were only four left of the volunteer fire company he founded in 1736, but Franklin dug out his bucket and convened a meeting. The American Philosophical Society, which sometimes held sessions in his dining room, elected Temple a new member in 1786, along with most of the intellectual friends Franklin had made in Europe over the years: le Veillard, la Rochefoucauld, Condorcet, Ingenhousz, and Cabanis. To apply the same earnest curiosity to "the arduous and complicated science of government" that the philosophical society applied to the science of nature, Franklin organized a companion group, the Society for Political Inquiries, whose members included his young activist friends such as Thomas Paine.

Franklin had reached an age when he no longer fretted about squandering his time. For hours on end, he would play cribbage or cards with friends, which caused him, he wrote Polly, to have brief twinges of guilt. "But another reflection comes to relieve me, whispering: 'You know the soul is immortal; why then should you be such a niggard of a little time, when you have a whole eternity before you?' So being easily convinced and, like other reasonable creatures, satisfied with a small reason when it is in favor of doing what I have a mind to, I shuffle the cards again, and begin another game."[5]

Finding the well-stocked farmers' market, which now extended to the third block of Market Street where he lived, an easier source of produce than growing his own, he turned his vegetable patch into a pocket Passy garden with gravel paths, shrubs, and a shady mulberry tree. As one visitor recorded the new domestic scene, "We found him in his garden, sitting up a grassplot, under a very large mulberry tree, with several other gentlemen and two or three ladies . . . The tea table was spread under the tree, and Mrs. Bache, who is the only daughter of the Doctor, and lives with him, served it out to the company. She had three of her children about her. They seemed to be excessively fond of their grandpapa."[6]

It was a lifestyle that kept the gout at bay and, for the time being, his kidney stones from worsening. He suffered pain only when he was walking or "making water," he wrote Veillard. "As I live temperately, drink no wine, and use daily the exercise of the dumb-bell, I flatter myself that the stone is kept from augmenting so much as it might otherwise do, and that I may still continue to find it tolerable. People who live long, who will drink the cup of life to the very bottom, must expect to meet with some of the usual dregs."

Twenty-two years earlier, he had personally overseen each detail of the construction of his new house on Market Street, and he even instructed Deborah from afar about the specifics of its decoration and furnishing. But he had lived in it for only brief intervals, and now he found it far too cramped for his extended family, club meetings, and entertaining. It was time, he decided, to embark on a new building spree.

Despite his age, he found the prospect enticing. He took joy in the details of design and craftsmanship, he had a passion for modern improvements and contrivances, and he relished the thrill of construction. As he wrote Veillard, he derived pleasure from overseeing the "bricklayers, carpenters, stone-cutters, painters, glaziers," whose craft he had first admired as a child in Boston. Plus, he knew that real estate was a good investment; housing values were rising fast, as were rents.[7]

His plan was to demolish three older houses he owned on Market Street and replace them with two larger ones. He had wooed Deborah in one of them and worked as a fledgling printer in another, but nostalgia was not among his stronger sentiments. He was forced to change his plans, however, by a challenge to their property lines. "My neighbor disputing my bounds, I have been obliged to postpone until that dispute is settled by law," he wrote his sister Jane in Boston. "In the meantime, the workmen and materials being ready, I have ordered an addition to the house I live in, it being too small for our growing family."

The new three-story wing, designed to meld seamlessly with the existing house, was thirty-three feet long and sixteen feet wide, which enlarged his space by a third. On the ground floor was a long dining room able to seat twenty-four, and on the third floor were new bedrooms. The finest feature, which connected by a passage to "my best old bedchamber," was a library that took up the entire second floor. With shelves from floor to ceiling, it accommodated 4,276 volumes, making it what one visitor claimed (with some exaggeration) "the largest and by far the best private library in America." As he confessed to Jane, "I hardly know how to justify building a library at an age that will soon oblige me to quit it, but we are apt to forget that we are grown old, and building is an amusement."[8]

Eventually he was able to build the two new houses as well, one of which became Benny's printing shop, and he designed an arched passageway between them into the courtyard in front of his own renovated home, which was set back from Market Street. All the new construction allowed him to put into practice the various fire safety ideas he had advocated over the years. None of the wooden beams in one room connected directly to those in another, the floors and stairs were tightly plastered, and a trapdoor opened to the roof so "one may go out and wet the shingles in case of a neighboring fire." He was satisfied to discover, during the renovation of his main house, that a bolt had melted the tip of its old lightning rod while he was in France, but the house had remained unscathed, "so that at length the invention has been of some use to the inventor."[9]

Besides all his books, his new library boasted a variety of scientific paraphernalia, including his electricity equipment and a glass machine that exhibited the flow of blood through the body. For his reading comfort, Franklin built a great armchair set on rockers with an overhead fan that was powered by a foot pedal. Among his musical instruments were an armonica, a harpsichord, a "glassichord" similar to his armonica, a viola, and bells.

From James Watt, the famed Birmingham steam engine maker, he imported, and made some improvements on, the first rudimentary copying machine. Documents would be written with a slow-drying ink made of gum arabic and then pressed on sheets of moist tissue paper to make copies for as long as the ink was still wet, usually a full day. Franklin, who had first used the machine in Passy, liked it so much that he ordered another that he gave to Jefferson.[10]

Franklin took special pride in one particularly handy invention, a mechanical arm that could retrieve and replace books from upper shelves. He wrote a description of it, filled with drawings and diagrams and instructive tips, that was as detailed as the scientific treatises he had written on his ocean crossing. It was typical of Franklin. Throughout his life, he loved immersing himself in minutiae and trivia in a manner so obsessive that it might today be described as geeky. He was meticulous in describing every technical detail of his inventions, be it the library arm, stove, or lightning rod. In his essays, ranging from his arguments against hereditary honors to his discussions of trade, he provided reams of detailed calculations and historical footnotes. Even in his most humorous parodies, such as his proposal for the study of farts, the cleverness was enhanced by his inclusion of mock-serious facts, trivia, calculations, and learned precedents.[11]

This penchant was on display in its most charming manner in a long letter he wrote to his young friend Kitty Shipley, daughter of the bishop, on the art of procuring pleasant dreams. It contained all of his theories, some more sound than others, on nutrition, exercise, fresh air, and health. Exercise should precede meals, he advised, not follow them. There should be a constant supply of fresh air in the bedroom; Methuselah, he reminded, always slept outdoors. He propounded a thorough, though not scientifically valid, theory of how air in a stifled room gets saturated and thus prevents people's pores from expelling "putrid particles." After a full discourse on the science and pseudoscience, he provided three important ways to avoid unpleasant dreams:

1. By eating moderately, less perspirable matter is produced in a given time; hence the bed-clothes receive it longer before they are saturated, and we may therefore sleep longer before we are made uneasy by their refusing to receive any more.
2. By using thinner and more porous bed-clothes, which will suffer the perspirable matter more easily to pass through them, we are less incommoded, such being longer tolerable.
3. When you are awakened by this uneasiness, and find you cannot easily sleep again, get out of bed, beat up and turn your pillow, shake the bed-clothes well, with at least twenty shakes, then throw the bed open and leave it to cool; in the meanwhile, continuing undressed, walk about your chamber till your skin has had time to discharge its load, which it will do sooner as the air may be dried and colder. When you

begin to feel the cool air unpleasant, then return to your bed, and you will soon fall asleep, and your sleep will be sweet and pleasant . . . If you happen to be too indolent to get out of bed, you may, instead of it, lift up your bed-clothes with one arm and leg, so as to draw in a good deal of fresh air, and by letting them fall force it out again. This, re-peated twenty times, will so clear them of the perspirable matter they have imbibed, as to permit your sleeping well for some time afterwards. But this latter method is not equal to the former. Those who do not love trouble, and can afford to have two beds, will find great luxury in rising, when they wake in a hot bed, and going into the cool one.

He concluded on a sweet note: "There is a case in which the most punctual observance of them will be totally fruitless. I need not men-tion this case to you, my dear friend, but my account of the art would be imperfect without it. The case is, when the person who desires to have pleasant dreams has not taken care to preserve, what is necessary above all things, A GOOD CONSCIENCE." [12]

Pennsylvania was prospering at the time. "The crops are plentiful," he wrote a friend, "working people have plenty of employ." Yet, as usual, the state's politicians were split into two factions. On one side were the populists, made up mainly of local shopkeepers and rural farmers, who supported the very democratic state constitution, with its directly elected unicameral legislature, that Franklin had helped write; on the other side were those more frightened of rabble rule, in-cluding middle- and upper-class property owners. Franklin fit philo-sophically in both camps, both sought his support, and both he obliged. So both nominated him for the state executive council and then its presidency, the equivalent of the governorship, to which he was elected almost unanimously. [13]

Pleased to find that he was still so popular, Franklin took great pride in his election. "Old as I am," he told a nephew, "I am not yet grown insensible with respect to reputation." To Bishop Shipley he conceded that "the remains of ambition from which I had imagined myself free" had successfully seduced him.

He also enjoyed the fact that, after years of watching his reputation be pricked by partisan attacks, he could gain prestige by being above the fray. "He has destroyed party rage in our state," gushed Benjamin Rush after dining with him, "or to borrow an allusion from one of his discoveries, his presence and advice, like oil upon troubled waters, have composed the contending waves of faction." It was a talent that would soon serve him and his nation very well.[14]

THE CONSTITUTIONAL CONVENTION OF 1787

The need for a new federal constitution became apparent, to those who wanted to notice, just a few months after the ratification of the Articles of Confederation back in 1781, when a messenger reached the Congress with the wondrous news of the victory at Yorktown. There was no money in the national treasury to pay the messenger's expenses, so the members had to pull coins from their own pockets. Under the Articles, the Congress had no power to levy taxes, or do much of anything else. Instead, it attempted to requisition money from the states, the way colonial leaders had once wished the king would do, and the states, as the king and his ministers had once feared, often did not respond.

By 1786, the situation was ominous. A former Revolutionary War officer named Daniel Shays led a rebellion of poor farmers in western Massachusetts against tax and debt collections, and there were worries that the anarchy would spread. The Congress, which was then meeting in New York, had been wandering from venue to venue, often unable to pay its bills or sometimes muster a quorum. The thirteen states were indulging in their independence not only from Britain but also from one another. New York imposed fees on all vessels coming from New Jersey, which retaliated by taxing a New York harbor lighthouse on Sandy Hook. Other states were in the process of being formed— including one called Franklin, later renamed Tennessee—that struggled to sort out their potential relationship with the existing states. When the settlers who wished to form the new state of Franklin sought his advice on how to deal with the rival claims of North Carolina, he told them to submit the whole matter to the Congress, which everyone knew would do little good.[15]

After Maryland and Virginia were unable to resolve some border and navigation disputes, a multistate conference was convened in Annapolis to address them along with larger issues of trade and cooperation. Only five states attended and little was accomplished, but James Madison and Alexander Hamilton, along with others who saw the need for a stronger national government, used the gathering to call for a federal convention, ostensibly designed merely to amend the Articles of Confederation. It was scheduled for Philadelphia in May 1787.

The stakes were enormous, as Franklin, who was selected as one of Pennsylvania's delegates, made clear in a letter he sent to Jefferson in Paris: "Our federal constitution is generally thought defective, and a convention, first proposed by Virginia, and since recommended by Congress, is to assemble here next month, to revise it and propose amendments . . . If it does not do good it will do harm, as it will show that we have not the wisdom enough among us to govern ourselves."[16]

So they gathered in the abnormally hot and humid summer of 1787 to draft, in deepest secrecy, a new American constitution that would turn out to be the most successful ever written by human hand. The men there formed, in Jefferson's famous assessment later, "an assembly of demi-gods." If so, they were mainly young ones. Hamilton and Charles Pinckney were 29. (Vain about his age as well as his wealth, Pinckney pretended to be but 24 so he could pass for the youngest member, who was in fact Jonathan Dayton of New Jersey, 26.) At 81, Franklin was the oldest member by fifteen years and exactly twice the average age of the rest of the members.[17]

When General Washington arrived in town on May 13, his first act was to pay a call on Franklin, who opened his new dining room along with a cask of dark beer to entertain him. Among the many roles that Philadelphia's celebrated sage played at the convention was that of symbolic host. His garden and shady mulberry tree, just a few hundred yards from the statehouse, became a respite from the debates, a place where delegates could talk over tea, hear Franklin's tales, and be calmed into a mood of compromise. Among the sixteen grand murals in the U.S. Capitol's Great Experiment Hall depicting scenes of historical importance, from the Mayflower Compact to the suffragette marches, is a garden scene of Hamilton, Madison, and James Wilson talking to Franklin under the shade of his mulberry tree.

If his health permitted and ambition desired, Franklin could have been the only person other than Washington with a chance of becoming the chairman of the convention. He chose instead to be the one to nominate Washington. Unfortunately, heavy rains and a flare-up of his kidney stones made him miss the opening day, May 25, so he asked another member of his delegation to nominate Washington. In his journal of the convention, Madison recorded that "the nomination came with particular grace from Pennsylvania, as Dr. Franklin alone could have been thought of as a competitor."

On Monday, May 28, Franklin arrived to take his seat at one of the fourteen round tables in the East Room of the statehouse, where he had spent so many years. According to some later accounts, it was a grand entrance: to minimize his pain, he was reportedly transported the block from his home in an enclosed sedan chair he had brought from Paris, which was carried by four prisoners from the Walnut Street jail. They held the chair aloft on flexible rods and walked slowly to prevent any painful jostling.[18]

Franklin's benign countenance and venerable grace as he took his seat every morning, and his preference for wry storytelling over argumentative oratory, added a calming presence. "He exhibits daily a spectacle of transcendent benevolence by attending the convention punctually," said Benjamin Rush, who added that Franklin had declared the convention "the most august and respectable assembly he was ever in."

Franklin could be doddering at times, a bit unfocused in his speeches, and occasionally baffling in a few of his suggestions. Still, the delegates usually respected him and always indulged him. This mix of feelings was tellingly recorded by one member, William Pierce of Georgia:

> Dr. Franklin is well known to be the greatest philosopher of the present age; all the operations of nature he seems to understand, the very heavens obey him, and the clouds yield up their lightning to be

imprisoned in his rod. But what claim he has to be a politician, posterity must determine. It is certain that he does not shine much in public council. He is no speaker, nor does he seem to let politics engage his attention. He is, however, a most extraordinary man, and tells a story in a style more engaging than anything I ever heard.

Over the ensuing four months, many of Franklin's pet proposals—a unicameral legislature, prayers, an executive council instead of president, no salaries for officeholders—were politely listened to and, sometimes with a bit of embarrassment, tabled. However, he brought to the convention floor three unique and crucial strengths that made him central to the historic compromise that saved the nation.

First, he was far more comfortable with democracy than most of the delegates, who tended to regard the word and concept as dangerous rather than desirable. "The evils we experience," declared Elbridge Gerry of Massachusetts, "flow from the excess of democracy." The people, Roger Sherman of Connecticut concurred, "should have as little to do as may be possible about government." Franklin was at the other end of the spectrum. Though averse to rabble rule, he favored direct elections, trusted the average citizen, and resisted anything resembling elitism. The constitution he had drafted for Pennsylvania, with its popularly elected single-chamber legislature, was the most democratic of all the new states'.

Second, he was, by far, the most traveled of the delegates, and he knew not only the nations of Europe but the thirteen states, appreciating both what they had in common and how they differed. As a postmaster he had helped bind America together. He was one of the few men equally at home visiting the Carolinas as Connecticut—both places where he had once franchised print shops—and he could discuss, as he had done, indigo farming with a Virginia planter and trade economics with a Massachusetts merchant.

Third, and what would prove most important of all, he embodied a spirit of Enlightenment tolerance and pragmatic compromise. "Both sides must part with some of their demands," he preached at one point, in a phrase that would be his mantra. "We are sent hither to *consult*, not to *contend*, with each other," he said at another. "His disarmingly candid manner masked a very complex personality," the con-

stitutional historian Richard Morris has written, "but his accommodating nature would time after time conciliate jarring interests."[19]

These three attributes proved invaluable in resolving the core issues facing the convention. The greatest of these was whether America would remain thirteen separate states or become one nation, or—if
the demigods could prove so ingenious—some magical combination
of both, as Franklin had first suggested in his Albany Plan of Union
back in 1754. This issue was manifest in various specific ways: Would
Congress be directly elected by the people or chosen by the state legislatures? Would representation be based on population or be equal for
each state? Would the national government or the state governments
be sovereign?

America was deeply split on this set of issues. Some people, Franklin initially among them, were in favor of creating a supreme national
government and reducing the states to a subordinate role. On the
other side were those fervently opposed to any surrender of state sovereignty, which had been enshrined in the Articles of Confederation.
The call for the convention expressly declared that its purpose would
be to revise the Articles, not abandon them. The most radical proponents of states' rights even refused to attend. "I smell a rat," declared
Patrick Henry. Samuel Adams justified his own absence by saying, "I
stumble at the threshold. I meet with a national government instead of
a federal union of sovereign states."[20]

The Virginia delegation, led by Madison and Edmund Randolph,
arrived in Philadelphia early and proceeded to do just what the states'
rights camp feared: they proposed scrapping the Articles entirely and
starting afresh with a new constitution for a strong national government. It would be headed by a very powerful House of Representatives
elected directly by the people based on proportional representation.
The House would select members of an upper chamber, the president,
and the judiciary.

Franklin had long favored a legislature with only one directly
elected house, seeing little reason to place checks on the democratic
will of the people, and he had designed such a system in Pennsylvania.
But in its first week the convention decided this was, in fact, too democratic by half. Madison recorded: " 'The national Legislature ought

to consist of two branches' was agreed to without debate or dissent, except that of Pennsylvania, given probably from complaisance to Dr. Franklin, who was understood to be partial to a single House of Legislation." One modification was made to the Virginia plan. To give the state governments some stake in the new Congress, the delegates decided that the upper chamber, dubbed the Senate after the Roman precedent, would be chosen by the state legislatures rather than by the House of Representatives. (This procedure remained in effect until 1913.)[21]

The central issue, however, remained unresolved. Would votes in the houses of Congress be in proportion to population or, as per the Articles of Confederation, equal for each state? The dispute was not only a philosophical one between proponents of a strong national government and those who favored protecting the rights of the states. It was also a power struggle: little states, such as Delaware and New Jersey, feared they would be overwhelmed by the big states such as Virginia and New York.

The debate grew heated, threatening to break up the convention, and on June 11 Franklin decided it was time to try to restore a spirit of compromise. He had written his speech in advance and because of his health asked another delegate to read it aloud. "Until this point [about] the proportion of representation came before us," he began, "our debates were carried on with great coolness and temper." After making his plea that members consult rather than contend, he expressed a sentiment that he had preached for much of his life, starting with the rules he had written for his Junto sixty years earlier, about the dangers of being too assertive in debate. "Declarations of a fixed opinion, and of determined resolution never to change it, neither enlighten nor convince us," he said. "Positiveness and warmth on one side, naturally beget their like on the other." He had personally been willing, he said, to revise many of his opinions, including the desirability of a unicameral legislature. Now it was time for all members to compromise.

Franklin went on to propose a few suggestions, some of them sensible, others rather odd. He defended the idea of proportional representation with the historical example of how Scotland, despite its smaller representation in the British Parliament, had avoided being overwhelmed by England. Then, with his love of detail, he provided a lengthy mathematical set of calculations showing how smaller states could garner enough votes to match the power of larger ones. There were other remedies to be considered. Perhaps the larger states could give up some of their land to the smaller ones. "If it should be found necessary to diminish Pennsylvania, I should not be averse to the giving a part of it to New Jersey, and another to Delaware." But if that was not feasible, he suggested an even more complex option: there could be equal tax contributions requisitioned from each state, and equal votes in Congress from each state on how to spend this money, then a supplemental requisition from larger states, with proportional votes in Congress on how to spend that fund.[22]

Franklin's speech was long, complex, and at times baffling. Were these all serious suggestions or were some of them merely theoretical discourses? Members seemed not to know. He made no motion to vote on his suggestion for adjusting borders or creating separate treasury funds, nor did any of the other delegates. More important than his specific ideas was his tone of moderation and conciliation. His speech, with its openness to new ideas and absence of one-sided advocacy, provided time for tempers to cool, and his call for creative compromises had an effect.

A few minutes later, Roger Sherman of Connecticut rose to suggest another possible approach: the House of Representatives would be apportioned by population and the Senate would have equal votes for each state. Samuel Johnson, also of that state, explained the thinking behind what would become known as the Connecticut Compromise. The new country was, in some ways, "one political society," but in other ways it was a federation of separate states, yet these two concepts need not conflict, for they could be combined as "halves of a unique whole." There was, however, little discussion of the plan. By a 6–5 vote, the idea was rejected, for the time being, in favor of proportional representation in both chambers.

As the days grew even hotter, so again did the dispute over representation. William Paterson of New Jersey proposed a counterplan, based on amending the Articles rather than supplanting them, that featured a single-house legislature in which each state, large or small, would have one vote. The larger states were able to defeat that idea, but the debate grew so intense that one Delaware delegate suggested that, if the large states sought to impose a national government, "the small ones will find some foreign ally of more honor and good faith, who will take them by the hand and do them justice."

Once again it was time for Franklin to try to restore equanimity, and this time he did so in an unexpected way. In a speech on June 28, he suggested that they open each session with a prayer. With the convention "groping as it were in the dark to find political truth," he said, "how has it happened that we have not hitherto once thought of humbly applying to the Father of lights to illuminate our understandings?" Then he added, in a passage destined to become famous, "The longer I live, the more convincing proofs I see of this truth—that God governs in the affairs of men. And if a sparrow cannot fall to the ground without his notice, is it probable that an empire can rise without his aid?"

Franklin was a believer, even more so as he grew older, in a rather general and at times nebulous divine providence, the principle that God had a benevolent interest in the affairs of men. But he never showed much faith in the more specific notion of special providence, which held that God would intervene directly based on personal prayer. So the question arises: Did he make his proposal for prayer out of a deep religious faith or out of a pragmatic political belief that it would encourage calm in the deliberations?

There was, as usual, probably an element of both, but perhaps a bit more of the latter. Franklin was never known to pray publicly himself, and he rarely attended church. Yet he thought it useful to remind this assembly of demigods that they were in the presence of a God far greater, and that history was watching as well. To succeed, they had to be awed by the magnitude of their task and be humbled, not assertive. Otherwise, he concluded, "we shall be divided by our little, partial, local interests, our projects will be confounded, and we ourselves shall become a reproach and a by-word down to future ages."[23]

Hamilton warned that the sudden hiring of a chaplain might frighten the public into thinking that "embarrassments and dissensions within the convention had suggested this measure." Franklin replied that a sense of alarm outside the hall might help rather than hurt the deliberations within. Another objection was raised: that there was no money to pay a chaplain. The idea was quietly shelved. On the bottom of his copy of his speech, Franklin appended a note of marvel: "The convention, except three or four persons, thought prayers unnecessary!"[24]

The time had come for Franklin to propose more earthly measures. Two days after his prayer speech—on Saturday, June 30—he helped to set in motion the process that would break the impasse and, to a large extent, shape the new nation. Others had discussed compromises, and now it was time to insist on one and to propose it.

First Franklin succinctly stated the problem: "The diversity of opinions turns on two points. If a proportional representation takes place, the small States contend that their liberties will be in danger. If an equality of votes is to be put in its place, the large States say their money will be in danger."

Then he gently emphasized, in a homespun analogy that drew on his affection for craftsmen and construction, the importance of compromise: "When a broad table is to be made, and the edges of planks do not fit, the artist takes a little from both, and makes a good joint. In like manner here, both sides must part with some of their demands."

Finally, he incorporated a workable compromise into a specific motion. Representatives to the lower House would be popularly elected and apportioned by population, but in the Senate "the Legislatures of the several States shall choose and send an equal number of Delegates." The House would have primary authority over taxes and spending, the Senate over the confirmation of executive officers and matters of state sovereignty.[25]

The convention proceeded to appoint a committee, which included Franklin, to draw up the details of this compromise, and by a close vote it was finally adopted, in much the form Franklin had proposed, on July 16. "This was Franklin's great victory in the Convention," declares Van Doren, "that he was the author of the compromise which held the delegates together."

That, perhaps, gives him a bit too much credit. He was not the author of the idea, nor the first to suggest it. It grew from proposals by

Sherman of Connecticut and others. Franklin's role, nonetheless, was crucial. He embodied the spirit and issued the call for compromise, he selected the most palatable option available and refined it, and he wrote the motion and picked the right moment to offer it. His prestige, his neutrality, and his eminence made it easier for all to swallow. The artisan had taken a little from all sides and made a joint good enough to hold together a nation for centuries.

A few days after he offered his compromise, Franklin hosted some of the delegates for tea in his garden, including Elbridge Gerry of Massachusetts, a leading skeptic of unfettered democracy. But Franklin's shaded garden was a place where controversies could be cooled. Gerry invited along a Massachusetts minister named Manasseh Cutler, a portly and congenial character who was in town pushing the territorial schemes of the Ohio Company, which he had helped found. In his journal Cutler noted that "my knees smote together" at the prospect of meeting the celebrated sage, but he was immediately put at ease by Franklin's unassuming style. "I was highly delighted with the extensive knowledge he appeared to have of every subject, the brightness of his memory, and clearness and vivacity of all his mental faculties, notwithstanding his age," Cutler recorded. "His manners are perfectly easy, and every thing about him seems to diffuse an unrestrained freedom and happiness. He has an incessant vein of humor, accompanied with an uncommon vivacity, which seems as natural and involuntary as his breathing."

Discovering that Cutler was an avid botanist, Franklin produced a curiosity he had just received, a ten-inch snake with two perfectly formed heads preserved in a vial. Imagine what would happen, Franklin speculated with amusement, if one head of the snake attempted to go to the left of a twig and the other head went to the right and they could not agree. He was about to compare this to an issue that had just been debated at the convention, but some of the other delegates stopped him. "He seemed to forget that everything in the convention was to be kept a profound secret," Cutler noted. "But the secrecy of convention matters was suggested to him, which stopped him, and deprived me of the story he was going to tell."

The point Franklin was about to make, no doubt, was the same one he had made in the Pennsylvania state convention in 1776, when he argued against a two-chamber legislature because it might fall prey to the fate of the fabled two-headed snake that died of thirst when its heads could not agree on which way to pass a twig. Indeed, in a paper he wrote in 1789 extolling Pennsylvania's unicameral legislature, he again referred to what he called "the famous political fable of the snake with two heads." He had come to accept, however, that in forging the compromise needed to create a national Congress, two heads could be better than one.[26]

On other issues as well, Franklin was usually on the side favoring fewer fetters on direct democracy. He opposed, for example, giving the president a veto over acts of Congress, which he saw as the repository of the people's will. Colonial governors, he reminded the delegates, had used that power to extort more influence and money whenever the legislature wanted a measure approved. When Hamilton favored making the president a near-monarch to be chosen for life, Franklin noted that he provided living proof that a person's life sometimes lasted longer than his mental and physical prime. Instead, it would be more democratic to relegate the president to the role of average citizen after his term. The argument that "returning to the mass of the people was degrading," he said, "was contrary to republican principles. In free Governments the rulers are the servants, and the people their superiors and sovereigns. For the former therefore to return among the latter was not to degrade but to promote them."

Likewise, he argued that Congress should have the power to impeach the president. In the past, when impeachment was not possible, the only method people had for removing a corrupt ruler was through assassination, "in which he was not only deprived of his life but of the opportunity of vindicating his character." Franklin also felt that it would be more democratic for executive power to reside with a small council, as it did in Pennsylvania, rather than one man. This was a hard debate to have with Washington sitting in the chair, as it was widely assumed that he would be the first president. So Franklin noted diplomatically that the first man to take the office would likely be benevolent, but the person who came next (perhaps he had a sense that it could be John Adams) might harbor more autocratic tendencies. On this issue Franklin lost, but the convention did decide to institutionalize the role of the Cabinet.

He also advocated, unsuccessfully, the direct election of federal judges, instead of permitting the president or Congress to select them. As usual, he made his argument by telling a tale. It was the practice in Scotland for judges to be nominated by that country's lawyers, who always selected the ablest of the profession in order to get rid of him and share his practice among themselves. In America, it would be in the best interest of voters "to make the best choice," which was the way it should be.[27]

Many of the delegates believed strongly that only those who owned substantial property should be eligible for office, as was the case in most states other than Pennsylvania. Young Charles Pinckney of South Carolina went so far as to propose that the wealth requirement for president should be $100,000, until it was pointed out that this might exclude Washington. Franklin rose and, in Madison's words, "expressed his dislike of everything that tended to debase the spirit of the common people." His democratic sensibilities were offended by any suggestion that the Constitution "should betray a great partiality to the rich." On the contrary, he said, "some of the greatest rogues I was ever acquainted with, were the richest rogues." Likewise, he spoke out against any property requirements on the right to vote. "We should not depress the virtue and public spirit of our common people." On these issues he was successful.[28]

On only one issue did Franklin take what could be considered the less democratic position, though he did not recognize it as such. Federal officials, he argued, should serve without pay. In *The Radicalism of the American Revolution,* historian Gordon Wood contends that Franklin's proposal reflected the "classical sentiments of aristocratic leadership." Even John Adams, generally less democratic in his outlook, wrote from London that under such a policy "all offices would be monopolized by the rich, the poor and middling ranks would be excluded and an aristocratic despotism would immediately follow."

Franklin, I think, did not intend for his proposal to be elitist or exclusionary, but instead saw it as a way to limit corrupting influences. In his many letters on the subject, he never considered, though he should have, that his plan might limit the jobs to those who could afford to work for free. Indeed, he seemed quite oblivious to this argument. Instead, he based his position on his faith in citizen volunteers and his long-standing belief that a pursuit of profit had corrupted English government. It was a case he had made in an exchange of letters with William Strahan three years earlier, and he used almost the exact same language on the floor of the convention:

> There are two passions which have a powerful influence in the affairs of men. These are *ambition* and *avarice;* the love of power and the love of money. Separately, each of these has great force in prompting men to action; but, when united in view of the same object, they have in many minds the most violent effects . . . And of what kind are the men that will strive for this profitable preeminence, through all the bustle of cabal, the heat of contention, the infinite mutual abuse of parties, tearing to pieces the best of characters? It will not be the wise and moderate, the lovers of peace and good order, the men fittest for the trust. It will be the bold and the violent, the men of strong passions and indefatigable activity in their selfish pursuits.

On this issue he found almost no support, and the idea was put aside with no debate. "It was treated with great respect," Madison recorded, "but rather for the author of it than from any conviction of its expediency or practicability."[29]

There were, through the long and hot summer, some occasions for humor. Gouverneur Morris of Pennsylvania, who wrote with a taut and serious pen but at times acted as the congressional jester, was dared by Hamilton, for the price of a dinner, to slap the austere and intimidating Washington on the shoulder and say, "My dear general, how happy I am to see you look so well!" Morris did, but after weathering the look from Washington's face declared that he would not do so again for a thousand dinners. Elbridge Gerry, arguing against a large standing army, lasciviously compared it to a standing penis: "An excellent assurance of domestic tranquility, but a dangerous temptation to foreign adventure."[30]

When it was all over, many compromises had been made, including on the issue of slavery. Some members were distressed because they felt that the final result usurped too much state sovereignty, others because they thought it did not create a strong enough national government. The cantankerous Luther Martin of Maryland sneered contemptuously that they had concocted a "perfect medley," and left before the final vote.

He was right, except for his contemptuous sneer. The medley was, indeed, as close to perfect as mortals could have achieved. From its profound first three words, "We the people," to the carefully calibrated compromises and balances that followed, it created an ingenious system in which the power of the national government as well as that of the states derived directly from the citizenry. And thus it fulfilled the motto on the nation's great seal, suggested by Franklin in 1776, of *E Pluribus Unum*, out of many one.

With the wisdom of a patient chess player and the practicality of a scientist, Franklin realized that they had succeeded not because they were self-assured, but because they were willing to concede that they might be fallible. "We are making experiments in politics," he wrote la Rochefoucauld. To Du Pont de Nemours he confessed, "We must not expect that a new government may be formed as a game of chess may be played, by a skillful hand, without a fault."[31]

Franklin's final triumph was to express these sentiments with a wry but powerful charm in a remarkable closing address to the convention. The speech was a testament to the virtue of intellectual tolerance and to the evil of presumed infallibility, and it proclaimed for the ages the enlightened creed that became central to America's freedom. They were the most eloquent words Franklin ever wrote—and perhaps the best ever written by anyone about the magic of the American system and the spirit of compromise that created it:

> I confess that I do not entirely approve this Constitution at present; but sir, I am not sure I shall never approve it: For, having lived long, I have experienced many instances of being obliged, by better information or fuller consideration, to change opinions even on important subjects, which I once thought right, but found to be otherwise. It is therefore that, the older I grow, the more apt I am to doubt my own judgment and pay more respect to the judgment of others.
>
> Most men, indeed as well as most sects in religion, think themselves in possession of all truth, and that wherever others differ from them, it is so far error. Steele, a Protestant, in a dedication, tells the Pope that

the only difference between our two churches in their opinions of the certainty of their doctrine is, the Romish Church is infallible, and the Church of England is never in the wrong. But, though many private persons think almost as highly of their own infallibility as of that of their sect, few express it so naturally as a certain French lady, who, in a little dispute with her sister said: "I don't know how it happens, sister, but I meet with nobody but myself that is *always* in the right."

In these sentiments, sir, I agree to this Constitution with all its faults—if they are such—because I think a general government necessary for us . . . I doubt, too, whether any other convention we can obtain may be able to make a better Constitution; for, when you assemble a number of men, to have the advantage of their joint wisdom, you inevitably assemble with those men all their prejudices, their passions, their errors of opinion, their local interests, and their selfish views. From such an assembly can a perfect production be expected?

It therefore astonishes me, sir, to find this system approaching so near to perfection as it does; and I think it will astonish our enemies, who are waiting with confidence to hear that our councils are confounded like those of the builders of Babel, and that our States are on the point of separation, only to meet hereafter for the purpose of cutting one another's throats. Thus I consent, sir, to this Constitution because I expect no better, and because I am not sure that it is not the best.

He concluded by pleading that, "for the sake of our posterity, we shall act heartily and unanimously." To that end, he made a motion that the convention adopt the device of declaring that the document had been accepted by all of the states, which would allow even the minority of delegates who dissented to sign it. "I cannot help expressing a wish that every member of the convention who may still have objections to it, would, with me, on this occasion, doubt a little of his own infallibility, and, to make manifest our unanimity, put his name to this instrument."[32]

And so it was that when Franklin finished, most of the delegates, even some with doubts, heeded his urgings and lined up by state delegation for the historic signing. As they did so, Franklin turned their attention to the sun carved on the back of Washington's chair and observed that painters often found it difficult to distinguish in their art a rising sun from a setting one. "I have," he said, "often in the course of the session, and the vicissitudes of my hopes and fears as to its issue, looked at that behind the President without being able to tell whether it was rising or setting. But now at length I have the happiness to know that it is a rising and not a setting sun."

According to a tale recorded by James McHenry of Maryland, he made his point in a pithier way to an anxious lady named Mrs. Powel, who accosted him outside the hall. What type of government, she asked, have you delegates given us? To which he replied, "A republic, madam, if you can keep it."[33]

The historian Clinton Rossiter has called Franklin's closing speech "the most remarkable performance of a remarkable life," and the Yale scholar Barbara Oberg calls it "the culmination of Franklin's life as a propagandist, persuader and cajoler of people." With his deft and self-deprecating use of double negatives—"I am not sure I shall never approve it," "I am not sure that it is not the best"—he emphasized the humility and appreciation for human fallibility that was necessary to form a nation. Opponents attacked Franklin's compromising approach as lacking in principle, yet that was the point of his message. "A stand for compromise," Oberg points out, "is not the stuff of heroism, virtue, or moral certainty. But it is the essence of the democratic process."[34]

Throughout his life, Franklin had, by his thoughts and activities, helped to lay the foundation for the democratic republic that this Constitution enshrined. He had begun as a young man by teaching his fellow tradesmen ways to become virtuous, diligent, and responsible citizens. Then he sought to enlist them in associations—Juntos, libraries, fire departments, neighborhood patrols, and militias—for their mutual benefit and the good of the common community. Later, he created networks, from the postal service to the American Philosophical Society, designed to foster the connections that would integrate an emerging nation. Finally, in the 1750s, he began pushing the colonies to gain strength through unity, to stand together for common purposes in a way that helped shape a national identity.

Since that time, he had been instrumental in shaping every major document that led to the creation of the new republic. He was the only person to sign all four of its founding papers: the Declaration of Independence, the treaty with France, the peace accord with Britain, and the Constitution. In addition, he devised the first federal scheme for America, the unfulfilled Albany Plan of 1754, under which the separate states and a national government would have shared power. And the Articles of Confederation he proposed in 1775 were a closer approximation of the final Constitution than were the weak and ill-fated alternative Articles adopted in 1781.

The Constitution, wrote Henry May in his book *The Enlightenment in America*, reflected "all the virtues of the moderate Enlightenment, and also one of its faults: the belief that everything can be settled by compromise." For Franklin, who embodied the Enlightenment and its spirit of compromise, this was hardly a fault. For him, compromise was not only a practical approach but a moral one. Tolerance, humility, and a respect for others required it. On almost every issue for more than two centuries, this supposed fault has served the Constitution, and the nation it formed, quite well. There was only one great issue that could not, then or later, be solved by constitutional compromise: slavery. And that indeed was the issue on which Franklin, as his life neared its end, chose to take an uncompromising stand.[35]

ENDGAME

Franklin's role in the miracle at Philadelphia could have been a fitting finale to a career spent creating the possibility of a free and democratic republic, and for most people, or at least most people of his era approaching 82, it would have been enough to sate any ambition. Now he could, if he wanted, retire from public life knowing that he was widely revered and had outlasted any enemies. Nevertheless, a month after personally presenting a copy of the new federal Constitution to the Pennsylvania Assembly, he accepted reelection for a third one-year term as the state's president. "It was my intention to decline serving another year as president, that I might be at liberty to take a trip to Boston in the spring," he wrote his sister. "I have now upwards of fifty years employed in public offices."

He would, in fact, never travel nor see his sister again. His kidney stones and her health, he noted, made it so they would have to be satisfied by letters rather than visits. In addition, as he freely admitted, his pride made him still appreciate public recognition. "It is no small pleasure to me, and I suppose it will give my sister pleasure, that after such long trial of me, I should be elected a third time by my fellow citizens," he wrote. "This universal and unbounded confidence of a whole people flatters my vanity much more than a peerage could do."

Franklin's letters to his sister were filled with such candid comments, especially during his later years. At one point he scolded that "your Post Office is very badly managed" and decried her propensity to get into little feuds. This led to an amusing riff on how the Franklins "were always subject to being a little miffy." What had happened, he asked, to the Folger cousins in Nantucket? "They are wonderfully shy. But I admire their honest plainness of speech. About a year ago I invited two of them to dine with me. Their answer was that they would—if they could not do better. I suppose they did better, for I never saw them afterwards." [36]

To Noah Webster, the famous lexicographer who had dedicated his *Dissertations on the English Language* to him, Franklin lamented the loose new word usages infecting the language, a common complaint of curmudgeonly writers but a bit atypical of the jovial Franklin, who had once taken pleasure in inventing new English words and, with even more pleasure, amusing the ladies of Paris with new French ones. "I find a verb formed from the substantive *notice;* 'I should not have *noticed* this, were it not that the gentleman, etc.' Also another verb from the substantive *advocate;* 'the Gentleman who *advocates* or who has *advocated* that motion, etc.' Another from the substantive *progress,* the most awkward and abominable of the three; 'the committee, having *progressed,* resolved to adjourn . . . If you should happen to be of my opinion with respect to these innovations, you will use your authority in reprobating them." [37]

He also finally resumed work on his autobiography. He had written 87 manuscript pages in Twyford in 1771, and then added 12 more in Passy in 1784. Writing steadily from August 1788 until May of the following year, he completed another 119 pages, which brought him up to his arrival in England as a colonial agent. "I omit all facts and transactions that may not have a tendency to benefit the young reader," he wrote to Vaughan. His purpose was still to provide a self-help manual for America's ambitious middle class by describing "my success in emerging from poverty" and "the advantages of certain modes of conduct which I observed." [38]

By now he was facing ever greater pain from his kidney stones, and he resorted to using laudanum, a tincture of opium and alcohol. "I am so interrupted by extreme pain, which obliges me to have recourse to opium, that between the effects of both, I have but little time in which I can write anything," he complained to Vaughan. He also worried that what he had written was not worth publishing. "Give me your candid opinion whether I had best publish it or suppress it," he asked, "for I am grown so old and feeble in mind, as well as body, that I cannot place any confidence in my own judgment." He had now begun to dictate the work to Benny rather than write it by hand, but he was able to complete only a few more pages.

Friends sent him various home remedies for kidney stones, including a suggestion from Vaughan, which amused Franklin, that a small dose of hemlock might work. At times, he could be cheerful enough about his maladies and repeat his maxim that those who "drink to the bottom of the cup must expect to meet some of the dregs," as he did to his old friend Elizabeth Partridge. He was still, he said, "joking, laughing and telling merry stories, as when you first knew me, a young man about fifty." [39]

Yet Franklin was becoming resigned to the fact that he did not have much longer to live, and his letters took on a tone of sanguine farewell. "Hitherto this long life has been tolerably happy," he wrote to Caty Ray Greene, the girl who had captured his mind and heart thirty-five years earlier. "If I were allowed to live it over again, I should make no objection, only wishing for leave to do what authors do in a second edition of their works, correct some of my errata." When Washington became president that year, Franklin wrote to him that it made him glad he was still alive: "For my own personal ease, I should have died two years ago; but, though those years have been spent in excruciating pain, I am pleased that I have lived them, since they have brought me to see our present situation." [40]

He was also sanguine about the revolution now welling up in his

beloved France. The explosion of democratic sentiments was producing "mischief and trouble," he noted, but he assumed that it would
lead to greater democracy and eventually a good constitution. So most
of his letters to his French friends were inappropriately lighthearted.
"Are you still living?" he wrote the French scientist Jean-Baptiste Le
Roy, his friend and Passy neighbor, in late 1789. "Or have the mob of
Paris mistaken the head of a monopolizer of knowledge for a monopolizer of corn, and paraded it about the streets upon a pole?" (It was
also in this letter that he famously noted that "nothing can be said to
be certain except death and taxes.") He assured Louis-Guillaume le
Veillard, his neighbor and closest friend in Passy, that it was all for the
good. "When the fermentation is over and the troubling parts subsided, the wine will be fine and good, and cheer the hearts of those
that drink it." [41]

Franklin was wrong, sadly wrong, about the French Revolution,
though he would not live long enough to learn it. Le Veillard would
soon lose his life to the guillotine. So would Lavoisier the chemist,
who had worked with him on the Mesmer investigation. Condorcet,
the economist who had accompanied Franklin to his famed meetings
with Voltaire, would be imprisoned and poison himself in his cell. And
la Rochefoucauld, who had translated the state constitutions for
Franklin and engaged him in a lively correspondence since his departure, would be stoned to death by a mob.

SLAVERY

In the very last year of his life, Franklin was to embark on one final
public mission, a moral crusade that would help ameliorate one of the
few blemishes on a life spent fighting for freedom. Throughout much
of the eighteenth century, slavery had been an institution that few
whites questioned. Even in brotherly Philadelphia, ownership continued to climb until about 1760, when almost 10 percent of the city's
population were slaves. But views had begun to evolve, especially after
the ringing words of the Declaration and the awkward compromises
of the Constitution. George Mason of Virginia, despite the fact that

he owned two hundred slaves, called the institution "pernicious" at the Constitutional Convention and declared that "every master of slaves is a petty tyrant; they bring the judgment of heaven on a country."

Franklin's views had been evolving as well. He had, as we have seen, owned one or two household slaves off and on for much of his life, and as a young publisher he had carried ads for slave sales. But he had also published, in 1729, one of the nation's first antislavery pieces and had joined the Associates of Dr. Bray to establish schools for blacks in America. Deborah had enrolled her house servants in the Philadelphia school, and after visiting it Franklin had spoken of his "higher opinions of the natural capacities of the black race." In his 1751 "Observations on the Increase of Mankind," he attacked slavery strongly, but mainly from an economic perspective rather than a moral one. In expressing sympathy for the Philadelphia abolitionist Anthony Benezet in the 1770s, he had agreed that the importation of new slaves should end immediately, but he qualified his support for outright abolition by saying it should come "in time." As an agent for Georgia in London, he had defended the right of that colony to keep slaves. But he preached, in articles such as his 1772 "The Somerset Case and the Slave Trade," that one of Britain's great sins against America was foisting slavery on it.

Franklin's conversion culminated in 1787, when he accepted the presidency of the Pennsylvania Society for Promoting the Abolition of Slavery. The group tried to persuade him to present a petition against slavery at the Constitutional Convention, but knowing the delicate compromises being made between north and south, he kept silent on the issue. After that, however, he became outspoken.

One of the arguments against immediate abolition, which Franklin had heretofore accepted, was that it was not practical or safe to free hundreds of thousands of adult slaves into a society for which they were not prepared. (There were about seven hundred thousand slaves in the United States out of a total population of four million in 1790.) So his abolition society dedicated itself not only to freeing slaves but also to helping them become good citizens. "Slavery is such an atrocious debasement of human nature that its very extirpation, if not performed with solicitous care, may sometimes open a source of serious evils," Franklin wrote in a November 1789 address to the public from the society. "The unhappy man, who has long been treated as a brute animal, too frequently sinks beneath the common standard of the human species. The galling chains that bind his body do also fetter his intellectual faculties and impair the social affections of his heart."

As was typical of Franklin, he drew up for the society a meticulously detailed charter and procedures "for improving the condition of free blacks." There would be a twenty-four-person committee divided into four subcommittees:

A Committee of Inspection, who shall superintend the morals, general conduct, and ordinary situation of the free Negroes, and afford them advice and instruction . . .

A Committee of Guardians, who shall place out children and young people with suitable persons, that they may (during a moderate time of apprenticeship or servitude) learn some trade or other business . . .

A Committee of Education, who shall superintend the school instruction of the children and youth of the free blacks. They may either influence them to attend regularly the schools already established in this city, or form others with this view . . .

A Committee of Employ, who shall endeavor to procure constant employment for those free Negroes who are able to work; as the want of this would occasion poverty, idleness, and many vicious habits.[42]

On behalf of the society, Franklin presented a formal abolition petition to Congress in February 1790. "Mankind are all formed by the same Almighty Being, alike objects of his care, and equally designed for the enjoyment of happiness," it declared. The duty of Congress was to secure "the blessings of liberty to the People of the United States," and this should be done "without distinction of color." Therefore, Congress should grant "liberty to those unhappy men who alone in this land of freedom are degraded into perpetual bondage."[43]

Franklin and his petition were roundly denounced by the defenders of slavery, most notably Congressman James Jackson of Georgia, who declared on the House floor that the Bible had sanctioned slavery and, without it, there would be no one to do the hard and hot work on plantations. It was the perfect setup for Franklin's last great parody, written less than a month before he died.

He had begun his literary career sixty-eight years earlier when, as a 16-year-old apprentice, he pretended to be a prudish widow named Silence Dogood, and he made a subsequent career of enlightening readers with similar hoaxes such as "The Trial of Polly Baker" and "An Edict from the King of Prussia." In the spirit of the latter of these essays, he anonymously published in a local newspaper, with appropriate scholarly source citations, a purported speech given by a member of the divan of Algiers one hundred years earlier.

It bore a scathing mirror resemblance to Congressman Jackson's speech. "God is great, and Mahomet is his prophet," it began realistically. Then it went on to attack a petition by a purist sect asking for an end to the practice of capturing and enslaving European Christians to work in Algeria: "If we forbear to make slaves of their people, who in this hot climate are to cultivate our lands? Who are to perform the common labors of our city, and in our families?" An end to the slavery of "infidels" would cause land values to fall and rents to sink by half.

> Who is to indemnify their masters for their loss? Will the state do it? Is our Treasury sufficient? . . . And if we set our slaves free, what is to be done with them? Few of them will return to their countries; they know too well the greater hardships they must there be subject to; they will not embrace our holy religion; they will not adopt our manners; our people will not pollute themselves by intermarrying with them. Must we maintain them as beggars in our streets, or suffer our properties to be the prey of their pillage? For men long accustomed to slavery will not work for a livelihood when not compelled.
>
> And what is there so pitiable in their present condition? . . . Here they are brought into a land where the sun of Islamism gives forth its light, and shines in full splendor, and they have an opportunity of making themselves acquainted with the true doctrine, and thereby saving their immortal souls . . . While serving us, we take care to provide them with every thing, and they are treated with humanity. The laborers in their own country are, as I am well informed, worse fed, lodged, and clothed . . .

How grossly are they mistaken in imagining slavery to be disallowed by the Koran! Are not the two precepts, to quote no more, "Masters, treat your Slaves with kindness; Slaves, serve your Masters with cheerfulness and Fidelity," clear proofs to the contrary? . . . Let us then hear no more of this detestable proposition, the manumission of Christian slaves, the adoption of which would, by depreciating our lands and houses, and thereby depriving so many good citizens of their properties, create universal discontent, and provoke insurrections.[44]

In his parody, Franklin recorded that the Algerian divan ended up rejecting the petition. Congress, likewise, decided that it did not have the authority to act on Franklin's abolition petition.

TO BED

It is not surprising that, at the end of their lives, many people take stock of their religious beliefs. Franklin had never fully joined a church nor subscribed to a sectarian dogma, and he found it more useful to focus on earthly issues rather than spiritual ones. When he narrowly escaped a shipwreck as he neared the English coast in 1757, he had joked to Deborah that, "Were I a Roman Catholic, perhaps I should on this occasion vow to build a chapel to some saint; but as I am not, if I were to vow at all, it should be to build a *lighthouse*." Likewise, when a town in Massachusetts named itself Franklin in 1785 and asked him to donate a church bell, he told them to forsake the steeple and build a library, for which he sent "books instead of a bell, sense being preferable to sound."[45]

As he grew older, Franklin's amorphous faith in a benevolent God seemed to become more firm. "If it had not been for the justice of our cause and the consequent interposition of Providence, in which we had faith, we must have been ruined," he wrote Strahan after the war. "If I had ever before been an atheist, I should now have been convinced of the Being and government of a Deity!"[46]

His support for religion tended to be based on his belief that it was useful and practical in making people behave better, rather than because it was divinely inspired. He wrote a letter, possibly sent in 1786 to Thomas Paine, in response to a manuscript that ridiculed religious devotion. Franklin begged the recipient not to publish his heretical treatise, but he did so on the grounds that the arguments could have harmful practical effects, not on the grounds that they were false. "You yourself may find it easy to live a virtuous life without the assistance afforded by religion," he said, "but think how great a proportion of mankind consists of weak and ignorant men and women, and of inexperienced and inconsiderate youth of both sexes, who have need of the motives of religion to restrain them from vice." In addition, he noted, the personal consequences for the author would likely be odious. "He that spits against the wind, spits in his own face." If the letter was indeed addressed to Paine, it had an effect. He had long been formulating the virulent attack on organized religious faith that he would later title *The Age of Reason*, but he held off publishing it for another seven years, until near the end of his life.[47]

The most important religious role Franklin played—and it was an exceedingly important one in shaping his enlightened new republic—was as an apostle of tolerance. He had contributed to the building funds of each and every sect in Philadelphia, including £5 for the Congregation Mikveh Israel for its new synagogue in April 1788, and he had opposed religious oaths and tests in both the Pennsylvania and federal constitutions. During the July 4 celebrations in 1788, Franklin was too sick to leave his bed, but the parade marched under his window. For the first time, as per arrangements that Franklin had overseen, "the clergy of different Christian denominations, with the rabbi of the Jews, walked arm in arm."[48]

His final summation of his religious thinking came the month before he died, in response to questions from the Rev. Ezra Stiles, president of Yale. Franklin began by restating his basic creed: "I believe in one God, Creator of the Universe. That he governs it by his Providence. That he ought to be worshipped. That the most acceptable service we render to him is doing good to his other children." These beliefs were fundamental to all religions; anything else was mere embellishment.

Then he addressed Stiles's question about whether he believed in Jesus, which was, he said, the first time he had ever been asked directly. The system of morals that Jesus provided, Franklin replied, was "the best the world ever saw or is likely to see." But on the issue of whether Jesus was divine, he provided a surprisingly candid and wry response. "I have," he declared, "some doubts as to his divinity; though it is a question I do not dogmatize upon, having never studied it, and think it needless to busy myself with it now, when I expect soon an opportunity of knowing the truth with less trouble." [49]

The last letter Franklin ever wrote was, fittingly, to Thomas Jefferson, his spiritual heir as the nation's foremost apostle of the Enlightenment's faith in reason, experiment, and tolerance. Jefferson had come to call at Franklin's bedside and provide news of their beleaguered friends in France. "He went over all in succession," Jefferson noted, "with a rapidity and animation almost too much for his strength." Jefferson praised him for getting so far in his memoirs, which he predicted would be very instructive. "I cannot say much of that," replied Franklin, "but I will give you a sample." Then he pulled out a page that described the last weeks of his negotiations in London to avert the war, which he insisted that Jefferson keep as a memento.

Jefferson followed up by asking about an arcane issue that needed resolving: Which maps had been used to draw America's western boundaries in the Paris peace talks? After Jefferson left, Franklin studied the matter and then wrote his final letter. His mind was clear enough to describe, with precision, the decisions they had made and the maps they had used regarding various rivers running into the Bay of Passamaquoddy. [50]

Soon after he finished the letter, Franklin's fever and chest pains began to worsen. For ten days he was confined to bed with a heavy cough and labored breathing. Sally and Richard Bache attended to him, as did Temple and Benny. Polly Stevenson was there as well, pressing him to make a clearer proclamation of his religious faith, pleased that he had a picture of the Day of Judgment by his bedside. Only once during that period was he able to rise briefly, and he asked that his bed be made up so that he could "die in a decent manner." Sally expressed hope that he was recovering, that he might live many years longer. "I hope not," he calmly replied. [51]

Then an abscess in his lung burst, making it impossible for him to talk. Benny approached his bed, and his grandfather reached out to hold his hand for a long time. At eleven that evening, April 17, 1790, Franklin died at the age of 84.

Back in 1728, when he was a fledgling printer imbued with the pride that he believed an honest man should have in his trade, Franklin had composed for himself, or at least for his amusement, a cheeky epitaph that reflected his wry perspective on his pilgrim's progress through this world:

> *The body of*
> *B. Franklin, Printer;*
> *(Like the cover of an old book,*
> *Its contents worn out,*
> *and stripped of its lettering and gilding)*
> *Lies here, food for worms.*
> *But the work shall not be lost:*
> *For it will, (as he believed) appear once more,*
> *In a new and more elegant edition,*
> *Revised and corrected*
> *By the Author.*[52]

Shortly before he died, however, he prescribed something simpler to be placed over the grave site that he would share with his wife. His tombstone should be, he wrote, a marble slab "six feet long, four feet wide, plain, with only a small molding round the upper edge, and this inscription: Benjamin and Deborah Franklin."[53]

Close to twenty thousand mourners, more than had ever before gathered in Philadelphia, watched as his funeral procession made its way to the Christ Church burying ground, a few blocks from his home. In front marched the clergymen of the city, all of them, of every faith.

CHAPTER SEVENTEEN

EPILOGUE

William Franklin: In his will, Franklin bequeathed to his only surviving son nothing more than some worthless land claims in Canada and the forgiveness of any debts he still owed him. "The part he acted against me in the late war, which is of public notoriety, will account for my leaving him no more of an estate he endeavored to deprive me of." William, who thought he had already paid off his debts by deeding over his New Jersey lands, complained about the "shameful injustice" of the will, and for the remaining twenty-five years of his life never returned to America. But he still revered his father's memory, and he did not permit himself another harsh public word about him. Indeed, when his own son, Temple, dithered in producing an edition of Franklin's life and writings, William began work on one of his own, which he hoped would honor his father by showing the "turn of his mind and variety of his knowledge." It was not to be. He had married his Irish landlady, Mary D'Evelyn, but after she died in 1811 he was a broken and lonely man. He died three years later, estranged from his son, suffering in what he called "that solitary state which is most repugnant to my nature."[1]

Temple Franklin: Having inherited a nice share of his grandfather's estate and all of his important papers, Temple returned to England in 1792 and reunited temporarily with his father. Still a charming but aimless rogue, he chafed under his father's pressure to get married and work on Franklin's papers, and he brought the family's dysfunctionality to new heights. He had another illegitimate child, a daughter named Ellen, whose mother was the younger sister of William's new wife, and then he broke bitterly with them all and ran away to Paris, leaving little Ellen Franklin to be raised by William, who was both her uncle and grandfather. For fourteen years, Temple neither reestablished contact with his father nor published the papers of his grandfather, even as unauthorized portions of the *Autobiography* appeared in France. Finally, in 1812, he wrote his father to say he was about to publish the papers and wanted to come to London to consult with him. William, who remembered the cool response he had gotten when he wrote a similar letter to his own father twenty-eight years earlier, was overjoyed. "I shall be happy to see you," he said, "not being able to bear the thought of dying in enmity with one so nearly connected." But Temple never came to England. Instead, in 1817, he published the *Autobiography* (without the final installment) and a haphazard collection of some of his grandfather's papers. He lived the next six years in Paris with yet another mistress, an Englishwoman named Hannah Collyer, whom he married a few months before he died in 1823. She later brought many of Franklin's precious papers back to London, where they were rediscovered in 1840 in the shop of a tailor who was using them as patterns. The papers that Temple abandoned in Philadelphia were scattered to various souvenir hunters until the American Philosophical Society began the process of collecting them in the 1860s.[2]

Sally and Richard Bache: Franklin's loyal daughter and her husband got most of his property, including the Market Street houses, on the condition that Richard "set free his Negro man Bob." (He did, but Bob took to drink, couldn't support himself, and asked to be restored to slavery; the Baches declined, but they let him live in their home for the rest of his life.) Sally was also given the Louis XVI miniature encircled with diamonds, with the stipulation that she not turn "any of those diamonds into ornaments either for herself or daughters and thereby introduce or countenance the expensive, vain and useless fashion of wearing jewels in this country." She sold the diamonds to fulfill her lifelong desire to see England. With her husband, she went to stay with William, with whom she had always remained close. On their return, the Baches settled on a farm in Delaware.

Benjamin Bache: Inheriting Franklin's printing equipment and many of his books, he followed in his grandfather's steps by launching, seventy years after the *New England Courant* was first published, a crusading Jeffersonian newspaper, *The American Aurora.* The paper became fiercely partisan on behalf of those who believed, with a passion that surpassed even Franklin's, in pro-French and democratic policies, and it attacked Washington and then Adams for creating imperial presidencies. It was, for a while, the most popular paper in America, and has been the subject of two recent books. His politics caused a rift with his parents, as did his decision to marry against their wishes a feisty woman named Margaret Markoe. In 1798, he was arrested for sedition and for libeling Adams, but before he could stand trial he died of yellow fever at age 29. By then he was so estranged from his parents that his sisters had to sneak away to see him during his final illness. Margaret promptly married her late husband's pressman, an argumentative Irishman named William Duane, and they kept the *Aurora* going. One of Benny's sisters, Deborah Bache, then married one of Duane's sons from his first marriage.[3]

Polly Stevenson: She inherited nothing more than a silver tankard from the man she had revered for thirty-three years, and she soon became disenchanted with all branches of his family and all things American. When her second son, Tom, went back to England (accompanied by Willie Bache, to study medicine), she wrote him longing letters about her desire to return home as well. But she died in 1795, before she had the chance. Tom ended up back in Philadelphia, where he became a successful doctor; his brother William and sister Eliza stayed in America as well, and they all raised happy families.

The aspiring tradesmen of Boston and Philadelphia: The most unusual provision in the codicil to Franklin's will was a trust he established. He noted that, unlike the other founders of the country, he was born poor and had been helped in his rise by those who supported him as a struggling artisan. "I wish to be useful even after my death, if possible, in forming and advancing other young men that may be serviceable to their country." So he designated the £2,000 he had earned as President of Pennsylvania—citing his often expressed belief that officials should serve without pay—to be split between the towns of Boston and Philadelphia and provided as loans, "at 5 percent per annum, to such young married artificers" who had served apprenticeships and were now seeking to establish their own businesses. With his usual obsession with detail, he described precisely how the loans and repayments would work, and he calculated that after one hundred years, the annuities would each be worth £131,000. At that time, the cities could spend £100,000 of it on public projects, keeping the remainder in the trust, which after another hundred years of loans and compounded interest would, he calculated, be worth £4,061,000. At that point, the money would go into the public treasury.

Did it work as he envisioned? In Boston it had to be modified as the apprenticeship system went out of fashion, but the loans were made according to the spirit of his bequest and, after one hundred years, the fund was worth about $400,000, a little bit less than he had calculated. At that point a trade school, Franklin Union (now the Benjamin Franklin Institute of Technology), was founded with three-fourths of the money plus a matching bequest from Andrew Carnegie, who considered Franklin a hero; the rest remained in the trust. A century later, that amount had grown to nearly $5 million, not quite the equivalent of £4 million but still a sizable sum. As per Franklin's will, the fund was then disbursed. After a legal struggle that was settled by an act of the legislature, the funds went to the Benjamin Franklin Institute of Technology.

In Philadelphia, the bequest did not accumulate quite as well. A century after his death, it totaled $172,000, about one-quarter of what he had projected. Of that sum, three-fourths went to establish Philadelphia's Franklin Institute, still a thriving science museum, with the remainder continued as a loan fund for young tradesmen, much of it given as home mortgages. A century later, in 1990, this fund had reached $2.3 million. Why was it less than half of what Boston had? One Philadelphia partisan charged that Boston had turned its fund into "a savings company for the rich." By focusing on loans to poor individuals, as Franklin intended, Philadelphia had not been as successful in getting repayments.

At that point, Philadelphia Mayor Wilson Goode suggested, one assumes jokingly, that the Ben Franklin money be used to pay for a party featuring *Ben* Vereen and Aretha *Franklin*. Others, more serious, proposed it be used to promote tourism, which caused a popular uproar. The mayor finally appointed a panel of historians, and the state divvied up the money in accordance with their general recommendations. Among the recipients were the Franklin Institute, a variety of community libraries and fire companies, and a group called the Philadelphia Academies that funds scholarships at vocational training programs in the city schools. When the 2001 scholarships were announced, a *Philadelphia Inquirer* columnist pointed out that the diversity among the thirty-four names—including Abimael Acaedevo, Muhammed Hogue, Zrakpa Karpoleh, David Kusiak, Pedro Lopez, and Rany Ly—would have delighted their benefactor. He most certainly would have smiled at one of the small but appropriate examples of his legacy that occurred at that year's Tour de Sol, a race of experimental cars. Some of these scholarship recipients from a poor high school in West Philadelphia used a $4,300 grant from the father of electricity to build a battery-powered car that won the race's Power of Dreams award.[4]

CHAPTER EIGHTEEN

CONCLUSIONS

HISTORY'S REFLECTIONS

"Mankind divides into two classes," the *Nation* magazine declared in 1868: the "natural-born lovers" and the "natural-born haters" of Benjamin Franklin. One reason for this split is that he does not, despite what some commentators claim, embody the American character. Instead, he embodies one aspect of it. He represents one side of a national dichotomy that has existed since the days when he and Jonathan Edwards stood as contrasting cultural figures.[1]

On one side were those, like Edwards and the Mather family, who believed in an anointed elect and in salvation through God's grace alone. They tended to have a religious fervor, a sense of social class and hierarchy, and an appreciation for exalted values over earthly ones. On the other side were the Franklins, those who believed in salvation through good works, whose religion was benevolent and tolerant, and who were unabashedly striving and upwardly mobile.

Out of this grew many related divides in the American character, and Franklin represents one strand: the side of pragmatism versus romanticism, of practical benevolence versus moral crusading. He was on the side of religious tolerance rather than evangelical faith. The side of social mobility rather than an established elite. The side of middle-class virtues rather than more ethereal noble aspirations.

During the three centuries since his birth, the changing assessments of Franklin have tended to reveal less about him than about the values of the people judging him and their attitudes toward a striving middle class. From an august historical stage filled with far less accessible founders, he turned to each new generation with a half-smile and spoke directly in whatever vernacular was in vogue, infuriating some and beguiling others. His reputation thus tended to reflect, or refract, the attitudes of each succeeding era.

In the years right after his death, as personal antagonisms faded, reverence for him grew. Even William Smith, who had battled him in the legislature and on the board of the Academy, gave a respectful eulogy at a memorial service in 1791, in which he dismissed their "unhappy divisions and disputes" and focused instead on Franklin's philanthropy and science. When his daughter afterward said she doubted he believed "one-tenth of what you said of old Ben lightning-rod," he merely laughed heartily.[2]

Franklin's other occasional antagonist, John Adams, likewise mellowed. "Nothing in life has mortified or grieved me more than the necessity which compelled me to oppose him so often as I have," he wrote in a remarkably anguished reassessment in 1811. His earlier harsh criticisms, Adams explained, were in some ways a testament to Franklin's greatness: "Had he been an ordinary man, I should never have taken the trouble to expose the turpitude of his intrigues." He even cast Franklin's lack of religious commitment, which he had once derided as verging on atheism, in a more favorable light: "All sects considered him, and I believe justly, a friend to unlimited toleration." At times, Adams charged, Franklin was hypocritical, a poor negotiator, and a misguided politician. But his essay also included some of the most nuanced words of appreciation written by any contemporary:

> Franklin had a great genius, original, sagacious and inventive, capable of discoveries in science no less than of improvement in the fine arts and the mechanical arts. He had a vast imagination . . . He had wit at will. He had a humor that, when he pleased, was delicate and delightful. He had a satire that was good-natured or caustic, Horace or Juvenal, Swift or Rabelais, at his pleasure. He had talents for irony, allegory

and fable that he could adapt with great skill to the promotion of moral and political truth. He was a master of that infantile simplicity which the French call naiveté, which never fails to charm.[3]

By this time, Franklin's view of the central role of the middle class in American life had triumphed, despite the qualms of those who felt that this represented a trend toward vulgarization. "By absorbing the gentility of the aristocracy and the work of the working class, the middling sorts gained a powerful moral hegemony over the whole society," historian Gordon Wood noted. He was describing America in the early 1800s, but he could also have been describing Franklin personally.

Franklin's reputation was further enhanced when his grandson Temple finally produced an edition of his papers in 1817. Adams wrote to Temple that his collection "seemed to make me live over again my life at Passy," which could have been read ambiguously by those who knew of their bitter feuding at Passy had he not added: "There is scarce a scratch of his pen that is not worth preserving." Francis, Lord Jeffrey, a founder of the *Edinburgh Review,* extolled Franklin's writings for their "homely jocularity," their attempt to "persuade the multitude to virtue," and above all for their emphasis on the humanistic values that defined the Enlightenment. "This self-taught American is the most rational, perhaps, of all philosophers. He never loses sight of common sense in any of his speculations."[4]

This Age of Enlightenment, however, was being replaced in the early 1800s by a literary era that valued romanticism more than rationality. With the shift came a profound reversal, especially among those of presumed higher sensibilities, in attitudes toward Franklin. The romantics admired not reason and intellect but deep emotion, subjective sensibility, and imagination. They exalted the heroic and the mystical rather than tolerance and rationality. Their haughty criticisms decimated the reputations of Franklin, Voltaire, Swift, and other Enlightenment thinkers.[5]

The great romantic poet John Keats was among the many who assaulted Franklin for his lowly sensibilities. He was, Keats wrote his brother in 1818, "full of mean and thrifty maxims" and a "not sublime man." Keats's friend and early publisher, the poet and editor Leigh Hunt, heaped scorn on Franklin's "scoundrel maxims" and charged that he was "at the head of those who think that man lives by bread alone." He had "few passions and no imagination," Leigh's indictment continued, and he encouraged mankind to a "love of wealth" that was stripped of "higher callings" or of "heart and soul." Along these lines, Thomas Carlyle, the Scottish critic so in love with romantic heroism, scorned Franklin as "the father of all Yankees," which was perhaps not as denigrating as Carlyle meant it to be.[6]

American transcendentalists such as Thoreau and Emerson, who shared the romantic poets' allergic reaction to rationalism and materialism, also found Franklin too mundane for their rarefied tastes. The more earthy and middle-class backwoodsmen still revered Franklin's *Autobiography*—it was the one book that Davy Crockett carried with him to his death at the Alamo—but a backwoodsman as refined as Thoreau had no place for it when heading off to Walden Pond. Indeed, the first chapter of his Walden journal, on economy, has tables and charts that subtly satirize those used by Franklin. Edgar Allen Poe, in his story "The Business Man," likewise poked glancingly at Franklin and other "methodical" men in describing the rise and methods of his aptly named antihero Peter Proffit.

Franklin appears by name in Herman Melville's semihistorical 1855 novel *Israel Potter*. In the narrative he comes across as a shallow spouter of maxims. But Melville, addressing the reader directly, apologized and noted that Franklin was not quite as one-dimensional as the book portrays him. "Seeking here to depict him in his less exalted habitudes, the narrator feels more as if he were playing with one of the sage's worsted hose than reverentially handling the honored hat which once oracularly sat on his brow." Melville's own judgment on Franklin was that for better or worse, he was very versatile. "Having carefully weighed the world, Franklin could act any part in it." He lists the dozens of pursuits in which Franklin excelled, and then he adds, in the quintessential romantic critique, "Franklin was everything but a poet." (Franklin would have agreed. He wrote that he "approved [of] amusing one's self with poetry now and then, so far as to improve one's language, but no further.")[7]

Emerson provided a similar mixed assessment. "Franklin was one of the most sensible men that ever lived," he wrote his aunt, and was "more useful, more moral and more pure" than Socrates. But he went on to lament, "Franklin's man is a frugal, inoffensive, thrifty citizen, but savors of nothing heroic." Nathaniel Hawthorne has one of his young characters complain that Franklin's maxims "are all about getting money or saving it," in response to which Hawthorne himself observes that there is some virtue in the sayings but that they "teach men but a small portion of their duties."[8]

Along with the rise of romanticism came a growing disdain, among those for whom "bourgeois" would become a term of contempt, for Franklin's beloved urban middle class and its shopkeeping values. It was a snobbery that would come to be shared by very disparate groups: proletarians and aristocrats, radical workers and leisured landowners, Marxists and elitists, intellectuals and anti-intellectuals. Flaubert declared that hatred of the bourgeoisie "is the beginning of all virtue," which was precisely the opposite of what Franklin had preached.[9]

But with the publication of fuller editions of his papers, Franklin's reputation began to revive. After the Civil War, the growth of industry and the onset of the Gilded Age made the times ripe for the glorification of his ideas, and for the next three decades he was the most popular subject of American biography. The 130 novels by Horatio Alger, which would eventually sell twenty million copies, made tales of virtuous boys who rose from rags to riches popular again. Franklin's reputation was also elevated by the emergence of that distinctly American philosophy known as pragmatism, which holds, as Franklin had, that the truth of any proposition, whether it be a scientific or moral or theological or social one, is based on how well it correlates with experimental results and produces a practical outcome.

Mark Twain, a literary heir who cloaked his humor in the same homespun cloth, had a wonderful time poking friendly fun at Franklin, who "prostituted his talents to the invention of maxims and aphorisms calculated to inflict suffering upon the rising generation of all subsequent ages . . . boys who might otherwise have been happy." But

Twain was actually a grudging admirer, and even more so were the great capitalists who took Franklin's maxims seriously.[10]

The industrialist Thomas Mellon, who erected a statue of Franklin in his bank's headquarters, declared that Franklin had inspired him to leave his family's farm near Pittsburgh and go into business. "I regard the reading of Franklin's *Autobiography* as the turning point of my life," he wrote. "Here was Franklin, poorer than myself, who by industry, thrift and frugality had become learned and wise, and elevated to wealth and fame . . . The maxims of 'poor Richard' exactly suited my sentiments. I read the book again and again, and wondered if I might not do something in the same line by similar means." Andrew Carnegie was similarly stimulated. Not only did Franklin's success story provide him guidance in business, it also inspired his philanthropy, especially his devotion to the creation of public libraries.[11]

Franklin was praised as "the first great American" by the definitive historian of that period, Frederick Jackson Turner. "His life is the story of American common-sense in its highest form," he wrote in 1887, "applied to business, to politics, to science, to diplomacy, to religion, to philanthropy." He also was championed by the period's most influential editor, William Dean Howells of *Harper's* magazine. "He was a very great man," Howells wrote in 1888, "and the objects to which he dedicated himself with an unfailing mixture of motive were such as concerned the immediate comfort of men and the advancement of knowledge." Despite the fact that he was "cynically incredulous of ideals and beliefs sacred to most of us," he was "instrumental in promoting the moral and material welfare of the race."[12]

The pendulum again swung against Franklin in the 1920s, as Gilded Age individualism fell out of intellectual favor. Max Weber famously dissected America's middle-class work ethic from a quasi-Marxist perspective in *The Protestant Ethic and the Spirit of Capitalism,* which quoted Franklin (and Poor Richard) extensively as a prime example of the "philosophy of avarice." "All Franklin's moral attitudes," wrote Weber, "are colored with utilitarianism," and he accused Franklin of believing only in "the earning of more and more money combined with the strict avoidance of all spontaneous engagement of life."

The literary critic Van Wyck Brooks distinguished between America's highbrow and lowbrow cultures, and he placed Franklin as the founder of the latter. He exemplified, Brooks said, a "catchpenny opportunism" and a "two-dimensional wisdom." The poet William Carlos Williams added that he was "our wise prophet of chicanery." And in his novel *Babbitt*, Sinclair Lewis belittled bourgeois values and civic boosterism. In a barb aimed at Franklin's oft-stated creed, Lewis wrote: "If you had asked Babbitt what his religion was, he would have answered in sonorous Boosters' Club rhetoric, 'My religion is to serve my fellow men, to honor my brother as myself, and to do my bit to make life happier for one and all.' "[13]

The most vicious and amusing—and in most ways, misguided—attack on Franklin came in 1923 from the English critic and novelist D. H. Lawrence. His essay is, at times, a stream-of-consciousness rant that assaults Franklin for the unromantic and bourgeois nature of the virtues reflected in his *Autobiography:*

> Doctor Franklin. Snuff-colored little man! Immortal soul and all! The immortal soul part was a sort of cheap insurance policy. Benjamin had no concern, really, with the immortal soul. He was too busy with social man . . . I do not like him.
>
> I can remember, when I was a little boy, my father used to buy a scrubby yearly almanac with the sun and moon and stars on the cover. And it used to prophesy bloodshed and famine. But also crammed in corners it had little anecdotes and humorisms, with a moral tag. And I used to have my little priggish laugh at the woman who counted her chickens before they were hatched and so forth, and I was convinced that honesty was the best policy, also a little priggishly. The author of these bits was Poor Richard, and Poor Richard was Benjamin Franklin, writing in Philadelphia well over a hundred years before. And probably I haven't got over those Poor Richard tags yet. I rankle still with them. They are thorns in young flesh.
>
> Because, although I still believe that honesty is the best policy, I dislike policy altogether; though it is just as well not to count your chickens before they are hatched, it's still more hateful to count them with gloating when they are hatched. It has taken me many years and countless smarts to get out of that barbed wire moral enclosure that Poor Richard rigged up . . .
>
> Which brings us right back to our question, what's wrong with Benjamin, that we can't stand him? . . . I am a moral animal. And I'm going

to remain such. I'm not going to be turned into a virtuous little automaton as Benjamin would have me . . . And now I, at least, know why I can't stand Benjamin. He tries to take away my wholeness and my dark forest, my freedom.

As part of the essay, Lawrence rewrote Franklin's thirteen virtues to make them more to his romantic liking. Instead of Franklin's definition of industry ("Be always employed in something useful") Lawrence substituted "Serve the Holy Ghost; never serve mankind." Instead of Franklin's definition of justice ("Wrong none by doing injuries"), Lawrence proclaimed, "The only justice is to follow the sincere intuition of the soul, angry or gentle."

It is a bracing essay, but it should be noted that Lawrence, in addition to having an odd and self-indulgent definition of justice, aimed his assault not on the real-life Franklin but on the character he created in Poor Richard and in the *Autobiography*. In addition, Lawrence got a few facts wrong, among them attributing to Franklin the maxim "Honesty is the best policy," which sounds like him but actually is from Cervantes, just as the one about not counting unhatched chickens is from Aesop.[14]

Lawrence's approach was echoed in a more substantive, if less dramatic, attack on Franklin's bourgeois Babbittry by Charles Angoff in his *Literary History of the American People*, published in 1931. Carlyle's description of Franklin as the father of all the Yankees was, Angoff declared, a "libel against the tribe" that had produced fine writers such as Hawthorne and Thoreau. "It would be more accurate to call Franklin the father of all the Kiwanians," Angoff sneered, and he was brutal about what he saw as the "low order" of Franklin's thinking:

> Franklin represented the least praiseworthy qualities of the inhabitants of the new world: miserliness, fanatical practicality, and lack of interest in what are usually known as spiritual things. Babbittry was not a new thing in America, but he made a religion of it, and by his tremendous success with it grafted it upon the American people so securely that the national genius is still suffering from it . . . Not a word about nobility, not a word about honor, not a word about grandeur of soul, not a word about charity of mind! . . . He had a cheap and shabby soul, and the upper levels of the mind were far beyond his reach.[15]

The Great Depression of the 1930s reminded people that the virtues of industry and frugality, of helping others and making sure that the community held together, did not deserve to be dismissed as trivial and mundane. Franklin's reputation again made a comeback. The pragmatist philosopher Herbert Schneider, in his book *The Puritan Mind*, pointed out that the previous attacks had mainly been on Poor Richard's preachings rather than on how Franklin really lived his life, which did not focus on the pursuit of wealth for its own sake.

Carl Van Doren, Schneider's colleague at Columbia, in 1938 fleshed out this point in his glorious literary biography of Franklin. "He moved through this world in a humorous mastery of it," Van Doren concluded. And the great historian of science, I. Bernard Cohen, began his lifelong work of showing that Franklin's scientific achievements placed him in the pantheon with Newton. Franklin's experiments, he wrote in 1941, "afforded a basis for the explanation for all the known phenomena of electricity."[16]

Franklin also became the patron saint of the self-help movement. Dale Carnegie studied the *Autobiography* when writing *How to Win Friends and Influence People*, which, after its publication in 1937, helped launch a craze that persists to this day for books featuring simple rules and secrets about how to succeed in business and in life. As E. Digby Baltzell, a sociologist of America's elite, has noted, Franklin's *Autobiography* was "the first and greatest manual of careerist Babbittry ever written."[17]

Stephen Covey, the guru of the genre, referred to Franklin's system in developing his bestseller *The Seven Habits of Highly Effective People*, and a national chain of stores now sell "FranklinCovey Organizers" and other paraphernalia featuring Franklin's ideas. By the beginning of the twenty-first century, the self-help shelves of bookstores were filled with titles such as *Ben's Book of Virtues: Ben Franklin's Simple Weekly Plan for Success and Happiness; Ben Franklin's 12 Rules of Management: The Founding Father of American Business Solves Your Toughest Problems; Benjamin Franklin's the Art of Virtue: His Formula for Successful Living; The Ben Franklin Factor: Selling One to One;* and *Healthy, Wealthy and Wise: Principals for Successful Living from the Life of Benjamin Franklin.*[18]

In the academic world, Franklin was the subject of generally favorable books as the three hundredth anniversary of his birth approached. In *The First American*, H. W. Brands of Texas A&M sympathetically described the evolution of Franklin's character in a solid and balanced narrative biography. "To genius he joined a passion for virtue," he concluded. In 2002, Edmund S. Morgan, the retired and revered Sterling Professor of History at Yale, wrote a wonderfully astute character analysis based on an exhaustive reading of Franklin's papers. "We may discover," Morgan declared, "a man with a wisdom about himself that comes only to the great of heart."[19]

In the popular imagination, Franklin came to be viewed as a figure of fun, rather than as the serious thinker admired by Hume or the political manipulator resented by Adams. During an era that was at times trivial and untroubled, filled with sexual winks and unfettered entrepreneurship, Franklin was enlisted into the spirit. He became a jovial lecher dabbling in statecraft in such plays as *1776* and *Ben Franklin in Paris*, a sprightly old spokesman for everything from cookies to mutual funds, and a genial sage whose adages were designed to entertain rather than intimidate aspiring young workers.

"Today we know Benjamin Franklin mainly from an old advertising image: an elderly man in knickers, long coat, and spectacles, with a bald crown and long hair—a zealot foolishly determined to fly a kite during a thunderstorm," the historian Alan Taylor has written. "He no longer arouses either controversy or adulation—merely laughter. We only dimly sense his importance in the nineteenth and early twentieth centuries as the paragon of, and the pattern for, American middle-class values."[20]

To the social commentator David Brooks, this anodyne version of Franklin embodies both the entrepreneurial and moral tenor of America at the beginning of the twenty-first century. He was the one historic figure from the American pantheon, Brooks wrote, "who would be instantly at home in an office park."

He'd probably join the chorus of all those techno-enthusiasts who claim that the internet and bio-tech breakthroughs are going to transform life on earth wonderfully; he shared that passion for progress. At the same time, he'd be completely at home with the irony and gen-

tle cynicism that is the prevailing conversational tone in those buildings . . .

But then, Franklin would be at home in much of contemporary
America. He'd share the values of the comfortably middle class; he was
optimistic, genial, and kind, and his greatest flaw was his self-approving
complacency. One can easily picture him traipsing through a shopping
mall enchanted by the cheerful abundance and the clever marketing. At
the same time, he'd admire all the effort young Americans put into civic
activism, and the way older Americans put religion to good use through
faith-based community organizations.

Franklin had been unfairly attacked over the years, Brooks concluded, by romantics whose real targets were capitalism and middle-
class morality. "But now the main problem is excess Franklinism,
and we've got to figure out how to bring to today's America the
tragic sense and the moral gravity that was so lacking in its Founding
Yuppie."[21]

THE LEDGER BOOK

This perceived lack of moral gravity and spiritual depth is the most
serious charge against Franklin. In both his life and his writings, he
sometimes displayed a lack of commitment, anguish, poetry, or soul. A
sentence he wrote to his sister Jane in 1771 captured this complacency
and dearth of passion: "Upon the whole, I am much disposed to like
the world as I find it, and to doubt my own judgment as to what would
mend it."[22]

His religious beliefs, especially early in life, were largely a calculus
of what credos would prove useful for people to believe, rather than an
expression of sincere inner convictions. Deism was appealing, but he
discovered it was not all that helpful, so he gave it a moral gloss and
seldom troubled his soul with questions about grace, salvation, the divinity of Christ, or other profound issues that did not lend themselves
to practical inquiry. He was at the other extreme from the anguished
soul-searching Puritans. As he had no factual evidence about what
was divinely inspired, he settled instead for the simple creed that the
best way to serve God was doing good to others.

His moral beliefs were likewise plain and earthly, focused on practical ways to benefit others. He espoused the middle-class virtues of a shopkeeper, and he had little interest in proselytizing about higher ethical aspirations. He wrestled more with what he called "errata" than he did with sin.

As a scientist, he had a feel for the mechanical workings of the world but little appreciation for abstract theories or the sublime. He was a great experimenter and clever inventor, with an emphasis on things useful. But he had neither the temperament nor the training to be a profound conceptualizer.

In most of the endeavors of his soul and mind, his greatness sprang more from his practicality than from profundity or poetry. In science he was more an Edison than a Newton, in literature more a Twain than a Shakespeare, in philosophy more a Dr. Johnson than a Bishop Berkeley, and in politics more a Burke than a Locke.

In his personal life as well, there was likewise a lack of soulful commitment and deep passion. He frequented many antechambers, but few inner chambers. His love of travel reflected the spirit of a young runaway, one who had run from his family in Boston, from Deborah when he first thought of marrying, and from William just before his wedding. Throughout his life he had few emotional bonds tying him to any one place, and he seemed to glide through the world the way he glided through relationships.

His friendships with men often ended badly: his brother James, his friends John Collins and James Ralph, his printing partners Samuel Keimer and Hugh Meredith. He was a sociable man who liked clubs that offered enlightening conversations and activities, but the friendships he formed with his fellow men were more affable than intimate. He had a genial affection for his wife, but not enough love to prevent him from spending fifteen of the last seventeen years of their marriage an ocean away. His relationship with her was a practical one, as was the case with his London landlady, Margaret Stevenson. With his many women admirers, he preferred flirting rather than making serious commitments, and he retreated into playful detachment at any sign of danger. His most passionate relationship was with his son William, but that fire turned into ice. Only to his grandson Temple did he show unalloyed affection.

He could also, despite his professed belief in the virtue of sincerity, come across as conniving. He wrote his first hoax at 16 and the last on his deathbed; he misled his employer Samuel Keimer when scheming to start a newspaper; he perfected indirection as a conversational artifice; and he utilized the appearance of virtue as well as its reality. "In a place and a time that celebrated sincerity while practicing insincerity, Franklin seemed far too accomplished at the latter," Taylor notes. "Owing to his smooth manner and shifting tactics, Franklin invited suspicions far beyond his actual intent to trick."[23]

All of which has led some critics to dismiss even Franklin's civic accomplishments as the mundane aspirations of a shallow soul. The apotheosis of such criticism is in Vernon Parrington's famous *Main Currents in American Thought:*

> A man who is less concerned with the golden pavements of the City of God than that the cobblestones on Chestnut Street in Philadelphia should be well and evenly laid, who troubles less to save his soul from burning hereafter than to protect his neighbors' houses by organizing an efficient fire-company, who is less regardful of the light that never was on sea or land than of a new-model street lamp to light the steps of a belated wayfarer—such a man, obviously, does not reveal the full nature of human aspiration.[24]

It is Parrington's haughty use of the word "obviously" that provides us with a good launching point for a defense of Franklin. "Obviously," perhaps, to Parrington and others of rarefied sensibility whose contributions to society are not so mundane as a library, university, fire company, bifocals, stove, lightning rod, or, for that matter, democratic constitutions. Their disdain is in part a yearning for the loftier ideals that could sometimes seem lacking in Franklin's soul. Yet it is also, in part, a snobbery about the earthly concerns and middle-class values that he appreciated.

So how are we, as Franklin the bookkeeper would have wished, to balance the ledger fairly? As he did in his own version of a moral calculus, we can list all the Pros on the other side and determine if, as I think is the case, they outweigh the Cons.

First we must rescue Franklin from the schoolbook caricature of a genial codger flying kites in the rain and spouting homespun maxims about a penny saved being a penny earned. We must also rescue him from the critics who would confuse him with the character he carefully crafted in his *Autobiography*.[25]

When Max Weber says that Franklin's ethics are based only on the earning of more money, and when D.H. Lawrence reduces him to a man who pinched pennies and morals, they betray the lack of even a passing familiarity with the man who retired from business at 42, dedicated himself to civic and scientific endeavors, gave up much of his public salaries, eschewed getting patents on his inventions, and consistently argued that the accumulation of excess wealth and the idle indulgence in frivolous luxuries should not be socially sanctioned. Franklin did not view penny saving as an end in itself but as a path that permitted young tradesmen to be able to display higher virtues, community spirit, and citizenship. "It is hard for an empty sack to stand upright," both he and Poor Richard proclaimed.[26]

To assess Franklin properly, we must view him, instead, in all his complexity. He was not a frivolous man, nor a shallow one, nor a simple one. There are many layers to peel back as he stands before us so coyly disguised, both to history and to himself, as a plain character unadorned by wigs and other pretensions.

Let's begin with the surface layer, the Franklin who serves as a lightning rod for the Jovian bolts from those who disdain middle-class values. There is something to be said—and Franklin said it well and often—for the personal virtues of diligence, honesty, industry, and temperance, especially when they are viewed as a means toward a nobler and more benevolent end.

The same is true of the civic virtues Franklin both practiced and preached. His community improvement associations and other public endeavors helped to create a social order that promoted the common good. Few people have ever worked as hard, or done as much, to inculcate virtue and character in themselves and their communities.[27]

Were such efforts mundane, as Parrington and some others charge? Perhaps in part, but in his autobiography, after recounting his effort to pave Philadelphia's streets, Franklin provided an eloquent defense against such aspersions:

> Some may think these trifling matters not worth minding or relat-
> ing; but when they consider that though dust blown into the eyes of a
> single person, or into a single shop on a windy day, is but of small im-
> portance, yet the great number of the instances in a populous city, and
> its frequent repetitions give it weight and consequence, perhaps they
> will not censure very severely those who bestow some attention to af-
> fairs of this seemingly low nature. Human felicity is produced not so
> much by great pieces of good fortune that seldom happen, as by little
> advantages that occur every day.[28]

Likewise, although a religious faith based on fervor can be inspiring, there is also something admirable about a religious outlook based
on humility and openness. Charles Angoff has charged that "his main
contribution to the religious question was little more than a good-
natured tolerance." Well, perhaps so, but the concept of good-natured
religious tolerance was in fact no small advance for civilization in the
eighteenth century. It was one of the greatest contributions to arise
out of the Enlightenment, more indispensable than that of the most
profound theologians of the era.

In both his life and his writings, Franklin became a preeminent
proponent of this creed of tolerance. He developed it with great
humor in his tales and with an earnest depth in his life and letters. In a
world that was then (as, alas, it still is now) bloodied by those who
seek to impose theocracies, he helped to create a new type of nation
that could draw strength from its religious pluralism. As Garry Wills
argued in his book *Under God,* this "more than anything else, made the
United States a new thing on earth."[29]

Franklin also made a more subtle religious contribution: he detached the Puritan spirit of industriousness from the sect's rigid
dogma. Weber, with his contempt for middle-class values, disdained
the Protestant ethic, and Lawrence felt that Franklin's demystified
version of it could not sate the dark soul. This ethic was, however, instrumental in instilling the virtue and character that built a nation.
"He remade the Puritan in him into a zealous bourgeois," writes John
Updike, whose novels explore these very themes, "and certainly this is
his main meaning for the American psyche: a release into the Enlightenment of the energies cramped under Puritanism." As Henry Steele

Commager declared in *The American Mind,* "In a Franklin could be merged the virtues of Puritanism without its defects, the illumination of the Enlightenment without its heat."[30]

So, does Franklin deserve the accolade, accorded by his great contemporary David Hume, of America's "first philosopher"? To some extent, he does. Disentangling morality from theology was an important achievement of the Enlightenment, and Franklin was its avatar in America. In addition, by relating morality to everyday human consequences, Franklin laid the foundation for the most influential of America's homegrown philosophies, pragmatism. His moral and religious thinking, when judged in the context of his actions, writes James Campbell, "becomes a rich philosophical defense of service to advance the common good." What it lacked in spiritual profundity, it made up for in practicality and potency.[31]

What about the charge that Franklin was too much of a compromiser instead of a heroic man of principle? Yes, he played both sides for a few years in the 1770s, when he was trying to mediate between England and America. Yes, he was somewhat squishy in dealing with the Stamp Act. He had taught himself as a young tradesman to avoid disputatious assertions, and his habit of benignly smiling while he listened to all sorts of people made him seem at times duplicitous or insinuating.

But once again, there's something to be said for Franklin's outlook, for his pragmatism and occasional willingness to compromise. He believed in having the humility to be open to different opinions. For him that was not merely a practical virtue, but a moral one as well. It was based on the tenet, so fundamental to most moral systems, that every individual deserves respect. During the Constitutional Convention, for example, he was willing to compromise some of his beliefs to play a critical role in the conciliation that produced a near-perfect document. It could not have been accomplished if the hall had contained only crusaders who stood on unwavering principle. Compromisers may not make great heroes, but they do make democracies.

More important, Franklin did in fact believe, uncompromisingly, in a few high principles—very important ones for shaping a new nation—that he stuck to throughout his life. Having learned from his brother a resistance to establishment power, he was ever unwavering in his opposition to arbitrary authority. That led him to be unflinching in opposing the unfair tax policies the Penns tried to impose, even when it would have served his personal advantage to go along. It also meant that, despite his desire to find a compromise with Britain during the 1770s, he adhered firmly to the principle that American citizens and their legislatures must not be treated as subservient.

Similarly, he helped to create, and came to symbolize, a new political order in which rights and power were based not on the happenstance of heritage but on merit and virtue and hard work. He rose up the social ladder, from runaway apprentice to dining with kings, in a way that would become quintessentially American. But in doing so he resolutely resisted, as a matter of principle, sometimes to a fur-capped extreme, taking on elitist pretensions.

Franklin's belief that he could best serve God by serving his fellow man may strike some as mundane, but it was in truth a worthy creed that he deeply believed and faithfully followed. He was remarkably versatile in this service. He devised legislatures and lightning rods, lotteries and lending libraries. He sought practical ways to make stoves less smoky and commonwealths less corrupt. He organized neighborhood constabularies and international alliances. He combined two types of lenses to create bifocals and two concepts of representation to foster the nation's federal compromise. As his friend the French statesman Turgot said in his famous epigram, *Eripuit cœlo fulmen sceptrumque tyrannis,* he snatched lightning from the sky and the scepter from tyrants.

All of this made him the most accomplished American of his age and the most influential in inventing the type of society America would become. Indeed, the roots of much of what distinguishes the nation can be found in Franklin: its cracker-barrel humor and wisdom; its technological ingenuity; its pluralistic tolerance; its ability to weave together individualism and community cooperation; its philosophical pragmatism; its celebration of meritocratic mobility; the idealistic streak ingrained in its foreign policy; and the Main Street (or Market Street) virtues that serve as the foundation for its civic values. He was egalitarian in what became the American sense: he approved of individuals making their way to wealth through diligence and talent, but opposed giving special privileges to people based on their birth.

His focus tended to be on how ordinary issues affect everyday lives, and on how ordinary people could build a better society. But that did not make him an ordinary man. Nor did it reflect a shallowness. On the contrary, his vision of how to build a new type of nation was both revolutionary and profound. Although he did not embody each and every transcendent or poetic ideal, he did embody the most practical and useful ones. That was his goal, and a worthy one it was.

Through it all, he trusted the hearts and minds of his fellow leather-aprons more than he did those of any inbred elite. He saw middle-class values as a source of social strength, not as something to be derided. His guiding principle was a "dislike of everything that tended to debase the spirit of the common people." Few of his fellow founders felt this comfort with democracy so fully, and none so intuitively.

From the age of 21, when he first gathered his Junto, he held true to a fundamental ideal with unwavering and at times heroic fortitude: a faith in the wisdom of the common citizen that was manifest in an appreciation for democracy and an opposition to all forms of tyranny. It was a noble ideal, one that was transcendent and poetic in its own way.

And it turned out to be, as history proved, a practical and useful one as well.

CAST OF CHARACTERS

JOHN ADAMS (1735–1826). Massachusetts patriot, second U.S. president. Worked with Franklin editing Jefferson's draft of the Declaration of Independence and negotiating with Lord Howe in 1776. Arrived in Paris April 1778 to work with Franklin as commissioner, left March 1779, returned February 1780, left for Holland August 1780, returned for final peace talks with Britain October 1782.

WILLIAM ALLEN (1704–1780). Pennsylvania merchant and chief justice who was initially a friend but broke with Franklin by supporting the Proprietors.

BENJAMIN "BENNY" FRANKLIN BACHE (1769–1798). Son of Sally and Richard Bache, traveled to Paris with grandfather Franklin and cousin Temple in 1776, sent to school in Geneva, learned printing in Passy, set up by Franklin as a printer in Philadelphia, published antifederalist paper *The American Aurora*, arrested for libeling President John Adams. Died of yellow fever at 29.

RICHARD BACHE (1737–1811). Struggling merchant who married Franklin's daughter, Sally, in 1767. They had seven children who survived infancy: Benjamin, William, Louis, Elizabeth, Deborah, Sarah, and Richard.

EDWARD BANCROFT (1745–1821). Massachusetts-born physician and stock speculator who met Franklin in London, became secretary to the American commission in France during the American Revolution, and turned out to be a British spy.

PIERRE-AUGUSTIN CARON DE BEAUMARCHAIS (1732–1799). Dramatic dramatist, stock speculator, and arms dealer. Helped arrange French aid to America during the Revolution and became a friend of Franklin's in Passy. Wrote *The Barber of Seville* in 1775 and *Figaro* in 1784.

ANDREW BRADFORD (1686–1742). Philadelphia printer and publisher of *American Weekly Mercury*, became a competitor of Franklin's and supported the Proprietary elite.

WILLIAM BRADFORD (1663–1752). Pioneering printer in New York whom Franklin met when running away from Boston and who introduced him to his son Andrew in Philadelphia.

ANNE-LOUISE BOIVIN D'HARDANCOURT BRILLON DE JOUY (1744–1824). Franklin's neighbor in Passy, an accomplished harpsichordist who became one of Franklin's favorite female friends. Wrote "Marche des Insurgents" to commemorate American victory at Saratoga.

WILLIAM PITT THE ELDER, EARL OF CHATHAM (1708–1778). As the "Great Commoner," was prime minister during Seven Years' War, 1756–63. Accepted peerage in 1766. Opposed repressive Tory measures. Negotiated with Franklin in early 1776, parking his carriage outside Mrs. Stevenson's boarding house.

JACQUES-DONATIEN LE RAY DE CHAUMONT (1725–1803). Merchant, aspiring war profiteer, and former slave trader. Franklin's landlord in Passy.

CADWALLADER COLDEN (1688–1776). New York politician and naturalist. Corresponded frequently with Franklin about experiments and science.

PETER COLLINSON (1694–1768). London merchant and scientist who helped Franklin set up the library and furnished him with electricity tracts and equipment.

MARIE-JEAN-ANTOINE-NICOLAS CARITAT, MARQUIS DE CONDORCET (1743–1794). Mathematician and biographer, contributor to Diderot's *Encyclopédie*. Franklin's close friend in Paris. Poisoned during the French Revolution.

SAMUEL COOPER (1725–1783). Boston politican and minister. An advocate of independence and close confidant of Franklin.

THOMAS CUSHING (1725–1788). Massachusetts politician and its speaker of the House 1766–74. A frequent correspondent of Franklin's and the recipient of the Hutchinson letters.

SILAS DEANE (1737–1789). Connecticut diplomat and merchant. Went to France in July 1776, just before Franklin, to solicit support. Became an ally of Franklin's but antagonized Arthur Lee, who accused him of corruption and helped to force his recall.

WILLIAM DENNY (1709–1765). British army officer who was the Penns' appointed governor 1756–59.

FRANCIS DASHWOOD, BARON LE DESPENCER (1708–1781). British politician and, from 1766 to 1781, the postmaster who protected and then had to fire his friend Franklin as the deputy postmaster for America. At his country house, Franklin had the pleasure of hearing his hoax "An Edict from the King of Prussia" fool people.

JOHN DICKINSON (1732–1808). Philadelphia politician who opposed Franklin in the fight with the Proprietors and was more cautious about independence. Wrote "Letters from a Pennsylvania Farmer," which Franklin (not knowing who was the author) helped publish in London.

JOHN FOTHERGILL (1712–1780). Quaker physician in London. Published Franklin's electricity papers in 1751 and served as his doctor in England. "I can hardly conceive that a better man has ever lived," Franklin once said.

ABIAH FOLGER FRANKLIN (1667–1752). Married Josiah Franklin in 1689 and had ten children, including Benjamin.

BENJAMIN FRANKLIN "THE ELDER" (1650–1727). The brother of Franklin's father Josiah. Encouraged his nephew (unsuccessfully) in poetry and preaching and came to live in Boston in 1715 as a retired widower.

DEBORAH READ FRANKLIN (1705?–1774). Franklin's loyal, common-law wife. May have been born in Birmingham, but was raised on Market Street in Philadelphia and never left that neighborhood for the rest of her life. First saw Franklin in October 1723 when he straggled off the boat into Philadelphia. Married John Rogers, who abandoned her. Entered common-law union with Franklin in 1730. Served as bookkeeper and manager of print shop. Defended home during Stamp Act riots. Two children: Francis "Franky," who died at age 4, and Sarah "Sally," who in many ways resembled her.

JAMES FRANKLIN (1697–1735). Franklin's brother and early master. Started *New England Courant* in 1721 and was a pioneer in provocative American journalism.

JANE FRANKLIN [MECOM] (1712–1794). Franklin's youngest sister and favorite sibling.

JOHN FRANKLIN (1690–1756). Franklin's brother. Became a soap and candle maker in Rhode Island and then (with Franklin's help) the postmaster in Boston. Franklin made a flexible catheter for him.

JOSIAH FRANKLIN (1657–1745). A silk dyer born in Ecton, England. Emigrated to America in 1683, where he became a candle maker. Had seven children by his first wife, Anne Child, and ten (inluding Benjamin Franklin) by his second wife, Abiah Folger Franklin.

SARAH "SALLY" FRANKLIN [BACHE] (1743–1808). Loyal only daughter. Married Richard Bache in 1767. Served as hostess and homemaker when Franklin returned to Philadelphia in 1776 and 1785. Like her mother, she never traveled to Europe with him, but she did travel to Boston with him in 1763.

[WILLIAM] TEMPLE FRANKLIN (ca. 1760–1823). Illegitimate son of William Franklin. Grandfather helped to raise and educate him, brought him back to America in 1775, took him to Paris in 1776, retained his loyalty in struggle with the boy's father. Had his own illegitimate children. Published a haphazard collection of his gandfather's writings.

WILLIAM FRANKLIN (ca. 1730–1813). Illegitimate son raised by Franklin. Accompanied him to England, became a Tory sympathizer, appointed royal governor of New Jersey, remained loyal to the Crown, and irrevocably split with his father.

JOSEPH GALLOWAY (ca. 1731–1803). Philadelphia politician and longtime ally of Franklin in fight with the Proprietors. His home, Trevose, was the site of a tense meeting between Franklin and his son. Remained loyal to the Crown and split with Franklin during the Revolution.

DAVID HALL (1714–1772). Recommended by William Strahan, moved from London in 1744 to become Franklin's shop foreman and in 1748 took over running the business as managing partner.

ANDREW HAMILTON (ca. 1676–1741). Speaker of the Pennsylvania Assembly for much of the 1730s. Defended John Peter Zenger in his libel trial and usually supported Franklin.

JAMES HAMILTON (1710–1783). Andrew's son. Governor of Pennsylvania 1748–54 and 1759–63. As a Mason, trustee of the Library Company and the Academy, he was Franklin's friend, but they were often politically opposed.

ANNE-CATHERINE DE LIGNIVILLE HELVÉTIUS (1719–1800). Franklin's close friend in Auteuil, near Passy. Franklin proposed marriage, more than half-seriously, in 1780. Widowed in 1771 from noted philosopher and wealthy farmer-general Claude-Adrien Helvétius.

LORD RICHARD HOWE (1726–1799). British admiral. Joined the Royal Navy at age 14 and became commander in America. First negotiated with Franklin secretly under cover of chess games at his sister's in late 1775. Met Franklin and Adams on Staten Island in September 1776.

WILLIAM HOWE (1729–1814). Younger brother of Admiral Lord Richard Howe. Fought in the French and Indian War and then the Battle of Bunker Hill. In 1775, replaced General Thomas Gage as the commander of British land troops in the colonies, serving under the overall command of his brother. Became Viscount Howe in 1799.

DAVID HUME (1711–1776). Scottish historian and philosopher. With Locke and Berkeley, one of the greatest British empirical analysts. Franklin befriended him in London and visited him in Edinburgh in 1759 and 1771.

THOMAS HUTCHINSON (1711–1780). Originally a friend of Franklin's and an ally at the Albany Conference of 1754. Became royal governor of Massachusetts in 1771. House burned during Stamp Act crisis, and Franklin wrote him sympathetically. But in 1773, Franklin got hold of some of his letters and sent them to allies in Massachusetts, which caused Franklin to face a grilling by British ministers in the Cockpit.

HENRY HOME, LORD KAMES (1696–1782). Scottish judge and moral philosopher, with interests in farming and science and history, whom Franklin first met on his 1759 trip to Scotland.

SAMUEL KEIMER (ca. 1688–1742). London printer. Moved to Philadelphia in 1722 and gave Franklin his first job there the following year. Franklin had a stormy relationship with him and became his competitor; Keimer left for Barbados in 1730.

SIR WILLIAM KEITH (1680–1749). Governor of Pennsylvania 1717–26. Became an unreliable patron to Franklin in 1724 and sent him to London without a letter of credit he had promised. Keith was fired when he defied the Proprietors. Eventually imprisoned as a debtor in the Old Bailey, where he died.

ARTHUR LEE (1740–1792). Virginia politician and diplomat. Began his personal opposition to Franklin while both were in London in late 1760s. His disputes with Franklin intensified when both were commissioners in Paris in 1777. Remained a Franklin foe along with his powerful brothers: William, Richard Henry, and Francis Lightfoot Lee.

JEAN-BAPTISTE LE ROY (1720–1800). French scientist. Shared Franklin's interest in electricity and became his close friend in Paris.

ROBERT LIVINGSTON (1746–1813). New York statesman, foreign secretary of the United States 1781–83.

JAMES LOGAN (1674–1751). Prominent Philadelphia Quaker and gentleman, whom Franklin befriended as an adviser to the library.

COTTON MATHER (1663–1728). Prominent Puritan clergyman and famed witch-hunter. Succeeded his father, Increase Mather, as pastor of Boston's Old North Church. His writings inspired Franklin's civic projects.

HUGH MEREDITH (ca. 1697–ca. 1749). Printer at Keimer's shop. Became a member of Franklin's Junto and then his first partner in 1728. But when he resumed drinking, Franklin bought him out in 1730, and he left for North Carolina.

ABBÉ ANDRÉ MORELLET (1727–1819). Economist, contributor to the *Encyclopédie,* and lover of wine. Met Franklin in 1772 at Lord Shelburne house party, where Franklin did his trick stilling waves with oil. Part of Madame Helvétius's circle.

ROBERT HUNTER MORRIS (ca. 1700–1764). The Penns' governor in Pennsylvania 1754–56. Fought with Franklin over taxing the Proprietors' estates. Son of New Jersey governor Lewis Morris.

JEAN-ANTOINE NOLLET (1700–1770). French scientist and electrician. Jealous opponent of Franklin's theories.

ISAAC NORRIS (1701–1766). Philadelphia merchant, speaker of the Assembly 1750–64; allied with Franklin in opposition to the Proprietors.

THOMAS PAINE (1737–1809). Failed corset-maker and a tax clerk in England. Charmed Franklin, who provided a letter of introduction to Richard Bache, which led to a job as a journalist and printer in Philadelphia. Wrote *Common Sense* in January 1776, which paved the way for the Declaration of Independence. Wrote *The Age of Reason,* but delayed publishing it until 1794, perhaps after Franklin warned that people would find it heretical.

JAMES PARKER (ca. 1714–1770). New York printer, fled an apprenticeship with William Bradford, and Franklin set him up in New York as a printing partner, local postmaster, and then comptroller of the postal system. Franklin corresponded with him about a plan for union before the Albany Conference.

JOHN PENN (1729–1785). Grandson of Pennsylvania founder William Penn. Served as his family's governer there for most of 1763–76. Went with Franklin to Albany Conference in 1754, solicited Franklin's help during Paxton Boys riots, but soon was a political foe over Proprietary rights and taxes.

THOMAS PENN (1702–1775). Son of William and uncle of John Penn. Became, in 1746, the primary Proprietor of Pennsylvania, based in London with his brother Richard. One of Franklin's foremost political enemies.

RICHARD PETERS (ca. 1704–1776). Anglican clergyman. Came to Pennsylvania in 1734 as the right hand of the Penn family. Became one of Franklin's adversaries even as they worked together building the Academy.

JOSEPH PRIESTLEY (1733–1804). Theologian who turned to science. Met Franklin in 1765. Wrote a history of electricity (1767) that stressed Franklin's work. Isolated oxygen and other gases.

SIR JOHN PRINGLE (1707–1782). Physician who became Franklin's close English friend and traveling companion.

CATHERINE "CATY" RAY [GREENE] (1731–1794). Met Franklin on his 1754 trip to New England and became his first major young female flirtation. Married in 1758 to William Greene, who became governor of Rhode Island, but remained a friend of Franklin and his family. (She signed her name "Caty," but Franklin tended to address her as "Katy" or "Katie.")

LOUIS-ALEXANDER, DUC DE LA ROCHEFOUCAULD (1743–1792). Scientist and nobleman. Translated the American state constitutions for publication in France at Franklin's request. Stoned to death during the French Revolution.

EARL OF SHELBURNE (1737–1805). English friend at whose house party Franklin did his oil-on-water trick. Later, colonial secretary and prime minister during Franklin's 1782 British-American peace talks.

JONATHAN SHIPLEY, BISHOP OF ST. ASAPH (1714–1788). Anglican bishop at whose house, Twyford, near Winchester, Franklin began his autobiography.

WILLIAM SHIRLEY (1694–1771). London lawyer. Moved to Boston as governor of Massachusetts 1741–57 and briefly as commander of British troops. He and Franklin corresponded after the Albany Conference of 1754 on the shape an American colonial union should take.

WILLIAM SMITH (1727–1803). English clergyman and writer. Recruited by Franklin in the early 1750s for the new Philadelphia Academy, where he was made provost. Became an ardent supporter of the Proprietors and bitterly split with Franklin.

MARGARET STEVENSON (1706–1783). Franklin's landlady on Craven Street, off the Strand, and occasional companion in London.

MARY "POLLY" STEVENSON [HEWSON] (1739–1795). Mrs. Stevenson's daughter. Longtime flirtatious young friend and intellectual companion to Franklin. Married in 1770 to medical researcher William Hewson. Widowed in 1774. Visited Franklin in Passy in 1785. Moved to Philadelphia in 1786 to be at his deathbed.

WILLIAM STRAHAN (1715–1785). London printer who became Franklin's close friend via letters before even meeting him in person. Sent David Hall to be his partner. Franklin wrote but did not send a famous "you are my enemy" letter to him during the American Revolution, but they actually remained friends.

CHARLES THOMSON (1729–1824). Irish-born teacher. Franklin gave him a job at the Philadelphia Academy and got him involved in Pennsylvania politics. Served as Franklin's eyes and ears while Franklin was in London. Later became the secretary to Congress 1774–89.

ANNE-ROBERT-JACQUES TURGOT (1727–1781). Economist, finance minister to Louis XVI, Franklin's friend and occasional rival for the affections of Madame Helvétius. Wrote the famous epigram: *Eripuit cœlo fulmen sceptrumque tyrannis,* He snatched lightning from the sky and the scepter from tyrants.

BENJAMIN VAUGHAN (1751–1835). Diplomat and associate of Lord Shelburne. Compiled many of Franklin's papers in 1779 and helped to negotiate with him the final peace treaties with Britain.

LOUIS-GUILLAUME LE VEILLARD (1733–1794). Proprietor of a famed water spa. Franklin's neighbor at Passy. Guillotined during the French Revolution.

CHARLES GRAVIER, COMTE DE VERGENNES (1717–1787). French foreign minister 1774–87, with whom Franklin negotiated an alliance.

THOMAS WALPOLE (1727–1803). British banker and MP, nephew of Prime Minister Robert Walpole. Formed with Franklin the Grand Ohio Co. to seek an American land grant and later speculated on stocks, using inside information from Edward Bancroft.

PAUL WENTWORTH (ca. 1740–1793). Britain's spymaster in France who recruited Edward Bancroft. Born in New Hampshire, moved to London in the 1760s, became rich on stocks and land purchases in Guyana, and met with Franklin in Paris in December 1777 to try to scuttle American treaty with France.

SAMUEL WHARTON (1732–1800). Philadelphia-born merchant. Moved to London in 1769 and became involved in land deal schemes and stock speculations with Thomas Walpole.

GEORGE WHITEFIELD (1714–1770). Evangelist. Joined the Wesley movement while at Pembroke College, Oxford. Made seven trips to America as one of the foremost of the Great Awakening revivalist preachers and was supported by Franklin in Philadelphia in 1739.

CHRONOLOGY

1706   Born in Boston on Jan. 17 (Jan. 6, 1705, Old Style).

1714   Attends Boston Latin.

1715   Attends Brownell's school.

1716   Begins working at father's candle shop.

1718   Apprenticed to brother James.

1722   Writes Silence Dogood essays.

1723   Runs away to Philadelphia. Works for Keimer.

1724   Moves to London.

1725   "A Dissertation on Liberty and Necessity, Pleasure and Pain"

1726   Returns to Philadelphia. Works with Denham.

1727   Rejoins Keimer's print shop.

1728   Opens his own print shop with Hugh Meredith.

1729   Writes Busy-Body essays. Buys *Pennsylvania Gazette*.

1730   Enters common-law marriage with Deborah Read. William born?

1731   Joins Freemasons. Founds library.

1732   Francis born. Launches *Poor Richard's Almanack*.

1733   Moral perfection project.

1735   Controversy over preacher Hemphill.

1736   Clerk of Pennsylvania Assembly. Francis dies. Forms Union Fire Co.

1737   Made Philadelphia postmaster.

1739   Becomes friends with evangelist Whitefield.

1741   Launches *General Magazine,* which fails. Designs stove.

1743   Sarah ("Sally") born. Launches American Philosophical Society.

1745   Collinson sends electricity pamphlets and glass tube.

1746   Summer of electricity experiments.

1747   Writes *Plain Truth*. Organizes militia.

1748   Retires from printing business.

1749   Writes proposal for the Academy (University of Pennsylvania).

1751   Electricity writings published in London. Elected to Pennsylvania Assembly.

1752   Kite and lightning experiment.

1753   Becomes joint postmaster for America. Carlisle Indian summit.

1754 French and Indian War begins. Albany Plan of Union.

1755 Supplies Gen. Braddock. Passes militia bill. Fights Proprietors.

1756 Night watchmen and street lighting bills passed.

1757 Leaves for London as agent. Writes "Way to Wealth" and last *Poor Richard's Almanack.* Moves in with Mrs. Stevenson on Craven Street.

1758 Visits Ecton to research ancestry with William.

1759 Visits northern England and Scotland. English and American troops capture Quebec.

1760 Urges Britain to keep Canada. Privy Council gives partial victory in fight with Penns. Travels in England with William.

1761 Travels to Flanders and Holland with William.

1762 Returns to Philadelphia. William made royal governor of New Jersey, marries.

1763 Begins new Market Street house. Postal inspection trip from Virginia to New England. French and Indian War ends.

1764 Paxton Boys crisis. Defeated in bitter Assembly election. Returns to London as agent.

1765 Stamp Act passes.

1766 Testifies against Stamp Act in Parliament. Act repealed. Partnership with David Hall expires.

1767 Townshend duties imposed. Travels to France.

1768 Wages press crusade in London on behalf of the colonies.

1769 Second visit to France.

1770 Townshend duties repealed except on tea. Made agent for Massachusetts.

1771 Showdown with Hillsborough. Begins *Autobiography.* Visits Ireland and Scotland. Meets son-in-law, Bache.

1772 Secretly sends purloined Hutchinson letters to Boston.

1773 Writes parodies "Rules by Which a Great Empire May Be Reduced to a Smaller One" and "Edict of the King of Prussia." Boston Tea Party.

1774 Cockpit showdown over Hutchinson letters. Dismissed as postmaster. Coercive Acts passed. Begins peace discussions with both Lord Chatham and Lord Howe. Deborah dies.

1775 Returns to Philadelphia. Battles of Lexington and Concord. Elected to Second Continental Congress. Proposes first Articles of Confederation.

1776 William removed as royal governor, imprisoned in Connecticut. Canada mission. Declaration of Independence. Meets with Lord Howe on Staten Island. Goes to France with Temple and Benny.

1777 Settles in Passy, feted throughout Paris.

1778 Treaties of alliance and commerce with France. William released from captivity and moves to loyalist New York.

1779 Becomes sole minister to France. Salons of Mesdames Brillon and Helvétius. John Paul Jones's *Bonhomme Richard* defeats the *Serapis.*

1780 Adams returns, then Franklin helps get him dismissed as commissioner. British capture Charleston.

1781   Adams returns to Paris again as minister to negotiate with Britain. Franklin is then appointed (with Jay and others) to join Adams in that commission. Cornwallis surrenders at Yorktown.

1782   Negotiates, with Adams and Jay, peace treaty with Britain. William returns to London.

1783   Balloon flights.

1784   Mesmer commission. Polly Stevenson visits Passy.

1785   Last meeting with William. Returns to Philadelphia.

1786   Builds addition to Market Street house.

1787   Constitutional Convention. Elected president of Pennsylvania Society for Promoting the Abolition of Slavery.

1790   Dies on Apr. 17 at age 84.

CURRENCY CONVERSIONS

Rough equivalents of eighteenth-century currencies in today's value based on price index comparisons of a bundle of consumer products:

1706

The British pound was the standard currency in America.

£1 in 1706 had the same purchasing power as £104 (or $161) in 2002.

A fine ounce of gold cost £4.35.

1750

The British pound was still the standard currency in America, but some colonies (including Pennsylvania at Franklin's behest) were printing paper currency denominated in pounds that varied somewhat in value.

£1 in 1750 had the same purchasing power as £103 (or $160) in 2002.

A fine ounce of gold cost £4.25.

1790

The dollar was becoming the standard currency in the United States, and an official exchange rate was established. The gold price of the pound remained fixed, but its consumer purchasing power had fallen.

The exchange rate was £1 equals $4.55 equals 23.5 French livres.

A fine ounce of gold cost £4.25 or $19.50.

£1 in 1790 had the same purchasing power as £70 in 2002.

$1 in 1790 had the same purchasing power as $19.26 in 2002.

The changes in purchasing power of the pound and dollar from 1790 are not comparable.

Sources: Economic History Services, eh.net/hmit ; John McCusker, *How Much Is That in Real Money?* (New Castle, Del.: Oak Knoll Press, 2001).

ACKNOWLEDGMENTS

Alice Mayhew at Simon & Schuster has been a diligent editor and gracious friend for twenty years and, now, three books. Her detailed notes and valuable edits on all my manuscripts are treasured possessions. She has always been rigorous about, among other things, shaping a logical narrative, and her energy in handling this book was unflagging and deeply appreciated. Amanda Urban at ICM has likewise been a valued friend and agent for all these years. She read my earliest drafts and offered good suggestions and warm encouragement, as well as an occasional guest room in which to work.

To help ensure that my facts were as correct as possible and that I did not inadvertently fail to give due citations, I hired Carole Le Faivre-Rochester to vet my manuscript, sources, and credit notes. For twenty-four years, she worked at the American Philosophical Society, which Franklin founded and which has done great work in preserving his papers, and she retired as the editor of that society in 2001. She was industrious in digging out material and making useful suggestions.

One of the joys of working on Franklin was meeting the generous and humorous Claude-Anne Lopez, who was a longtime editor at Yale compiling his papers and is the author of many delightful books and articles about him. She graciously agreed to read parts of the manuscript and edited the three chapters on his years in France, about which she is both an expert and an enthusiast.

Ms. Lopez suggested that I try to dig out information about Edward Bancroft's spying activities on Franklin. To help in that task, I hired Susan Ann Bennett, a researcher in London who, among other things, wrote "Benjamin Franklin of Craven Street" when she was a curator at the RSA (formerly, the Royal Society of Arts). I am very grateful for her diligent work, transcriptions, and intelligent sleuthing at the British Library, where some of Bancroft's reports in code and invisible ink are stored.

I am also grateful to the editors at Yale who continue the task of producing what I think must be the greatest collection of anyone's papers ever. Their thirty-seventh volume, which goes through August 1782, is due out at the same time as this book and should be bought by everyone interested in Franklin. They were gracious in letting me study their manuscript of that work as well as their early drafts of volumes 38, 39, and 40. I particularly enjoyed a vibrant lunch I had in New

Haven with Ms. Lopez and some core members of the current team, including Ellen Cohen, Judith Adkins, Jonathan Dull, Karen Duval, and Kate Ohno.

Also at that lunch was the justly venerated Edmund Morgan, retired Sterling Professor of History at Yale, who had written his own wonderful book analyzing Franklin and his papers. Professor Morgan has been kindly, beneficent, generous, and exceedingly helpful in the tradition of our subject. He graciously offered to read parts of my manuscript, and he provided suggestions and encouragement about my theme and concluding chapter. I tried to take a different approach from his by writing a chronological narrative biography, but I do not pretend to have matched his insights. Those who find my book interesting, and more important those who don't, should buy and read his, if they haven't already.

Márcia Baliscano is the director of the Franklin House on Craven Street in London, soon to be (we all hope) a fitting museum. With enormous skill and intellectual rigor, along with a diligence that would have dazzled even Franklin, she painstakingly dissected my entire manuscript and made scores of invaluable suggestions. In addition, she was very helpful in hosting me on Craven Street, and she did her duty by energetically enlisting me and others to her cause. One of her board members is Lady Joan Reid, a great repository of Franklin information. I deeply appreciate her willingness to volunteer for the arduous task of reading my manuscript and being both meticulous and unflinching in her crusade to separate facts from lore. In doing so, she expended not only an enormous amount of time and intellectual energy, but also a huge pile of colored Post-it notes filled with suggestions. Someday, I hope, she will write a book about Franklin's London circle of friends.

Part of the pleasure of writing about Franklin is meeting his aficionados. Foremost among them is a group called the Friends of Franklin, based in Philadelphia, which hosts lunches, organizes seminars, and publishes the delightful *Franklin Gazette*. (To join, go to www.benfranklin2006.org) I want to thank Kathleen DeLuca, the executive secretary, for her hospitality. The group is working with the Franklin Institute, the American Philosophical Society, the Library Company of Philadelphia, the Philadelphia Museum of Art, the University of Pennsylvania, and the Pew Charitable Trust to organize a celebration and exhibition, under the direction of Connover Hunt, that will culminate with Franklin's three hundredth birthday in January 2006.

I am deeply indebted to Strobe Talbott, who has long been a friend and inspiration. He helped to shape and carefully edit both *The Wise Men*, which I coauthored in 1986, and a biography of Henry Kissinger that I published in 1992. This time, he volunteered again to read my manuscript, and he came back with a wealth of helpful suggestions and comments. Stephen Smith, one of the most deft editors I have ever known, also read the entire manuscript and offered useful perspectives and ideas. Evan Thomas, my coauthor on *The Wise Men*, spotted some mistakes I made about John Paul Jones, about whom he has written a great book. Steven Weisman read a draft and provided very insightful suggestions. Many other friends have given wise counsel, among them: James Kelly, Richard Stengel, Priscilla Painton and Tim Smith, Elisabeth Bumiller, Andrew and Betsy Lack, David and Sherrie Westin.

Elliot Ravetz, my former assistant at *Time*, helped me get started by giving me my first collection of Franklin papers, inspired me later with a bust of Franklin, offered comments on my manuscript, and has been an earnest compatriot. I am also grateful to Tosca Laboy and Ashley Van Buren at CNN, who are both truly wonderful people.

My father and stepmother, Irwin and Julanne Isaacson, also read and edited my manuscript. They are, along with my late mother, Betsy Isaacson, the smartest people I have ever known.

Most of all, I am grateful to my wife, Cathy, and daughter, Betsy. Cathy read through what I wrote with enormous care and was invaluable in sharpening the themes and spotting some problems. But that is merely a tiny fraction of what she did as my partner in this book and in life. As for Betsy, after a bit of prodding, she faithfully plowed through some of the manuscript. Parts of it she admitted were interesting (as befitting a 12-year-old, she liked the section on ballooning) and other parts (like that on the Constitutional Convention) she declared boring, which I guess was a help, especially to readers who were thus treated to shortened versions of a few of these sections. They both make everything not only possible but worthwhile.

None of these people, of course, deserve blame for any errors or lapses that I have undoubtedly made. In a May 23, 1785, letter to his friend George Whatley, Franklin said about his life, "I shall not object to a new edition of mine; hoping however that the errata of the last may be corrected." I feel the same of this book.

SOURCES AND ABBREVIATIONS

Except where otherwise noted, Franklin's writings cited are in the Franklin Papers edited at Yale (see below) and the CD-ROM by the Packard Humanities Institute.

In using Internet addresses, please note that the periods, commas, hyphens, and semicolons used below to separate entries should not be included as part of a URL.

ABBREVIATIONS USED IN SOURCE NOTES

People

BF	=	Benjamin Franklin
DF	=	Deborah Franklin, wife
JM	=	Jane Franklin Mecom, sister
MS	=	Margaret Stevenson, London landlady
PS	=	Mary "Polly" Stevenson [Hewson], landlady's daughter
RB	=	Richard Bache, son-in-law
SF	=	Sarah "Sally" Franklin [Bache], daughter
TF	=	[William] Temple Franklin, grandson
WF	=	William Franklin, son

Franklin's Writings

Autobiography = *The Autobiography of Benjamin Franklin*.

For the reader's convenience, page citations refer to the most commonly available edition, the Signet Classic paperback (New York: Penguin Putnam, 2001), which is primarily based on a version prepared by Max Farrand (Berkeley: University of California Press, 1949).

There are more than 150 editions of this classic. The one that best shows his revisions is the "Genetic Text" edited by J. A. Leo Lemay and P. M. Zall (Knoxville: University of Tennessee Press, 1981), which is also to be found in the Norton Critical Edition, edited by Lemay and Zall (New York: Norton, 1986), referred to in the notes below as the Lemay/Zall Autobiography and Norton Autobiography, respectively. The authoritative edition produced by Leonard Labaree and the other editors of the Franklin Papers at Yale (New Haven: Yale University Press, 1964), referred to below as the Yale Autobiography, is based directly on Franklin's handwritten manuscript and includes useful annotations and a history of various versions.

Searchable electronic versions of the autobiography can be found on the Internet at ushistory.org/franklin/autobiography/index.htm ; cedarcottage.com/eBooks/ benfrank.rtf ; earlyamerica.com/lives/franklin/index.html ; odur.let.rug.nl/~usa/B/ bfranklin/frank.htm ; etext.lib.virginia.edu/toc/modeng/public/Fra2Aut.html ; eserver.org/books/franklin/.

Lib. of Am. = *Benjamin Franklin Writings*
with notes by J. A. Leo Lemay (New York: Library of America, 1987). This 1,560-page volume has an authoritative collection of Franklin's most important writings along with source notes and annotations. It includes important revisions to the Franklin canon by Lemay that update the work of the Yale editors of Franklin's papers. A searchable electronic version of much of the text is on the Internet at www.historycarper.com/resources/twobf1/contents.htm .

Pa. Gazette = The *Pennsylvania Gazette*
Searchable electronic versions are on the Internet at www.accessible.com/ about.htm ; etext.lib.virginia.edu/pengazet.html ; www.historycarper.com/re sources/ twobf2/pg29-30.htm .

Papers = *The Papers of Benjamin Franklin*
(New Haven: Yale, 1959–). This definitive and extraordinary series of annotated volumes, produced at Yale in conjunction with the American Philosophical Society, was begun under Leonard Labaree. Recent members of the distinguished team of editors include Ellen Cohn, Judith Adkins, Jonathan Dull, Karen Duval, Leslie Lindenauer, Claude-Anne Lopez, Barbara Oberg, Kate Ohno, and Michael Sletcher. By 2003, the team had reached volume 37, which goes through August 1782. All correspondence and writings cited below, unless otherwise noted, refer to versions in the Papers. See: www.yale.edu/franklinpapers .

Papers CD = CD-ROM of the *Papers of Benjamin Franklin*
prepared by the Packard Humanities Institute in cooperation with the Yale editors. These include all of Franklin's known writings, including material from 1783 to 1790 that has not yet been published. It is searchable by phrase, correspondent, and chronology, but it does not include the valuable annotations by the Yale editors. I am grateful to David Packard and his staff for giving me a version of the CD-ROM before its release.

Poor Richard's = *Poor Richard's: An Almanack*
by Benjamin Franklin. Many versions are available, and quotations are cited by year in the notes below. Searchable electronic versions can be found on the Internet at www.sage-advice.com/Benjamin_Franklin.htm ; www.ku.edu/carrie/stacks/au thors.franklin.html ; itech.fgcu.edu/faculty/wohlpart/alra/franklin.htm ; and www. swarthmore.edu/SocSci/bdorsey1/41docs/52-fra.html .

Silence Dogood = The Silence Dogood essays
The complete editions of the *New England Courant,* including these essays, are at ushistory.org/franklin/courant .

Smyth *Writings = The Writings of Benjamin Franklin*
edited by Albert Henry Smyth, first published in 1907 (New York: Macmillan, 1905–7; reprinted New York: Haskell House, 1970). Until the Yale editions, this 10-volume work had been a definitive collection of Franklin's papers.

Sparks = *The Works of Benjamin Franklin* and the *Life of Benjamin Franklin*
by Jared Sparks (Boston: Tappan, Whittemore and Mason, 1840). Sparks was a Harvard history professor and president who published a 10-volume collection of Franklin's papers and a biography in 1836–40; www.ushistory.org/franklin/biography/index.htm .

Temple *Writings = Memoirs of the Life and Writings of Benjamin Franklin*
by [William] Temple Franklin, 3 volumes (London: Henry Colburn, 1818).

Other Frequently Cited Sources

Adams Diary = *The Diary and Autobiography of John Adams*
edited by L. H. Butterfield (Cambridge: Harvard University Press, 1961).

Adams Letters = *Adams Family Correspondence*
edited by L. H. Butterfield (Cambridge: Harvard University Press, 1963–73).

Aldridge *French = Franklin and His French Contemporaries*
by Alfred Owen Aldridge (New York: NYU Press, 1957).

Aldridge *Nature = Benjamin Franklin and Nature's God*
by Alfred Owen Aldridge (Durham, N.C.: Duke University Press, 1967).

Alsop = *Yankees at the Court*
by Susan Mary Alsop (Garden City, N.Y.: Doubleday, 1982).

Bowen = *The Most Dangerous Man in America*
by Catherine Drinker Bowen (Boston: Little, Brown, 1974).

Brands = *The First American*
by H. W. Brands (New York: Doubleday, 2000).

Buxbaum = *Benjamin Franklin and the Zealous Presbyterians*
by Melvin Buxbaum (University Park: Pennsylvania State University Press, 1975).

Campbell = *Recovering Benjamin Franklin*
by James Campbell (Chicago: Open Court, 1999).

Clark = *Benjamin Franklin*
by Ronald W. Clark (New York: Random House, 1983).

Cohen = *Benjamin Franklin's Science*
by I. Bernard Cohen (Cambridge: Harvard University Press, 1990).

Faÿ = *Franklin: The Apostle of Modern Man*
by Bernard Faÿ (Boston: Little, Brown, 1929).

Fleming = *The Man Who Dared the Lightning*
by Thomas Fleming (New York: Morrow, 1971).

Hawke = *Franklin*
by David Freeman Hawke (New York: Harper & Row, 1976).

Jefferson Papers = *Papers of Thomas Jefferson*
edited by Julian Boyd (Princeton: Princeton University Press, 1950–).

Lemay *Internet Doc* = "Benjamin Franklin: A Documentary History"
by J. A. Leo Lemay, University of Delaware, www.english.udel.edu/lemay/
franklin .

Lemay *Reappraising* = *Reappraising Benjamin Franklin*
edited by J. A. Leo Lemay (Newark: University of Delaware Press, 1993).

Lopez *Cher* = *Mon Cher Papa*
by Claude-Anne Lopez (New Haven: Yale University Press, 1966).

Lopez *Life* = *My Life with Benjamin Franklin*
by Claude-Anne Lopez (New Haven: Yale University Press, 2002).

Lopez *Private* = *The Private Franklin*
by Claude-Anne Lopez and Eugenia Herbert (New York: Norton, 1975).

McCullough = *John Adams*
by David McCullough (New York: Simon & Schuster, 2001).

Middlekauff = *Benjamin Franklin and His Enemies*
by Robert Middlekauff (Berkeley: University of California Press, 1996).

Morgan *Franklin* = *Benjamin Franklin*
by Edmund S. Morgan (New Haven: Yale University Press, 2002).

Morgan *Devious* = *The Devious Dr. Franklin: Benjamin Franklin's Years in London*
by David Morgan (Macon, Ga.: Mercer University Press, 1996).

Parton = *Life and Times of Benjamin Franklin*
by James Parton, 2 volumes (New York: Mason Brothers, 1865).

PMHB = *Pennsylvania Magazine of History and Biography*

Randall = *A Little Revenge*
by Willard Sterne Randall (New York: William Morrow, 1984).

Sanford = *Benjamin Franklin and the American Character*
edited by Charles Sanford (Boston: Heath, 1955).

Sappenfield = *A Sweet Instruction: Franklin's Journalism as a Literary Apprentice-ship*
by James Sappenfield (Carbondale: Southern Illinois University Press, 1973).

Schoenbrun = *Triumph in Paris*
by David Schoenbrun (New York: Harper & Row, 1976).

Skemp *William* = *William Franklin*
by Sheila Skemp (New York: Oxford University Press, 1990).

Skemp *Benjamin* = *Benjamin and William Franklin*
by Sheila Skemp (New York: St. Martin's, 1994).

Smith = *Franklin and Bache: Envisioning the Enlightened Republic*
by Jeffery A. Smith (New York: Oxford University Press, 1990).

Stourzh = *Benjamin Franklin and American Foreign Policy*
by Gerald Stourzh (Chicago: University of Chicago Press, 1954).

Tourtellot = *Benjamin Franklin: The Shaping of Genius, the Boston Years*
by Arthur Tourtellot (Garden City, N.Y.: Doubleday, 1977).

Van Doren = *Benjamin Franklin*
by Carl Van Doren (New York: Viking, 1938). The page numbers are the same in the Penguin USA paperback edition, 1991 and subsequent reprints.

Walters = *Benjamin Franklin and His Gods*
by Kerry S. Walters (Urbana: University of Illinois Press, 1998).

Wright = *Franklin of Philadelphia*
by Esmond Wright (Cambridge: Harvard University Press, 1986).

NOTES

CHAPTER 1

1. For a description of the writing of the *Autobiography*, see pages 254–57 and chapter 11 note 5 on page 542.

2. David Brooks, "Our Founding Yuppie," *Weekly Standard*, Oct. 23, 2000, 31. The word "meritocracy" is an argument-starter, and I have employed it sparingly in this book. It is often used loosely to denote a vision of social mobility based on merit and diligence, like Franklin's. The word was coined by British social thinker Michael Young (later to become, somewhat ironically, Lord Young of Darlington) in his 1958 book *The Rise of the Meritocracy* (New York: Viking Press) as a dismissive term to satirize a society that misguidedly created a new elite class based on the "narrow band of values" of IQ and educational credentials. The Harvard philosopher John Rawls, in *A Theory of Justice* (Cambridge: Harvard University Press, 1971), 106, used it more broadly to mean a "social order [that] follows the principle of careers open to talents." The best description of the idea is in Nicholas Lemann's *The Big Test: The Secret History of the American Meritocracy* (New York: Farrar, Straus & Giroux, 1999), a history of educational aptitude tests and their effect on American society. In Franklin's time, Enlightenment thinkers (such as Jefferson in his proposals for creating the University of Virginia) advocated replacing the hereditary aristocracy with a "natural aristocracy," whose members would be plucked from the masses at an early age based on "virtues and talents" and groomed for leadership. Franklin's idea was more expansive. He believed in encouraging and providing opportunities for all people to succeed as best they could based on their diligence, hard work, virtue, and talent. As we shall see, his proposals for what became the University of Pennsylvania (in contrast to Jefferson's for the University of Virginia) were aimed not at filtering a new elite but at encouraging and enriching all "aspiring" young men. Franklin was propounding a more egalitarian and democratic approach than Jefferson by proposing a system that would, as Rawls (p. 107) would later prescribe, assure that "resources for education are not to be allotted solely or necessarily mainly according to their return as estimated in productive trained abilities, but also according to their worth in enriching the personal and social life of citizens." (Translation: He cared not simply about making

society as a whole more productive, but also about making each individual more enriched.)

CHAPTER 2

1. Autobiography 18; Josiah Franklin to BF, May 26, 1739; editor's note in Papers 2:229; Tourtellot 12. Franklin provides a footnote in the Autobiography showing how the noun and surname "franklin" was used in fifteenth-century England. Some analysts, as well as his French fans, have pointed out that Franquelin was a common name in the province of Picardie, France, in the fifteenth century, and his ancestors may have come from there. His father, Josiah Franklin, wrote, "Some think we are of a French extract which was formerly called Franks; some of a free line (frank line), a line free from that vassalage which was common to subjects in the days of old; some from a bird of long red legs." Franklin's own assessment that his surname came from the class of English freemen called *franklins* is almost surely the correct explanation, and just as important, it was the one he believed. The *Oxford English Dictionary* defines *franklin* as "A class of landowners, of free but not noble birth, and ranking next below the gentry." It is derived from the Middle English word *frankeleyn,* meaning a freeman or freeholder. See Chaucer's "The Franklin's Tale," or "The Frankeleyn's Tale," www.librarius.com/ cantales.htm .

2. Autobiography 20; Josiah Franklin to BF, May 26, 1739. The tale of the Bible and stool is in the letter from Josiah Franklin, but BF writes that he heard it from his uncle Benjamin. For a full genealogy, see Papers 1:xlix. The Signet edition of the Autobiography, based on a version prepared by Max Farrand (Berkeley: University of California Press, 1949), uses a somewhat different phrase: "Our humble family early embraced the Reformation."

3. As David McCullough does in *Truman* (New York: Simon & Schuster, 1992) and Robert Caro in *The Path to Power* (New York: Knopf, 1982).

4. Autobiography 20; "A short account of the Family of Thomas Franklin of Ecton," by Benjamin Franklin the elder (uncle of BF), Yale University Library; Benjamin Franklin the Elder's commonplace book, cited in Papers, vol. 1; Tourtellot 18.

5. BF to David Hume, May 19, 1762.

6. Tourtellot 42.

7. John Winthrop, "A Model of Christian Charity" (1630), www.winthrop society.org/charity.htm ; Perry Miller, *Errand into the Wilderness* (Cambridge: Harvard University Press, 1956). See also Andrew Delbanco, *The Puritan Ordeal* (Cambridge: Harvard University Press, 1989); Edmund Morgan, *Visible Saints: The History of a Puritan Idea* (New York: NYU Press, 1963); Herbert Schneider, *The Puritan Mind* (Ann Arbor: University of Michigan Press, 1958).

8. Perry Miller, "Benjamin Franklin and Jonathan Edwards," in *Major Writers of America* (New York: Harcourt Brace, 1962), 84; Tourtellot 41; Cotton Mather, "A Christian at His Calling," 1701, personal.pitnet.net/primarysources/mather.html ;

Poor Richard's, 1736 (drawn from Aesop's "Hercules and the Wagoner," ca. 550 B.C., and Algernon Sidney's *Discourses on Government*, 1698, among other antecedents).

9. Tourtellot 47–52; Nian Sheng Huang, "Franklin's Father Josiah: Life of a Colonial Boston Tallow Chandler, 1657–1745" (Philadelphia: Transactions of the American Philosophical Society, 2000) vol. 90, pt. 3.

10. Lemay *Internet Doc* for 1657–1705; a drawing of the house is in Papers 1:4.

11. Edmund Morgan, *The Puritan Family* (New York: Harper & Row, 1966); Mark Van Doren and Samuel Sewall, eds., *Samuel Sewall's Diary* (New York: Macy-Masius, 1927), 208.

12. Autobiography 24.

13. Autobiography 25, 91.

14. Tourtellot 86; Lopez *Private* 5–7.

15. Alexander Starbuck, *The History of Nantucket* (New York: Heritage, 1998), 53, 91, cited in Tourtellot 104.

16. Peter Folger, "A Looking Glass for the Times," reprinted in Tourtellot 106; Autobiography 23.

17. The genealogy of the Franklin and Folger families is in Papers 1:xlix.

18. Autobiography 23. The Farrand/Signet edition uses the phrase: "that which was not honest could not be truly useful."

19. BF to Barbeu Dubourg, April 1773; Tourtellot 161.

20. BF to Madame Brillon, Nov. 10, 1779 (known as the bagatelle of The Whistle); Autobiography 107; Pierre Jean Georges Cabanis, in *Complete Works* (Paris: Bossange frères, 1823), 5:222, records it as a lesson learned from his family.

21. Autobiography 24; Lopez *Private* 7.

22. Benjamin Franklin the elder, "To My Name, 1713," Paper 1:3–5; BF to JM, July 17, 1771; Parton 32–38; Tourtellot 139–40; Autobiography 20.

23. Autobiography 22; BF to JM, July 17, 1771; Lopez *Private*, 9.

24. Autobiography 22; Tourtellot 156. Boston Latin School was then generally called the South Grammar School.

25. Temple *Writings*, 1: 447.

26. Autobiography 25–26.

27. Autobiography 27; *Boston Post*, Aug. 7, 1940, cited in Papers 1:6–7. No authenticated copies of these two poems are known to have survived. The Franklin Papers 1:6–7 quote a few possible verses that may have been his.

28. Lemay *Internet Doc* for 1719–20, citing *Early Boston Booksellers*, by George Emery Littlefield (Boston: Antiquarian Society, 1900), 150–55; Tourtellot 230–32. Franklin incorrectly states that the *Courant* was the second newspaper in Boston. See Yale Autobiography 67n.

29. Perry Miller, *The New England Mind: From Colony to Province* (Cambridge: Harvard University Press, 1983), 344. See also E. Digby Baltzell, *Puritan Boston and Quaker Philadelphia* (New York: Free Press, 1979).

30. John Blake, "The Inoculation Controversy in Boston: 1721–1722," *New England Quarterly* (1952): 489–506; *New England Courant*, Aug. 7, 1721, and following, ushistory.org/franklin/courant ; Tourtellot 252.

31. Lemay *Internet Doc* for 1721; Perry Miller, *The New England Mind: From Colony to Province*, 337.

32. Autobiography 26. Analysis of Franklin's childhood reading can be found in Parton 1:44–51, 60–72; Ralph Ketcham, *Benjamin Franklin* (New York: Washington Square Press, 1965), 8–31; Tourtellot 166.

33. Autobiography 27; BF to Samuel Mather, July 7, 1773, May 12, 1784; John Bunyan, *Pilgrim's Progress*, 1678, www.ccel.org/b/bunyan/progress/; Plutarch, *Parallel Lives*, ca. A.D. 100, ibiblio.org/gutenberg/etext96/plivs10.txt ; Cotton Mather, *Bonifacius*, also known as *Essays to Do Good* and *An Essay upon the Good*, 1710, edweb.sdsu.edu/people/DKitchen/new_655/mather.htm ; Tourtellot 187–89.

34. Daniel Defoe, *An Essay upon Projects*, 1697, ibiblio.org/gutenberg/etext03/esprj10.txt ; Tourtellot 185.

35. Autobiography 28.

36. *The Spectator,* Mar. 13, 1711, harvest.rutgers.edu/projects/spectator/markup.html ; Autobiography 29.

37. *The Spectator,* Mar. 1, 1711; Silence Dogood #1, Apr. 2, 1722; Silence Dogood #2, Apr. 16, 1722; Silence Dogood #3, Apr. 30, 1722; ushistory.org/franklin/courant ; Papers 1:8–11. These dates, unlike others, are in the Old Style because they refer to editions of the *Courant* as dated at the time.

38. Silence Dogood #4, May 14, 1722; *The Spectator*, Mar. 3, 1711.

39. Autobiography 34; *New England Courant*, June 18, 25, July 2, 9, 1722. The excerpt is from *The London Journal.*

40. *New England Courant,* July 16, 23, 1722.

41. *New England Courant,* Sept. 14, 1722, Feb. 11, 1723; Autobiography 33. Franklin compresses the chronology by recalling that his name went on top of the paper right after his brother's release from jail, which was in July 1722; in fact, it occurred after James got into another dispute in January 1723. Oddly, his name remained atop the paper until at least 1726, which was three years after he had run away to Philadelphia. See *New England Courant,* June 25, 1726, and Yale Autobiography 70n.

42. Autobiography 34–35.

43. Claude-Anne Lopez, an editor of Franklin's papers at Yale, discovered a scrap of paper on which Franklin, in 1783, jotted down some dates and places designed to pinpoint his itinerary of sixty years earlier. In the Norton edition of the Autobiography, J. A. Leo Lemay and P. M. Zall note that the only boat leaving Boston for New York that week was a sloop on September 25. Franklin's editing of the "naughty girl" passage is noted in the Signet edition, 35. James Franklin's forlorn ad appears in *New England Courant,* Sept. 30, 1723.

CHAPTER 3

1. *The Way to Health* was written by Thomas Tryon (1634–1703) and first published in 1683; Autobiography 29.

2. Autobiography 49.

3. Autobiography 38.

4. Autobiography 79; Jonathan Yardley, review of Edmund Morgan's *Benjamin Franklin*, in *Washington Post Book World*, Sept. 15, 2002, 2.

5. Autobiography 41.

6. Autobiography 52.

7. Autobiography 42. Franklin later politely revised the phrase in his autobiography to read, "stared with astonishment." Lemay/Zall Autobiography provides a complete look at the original manuscript and all of its revisions. The governors sent to Pennsylvania were sometimes referred to as lieutenant governors.

8. Franklin recounted this tale twice to Mather's son: BF to Samuel Mather, July 7, 1773, and May 12, 1784.

9. Autobiography 104.

10. Autobiography 48.

11. Autobiography 54.

12. Autobiography 55–58.

13. "A Dissertation on Liberty and Necessity, Pleasure and Pain," 1725, Papers 1:58; Campbell 101–3.

14. Autobiography 70; Campbell 91–135.

15. Autobiography 92; Poor Richard Improved, 1753; Papers 4:406. See also Alfred Owen Aldridge, "The Alleged Puritanism of Benjamin Franklin," in Lemay *Reappraising* 370; Aldridge *Nature;* Campbell 99. For good descriptions of the evolution of Franklin's religious thought, see Walters; Buxbaum. See also chapter 7 of this book.

16. Autobiography 63.

17. "Plan of Conduct," 1726, Papers 1:99; Autobiography 183.

18. "Journal of a Voyage," July 22–Oct. 11, 1726, Papers 1:72–99. The idea that "affability and sociability" were core tenets of the Enlightenment is explained well in Gordon Wood, *The Radicalism of the American Revolution* (New York: Random House, 1991), 215–6.

CHAPTER 4

1. Autobiography 64. For overviews of life in Philadelphia, see Carl Bridenbaugh and Jessica Bridenbaugh, *Rebels and Gentlemen: Philadelphia in the Age of Franklin* (New York: Oxford University Press, 1942); E. Digby Baltzell, *Puritan Boston and Quaker Philadelphia* (New York: Free Press, 1979). For a good overview of Franklin's work as a printer, see C. William Miller, *Benjamin Franklin's Philadelphia Printing 1728–1766* (Philadelphia: American Philosophical Society, 1974).

2. The chronology in the Autobiography is not quite correct. Denham took ill in the spring of 1727 but did not die until July 1728. Lemay/Zall Autobiography 41.

3. Autobiography 69; Brands 87–89; Van Doren 71–73.

4. Autobiography 71–79; Brands 91; Lemay/Zall Autobiography 49. The

Quaker history was written by William Sewel. Franklin records that he published forty sheets of folio, which would have been 160 pages, but in fact he produced 178 pages and Keimer the remaining 532 pages.

5. Last Will and Codicil, June 23, 1789, Papers CD 46:u20.

6. Whitfield J. Bell Jr., *Patriot Improvers* (Philadelphia: American Philosophical Society, 1999), vol. 1; Autobiography 72–73; "On Conversation," Pa. Gazette, Oct. 15, 1730. Dale Carnegie, in his book *How to Win Friends and Influence People* (1937; New York: Pocket Books, 1994), draws on Franklin's rules for conversation. Carnegie's first two rules for "How to Win People to Your Way of Thinking" are: "The only way to get the best of an argument is to avoid it" and "Show respect for the other person's opinions. Never say, 'You're wrong.' " In his section on "How to Change People without Giving Offense or Arousing Resentment," he instructs: "Call attention to people's mistakes indirectly" and "Ask questions instead of giving direct orders." Carnegie's book has sold more than 15 million copies.

7. Autobiography 96; "Rules for a Club for Mutual Improvement," 1727; "Proposals and Queries to be Asked the Junto," 1732.

8. BF to Samuel Mather, May 17, 1784; Van Doren 75; Cotton Mather, "Religious Societies," 1724; Lemay/Zall Autobiography 47n. See also Mitchell Breitwieser, *Cotton Mather and Benjamin Franklin* (Cambridge: Cambridge University Press, 1984).

9. Autobiography 74; *American Weekly Mercury*, Jan. 28, 1729 (Shortface and Careful); Papers 1:112; Brands 101; Van Doren 94; Sappenfield 49–55.

10. Busy-Body #1, *American Weekly Mercury*, Feb. 4, 1729; Sappenfield 51; *The Universal Instructor . . . and Pennsylvania Gazette*, Feb. 25, Mar. 13, 1729; Papers 1:115–27.

11. Busy-Body #3, *American Weekly Mercury*, Feb. 18, 1729; Busy-Body #4, *American Weekly Mercury*, Feb. 25, 1789; Busy-Body #8, *American Weekly Mercury*, Mar. 28, 1729. Lemay's masterly notes in the Library of America's edition of Franklin's *Writings* (p. 1524) describe which parts Franklin wrote and what was withdrawn in Busy-Body #8.

12. "A Modest Enquiry into the Nature and Necessity of a Paper Currency," Apr. 3, 1729; Autobiography 77–78. Franklin draws on William Petty's 1662 work, *A Treatise of Taxes and Contributions*, www.socsci.mcmaster.ca/~econ/ugcm/3113/petty/taxes.txt .

13. "The Printer to the Reader," Pa. Gazette, Oct. 2, 1729.

14. "Printer's Errors," Pa. Gazette, Mar. 13, 1730.

15. Pa. Gazette, Mar. 19, 1730; Autobiography 75.

16. "Apology for Printers," Pa. Gazette, June 10, 1731; Clark 49; Isaiah Thomas, *The History of Printing in America* (1810; Albany: Munsell, 1874), 1: 237.

17. Pa. Gazette, June 17, 24, July 29, 1731, Feb. 15, June 19, July 3, 1732.

18. Pa. Gazette, Oct. 24, 1734; not in the Yale Papers, but later ascribed to the Franklin canon by Lemay, see Lib. of Am. 233–34.

19. Pa. Gazette, Sept. 7, 1732. For an analysis of Franklin's journalistic treatment of crime and scandal, see Ronald Bosco, "Franklin Working the Crime Beat," Lemay *Reappraising*, 78–97.

20. Pa. Gazette, Sept. 12, 1732, Jan. 27, 1730.

21. "Death of a Drunk," Pa. Gazette, Dec. 7, 1732; "On Drunkenness," Feb. 1, 1733; "A Meditation on a Quart Mugg," July 19, 1733; "The Drinker's Dictionary," Jan. 13, 1737. In Silence Dogood #12 (Sept. 10, 1722), Franklin had his sassy widow defend moderate drinking and condemn excess, drawing on Richard Steele's essays in London's *Tatler.* See Robert Arnor, "Politics and Temperance," in Lemay *Reappraising,* 52–77.

22. Pa. Gazette, Sept. 23, 1731.

23. Autobiography 34, 80, 72; "Anthony Afterwit," Pa. Gazette, July 10, 1732.

24. Autobiography 64, 81; Faÿ 135; Brands 106–9; Lopez *Private,* 23–24; BF to Joseph Priestley, Sept. 19, 1772; Poor Richard's, 1738. The first volume of the Papers 1:1xii in 1959 said Deborah was born in Philadelphia in 1708, but that thinking was revised after Francis James Dallett published a paper the following year called "Dr. Franklin's In-Laws," which is cited in Papers 8:139. Dallett's evidence indicates that Deborah was born in 1705 or 1706, maybe in Philadelphia but more likely in Birmingham, from which she emigrated to Philadelphia with her family in about 1711. See Edward James et al., *Notable American Women 1607–1950* (Cambridge: Harvard University Press, 1971), 1:663, entry on Deborah Franklin by Leonard Labaree, the initial editor of the Yale Papers. If she did cross the ocean at age 5 or so, it may have caused her lifelong aversion to ever crossing (or even seeing) it again. For a good analysis, see J. A. Leo Lemay, "Recent Franklin Scholarship," *PMHB* 76.2 (Apr. 2002): 336.

25. BF to "honoured mother" Abiah Franklin, Apr. 12, 1750; Lemay *Internet Doc* for 1728; Parton 1:177, 198–99; Randall 43; Skemp *William,* 4–5, 10; Brands 110, 243; *Gentleman's Magazine* (1813), in Papers 3:474n. The Yale editors of Franklin's papers say in volume 1 (published in 1959) that William was born circa 1731, but by volume 3 (published in 1961) they note the controversy (Papers 3:89n) and suggest that perhaps he was born earlier; however, in their edition of the Autobiography, published in 1964, they reiterate "circa 1731" as the year of his birth.

26. Van Doren 93, 231; Brands 110, 243. See also Charles Hart, "Who Was the Mother of Franklin's Son?" *PMHB* (July 1911): 308–14; Paul Leicester Ford, *Who Was the Mother of Franklin's Son?* (New York: Century, 1889).

27. Van Doren 91; Lopez *Private,* 22–23; Clark 41; Roberts letter, Papers 2:370n.; Bell, *Patriot Improvers,* 1:277–80.

28. Autobiography 92; BF to JM, Jan. 6, 1727; Poor Richard's, 1733.

29. "Anthony Afterwit," Pa. Gazette, July 10, 1732; "Celia Single," Pa. Gazette, July 24, 1732.

30. "Rules and Maxims for Promoting Matrimonial Happiness," Pa. Gazette, Oct. 8, 1730, Lib. of Am. 151. This piece is not included by the Yale editors, but Lemay and others subsequently attributed it to Franklin.

31. Lopez *Private,* 31–37; BF to James Read, Aug. 17, 1745; "A Scolding Wife," Pa. Gazette, July 5, 1733.

32. BF to Deborah Franklin, Feb. 19, 1758; "I Sing My Plain Country Joan," 1742; Francis James Dallett, "Dr. Franklin's In-Laws," cited in Papers 8:139;

Leonard Labaree, "Deborah Franklin," in *Notable American Women 1607–1950*, ed. Edward James et al. (Cambridge: Harvard University Press 1971), 1:663.

33. Autobiography 112; BF to JM, Jan. 13, 1772; Pa. Gazette, Dec. 23–30, 1736; Van Doren 126; Clark 43; Brands 154–55. Franklin had editorialized in favor of smallpox inoculations in his paper before Francis was born: Pa. Gazette, May 14, 28, 1730, Mar. 4, 1731.

34. "The Death of Infants," Pa. Gazette, June 20, 1734, ascribed to the Franklin canon by Lemay, Lib. of Am. 228.

35. Franklin writes in the Autobiography (p. 92) that he was "educated as a Presbyterian," but the Puritan sect in Boston into which he was baptized in fact became what is now called the Congregational Church. Both Presbyterians and Congregationalists generally follow the doctrines of John Calvin. See Yale Autobiography 145n. For more on Jedediah Andrews, see Richard Webster, *A History of the Presbyterian Church in America, from Its Origin until the Year 1760* (Philadelphia: J. M. Wilson, 1857), 105–12. For more on Franklin and the Presbyterians, see chapter 5, n. 7.

36. Autobiography 92–94.

37. Deism can be an amorphous concept. Despite his qualms about the consequences of unenhanced deism, Franklin did not shy from the word in labeling his beliefs. I use the word, as he did, to describe the Enlightenment-era philosophy that (1) rejects the belief that faith depends on received or revealed religious doctrines; (2) does not emphasize an intimate or passionate spiritual relationship with God or Christ; (3) believes in a rather impersonal Creator who set in motion the universe and all its laws; (4) holds that reason and the study of nature tells us all we can know about the Creator. See Walters; "Franklin's Life in Deism," in Campbell 110–26; Kerry Walters, *The American Deists* (Lawrence: University of Kansas Press, 1992); Buxbaum; A. Owen Aldridge, "Enlightenment and Awakening in Franklin and Edwards," in *Benjamin Franklin, Jonathan Edwards*, ed. Barbara Oberg and Harry Stout (New York: Oxford University Press, 1997), 27–41; Aldridge, "The Alledged Puritanism of Benjamin Franklin," in Lemay *Reappraising*, 362–71; Aldridge, *Nature;* Douglas Anderson, *The Radical Enlightenments of Benjamin Franklin* (Baltimore: Johns Hopkins University Press, 1997); Baltzell, *Puritan Boston and Quaker Philadelphia;* Larzer Ziff, *Puritanism in America* (New York: Viking, 1973); Donald Meyer, "Franklin's Religion," in *Critical Essays*, ed. Melvin Buxbaum (Boston: Hall, 1987), 147–67; Perry Miller, *Nature's Nation* (Cambridge: Harvard University Press, 1967); Mark Noll, *America's God* (New York: Oxford University Press, 2002); Simon Blackburn, *The Oxford Dictionary of Philosophy* (Oxford: Oxford University Press, 1994).

38. "Articles of Belief and Acts of Religion," Nov. 20, 1728, Papers 1:101.

39. Walters 8, 84–86. Walters's book is the most direct argument that Franklin was not espousing a literal polytheism. The opposite view is expressed in A. Owen Aldridge's comprehensive *Benjamin Franklin and Nature's God*. Read figuratively, Franklin seems to be saying that different denominations and religions each have their own gods: there is the God of the Puritans, who is different from Franklin's own God, or the God of the Methodists, of the Jews, of the Anabaptists, or, for that

matter, of the Hindus, Muslims, and ancient Greeks. These different gods arise because of differing perspectives (producing what Walters calls Franklin's "theistic perspectivism"). Franklin believed that the idea of a God as Creator and first cause is common to all religions, and thus can be assumed true. But different religions and sects add their own expressions and concepts, none of which we can really know to be true or false, but that lead to the existence of a multiplicity of gods that allow a more personal relationship with their believers. This interpretation comports with Franklin's comment in his essay that these gods can sometimes disappear as times and cultures evolve. "It may be that after many ages, they are changed and others supply their places."

40. "On the Providence of God in the Government of the World," Papers 1:264. The Yale editors posit 1732 as its date. A. Owen Aldridge, Leo Lemay, and others persuasively argue, based on a letter Franklin later wrote about it, that it was actually 1730; BF to Benjamin Vaughan, Nov. 9, 1779. See Aldridge *Nature*, 34–40; Lemay *Internet Doc* for 1730. The Library of America edition of Franklin's writings accepts the 1730 date. Wilhelm Niesel, *The Theology of Calvin* (Philadelphia: Westminster Press, 1956), 70; John Calvin, *Commentaries*, "On Paul's Epistle to the Romans" (1539), www.ccel.org/c/calvin/comment3/comm_vol38/htm/TOC.htm .

41. Walters 98; Campbell 109–11; Aldridge *Nature*, 25–38; BF to John Franklin, May 1745.

42. "A Witch Trial at Mount Holly," Pa. Gazette, Oct. 22, 1730.

43. BF to Josiah and Abiah Franklin, Apr. 13, 1738. When his beloved sister Jane also conveyed her misgivings about his emphasis on good works rather than prayer, he offered a similar mix of explanation and mild reassurance. "I am so far from thinking that God is not to be worshipped that I have composed and wrote a whole book of devotions for my own use," he says, and then urges tolerance. "There are some things in your New England doctrines and worship which I do not agree with, but I do not therefore condemn them . . . I would only have you make me the same allowances." BF to JM, July 28, 1743.

44. Autobiography 94–105, 49; D. H. Lawrence, "Benjamin Franklin," in *Studies in Classic American Literature* (New York: Viking, 1923), 10–16, xroads. virginia.edu/~HYPER/LAWRENCE/dhlch02.htm .

45. Randy Cohen, "Best Wishes," *New York Times Magazine*, June 30, 2002; David Brooks, *Bobos in Paradise* (New York: Simon & Schuster, 2000), 64; Morgan *Franklin*, 23; Autobiography 104.

46. Autobiography 94–105, 49; Sappenfield 187–88; Lopez *Private*, 24; Lopez *Cher*, 277. The French friend was the scientist Pierre-Georges Cabanis, *Complete Works* (Paris: Bossange frères, 1825), 2:348.

47. Cotton Mather, "Two Brief Discourses," 1701; A. Whitney Griswold, "Two Puritans on Prosperity," 1934, in Sanford 42; Campbell 99, 166–74; Ziff, *Puritanism in America*, 218; Aldridge, "The Alleged Puritanism of Benjamin Franklin," in Lemay *Reappraising*, 370; Lopez *Private*, 104. Perry Miller notes: "This child of New England Puritanism simply dumped the whole theological preoccupation overboard; but, not the slightest ceasing to be a Puritan, went about his business"; see "Ben Franklin, Jonathan Edwards," *Major Writers of America* (New York: Har-

court Brace, 1962), 86. See chapter 4, n. 37 for sources on deism and the Enlightenment.

48. See chapter 18 for details of the Romantic-era view of Franklin.

49. John Updike, "Many Bens," *The New Yorker*, Feb. 22, 1988, 115; Henry Steele Commager, *The American Mind* (New Haven: Yale University Press, 1950), 26.

The strongest argument that Franklin was a pure exemplar of the Enlightenment is in historian Carl Becker's masterful essay on him in the *Dictionary of American Biography* (New York: Scribner's, 1933), in which he called Franklin "a true child of the Enlightenment, not indeed of the school of Rousseau, but of Defoe and Pope and Swift, of Fontenelle and Montesquieu and Voltaire. He spoke their language, although with a homely accent . . . He accepted without question all the characteristic ideas [of the Enlightenment]: its healthy, clarifying skepticism; its passion for freedom and its humane sympathies; its preoccupation with the world that is evident to the senses; its profound faith in common sense, in the efficacy of Reason for the solution of human problems and the advancement of human welfare." See also Stuart Sherman, "Franklin and the Age of Enlightenment," in Sanford.

50. Autobiography 139; Albert Smyth, *American Literature* (Philadelphia: Eldredge, 1889), 20; BF to Benjamin Vaughan, Nov. 9, 1779; BF to DF, June 4, 1765. For additional words of disgust about metaphysics, see BF to Thomas Hopkinson, Oct. 16, 1746. For a fuller assessment of Franklin's religious and moral beliefs, see the final chapter of this book. The ideas here draw in part from the following: Campbell 25, 34–36, 137, 165, 169–72, 286; Charles Angoff, *Literary History of the American People* (New York: Knopf, 1931), 295–310; Van Wyck Brooks, *America's Coming of Age* (Garden City, N.Y.: Anchor, 1934), 3–7; Lopez *Private*, 26; Alan Taylor, "For the Benefit of Mr. Kite," *The New Republic*, Mar. 19, 2001, 39; Vernon Parrington, *Main Currents in American Thought* (New York: Harcourt, 1930), 1:178; David Brooks, "Our Founding Yuppie," *The Weekly Standard*, Oct. 23, 2000, 31. "In its naive simplicity this hardly seems worthy of study as a philosophy," writes Herbert Schneider, "yet as a moral regime and outline of the art of virtue, it has a clarity and a power that command respect." Herbert Schneider, *The Puritan Mind* (Ann Arbor: University of Michigan Press, 1958), 246.

51. Alan Taylor, "For the Benefit of Mr. Kite," 39.

52. Poor Richard's 1733–58, by Franklin, plus editor's note in Papers 1:280; Faÿ 159–73; Sappenfield 121–77; Brands 124–31. There was also a real Richard Saunders who appears in the account books as a customer of Franklin's. Van Doren 107.

53. Pa. Gazette, Dec. 28, 1732.

54. Poor Richard's, 1733; Autobiography 107.

55. Poor Richard's, 1734, 1735; Titan Leeds's *American Almanack*, 1734; Jonathan Swift, "Predictions for the Ensuing Year by Isaac Bickerstaff, esq.," 1708, ftp://sailor.gutenberg.org/pub/gutenberg/etext97/bstaf10.txt . Swift's piece was a parody of an almanac by John Partridge; he predicted Partridge's death, and then engaged in a running jest similar to the one Franklin perpetrated on Leeds.

56. Poor Richard's, 1734, 1735, 1740; Papers 2:332n; Sappenfield 143; Brands 126.

57. Poor Richard's, 1736, 1738, 1739. See also the verses by "Bridget Saunders, my duchess" about lazy men in 1734 ("God in his mercy may do much to save him/ But woe to the poor wife whose lot is to have him"), which "Poor Richard" prints as a response to his own 1733 verses about lazy women.

58. Mark Twain, "The Late Benjamin Franklin," *The Galaxy*, July 1870, www.twainquotes.com/Galaxy/187007e.html ; Groucho Marx, *Groucho and Me* (New York: Random House, 1959), 6.

59. For an exhaustive study of the provenance of "early to bed and early to rise" see Wolfgang Mieder, "Early to Bed and Early to Rise," in the Web-based journal *De Proverbio*, www.utas.edu.au/docs/flonta/DP,1,1,95/FRANKLIN.html . *Bartlett's Familiar Quotations* (1882; Boston: Little, Brown, 2002) in its thirteenth edition (1955) and previous editions attributes the phrase to Franklin but also cites John Clarke's *Proverbs* (1639); it drops the reference to Clarke in subsequent editions.

60. The most detailed work on the origins of the maxims is Robert Newcombe, "The Sources of Benjamin Franklin's Sayings of Poor Richard," Ph.D. diss., University of Maryland, 1957. See also Papers 1:281–82; Van Doren 112–13; Wright 54; Frances Barbour, *A Concordance to the Sayings in Franklin's Poor Richard* (Detroit: Gale Research, 1974). Franklin's greatest reliance is on Jonathan Swift, James Howell's *Proverbs* (1659), and Thomas Fuller's *Gnomologia* (1732).

61. Philomath (BF), "Talents Requisite in an Almanac Writer," Pa. Gazette, Oct. 20, 1737. "Philomath" was a term used for almanac writers.

62. *Poor Richard Improved*, 1758.

63. Autobiography 107; Wright 55; Van Doren 197; D. H. Lawrence, "Benjamin Franklin," 14; BF to William Strahan, June 2, 1750; Poor Richard's, 1743.

CHAPTER 5

1. Poor Richard's, 1744; "Appeal for the Hospital," Pa. Gazette, Aug. 8, 1751; Alexis de Tocqueville, *Democracy in America* (1835; New York: Doubleday, 1969), 513; "Inside Main Street USA," *New York Times*, Aug. 27, 1995; John Van Horne, "Collective Benevolence for the Common Good," in Lemay *Reappraising*, 432. The two books that most influenced Franklin to form associations for the public good were Daniel Defoe's *An Essay upon Projects* (1697) and Cotton Mather's *Bonifacius: Essays to do Good* (1710).

2. Autobiography 90–91, 82; Faÿ 149; "The Library Company of Philadelphia," www.librarycompany.org ; Morgan *Franklin*, 56. The list of first books is in *PMHB* 300 (1906): 300.

3. "Brave Men at Fires," Pa. Gazette, Dec. 1, 1733; Autobiography 115; "On Protection of Towns from Fire," Pa. Gazette, Feb. 4, 1735; notice in Pa. Gazette, Jan. 27, 1743; Van Doren 130; Brands 135–37; Hawke 53.

4. Autobiography 115; Brands 214.

5. Faÿ 137; Pa Gazette, Dec. 30, 1730; Clark 44; Pennsylvania Grand Lodge Web site, www.pagrandlodge.org ; Julius Sachse, *Benjamin Franklin's Account with the Lodge of Masons* (Kila, Mont.: Kessinger, 1997).

6. Van Doren 134; Faÿ 180; Brands 152–54; BF to Joseph and Abiah Franklin, Apr. 13, 1738; Pa. Gazette, Feb. 7 (dated Feb. 15), 1738.

7. Autobiography 111; "Dialogue Between Two Presbyterians," Pa. Gazette, Apr. 10, 1735; "Observations on the Proceedings against Mr. Hemphill," July 1735, Papers 2:37; BF, "A Letter to a Friend in the Country," Sept. 1735, Papers 2:65; Jonathan Dickinson, "A Vindication of the Reverend Commission of the Synod," Sept. 1735, and "Remarks Upon the Defense of Rev. Hemphill's Observations," Nov. 1735; "A Defense of Mr. Hemphill's Observations," Oct. 1735. The pieces by Franklin, along with annotations about the affair and Dickinson's presumed authorship of the essays attributed to him, are in Papers 2:27–91. Franklin's fascinating battle over Hemphill has been recounted in many good historical studies, from which this section draws: Bryan LeBeau, "Franklin and the Presbyterians," *Early American Review* (summer 1996), earlyamerica.com/review/summer/franklin/; Merton Christensen, "Franklin on the Hemphill Trial: Deism versus Presbyterian Orthodoxy," *William and Mary Quarterly* (July 1953): 422–40; William Barker, "The Hemphill Case, Benjamin Franklin and Subscription to the Westminster Confession," *American Presbyterians* 69 (winter 1991); Aldridge *Nature,* 86–98; Buxbaum 93–104.

8. Campbell 97; Barbara Oberg and Harry Stout, eds., *Benjamin Franklin, Jonathan Edwards* (New York: Oxford University Press, 1997), 119; Carl Van Doren, *Benjamin Franklin and Jonathan Edwards* (New York: Scribner's, 1920), introduction; Jonathan Edwards, "Sinners in the Hands of an Angry God," delivered at Enfield, Conn., July 8, 1741, douglass.speech.nwu.edu/edwa_a45.htm ; Jack Hitt, "The Great Divide: It's Not Left and Right. It's Meritocrats and Valuecrats," *New York Times Magazine,* Dec. 31, 2000, 14.

9. Pa. Gazette, Nov. 15, 1739, May 22, 1740, June 12, 1740; Autobiography 116–20; Buxbaum 93–142; Brands 138–48; Hawke 57. Buxbaum presents an exhaustive analysis of all the items Franklin printed on Whitefield.

10. Frank Lambert, "Subscribing for Profits and Piety," *William and Mary Quarterly* (July 1993): 529–48; Harry Stout, "George Whitefield and Benjamin Franklin," *Massachusetts Historical Society* 103 (1992):9–23; David Morgan, "A Most Unlikely Friendship," *The Historian* 47 (1985): 208–18; Autobiography 118.

11. "Obadiah Plainman," Pa. Gazette, May 15, 29, 1740, Lib. of Am. 275–83, 1528; *American Weekly Mercury,* May 22, 1740. The editors of the Yale Papers do not include the Obadiah Plainman letters as Franklin's. But Leo Lemay convincingly argues that he wrote them, and he included them in the Library of America collection. Likewise, it seems possible that Franklin, as was his wont, stoked the controversy by writing the opposing letters from "Tom Trueman."

12. "Letter to a Friend in the Country" and "Statement of Editorial Policy," Pa. Gazette, July 24, 1740; Autobiography 118.

13. "Obituary of Andrew Hamilton," Pa. Gazette, Aug. 6, 1741; "Half-Hour's Conversation with a Friend," Pa. Gazette, Nov. 16, 1733.

14. Sappenfield 86–93; Autobiography 113–14.

15. C. William Miller, *Benjamin Franklin's Philadelphia Printing: A Descriptive Bibliography* (Philadelphia: American Philosophical Society, 1984), 32; James Green, *Benjamin Franklin as Publisher and Bookseller*, in Lemay *Reappraising*, 101. Green was a distinguished curator at the Library Company, and his notes on exhibitions of Franklin's books are useful.

16. Walter Isaacson, "Info Highwayman," *Civilization* (Mar. 1995): 48; Autobiography 114.

17. Sappenfield 93–105; Pa. Gazette, Nov. 13, Dec. 11, 1740; *American Weekly Mercury*, Nov. 20, 27, Dec. 4, 18, 1740; Papers, vol. 2; Frank Mott, *A History of American Magazines* (New York: Appleton, 1930), 1:8–27.

18. BF to Abiah Franklin, Oct. 16, 1747, Apr. 12, 1750; Lopez *Private*, 70–79; Autobiography 109; BF to William Strahan, June 2, 1750, Jan. 31, 1757; Clark 62, 139; Mrs. E. D. Gillespie (daughter of Sally Franklin Bache), *A Book of Remembrance* (Philadelphia: Lippincott, 1901), cited in Clark 17; Silence Dogood #5, *New England Courant*, May 28, 1722; DF to Margaret Strahan, Dec. 24, 1751; "A Petition of the Left Hand," 1785, in Lib. of Am. 1115 and Papers CD 43:u611.

In addition to half-seriously trying to fix Sally up with Strahan's son Billy, Franklin hoped his son, William, would marry Polly Stevenson, the daughter of his London landlady; that his grandson William Temple Franklin would marry the son of his Paris lady friend Mme. Brillon; and that Sally's son Benjamin Bache would marry Polly Stevenson's daughter. A harsher assessment of Franklin's treatment of Sally and the education he provided her can be found in an essay by Larry Tise, "Liberty and the Rights of Women," in the collection he edited, *Benjamin Franklin and Women* (University Park: Pennsylvania State University Press, 2000), 37–49.

19. Lopez *Private*, 34; Poor Richard's, 1735. "Reply to a Piece of Advice," Pa. Gazette, Mar, 4, 1735, praises marriage and children. The Yale editors of Franklin Papers tentatively attribute it to him, partly because it is signed "A.A.," initials he often used. Papers 2:21.

20. "Advice to a Young Man on the Choice of a Mistress," also known as "Old Mistress Apologue," June 25, 1745. A description of its publishing history is in Papers 3:27–31, and in the introduction to Larry Tise, *Benjamin Franklin and Women*.

21. "Speech of Polly Baker," *General Advertiser*, Apr. 15, 1747; Sappenfield 64. Franklin revealed his authorship in about 1778 at a dinner with the Abbé Raynal in Paris, where the authenticity of the famous speech was being debated. Franklin told the group, "I am going to set you straight. When I was young and printed a newspaper, it sometimes happened, when I was short of material to fill my sheet, that I amused myself by making up stories, and that of Polly Baker is one of the number." Papers 3:121–22.

22. "A Proposal for Promoting Useful Knowledge," May 14, 1743, Papers 2:378; *The Beginnings of the APS* (Philadelphia: APS Proceedings, 1944), 277–89; Edward C. Carter III, *One Grand Pursuit* (Philadelphia: American Philosophical Society, 1993); American Philosophical Society, www.amphilsoc.org .

Franklin had a love for writing very detailed charters, rules, and procedures for organizations. Among the groups he did this for were the Junto, Masonic lodge, fire company, police patrol, American Philosophical Society, Pennsylvania militia, Academy, postal service, and society for the abolition of slavery. This penchant also helped him draw up the Albany plan for union, the discipline regulations for the colonial army, and the first proposed articles of confederation.

23. Autobiography 121–23; "Plain Truth," Nov. 17, 1747; "Form of Association," Nov. 24, 1747; Papers 3:187, with historical notes. See chapter 4 for the issue of whether William was 16 or perhaps a bit older.

24. Autobiography 123; Richard Peters to Thomas Penn, Nov. 29, 1747, Papers 3:214; Penn to Peters, Mar. 30, June 9, 1748, Papers 3:186; "The Necessity of Self Defense," Pa. Gazette, Dec. 29, 1747 (in Lib. of Am. but not Yale papers); Brands 179–88; Wright 77–81; Hawke 75–80.

25. Wright 52; Van Doren 122; Autobiography 120, 92; "Articles of Agreement with David Hall," Jan. 1, 1748; Brands 188, 380; Clark 62; BF to Abiah Franklin, Apr. 12, 1750; BF to Cadwallader Colden, Sept. 29, 1748; Poor Richard's, 1744.

The year he retired, Franklin wrote and published an essay called "Advice to a Young Tradesman, Written by an Old One," in which he restated much of the philosophy of Poor Richard and the Autobiography: "The way to wealth, if you desire it, is as plain as the way to market. It depends chiefly on two words, Industry and Frugality; i.e., waste neither time nor money, but make the best use of both." Papers 3:304.

26. Gordon S. Wood, *The Radicalism of the American Revolution* (New York: Random House, 1991), 77, 85–86, 199. I tend to disagree with Wood's thesis to the extent that he portrays Franklin as a man of aristocratic aspirations whose leather-apron image was mainly affected after his social ambitions were dashed. The evidence in favor of giving more weight than Wood does to the view of Franklin as a proud member of the middle class is, I hope, detailed throughout this book. Even during the period right after his retirement, which Wood says was the prime period of his "aristocratic" aspirations, Franklin's politics remained rather populist and his civic endeavors had a common touch. Nevertheless, Wood provides an interesting assessment that merits consideration as a counterpoint to the approach taken by other historians. And because Wood contends that Franklin's aristocratic attitude was manifest primarily during the period from 1748 to the late 1760s (plus when he advocated at the Constitutional Convention that officeholders serve without pay), his thesis can be given weight without entirely rejecting the view that for most of his life Franklin was, as he claimed, a proud part of "we, the middling people." Wood also uses a somewhat broader definition of aristocracy than others do; he includes in it not only titled nobility and hereditary classes but also wealthy commoners who hold themselves out to be gentlemen. Wood's thesis reminds us, correctly I think, that one of Franklin's goals, beginning with his creation of the lending library, was to help members of the middling class take on some of the qualities of the enlightened gentry. (It should also be noted that the classical definition of aristocracy denoted a system of rule by the best, rather than a hereditary class system of social hierarchy and titles based on birth, which is what the term came to mean in England by Franklin's time.)

27. Wayne Craven, "The British and American Portraits of Benjamin Franklin," in Lemay *Reappraising*, 249; Charles Sellers, *Benjamin Franklin in Portraiture* (New Haven: Yale University Press, 1962); Poor Richard's, 1748.

CHAPTER 6

1. Dudley Herschbach, "Dr. Franklin's Scientific Amusements," *Harvard Magazine* (Nov. 1995): 36, and in the *Bulletin of the American Academy of Arts and Sciences* (Oct. 1994): 23. Herschbach, the Baird Professor of Science at Harvard, won the Nobel Prize for chemistry in 1958.

The most important academic studies on Franklin's science were done by the eminent scientific historian Harvard's I. Bernard Cohen. These include *Benjamin Franklin's Science* (Cambridge: Harvard University Press, 1990); *Science and the Founding Fathers* (New York: Norton, 1995), and *Franklin and Newton* (Philadelphia: American Philosophical Society, 1956). Also useful are Charles Tanford, *Ben Franklin Stilled the Waves* (Durham, N.C.: Duke University Press, 1989); Nathan Goodman, ed., *The Ingenious Dr. Franklin* (Philadelphia: University of Pennsylvania Press, 1931), which is a collection of Franklin's scientific letters and essays; J. L. Heilbron, "Franklin as an Enlightened Natural Philosopher," and Heinz Otto Sibum, "The Bookkeeper of Nature," in Lemay *Reappraising*.

2. "Magic Squares," BF to Peter Collinson, 1750; BF to PS, Sept. 20, 1761; Cohen 159–71; Brands 630. Cohen dates the heat experiments of Franklin and Breintnall from 1729 to 1737 based on letters and Junto notes, and traces the theories back to Newton and Boyle, accounts of which Franklin had read.

3. "An Account of the New Invented Pennsylvania Fire-Places," 1744, Papers 2:419–46 (with historical notes by the paper's editors); Autobiography 128; Lemay *Reappraising*, 201–3; letter to the *Boston Evening Post*, Sept. 8, 1746, first rediscovered and noted in Lemay *Internet Doc* for 1746; Brands 167; Samuel Edgerton Jr., "The Franklin Stove," in Cohen 199–211. Edgerton, an art historian at the University of Pennsylvania, shows that the stove was not as practical or popular as other historians assume.

4. BF to John Franklin, Dec. 8, 1752; "Origin of Northeast Storms," BF to Jared Eliot, Feb. 13, 1750; BF to Jared Eliot, July 16, 1747; BF to Alexander Small, May 12, 1760; John Cox, *The Storm Watchers* (New York: Wiley, 2002), 5–7.

5. Cohen 40–65; BF to Collinson, Mar. 28, 1747; Autobiography 164; Bowen 47–49. Cohen provides detailed evidence on the dates of Dr. Spencer's lectures, their content, Collinson's gift, and the errors Franklin made in later recalling the chronology.

6. BF to Collinson, May 25, July 28, 1747, Apr. 29, 1749; Cohen 22–26; I. Bernard Cohen, *Franklin and Newton*, 303; Clark 71. J. L. Heilbrun and Heinz Otto Sibum, in Lemay's *Reappraising*, 196–242, emphasize the "bookkeeping" nature of Franklin's theories.

7. BF to Collinson, Apr. 29, 1749, Feb. 4, 1750; Brands 199; Thomas Pynchon, *Mason & Dixon* (New York: Holt, 1997), 294.

8. BF to John Lining, Mar. 18, 1755; BF to Collinson, Mar. 2, 1750; BF to John Winthrop, July 2, 1768; Hawke 86–88; Cohen 121; Van Doren 156–70; Brands 198–202. Andrew White, "History of Warfare of Science with Theology in Christendom," www.human-nature.com/reason/white/chap11.html . Among those, in addition to Newton, who had already noted the similarities between electrical sparks and lightning were Francis Hauksbee, Samuel Wall, John Freke, Johann Heinrich Winkler, and Franklin's antagonist the Abbé Nollet; see Clark 79–80. None, however, had proposed serious experiments to assess the hypothesis.

9. BF to John Mitchell, Apr. 29, 1749.

10. BF to Collinson, July 29, Mar. 2, 1750.

11. *The Gentleman's Magazine,* Jan., May 1750; *Experiments and Observations on Electricity, Made at Philadelphia in America, by Mr. Benjamin Franklin* (London: 1750, 1756, and subsequent editions); Abbé Guillaume Mazéas to Stephen Hales, May 20, 1752, Papers 4:315 and *Philosophical Transactions of the Royal Society* (1751–52); Autobiography 165–67; Clark 3–5, 83; Cohen 70–72.

12. "The Kite Experiment," Pa. Gazette, Oct. 19, 1752; Papers 4:360–65 has a footnote explaining historical issues; Pa. Gazette, Aug. 27, Oct. 19, 1752; Cohen 68–77; Joseph Priestley, *The History and Present State of Electricity* (1767), www.ushistory.org/franklin/kite/index.htm ; Hawke 103–6.

13. Cohen 66–109; Van Doren 164; Tom Tucker, *Bolt of Fate* (New York: Public Affairs, 2003). Tucker charges that "It's possible that . . . Franklin dreamed up his own kite claim" and that it was all a "hoax" akin to his literary ones. His book does not address the detailed evidence I. Bernard Cohen cites on this question and is, I think, unpersuasive. Franklin's kite description is in no ways similar to his literary hoaxes, and if untrue would have been an outright lie rather than a hoax. Tucker also makes the odd allegation that Franklin's description of his sentry box experiment was a death threat to the president of London's Royal Society. He also charges that Franklin may have been lying when he publicly reported in 1752 that two lightning rods had been erected on public buildings in Philadelphia that summer (a report that was published in the Royal Society's journal and would, it seems, have been challenged at the time if it were false). The comprehensive analysis by Cohen, a professor of the history of science who is the foremost authority on Franklin's electricity work, addresses fully and more convincingly the issues surrounding Franklin's sentry box, kite, and lightning rods. Other articles about whether Franklin flew the kite that summer include Abbott L. Rotch, "Did Franklin Fly His Electrical Kite before He Invented the Lighting Rod?" *American Antiquarian Society Proceedings,* 1907; Alexander McAdie, "The Date of Franklin's Kite Experiment," *American Antiquarian Society Proceedings,* 1925.

14. Cohen 66–109; Van Doren 165–70. Van Doren says that the possibility that Franklin fabricated or embellished his kite experiment would be "quite out of keeping with his record in science, in which he elsewhere appears always truthful and unpretending."

15. BF to Collinson, Sept. 1753; BF to DF, June 10, 1758; Dudley Herschbach, "Ben Franklin's Scientific Amusements," *Harvard Magazine* (Nov. 1995): 44; BF to Cadwallader Colden, Apr. 12, 1753; BF to Royal Society, May 29, 1754.

16. BF to Collinson, July 29, 1750; Van Doren 171; J. J. Thompson, *Recollections and Reflections* (London: Bell, 1939), 252; BF to Cadwallader Colden, Oct. 11, 1750; Turgot epigram, 1781: *Eripuit cœlo fulmen, sceptrumque tyrannis.*

CHAPTER 7

1. "On the Need for an Academy," Pa. Gazette, Aug. 24, 1749; "Proposals Relating to the Education of Youth in Pennsylvania," Oct. 1749; BF to Cadwallader Colden, Nov. 1749; Constitutions of the Publick Academy, Nov. 13, 1749; Autobiography 121, 129–31; Van Doren 193; University of Pennsylvania history, www.archives.upenn.edu/histy/genlhistory/brief.html . (The school was originally called the Academy of Philadelphia, then the College of Philadelphia, then in 1779 it was taken over by the state and became the University of the State of Pennsylvania, and finally in 1791 it was named the University of Pennsylvania.)

2. "Appeal for the Hospital," Pa. Gazette, Aug. 8, 1751; Autobiography 134.

3. BF to Peter Collinson, May 9, 1753; Stuart Sherman, "Franklin and the Age of Enlightenment," in Sanford 75. See also chapter 4, n. 49.

For more on Franklin's political thought, see Paul Conner, *Poor Richard's Politicks* (New York: Oxford University Press, 1965), and Francis Jennings, *Benjamin Franklin: Politician* (New York: Norton, 1996).

4. "Observations Concerning the Increase of Mankind," 1751, Papers 4:225; Conner 69–87; Hawke 95.

5. "Felons and Rattlesnakes," Pa. Gazette, May 9, 1751.

6. "Observations Concerning the Increase of Mankind," 1751; BF to Abiah Franklin, Apr. 12, 1750; John Van Horne, "Collective Benevolence," in Lemay *Reappraising,* 433–36; Lopez *Private,* 291–302.

7. BF to John Waring, Dec. 17, 1763.

8. BF to Peter Collinson, May 9, 1753.

9. Autobiography 131.

10. Autobiography 132.

11. Autobiography 132; Report of the Treaty of Carlisle, Nov. 1, 1753; Minutes of the Provincial Council of Pennsylvania, Nov. 15, 1753.

12. Autobiography 140; BF to Collinson, May 21, 1751; John Franklin to BF, Nov. 26, 1753; "Procedures for Postmasters," 1753, Papers 5:162–77; post office finances, Aug. 10, 1753, Papers 5:18; Wright 85; Hawke 114; Brands 243–45; Clark 100; Lopez *Private,* 53.

13. BF to James Parker, Mar. 20, 1751; Pa. Gazette, May 9, 1754.

14. "Commission to Treat With the Indians," Pa. Assembly, May 13, 1754, Papers 5:275; "Short Hints towards a Scheme for Uniting the Northern Colonies," in BF to James Alexander and Cadwallader Colden, June 8, 1754, Papers 5:335.

15. BF to Peter Collinson, July 29, 1754; BF to Cadwallader Colden, July 14, 1754; "Plan of Proposed Union," July 10, 1754; Autobiography 141–42; BF to William Shirley, Dec. 4, 22, 1754.

For overviews: Bernard Bailyn, *The Ordeal of Thomas Hutchinson* (Cambridge:

Harvard University Press, 1974); Robert Newbold, *The Albany Congress and Plan of Union* (New York: Vantage, 1955), 95–105; Morgan *Franklin*, 83–90; Hawke 116–23; Brands 234–40; Wright 89–94. The most colorful popular account is in Catherine Drinker Bowen, *The Most Dangerous Man in America* (Boston: Little, Brown, 1974), 91–162.

There is a scholarly dispute on how to apportion credit for the final plan between Franklin and Hutchinson. In a letter years later, Hutchinson referred to it as his plan, but in a history book he wrote that "the plan for a general union was projected by Benjamin Franklin." Indeed, the final plan was very similar in structure and phrasing to the "Short Hints" paper that Franklin prepared before arriving at Albany. See Papers 5:335; Wright 92. For a pro-Hutchinson view, see Lawrence Gipson, *The British Empire before the American Revolution* (New York: Knopf, 1936–69), 5:126–38.

16. BF to John Franklin, Mar. 16, 1755; BF to Catherine Ray, Mar. 4, Mar.–Apr., Sept. 11, Oct. 16, 1755; Catherine Ray to BF, June 28, 1755. (She signed her name "Caty," but Franklin tended to address her as "Katy" or "Katie.")

17. The best analysis is in Lopez *Private*, 55–57, and Lopez *Life*, 25–29. The quote from Lopez is from the former book, but it is repeated in similar form in the latter. See also William Roelker, *Benjamin Franklin and Catherine Ray Greene* (Philadelphia: American Philosophical Society, 1949). Also worth noting is J. A. Leo Lemay's astute analysis in *PMHB* 126:2 (Apr. 2002): 336: "Biographers who read Franklin's flirtations as serious attempts to have sexual affairs seem to me to be either unsophisticated about human psychology or as prudish as John Adams in Paris."

18. BF to Catherine Ray, Mar. 2, 1789.

19. Autobiography 143–47; Hawke 124–62; BF to Peters, Sept. 17, 1754; BF to Collinson, Aug. 25, 1755.

20. Autobiography 151–52, 148–51; "Advertisement for Wagons," Apr. 26, 1755; Papers 6:19. (It is misdated in the Autobiography.)

21. BF to Peter Collinson, June 26, 1755; Autobiography 144; Robert Hunter Morris to Thomas Penn, June 16, 1755.

22. Autobiography 154–56; Assembly reply to Governor Morris, Aug. 8, 19, Nov. 11, 1755.

23. Autobiography 156; Brands 262; Pa. Gazette, Dec. 18, 1755; BF to James Read, Nov. 2, 1755; BF to Richard Partridge, Nov. 27, 1755.

24. BF to DF, Jan. 25, 1756; Autobiography 160–62; Brands 267–69; J. Bennett Nolan, *General Benjamin Franklin* (Philadelphia: University of Pennsylvania Press, 1936), 62.

25. Autobiography 162–63; Brands 270–71; BF to Collinson, Nov. 5, 1756.

26. BF to George Whitefield, July 2, 1756; BF to DF, Mar. 25, 1756; Autobiography 169; Assembly reply, by BF, Oct. 29, 1756; Assembly appointment of Franklin, Jan. 29, Feb. 3, 1757, Papers 7:109; Wright 105; Thomas Penn to Richard Peters, May 14, 1757.

CHAPTER 8

1. BF to William Brownrigg, Nov. 7, 1773; "Everything is soothed by oil," Pliny the Elder (A.D. 23–79) wrote in his work *Natural History*, book 2, section 234. He was, in addition to being a scientist and senator, a commander of the Roman imperial fleet near Naples, and was killed at an eruption of Mount Vesuvius.

2. BF to DF, July 17, 1757; Autobiography 175–77.

3. Lopez *Private*, 86.

4. The Craven Street house where Franklin spent most of his time, now number 36, still exists, and in 2003 work began on converting it into a small museum. The plan is to have each of the tiny rooms feature a different aspect of his stay in London: his diplomacy, science, social life, and writings. The house, which has a nineteenth-century brick façade but is otherwise structurally similar to the way it was in Franklin's time, is a few hundred yards from Charing Cross station and Trafalgar Square. www.thersa.org/franklin/default.html ; www.rsa.org.uk/projects/project_closeup.asp?id=1001 ; www.cs.mdx.ac.uk/wrt/Siteview/project.html .

5. BF to PS May 4, 1759, and undated 1759, May 1, Sept. 13, 1760.

6. BF to PS, Sept. 13, 1759, May 1, June 11 (includes the "prudent moderation" excerpt), Sept. 13, and undated Nov., 1760; PS to BF, June 23, 1760, undated Aug., and Sept. 16, 1760. See also their letters throughout 1761–62.

7. BF to PS, Jan. 27, 1783; Wright 110; Clark 140; Lopez *Private*, 83; Randall 123.

8. William Strahan to DF, Dec. 13, 1757.

9. BF to DF, Jan. 14, Feb. 19, June 10, 1758; Lopez *Private*, 80; Clark 142–43, 147.

10. BF to DF, Nov. 22, Dec. 3, 1757, June 10, 1758, June 27, 1760; Lopez *Private*, 172.

11. Verner Crane, "The Club of Honest Whigs," *William and Mary Quarterly* 23 (1966): 210; Leonard Labaree, "Benjamin Franklin's British Friendships," *Proceedings of the American Philosophical Society* 108 (1964): 423; Clark 142; Brands 279; Morgan *Devious*, 15; Hawke 163.

12. Strahan to DF, Dec. 13, 1757; BF to DF, Nov. 27, 1757.

13. Wright 114–15, 216–17.

14. Thomas Penn to Richard Peters, May 14, 1757.

15. Autobiography 177–79.

16. Autobiography 178.

17. Autobiography 179; "Heads of Complaint," BF to the Penns, Aug. 20, 1757; answer to "Heads of Complaint" by Ferdinand John Paris, Nov. 28, 1758, Papers 8:184; Cecil Currey, *Road to Revolution* (Garden City, N.Y.: Anchor, 1968), 35.

18. "Pennsylvania Charter of Privileges," Oct. 28, 1701, www.constitution.org/bcp/penncharpriv.htm ; BF to Isaac Norris, Jan. 14, 1758; Clark 144; Middlekauff 65–66; Brands 301.

19. Thomas Penn to Richard Peters, July 5, 1758; BF to Joseph Galloway, Feb. 17, 1758; Brands 302; Wright 117.

20. WF to the Printer of the *Citizen,* from the Pennsylvania Coffee-house in London, Sept. 16, 1757.

21. BF to DF, June 10, 1758; Skemp *William,*30–31.

22. Lopez *Private,* 61–69; Skemp *William,* 24–26, 37; Randall 102–15; WF to Elizabeth Graeme, Feb. 26, Apr. 7, Dec. 9, 1757; WF to Margaret Abercrombie, Oct. 24, 1758. *The True Conduct of Persons of Quality* was written by Nicolas Rémond des Cours and translated from the French and published in London in 1694.

23. BF to Abiah Franklin, Apr. 12, 1750; WF to BF, Sept. 3, 1758.

24. BF to DF, Sept. 6, 1758, Aug. 29, 1759.

25. Dr. Thomas Bray, "Society for the Propagation of the Gospel in Foreign Parts Among the Negroes in the Colonies," docsouth.dsi.internet2.edu/church/pierre/pierre.html ; BF to John Lining, Apr. 14, 1757, June 17, 1758; BF to Cadwallader Colden, Feb. 25, 1763.

26. BF to DF, Sept. 6, 1758.

27. Answer to Heads of Complaint by Ferdinand John Paris, Nov. 28, 1758; Thomas and Richard Penn to the Assembly, Nov. 28, 1758; BF to Isaac Norris, Jan. 19, 1759. See Papers 8:178–86; Middlekauff 68–70; Hawke 173; Morgan *Devious,* 38.

28. Morgan *Franklin,* 102, 130; Gordon Wood, "Wise Men," *New York Review,* Sept. 26, 2002, 44. In this review of Morgan's book, Wood argues that Franklin's actions can be readily explained by his loyalty to the Crown, and he faults Morgan for being blinded by hindsight when he accuses Franklin of blindness. "His account of Franklin seems at times subtly infused with what historians call 'whiggism,' the anachronistic foreshortening that makes the past an anticipation of the future," Wood writes. On balance, I feel that Franklin's anger at the Proprietors did, in fact, cause him to lose his perspective at a time when others, both supporters and foes of the Penns, were able to see more clearly that there was not enough support on either side of the ocean to turn Pennsylvania into a royal colony and that the fundamental problem was the general attitude among British leaders that the colonies ought to be economically and politically submissive.

29. BF to the Privy Council, Sept. 20, 1758; Hawke 176.

30. BF to Thomas Leech, May 13, 1758; Hawke 169, 177; Papers 8:60.

31. Autobiography 180; Report of the Board of Trade, June 24, 1760, in Papers 9:125–73; Privy Council order, Sept. 2, 1760; Morgan *Devious,* 56–57; Middlekauff 73.

32. Brands 305–6; "A Parable on Brotherly Love," 1755, Papers 6:124; BF to Lord Kames, May 3, 1760.

33. BF to David Hume, May 19, 1762.

34. BF to David Hume, Sept. 27, 1760; David Hume to BF, May 10, 1762.

35. BF to Lord Kames, Jan. 3, 1760; Brands 287; St. Andrew's citation, Oct. 1, 1759, Papers 8:277.

36. BF to DF, Mar. 5, 1760.

37. Temple Franklin's tombstone refers to his birthdate as Feb. 22, 1762, but

family correspondence indicates that he was born in February 1760. Lopez *Private*, 93; Van Doren 290.

38. BF to Jared Ingersoll, Dec. 11, 1762; WF to SF, Oct. 10, 1761.

39. "Humorous Reasons for Restoring Canada," London *Chronicle*, Dec. 27, 1759; "The Interest of Great Britain Considered," Apr. 1760, Papers 9:59–100; Jack Greene, "Pride, Prejudice and Jealousy," in Lemay *Reappraising*, 125.

40. BF to William Strahan, Aug. 23, 1762.

41. Aldridge *French*, 169, from Pierre Cabanis, *Complete Works* (Paris: Bossange frères, 1825), 5:222.

42. Temple Franklin, "Memoirs of Benjamin Franklin," 1:75; Randall 180; Skemp *William*, 38; Brands 328; BF to JM, Nov. 25, 1752; BF to PS, Aug. 11, 1762.

43. BF to John Pringle, Dec. 1, 1762.

CHAPTER 9

1. Skemp *William*, 48; Thomas Penn to James Hamilton, Sept. 1762; Clark 170.

2. BF to Benjamin Waller, Aug. 1, 1763.

3. BF to Lord Bessborough, Oct. 1761; Lopez *Private*, 100; BF to DF, June 16, 1763.

4. BF to PS, June 10, 1763; Lopez *Private*, 100.

5. Hawke 202; BF to JM, June 19, 1763; BF to Catherine Ray Greene, Aug. 1, 1763; BF to William Strahan, Aug. 8, 1763.

6. Lopez *Private*, 114; WF to William Strahan, Apr. 25, 1763; BF to William Strahan, Dec. 19, 1763.

7. BF to Peter Collinson, Dec. 19, 1763; "A Narrative of the Late Massacres, in Lancaster County, of a Number of Indians, Friends of this Province, by Persons Unknown," Jan. 1764; Van Doren 307; Hawke 208; Brands 352.

There is an interesting historical dispute over Franklin's sympathies for the Indians and prejudice toward the frontier Presbyterians and ethnic Germans. Buxbaum 185–219 is among those who play up Franklin's prejudice toward Presbyterians and take him to task for making the Indians seem "human beings not essentially different from Englishmen." Brooke Hindle, in "The March of the Paxton Boys," *William and Mary Quarterly* (Oct. 1946), takes a similar approach. They are opposed by Francis Jennings in *Benjamin Franklin: Politician* (New York: Norton, 1996), 158–59. He calls Buxbaum "learnedly confused" and accuses Hindle of "absolute ignorance" and of making "bigoted asinine" comments.

8. BF to John Fothergill, Mar. 14, 1764; BF to Richard Jackson, Feb. 11, 1764; Hawke 208.

9. BF to Lord Kames, June 2, 1765; John Penn to Thomas Penn, May 5, 1764; BF to John Fothergill, Mar. 14, 1764; Hawke 211; Brands 356; Van Doren 311.

10. Assembly reply to the governor, Mar. 24, 1764.

11. Van Doren 314; Buxbaum 192; Cecil Currey, *Road to Revolution* (Garden City, N.Y.: Anchor, 1968), 58.

12. Resolutions of the Pennsylvania Assembly, Mar. 24, 1764; "Cool Thoughts on the Present Situation of Our Public Affairs," Apr. 12, 1764; BF to Richard Jackson, Mar. 14, 29, Sept. 1, 1764; BF to William Strahan, Mar. 30, 1764; J. Philip Gleason, "A Scurrilous Election and Franklin's Reputation," *William and Mary Quarterly* (Oct. 1961); Brands 357; Van Doren 313; Morgan *Devious,* 80–83. The anti-Franklin pamphlets are in Papers 11:381.

13. Hawke 225; Brands 358; Van Doren 316; Buxbaum 12; "Remarks on a Late Protest," Nov. 5, 1764.

14. BF to Richard Jackson, May 1, 1764; BF to SF, Nov. 8, 1764; Hawke 222–26.

CHAPTER 10

1. BF to PS, Dec. 12, 1764.

2. BF to DF, Dec. 27, 1764, Feb. 9, 14, 1765. For good overviews on Franklin's mission, see Middlekauff; Morgan *Devious;* Cecil Currey, *Road to Revolution* (Garden City, N.Y.: Anchor, 1968); Theodore Draper, *The Struggle for Power* (New York: Times Books, 1996); Edmund Morgan and Helen Morgan, *The Stamp Act Crisis* (Chapel Hill: University of North Carolina Press, 1953).

3. BF to PS, July 20, 1768; PS to BF, Sept. 26, 1768; Noah Webster to BF, May 24, 1786; BF to Webster, June 18, 1786; Van Doren 426; Noah Webster, *Dissertations on the English Language: With Notes, Historical and Critical, to Which Is Added, by Way of Appendix, an Essay on a Reformed Mode of Spelling, with Dr. Franklin's Arguments on That Subject* (Boston: Isaiah Thomas, 1789), edweb.sdsu.edu/people/DKitchen/new_655/webster_language.htm .

4. Lopez *Private,* 152; WF to BF, Jan. 2, 1769; PS to Barbara Hewson, Oct. 4, 1774; PS to BF, Sept. 5, 1776.

5. Cadwalader Evans to BF, Mar. 15, 1765; John Penn to Thomas Penn, Mar. 16, 1765; Morgan *Devious,* 94.

6. BF to Joseph Galloway, Oct. 11, 1766; Morgan *Devious,* 102. Morgan and Morgan, *The Stamp Act Crisis,* 89–91; Brands 360–63; Van Doren 320.

7. BF to John Hughes, Aug. 9, 1765; Morgan *Devious,* 106; Thomas Penn to William Allen, July 13, 1765.

8. BF to Charles Thomson, July 11, 1765; Morgan *Devious,* 105; Charles Thomson to BF, Sept. 24, 1765; John Hughes to BF, Sept. 17, 1765.

9. David Hall to BF, Sept. 6, 1765; Morgan *Devious,* 106; Wright 188.

10. Samuel Wharton to BF, Oct. 13, 1765; John Hughes to BF, Sept. 12, 1765; DF to BF, Sept. 22, 1765; Morgan *Devious,* 107; BF to DF, Nov. 9, 1765; Brands 368.

11. Patrick Henry to the Virginia House of Delegates, May 30, 1765; BF to John Hughes, Aug. 9, 1765; Thomas Hutchinson to BF, Nov. 18, 1765; Brands 368.

12. BF to Pennsylvania Assembly committee, Apr. 12, 1766; Thomas Penn to John Penn, Nov. 30, 1765.

13. BF to David Hall, Nov. 9, 1765; BF to Joseph Galloway, Oct. 11, 1766; John Fothergill to James Pemberton, Feb. 27, 1766; "Defense of Indian Corn and a Reply," *The Gazetteer,* Jan. 2, 15, 1766.

14. *Public Advertiser,* May 22, 1765, Jan. 2, 1766.

15. William Warner, "Enlightened Anonymity," University of California Santa Barbara, lecture, Mar. 8, 2002, dc-mrg.english.ucsb.edu/conference/2002/documents/william_warner_anon.html .

16. BF to JM, Mar. 1, 1766; BF to WF, Nov. 9, 1765; Brands 373; Hawke 235–37.

17. BF to unknown recipient, Jan. 6, 1766; see also BF to Cadwalader Evans, May 1766; Wright 187; Van Doren 333.

18. Testimony to the House of Commons, Feb. 13, 1766, Papers 13:129–62; Brands 374–76; Van Doren 336–52.

19. William Strahan to David Hall, May 10, 1766; Joseph Galloway to BF, May 23, June 7, 1766; Charles Thomson to BF, May 20, 1766; Van Doren 353; Clark 195; Hawke 242.

20. BF to DF, Apr. 6, 1766.

21. DF to BF, Feb. 10, Oct. 8, 13, 1765; BF to DF, June 4, 1765; Lopez *Private,* 126.

22. David Hall to BF, Jan. 27, 1767; BF to Hall, Apr. 14, 1767.

23. BF to DF, June 22, 1767.

24. Lopez *Private,* 134, citing E. D. Gillespie, *A Book of Remembrance* (Philadelphia: Lippincott, 1901), 25.

25. DF to BF, Apr. 25, 1767; BF to DF, May 23, June 22, 1767; Brands 390; Hawke 255.

26. WF to BF, May 1767; RB to BF, May 21, 1767; Brands 391.

27. BF to RB, Aug. 5, 1767; BF to DF, Aug. 5, 1767.

28. MS to DF, Sept. 18, 1767; Lopez *Private,* 139.

29. BF to DF, Aug. 28, 1767; BF to PS, Sept. 14, 1767.

30. BF to PS, Aug. 28, 1767; Van Doren 367–69.

31. BF to DF, Nov. 2, 17, 1767; BF to PS, Oct. 9, 1767; Brands 395–96; Van Doren 368; Hawke 258.

32. JM to BF, Dec. 1, 1767; BF to JM, Feb. 21, 1768.

33. BF to RB, Aug. 13, 1768; BF to DF, Aug. 9, 1768; Lopez *Private,* 141.

34. BF to DF, Jan. 26, 1769; Thomas Bond to BF, June 7, 1769; DF to BF, Nov. 27, 1769; Van Doren 404; Lopez *Private,* 143; Brands 456.

35. PS to BF, Sept. 1, 1769; BF to PS, Sept. 2, 1769, May 31, 1770; Lopez *Private,* 154.

36. "Craven Street Gazette," Sept. 22–25, 1770, in Papers 17:220–26.

37. BF to Barbeu Dubourg, July 28, 1768; Lopez *Private,* 27.

38. BF to MS, Nov. 3, 1772, misdated 1767 in Papers.

39. "A Friend to Both Countries," London *Chronicle,* Apr. 9, 1767; "Be-

nevolous," London *Chronicle,* Apr. 11, 1767; Brands 386; Hawke 252; Cecil Currey, *Road to Revolution,* 222.

40. "Causes of the American Discontents before 1768," London *Chronicle,* Jan. 7, 1768. Although it was anonymous, Franklin indicated his authorship by using as an epigram a line he had used in his 1760 piece on "The Interest of Great Britain Considered": "The waves never rise but when the winds blow." With his interest in waves, both scientific and political, he enjoyed this metaphor.

41. "Preface to Letters from a Farmer," by N.N. (BF), May 8, 1768, Papers 15:110; BF to WF, Mar. 13, 1768.

42. BF to Joseph Galloway, Jan. 9, 1768; BF to WF, Jan. 9, 1768; BF to unknown recipient, Nov. 28, 1768; Lib. of Am. 839; Clark 211.

43. BF to Joseph Galloway, July 2, Dec. 13, 1768; BF to WF, July 2, 1768; Hawke 263, 268; Brands 408.

44. To Thomas Crowley, by "Francis Lynn" (BF), *Public Advertiser,* Oct. 21, 1768; "On Civil War," signed N.N. (BF), *Public Advertiser,* Aug. 25, 1768; "Queries," by "NMCNPCH" (BF), London *Chronicle,* Aug. 18, 1768; "On Absentee Governors," by Twilight (BF), *Public Advertiser,* Aug. 27, 1768.

45. "An American" (BF) to the *Gazetteer,* Jan. 17, 1769; "A Lion's Whelp," *Public Advertiser,* Jan. 2, 1770.

46. BF to William Strahan, Nov. 29, 1769.

47. BF to Charles Thomson, Mar. 18, 1770; BF to Samuel Cooper, June 8, 1770.

48. Franklin's account of audience with Hillsborough, Jan. 16, 1771, Papers 18:9; Hawke 290; Brands 431–34.

49. BF to Samuel Cooper, Feb. 5, June 10, 1771; Strahan to WF, Apr. 3, 1771; BF to Massachusetts Committee of Correspondence, May 15, 1771; Hawke 294–95; Van Doren 387–88.

50. BF to Thomas Cushing, June 10, 1771; Arthur Lee to Sam Adams, June 10, 1771, in Richard Henry Lee, *The Life of Arthur Lee* (Boston: Wells and Lilly, 1829); Samuel Cooper to BF, Aug. 25, 1771; Brands 437–38.

CHAPTER 11

1. BF to William Brownrigg, Nov. 7, 1773; Charles Tanford, *Ben Franklin Stilled the Waves* (Durham, N.C.: Duke University Press, 1989), 29; Van Doren 419.

2. Jonathan Williams (BF's nephew), "Journal of a Tour Through Northern England," May 28, 1771, Papers 18:113; BF to Thomas Cushing, June 10, 1771; BF to DF, June 5, 1771; Hawke 295; Brands 438.

3. BF to Jonathan Shipley, June 24, 1771.

4. BF to JM, July 17, 1771; BF to Samuel Franklin, July 19, 1771.

5. John Updike, "Many Bens," *New Yorker,* Feb. 22, 1988, 112; Charles Angoff, *A Literary History of the American People* (New York: Knopf, 1931); Van Doren 415.

Lemay/Zall Autobiography provides a complete look at the original manuscript and all of its revisions. The edition produced by Leonard Labaree and the other editors of the Franklin Papers at Yale (New Haven: Yale University Press, 1964) is authoritative, filled with useful annotations, and has an introduction that gives a good history of the manuscript. Carl Van Doren, *Benjamin Franklin's Autobiographical Writings* (1945; New York: Viking, 2002), 208–11, and Van Doren's biography of Franklin, 414–15, describe Franklin's process of writing. Also valuable are various articles by J. A. Leo Lemay: "The Theme of Vanity in Franklin's Autobiography," in Lemay *Reappraising,* 372, and "Franklin and the Autobiography," *Eighteenth Century Studies* (1968): 200. For good analyses of the manuscript, which is available at the Huntington Library, see P. M. Zall, "The Manuscript of Franklin's Autobiography," *Huntington Library Quarterly* 39 (1976); P. M. Zall, "A Portrait of the Autobiographer as an Old Artificer," in *The Oldest Revolutionary,* ed. J. A. Leo Lemay (Philadelphia: University of Pennsylvania Press, 1976), 53. The Norton Critical edition (New York: Norton, 1968), which was edited by Lemay and Zall, contains a bibliography of scholarly articles as well as excerpts of criticism. See also Ormond Seavey, *Becoming Benjamin Franklin: The Autobiography and the Life* (University Park: Pennsylvania State University Press, 1988); Henry Steele Commager, introduction to the Modern Library edition (New York: Random House, 1944); Daniel Aaron, introduction to the Library of America edition (New York: Vintage, 1990).

The memoir written by Lord Herbert of Cherbury (1583–1648) had been published by Franklin's friend Horace Walpole in 1764, seven years before Franklin began his own work. Gilbert Burnet was a great English clergyman and historian who described the revolution of 1688 in his *History of My Own Time,* a copy of which was owned by Franklin's Library Company.

6. BF to Anna Shipley, Aug. 13, 1771; BF to Georgiana Shipley, Sept. 26, 1772; BF to DF, Aug. 14, 1771; Van Doren 416–17.

7. BF to Thomas Cushing, Jan. 13, 1772; BF to Joshua Babcock, Jan. 13, 1772; Brands 440.

8. BF to Thomas Cushing, Jan. 13, 1772; BF to WF, Jan. 30, 1772.

9. J. Bennett Nolan, *Benjamin Franklin in Scotland and Ireland* (Philadelphia: University of Pennsylvania Press, 1956). This small book is a detailed and well-researched account of Franklin's activities on these trips. There is some disagreement about whether Adam Smith showed Franklin chapters of the *Wealth of Nations,* published in 1776, but one of Smith's relatives said this was the case.

10. PS to BF, Oct. 31, 1771; SF to RB, Dec. 2, 1771; RB to DF, Dec. 3, 1771; Mary Bache to BF, Dec. 3, 1771, Feb. 5, 1772; Lopez *Private,* 143–44.

11. BF to DF, Jan. 28, 1772; BF to SF, Jan. 29, 1772; Lopez *Private,* 146; RB to BF, Apr. 6, 1773; Van Doren 392; Brands 455.

12. BF to DF, Oct. 3, 1770; BF to PS, Nov. 25, 1771; BF to DF, Feb. 2, 1773; Brands 456; Van Doren 404, 411.

13. BF to William Brownrigg, Nov. 7, 1773; Stanford 78–80; C. H. Giles, "Franklin's Teaspoon of Oil," *Chemistry & Industry* (1961): 1616–34; Stephen Thompson, "How Small Is a Molecule?" *SHiPS News,* Jan. 1994, www1.umn.edu/ships/words/avogadro.htm ; "Measuring Molecules: The Pond on Clapham Common," www.rosepetruck.chem.brown.edu/Chem10-01/Lab3/Chem10_lab3.htm .

14. BF to Benjamin Rush, July 14, 1773.

15. BF to WF, Aug. 19, 1772.

16. BF to Cadwalader Evans, Feb. 20, 1768.

17. BF to John Pringle, May 10, 1768.

18. BF to Peter Franklin, May 7, 1760.

19. BF to Giambatista Beccaria, July 13, 1762; www.gigmasters.com/armonica/index.asp .

20. Franklin to Collinson, May 9, 1753.

21. Medius (BF), "On the Labouring Poor," *The Gentleman's Magazine*, Apr. 1768.

22. Campbell 236.

23. "A Conversation on Slavery," *Public Advertiser*, Jan. 30, 1770.

24. Lopez *Private*, 292–98; Gary Nash, "Slaves and Slaveowners in Colonial Philadelphia," *William and Mary Quarterly* (Apr. 1973): 225–56. Lopez and Herbert say that one out of five families owned slaves, which is wrong; however, it is true that slaves accounted for roughly one-fifth of the population in 1790, which is not quite the same thing. According to the 1790 census, the first conducted in America, the country had a population of 3,893,874, of which 694,207 were slaves. There were 410,636 families, of which 47,664 owned slaves. In 1750, it is estimated there were 1.2 million people in the thirteen colonies, of which 236,000 were slaves. See fisher.lib.virginia.edu/census/; www.eh.net/encyclopedia/wahl.slavery.us.php; Stanley Engerman and Eugene Genovese, *Race and Slavery in the Western Hemisphere: Quantitative Studies* (Princeton: Princeton University Press, 1975).

25. Anthony Benezet to BF, Apr. 27, 1772; BF to Anthony Benezet, Aug. 22, 1772; BF to Benjamin Rush, July 14, 1773; "The Somerset Case and the Slave Trade," London *Chronicle*, June 20, 1772; Lopez *Private*, 299.

26. BF to WF, Jan. 30, Aug. 19, 1772.

27. BF to WF, Aug. 17, 1772, July 14, 1773; BF to Joseph Galloway, Apr. 6, 1773; Van Doren 394–98.

28. BF to Thomas Cushing, Dec. 2, 1772; BF, *Tract Relative to the Affair of the Hutchinson Letters*, 1774, Papers 21:414. An excellent account of the affair is in Bernard Bailyn, *The Ordeal of Thomas Hutchinson* (Cambridge: Harvard University Press, 1974), 221–49. See also Brands 452; Van Doren 461; Wright 224.

29. BF to Thomas Cushing, Mar. 9, May 6, 1773.

30. "Rules by Which a Great Empire May Be Reduced to a Small One," *Public Advertiser*, Sept. 11, 1773.

31. "An Edict by the King of Prussia," *Public Advertiser*, Sept. 23, 1773.

32. Baron Le Despencer, "Franklin's Contributions to an Abridged Version of a Book of Common Prayer," Aug. 5, 1773, Dashwood Papers, Bodleian Library, Oxford, Papers 20:343; "A New Version of the Lord's Prayer," Papers 15:299; BF to WF, Oct. 6, 1773. Sir Francis Dashwood became Lord Le Despencer in 1763.

33. BF to Joseph Galloway, Nov. 3, 1773; BF to Thomas Cushing, Feb. 2, 1774.

34. BF to Thomas Cushing, July 25, 1773; BF to London *Chronicle*, Dec. 25, 1773, Papers 20:531; BF, *Tract Relative to the Affair of the Hutchinson Letters*, 1774, Papers 21:414; Bailyn, *The Ordeal of Thomas Hutchinson*, 255.

35. BF to Thomas Cushing, Feb. 15, 1774; BF to Thomas Walpole, Jan. 12, 1774; Van Doren 462–63.

36. The record of hearings and the speech by Wedderburn, Jan. 29, 1774, are in Papers 21:37. There are numerous reconstructions, notably, Fleming 248–50; Hawke 324–27; Brands 470–74; Van Doren 462–76.

37. BF to Thomas Cushing, Feb. 15, 1774; BF to WF, Feb. 2, 1774; BF to JM, Feb. 17, 1774.

38. BF to Jan Ingenhousz, Mar. 18, 1774; "A Tract Relative to the Hutchinson Letters," 1774, Papers 21:414; Hawke 327; Van Doren 477.

39. Homo Trium Literarum (A Man of Letters, BF), "The Reply," *Public Advertiser*, Feb. 16, 1774; Boston *Gazette*, Apr. 25, 1774; Brands 477–78.

40. *Public Advertiser*, Apr. 15, May 21, 1774.

41. BF to RB, Feb. 17, 1774; Hawke 329; BF to JM, Sept. 26, 1774.

42. WF to BF, May 3, 1774; WF to Lord Dartmouth, May 31, 1774; Lord Dartmouth to WF, July 6, 1774; Randall 282–84.

43. BF to WF, June 30, May 7, 1774. The May 7 letter is dated 1775, and many authors accept that it was written then, which was just a couple of days after Franklin's arrival back in America. In fact, it seems to be misdated, as the Yale editors have concluded. On May 7, 1775, a Sunday, he did not write any other letters, but on May 7, 1774, he was busily engaged in correspondence. The letter fits into the pattern of letters he was writing at that time.

44. BF to undisclosed recipient, July 27, 1774; BF to Thomas Cushing, Mar. 22, 1774; WF to BF, July 5, 1774; BF to WF, Sept. 7, Oct. 12, 1774.

45. BF to DF, Sept. 10, 1774; WF to BF, Dec. 24, 1774.

46. "Journal of the Negotiations in London," BF to WF, Mar. 22, 1775, in Papers 21:540; Sparks, ch. 8.

47. Morgan *Devious*, 241.

48. This section is drawn from Franklin's Mar. 22, 1775, journal (cited above) of negotiations and the notes he inserted into it, Papers 21:540. Also, BF to Charles Thomson, Feb. 5, Mar. 13, 1775; BF to Thomas Cushing, Jan. 28, 1775; BF to Joseph Galloway, Feb. 5, 25, 1775; Thomas Walpole to BF, Mar. 16, 1775; Van Doren 495–523.

49. BF to Charles Thomson, Feb. 5, 1775.

50. Van Doren 521, citing J. T. Rutt, ed., *The Life and Correspondence of Joseph Priestley* (1817; New York: Thoemmes Press, 1999), 1:227.

CHAPTER 12

1. "Benjamin Franklin and the Gulf Stream," podaac.jpl.nasa.gov/kids/history.html .

2. BF to TF, June 13, 1775; Brands 499.

3. Adams Diary 2:127; William Rachel, ed., *Papers of James Madison* (Chicago: University of Chicago Press, 1962), 1:149; Lopez *Private*, 200; Van Doren 530; Hawke 351; Brands 499.

4. BF to Joseph Galloway, Feb. 25, May 8, 1775; Van Doren 527; Peter Hutchinson, ed., *The Diary of Thomas Hutchinson* (1884; Boston: Houghton Mifflin, 1991), 2:237.

5. WF to William Strahan, May 7, 1775. There is some uncertainty about when the Franklins first reunited. Some assume it was within days of Benjamin Franklin's return, though I find no evidence for this. See Hawke 292, and Clark 273. Sheila Skemp, in two books about William Franklin, concludes that William remained in New Jersey until the end of the May 15–16 legislative session and traveled to Pennsylvania for the first time shortly thereafter. See Skemp *William*, 167, 173; Skemp *Benjamin*, 127. Brands 524 accepts that chronology. Also, see ch. 11 n. 43 regarding the May 7 letter from Benjamin to William Franklin that some authors (notably Hawke 349), though not the Yale editors, date as being written in 1775, just after Franklin's arrival.

6. Peter Hutchinson, *The Diary of Thomas Hutchinson*, 2: 237; Hawke 349; Skemp *William*, 173–79; Fleming 292; Lopez *Private*, 199. See also Bernard Bailyn, *The Ordeal of Thomas Hutchinson* (Cambridge: Harvard University Press, 1974).

7. BF to William Strahan, unsent, July 5, 1775; BF to Strahan, July 7, 1775, quoted by Strahan to BF, Sept. 6, 1775.

8. William Strahan to BF, July 5, Sept. 6, Oct. 4, 1775; BF to Strahan, Oct. 3, 1775; Lopez *Private*, 198; Clark 276–77.

9. BF to Jonathan Shipley, July 7, 1775.

10. BF to Joseph Priestley, July 7, 1775.

11. "Intended Vindication and Offer from Congress to Parliament," July 1775, in Smyth *Writings*, 412–20 and Papers 22:112; Proposed preamble, before Mar. 23, 1776, Papers 22:388.

12. Adams to Abigail Adams, July 23, 1775; Brands 500; Hawke 354.

13. "Proposed Articles of Confederation," July 21, 1775, Papers 22:120; www.yale.edu/lawweb/avalon/contcong/07-21-75.htm ; Articles of Confederation of the United Colonies of New England, May 19, 1643, religiousfreedom.lib. virginia.edu/sacred/colonies_of_ne_1643.html .

14. WF to BF, Aug. 14, Sept. 6, 1775; Lopez *Private*, 202; Skemp *William*, 181.

15. BF to MS, July 17, 1775; Lopez *Private*, 201; Dorothea Blount to BF, Apr. 19, 1775.

16. BF to Joseph Priestley, July 7, 1775; BF to Charles Lee, Feb. 11, 1776; Van Doren 532–36.

17. BF to David Hartley, Oct. 3, 1775; BF to Joseph Priestley, July 7, Oct. 3, 1775.

18. Minutes of Conference with General Washington, Oct. 18–24, 1775, in Papers 22:224.

19. BF to RB, Oct. 19, 1775.

20. Abigail to John Adams, Nov. 5, 1775, Adams Letters, 1:320; Van Doren 537.

21. Lopez *Private*, 204; JM to Catherine Ray Greene, Nov. 24, 1775.

22. JM to Catherine Ray Greene, Nov. 24, 1775; Elizabeth Franklin to TF, Nov. 9, 1775.

23. "The Rattle-Snake as a Symbol of America," by An American Guesser (BF), Pa. Journal, Dec. 27, 1775; www.crwflags.com/fotw/flags/us-ratt.html .

24. WF to TF, Mar. 14, June 3, 1776; WF to Lord Germain, Mar. 28, 1776; BF to Josiah Quincy, Apr. 15, 1776.

25. Franklin's Journal in Passy, Oct. 4, 1778; BF to Charles Carroll and Samuel Chase, May 27, 1776; Allan Everest, ed., *The Journal of Charles Carroll* (1776; New York: Champlain–Upper Hudson Bicentennial Commission, 1976), 50; BF to John Hancock, May 1, 8, 1776; BF to George Washington, June 21, 1776; Brands 506–8; Van Doren 542–46; Clark 281–84.

26. BF to RB, Sept. 30, 1774; Thomas Paine, *Common Sense*, Feb. 14, 1776, www.bartleby.com/133/.

27. WF to TF, June 25, 1776; Skemp *William*, 206–15.

28. The literature on the writing of the Declaration of Independence is voluminous. This section draws from Pauline Maier, *American Scripture* (New York: Knopf, 1997); Garry Wills, *Inventing America* (Garden City, N.Y.: Doubleday, 1978); and Carl Becker, *The Declaration of Independence* (New York: Random House, 1922; Vintage paperback, 1970). See also McCullough, 119–36; Adams Diary 2:392, 512–15; Jefferson to James Madison, Aug. 30, 1823, in Jefferson Papers 10:267–69; drafts and revisions of the Declaration of Independence, www. walika.com/sr/drafting.htm . See also n. 34 below.

29. Adams Diary 3:336, 2:512–15; Jefferson Papers 1:299; Maier 100; "Thomas Jefferson's Recollection," www.walika.com/sr/jeff-tells.htm .

30. Maier, *American Scripture*, 38.

31. Sparks, ch. 9 n. 62; Preamble to a Congressional Resolution, Papers 22:322. The document in Sparks's work is more complete than the one in the Franklin papers.

32. Becker, *The Declaration of Independence*, 24–25; Adams Diary 2:512; Jefferson Papers 7:304.

33. Jefferson to BF, June 21, 1776.

34. The "original rough draught" of the Declaration shows the evolution of the text from the initial "fair copy" draft by Thomas Jefferson to the final text adopted by Congress. It can be viewed at the Library of Congress and on the Internet at www.loc.gov/exhibits/treasures/trt001.html and www.lcweb.loc.gov/exhibits/ declara/declara4.html . See also odur.let.rug.nl/~usa/D/1776-1800/independence/ doitj.htm and www.walika.com/sr/drafting.htm .

I am grateful to Gerhard Gawalt, the historian of the Library of Congress, for personally showing me the "original rough draft" and sharing his knowledge about each of the edit changes. I am also grateful to James Billington, Librarian of Congress, and Mark Roosa, the director of preservation, who arranged the presentation. Dr. Gawalt has edited and written a preface to an updated version of a useful illustrated book showing the various drafts: Julian Boyd, *The Declaration of Independence: The Evolution of the Text* (1945; Washington, D.C.: Library of Congress, 1999).

35. Franklin's alterations are noted in Becker, *The Declaration of Independence,* 142; Van Doren 550; Maier, *American Scripture,* 136. See also Wills, *Inventing America,* 181 and passim. Wills does not discuss Franklin's role in changing Jefferson's words to "self-evident," but he does discuss the definition used by Locke. Wills also gives a fascinating analysis of the influences of the Scottish Enlightenment philosophers.

36. Maier, *American Scripture,* appendix C, 236–40, shows all of the revisions made by Congress. Garry Wills argues that the changes made did not improve the document as much as other scholars have contended; Wills, *Inventing America,* 307 and passim.

37. Thomas Jefferson to Robert Walsh, Dec. 4, 1818, Jefferson Papers 18:169.

38. Sparks 1:408, ch. 9.

39. Franklin speech of July 31, 1776, in Adams Diary 2:245; Van Doren 557–58.

40. Smyth *Writings,* 10:57; Papers CD 46:u344 has the speech reused in his Nov. 3, 1789, remarks on the Pennsylvania Constitution. For a description of Franklin's design of the Great Seal, see James Hutson, Sara Day, and Jaroslav Pelikan, *Religion and the Founding of the American Republic* (Washington, D.C.: Library of Congress, 1998), 50–52; Jefferson Papers, LCMS-27748, 181–82.

41. Richard Howe to BF, written June 20, sent July 12, 1776.

42. BF to Lord Howe, July 30, 1776.

43. Howe's remarks in Papers 22:518; Richard Howe to BF, Aug. 16, 1776.

44. Adams Diary 3:418.

45. Many accounts were written of the Staten Island summit: the notes of Henry Strachey (Howe's secretary) in the New York Public Library and reprinted elsewhere; report to Congress of the committee to confer with Lord Howe, in Smyth *Writings,* 6:465 and elsewhere; Adams Diary 3:79, 3:418–22; Papers 22:518–20; Howe's report to Lord Germain, Sept. 20, 1776, in the London Public Records Office and reprinted in *Documents of the American Revolution* (Dublin: Irish Academic Press, 1981); John Adams to Abigail Adams, Sept. 14, 1776, in Adams Letters 2:124. See also Parton 2:148; Van Doren 558–62; Clark 287–91; Brands 518–19; McCullough 156–58.

46. Alsop 30–31.

47. BF to Benjamin Rush, Sept. 27, 1776.

48. "Sketch of Propositions for Peace," written sometime between Sept. 26 and Oct. 25, 1776, Papers 22:630; Smyth *Writings,* 454; Cecil Currey, *Code Number 72* (Englewood Cliffs, N.J.: Prentice-Hall, 1972), 73; Van Doren 553.

49. Currey *Code Number 72,* 77–78; Edward Hale Sr. and Edward Hale Jr., *Franklin in France* (Boston: Roberts Brothers, 1888), 1:67.

50. Elizabeth Franklin to SF, July 12, 1776; Elizabeth Franklin to TF, July 16, 1776.

51. BF to TF, Sept. 19, 1776; Elizabeth Franklin to BF, Aug. 6, 1776; Skemp *William,* 217.

52. BF to TF, Sept. 19, 22, 1776; TF to BF, Sept. 21, 1776.

53. BF to TF, Sept. 28, 1776; WF to Elizabeth Franklin, Nov. 25, 1776.

54. BF to RB, June 2, 1779.

CHAPTER 13

1. Franklin's Passy journal, Oct. 4, 1778; BF to SF, May 10, 1785; BF to John Hancock, Dec. 8, 1776. He was writing to Hancock in his capacity as president of Congress.

Franklin's social life in Paris has, not suprisingly, inspired many books. The most delightful include Lopez *Cher;* Aldridge *French;* Alsop; Schoenbrun. An older work of some value is Edward Hale Sr. and Edward Hale Jr., *Franklin in France* (Boston: Roberts Brothers, 1888). It was also the subject of a musical, *Ben Franklin in Paris,* by Mark Sandrich Jr. and Sidney Michaels, which premiered Oct. 27, 1964, and ran for 215 performances.

2. BF to SF, June 3, 1779; Aldridge *French,* 43; Van Doren 632. The tale of the chamber pot given by the king to Comtesse Diane de Polignac comes from the memoirs of Madame Henriette de Campan, the lady-in-waiting to Marie-Antoinette. It is well enough known that it was told by the French ambassador at a ceremony in the Benjamin Franklin room of the U.S. State Department; see: www.info-france-usa.org/news/statmnts/1998/amba0910.asp. However, Claude-Anne Lopez tells me, "It comes from a very unreliable source, a snobbish sourpuss, and my guess is that it's not true." That said, Lopez included it without qualification in her own book, Lopez *Cher,* 184.

3. *The Boston Patriot,* May 15, 1811, in Charles Francis Adams, ed., *The Works of John Adams* (Boston: Little, Brown, 1856) 1:660; Lopez *Cher,* 13; Wright 270.

4. Aldridge *French,* 23, 66, 115, 43, 61; Voltaire, "Letters on England" (1733), www.literatureproject.com/letters-Voltaire ; Van Doren 570; Abbé Flamarens to *Mèmoires Secret,* Jan. 17, 1777.

5. BF to Emma Thompson, Feb. 8, 1777; BF to PS, Aug. 28, 1767.

6. BF to Josiah Quincy, Apr. 22, 1779; BF to Elizabeth Partridge, Oct. 11, 1776.

7. BF to MS, Jan. 25, 1779; Alsop 76–94; Lopez *Cher,* 123–36; Aldridge *French,* 196–99. Temple's letter is from Randall 455, citing TF to SF, Nov. 25, 1777. The quote from Madame Chaumont is from Adams Diary 4:64. I am grateful to Professor Thomas Schaeper of St. Bonaventure University for his help and his delightful, though hard to find, biography of Franklin's landlord, *France and America in the Revolutionary Era: The Life and Times of Jacques-Donatien Leray de Chaumont* (Providence, R.I.: Berghahn, 1995).

8. Arthur Lee to Richard Lee, Sept. 12, 1778; BF to Congress, Dec. 7, 1780; Charles Isham, *The Silas Deane Papers* (New York: New-York Historical Society, 1890). For more on the Silas Deane papers in the Connecticut Historical Society in Hartford and a biographical sketch, see www.chs.org/library/ead/htm_faids/deans1789.htm#OB1.3 .

9. BF to Arthur Lee, Apr. 3 (unsent), 4, 1778; Van Doren 598.

10. "Petition of the Letter Z," 1778, Papers 28:517.

11. "Instructions to Silas Deane," Mar. 2, 1776, from Congress's Committee of Secret Correspondence, signed by BF and others and apparently written by BF, Papers 22:369; Sidney Edelstein, "Notes on the Wet-Processing Industry: The Dual Life of Edward Bancroft," *American Dyestuff Reporter* (Oct. 25, 1954).

12. "Engagement of Dr. Edwards to correspond with P. Wentworth and Lord Stormont, and the means of conducting that correspondence," Dec. 13, 1776, British Library, London, Auckland Papers, additional manuscripts 34,413 (hereafter cited as Auckland Papers, Add Mss); Edward Bancroft memo to the Marquis of Camarthen, Sept. 17, 1784, Foreign Office papers, 4:3, Public Records Office, London.

Some of the material is available in *Material Relating to the American Revolution from the Auckland Papers* (Yorkshire, England: EP Microform, 1974) and in Benjamin Stevens, ed., *Facsimiles of Manuscripts in European Archives Relating to America, 1773–1783* (25 volumes published in 1898, copies in the Franklin collection in Yale's Sterling Library). Please note the acknowledgment to Susan Ann Bennett, who provided research help in London finding and transcribing some of the documents cited in this section.

I am also grateful to the Central Intelligence Agency's Center for the Study of Intelligence for providing the declassified paper by John Vaillancourt, "Edward Bancroft (@Edwd.Edwards) Estimable Spy," *Studies in Intelligence* (winter 1961): A53–A67. See also Lewis Einstein, *Divided Loyalties* (Boston: Ayer, 1933), 3–48; Cecil Currey, *Code Number 72* (Englewood Cliffs, N.J.: Prentice-Hall, 1972); Samuel Bemis, "The British Secret Service and the French-American Alliance," *American Historical Review* 29.3 (Apr. 1924). There is also a historical novel, fun but heavily fictionalized, on Bancroft: Arthur Mullin, *Spy: America's First Double Agent, Dr. Edward Bancroft* (Santa Barbara, Calif.: Capra Press, 1987).

Currey argues that Franklin's loyalties (and Deane's) were also suspect. It's an interesting and fact-filled book, but I think its analysis is unconvincing. Jonathan Dull, in *Franklin the Diplomat* (Philadelphia: Transactions of the American Philosophical Society, 1982), 1:72, 36, and passim, convincingly argues that Franklin was oblivious to Bancroft's dealings and that Deane was involved in stock speculating but not in spying with Bancroft.

13. Auckland papers, Add Mss 34413, f330 and 402; 46490, f64; 34413, f405–7; Paul Wentworth to the Earl of Suffolk (the minister in charge of the northern department), quoting a secret letter from "Dr. Edwards," Sept. 19, 1777, in the Stevens *Facsimiles* at Yale noted above.

14. Silas Deane to Robert Morris for Congress, Mar. 16, 1777; Isham, *The Silas Deane Papers*, 2:24.

15. Arthur Lee to BF and John Adams, Feb. 7, 1779; Auckland Papers, Add Mss, 46490, f52 and f57.

16. Juliana Ritchie to BF, Jan. 12, 1777; BF to Juliana Ritchie, Jan. 19, 1777.

17. Alsop 20.

18. Dull, *Franklin the Diplomat*, 1:72, 9; Alsop 35–40, from Henri Doniol, *His-*

tory of the Participation of France in the Establishment of the United States (Paris: Imprimerie Nationale, 1866), 1:244.

The best overviews of Franklin's diplomacy in France, in addition to Dull's book cited above, include Jonathan Dull, *A Diplomatic History of the American Revolution* (New Haven: Yale University Press, 1987); Jonathan Dull, *The French Navy and American Independence* (Princeton: Princeton University Press, 1975); Richard Morris, *The Peacemakers* (New York: Harper & Row, 1965); Samuel Flagg Bemis, *The Diplomacy of the American Revolution* (New York: Appleton, 1935); Stourzh; Ronald Hoffman and Peter Albert, eds., *Diplomacy and Revolution* (Charlottesville: University of Virginia Press, 1981). For original documents, see Francis Wharton, ed., *Revolutionary Diplomatic Correspondence of the United States* (Washington, D.C.: GPO, 1889). See also Orville Murphy, *Charles Gravier, Comte de Vergennes* (Albany: State University of New York Press, 1982).

19. Vergennes, Dec. 28, 1776, in Papers 23:113n; Vergennes to the Marquis de Noailles, Jan. 10, 1777, in Clark 306.

20. BF to Vergennes, Jan. 5, 1777; Doniol, *History of the Participation of France*, 1:20; Stourzh 137.

21. Bernard Bailyn, *Realism and Idealism in American Foreign Policy* (Princeton: Institute of Advanced Studies, 1994), 13, reprinted in Bernard Bailyn, *To Begin the World Anew* (New York: Knopf, 2003).

22. BF to Committee of Secret Correspondence, Apr. 9, 1777; BF to Samuel Cooper, May 1, 1777; Brands 532; Stourzh 3. For a contemporary discussion of "hard power" versus "soft power," see Joseph Nye, *The Paradox of American Power* (New York: Oxford University Press, 2002). The "city upon a hill" image comes from Jesus' Sermon on the Mount, Matthew 5:14: "Ye are the light of the world. A city that is set on an hill cannot be hid." It was used by John Winthrop in the sermon, "A Model of Christian Charity," that he preached on Mar. 22, 1630, on the *Arabella* while heading to America. Ronald Reagan used the image throughout his political career, most notably as the title of a Jan. 25, 1974, speech to the Conservative Political Action Committee, in his first 1980 debate with Jimmy Carter, in a 1980 debate with John Anderson, in his 1984 speech to the Republican Convention, and in his 1989 farewell speech.

23. "The Sale of the Hessians," Feb. 18, 1777, Lib. of Am. 917; Papers 23:480; Van Doren 577. I am grateful to Claude-Anne Lopez for pointing out to me the weak French pun.

24. Alsop 77; *New Jersey Gazette*, Oct. 2, 1777, quoted in Clark 325.

25. William Parsons to BF, Aug. 4, 1778; Mrs. Parsons to BF, Aug. 12, 17, Oct. 2, Nov. 2, 1778; BF to Mrs. Parsons, Aug. 12, 1778; BF to George Washington, Mar. 29, Sept. 4, 1777; Washington to BF, Aug. 17, 1777; "Model of a Letter of Recommendation," by BF, Apr. 2, 1777; Van Doren 578; Clark 335. In the Sept. 4, 1777, letter to Washington, Franklin refers to Baron von Steuben as Baron de Steuben and inflates his rank from captain to lieutenant general. The spy Bancroft reported back to London that they had "received a resolve of Congress directing all their ministers" to discourage French mercenaries unless they spoke English, which "may enable us to cut short the solicitation with which we have for a long time al-

most been persecuted to death by thousands of officers wanting employment in America"; Edward Bancroft to Paul Wentworth, June 1777, Auckland papers, Add MSS 46490, f64.

26. Arthur Lee's journal, Nov. 27, 1777, in Richard Lee, *Life of Arthur Lee* (Boston: Wells and Lilly, 1829), 1:354; Hale and Hale, *Benjamin Franklin in France*, 1:159; Papers 25:234n.

27. Franklin statement, Dec. 4, 1777; BF to Vergennes, Dec. 4, 1777; Lee, *Life of Arthur Lee*, 1:357; Alsop 93–94; Doniol, *History of the Participation of France*, 2:625. See also Dull, *A Diplomatic History of the American Revolution*, 89. Dull argues that for months the French had been planning to enter the war against Britain in early 1778 once their naval rearmament program permitted; the American victory at Saratoga, he contends, was not a major factor. Others dispute this view. See Claude Van Tyne, "Influences Which Determined the French Government to Make Their Treaty with America," *American Historical Review* 21 (1915–16): 528, cited by Dull.

28. Alsop 103; Cecil Currey, *Code Number 72* (Englewood Cliffs, N.J.: Prentice-Hall, 1972), 175–92. Currey devotes an entire chapter to the Wentworth meeting. It seems somewhat overdrawn in its assessment of Franklin's duplicity, but it is carefully annotated and researched. See also James Perkins, *France and the American Revolution* (New York: Franklin, 1970), 203–4.

29. Paul Wentworth to William Eden, Dec. 25, 1777, Jan. 7, 1778; Van Doren 592; Currey, *Code Number 72*, 186; Dull, *Franklin the Diplomat*, 29.

30. BF to Thomas Cushing, for Congress, Feb. 27, 1778.

31. R. M. Bache, "Franklin's Ceremonial Coat," *PMHB* 23 (1899); 444–52, quote is on 450.

32. Edward Bancroft to Paul Wentworth, as deciphered, Jan. 22, 28, 1778, Auckland Papers, Add Mss 46491, f1 and f1b; Edward Bancroft memo to the Marquis of Camarthen, Sept. 17, 1784, Foreign Office papers 4:3, Public Records Office, London; Edward Bancroft to Thomas Walpole, under cover to Mr. White, with two pages of invisible ink, Nov. 3, 1777, Auckland Papers, Add Mss 34414, f.304; Edward Bancroft note, unsigned and undated, sent to Samuel Wharton, with two pages of white ink, November 1777, Auckland Papers, Add Mss 34414, f.306; Samuel Wharton letters to Edward Bancroft, 1778, Auckland Papers, Add Mss 321, ff6–35; Silas Deane's accounts with Edward Bancroft, Feb, 1778, Aug. 1779, the Connecticut Historical Society, Hartford, series 4, folder 9.12.

Jonathan Dull discusses Bancroft's stock manipulations in *Franklin the Diplomat*, 33–36, and notes that Silas Deane, although in his opinion not a spy, was also able to make money by speculating with Wharton on Bancroft's inside information. Also in on the scheme was Thomas Walpole, the wealthy and well-connected London banker who had tried with Franklin to win a land grant in Ohio. Deane died of poisoning in 1789 as he was preparing to sail from London to Canada, and some have speculated that he was murdered by Bancroft, an expert in poisons.

33. Lopez *Cher*, 179–83; Alsop 108–10; Van Doren 595; Clark 341.

34. Van Doren 593; Edmund Morgan, *The Birth of the Republic* (Chicago: University of Chicago Press, 1956), 83; Gordon Wood, "Not So Poor Richard," *The*

New York Review of Books, June 6, 1996; Samuel Cooper to BF, May 14, 1778. See also Samuel Cooper to BF, July 1, 1778, in which the Boston clergyman describes how the treaty thwarted England's attempts to lure Congress into a reconciliation and how information sent by Franklin and Adams about a British convoy of eleven warships would be passed along, presumably to warn French admiral d'Estaing.

CHAPTER 14

1. Edward Bancroft, "most secret extracts," Apr. 2, 16, 1778, British Library, Auckland papers, Add MSS 34413, f405–7; Middlekauff 171; McCullough 197, 204, 208, 239. Middlekauff's chapter on Adams in his book, pp. 171–202, is a vivid look at the vagaries of their relationship. McCullough, 210–15, provides an author-itative assessment of their feelings about each other, with some deference to Adams.

2. Adams to James Lovell, Feb. 20, 1779, Adams Letters 4:118–19; Mid-dlekauff 189.

3. Lopez *Private,* 237; Lopez *Cher,* 9. The quote is from Pierre-Jean-Georges Cabanis, *Complete Works* (Paris: Bossange frères, 1825), 2:267.

4. Brands 547–48; Adams Diary 2:391, 4:69.

5. BF to Robert Livingston, July 22, 1783.

6. Diderot, editor, *Enyclopédie,* www.lib.uchicago.edu/efts/ARTFL/projects/encyc/; Alsop 13; Harold Nicolson, *The Age of Reason* (London: Constable, 1960), 268.

7. Most accounts say, I think mistakenly, that it was Temple who received the benediction. Smith 60, 187 traces the mystery and convincingly concludes that the "boy" was actually his younger grandson Benny, who was 7 at the time, rather than Temple, who was about 18. Aldridge *French,* 10, says it was Temple, but in his later writings, including *Voltaire and the Century of Light* (Princeton: Princeton University Press, 1975), 399, he revises his opinion. Claude-Anne Lopez tells me that Temple used a wax seal with the phrase "God and Liberty," which leads her to be-lieve it may have been Temple. See also Voltaire to the Abbé Gaultier, Feb. 21, 1778, in *The Works of Voltaire* (Paris: Didot, 1829), 1:290; Hutchinson Diary and Letters 2:276. The newspaper quoted is *Les Memoirs Secret,* Feb. 22, 1778, in Aldridge *French,* 10.

8. Aldridge *French,* 12; Adams Diary 3:147; Van Doren 606.

9. Lopez *Life,* 148–57; Van Doren 655–56; Lemay *Reappraising,* 145.

10. Lopez *Cher,* 34, 29. As one of the Yale editors, Lopez's specialty was analyz-ing Franklin's papers from his period in France. Her translations, astute assess-ments, and personal discussions with me informed this chapter.

11. Madame Brillon to BF, July 30, 1777.

12. Madame Brillon to BF, Mar. 7, 1778; BF to Madame Brillon, Mar. 10, 1778.

13. Madame Brillon to BF, May 3, 8, 1779; Lopez *Cher,* 40, 61–62; Adams Let-ters 4:46; Brands 552.

14. BF to Madame Brillon, July 27, 1778. Lib. of Am. uses a version dated 1782,

and some sources have the final article worded differently. The version I have used is from the Yale Papers and the American Philosophical Society; Papers 27:164.

15. Madame Brillon to BF, Mar. 16, 17, 18, Apr. 26, June 9, July 27, Sept. 13, 17, 1778; BF to Madame Brillon, July 27, Sept. 1, 15, 1778.

16. Madame Brillon to BF, Sept. 13, 1778; BF to Madame Brillon, Sept. 15, 1778; Lopez *Cher,* 29–121.

17. "The Ephemera," Sept. 20, 1778, Lib. of Am. 922; A. Owen Aldridge, "Sources for Franklin's Ephemera," *New England Quarterly* 27 (1954): 388.

18. BF to Madame Brillon, Nov. 29, 1777; Madame Brillon to BF, Nov. 30, 1777 (the chess game partner was their neighbor Louis-Guillaume le Veillard); Papers 25:204, 25:218); Madame Brillon to BF, Dec. 10, 15, 20, 1778; BF to Madame Brillon, Dec. 11?, 1778.

19. Lopez *Cher,* 243–48. Lopez draws on Antoine Guillois, *Le Salon de Madame Helvétius* (Paris: Calmann Levy, 1894). Claude-Adrien Helvétius, *De l'Esprit* (Paris, 1758; English translation, *Essays on the Mind,* London, 1759); it was publicly burned in Paris but also one of the most widely read books of its time. See gallica.bnf.fr/Fonds_textes/T0088614.htm ; www.aei.ca/~anbou/mhelv.html .

20. Aldridge *French,* 162; Gilbert Chinard, "Abbé Lefebvre de la Roche's Recollections of Benjamin Franklin," *Proceedings of the American Philosophical Society* (1950).

21. BF to Madame Helvétius, Oct. 31, 1778.

22. Aldridge *French,* 165; Adams Papers 2:55.

23. BF to Madame Helvétius, through Cabanis, Sept. 19, 1779. It is possible that Poupon was a cat, but we know she had a dog and this is more likely.

24. "The Flies," Papers 34:220; Lib. of Am., 991 (the date of this piece is unkown and in dispute); Lopez *Cher,* 260. See also Lopez *Cher,* 371n.32 arguing that some biographers "overdramatize" Franklin's proposal to Madame Helvétius whereas others discount it too much.

25. "The Elysian Fields," Dec. 7, 1778, Lib. of Am. 924.

26. Turgot to Pierre du Pont de Nemours, June 24, 1780, in Lopez *Cher,* 170.

27. BF to Thomas Bond, Mar. 16, 1780.

28. Aldridge *French,* 183. For a good assessment, see Richard Amacher, *Franklin's Wit and Folly: The Bagatelles* (New Brunswick, N.J.: Rutgers University Press, 1953).

29. Poem from Madame Brillon to BF, Oct., 1780, translation in Lopez *Cher,* 78; "Dialogue with the Gout," Oct. 22, 1780.

30. Madame Brillon to BF, Nov. 18, 26, 1780; Lopez *Cher,* 79–81; Aldridge *French,* 166.

31. Lopez *Cher,* 25–26.

32. "Conte," dated Dec. 1778 in Papers 28:308 and early 1779 by Lemay in Lib. of Am. 938; Aldridge *French,* 173; Lopez *Cher,* 90.

33. Abbé Flamarens, Jan. 15, 1777, in Aldridge *French,* 61.

34. "The Morals of Chess," June 28, 1779; Papers 29:750–56 also includes the Junto notes he made in 1732. See also Jacques Barbeu-Dubourg to BF, July 3, 1779, which mentions a "refutation" of Franklin's points.

35. Aldridge *French,* 197; Jefferson Papers 18:168.

36. "An Economical Project," *Journal of Paris,* Apr. 26, 1784; Poor Richard's, 1735. See also http://www.standardtime.com ; http://www.energy.ca.gov/daylight saving.html ; http ://webexhibits.org/daylightsaving .

37. Aldridge *French,* 178

38. "To the Royal Academy of ***," May 19, 1780, or after, Lib. of Am. 952. See also, Carl Japsky, ed., *Fart Proudly* (Columbus, Ohio: Enthea Press, 1990).

39. BF to the Abbé Morellet, ca. July 5, 1779.

40. SF to BF, Jan. 17, 1779; BF to SF, June 3, 1779. General Howe had been re-placed by Sir Henry Clinton, who evacuated his British troops from Philadelphia in May 1778 to concentrate on the defense of New York. General Washington tried and failed to stop the British in a battle in Monmouth County, New Jersey, and Clinton's troops safely ensconced themselves in New York.

41. SB to BF, Sept. 14, 1779; BF to SB, Mar. 16, 1780. See the poignant chapter "No Watch for Benny, No Feathers for Sally," in Lopez *Private,* 215–32.

42. SF to BF, Jan. 17, Sept. 25, 1779, Sept. 8, 1780; BF to SF, June 3, 1779.

43. RB to BF, July 28, 1780; SF to BF, Sept. 9, 1780; BF to RB and SF, Oct. 4, 1780.

44. BF to SF, June 3, 1779.

45. BF to Benjamin Bache, Aug. 19, 1779, Apr. 16, 1781. For a well-researched and insightful assessment of their relationship, see Smith, in particular 67–70, 77–82. Also Lopez *Private,* 221–30.

46. BF to Benjamin Bache, Jan. 25, 1782. See also May 3, 30, Aug. 19, 1779, July 18, 1780. Gabriel Louis de Marignac to BF, Nov. 20, 1781.

47. Catherine Cramer to BF, May 15, 1781; RB to BF, July 22, 1780.

48. BF to Benjamin Bache, Sept. 25, 1780; SB to BF, Jan. 14, 1781.

49. Benjamin Bache to BF, Jan. 30, 1783; BF to Benjamin Bache, May 2, 1783; BF to Johonnot, Jan. 26, 1782.

50. BF to the Brillons, Apr. 20, Oct. 30, 1781; Madame Brillon to BF, Apr. 20, Oct. 20, 1781; Lopez *Cher,* 91–101.

CHAPTER 15

1. BF to James Lovell (for Congress), July 22, 1778; Richard Bache to BF, Oct. 22, 1778; Van Doren 609.

2. BF to John Adams, Apr. 3, 24, May 10, June 5, 1779; John Adams to BF, Apr. 13, 29, May 14, 17, 1779; Middlekauff 190–92; McCullough 210–14; Schoenbrun 229.

3. RB to BF, Oct. 8, 22, 1778; BF to RB, June 2, 1779; BF to SF, June 3, 1779.

4. BF to Lafayette, Mar. 22, Oct. 1, 1779; Lafayette to BF, July 12, 1779; Lafayette to TF, Sept. 7, 1779. See also Harlowe Giles Unger, *Lafayette* (New York: Wiley, 2002).

5. BF to Lafayette, Mar. 22, 1779; BF to John Paul Jones, May 27, June 1, 10, 1778. See also Evan Thomas, *John Paul Jones* (New York: Simon & Schuster, 2003).

Evan Thomas graciously provided an early copy of his manuscript, which helped inform this section, and he read and helped to correct this section.

6. Samuel Eliot Morison, *John Paul Jones* (Annapolis, Md.: Naval Institute Press, 1959), 156 and passim. Alsop 176 also says that "all the world knew of the love affair between the dashing officer and Madame de Chaumont." But Evan Thomas in his biography points out that there is no concrete evidence of this.

7. John Paul Jones to BF, Mar. 6, 1779; BF to Jones, Mar. 14, 1779.

8. BF to John Paul Jones, Apr. 27, 1779; Jones to BF, May 1, 1779.

9. John Paul Jones to BF, May 26, Oct. 3, 1779; BF to Jones, Oct. 15, 1779. As Evan Thomas points out, it is very unclear whether Jones actually uttered his famous "I have not yet begun to fight."

10. Vergennes to Adams, Feb. 15, 1780; McCullough 232.

11. BF to George Washington, Mar. 5, 1780.

12. BF to David Hartley, Feb. 2, 1780.

13. For Franklin's use of the phrase "no bad peace or good war," see BF to Jonathan Shipley, June 10, 1782; BF to Joseph Banks, July 27, 1783; BF to Josiah Quincy, Sept. 11, 1783; BF to Rodolphe-Ferdinand Grand, Mar. 5, 1786.

14. BF to Arthur Lee, Mar. 21, 1777; Stourzh 160; BF to Robert Livingston, Mar. 4, 1782.

15. John Adams to Congress, Apr. 18, 1780, Adams Letters 3:151; Vergennes to John Adams, July 29, 1780, Adams Letters 3:243; McCullough 241.

16. Vergennes to BF, July 31, 1780; BF to Vergennes, Aug. 3, 1780; BF to Samuel Huntington (for Congress), Aug. 9, 1780. Adams was still rehashing this disagreement decades later in an article in the *Boston Patriot*, May 15, 1811; see Stourzh 159.

17. BF to John Adams, Oct. 2, 1780, Feb. 22, 1781. Adams replied with a gloomy camaraderie, saying he had accepted some bills "relying on your virtues and graces of Faith and Hope." John Adams to BF, Apr. 10, 1781.

18. Washington to BF, Oct. 9, 1780; BF to Vergennes, Feb. 13, 1781.

19. For currency conversion data see page 507. See also: Thomas Schaeper, *France and America in the Revolutionary Era* (Providence: Bergham Books, 1995), 348; John McCusker, *How Much Is That in Real Money?* (New Castle, Del.: Oak Knoll Press, 2001); Economic History Services, http://eh.net/hmit/; Inflation Conversion Factors, www.orst.edu/Dept/pol_sci/fac/sahr/cf166502.pdf .

20. Ralph Izard to Richard Lee, Oct. 15, 1780; Vergennes to la Luzerne, Feb. 19, 1781; Stourzh 153; BF to Samuel Huntington (for Congress), Mar. 12, 1781.

21. Vergennes to la Luzerne, Dec. 4, 1780; Stourzh 167.

22. Stourzh 168; BF to Samuel Huntington (for Congress), Sept. 13, 1781.

23. BF to William Carmichael, Aug. 24, 1781; BF to John Adams, Oct. 12, 1781.

24. BF to Robert Morris, Mar. 7, 1782.

25. Madame Brillon to BF, Jan. 20, Feb. 1, 1782; BF to Shelburne, Mar. 22, Apr. 18, 1782; BF to Vergennes, Apr. 15, 1782. See also BF to WF, Sept. 12, 27, Oct. 11, 1766, June 13, Aug. 28, 1767, for discussions of Franklin's early meetings with Shelburne.

26. "Journal of Peace Negotiations," May 9–July 1, 1782, Papers CD 37:191. This forty-page journal is a detailed description of all the talks and meetings Franklin had up until an attack of the gout caused him to quit keeping the journal on July 1. The following narrative is drawn from this journal as well as the letters he included in it.

Much of this information is also based on the forthcoming volume 37 of the Franklin Papers, due to be published in late 2003, which covers March 16–September 15, 1782. It adds notes and assessments about Franklin's writings, which were already available on the Papers CD and elsewhere. I am grateful to the Yale editors for letting me read the manuscript in the fall of 2002. The editors also provided access to the drafts of volumes 38 and 39, due out in 2004, which cover the conclusion of the negotiations.

27. "Supplement to the *Boston Independent Chronicle*," a hoax by BF, Mar. 12, 1782. The Yale editors provide a detailed assessment of this document for the forthcoming volume 37 of the Papers. Among the people he sent it to was James Hutton, an English friend, who replied, "That article in the Boston paper must be romance, all of it invention, cruel forgery I hope and believe. Bales of scalps!!! Neither the King nor his old ministers . . . are capable of such atrocities." Nevertheless, at least one London magazine (*Public Advertiser*, Sept. 27, 1782) reprinted parts of it as true. BF to James Hutton, July 7, 1782; James Hutton to BF, July 23, 1782, Papers 37:443, 37:503.

28. "Journal of Peace Negotiations"; Shelburne to BF, Apr. 28, 1782; Charles Fox to BF, May 1, 1782.

29. Richard Morris, *The Peacemakers* (New York: Harper & Row, 1965), 274, points out that Grenville and Oswald did not report Franklin's strong refusals to consider a separate peace, but instead reported back hints that he might be open to it.

30. BF to John Adams, June 2, 1782.

31. "Journal of Peace Negotiations"; BF to Shelburne, Apr. 18, May 10, 13, 1782; Shelburne to BF, Apr. 28, 1782; BF to Charles James Fox, May 10, 1782; BF to John Adams, Apr. 20, May 2, 8, 1782; BF to Henry Laurens, Apr. 20, 1782.

32. BF to Robert Livingston, June 25, 29, 1782; BF to Richard Oswald, June 25, 1782. Franklin's journal ends July 1.

33. Richard Oswald to Lord Shelburne, July 10, 1782; BF to Richard Oswald, July 12, 1782; BF to Vergennes, July 24, 1782.

34. Lord Shelburne to Richard Oswald, July 27, 1782; Wright 314.

35. John Jay to Robert Livingston, Sept. 18, Nov. 17, 1782; Stourzh 178; BF to Lafayette, Sept. 17, 1782.

36. Vergennes to la Luzerne, Dec. 19, 1782; McCullough 280.

37. Middlekauff 197; Herbert Klinghoffer, "Matthew Ridley's Diary during the Peace Negotiations of 1782," *William and Mary Quarterly* 20.1 (January 1963): 123; John Adams to Edmund Jennings, July 20, 1782, in McCullough 276; Adams Letters 3:38; Wright 315.

38. John Adams to BF, Sept. 13, 1783; McCullough 277; Wright 316; Stourzh 177; BF to Robert Livingston, July 22, 1783.

39. BF to John Jay, Sept. 10, 1783; John Adams to BF, Sept. 13, 1783; McCullough 282.

40. Samuel Cooper to BF, July 15, 1782; Robert Livingston to BF, June 23, 1782; BF to Richard Oswald, July 28, 1782; Fleming 455.

41. Benjamin Vaughan to Lord Shelburne, July 31, Dec. 10, 1782.

42. "Apologue," Nov. 1782, Lib. of Am. 967; Smyth *Writings,* 8:650.

43. Adams Diaries 3:37; Middlekauff 198; Klinghoffer, "Matthew Ridley's Diary," 132.

44. Vergennes to la Luzerne, Dec. 19, 1782; Vergennes to BF, Dec. 15, 1782.

45. BF to Vergennes, Dec. 17, 1782; Stourzh 178. The dispute, it so happens, hardly remained a secret: Edward Bancroft, still a spy, promptly sent the letter to the British ministers.

46. Vergennes to la Luzerne, Dec. 19, 1782. A few months later, when Foreign Secretary Robert Livingston asked him about the French objections, Franklin replied, "I do not see, however, that they have much reason to complain of that Transaction. Nothing was stipulated to their Prejudice, and none of the Stipulations were to have Force, but by a subsequent Act of their own . . . I long since satisfied Count de Vergennes about it here. We did what appeared to all of us best at the Time, and, if we have done wrong, the Congress will do right, after hearing us, to censure us." Franklin told Livingston he felt that the French advice on fishing rights was merely designed to assure that a deal was made. Adams felt the French were making the suggestions because they did not want America to succeed in getting the fishing rights. It is in this letter that Franklin chides Adams for his lack of gratitude toward France and calls him "in some things completely out of his senses." BF to Robert Livingston, July 22, 1783.

47. Van Doren 696–97.

48. BF to PS, Jan. 27, 1783; BF to Joseph Banks, July 27, 1783.

49. BF to Benjamin Bache, June 23, 1783; Robert Pigott to BF, June 27, 1783; Smith 79.

50. Dorcas Montgomery to SB, July 23, 1783; BF to PS, Sept. 7, 1783; BF to SF, July 27, 1783; Benjamin Bache to RB and SF, Oct. 30, 1783; Smith 80–82.

51. BF to PS, 1782, Jan. 8, Sept. 7, 1783; PS to BF, Sept. 28, 1783.

52. BF to PS, Dec. 26, 1783; BF to RB, Nov. 11, 1783; Van Doren 709.

53. BF to Robert Livingston, July 22, 1783; Lopez *Cher,* 314.

54. BF to Joseph Banks, Aug. 30, Nov. 21, Dec. 1, 1783. A vivid account of the ballooning race and craze is in Lopez *Cher,* 215–22, which cites Gaston Tissandier, *Histoire des ballons et des aéronautes célèbres, 1783–1800* (Paris: Launette, 1887). See also Lopez *Private,* 267; www.ballooning.org/ballooning/timeline.html ; www. balloonzone.com/history.html .

55. Joseph Banks to BF, Nov. 7, 1783; BF to Joseph Banks, Nov. 21, 1783; BF to Jan Ingenhousz, Jan. 16, 1784; Lopez *Cher,* 222, contains Franklin's parody letter.

56. BF to SF, Jan. 26, 1784.

57. "Information to Those Who Would Remove to America," Feb. 1784; Lib. of Am. 975; Morgan *Franklin,* 297. In a letter to me commenting on some draft sections of this book, Edmund Morgan noted: Franklin's "description is mainly accu-

rate but at the same time a statement of what he values in the country and hopes to see perpetuated or magnified" (Dec. 2, 2002).

58. BF to Benjamin Vaughan, July 26, 1784.

59. BF to Robert Morris, Dec. 25, 1783; BF to Benjamin Vaughan, Mar. 14, 1785.

60. BF to Strahan, Jan. 24, 1780, Feb. 16, Aug. 19, 1784.

61. Lopez *Cher,* 277–79; Pierre Cabanis, *Complete Works* (Paris: Bossange frères, 1825), 2:348.

62. BF to George Whatley, Aug. 21, 1784, May 23, 1785.

63. BF to TF, Aug. 25, 1784. There are many books and articles on Mesmer. The best, as it relates to Franklin, is the chapter in Lopez *Life,* 114–26. See also Robert Darnton, *Mesmerism and the End of the Enlightenment in France* (Cambridge: Harvard University Press, 1968); Lopez *Cher,* 163–73; Van Doren 713–14.

64. Willard Sterne Randall, *Thomas Jefferson* (New York: Henry Holt, 1993), 370–400; John Adams to Robert Livingston, May 25, 1783, James Madison to Thomas Jefferson, Feb. 11, 1783, Jefferson to Madison, Feb. 14, 1783, all quoted in Middlekauff 200–201.

65. WF to BF, July 22, 1784.

66. BF to WF, Aug. 16, 1784.

67. BF to TF, Oct. 2, 1784; Lopez *Private,* 258.

68. BF to PS, Mar. 19, Aug. 15, 1784.

69. Lopez *Private,* 272.

70. PS to BF, Oct. 25, 1784; PS to Barbara Hewson, Jan. 25, 1785; Lopez *Private,* 269.

71. BF to PS, July 4, 1785; BF to JM, July 13, 1785; BF to David Hartley, July 5, 1785.

72. Vergennes to François Barbé de Marbois, May 10, 1785; BF to John Jay, Sept. 21, 1785.

73. Lopez *Cher,* 137–39; Lopez *Private,* 275; Fawn Brodie, *Thomas Jefferson* (New York: Norton, 1974), 425.

74. Franklin trip journal, July 13–28, 1785, Papers CD 43:310.

75. WF to SF, Aug. 1, 1785; Temple *Writings,* 2:165. In a letter to John Jay, Sept. 21, 1785, he describes how Shipley and others visited him in Southampton, but does not mention William.

CHAPTER 16

1. "Maritime Observations," BF to David Le Roy, Aug. 1785, Papers CD 41:384.

2. "Causes and Cure of Smoky Chimneys," BF to Jan Ingenhousz, Aug. 28, 1785; "Description of a New Stove," by BF, Aug. 1785, Papers CD 43:380.

3. BF journal, Sept. 14, 1785, unpublished, Papers CD 43:310; BF to John Jay, Sept. 21, 1785.

4. BF to Jonathan Shipley, Feb. 24, 1786.

5. BF to Polly Stevenson, May 6, 1786.

6. Manasseh Cutler, diary excerpt of July 13, 1787, in Smyth *Writings,* 10:478.

7. BF to Louis-Guillaume le Veillard, Apr. 15, 1787; BF to Ferdinand Grand, Apr. 22, 1787.

8. BF to JM, Sept. 21, 1786; Manasseh Cutler, diary excerpt of July 13, 1787, in Smyth *Writings,* 10:478. When he died, the 4,276 volumes in his library were valued at just over £184. See "An inventory and appraisement of the goods and chattels of the estate of Benjamin Franklin," Bache papers, Castle Collection, American Philosophical Society, Philadelphia.

9. BF to JM, Sept. 20, 1787; BF to Professor Landriani, Oct. 14, 1787.

10. BF to James Woodmason, July 25, 1780, in which he discusses with the London stationer the "new-invented art of copying" and orders three rudimentary machines from him for delivery to Passy. The machines from Woodmason came from Watt's factory, and the stationer insisted that Franklin pay in advance before they were ordered. In a letter of Nov. 1, 1780, he tells Franklin he is sending three new machines and provides instructions for how to use the ink; Papers CD 33:579. See also Copying machine history, http://www.inc.com/articles/it/computers_networks/peripherals/2000.html .

11. "Description of An Instrument for Taking Down Books from High Shelves," Jan. 1786, Papers CD 43:873; Lib. of Am. 1116.

12. BF to Catherine (Kitty) Shipley, May 2, 1786; Lib. of Am. 1118.

13. BF to David Hartley, Oct. 27, 1785.

14. BF to Jonathan Williams, Feb. 16, 1786; to Jonathan Shipley, Feb. 24, 1786; Brands 661.

15. BF to William Cocke, Aug. 12, 1786.

16. BF to Thomas Jefferson, Apr. 19, 1787.

17. www.nara.gov/exhall/charters/constitution/confath.html .

Much of the following relies on Max Farrand, ed., *Records of the Federal Convention* (New Haven: Yale University Press, 1937) and, in particular, *Madison's Journals.* There are many editions of this masterful narrative. Among the most convenient are the searchable versions on the Web, including www.yale.edu/lawweb/avalon/debates/debcont.htm , and www.constitution.org/dfc/dfc_000.htm .

For good analysis of Franklin's role at the convention, see William Carr, *The Oldest Delegate* (Newark: University of Delaware Press, 1990); Gordon Wood, *The Creation of the American Public* (Chapel Hill: University of North Carolina Press, 1969); Clinton Rossiter, *1787: The Grand Convention* (New York: Macmillan, 1966); Catherine Drinker Bowen, *Miracle at Philadelphia* (Boston: Little, Brown, 1966); Richard Morris, *The Forging of the Union* (New York: Harper & Row, 1987).

18. The oft-told story of Franklin arriving at the convention in a sedan chair is described most vividly in Catherine Drinker Bowen's *Miracle at Philadelphia,* 34. See also Smyth *Writings,* 10:477; Brands 674; Van Doren 741. The careful scholar J. A. Leo Lemay writes that no evidence exists that Franklin was carried in a sedan chair to any meeting of the convention. See Lemay, "Recent Franklin Scholarship,

with a Note on Franklin's Sedan Chair," *PMHB* 76:2 (Apr. 2002): 339–40. In fact, however, there is an unpublished letter written by his daughter, Sally, to his grandson Temple during the convention in which she reports: "Your Grand Father was just getting into his Chair to go to convention when I told him I had received your letter" (SB to TF, undated in 1787, Papers CD 45:u350). We know that Franklin was feeling poorly at the outset of the convention, though not throughout it, and also that he owned a sedan chair. The list of items in his estate ("An inventory and appraisement of the goods and chattels of the estate of Benjamin Franklin," Bache papers, Castle Collection, American Philosophical Society, Philadelphia) lists a "Sedan Chair" valued at £20, and it is also listed as part of the items sold from Franklin's house on May 25, 1792, two years after his death (*Dunlap's American Daily Advertiser,* May 21, 1792, copy in the American Philosophical Society, also reprinted in *PMHB* 23 [1899]: 123). We also know that a friend requested permission to borrow "his sedan chair" in 1788 (Mrs. Powel to BF, unpublished, June 16, 1788, Papers CD 45:558). Thus, I think it is reasonable to believe the reports that he was carried in the chair to the convention that first day, May 28. However, Lemay makes the good point that it is unlikely that he regularly used the sedan chair to get to the convention. As Franklin wrote to his sister in September, "The daily exercise of going and returning from the state house has done me good" (BF to JM, Sept. 20, 1787, Papers CD, 45:u167). One friend wrote in late 1786, "Except for the stone, which prevents his using exercise except in walking in the house up and down stairs and sometime to the state-house, [he] still retains his health, spirits and memory" (Samuel Vaughan to Richard Price, Nov. 4, 1786, *Massachusetts Historical Society Proceedings*, 21.17 [May 1903]: 355).

19. Benjamin Rush to Richard Price, June 2, 1787, *Massachusetts Historical Society Proceedings* 21.17 (May 1903): 361. For Pierce's speech, see Farrand's Records of the Convention, 3:91; Franklin speeches, June 30, June 11, Madison's journal; Morris, *The Forging of the Union,* 272.

20. Bowen 18.

21. Madison journal, May 31, 1787.

22. Madison journal, June 11, 1787.

23. Madison journal, June 28, 1787.

24. "Motion For Prayers," by BF, June 28, 1787; Madison's journal, Farrand, 1:452; Papers CD 45:u77; Smyth *Writings,* 9:600.

25. Madison journal, June 30, 1787.

26. Manasseh Cutler journal, July 13, 1787, in Smyth *Writings,* 10:478; "Queries and Remarks Respecting Alterations in the Constitution of Pennsylvania," Nov. 3, 1789, Smyth *Writings,* 10:57.

27. Madison journal, July 26, 20, June 5, 1787.

28. Madison journal, Aug. 7, 10, 1787.

29. Madison journal, June 2, 1787; BF to Benjamin Strahan, Feb. 16, Aug. 19, 1784; Gordon S. Wood, *The Radicalism of the American Revolution* (New York: Random House, 1991), 199. See also chapter 5 n. 25; McCullough 400.

30. Farrand's Records of Convention, 3:85; Samuel Eliot Morison, *Oxford History of the American People* (New York: Oxford University Press, 1965), 1:398.

31. BF to la Rochefoucauld, Oct. 22, 1788; BF to Pierre Du Pont de Nemours, June 9, 1788.

32. Franklin closing speech, Sept. 17, 1787, Papers CD 45:ul61. There are a few versions of this speech, including a draft version, a copy, and Madison's notes, each with minor variations. The one quoted here is that used by the Yale editors of Franklin's papers.

33. Farrand's Records of Convention, 3:85; see memory.loc.gov/ammem/amlaw/lwfr.html .

34. Barbara Oberg, "Plain, Insinuating, Persuasive," in Lemay *Reappraising*, 176, 189; Rossiter, *1787: The Grand Convention*, 234.

35. Roger Rosenblatt, *Where We Stand* (New York: Harcourt, 2002), 70, citing Henry May, *The Enlightenment in America* (New York: Oxford University Press, 1976). The only major founding document Franklin did not sign was the Articles of Confederation, as he was then in France. Roger Sherman signed the Declaration of Independence, the Articles of Confederation, and the Constitution, as well as the Declaration of 1774, but he did not sign either of the treaties.

36. BF to JM, Nov. 4, 1787, Aug. 3, 1789.

37. BF to Noah Webster, Dec. 26, 1789.

38. BF to Benjamin Vaughan, Oct. 24, 1788; see also BF to Louis-Guillaume Le Veillard, Oct. 24, 1788.

39. BF to Benjamin Vaughan, June 3, Nov. 2, 1798; BF to Elizabeth Partridge, Nov. 25, 1788.

40. BF to Catherine Ray Greene, Mar. 2, 1789; BF to George Washington, Sept. 18, 1789.

41. BF to Jean Baptiste Le Roy, Nov. 13, 1789; BF to Louis-Guillaume le Veillard, Oct. 24, 1788.

42. "An Address to the Public," Nov. 9, 1789, Smyth *Writings*, 10:66. Mason quote is in Farrand's Records of the Convention, 2:370.

43. Pennsylvania Society for the Abolition of Slavery, Petition to Congress, by BF, Feb. 12, 1790.

44. "Sidi Mehemet Ibrahim on the Slave Trade," BF to *Federal Gazette*, Mar. 23, 1790.

45. See chapter 11; BF to Richard Price, Mar. 18, 1785.

46. BF to William Strahan, Aug. 19, 1784.

47. BF to unknown recipient, July 3, 1786, Smyth *Writings*, 9:520; the same letter, dated Dec. 13, 1757, Papers 7:293; Thomas Paine, *The Age of Reason*, first fully published in 1794, www.ushistory.org/paine/; libertyonline.hypermall.com/Paine/AOR-Frame.html .

The Yale editors of the Franklin Papers note, "Both the date and the addressee of this letter have been subjects of much difference of opinion. Each of the three surviving manuscript versions bears a different date line. That on the draft, in Franklin's hand, has been heavily scratched out, probably long after the letter was written, by someone other than Franklin." That draft, now at the Library of Congress, has a note by Franklin calling it "Rough of letter dissuading ——— from publishing his piece." Jared Sparks, one of the earliest editors and biographers, deciphered the blacked-out line as "Phila., July 3, 1786," and he published it as addressed to Thomas Paine (Sparks 10:281). Sparks writes, "When a skeptical writer, who is supposed to have been Thomas Paine, showed him in manuscript a work written against religion, he urged him earnestly not to publish it, but to burn it; objecting to his arguments as fallacious, and to his principles as poisoned with the seeds of vice, without tending to any imaginable good." John Bigelow in *The Works of Benjamin Franklin* (New York: Putnam's, 1904) and Smyth *Writings*, 9:520, also use that date. For a contrary assessment written by a student of Sparks's, see Moncure Conway, *The Life of Thomas Paine* (New York: Putnam's, 1892), vii–viii.

The Yale editors (Papers 7:293n, published in 1963) called that dating "plausible" but give six other possible years, ranging from 1751 to 1787. They tentatively use the 1757 date based on a transcription in French that appears to have been written and dated by the clerk Franklin used while living in Passy. In their note, however, they say, "The editors have not been able to identify any particular 'infidel' who might have sent Franklin a manuscript in 1757, nor have they located any particular tract which might be evidence that his advice against publication was disregarded." The Yale editors, when I asked them in 2002, said that they remain uncertain about the date. In a letter to me commenting on some draft sections of this book, Dec. 2, 2002, Edmund Morgan wrote, "Your suggestion that it was written in 1786 to Paine makes more sense to me than the reasons offered by the former editors for placing it in 1757."

My belief that the 1786 date is likely and that it was sent to Paine is based on the following. As early as 1776, Paine had expressed his "contempt" for the Bible and told John Adams, "I have some thoughts of publishing my thoughts on religion, but I believe it will be best to postpone it to the latter part of my life" (John Keane, *Tom Paine* [Boston: Little, Brown, 1995], 390). By 1786, Paine was writing frequently to Franklin (Sept. 23, Dec. 31, 1785, Mar. 31, June 6, 14, 1786) and even using the courtyard in front of Franklin's house to display a bridge design Paine had made. In *The Age of Reason,* Paine favorably mentions Franklin five times ("The Proverbs which are said to be of Solomon's . . . [are] not more wise and economical than those of the American Franklin"). He echoes the more general aspects of Franklin's deist creed by saying that he believes in God and that the "moral duty of man" is to practice God's beneficence "toward each other." But he also engages in many heretical attacks on organized religion that would have elicited Franklin's cautious response. He says that churches "appear to me to be no other than human inventions set up to terrify and enslave mankind and monopolize power and profit." He also says that "the theory of what is called the Christian church sprung out of the tale of heathen mythology" and decries Christian theology for its "absurdity." And he begins his book by indicating that he had considered publishing his thoughts earlier but was dissuaded: "It has been my intention, for several years past, to publish my thoughts upon religion. I am well aware of the difficulties that attend the subject, and from that consideration had reserved it to a more advanced period of life."

48. Archives of Congregation Mikveh Israel, Apr. 30, 1788 (Franklin's gift is one of the three largest of forty-four, and he is on top of the subscriber list), www.mikvehisrael.org/gifs/frank2.jpg ; BF to John Calder, Aug. 21, 1784.

49. BF to Ezra Stiles, Mar. 9, 1790.

50. BF to Thomas Jefferson, Apr. 8, 1790.

51. Reports of Dr. John Jones and Benjamin Rush, in Sparks and elsewhere; Pa. Gazette, Apr. 21, 1790; Benjamin Bache to Margaret Markoe, May 2, 1790.

52. Epitaph, 1728; this is the version Temple Franklin published. See Papers CD 41:u539. Franklin also produced slightly edited versions, including one that ends "Corrected and amended/By the author" (Papers 1:109a).

53. Last will and testament, plus codicil, June 23, 1789, Papers CD 46:u20.

CHAPTER 17

1. Last will and testament, plus codicil, June 23, 1789, Papers CD 46:u20; Skemp *William*, 275. The will and codicil are at www.sln.fi.edu/franklin/family/ lastwill.html .

2. WF to TF, July 3, 1789; Skemp *William*, 275; Lopez *Private*, 309. A full and authorized English edition of Franklin's autobiography was not published until 1868.

3. The two great books on Benjamin Bache and his paper are Jeffery A. Smith, *Franklin and Bache: Envisioning the Enlightened Republic* (New York: Oxford University Press, 1990), and Richard Rosenfeld, *American Aurora* (New York: St. Martin's, 1997). See also Bernard Faÿ, *The Two Franklins* (Boston: Little, Brown, 1933).

4. Patricia Nealon, "Ben Franklin Trust to Go to State, City," *Boston Globe*, Dec. 7, 1993, A22; Clark DeLeon, "Divvying Up Ben," *Philadelphia Inquirer*, Feb. 7, 1993, B2; Tom Ferrick Jr., "Ben Franklin's Gift Keeps Giving," *Philadelphia Inquirer*, Jan. 27, 2002, B1; Tour de Sol Web site, www.nesea.org/transportation/ tour ; *The Franklin Gazette*, printed by the Friends of Franklin Inc., www. benfranklin2006.org (spring 2002); Philadelphia Academies Annual Report 2001 and Web site, www.academiesinc.org . Web sites on Franklin's bequest include www.philanthropyroundtable.org/magazines/2000-01/lastpage.html ; www.cs.app state.edu/~sjg/class/1010/wc/finance/benfranklin.html ; www.lehighvalleyfounda tion.org/support.html#BenFranklin .

CHAPTER 18

1. *The Nation*, July 9, 1868, reprinted in Norton Autobiography 270. See also Nian-Sheng Huang, *Benjamin Franklin in American Thought and Culture, 1790–1990* (Philadelphia: American Philosophical Society, 1994).

2. The Provost Smith papers, *Pennsylvania Gazette*, Apr. 1997, www.upenn. edu/gazette/0497/.

3. John Adams, *Boston Patriot*, May 15, 1811.

4. Gordon Wood, *The Radicalism of the American Revolution* (New York: Vintage, 1991), 347; John Adams to TF, May 5, 1817; Francis, Lord Jeffrey, *Edinburgh Review* 8 (1806), in Norton Autobiography 253. Jeffrey was reviewing an earlier unauthorized edition of the writings and autobiography.

5. Robert Spiller, "Franklin and the Art of Being Human," *Proceedings of the American Philosophical Society* 100.4 (Aug. 1956): 304.

6. John Keats to George and Georgiana Keats, Oct. 31, 1818; Leigh Hunt, *Autobiography* (New York: Harper, 1850), 1:130–32; both reprinted in Norton Autobiography 257, 266.

7. Herman Melville, *Israel Potter* (1855; New York: Library of America, 1985), chapter 8, http://www.melville.org/hmisrael.htm ; Autobiography 45.

8. Emerson's Journals 1:375, quoted in Campbell 35; Nathaniel Hawthorne, *Works,* 12:189, cited in Yale Autobiography 13.

9. David Brooks, "Among the Bourgeoisophobes," *The Weekly Standard,* Apr. 15, 2002.

10. Mark Twain, "The Late Benjamin Franklin," *The Galaxy,* July 1870.

11. Jim Powell, "How Benjamin Franklin's *Autobiography* inspired all kinds of people to help themselves," www.libertystory.net/LSCONNFRAN.htm .

12. Frederick Jackson Turner, essay in *The Dial,* May 1887; William Dean Howells, "Editor's Study," *Harper's,* Apr. 1888; reprinted in Norton Autobiography.

13. Max Weber, *The Protestant Ethic and the Spirit of Capitalism,* first published (in German) in 1904 and revised in 1920 (New York: Harper Collins, 1930), 52–53; Van Wyck Brooks, *America's Coming of Age,* originally published in 1915 as an essay (Garden City, N.Y.: Doubleday, 1934); William Carlos Williams, *In the Grain* (New York: New Directions, 1925), 153; Sinclair Lewis, *Babbitt,* first published in 1922, chapter 16, section 3, see www.bartleby.com/162/16.html .

14. D. H. Lawrence, "Benjamin Franklin," *Studies in Classic American Literature* (New York: Viking, 1923), 10–16, xroads.virginia.edu/~HYPER/LAWRENCE/dhlch02.htm ; Cervantes, *Don Quixote,* part 2, chapter 33; Aesop, "The Milkmaid and the Pail." Franklin did cite the maxim "Honesty is the best policy" in a letter to Edward Bridgen, Oct. 2, 1779, but it was part of a list of maxims that could be on coins, and he did not claim it as his own.

15. Charles Angoff, *A Literary History of the American People* (New York: Knopf, 1931), 296–308.

16. Herbert Schneider, *The Puritan Mind* (New York: Henry Holt, 1930); Van Doren 782; I. Bernard Cohen, *Benjamin Franklin's Experiments* (Cambridge: Harvard University Press, 1941), 73.

17. For more on Dale Carnegie's *How to Win Friends and Influence People* (1937; New York: Pocket Books, 1994), see ch. 4 n. 6, above; E. Digby Baltzell, *Puritan Boston and Quaker Philadelphia* (New York: Free Press, 1979), 55.

18. FranklinCovey Web site, www.franklincovey.com ; Grady McAllister, "An Unhurried Look at Time Management," vasthead.com/Time/tm_papl.html. Peter Jennings and Todd Brewster, *In Search of America* (New York: Hyperion, 2002), chapter 3, reports on an interesting class discussion by Baylor professor Blaine McCormick about Franklin as the founding father of business books.

19. Brands 715; Morgan *Franklin*, 314.

20. Alan Taylor, "For the Benefit of Mr. Kite," *The New Republic*, Mar. 19, 2001, 39. The play *1776*, by Sherman Edwards and Peter Stone, opened at Broadway's 46th Street Theater on Mar. 16, 1969, ran for 1,217 performances, and was made into a film in 1972; Howard Da Silva played Franklin on both stage and screen. *Ben Franklin in Paris*, by Mark Sandrich Jr. and Sidney Michaels, opened at the Lunt-Fontanne Theater on Oct. 27, 1964, and ran for 215 performances with Robert Preston playing Franklin.

21. David Brooks, "Our Founding Yuppie," *The Weekly Standard*, Oct. 23, 2000, 32, 35.

22. BF to JM, July 17, 1771.

23. Taylor, "For the Benefit of Mr. Kite," 39.

24. Vernon Parrington, *Main Currents in American Thought* (New York: Harcourt, 1930), 1:178.

25. Taylor, "For the Benefit of Mr. Kite," 39.

26. Poor Richard's, 1750; BF to Louis Le Veillard, Mar. 6, 1786; Autobiography 107 (all use the "empty sack" line).

27. Brooks, "Our Founding Yuppie," 35.

28. Autobiography 139.

29. Angoff, *A Literary History of the American People*, 306; Garry Wills, *Under God* (New York: Simon & Schuster, 1990), 380.

30. Henry Steele Commager, *The American Mind* (New Haven: Yale University Press, 1950), 26; John Updike, "Many Bens," *New Yorker*, Feb. 22, 1988, 115.

31. David Hume to BF, May 10, 1762; Campbell 356.

INDEX

ABOUT THE AUTHOR

Walter Isaacson is the president of the Aspen Institute. He has been the chairman and CEO of CNN and the managing editor of *Time* magazine. He is the author of *Kissinger: A Biography* and the coauthor, with Evan Thomas, of *The Wise Men: Six Friends and the World They Made.* He lives with his wife and daughter in Washington, D.C.

ILLUSTRATION CREDITS

Numbers in roman type refer to illustrations in the insert; *italics* refer to book pages.

Courtesy of The Bostonian Society/Old State House: 1
American Philosophical Society: 2, 11, 12, 17, 21, 26, 29
Private Collection: 3, 6
The Metropolitan Museum of Art, Catharine Lorillard Wolfe Collection, Wolfe
    Fund, 1901 (01.20). Photograph © 1998 The Metropolitan Museum of
    Art: 4
© Réunion des Musées Nationaux/Art Resource, NY: 5, 27
The Papers of Benjamin Franklin, Yale University Library: 7, *endpapers*
Philadelphia Museum of Art: Gift of Mr. and Mrs. Wharton Sinkler: 8
Courtesy of the Chapin Library of Rare Books, Williams College: 9, *131*
Franklin Collection, Yale University Library: 10, 28, 30
© Bettmann/Corbis: 13, 16, 19
Courtesy of the Harvard University Portrait Collection, Bequest of Dr. John
    Collins Warren, 1856: 14
Courtesy of The Historical Society of Pennsylvania Collection, Atwater Kent
    Museum of Philadelphia: 15, 24
By courtesy of the National Portrait Gallery, London: 18
Courtesy of the Pennsylvania Academy of Fine Arts, Philadelphia. Gift of Maria
    McKean Allen and Phebe Warren Downes through the bequest of their
    mother Elizabeth Wharton McKean: 20
© Huntington Library/SuperStock: 22
Library of Congress: 23
The Metropolitan Museum of Art, The Friedsam Collection, Bequest of Michael
    Friedsam, 1931 (32.100.132). Photograph © 1981 The Metropolitan
    Museum of Art: 25
Courtesy of the Winterthur Museum, Gift of Henry Francis du Pont: 31
The Architect of the Capitol: 32

Additional photo research by Alexandra Truitt and Jerry Marshall, Picture
    Research & Editing.

A NOTE ON TYPE

This book is set in Adobe Caslon type, designed in 1990 by Carol Twombly, which is known for its elegance, dignity, regularity, and legibility. It is based on a typeface originally created in the early 1720s by the preeminent London punch-cutter and type-maker William Caslon. Benjamin Franklin imported Caslon's type for his print shop in Philadelphia, championed it, and chose it for the first printing of the Declaration of Independence.

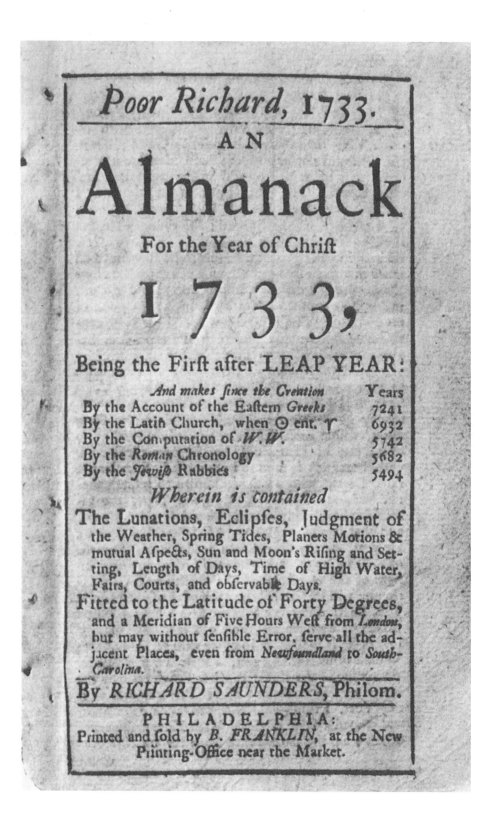

Poor Richard, 1733.

A N
Almanack

For the Year of Christ

1733,

Being the Firſt after LEAP YEAR:

And makes ſince the Creation	Years
By the Account of the Eaſtern *Greeks*	7241
By the Latin Church, when ☉ ent. ♈	6932
By the Computation of *W. W.*	5742
By the *Roman* Chronology	5682
By the *Jewiſh* Rabbies	5494

Wherein is contained

The Lunations, Eclipſes, Judgment of the Weather, Spring Tides, Planets Motions & mutual Aſpects, Sun and Moon's Riſing and Setting, Length of Days, Time of High Water, Fairs, Courts, and obſervable Days.
Fitted to the Latitude of Forty Degrees, and a Meridian of Five Hours Weſt from *London,* but may without ſenſible Error, ſerve all the adjacent Places, even from *Newfoundland* to *South-Carolina.*

By *RICHARD SAUNDERS,* Philom.

PHILADELPHIA:
Printed and ſold by *B. FRANKLIN,* at the New Printing-Office near the Market.